Utah

MAYA SILVER

Contents

sunrise at Arches National Park

WELCOME TO

Utah

Few places on earth combine such spectacular—and diverse—terrain as Utah. To the north, the Wasatch Range dominates the landscape. In winter, legendary light powder draws skiers and snowboarders to resorts in the Cottonwood Canyons outside Salt Lake and Park City's sought-after slopes. When the snow melts, hundreds of trail miles for hiking and mountain biking bloom with wildflowers.

Down south is a world apart, where the Colorado Plateau's colorful canyons and red-rock desert propel you into a state of awe. Sublime Zion Canyon, the hoodoos of Bryce, Capitol Reef's desert backcountry, the rock rainbows of Arches, Canyonlands' endless vistas and roads—each national park brings something unique to the adventurer's table. In between the stars of southern Utah are more places to explore: the vast canyon country of Grand Staircase-Escalante National Monument, the archaeological tapestry of Bears Ears National Monument, quirky state parks, and dinosaur relics.

One more topographic piece of the puzzle is the capitol's namesake: the Great Salt Lake. This remnant of a vast ancient lake is home to hundreds of bird species and is critically endangered, as drought worsens and water use grows.

Utah is also the seat of Mormonism. The first Latter-day Saints (LDS) pioneers arrived in 1847. You'll notice the presence of "the local religion" in some places more than others. Temple Square—the church headquarters—commands downtown Salt Lake. Cities such as Provo and St. George feel very LDS, while places like Park City and Moab don't.

If you're intrigued by dramatic canyons, majestic mountains, glistening salt flats, ancient rock art, dinosaur footprints, and adventure, Utah is the place to be.

Lake Blanche in Big Cottonwood Canyon

10 TOP
EXPERIENCES

1 Skiing and snowboarding in the deep powder of **Big** or **Little Cottonwood Canyon** (pages 82 and 91), **Park City Mountain** (page 131), or **Deer Valley** (page 134).

2 Exploring canyons, arches, hoodoos, and more at Utah's five national parks—**Zion** (page 176), **Bryce** (page 201), **Capitol Reef** (page 287), **Arches** (page 346), and **Canyonlands** (page 356).

3 Mountain biking, rock climbing, hiking, camping, slickrock wandering, and dining in **Moab,** the town that revolves around adventure (page 319).

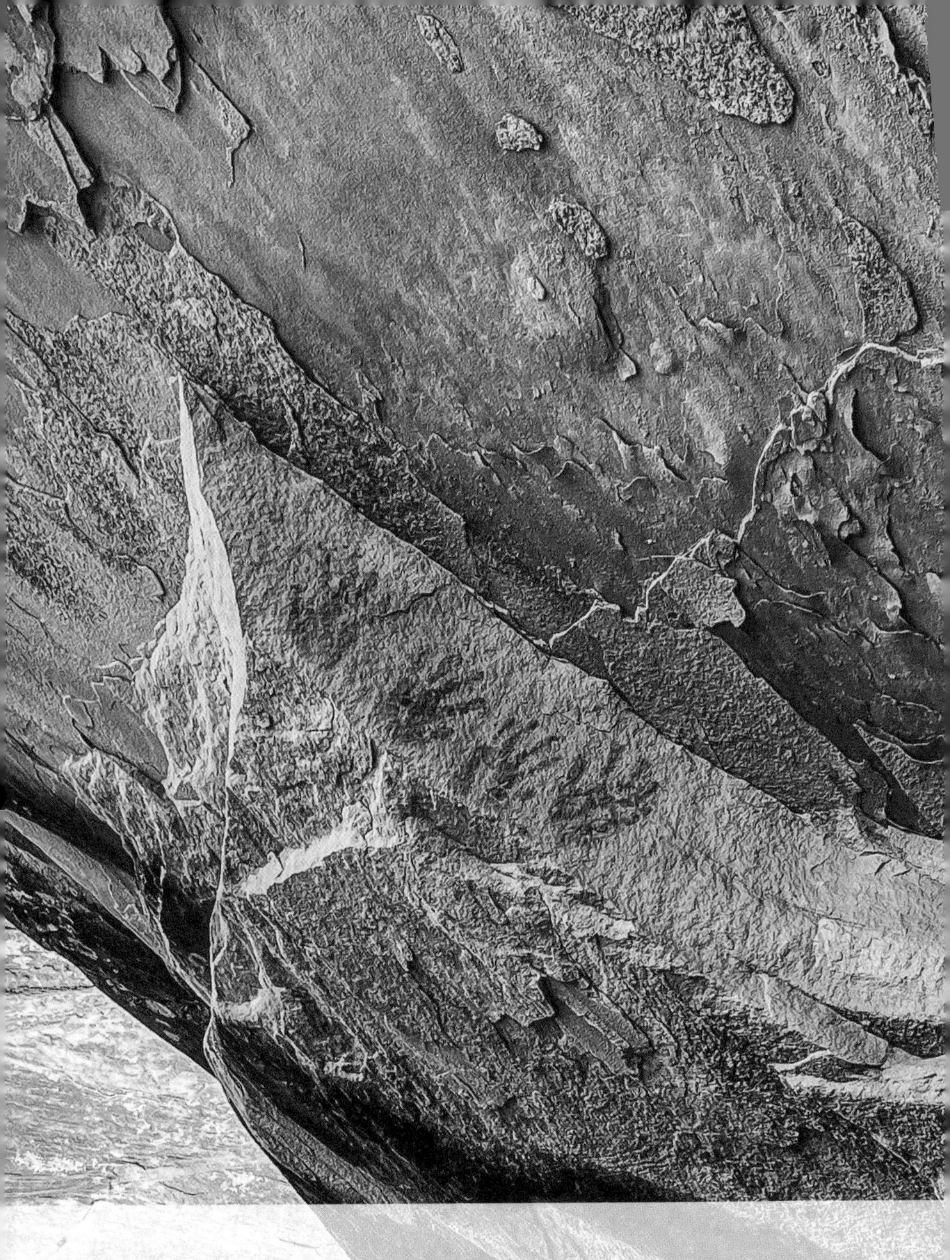

4 Going back in time at archaeological sites and rock-art panels at **Bears Ears National Monument** (page 384).

5 Encountering the otherworldly features of the Great Salt Lake, especially the **Bonneville Salt Flats** (page 106) and the legendary **Spiral Jetty** rock art (page 120).

6 Venturing into Utah's mountains to summit **the tallest point in the state** (page 420) or hike to the top of **its most popular peak** (page 162).

7 Discovering Utah's own Hollywood at **Sundance** (page 160), home of the buzzy winter film festival, year-round movie screenings, and the namesake resort formerly owned by Robert Redford.

8 Cycling Salt Lake City's classic **Emigration Canyon Road** (page 61) or Park City's **350 miles of single-track** (page 140).

9 Canyoneering at nontechnical **Peek-a-boo and Spooky Slot Canyons** (page 273) or Zion's **Narrows** (page 188).

10 Discovering dinosaur footprints and bones and traces of the Fremont and Ancestral Puebloan people preserved in **Utah's ancient rocks** (page 22).

Planning Your Trip

WHERE TO GO

Salt Lake City and Northern Utah

Home to a major university, seat of a major religion, gateway to adventure—sometimes Utah's capital seems a little at odds with itself. As far as capitals go, Salt Lake is small and easy to get to know in a few days. A little over 30 minutes due north of Salt Lake, the former railroad hub of **Ogden** offers small-town charm and great skiing, too. The city's namesake is about 20 miles (32 km) to the west, and **Antelope Island State Park** makes for a wild and beautiful way to experience the lake's ecosystem. The "backyards" of Salt Lake City are **Big and Little Cottonwood Canyons,** which are about 20 minutes southeast of downtown. Each canyon is home to two ski resorts and, come summer, beautiful trails and camping.

Park City and the Wasatch Back

As far as mountain towns go, Park City is among the swankiest. Chalk it up to regal **Deer Valley,** the annual **Sundance Film Fest,** or the massive terrain of **Park City Mountain,** which attracts skiers from across the globe. In "Old Town" Park City, you'll find upscale amenities, fine dining, a plethora of art galleries, and year-round events. Come summer, the mountains and ski areas offer great hiking and mountain biking. The Wasatch Back area—the back side of the Wasatch Range—also includes the nearby towns

a rainbow over Mount Timpanogos

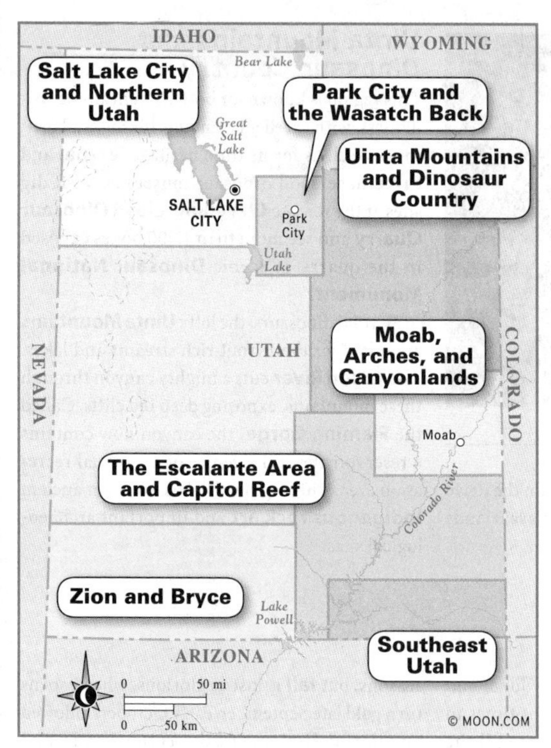

of **Heber** and **Midway,** where you'll find family-friendly activities and Swiss heritage. And farther southwest lies beautiful **Sundance Resort** at the foothills of Utah's most popular summit: **Mount Timpanogos.**

Zion and Bryce

With steep canyons featuring towering walls hung with improbable gardens and lined with cottonwood trees, **Zion National Park** is all about stunning contrasts. The highlights and easily accessible trails along the touristy scenic drive are worth battling crowds for—enhance your experience by touring the drive on bike or e-bike rather than shuttle bus. And don't skip other quieter sections of the park like **Kolob Canyons.**

A couple hours' drive from Zion, **Bryce Canyon National Park** is famed for its breathtaking amphitheater filled with red and pink hoodoos—delicate spires of stone rising from a steep mountainside. Nearby, **Cedar Breaks National Monument** has similar formations without the crowds.

The Escalante Area and Capitol Reef

The **Grand Staircase-Escalante National Monument** largely preserves the dry washes and slot canyons trenched by the Escalante River and its tributaries. Long-distance hikers descend into the deep, narrow river channels here to experience the near-mystical harmony of flowing water and stone. East of this massive monument, **Capitol Reef** is home to canyons, arches, and historic orchards where you can pick your own fruit.

Moab, Arches, and Canyonlands

Adventure-centric **Moab** is the recreational hub of southeastern Utah, known for its mountain bike lifestyle and great dining and lodging. The beauty is more bizarre at **Arches National Park,** where hundreds of rock arches provide windows into the landscape. In vast **Canyonlands National Park,** the Colorado River begins to tunnel its mighty—and eventually grand—canyon through an otherworldly landscape of red sandstone.

Southeast Utah

Perhaps the least-visited stretch of Utah in this guide, the southeastern corner of the state is home to the new **Bears Ears National Monument,** which preserves over a million acres of land considered sacred by several local tribes. Here you'll find intriguing archaeological sites, rock art, gorgeous hiking, and great scenic drives. Nearby **Hovenweep National Monument** protects

mule's ears near Park City

800-year-old villages, and to the south, the drive through **Monument Valley** across Navajo lands offers stunning cinematic landscapes.

Uinta Mountains and Dinosaur Country

This region is known for both its high alpine wilderness, with excellent camping, hiking, and fishing, as well as for its dino heritage. **Vernal** and **Price** have good dinosaur museums. Visit dig sites at the remote **Cleveland-Lloyd Dinosaur Quarry** and see more than 1,000 bones exposed in the quarry at scenic **Dinosaur National Monument.**

Beyond dinosaurs, the lofty **Uinta Mountains** are noted for their trout-rich streams and lakes. The **Green River** cuts a mighty canyon through these mountains, exposing deep red cliffs. Called the **Flaming Gorge,** the canyon now contains a reservoir that's the center of a national recreation area. This region also has excellent ancient **Indigenous rock art** and important archaeological sites.

WHEN TO GO

In southern Utah, **spring** (Apr.-early June) and **fall** (Sept.-Oct.) are the most pleasant times to visit, but the same spring showers that fill the desert with wildflowers can also dampen trails and turn dirt roads to absolute muck. Arm yourself with insect repellent late spring-midsummer.

In Park City, **winter** and **summer** are peak seasons, but **fall** is just as glorious, when aspens turn gold late September-early October, followed by colorful displays of oaks, cottonwoods, and other deciduous plants in lower canyons.

petroglyphs in Bears Ears National Monument

Except in the mountains, **summer** heat can rapidly drain your energy. In Canyonlands, Arches, Moab, and Salt Lake City, summer temperatures can easily top 100°F (38°C). Bryce, at 6,600-9,100 feet (2,012-2,774 m), is a good summertime bet, as are the Uinta Mountains and the Flaming Gorge area in northeastern Utah. Thunderstorms are fairly common late July-early September across the state, and they bring the threat of flash floods, especially in slot canyons.

Travel doesn't let up in **winter**—the ski areas here are some of the nation's best, and most are easy to get to from Salt Lake City. For those who don't mind the cold, this can also be a gorgeous and quieter time to visit southern Utah. Wherever you're traveling in winter, inquire about travel conditions, as snow and ice close some roads and trails at higher elevations.

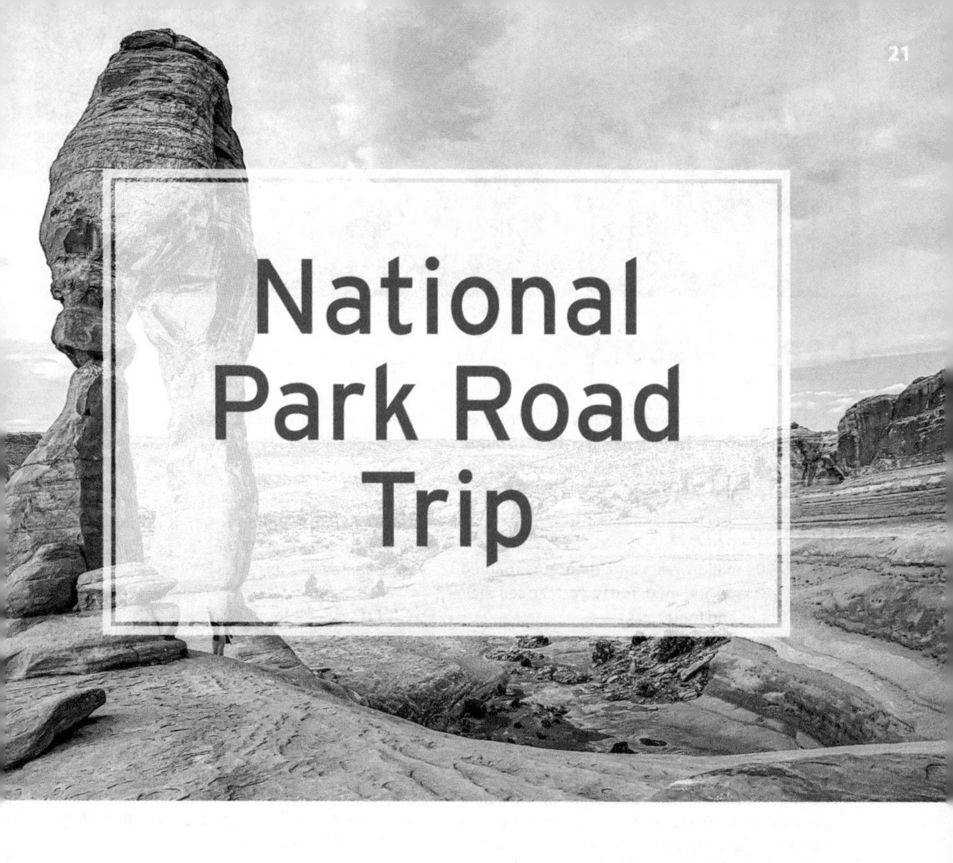

National Park Road Trip

Despite their proximity, visiting all of Utah's national parks is a bit complicated because of the **rugged terrain** and lack of direct routes between them. While you'll be doing a lot of **driving,** it's all scenic and worth it to see each park's unique sights, from Arches' namesake and Bryce's hoodoos to the panoramas of Canyonlands.

Day 1

Start in Moab and head a few miles north to **Arches National Park.** Visit a few sites along the park road and hike to the famed **Delicate Arch.** Settle into your reserved campsite at **Devils Garden** and take a short evening hike to **Broken Arch.**

Day 2

Devote Day 2 to exploring **Canyonlands' Island in the Sky District,** taking in the astonishing vista points (particularly Grand View Point, perched high above the Colorado River) and saving time for a hike to Mesa Arch. Camp at nearby **Dead Horse Point State Park** and explore the mountain biking there.

Day 3

Head into Moab for an early breakfast, then go south on US 191. Pull off US 191 south of Moab 40 miles (64 km) and drive toward the **Needles District** of Canyonlands. It's 38 miles (61 km) to the park gate (which will add considerably to the 115-mile (185-km) straight shot down US 191),

Deep History

A lot of history is preserved in Utah's ancient rocks. **Dinosaur footprints and bones** abound, alongside traces of the **Fremont** and **Ancestral Puebloan** people who lived here centuries ago.

JURASSIC UTAH

About 145-200 million years ago, dinosaurs roamed these lands of sand and mud. Today, you can see their fossilized bones and footprints.

- **Utah Museum of Natural History:** Amid all the dinosaur bones in this Salt Lake City museum is a good video exhibit featuring paleontologists explaining theories about the formation of the Cleveland-Lloyd Dinosaur Quarry (page 55).
- **St. George Dinosaur Discovery Site at Johnson Farm:** This is one of the world's best dinosaur tracks sites. Recently discovered tracks show early Jurassic dinosaurs running across the former lake beds here (page 233).
- **USU Eastern Prehistoric Museum:** The locally dug fossils here include the Utahraptor (remember *Jurassic Park*?). After the museum, in downtown Price, drive east from Huntington to the Cleveland-Lloyd Dinosaur Quarry and visit the excavation site (page 438).
- **Utahraptor State Park:** Created in 2021, this state park just outside Moab preserves Dalton Wells Quarry, among other historic sites, where the Utahraptor was first discovered in 1991 (page 323).
- **Utah Field House Museum:** Check out a great collection of dinosaur bones and fossilized plants and mammals. Head north from this Vernal museum to the northern edge of Red Fleet State Park and take a 3-mile (4.8-km) round-trip hike to see dinosaur tracks (page 423).
- **Dinosaur National Monument:** The monument's Quarry Exhibit Hall is built around a cliff face that has been excavated to expose about 1,500 dinosaur bones, including those of the stegosaurus. It's a short drive east of Vernal (page 428).
- **Big Water Visitor Center:** At the southern edge of the Kaiparowits Plateau, east of Kanab, this spiral-shaped building is home to bones from a 75-million-year-old, 30-foot-long (9-m) duck-billed dinosaur (page 258).

PICTOGRAPHS AND PETROGLYPHS

Searching out pictographs (drawings painted on rock) and petroglyphs (images carved into stone) will lead you far off the beaten path and deep into canyons that were once central for Utah's ancient inhabitants.

- **Nine Mile Canyon:** Drive the now-paved road from Price to Utah's largest concentration of excellent rock-art panels and ancient grain caches tucked into the cliffs (page 440).
- **Sego Canyon:** North of Moab on I-80, Sego Canyon is a vast gallery of prehistoric art, where you'll find hundreds of etched images (page 452).
- **Fremont Petroglyphs:** Petroglyphs of horned mountain sheep and humans in feathered headdresses are easily viewed from a parking area along Highway 24 in Capitol Reef National Park (page 289).
- **BLM Newspaper Rock:** This concentrated showcase of rock art sits 12 miles (19.2 km) west of US 191 on the entrance road for Canyonlands' Needles District, and just outside the Indian Creek section of Bears Ears National Monument (page 391).
- **Great Gallery:** In Canyonlands' remote Horseshoe Canyon Unit, human-size images of ghost spirits cover the walls of what was clearly a sacred place (page 377).

Above: an owl and other petroglyph figures up Nine Mile Canyon

but good hiking awaits. If you're short on time, follow the park access road for 12 miles (19.3 km) from the highway to **BLM Newspaper Rock Historical Monument,** one of Utah's finest and most accessible petroglyph sites. Head back to US 191, drive south to just past Blanding and head east on Highway 95 across Cedar Mesa to the campground at **Natural Bridges National Monument.**

Day 4

From Natural Bridges, it's a pretty 100-mile (161-km) easy drive north on Highway 95 to Hanksville and west 28 miles (45 km) on Highway 24 to **Capitol Reef,** one of the National Park Service's unsung heroes, with scenery to match the other Utah parks but fewer visitors, a grassy campground, and a fruit orchard.

Day 5

From Capitol Reef, follow Highway 12 south to **Grand Staircase-Escalante National Monument.** The 61-mile (98-km) trip between the towns of Torrey and Escalante is one of the most scenic routes in all of Utah—plan on more than an hour of driving time. Take in all the scenery and sights, including a visit to the restored Ancestral Puebloan village at **Anasazi State Park** and a hike across slickrock up **Lower Calf Creek Falls Trail** to a stunning waterfall.

Day 6

Explore more of the Escalante River canyons. Drive 12.5 miles (20.1 km) southeast on Highway 12 and turn onto the dirt Hole-in-the-Rock Road to traipse around **Devils Garden.** You can also visit the slot canyons of **Dry Fork of Coyote Gulch,** 26 bumpy miles (42 km) south of Highway 12.

hoodoos at Bryce Canyon National Park

Day 7

From Escalante, continue west 42 miles (68 km) on Highway 12 to **Bryce Canyon National Park.** Spend the day driving, riding the park shuttle, or biking to vista points and exploring hoodoos from trailheads along the road.

Days 8-9

Get up in time to see the rising sun light up the hoodoos, then drive west on Highway 12 to US 89, and south from there to Highway 9. At Highway 9, turn west and enter **Zion National Park** via **Zion-Mount Carmel Highway** (Bryce to Zion is 86 mi/138 km). Settle into your campsite or the lodge (reserve in advance), then ride the park shuttle or bike the scenic drive to see Zion's highlights.

Zion-Mount Carmel Highway

Starting point: *Zion National Park visitor center*
Ending point: *Junction of Hwy. 9 and US 89*
Mileage: *24.5 miles (39 km) one-way*
Driving time: *2 hours*

From Zion Canyon, this road climbs through a series of switchbacks, passes through a crazy long tunnel and provides access to the canyons and high plateaus to the east. Take the easy 1-mile (1.6-km) round-trip Canyon Overlook Trail to peer down at the huge Great Arch of Zion and stop to admire Checkerboard Mesa, a huge lump of hatch-marked sandstone right at the road's edge. From the end point, head north to Bryce Canyon National Park.

Utah Scenic Byway: Potash Road

Starting point: *Junction of US 191 and Hwy. 279, 3.5 miles (5.6 km) north of Moab*
Ending point: *Moab Salt Plant*
Mileage: *17 miles (27.4 km) one-way*
Driving time: *1-2 hours*

Just outside Moab, Potash Road (Hwy. 279) goes downstream along the west side of the Colorado River Canyon, past towering sandstone cliffs dotted with rock climbers, prehistoric rock art, arches, and hiking trails. The pavement ends at the Moab Salt Plant, where mining operations inject water underground to dissolve potash and other chemicals, then pump the solution into evaporation ponds.

Capitol Reef: The Scenic Drive

Starting/Ending point: *Capitol Reef National Park visitor center*
Mileage: *21 miles (34 km) round-trip*
Driving time: *1.5-2 hours*

Head into the heart of Capitol Reef National Park on this short but scenic excursion. The road passes the early settlement of Fruita and its

Fall Foliage

Utah's brief leaf-peeping season runs roughly from September through early October. While heading up any canyon into the Wasatch Range will reward you with a splash of color, these drives are particularly stunning. In dry years, colors may be less spectacular, especially at lower elevations.

- **Alpine Scenic Loop:** Take a winding drive up **Mount Timpanogos,** north of Provo. The aspen grove near the summit is the highlight of the drive. Be sure to visit Cascade Springs, which sparkles in the early October light (page 159).
- **Mirror Lake Highway:** Head up at least as far as Provo River Falls for huge swaths of yellow, orange, and red aspens. Make a day of it by going to Mirror Lake for a paddle or a hike (page 418).
- **Big Cottonwood Canyon:** Short on time? Drive from Salt Lake City up to Solitude and Brighton ski areas. Make it a road trip by continuing across Guardsman Pass to Park City or Heber City, past a tapestry of red, yellow, and green (page 82).
- **Boulder Mountain:** The Aquarius Plateau is North America's highest timbered plateau, and in early September, it bursts with color (page 286).
- **Capitol Reef National Park:** Capitol Reef is Utah's best national park for fall color. The trees along the Fremont River change a little later than those at higher elevations. Visit in October, when the orchard's apples will be primed for picking. If you have more time, visit nearby Pando, a massive aspen clone that's considered the world's largest organism (pages 289 and 304).

orchards, then climbs out of the Fremont River past tilted layers of rock. Stop to wander into the dry channels of the Grand Wash and Capitol Gorge. Once the area's main highway, Capitol Gorge is now a hiking trail between tall sandstone walls, leading to petroglyphs and early settler signatures carved into the rock walls.

Alpine Loop Scenic Drive

Starting point: *American Fork Canyon, Hwy. 92 east of Highland*

Ending point: *Junction of US 189 and Hwy. 92*

Mileage: *20 miles (32 km) one-way*

Driving time: *1-3 hours*

From its start at the mouth of American Fork Canyon just outside Salt Lake City, the road climbs through a stunning canyon past Timpanogos Cave National Monument—stop for a cave tour if you have time. It then ascends to an 8,000-foot (2,438-m) summit with views of Mount Timpanogos. Just past the summit, take the turnoff to Cascade Springs to see spring water gush from the ground and flow down a series of lushly vegetated travertine terraces. Back on the main scenic drive, the road continues through a grove of aspen trees, passes Sundance Resort (worth a stop), and descends to Provo Canyon. Pay the $6 fee at ticket booths at either end of the drive. Snow usually closes the road from late October until late May.

Highway 12 Scenic Byway

Starting point: *Junction of US 89 and Hwy. 12, near Panguitch*

Ending point: *Junction of Hwy. 12 and Hwy. 24, Torrey*

Mileage: *123 miles (198 km) one-way*

Driving time: *4 hours-1 week*

This "All-American Road" from US 89 packs in more parks, monuments, and geology than just about any other road in the country. Beginning near Panguitch just outside Bryce, it leads to Highway 24 in Torrey, past red-rock arches in Red Canyon and the edge of Bryce Canyon National Park. It continues east through the northern edge of Grand Staircase-Escalante National Monument across the Hells Backbone bridge to Boulder and one of Utah's best restaurants. Finally, the road turns north to cross over Boulder Mountain,

Highway 12 winds its way through desert country near Hells Backbone.

Mountain Biking

Utah is a mountain biker's dream. From high alpine single-track to desert slickrock, you'll find a bit of everything.

In **Park City,** riders can pedal over 350 miles (565 km) of a growing trail system rated gold by the International Mountain Bike Association. (There are only four gold-rated ride centers in the world.)

A few classic rides include biking the **Wasatch Crest** (with or without a shuttle) and **Mid-Mountain Trail.** For the best lift-serviced riding in the mountains, head to **Deer Valley Resort,** for technical terrain and massive berms, or **Snowbird,** for a long, sweeping descent via the aerial tram. The best time to ride in Utah's northern mountains is generally June-October.

The other world-class mountain biking destination in the state is **Moab,** where riders come from all over to experience pedaling on slickrock. The **Slickrock Bike Trail** gets all the attention, but there are plenty of less-crowded rides featuring slickrock riding, too. The classic epic ride here is the **Whole Enchilada,** which begins up in the La Sal Mountains and drops some 7,000 feet (2,134 m) into Grandstaff Canyon, just outside town. The best time for desert riding is mid-March-late May, then again in mid-September-October.

You'll also find single-track in Salt Lake City, Vernal, and just outside Bryce Canyon National Park.

then practically lands in the lap of Capitol Reef National Park. You'll pass cliffs, spires, petroglyphs, and views of the Grand Staircase and much of the Colorado Plateau.

Notom-Bullfrog Road

Starting point: *Hwy. 24 at eastern edge of Capitol Reef National Park*
Ending point: *Bullfrog Marina, Lake Powell*
Mileage: *70 miles (113 km) one-way*
Driving time: *3 hours*

The views of the eastern edge of Capitol Reef's Waterpocket Fold are a highlight of this fair-weather, partially paved road from the eastern edge of the national park to Bullfrog Marina on Lake Powell. The drive is long and slow but beautiful, crossing the colorful hills of the Morrison Formation with the snowcapped Henry Mountains to the east. Consider taking the whole day to hike into relatively uncrowded dry washes and slot canyons. From Bullfrog, you can head back north on a paved road to Hanksville and Goblin Valley State Park. This road can also be driven as part of an epic 125-mile loop, together with Burr Trail and Highway 12. Camping can be found along the Notom-Bullfrog as well.

Shafer Trail Road

Starting point: *Just before the entrance to Canyonlands' Island in the Sky District*
Ending point: *Junction of Potash Road and White Rim Road*
Mileage: *19.3 miles (31 km) one-way*
Driving time: *1 hour (one-way)*

This challenging dirt road descends 1,500 feet (457 m) from the mesa top of Canyonlands' Island in the Sky District via a long-traveled path—first a Native American route, then a cattleman trail, later a uranium mining road, and now a recreational thrill. Considered the first section of White Rim Road, Shafer Trail Road connects with the rest of White Rim Road and Potash Road below. You can drive it in either direction, or do it as a round-trip drive. High-clearance 4WD vehicles are required and road conditions can vary considerably, so contact a ranger beforehand. Drive cautiously and yield to uphill vehicles. This is also a fun mountain bike ride if you're up for the challenge, even if you don't plan to continue on White Rim for a multiday bikepacking epic.

Mirror Lake Highway

Starting point: *Kamas (Hwy. 150)*
Ending point: *Wyoming state line*
Mileage: *55 miles (89 km) one-way*
Driving time: *2-3 hours*

Just 30 minutes from Park City, the forested Uinta Mountains are a rare east-west range, where you can stop to see Provo River Falls, 10,620-foot (3,237-m) Bald Mountain Pass, and idyllic Mirror Lake. Plenty of scenic viewpoints, trails, and campgrounds make it possible to spend a few days here. You'll also find over 1,000 high alpine lakes across these mountains, over half of which offer good fishing. The Uintas are an excellent backpacking spot, with plenty of long trails through the High Uintas Wilderness—the 96-mile (155-km) Highline Trail is a classic. Buy a $6 pass at the kiosk near the start of the drive.

1: Notom-Bullfrog Road **2:** Mirror Lake Highway leads from Utah to Wyoming through the Uinta Mountains.

Choose Your Best Ski Experience

Resort	Description	Facilities
Big Cottonwood Canyon		
Solitude **800/748-4754** **www.solitudemountain.com**	Uncrowded skiing with old-world vibes and great terrain for blue/black skiers	Ample accommodations and some dining options
Brighton **801/532-4731** **www.brightonresort.com**	A laid-back, local's favorite resort that's entirely accessed via high-speed quads (the only Utah resort that can make this claim)	One lodging option and a few casual dining options
Little Cottonwood Canyon		
Snowbird **800/232-9542** **www.snowbird.com**	An adventurous skier's dream, with great snow and challenging terrain	Plenty of lodging and fun, memorable restaurant options; a full spa on- site
Alta **801/359-1078** **www.alta.com**	A rustic, old-world resort without the hustle, bustle, and commodification of many other mountains	Good lodging options, but fewer dining options than some other resorts; limited shopping/nightlife
Park City		
Park City Mountain **435/649-8111** **www.parkcitymountain.com**	Utah's destination-worthy, Vail-owned resort, and the largest ski resort (for inbounds terrain) in the Lower 48	Extensive lodging, dining, and après options with two distinct base areas
Deer Valley **800/424-3337** **www.deervalley.com**	Utah's poshest ski resort, known for crisp corduroy (groomed runs) and a well-balanced mix of terrain	Extensive high-end lodging, dining, and après options; limited affordable/casual facilities
Sundance		
Woodward **435/658-2648** **www.woodwardparkcity.com**	A small, newer mountain right off the highway in between Park City and Salt Lake City, mostly known for its terrain park features	No accommodations and limited casual dining available

Price (for a full-day adult ticket)	Pros	Cons
$115-159	Lots of intermediate and advanced terrain, including great tree skiing; low-key, European-style vibe; extensive Nordic skiing center	Limited beginner terrain; smaller than nearby mountains; paid parking only
$89-119	Balanced mix of runs, including great terrain parks and open bowls; affordable; snowboarding-friendly; excellent night skiing	Limited expert terrain; smaller than nearby mountains; limited facilities
$167-196	Great snow and fun terrain; legendary open bowls; one-of-a-kind party vibe; typically stays open later than other resorts (often as late as July 4)	Not a great spot for beginners; poor visibility is common; access road often closes during/after big storms for avalanche control
$159-179	Great challenging terrain; legendary powder skiing; independent and old-fashioned vibe	Snowboarding not allowed; limited beginner terrain; access road often closes during/after big storms for avalanche control; paid parking only
$101-299	Massive terrain; balanced and wide-ranging mix of runs; diverse and abundant facilities	Limited expert terrain; often crowded with long lift lines, especially during holiday weekends; expensive
$189-259	Great groomed skiing; diverse mix of runs, including expert terrain; world-class facilities	Expensive tickets and amenities; snowboarding not allowed; no terrain park
$99-159	Great features for practicing tricks; good, more affordable lessons for kids or beginners; easy to get to	Limited terrain; highway views

Choose Your Best Ski Experience (co

Resort	Description	Facilities
Sundance (continued)		
Sundance Resort **801/223-4849** **www.sundanceresort.com**	Laid-back skiing with a good mix of terrain in a gorgeous landscape resembling the Alps	Located adjacent to the destination-worthy Sundance Resort, with several dining options
Ogden Valley		
Snowbasin **888/437-5488** **www.snowbasin.com**	An awesome all-around mountain with endless runs and a balanced mix of terrain	No on-site accommodations and more limited dining options than other resorts
Powder Mountain **801/745-3772** **www.powdermountain.com**	A massive, laid-back ski area with extensive resort-accessed backcountry terrain	One lodging option and a few dining options
Nordic Valley **385/298-0155** **www.nordicvalley.ski**	A small family-friendly ski area that's great for a casual day on the hill or for beginners	No on-site accommodations; one casual dining option
And Beyond		
Beaver Mountain **435/753-0921** **www.skithebeav.com**	A small ski area in between the town of Logan and Bear Lake, a couple hours from Salt Lake City	No on-site lodging; one casual dining option
Brian Head **435/677-2035** **www.brianhead.com**	A small ski area where you'd least expect it (southern Utah!), with fine beginner and advanced terrain	A couple lodging options and limited dining
Backcountry Skiing		
Utah Avalanche Center **www.utahavalanchecenter.org**	With its light and abundant snow, and massive swaths of public land, Utah has excellent backcountry skiing.	There are several catskiing and heliskiing operations for those who'd rather not work for their turns. You can also find several guiding services if you need gear and/or expertise.

Price (for a full-day adult ticket)	Pros	Cons
$129	Beautiful natural setting and on-site amenities; well-balanced mix of runs; dedicated Nordic center	Limited expert terrain; smaller than other Utah mountains
$135-195	Excellent mix of terrain, from beginner to expert; speedy lifts; family-friendly vibe	Not quite as much snow as other Utah resorts; fewer facilities
$119-159	Well-balanced mix of difficulty level; controlled number of skiers per day; excellent resort-accessed backcountry	Fewer facilities; may be difficult to get a ticket
$45-50	Good mix of terrain; casual, inclusive, vibe; very affordable	Limited terrain; limited facilities
$60	Laid-back skiing; less crowded than the Wasatch Mountains; affordable	Smaller than most Utah mountains; limited facilities
$28-89	Good mix of terrain; laid-back vibe; very affordable; proximity to Zion and Bryce	Smaller than other Utah resorts
n/a	Fresh, untracked powder; usually no crowds or lines; no lift ticket required; free	Avalanche risk; requires specialized gear and knowledge; for advanced skiers only

A New Ski Resort on the Way

Just south of Deer Valley, **Mayflower Mountain Resort** is currently under development. Projected to open for the winter of 2025-2026, Mayflower will be operated by Deer Valley Resort, adding 3,700 acres (1,497 ha) to its existing 2,000-some (809 ha) acres. It's expected that the number of runs will more than double. It's unclear as of now whether both resorts will be available via one ticket or how this will impact Deer Valley lift ticket rates, but it will be a major change to the skiing landscape of Park City.

Best Hiking Trails

The Zion Narrows (Bottom Up)

Distance: *9.4 miles (15.1 km) round-trip*
Duration: *8 hours*
Elevation gain: *200 feet (61 m)*
Effort: *strenuous*
Trailhead: *end of Riverside Walk*
Shuttle Stop: *Temple of Sinawava*

At the end of Zion National Park's scenic drive, hike through the waters of the Virgin River up Zion Canyon as it reaches its narrowest point. The mystical lighting, sense of adventure required, and otherworldly hanging gardens lining the canyon walls make this hike worth the hype. While you'll find hordes of other hikers at the mouth of the canyon, crowds thin quickly the farther you go. Early summer (mid-June-mid-July) and early autumn (mid-Sept.-mid-Oct.) are the best windows, and you'll want to wear sturdy boots and bring poles for balance—you can rent this equipment in nearby Springdale. Check conditions before you go, as sometimes water levels are too high or cyanobacteria blooms make the water toxic.

Bryce Under-the-Rim Trail

Distance: *23 miles (37 km) one-way*
Duration: *2 days or longer for the full hike*
Elevation gain: *1,500 feet (457 m)*
Effort: *strenuous*
Trailheads: *Bryce Point, Rainbow Point*
Shuttle Stops: *Bryce Point, Rainbow Point*

This breathtaking tour of Bryce Canyon National Park winds 23 miles (37 km) from Bryce Point up to Rainbow Point, the park's highest point. Located in Bryce's wilderness, this trail is far quieter and more serene than others in the park. The trail takes you through stunning hoodoo scenery, canyons, and ponderosa groves. Day hikers can hike up as far as they want, then turn around for an out-and-back journey; several connecting trails also make it easy to exit the trail at different points and take the shuttle back to Bryce Point. Backpackers can camp at one of seven designated campsites and hop on the park shuttle back down.

Delicate Arch Trail

Distance: *3 miles (4.8 km) round-trip*
Duration: *2 hours*
Elevation gain: *500 feet (152 m)*
Effort: *moderate-strenuous*
Trailhead: *Wolfe Ranch*

Crowded for good reason, the hike to the base of the iconic Delicate Arch is one of the highlights of a visit to Arches National Park. After about 20-30 minutes of easy, uneventful hiking, the trail transitions to steep slickrock and the views open up across the park to the La Sal Mountains in the distance. Just before the end of the trail, walk up to the small, decidedly indelicate Frame Arch for a picture-perfect view of the final destination. Standing at the base of Delicate Arch is a magical moment: The arch rises out of the barren, almost lunar rock face, at the edge of a sandstone amphitheater overlooking the Colorado River valley. Do this hike at dawn or dusk for minimal crowds and the best light.

Lower Calf Creek Trail

Distance: *6 miles (9.6 km) round-trip*
Duration: *4 hours*
Elevation gain: *250 feet (76 m)*
Effort: *easy-moderate*
Trailhead: *Calf Creek Campground (day-use $5), 16 miles (26 km) east of Escalante on Hwy 12*

In Grand Staircase-Escalante National Monument, the Escalante River defines much of the landscape, and Calf Creek is one of its many tributaries. This out-and-back trail follows the creek through peaceful desert terrain and past a dramatic alcove to a stunning waterfall. The trailhead sits right off the highway, so it's one of the more accessible adventures in Grand Staircase-Escalante. From the parking area just off Highway 12, the trail winds between high Navajo sandstone cliffs streaked with desert varnish, where you'll see beaver ponds, a petroglyph of three figures holding hands, and ultimately, the misty 126-foot-high (38-m) Lower Calf Creek Falls.

hiking into the Narrows in Zion Canyon

Aspen Grove Trail to Mount Timpanogos

Distance: *16.6 miles (26.6 km) round-trip*
Duration: *8-10 hours*
Elevation gain: *4,900 feet (1,494 m)*
Effort: *strenuous*
Passes/Fees: *$10 to park*
Trailhead: *Theater in the Pines Picnic Area*

Just past Sundance Resort along the Alpine Scenic Loop, this is one of two trails leading to the 11,753-feet (3,582-m) summit of Mount Timpanogos, the second-highest peak in the Wasatch Range. This is a beautiful, challenging trek that leads past multiple waterfalls, wildflower fields, and vibrant lakes, with mountain goats frequently sighted along the way. Oddly, the first mile or so of the trail is paved. Once you reach the first waterfall, continue about 5 miles (8 km) to see **Emerald Lake.** The **Summit Trail** branches off west of Emerald Lake, climbs a steep slope, and follows a jagged ridge to the top. Hiking season is mid-July-mid-October. In winter and spring, Timpanogos is covered in snow, requiring specialized equipment to summit. On heavy snow years, snowfields can linger all summer, and hikers will want Yaktrax and poles—check local trail reports before you go.

Brighton Lakes Trail

Distance: *6 miles (9.6 km) round-trip*
Duration: *3 hours*
Elevation gain: *1,673 feet (510 m)*
Effort: *moderate*
Passes/Fees: *$10 to access road to trailhead*
Trailhead: *Silver Lake Loop trailhead*

Winding through gorgeous alpine lake country in Big Cottonwood Canyon just outside Salt Lake City, this trail begins behind Brighton Lodge. **Silver Lake** has a boardwalk, giving full access to fishing docks. The trail crosses wildflower-filled meadows, then climbs to Brighton Overlook, 1 mile (1.6 km) from the start. Dog Lake, surrounded by old mine dumps, lies 200 yards (183 m) to the south. Continue on the main trail 0.5 mile (0.8 km) to large and deep Lake Mary, below Mount Millicent. Lake Martha is another 0.5 mile (0.8 km) up the trail, and Lake Catherine just 1 mile (1.6 km) farther. Total elevation gain for the 3-mile (4.8-km) hike to Lake Catherine is 1,200 feet (366 m). Hikers can also go another 0.5 mile (0.8 km) to Catherine Pass and descend 1.5 miles (2.4 km) to Albion Basin in Little Cottonwood Canyon. Sunset Peak (10,648 ft/3,246 m) can be climbed by following a 0.5-mile (0.8-km) trail from the pass.

hiking toward Dog Lake on the Brighton Lakes Trail

Best Breweries and Distilleries

Salt Lake City

Squatters Pub Brewery

147 W. Broadway, 801/363-2739, www.saltlakebrewingco.com

Now owned locally under Salt Lake Brewing Co., Squatters and its original sister brewery Wasatch Beers lay claim to oldest continuously operating brewery in Utah. Known for its award-winning lineup of beers and spunky seasonals, Squatters also brews perennial favorites like Polygamy Nitro Porter and Ghostrider IPA.

TF Brewing

936 S. 300 W., Salt Lake City, 385/270-5972, www.tfbrewing.com

Short for Templin Family, TF pays homage to the German style of beermaking: long, slow processes using the best ingredients. TF puts out classics like Kellerbier and exercises more creative muscle with brews like its watermelon gose. Enjoy your Deutschland pint on the homey, convivial patio with fire pits and strung lighting.

Epic Brewing

825 S. State St., 801/906-0123, www.epicbrewing.com

Epic got its start in 1992—the early days of Utah brewing—and went on to re-headquarter to Denver, where alcohol laws are decidedly looser. With exposed brick and a social vibe, the Epic Utah taproom serves its many award-winning classic and experimental styles, from the Spiral Jetty IPA to its ever-evolving lineup of sours.

Tastiest Sweets

Utah loves its sweets. Award-winning chocolate bars. Pastry cases that would make Mary Berry swoon. Startup cookie brands gone global (looking at you, sugary Crumbl). The crown-jewel of patisserie in the state is **Gourmandise,** a Salt Lake café with elaborate cakes, pastries, petit fours, and more elegant sweets. Over in Park City, **Windy Ridge Bakery** also stocks an impressive pastry case—don't miss the flourless chocolate cake and pies. Stop by nearby **Ritual Chocolate Café** to enjoy a soul-warming sipping chocolate and pick up some souvenir bars. Up in the Bear Lake area, search out treats made with the local raspberry harvest, like a raspberry milkshake at **Crepes and Coffee.** On a hot Utah day, there's nothing better than a cone at Ogden's **Farr Better Ice Cream,** which has been scooping for over a century. Delicious doughnuts abound across the state, and we love the creative spread at **Doughbird** in Moab.

Park City's Alpine Distilling

Proper Brewing

857 S. Main St., 801/953-1707, www.properbrewingco.com

Proper curates a well-rounded beer list plus a few experimental styles for good measure. Outside-the-box brews include a gose with coriander and a plum ale aged in pinot noir barrels. Don't miss some sips of the Czech Your Head Bohemian-style pilsner. Proper is also known for serving one of the best burgers in the city, and now operates several pubs across Salt Lake and in Moab.

Park City

High West Distillery

27649 Old Lincoln Hwy., Wanship, 435/649-8300, www.highwest.com

An institution of the town, High West is known for its hearty whiskeys, particularly its American Prairie Bourbon, Rendezvous Rye, and Campfire (a blend of Scotch, bourbon, and rye—for intrepid imbibers only). This locally established distillery also spins out coveted limited releases and bottled whiskey cocktails. You can tour the distillery, sample a flight, and have a decadent brunch at its headquarters in Wanship, or enjoy the wares alongside great fare at the High West Saloon in Old Town.

Alpine Distilling

364 Main St., Park City, 435/200-9537, www.alpineparkcity.com

While technically headquartered a few miles from Old Town, this is the best spot to go to try Alpine's award-winning gin and other inventive botanical spirits. Alpine has also begun distilling some whisky and is known for using low-waste practices. Around the corner from the Main Street bar, you'll find a hip "Pleasure Club" serving inventive cocktails with Alpine spirits, too.

Ogden

Roosters Brewing

253 25th St., 801/627-6171, www.roostersbrewingco.com

One of the liveliest places along Ogden's Historic 25th Street, Roosters has been at it since the mid-1990s. With six flagship beers, like a Blood Orange IPA and a Niner Bock, rotating seasonals, and more creative brews on tap, Roosters has a well-rounded lineup. In town, this is a popular brunch and dinner spot alike. Roosters also operates a B Street Taproom on the outskirts of town.

Southern Utah

Moab Brewery

686 S. Main St., 435/259-6333, www.themoabbrewery.com

This brewpub is where Moab toasts to a day of adventure—over the classic Johnny's IPA or a Moab Especial (golden wheat). This is also one of the state's oldest breweries, dating back to 1996, when Moab had yet to become the bustling adventure town it is today. The brewery has branched out to begin distilling a wide-ranging portfolio of liquor, from single-malt whiskey and vodka to agave.

Best Family Activities

A canyon, forest, or river all make great places to let the little ones explore, but if you're looking for kid-oriented activities, there are plenty of options.

DINOSAURS AND NATURAL HISTORY

- For the T. rex-obsessed, the desert calls. Twenty minutes from Dinosaur National Monument at the **Utah Field House Museum,** life-size models stalk the grounds of its Dinosaur Gardens, while fossils and skeletons fill the Jurassic Hall. You'll also find good dino fun at the **Eccles Dinosaur Park** in Ogden, at Salt Lake's **Natural History Museum of Utah,** and at **Moab Giants.**

HISTORIC SITES

- A couple other surefire hits with kids are the **Heber Valley Historic Railroad,** with rides featuring Old West performances and local history, and **Wheeler Historic Farm** in Murray, with hayrides, sleigh rides, and a pumpkin patch.

ADVENTURE AND SPORTS

- Come summer, several of Utah's ski resorts also turn into adventure hubs for kids, with alpine slides, mountain coasters, and rock climbing walls—**Snowbird** and **Park City Mountain** are the places to go. While most resorts offer kids' lessons and good bunny hills for pint-sized skiers, **Nordic Valley** near Ogden is a particularly family-friendly option with easy terrain and affordable lift tickets.

Salt Lake City and Northern Utah

Base camp for skiers, climbers, cyclists, and more outdoorists. Headquarters of the Church of Jesus Christ of Latter-day Saints. Home to a growing LGBTQ+ population. Site of several large universities. Utah's capital is complex and evolving.

While the mountain-ringed scenery remains the same, the cultural identity of Salt Lake City has changed dramatically since it became the state capital in 1856, going from an agricultural religious settlement to a place where Latter-day Saints are no longer in the majority. The city has also become a blue island in a red state, frequently electing female leaders, including an openly gay mayor. In fact, 4.7 percent of Salt Lake residents identify as LGBTQ+, according to a 2021 Gallup

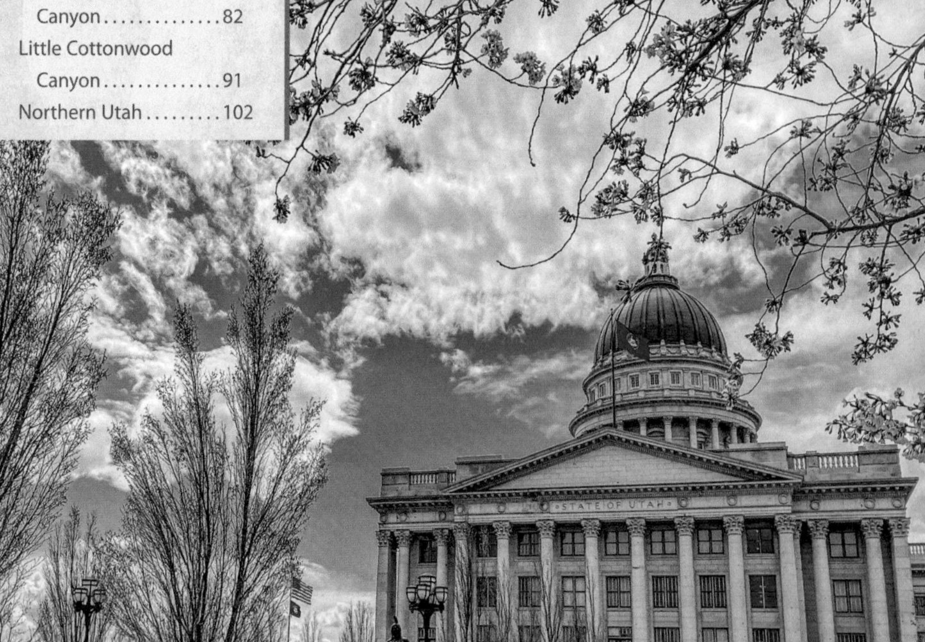

Highlights

Look for ★ to find recommended sights, activities, dining, and lodging.

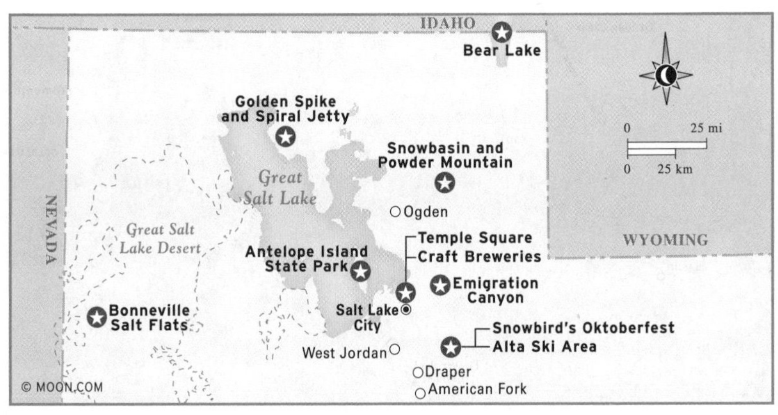

★ **Temple Square:** LDS or not, Temple Square's monuments, museums, and historic sites nearby provide a window into one of the few religions established in the United States. (page 48).

★ **Emigration Canyon:** Right from downtown, pedal into the foothills up scenic Emigration Canyon to a viewpoint overlooking a reservoir, stopping at iconic Ruth's Diner on the way back (page 61).

★ **Craft Breweries:** From TF Brewing to Epic, Utah brewers have something to prove—and their efforts are paying off (page 73).

★ **Snowbird's Oktoberfest:** Mid-August-mid-October, Snowbird hosts this German fest on weekends. Pre-game your stein with a foliage-filled hike or scenic aerial tram ride (page 94).

★ **Alta Ski Area:** Old-fashioned T-bars, a ban on snowboarding, and just about nothing fancy make skiing Alta both controversial and a blast from the sport's past—see why locals call themselves Altaholics (page 96).

★ **Antelope Island State Park:** Hundreds of species of birds, wild bison, pronghorn antelope, and more animals await along the scenic drive and trails of the Great Salt Lake's biggest island (page 103).

★ **Bonneville Salt Flats:** Find out how fast you can push that speedometer, catch the pro racers in August at Speed Week, or just wander this bizarre landscape bordering Nevada (page 106).

★ **Snowbasin and Powder Mountain:** Evade the crowds of Salt Lake's Cottonwood Canyons and Park City at the expansive, quieter resorts of the Ogden Valley (pages 113 and 116).

★ **Golden Spike and Spiral Jetty:** At the northern end of Great Salt Lake, relive railroad history at the Golden Spike, where the transcontinental rail lines were officially joined, then wander Spiral Jetty (page 118).

★ **Bear Lake:** Half in Idaho, half in northeast Utah, this vibrant blue lake is an idyllic spot to boat, fish, or enjoy a beach day (page 122).

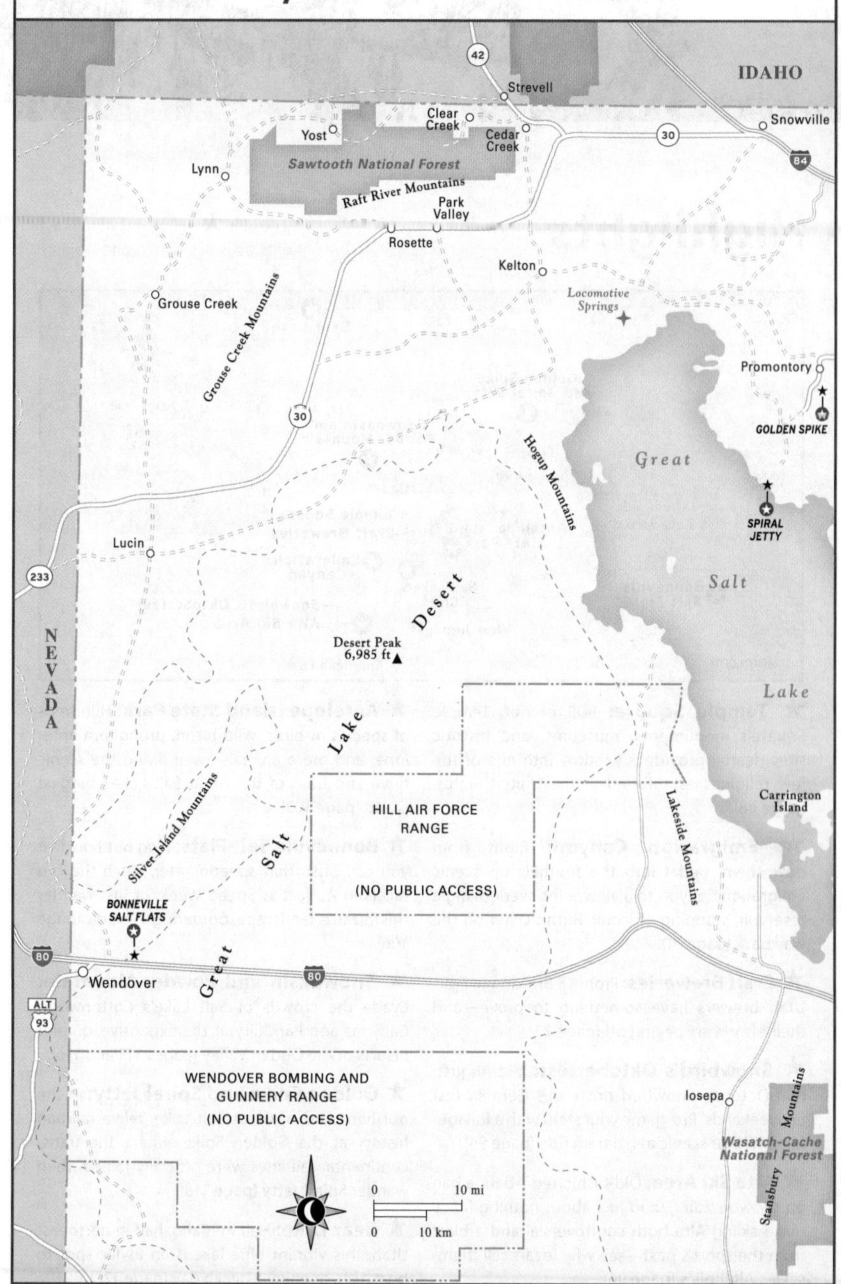
Salt Lake City and Northern Utah
IDAHO
42
Strevell
Clear Creek
Cedar Creek
30
Snowville
84
Yost
Sawtooth National Forest
Lynn
Raft River Mountains
Park Valley
Rosette
Kelton
Locomotive Springs
Grouse Creek
Grouse Creek Mountains
Promontory
GOLDEN SPIKE
Great
Hogup Mountains
SPIRAL JETTY
Lucin
233
Salt
Desert
Desert Peak
6,985 ft
NEVADA
Lake
Great Salt Lake Desert
Silver Island Mountains
HILL AIR FORCE RANGE
(NO PUBLIC ACCESS)
Carrington Island
Lakeside Mountains
BONNEVILLE SALT FLATS
80
Wendover
ALT 93
WENDOVER BOMBING AND GUNNERY RANGE
(NO PUBLIC ACCESS)
Iosepa
Stansbury Mountains
Wasatch-Cache National Forest
0
10 mi
0
10 km

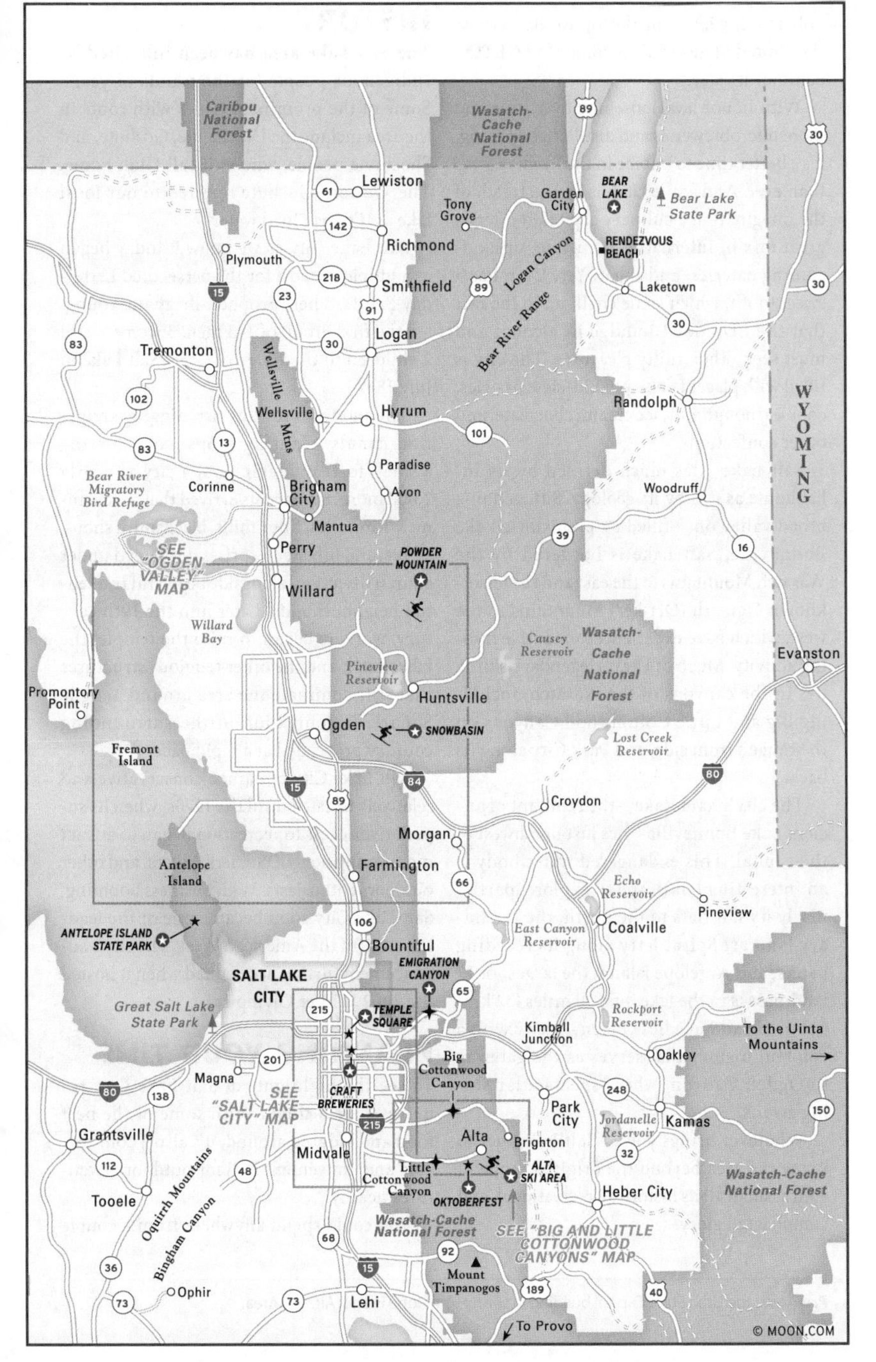
Caribou National Forest
Wasatch-Cache National Forest
Lewiston
Tony Grove
Garden City
BEAR LAKE
Bear Lake State Park
Richmond
Plymouth
Logan Canyon
RENDEZVOUS BEACH
Smithfield
Laketown
Logan
Bear River Range
Tremonton
Wellsville Mtns
Wellsville
Hyrum
Randolph
WYOMING
Paradise
Bear River Migratory Bird Refuge
Corinne
Brigham City
Avon
Woodruff
Mantua
Perry
SEE "OGDEN VALLEY" MAP
POWDER MOUNTAIN
Willard
Willard Bay
Causey Reservoir
Wasatch-Cache National Forest
Pineview Reservoir
Evanston
Promontory Point
Huntsville
Ogden
SNOWBASIN
Fremont Island
Lost Creek Reservoir
Croydon
Morgan
Antelope Island
Farmington
Echo Reservoir
Pineview
ANTELOPE ISLAND STATE PARK
East Canyon Reservoir
Coalville
Bountiful
EMIGRATION CANYON
SALT LAKE CITY
Great Salt Lake State Park
TEMPLE SQUARE
Rockport Reservoir
Kimball Junction
To the Uinta Mountains
Oakley
Magna
Big Cottonwood Canyon
SEE "SALT LAKE CITY" MAP
CRAFT BREWERIES
Park City
Kamas
Grantsville
Jordanelle Reservoir
Midvale
Alta
Brighton
Oquirrh Mountains
Little Cottonwood Canyon
ALTA SKI AREA
Tooele
OKTOBERFEST
Heber City
Wasatch-Cache National Forest
Bingham Canyon
Wasatch-Cache National Forest
SEE "BIG AND LITTLE COTTONWOOD CANYONS" MAP
Mount Timpanogos
Ophir
Lehi
To Provo
© MOON.COM

poll, making it among the top 10 cities across the United States when it comes to LGBTQ+ community size.

With liquor laws loosening over time and more microbreweries and distilleries opening, it's a better time to imbibe in the Beehive State than ever. And while Utah is by no stretch of the imagination a culinary capital, it offers a great mix of international cuisine, up-and-coming eateries, and sugar. Yes, Utah has a sweet tooth, which some chalk up to the fact that the LDS don't indulge in alcohol and must seek other guilty pleasures. The city is filled with places to enjoy world-class pastries, cookies, doughnuts, ice cream, chocolate, and other confections.

Salt Lake is as much defined by its in habitants as it is by its geology. Situated in a broad valley once filled by prehistoric Lake Bonneville, Salt Lake is bordered by the Wasatch Mountains to the east and the lesser-known Oquirrh (OH-ker) Mountains to the west, which have experienced extensive mining activity. Much of Utah's legendary skiing lies in the canyons of the Wasatch, including Big and Little Cottonwood Canyons on the range's front side, and Park City along its back.

The city's namesake—the remnant of ancient Lake Bonneville—lies just northwest of the capital. This endangered water body is an interesting landscape to explore, particularly its salt flats to the north, the legendary land art Spiral Jetty along its receding banks, and Antelope Island, the largest of 17 landmasses in the lake. Just 20 miles (32 km) north of Salt Lake lies Ogden—a city with a colorful history that serves as the gateway to Ogden Canyon, where spectacular skiing awaits.

Whatever brings you to Salt Lake, get to know the area beyond the original scope of your visit, in all its historical, recreational, and complicated glory.

HISTORY

The Salt Lake area has been inhabited by Indigenous people for thousands of years. Some of the prominent tribes with roots in the area include the Ute, Paiute, Goshute, and Shoshone people, who still call Utah home. The Western Goshute referred to our local lake as ti'ts-pa ("bad water").

Salt Lake City as we know it today began as a utopic outpost for the persecuted Latter-day Saints. Their prophet, Brigham Young, led the first group of 143 men, 3 women, and 2 children to the valley of Great Salt Lake in July 1847.

The pioneers set to work digging irrigation canals, planting crops, constructing a small fort, and laying out a city as nearly 2,000 more immigrants arrived that first summer. Tanneries, flour mills, blacksmith shops, stores, and other enterprises developed under church direction, alongside beautiful residential neighborhoods. Later into the 19th century, workers began to raise the temple, the tabernacle, and the other religious structures that still dominate the area around Temple Square. Colonization of the surrounding country proceeded at a rapid pace.

Salt Lake City remained conservative and relatively isolated until the 1970s, when its superlative access to recreation began to attract more young non-LDS skiers, hikers, and other outdoors enthusiasts. With business booming, Salt Lake City soon became one of the leading cities of the American West. The city's advancement further accelerated when it hosted the 2002 Winter Olympics.

PLANNING YOUR TIME

To see the highlights of Salt Lake City requires **2 or 3 days.** With some of the best food and lodging around, it's also a comfortable and convenient hub for outdoor adventures nearby.

You could spend anywhere from a couple

Previous: the Utah State Capitol building in spring; Antelope Island; Alta Ski Area.

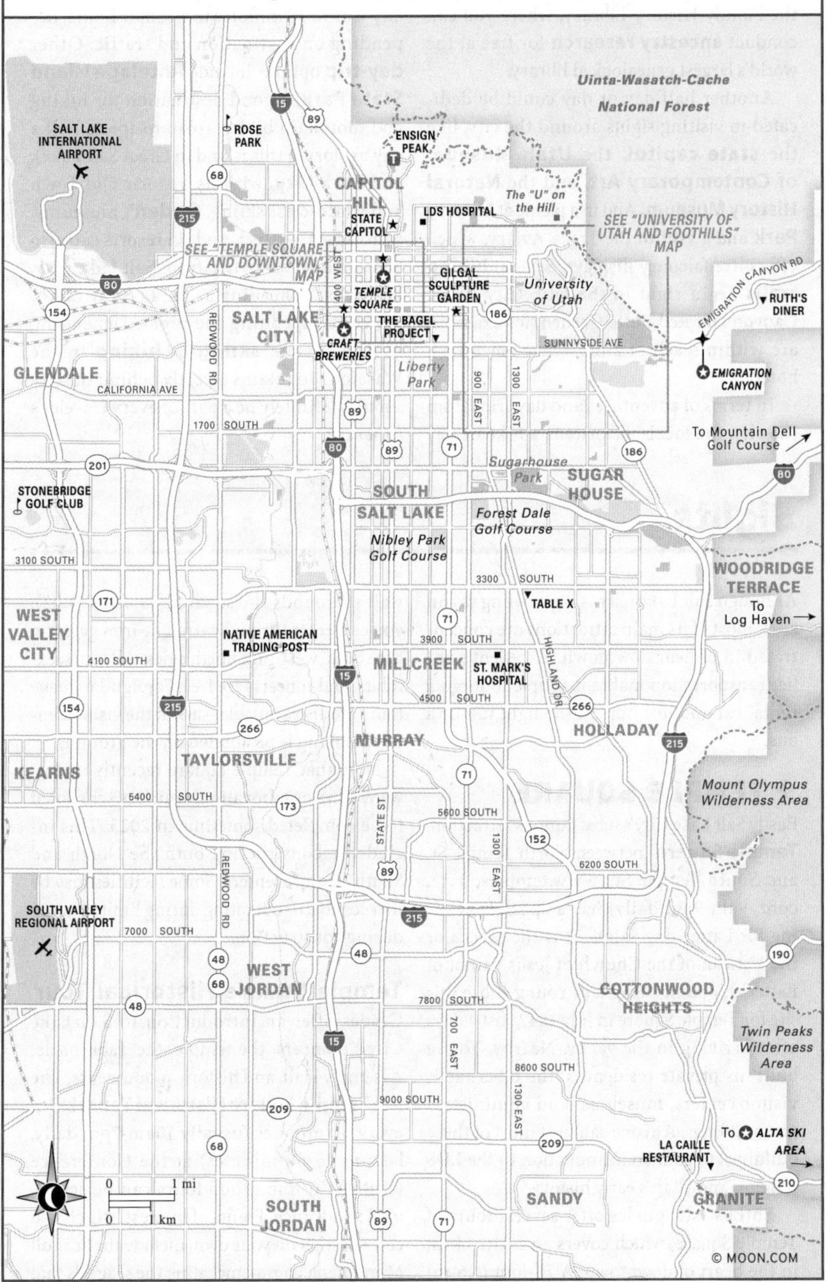
Salt Lake City
Uinta-Wasatch-Cache National Forest
SALT LAKE INTERNATIONAL AIRPORT
ROSE PARK
ENSIGN PEAK
CAPITOL HILL
STATE CAPITOL
LDS HOSPITAL
The "U" on the Hill
SEE "UNIVERSITY OF UTAH AND FOOTHILLS" MAP
SEE "TEMPLE SQUARE AND DOWNTOWN" MAP
400 WEST
TEMPLE SQUARE
GILGAL SCULPTURE GARDEN
University of Utah
EMIGRATION CANYON RD
RUTH'S DINER
SALT LAKE CITY
THE BAGEL PROJECT
CRAFT BREWERIES
REDWOOD RD
SUNNYSIDE AVE
EMIGRATION CANYON
GLENDALE
Liberty Park
CALIFORNIA AVE
900 EAST
1300 EAST
1700 SOUTH
To Mountain Dell Golf Course
Sugarhouse Park
SUGAR HOUSE
STONEBRIDGE GOLF CLUB
SOUTH SALT LAKE
Forest Dale Golf Course
Nibley Park Golf Course
3100 SOUTH
3300 SOUTH
WOODRIDGE TERRACE
TABLE X
To Log Haven
WEST VALLEY CITY
NATIVE AMERICAN TRADING POST
3900 SOUTH
4100 SOUTH
MILLCREEK
ST. MARK'S HOSPITAL
HIGHLAND DR
4500 SOUTH
HOLLADAY
MURRAY
TAYLORSVILLE
KEARNS
Mount Olympus Wilderness Area
5400 SOUTH
5600 SOUTH
STATE ST
6200 SOUTH
SOUTH VALLEY REGIONAL AIRPORT
7000 SOUTH
WEST JORDAN
7800 SOUTH
COTTONWOOD HEIGHTS
700 EAST
Twin Peaks Wilderness Area
8600 SOUTH
9000 SOUTH
To ALTA SKI AREA
LA CAILLE RESTAURANT
SANDY
GRANITE
SOUTH JORDAN
0 1 mi
0 1 km
© MOON.COM

hours to a full day visiting Temple Square, including its museums, historic sites, and even the Family History Library, where you can conduct **ancestry research** for free at the world's largest genealogical library.

Another half day or day could be dedicated to visiting sights around the city, like the **state capitol,** the **Utah Museum of Contemporary Art,** and the **Natural History Museum.** Add in a picnic at **Liberty Park** and a visit to the Tracy Aviary, which offers live falconry displays. Several **hiking trails** begin right in the city: City Creek Canyon and Red Butte Garden, for example, are within reach of almost any downtown hotel.

In terms of adventures and day trips from the city, the locals' favorite is a hike or day of skiing up **Big or Little Cottonwood Canyons,** which can be reached from the city within 30 minutes to a couple hours, depending on destination and traffic. Other **day-trip** options include **Antelope Island State Park,** a good destination for hiking and mountain biking (plan to spend half a day exploring this island in Great Salt Lake), and **Park City,** with its historic Old Town and world-class skiing. **Ogden**'s museums, historic main street, and ski resorts can also be visited as a side trip from Salt Lake City, but if you're heading as far as **Bear Lake,** it's worth spending the night. Depending on the season, **skiing** or **hiking** in the Wasatch Mountains directly behind the city should definitely be a part of every traveler's itinerary.

Sights

Although Salt Lake City is a sprawling urban area, most of its main attractions are concentrated in or near downtown. Excellent public transportation makes it simple to forgo a rental car and just hop on the light rail or a bus.

★ TEMPLE SQUARE

Easily Salt Lake City's most famous attraction, **Temple Square** (between North Temple St. and South Temple St., www.templesquare.com, 9am-9pm daily) has a special meaning for Latter-day Saints: It is the Mecca or the Vatican of the Church of Jesus Christ of Latter-day Saints. Brigham Young chose this site for Temple Square in July 1847, just 4 days after arriving in the valley. Nearby, Young built his private residences, the tabernacle, visitor centers, museums, and administrative buildings. Anyone can visit most of these buildings to gain an introduction to the LDS religion and Utah's early history.

Enthusiastic guides offer several tours of Temple Square, which covers an entire block in the heart of downtown. A 15-foot (4.6-m) wall surrounds the square's 10 acres (4 ha); you can enter through wrought-iron gates on the south, west, and north sides. All tours, exhibits, and concerts are free. Foreign-language tours are also available—ask at the visitor center. Smoking is prohibited on the grounds.

Note that Temple Square recently underwent a major renovation, which is scheduled to be completed sometime in 2025. This included reconstructing both the North and South Visitor Centers. Some facilities may be inaccessible or operating during limited hours during construction.

Temple Square Historical Tour

Guides offer an introduction to Salt Lake City's pioneers, the temple, the Tabernacle, Assembly Hall, and historic monuments. The free **Temple Square Historical Tours** begin every 30 minutes (usually 10am-7pm daily, lasting 45-60 minutes) at the Conference Center. Custom group tours can be scheduled in advance. Points of interest, which you can also visit on your own, include the Seagull Monument, commemorating the seagulls that

Temple Square and Downtown

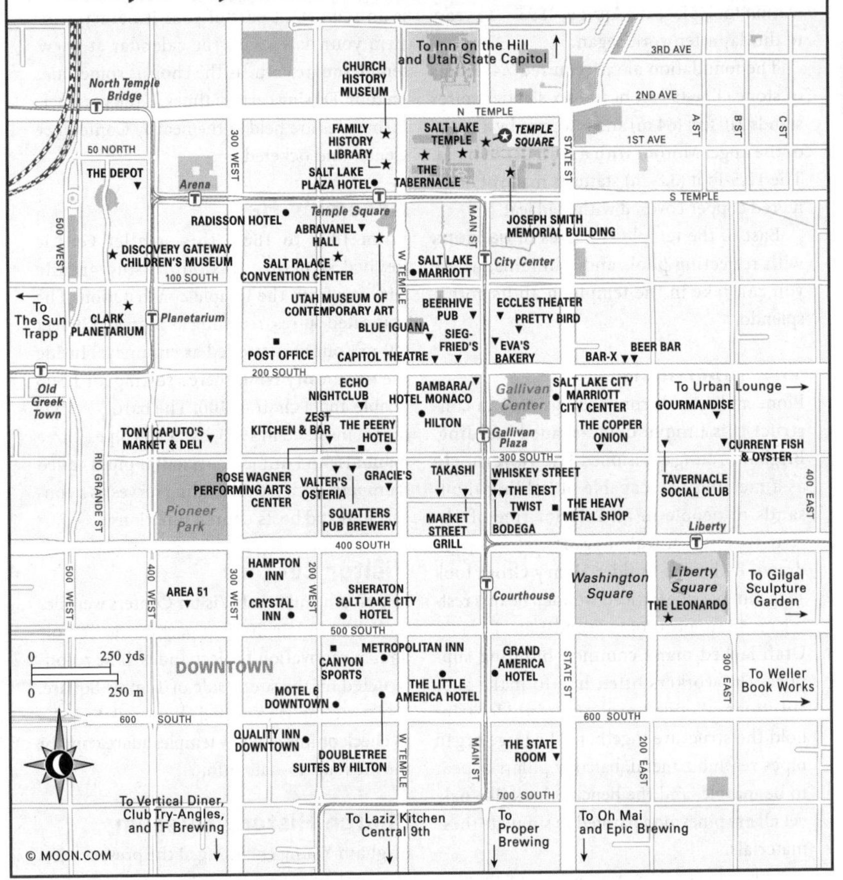

devoured the cricket plague in 1848; a bell from the abandoned Nauvoo Temple; sculptures of Christ, church leaders, and handcart pioneers; an astronomy observation site; and a meridian marker (outside the walls at Main St. and South Temple St.) from which surveyors mapped out Utah.

The Salt Lake Temple and Gardens

According to the LDS faith, baptisms, marriages, and other family ceremonies that take place inside a temple will last beyond death and into eternity, and the **Salt Lake Temple** is used only for these special functions. Regular Sunday services take place in local stake or ward buildings—in fact, the temple is closed on Sundays. Only LDS members in good standing may enter the temple, but you can get a good look at the temple's east facade from the Main Street gates.

While the plan for Salt Lake City's temple came to Brigham Young as a vision when he still lived in Illinois, construction officially commenced in 1853 with help from church architect Truman O. Angell. Workers chiseled granite blocks from Little Cottonwood Canyon, 20 miles (32 km) southeast of the city, then hauled them with oxen and later by rail for shaping at the temple site. The temple dedication took place on April 6, 1893—40 years to the day after work began.

The foundation alone required 7,478 tons of stone. The tallest of the six slender spires stands 210 feet (64 m) and is topped by a statue of the angel Moroni with a trumpet in hand. The 12.5-foot (3.8-m) statue is made of hammered copper covered with gold leaf.

East of the temple are acres of **gardens** with reflecting pools and fountains, where you can take in the temple in all its gothic splendor.

The Tabernacle

Pioneers labored from 1863 to 1867 to construct this unique dome-shaped building. Brigham Young envisioned **The Tabernacle** as a meeting hall capable of holding thousands of people in an interior free of obstructing structural supports. His design, drawn by bridge-builder Henry Grow, took shape in massive latticed wooden beams resting on 44 supports of red sandstone. Because Utah lacked many common building supplies, the workers often had to make substitutions. Wooden pegs and rawhide strips hold the structure together. The large organ pipes resemble metal, balcony pillars appear to be marble, and the benches look like oak, yet all are pinewood painted to simulate these materials.

The Tabernacle is renowned for its phenomenal acoustics, thanks to its smooth arched ceiling. Its massive pipe organ is regarded as one of the finest ever built. From 700 pipes when constructed in 1867, the organ has grown to about 12,000 pipes, five manuals, and one pedal keyboard. **Daily recitals** (www.thetabernaclechoir.org, noon and 2pm Mon.-Sat., 2pm Sun.) demonstrate the instrument's capabilities. The renowned **Mormon Tabernacle Choir,** 360 voices strong, is heard on the Sunday-morning national radio show *Music and the Spoken Word.* Visitors can attend choir rehearsals at 7:30pm Thursday or the broadcast performance at 9:30am Sunday (be seated by 9:15am); both are free. If attending performances in the Tabernacle is an important part of your itinerary, confirm your dates with the calendar at www.templesquare.com, as the choir is sometimes on tour. During certain times of the year, performances are held at the nearby Conference Center and ticketed.

Assembly Hall

From 1877 to 1882, this smaller Gothic Revival structure was built using granite left over from the temple construction. The truncated spires, reaching as high as 130 feet (40 m), once functioned as chimneys. Inside the **Assembly Hall,** there's seating for 1,500 people and a choir of 100. The baroque-style organ, installed in 1983, has 3,500 pipes, three manuals, and unique horizontal pipes called trumpets. Today, the building serves as a concert hall and hosts church functions.

Visitor Centers

The North and South Visitor Centers were demolished in late 2021 as part of the Temple Square renovation project and will be reconstructed on the south side of Temple Square. Construction is expected through late 2025, so check online at www.templesquare.com for the most up-to-date info.

Church History Museum

Brigham Young encouraged the preservation of church history, especially when he saw that Salt Lake City's pioneering era was drawing to a close. The **Church History Museum** (45 N. West Temple St., 801/240-3310, 10am-6pm Mon. and Fri.-Sat., 10am-8pm Tues.-Thurs., closed most federal holidays, free) houses a collection of church artifacts that includes the plow that cut the first furrows in Great Salt Lake Valley. Perhaps the most striking piece is the gilded 11.5-foot (3.5-m) statue of Moroni that crowned a Washington, DC chapel from 1933 to 1976. Step outside to see the 1847 log cabin, one of only two surviving from

1: Temple Square **2:** the dome-shaped Tabernacle

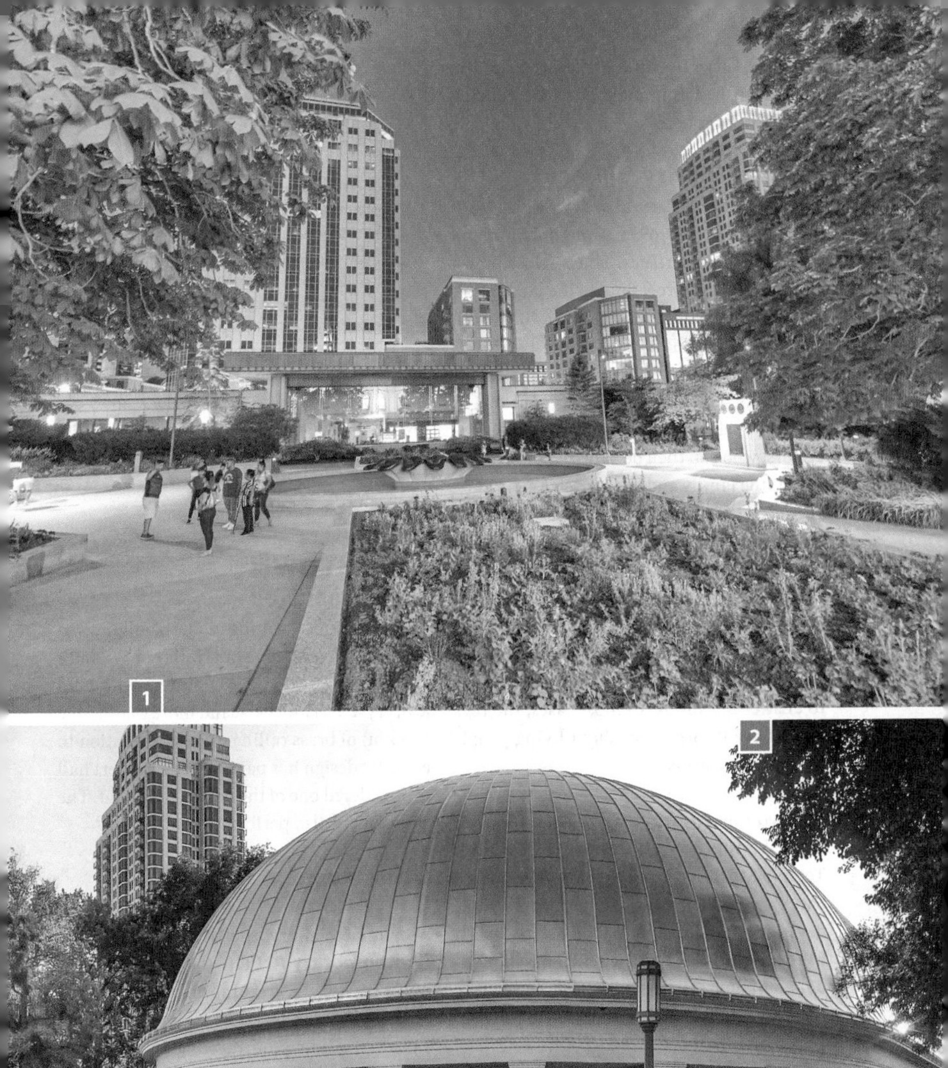

Salt Lake City's beginnings. The interior has been furnished as it might have been during the first winter here.

Family History Library

The **Family History Library** (35 N. West Temple St., 801/240-6996, 9am-6pm Mon. and Fri.-Sat., 9am-8pm Tues.-Thurs., closed most federal holidays, free) houses the largest collection of genealogical records in the world. Library workers have made extensive travels to many countries to microfilm documents and books. The LDS Church has gone to this effort to enable members to identify their ancestors, who can then be baptized by proxy to seal in the family and the church for eternity. However, the spirits for whom these baptisms are performed are said to have a choice of accepting or rejecting the baptism.

The library is open to the public. If you'd like to research your family tree, bring any information you have and get the library's booklet *A Guide to Research.* Staff is on hand to answer questions. In most cases, the files won't have information about living people for privacy reasons.

If you are new to genealogical investigation, you may want to start your research at the **FamilySearch Center** (15 E. South Temple St., 801/240-4085, 8am-8pm Mon.-Sat., 1pm-8pm Sun., closed most federal holidays), on the main floor in the **Joseph Smith Memorial Building.** The center has individual computer stations with access to family history resources, and staff is available to help you free of charge.

Eagle Gate

A modern replacement for the original 1859 gate, the **Eagle Gate** spans State Street just north of South Temple Street. It once marked the entrance to Brigham Young's property, which included City Creek Canyon. The bronze eagle has a 20-foot (6.1-m) wingspan and weighs two tons. The present gate, designed by Brigham Young's grandson, architect George Cannon Young, was dedicated in 1963.

Salt Lake City Connect Pass

If "all of the above" is your approach to trip-planning, consider investing in a **Connect Pass** (www.visitsaltlake.com) to gain entrance to 18 attractions, including the Natural History Museum, Red Butte Garden, and Hogle Zoo, as well as a few outside the city, like Thanksgiving Point and Utah Olympic Park. Ambitious visitors can cram as many activities as possible with a 1-day pass ($55 adults, $45 ages 3-12) or opt for 2- and 3-day passes for a little more. After purchase online, passes show up on a smartphone or can be printed.

DOWNTOWN

Abravanel Hall

One of the most striking modern buildings in Salt Lake City, **Abravanel Hall** (123 W. South Temple St., 801/355-2787) glitters with gold leaf, crystal chandeliers, and more than a mile (1.6 km) of brass railing. Careful attention to acoustic design has paid off: The concert hall is considered one of the best in the world. The Utah Opera also performs here.

Utah Museum of Contemporary Art

A civic art gallery, the **Utah Museum of Contemporary Art** (20 S. West Temple St., 801/328-4201, www.utahmoca.org, 11am-6pm Wed.-Sat., suggested $8 donation) hosts a changing lineup of traveling and thematic exhibits, including painting, photography, sculpture, ceramics, and conceptual art. Diverse art classes and workshops are scheduled along with films, lectures, poetry readings, concerts, and theater.

Salt Palace Convention Center

The enormous **Salt Palace Convention Center** (along West Temple St., between 200 South and South Temple St., 801/534-4777) is one of the largest convention centers in the West, with 515,000 square feet (47,845 sq m) of exhibit space and 164,000 square feet (15,236 sq m) of meeting space, including a 45,000-square-foot (4,181-sq-m) ballroom and 66 meeting rooms. Even in the sprawling scale of downtown Salt Lake City, this is a big building. The center houses the Salt Lake Convention and Visitors Bureau and the **Visitor Information Center** (90 S. West Temple St., 801/534-4900, www.visitsaltlake.com, 10am-5pm Mon.-Sat.).

Clark Planetarium

A planetarium and science center, the **Clark Planetarium** (110 S. 400 W., 801/456-7827, www.clarkplanetarium.org, 10am-7pm Sun.-Thurs., 10am-10:45pm Fri.-Sat., check website for hours of the Hansen Dome Theatre, most exhibits free, IMAX movies $9), in the Gateway shopping center, offers a 3D IMAX theater with a five-story screen, plus popular family-oriented science and space exhibits. Don't miss a show at the Hansen Dome Theatre, which employs state-of-the-art technology to project a star show on a 360-degree 55-foot (17-m) dome. Also in the Star Theatre are *Cosmic Light Shows,* which combine computer animation, special effects, and a 12,000-watt digital surround-sound system.

The Leonardo

A contemporary museum of science and culture, **The Leonardo** (209 E. 500 S., 801/531-9800, www.theleonardo.org, 10am-7pm Tues.-Sat., general admission $12 adults, $9 seniors, students, and military, $8 ages 3-12; tickets to special exhibitions may be extra) is housed in the former Salt Lake City Public Library. The Leo, as it's called, has permanent exhibits on science, technology, engineering, art, and math but is largely known for hosting traveling exhibits such as the *Dead Sea Scrolls* and *Van Gogh 360.*

Gilgal Gardens

Take a turn down a random alley in a residential neighborhood and discover some of the strangest sculptures in Salt Lake City—or just about anywhere. **Gilgal Sculpture Garden** (749 E. 500 S., 801/972-7860, http://gilgalgarden.org, 8am-8pm daily Apr.-Sept., 9am-5pm daily Oct.-Mar., free) was the passion project of mason and LDS bishop Thomas Battersby Child Jr., who worked on the 12 sculptures and 70 stone engravings from 1945 right up until his dying day in 1963.

The small garden takes its name from a biblical site where Israelites camped, likely translated from a Hebrew word for "circle of stones." You'll find everything from a quartzite sphinx to a face and body parts strewn across moss-covered stone (a giant in the biblical King Nebuchadnezzar's dream). While many of the Gilgal carvings are religiously inspired, the garden has an eclectic vibe that appeals to the religious, the spiritual, and the agnostic alike.

SOUTH OF DOWNTOWN

Liberty Park

Southeast of downtown, the large **Liberty Park** (bounded by 900 South, 1300 South, 500 East, and 700 East) is the jewel of the city's public park system with recreational facilities, the Tracy Aviary, a small contemporary folk-art museum (free), and 80 acres (32 ha) of grass and shaded boulevards. A fun addition to the park is a conceptual "map" of northern Utah that re-creates the rivers, lakes, and mountains as a series of fountains and wading pools.

The **Children's Garden**—a playground, amusement park, snack bar, and pond with rental boats (all spring-fall)—sits in the southeast corner of the park. The tennis center on the park's west side offers 16 lighted courts and instruction; an outdoor swimming pool adjacent to the tennis center is open in summer.

Tracy Aviary

Birds have taken over the southwest corner of Liberty Park. **Tracy Aviary** (589 E. 1300 S., 801/596-8500, www.tracyaviary.org, 9am-5pm daily, open until 8pm on Mon. June-Aug., $13 adults, $11 students, seniors, and military, $9 ages 3-12) houses more than 400 birds of 135 species and offers shows with trained free-flying birds such as falcons. Birds on display include majestic golden and bald eagles, showy flamingos and peacocks, the hyacinthine macaw (the world's largest parrot), the golden pheasant of China, and hundreds more. Emus from Australia prance across fields, while ducks, swans, and other waterfowl keep to the ponds. You'll also get to meet Utah's only native vulture: the turkey vulture.

Bird shows, which can include demonstrations or bird identification lessons, are usually held Tuesday-Sunday. They change from day to day and season to season, so check the website to verify what's scheduled.

The Chase Mill

Just north of the aviary entrance, the Chase Mill was built by Isaac Chase in 1852 and is one of the oldest buildings in the valley. Free flour from the mill saved many families during the famine of 1856-1857. The mill is open daily as a historic monument. Formal gardens are north of the mill.

CAPITOL HILL

State Capitol

Utah's granite **State Capitol** (300 North and State St., 801/538-3000, http://utahstatecapitol.utah.gov, 7am-8pm Mon.-Thurs., 7am-6pm Fri.-Sun. and holidays) occupies a prominent spot on a hill just north of downtown, and anyone can visit during operating hours for a self-guided tour. The architectural style may look familiar: The building was patterned after the national capitol. The interior, with its Ionic columns, is made of polished marble from Georgia.

Murals depict early explorers and pioneers. Smaller paintings and statues show all the territorial and state governors, along with prominent Utah figures of the past. The Gold Room, used for receiving dignitaries, provides a formal setting graced by chandeliers, wall tapestries, elegant furniture, and cherubs on the ceiling. Enter the chambers of the House of Representatives, Senate, and Supreme Court from the mezzanine. Photo exhibits of the state's scenic and historic spots, mining, agriculture, and beehive memorabilia line hallways on the ground floor.

Forty acres (16 ha) of manicured parks and monuments surround the capitol. From the steps leading to the building, you can look out over Salt Lake City and straight down State Street, which runs south about 28 miles (45 km) without a curve. From near the Mormon Battalion Monument, east of the capitol, steps lead down into a small canyon and **Memory Grove,** another war memorial, and a series of streamside parks.

Ensign Peak

Just over a mile (1.6 km) north of the Utah State Capitol lies the trailhead for **Ensign Peak** (1.8 mi/2.9 km out-and-back, 380 ft/116 m elevation gain, easy). This short trail travels to the top of the mini mountain due north of the capitol building. At the top of Ensign Peak, take in sweeping views of the city from the point at which Brigham Young once stood upon arriving in the area. This makes for a great spot to take in the sunset and, soon after, the lights of downtown below. To access the trailhead, travel north on East Capitol Boulevard for about a mile (1.6 km) and turn left on Ensign Vista Drive; the trailhead is on your right.

Council Hall

The venerable **Council Hall** lies across the street from the capitol. Dedicated in 1866, the brick building served as the city hall and a meeting place for the territorial and early state legislatures. Council Hall used to stand downtown before being moved here in 1963. It is now the home of the **Utah Office of Tourism** (www.visitutah.com).

UNIVERSITY OF UTAH AND FOOTHILLS

University of Utah

In 1850, just two-and-a-half years after reaching the Salt Lake Valley, the first colonists established the University of Deseret, using

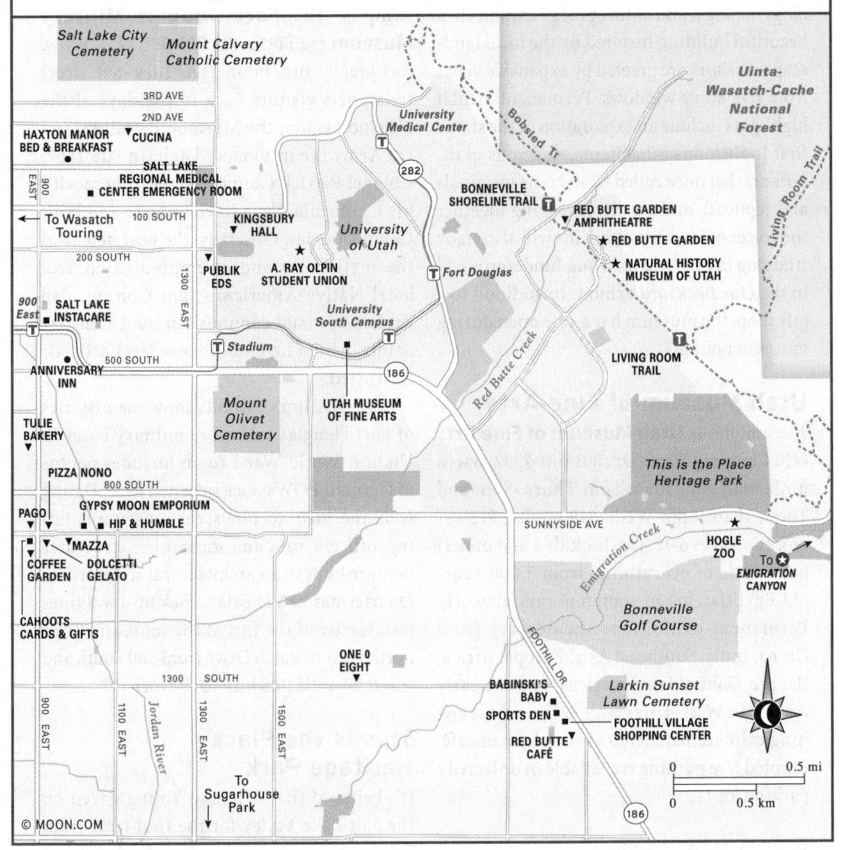

books they'd brought along from Nauvoo, Illinois. It was renamed the **University of Utah** (201 Presidents Circle, 801/581-7200) in 1892 and now has a 1,500-acre (607-ha) campus.

Over 32,000 students are enrolled within its 18 colleges and schools. The adjacent **Research Park** is a partnership of the university and private enterprise. Visitors are welcome at cultural and sporting events, libraries, the bookstore, the movie theater, and Olpin Union food services. Most recreational facilities are reserved for students. For a campus map, a list of scheduled events, and other information, drop by the **Park Building** (801/581-6515) at the top of President's Circle, or the **Olpin Union** (801/581-5888), just north of Central Campus Drive. Limited on-campus parking is available at metered spots and in pay lots next to the Olpin Union and the Marriott Library. Free parking can be found off campus on residential streets.

Utah Museum of Natural History

The impressive **Utah Museum of Natural History** (301 Wakara Way, 801/581-6927, http://nhmu.utah.edu, 10am-5pm Thurs.-Tues., 10am-9pm Wed., $20 adults, $18 ages

13-24 and over age 64, $15 ages 3-12, free 2 and under) has an excellent collection of geology, biology, and anthropology exhibits in a beautiful building inspired by the local landscape. Visitors are greeted by expansive views from five-story windows. Permanent exhibit highlights include an exploration of the state's first Indigenous inhabitants, skeletons of dinosaurs that once called Utah home (originals and replicas), and a gallery weaving together the voices of Utah's tribes. Kids will also enjoy studying insects and crawling "underground" in the *Our Backyard* exhibit. In addition to a gift shop, the museum has a café open during museum hours.

Utah Museum of Fine Arts

The ambitious **Utah Museum of Fine Arts** (410 Campus Center Dr., 801/581-7332, www.umfa.utah.edu, 10am-5pm Thurs.-Sun. and Tues., 10am-8pm Wed., $18 adults, $15 seniors and ages 6-18, free for kids 5 and under) has a little of everything, from 5,000-year-old Egyptian art to contemporary artwork. Permanent exhibitions include art from China, India, Southeast Asia, Europe, Africa, the pre-Columbian Americas, and the early American West. Three large galleries host visiting exhibitions; there's also a pleasant café. Limited free parking is available in university parking lot 11.

Red Butte Garden and Arboretum

Utah's largest botanical garden, the **Red Butte Garden and Arboretum** (300 Wakara Way, 801/581-4747, www.redbuttegarden.org, 9am-9pm daily May-Aug., 9am-7:30pm daily Apr. and Sept., 9am-5pm daily Oct.-Mar., $14 adults, $12 seniors, $7 ages 3-17, free access to hiking trails in the natural area) offers 30 acres (12 ha) of floral displays, ponds, waterfalls, and 4 miles (6.4 km) of mountain nature trails in a 200-acre (81-ha) natural area. The garden visitor center features botanical gifts and books, and the Courtyard Garden is an excellent place for a family picnic.

Fort Douglas Military Museum

On the outskirts of the University of Utah campus, the **Fort Douglas Military Museum** (32 Potter St., 801/581-1251, www.fortdouglas.org, noon-5pm Tues.-Sat., free) transports visitors back to the days of the Nauvoo Legion, the Mormon Battalion, and US Army life in pioneer Utah. In late 1862, Colonel Patrick Connor marched here with his California-Nevada volunteers and built Camp Douglas. Officially, the post defended the mail route and attempted to control local Native Americans, but Connor also kept an eye (and cannons) on the Latter-day Saints, whom he and other federal officials distrusted.

The museum's exhibits show the histories of Fort Douglas and other military bases in Utah. A World War I room includes photos of German POWs once interned here. Dating from the 1870s to 1880s, the museum building, officers' row, and some other structures here are built in an architectural style termed Quartermaster Victorian. Pick up a walking-tour leaflet of the fort at the museum. Turn north onto Wasatch Drive from 500 South and travel 0.5 mile (0.8 km) to the fort.

This Is the Place Heritage Park

It's believed that Brigham Young gazed on the Salt Lake Valley for the first time from this spot, now known as **This Is the Place Heritage Park** (2601 Sunnyside Ave., 801/582-1847, www.thisistheplace.org, park and visitor center 10am-5pm Mon.-Sat., $19 adults, $17 seniors, $15 ages 3-11), southeast of the University of Utah near the mouth of Emigration Canyon. Young then said, "This is the right place. Drive on." Exactly 100 years later, on July 24, 1947, a crowd gathered to dedicate *This Is the Place* monument. The park has 12-foot (3.7-m) bronze statues of Young and other church leaders, a pleasant picnic area, and a monument honoring not only the LDS pioneers, but also the Catholic missionaries from Spain, fur trappers, government explorers, and California immigrants who helped found an empire in "the top of the mountains."

The main attraction, however, is a family-oriented re-created Utah pioneer village. Springtime here is known as "baby animal season." In summer, it comes alive with farming and crafts demonstrations and wagon and pony rides. In addition, three mini trains loop around the park. Most of the two dozen buildings that were moved here are originals, some of the first in the valley. Some notable structures include Brigham Young's Forest farmhouse and the Charles Rich house, designed in the 1850s for polygamous family living.

Hogle Zoo

Utah's state zoo, **Hogle Zoo** (2600 E. Sunnyside Ave., 801/584-1700, www.hoglezoo.org, 9am-6pm daily, $22 adults, $18 ages 3-12, winter fees $2 lower), is on the eastern edge of town across from This Is the Place Heritage Park. Kids can ride the **miniature train** (spring-fall, $3) and see the *African Safari* exhibit. The elephants, rhinos, and many other large-animal enclosures have natural settings. A few highlights include the polar bears and sea lions of the *Rocky Shores* exhibit, and an endangered red panda in the *Asian Highlands* exhibit.

Sports and Recreation

All you need to do is look around to get a sense of just how close the mountains and the adventures therein are to the city. Even on a short visit to the Salt Lake area, you can enjoy a hike or bike ride up a mountain canyon.

PARKS

For information about the city's park system, contact the Parks and Recreation office (801/972-7800, www.slcgov.com/cityparks); for county park information, call 801/468-2560 (https://slco.org/parks).

City Creek Canyon

In the city itself, a pleasant route for a stroll or jog follows **City Creek Canyon,** a shady stream-filled ravine just east of the state capitol. The narrow road that runs up the canyon extends more than 5 miles (8 km), and gains over 750 feet (229 m) in elevation, from its beginning at Memory Grove, just northeast of the intersection of East North Temple Street and State Street, to Rotary Park at the top of the canyon. Since pioneer days, people have obtained precious water from City Creek and enjoyed its diverse vegetation, wildlife, and scenery. Because City Creek is still part of the city's water supply, regulations exclude dogs, horses, and overnight camping. You can walk dogs here, but they must be on leash at all times.

The big attraction for many visitors is a stop at one of the picnic areas along the road. Picnickers can reserve sites (801/483-6705). Sites are sometimes available on a first-come, first-served basis; midweek is best. Picnic permits cost $3 and up, depending on the size of the group.

Hikers and runners may travel on the road anytime. In summer (Memorial Day-Sept. 30), bicyclists may enter only on odd-numbered days. Motorized vehicles are allowed on holidays and on even-numbered days during summer; a gate at the bottom controls entry. During the rest of the year, no motorized vehicles are allowed, but cyclists can use the road daily (except for a brief pause for deer-hunting season), weather permitting. A $3 charge applies if you drive through to the trailhead at the upper end (no reservation needed).

Liberty Park

There are many reasons to hang out at **Liberty Park** (bounded by 900 South, 1300 South, 500 East, and 700 East, 801/538-2062), southeast of downtown, including Tracy Aviary, a kids' play area, and acres of shade and lawn. The park also has a tennis center

NATURAL HISTORY MUSEUM OF UTAH
RIO TINTO CENTER · THE UNIVERSITY OF
1
FAMILY HISTORY
2
3
UTAH'S HOGLE ZOO

Salt Lake City for Kids

DISCOVERY GATEWAY

You'll find engaging interactive activities designed to inspire learning and fun at the **Discovery Gateway Children's Museum** (Gateway complex, 444 W. 100 S., 801/456-5437, www.discoverygateway.org, 10am-6pm Mon. and Wed.-Sat., noon-6pm Sun., $13.50 adults, $12.50 kids). Kids get to put on plays, host the morning TV news, make short, animated films, and engage in many other activities. They can also take part in a mock Life Flight, or rescue operation, in an authentic life-size helicopter.

LAGOON AMUSEMENT PARK AND PIONEER VILLAGE

History, recreation, and rides come together at **Lagoon Amusement Park and Pioneer Village** (375 Lagoon Dr., Farmington, 801/451-8000, www.lagoonpark.com), 16 miles (26 km) north of Salt Lake City. Lagoon traces its history back to 1887, when bathers came to Lake Park on the shores of Great Salt Lake, 2 miles (3.2 km) west of its present location. The vast Lagoon Amusement Park area includes roller-coaster rides, a giant Ferris wheel, and other midway favorites. There are also musical performances and miniature golf. Lagoon A Beach provides thrilling waterslides and landscaped pools.

Pioneer Village brings the past alive with authentic 19th-century buildings, stagecoach and steam train rides, a Ute museum, a carriage museum, and many other exhibits. Wild West shootouts take place several times daily. Food booths are scattered throughout the park, or you can dine at the Gaslight Restaurant near the Opera House.

Hours vary depending on month and whether it's a weekday or weekend, but the park usually opens at 10am and closes anywhere between 6pm and 11pm. Lagoon is also closed seasonally November-late March, and mostly only operates on weekends March-May and mid-August-October. Check online for the most updated schedule. An all-day ride pass is $93 from 48 inches tall to 65 years old, $88 for seniors, and $75 for those under 48 inches tall. The all-day pass includes Lagoon A Beach, but be prepared to pay extra for special rides (although plenty of rides are included in the day pass). Parking is $20. Take I-15 to the Lagoon exit and follow the signs.

WHEELER HISTORIC FARM

Kids will enjoy a visit to the **Wheeler Historic Farm** (6351 S. 900 E., Murray, 385/468-1755, https://slco.org/wheeler-farm, dawn-dusk daily, free admission) to experience milking cows, gathering eggs, churning butter, and feeding animals. The farm also hosts hayrides in summer, sleigh rides in winter, a pumpkin patch in fall, and a summer Sunday market. Henry and Sariah Wheeler started the farm in 1886 and developed it into a prosperous dairy and ice-making operation. Tour guides take you through the Wheelers' restored Victorian house, built 1896-1898, the first in the county with an indoor bathroom (tours 11am and 1pm Mon.-Fri. May-Oct., $4 adults, $2 ages 3-12). The Rosebud Country Store sells crafts and snacks.

The Salt Lake County Recreation Department operates the farm and offers special programs for both youngsters and adults. There's no admission charged to visit the farm, but you'll pay for individual activities.

on the west side with 16 lighted courts, and an adjacent outdoor swimming pool that's open in summer. During the sweltering Salt Lake summer, the shady boulevards provide a cool spot for jogging. You'll find horseshoe pits to the north of the park's historic Chase House.

1: Utah Museum of Natural History 2: Family History Library 3: Hogle Zoo

Sugarhouse Park

On the southeast edge of the city, LDS pioneers began manufacturing beet sugar in 1851 at **Sugarhouse Park** (1300 East and 2100 South, 801/467-1721)—the unprofitable venture was ultimately abandoned. Today, expanses of rolling grassland in this 113-acre (46-ha) park are ideal for picnics, strolling, and running. The park has a playground and fields for baseball, soccer, and football. In winter, the hills provide good sledding and tubing. A lake attracts seagulls and other birds. Sweet scents rise from the Memorial Rose Garden in the northeast corner.

Mill Creek Canyon

Great mountain biking, picnic areas, and hiking possibilities lie along Mill Creek, just outside Salt Lake City. You can bring your dog along, too—this is one of the few canyons where pets are welcome. In fact, odd-numbered days are designated leash-free here. Obey posted regulations when you begin your hike. Bicycles are allowed in Mill Creek Canyon only on even-numbered days, the days when dogs must be leashed. A $3 fee is collected as you exit the canyon. Reach Mill Creek Canyon Road from 3800 Wasatch Boulevard.

Picnic sites are free and available on a first-come, first-served basis; most lack water. The first one, **Church Fork Picnic Area,** is 3 miles (4.8 km) in at an elevation of 5,700 feet (1,737 m); **Big Water Picnic Area** is the last, 8.8 miles (14.1 km) up at an elevation of 7,500 feet (2,286 m).

HIKING

A popular hike from the trailhead at City Creek Canyon Road's end (elev. 6,050 ft/1,844 m) is **City Creek Meadows,** 4 miles (6.4 km) away and 2,000 feet (610) higher. After 1.5 miles (2.4 km), you'll pass Cottonwood Gulch on the left; a side trail leads up the gulch to an old mining area. After another 0.5 mile (0.8 km) on the main trail, a spring off to the right in a small meadow is the last reliable source of drinking water. During the next mile, the trail grows steeper and winds through aspen groves, then passes two shallow ponds. The trail becomes indistinct here, but you can continue 1 mile (1.6 km) northeast to the meadows (elev. 8,000 ft/2,438 m); maps and compass will help. For splendid views of the Wasatch Range, climb north 0.5 mile (0.8 km) from the meadows up the ridge to where Davis, Salt Lake, and Morgan Counties meet. Hikers also enjoy shorter strolls from the trailhead along the gentle lower section of trail.

Salt Lake Overlook on Mill Creek Canyon's **Desolation Trail** is a good hiking destination for families. The trail climbs 1,200 vertical feet in 2 miles (3.2 km), gaining views of Salt Lake Valley. Begin from the lower end of Box Elder Picnic Area (elev. 5,760 ft/1,756 m), on the south side of the road. You can continue on Desolation Trail beyond the overlook to higher country near the timberline and go all the way to Desolation Lake (19 mi/31 km). The trail runs near the ridgeline separating Mill and Big Cottonwood Canyons, connecting with many trails from both canyons. Much of this high country lies in the Mount Olympus Wilderness. See the 7.5-minute topo maps for Mt. Aire and Park City West.

Alexander Basin Trail winds to a beautiful wooded glacial bowl below Gobblers Knob; the trailhead (elev. 7,080 ft/2,158 m) is on the south side of the road, 8 miles (12.9 km) up Mill Creek Canyon, 0.8 mile (1.3 km) beyond Clover Springs Picnic Area. The moderately difficult trail begins by paralleling the road northwest for a few hundred feet, then turns southwest through switchbacks for 1 mile (1.6 km) to the beginning of Alexander Basin (elev. 8,400 ft/2,560 m). The trail to Bowman and Porter Forks turns right here, but continue straight 0.5 mile (0.8 km) for the meadows of the upper basin (elev. 9,000 ft/2,743 m). The limestone rock here contains many fossils, mostly shellfish. From the basin, it's possible to scramble to the summit of Gobblers Knob (elev. 10,246 ft/3,123 m). The name comes from an attempt by mine owners to raise turkeys after their ore played out; the venture ended when bobcats ate all the birds. See the 7.5-minute topo map for Mt. Aire.

TOP EXPERIENCE

ROAD BIKING

★ Emigration Canyon

Arguably the most popular road bike ride in Salt Lake City is the climb up Emigration Canyon (16 mi/26 km round-trip, 1.5-2.5 hours depending on pace, 1,350 ft/411 m elevation gain, difficult). Many begin this out-and-back ride from Rotary Park in the Foothills, but it could easily be started from the University of Utah campus or any point within the city. The smooth road navigates its way east of Salt Lake up a curvy road through residential neighborhoods to the top of Little Mountain Summit, where you can behold Little Dell and East Dell Reservoirs—a glorious sight in fall. Due to the exposure and steep climb, this ride is best done at sunrise or sunset in the summer or in the autumn.

This is the route through which LDS pioneers first arrived in the Salt Lake area. This canyon also serves as a longer, scenic route between Park City and Salt Lake City, and is very popular with road cyclists and runners. From Park City, you can reach the canyon via a direct exit off I-80. In the valley of the canyon sits Little Dell Reservoir, where anglers and picnickers alike come in summer. From Salt Lake City's Foothills just south of the University of Utah campus, Sunnyside Avenue heads east and turns into Emigration Canyon Road, which travels through the canyon.

MOUNTAIN BIKING

Bikers should follow **Alexander Basin Trail** to the end of Mill Creek Canyon Road, then take **Big Water Trail.** At 1.5 miles (2.4 km), Big Water intersects with **Great Western Trail,** which follows a ridgetop 3,000 miles (4,830 km) from Canada to Mexico. Bikers can turn off Big Water Trail and follow Great Western to the ridgetop divide overlooking Park City Mountain Resort. Here, the route turns south and follows **Wasatch Crest Trail** along the ridge and around the head of the upper Mill Creek basin. To avoid conflicts with hikers, Big Water, Little Water, and the Great Western Trail are closed to mountain bikes on odd-numbered days.

WINTER SPORTS

Skiing has always been Utah's biggest recreational draw, and as host of the 2002 Winter Olympics, the Salt Lake City area drew the attention of international skiing and winter sports lovers. Summer visitors will find lots to like after the snow melts, when many ski areas offer lift-serviced mountain biking, hiking, and other warm-weather activities.

Downhill Skiing

Utah's "Greatest Snow on Earth" is close at hand. Within an hour's drive (barring pow day traffic) from Salt Lake City, you can be at one of 10 downhill areas in the Wasatch Range, each with its own character and distinctive terrain. For most resorts, the season runs from about Thanksgiving through mid-April—though one resort in particular has been known to hang on until early July. You'll find great info on passes, tickets, deals, trail maps, lodging, and more for all of Utah's resorts at www.skiutah.com, which is operated by the Utah Ski and Snowboard Association.

Salt Lake City-area ski resorts are grouped quite close together. Although they are in different drainages, Solitude and Brighton in Big Cottonwood Canyon, along with Snowbird and Alta in Little Cottonwood Canyon, all share the high country of the Wasatch Mountains with the ski areas of Park City and Deer Valley. There is no easy or quick route among the three different valleys, however, and traffic and parking can be a massive hassle. Luckily, there are plenty of options for convenient public transportation from Salt Lake City to ski areas and among the resorts themselves.

Alternatively, you can ski between the various ski areas with **Ski Utah Interconnect** (801/534-1907, www.skiutah.com/explore/the-interconnect-tour, $475 per day), which provides a guide service for backcountry touring among Wasatch Front ski areas. Skiers should be experienced and in good physical condition

Renting vs. Demoing Gear

If you're wondering what the difference is between renting and demoing gear—whether for biking or skiing—it boils down to intention and quality. A gear shop's rental stock is usually a little beat up and older, especially at the end of a season, but will do the trick if you just want to get out. For this reason, rentals are less expensive. The idea behind demoing gear is that the user is usually looking to buy and wants to try out some of the latest models before committing to a purchase. Demo stock is thus usually newer and higher quality—and more expensive.

because of the high elevations (around 10,000 ft/3,048 m) and traversing involved. Touring is with downhill equipment. Tours depart daily from Deer Valley or Snowbird, and pass through Park City Mountain, Solitude, Brighton, and Alta. The rates include the guide services, lunch, and all lift tickets.

Cross-Country Skiing

During heavy snowfall, Salt Lake City parks and streets become impromptu cross-country ski trails, and any snowed-under Forest Service road in the Wasatch Range is fair game for cross-country skiers. The **Mill Creek Canyon** Road is a favorite. If you don't mind cutting a trail or skiing ungroomed snow, ask at ski-rental shops for hints on where the backcountry snow is good.

Otherwise, there are numerous groomed cross-country ski areas in the Salt Lake City area. The **Mountain Dell Golf Course** in Parley's Canyon (off I-80 toward Park City) is a favorite place to make tracks. There are cross-country facilities at Alta and Solitude ski resorts, as well as at the White Pine Touring Center and Round Valley in Park City.

GOLF

Salt Lake City claims to have the highest number of golf courses per capita in the nation, with more than a dozen in the metro area. There's a course for every level of expertise, from city-owned 9-hole courses for beginners to championship-level courses like the 27-hole private **Stonebridge Golf Club** (4415 Links Dr., West Valley City, 801/957-9000, www.golfstonebridgeutah.com) and the 36-hole par 71 or 72 public **Mountain Dell Golf Course** (I-80 exit 134, 801/582-3812, www.mountaindellgc.com), each offering challenging terrain and mountain views. Other courses include **Bonneville** (954 Connor St., 801/583-9513, 18 holes, par 72), east of downtown; **Forest Dale** (2375 S. 900 E., 801/483-5420, 9 holes, par 36), near Sugarhouse Park; **Nibley Park** (2730 S. 700 E., 801/483-5418, 9 holes, par 34); **Glendale** (1603 W. 2100 S., 801/974-2403, 18 holes, par 72); and **Rose Park** (1386 N. Redwood Rd., 801/596-5030, 18 holes, par 72), northwest of downtown.

OUTFITTERS

Canyon Sports (517 S. 200 W., 801/322-4220, www.canyonsports.com, 10am-6pm daily, extended hours during ski season Nov.-Apr.) has been in the business of outfitting adventures for over 25 years. This downtown rental shop offers year-round rentals, including ski gear (starting at $30 per day), mountain bikes (starting at $55 per day), tents, and paddleboards (starting at $30 per day). You can also purchase discount ski lift tickets to resorts in the Cottonwood Canyons, as well as get your own gear tuned and repaired.

The story of **Wasatch Touring** (702 E. 100 S., 801/359-9361, www.wasatchtouring.com, 9am-7pm Mon.-Sat., mountain bikes starting at $50 per day, touring skis starting at $45 per day for skis and boots) begins in 1968, when the future owners took a ski trip to Utah and got blissfully socked in by a fierce winter storm at Alta Ski Area. Four years later, they moved to Salt Lake City and opened a backcountry specialty ski rental shop, the first of its kind in the city. Wasatch Touring sells, demos, and rents equipment for skiing, biking, water sports, and more.

Since 1972, **Sports Den** (1350 Foothill Dr., 801/582-5611, www.sportsden.com, 8am-7pm Mon.-Sat., 8am-6pm Sun., mountain bikes starting at $40 per day, ski rentals starting at $30 per day) has been helping people get out on bikes and skis in the Wasatch at competitive prices. With gear for sale, rent, and demo—as well as tuning and repair services—Sports Den is a great one-stop shop for all skiing and biking adventures. The shop also vends discounted tickets to nearby ski resorts, including Deer Valley, Snowbasin, Alta, and Snowbird.

Entertainment and Events

Salt Lake City may not be a world-class destination for music or the arts, but there's a good variety of high-quality arts and cultural institutions. Classical concert halls, choirs, jazz, blues, and alternative music clubs and dance bars are also numerous. In short, there's a lot more going on here than you might think.

Local publications are the best places to check for information on what's happening. The ***City Weekly*** (www.cityweekly.net) is the largest and most comprehensive free newspaper, with ample arts and entertainment coverage. The ***Deseret News*** (www.deseretnews.com) and ***Salt Lake Tribune*** (www.sltrib.com), both have listings in their Friday Weekend and Sunday Art and Entertainment sections. The **Salt Lake Convention and Visitors Bureau** (www.visitsaltlake.com) also has online listings of events and entertainment options.

THE ARTS

Most of Salt Lake City's top-flight music and arts performances are staged in a handful of premier venues. When you know the dates of your visit, check out the **Salt Lake County Center for the Arts** (801/355-2787, https://artsaltlake.org), which handles information and ticketing for most of the city's arts offerings.

One of the city's main performance spaces is the **Capitol Theatre** (50 W. 200 S., 801/344-2787), a glittering vaudeville house from the turn of the 20th century that's been refurbished into an elegant concert hall. **Abravanel Hall** (123 W. South Temple St., between the Salt Palace and Temple Square, 385/468-1010) has world-class acoustics and is home to the Utah Symphony and other classical music performances. The **Rose Wagner Performing Arts Center** (138 W. Broadway, 801/355-2787) has three performance spaces, where several local dance and theater troupes perform.

Downtown, the state-of-the-art **Eccles Theater** (131 S. Main St., 385/468-1010, www.saltlakecountyarts.org/eccles-theater) holds a 2,500-seat hall that hosts touring Broadway shows and other popular events, alongside a black box theater, a six-story grand lobby, and an outdoor plaza and galleria.

In **Temple Square** (800/537-9703), the Tabernacle and the Assembly Hall host various classical and religious concerts, including performances by the famed Mormon Tabernacle Choir.

Theater and Concerts

Pioneer Theatre Company (801/581-6961, www.pioneertheatre.org), one of Salt Lake City's premier theater troupes, offers a seven-show season running September-May. The company performs a mix of contemporary plays, classics, and musicals. Although the company operates from the University of Utah's **Pioneer Memorial Theatre** (300 South and University St.), it is not part of the university itself. The Pioneer Memorial

Theatre is also the site of University of Utah student productions and the Young People's Theatre for children.

The city's cutting-edge theater group is the **Salt Lake Acting Company** (168 W. 500 N., 801/363-7522, www.saltlakeactingcompany.org). This well-established troupe doesn't shy away from controversy: Its excellent production of Tony Kushner's *Angels in America* raised eyebrows and stirred strong reactions. Besides presenting new works from around the world, the company also stages plays by local playwrights.

At the **Desert Star Playhouse** (4861 S. State St., Murray, 801/266-2600, www.desertstar.biz), you'll find musical comedy revues and cabaret-style comedy skits, such as *My Big Fat Utah Wedding* or *Indiana Bones: Raiders of the Wall Mart.*

In June, the **Gina Bachauer Piano Competitions** (801/297-4250, www.bachauer.com) take over Salt Lake City. Competitions are divided into three categories based on age. Dozens of young pianists from around the world compete for recording contracts during a two-week-long series of performances, including with the Utah Symphony for finalists.

Temple Square Concert Series

The free concert series at **Temple Square** (801/240-3323, www.templesquare.com) presents hundreds of performances a year for the public—LDS and non-LDS alike are welcome. You might hear chamber music, a symphony, operatic selections, choral works, piano solos, organ works, a brass band, or a percussion ensemble.

The renowned 360-voice **Mormon Tabernacle Choir** sings at 9:30am Sunday morning (you must be seated by 9:15am and stay the whole time). You can also drop in for the more informal choir rehearsal at 7:30pm on Thursday evenings or catch the Mormon Youth Symphony rehearsals in the Tabernacle 8pm-9:30pm Wednesday evenings and the Youth Chorus rehearsals 8pm-9:30pm Tuesday evenings. June-August and December, rehearsals and broadcasts are held across the street in the Conference Center, which can accommodate the larger summer and Christmas season crowds.

The Temple Square Concert Series presents complimentary hour-long concerts featuring local and international artists at 7:30pm every Friday and Saturday evening in the Assembly Hall. Tickets are not required, but attendees must be age eight and older. June-August, the Temple Square Concert Series presents Concerts in the Park, held in the Brigham Young Historic Park (southeast corner of State St. and 2nd Ave.). These outdoor concerts begin at 7:30pm on Tuesday and Friday evenings.

Organists demonstrate the sounds and versatility of the Tabernacle's famous instrument in 30-minute **organ recitals** (noon and 2pm Mon.-Sat., 2pm Sun.).

Summer Concerts and Festivals

Come summer, Salt Lake City is filled with free concerts at local parks and public spaces. Check local media or the visitor center for details on ongoing concert series.

Gallivan Center Concerts and Films features free evening concerts on Wednesday nights at the downtown Gallivan Center (Main St. and 200 South, 801/535-6110, www.thegallivancenter.com/events.htm).

FESTIVALS AND EVENTS

Concerts, festivals, shows, rodeos, and other special events happen here nearly every day in summer, and the **Salt Lake Convention and Visitors Bureau** (90 S. West Temple St., 801/534-4900, www.visitsaltlake.com) can tell you what's going on. Also check the visitor bureau's *Salt Lake Visitors Guide* for intel on annual happenings.

The first weekends of April and October, the LDS church stages the **General Conference of the Church of Jesus Christ**

1: Eccles Theater 2: a concert at the Gallivan Center

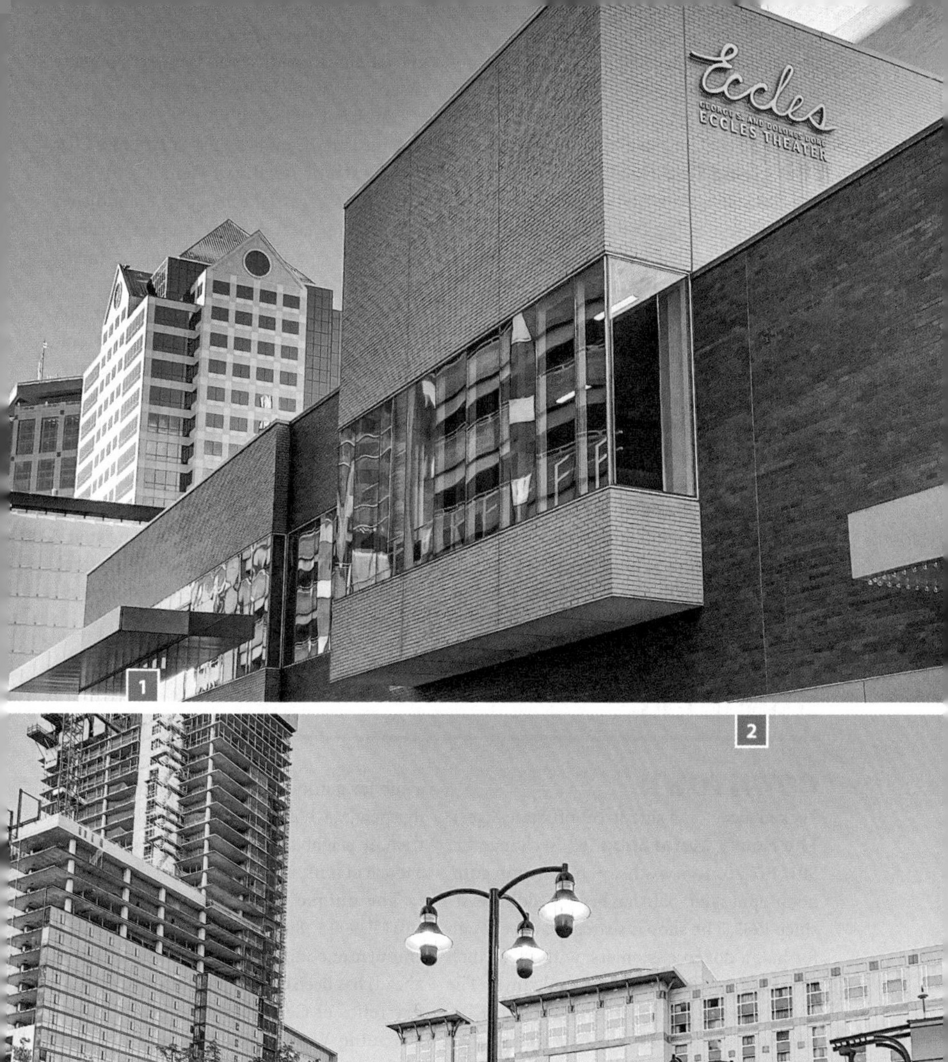
Eccles
GEORGE S. AND DOLORES DORÉ
ECCLES THEATER
1

2
Death Cab for Cutie
Father John Misty
Soccer Mommy

of Latter-day Saints at Temple Square. Hotel rooms are in short supply during this time.

During the third weekend of May, the free, 3-day **Living Traditions Festival** (State St. and 400 South, http://livingtraditionsfestival.com) celebrates the customs of all who call Utah home with fine arts, crafts, dance, music, food, and kids' activities from over 90 different cultures.

The **Utah Arts Festival** (801/322-2428, http://uaf.org) takes place the last weekend in June and includes lots of music, dance, readings, art demonstrations, craft sales, and food booths. The event is held at **Library Square** (200 E. 400 S.).

In July, the **Days of '47** (801/257-7959, www.daysof47.com) commemorates the arrival of LDS pioneers on July 24, 1847, with a huge 24th of July Pioneer Parade in the heart of downtown (the day is a state holiday), a marathon, fireworks, and the year's biggest rodeo, held at the Delta Center.

Check out high-quality crafts, food trucks, and music at the mid-August **Craft Lake City DIY Festival** (Gallivan Center, 801/906-8521, https://craftlakecity.com). In addition to shopping, festival-goers can participate in workshops (many fill up; sign up online in advance).

The **Greek Festival** (Hellenic Center, 300 S. 300 W., 801/328-9681) celebrates Greek culture with food, music, folk dancing, and tours of the historic Holy Trinity Greek Orthodox Cathedral during the weekend after Labor Day. The **Utah State Fair** (North Temple St. and 1000 West, 801/538-8400, www.utahstatefair.com), held at the state fairgrounds in September, is a celebration of the state's agricultural heritage featuring rodeos, livestock competitions, arts and crafts exhibits, musical entertainment, and a midway carnival.

Shopping

DOWNTOWN

Tucked away on a side street off State Street, **The Heavy Metal Shop** (63 Exchange Pl., 801/467-7071, www.heavymetalshop.com, noon-6pm Wed.-Sat.) has been "peddlin' evil" since 1987. The shop is scarcely large enough for half a dozen customers, with every inch of real estate dominated by metal vinyls. The shop is owned by local legend Kevin Kirt, who sort of resembles the title character of *Wayne's World,* gracefully aged. If you don't own a record player, you can still buy "The Heavy Metal Shop" shirt—a timeless tee worn by the likes of Alice Cooper.

9TH AND 9TH

If you like your shopping experience to be less mall-like and more organic, the 9th (900 E.) and 9th (900 S., also known as Harvey Milk Blvd.) neighborhood, just upstream of downtown, is a hub for quirky boutiques that you could easily spend a whole day browsing. This family-friendly neighborhood is very walkable, sports a touch of funk, and also has great dining.

The unique **Gypsy Moon Emporium** (1011 E. 900 S., 801/521-9100, www.gypsymoonemporium.com, by appointment only, call ahead) has been carrying ancient and present-day relics of Celtic culture since 1986 in a charming Victorian cottage. For gag gifts, Utah paraphernalia, and other unique souvenirs, head to **Cahoots** (878 E. 900 S., 801/538-0606, www.cahootssaltlake.com, 10am-9pm daily). And if it's women's clothing you're looking for, shop the racks of casual, on-trend apparel at **Hip & Humble** (1043 E. 900 S., 801/467-3130, https://hipandhumble.com, noon-7pm Mon.-Sat., noon-5pm Sun.), which also carries select home decor, gifts, and dish towels with attitude.

CENTRAL CITY

One locally beloved, historic shop at Trolley Square is **Weller Book Works** (607 Trolley Square, 801/328-2586, www.wellerbookworks.com, 10am-8pm Mon.-Thurs., 10am-9pm Fri.-Sat.), which has been helping Salt Lake discover great reads since 1929. Established by Gustav Weller, a German immigrant and LDS convert, the shop originally specialized in Latter-day Saints reading and went by the name Zion's Bookstore. Today, this two-floor shop serves up a mix of new, used, and rare books, plus a New West section highlighting local writers of Western history and culture.

WEST OF THE CENTER

The **Native American Trading Post** (3971 S. Redwood Dr., 801/952-0184, 10am-7pm Mon.-Sat., 10am-6pm Sun.) got its start as a flea market in 1987, before expanding to the large brick-and-mortar it is today. While it's not Indigenous-owned, the Trading Post supports Indigenous artists and artisans, selling everything from rugs and herbs to flour for fry bread. The Trading Post has come to serve as an unofficial hub of all things Native American in Salt Lake—a bulletin posts upcoming community events, and the store supports causes like the Adopt-a-Native-Elder program.

SUGARHOUSE

The Sundance Catalog got its start when guests of Sundance Resort—located about an hour from Salt Lake in Provo Canyon—would ask the staff where they could find products from the Sundance general store closer to home. Thus, a mail-order catalog was born in 1989. The catalog still exists and has branched out to a handful of stores scattered around the country, as well as Salt Lake City's own **Sundance Outlet** (Sugarhouse Shopping Center, 2201 Highland Dr., 801/487-3400, www.sundancecatalog.com, 10am-8pm Mon.-Sat., noon-5pm Sun.). The inventory spans men's and women's clothing, decor, and other knickknacks, all inspired by the refined Southwestern aesthetic of Sundance Resort.

Lusting after a new ski jacket or fleece from "Patagucci"—as Patagonia is jokingly dubbed for its steep prices—but don't want to shell out? Head to the **Patagonia Outlet** (2292 Highland Dr., 801/466-2226, www.patagonia.com, 10am-7pm Mon.-Fri., 10am-6pm Sat., 11am-6pm Sun.), where you'll find a mix of current and past-season styles on sale and clearance. This store also serves as a local community hub for everything from environmental speakers to yoga, so check the events calendar before you go.

Throw it back to the 1950s and 1960s at **Retro Betty** (2821 S. 2300 E., 801/467-2222, www.retrobettyslc.com, 10am-7pm Mon.-Sat., 10am-6pm Sun.), about a mile (1.6 km) southeast of Sugarhouse. Whether you're just reviving your wardrobe or costume shopping, discover vintage threads like a red polka-dot mermaid skirt or bowler shirt. You can also go retro with funky socks, stationery, gifts, and accessories.

Food

There are some great eats to be found in Salt Lake City—and at a more reasonable bang for your buck than what you might find in San Francisco, New York, or other US food destinations. You'll find some great fine-dining spots, wide-ranging international food, and excellent bakeries. Some of the most authentic cuisine is in South Salt Lake and at Food Truck Thursday at the Gallivan Center.

In Salt Lake, you can get everything from Middle Eastern cuisine and Pacific Island dishes to Peruvian food prepared by second- or third-generation Americans, immigrants, and refugees who have made Salt Lake City their home. When it comes to sweets, there are plenty of bakeries, ice cream shops, and other sweets throughout the city.

TEMPLE SQUARE AND DOWNTOWN

American

Just north of downtown in the so-called Marmalade District, the small but classy **Arlo Restaurant** (271 Center St., 385/266-8845, www.arlorestaurant.com, 5:30pm-9pm Wed.-Sun., $8-45) offers a weekly changing menu with contemporary, seasonal preparations featuring local produce and meats. Expect a couple pasta choices (garganelli with butternut squash, lime ricotta, hazelnuts, and marigolds), a savory tart, salads, and two or three mains. In good weather, a lovely patio invites al fresco dining.

Owned by local celeb chef Viet Pham—a winner of *Iron Chef America*—**Pretty Bird** (146 Regent St., www.prettybirdchicken.com, 11am-9pm Mon.-Sat., $14 for a sandwich) keeps things simple with Nashville-style hot chicken. Make it a combo with some cider slaw, and decide how much heat you can handle.

Fine Dining

★ **The Copper Onion** (111 E. Broadway, 801/355-3282, http://thecopperonion.com, 11:30am-3pm and 5pm-10pm Mon-Fri., 10:30am-3pm and 5pm-10pm Sat.-Sun., $15-28) always gets a mention when people talk about the best restaurant in Salt Lake City. Emphasizing full-flavored New American cooking, Copper Onion offers small and large plates, with beautifully orchestrated dishes like pork chop with farro, wild mushrooms, and pumpkin seed. For the quality, the prices are reasonable.

★ **Bambara** (202 S. Main St., 801/363-5454, http://bambara-slc.com, 7am-2pm and 5pm-9:30pm daily, $28-58), in the Hotel Monaco, is a downtown fixture and easily one of the most beautiful dining rooms in the city. The menu emphasizes the freshest and most flavorful local meat and produce, with preparations in a wide-awake New American style that's equal parts tradition and innovation.

Mexican and Southwestern

A local favorite, **Blue Iguana** (165 S. West Temple St., 801/410-0968, www.blueiguanarestaurant.net, 11am-9pm Mon.-Thurs., 11am-10pm Fri.-Sat., 4pm-9pm Sun., $10-19) offers Mexican plates—and specialty moles—in a lively basement dining room or a pleasant courtyard. You'll also find good margaritas, standard versions and spins on the cocktail alike.

Asian

Salt Lake City has several excellent Asian restaurants, but for the best and freshest sushi, go to **Takashi** (18 W. Market St., 801/519-9595, http://takashisushi.com, 11:30am-2pm and 5:30pm-10pm Mon.-Fri., 5:30pm-10pm Sat., sushi rolls $6-20). Takashi's non-seafood dishes, like its ribs, are also excellent.

Breakfast and Bakeries

If your idea of breakfast is a French pastry and shot of espresso, head to **Eva's Bakery** (155 S.

Utah's Mixed Soda Craze

You may notice a beverage vendor not commonly found throughout most of the United States: mixed sodas. Since coffee is outlawed by the church for those of the LDS faith, the way to start the day is with a soda or—even better—a **soda mixer.** These soda mocktails entail one or more sodas mixed with Torani syrups and other flavorings. You'll find them readily available throughout Salt Lake City and much of Utah, often via the convenience of a drive-thru.

Main St., 801/355-3942, http://evasbakeryslc.com, 9am-7pm Tues.-Fri., 9am-6pm Sat., 10am-6pm Sun.) for marvelous croissants, artisanal breads, soups, and sandwiches.

For a more elaborate patisserie selection—think stunning cakes and petit four à la *The Great British Bake Off*—ogle the display at **Gourmandise** (250 S. 300 E., 801/328-3330, www.gourmandise.com, 8am-10pm Mon.-Thurs., 8am-11pm Fri.-Sat., 9am-2pm Sun., pastries starting at $4).

Italian

Charming Valter and his attentive staff make every dinner at ★ **Valter's Osteria** (173 Broadway, 801/521-4563, http://valtersosteria.com, 5:30pm-10pm Tues.-Sat., $16-35) memorable in the best of ways. Valter's interpretations of his grandmother's Italian cooking can't be beat—try the sampler of house-made flavorful ravioli and delicate gnocchi.

Steak and Seafood

The **Market Street Grill** (48 Market St., 801/322-4668, https://marketstreetgrill.com, 8am-2pm and 5pm-9pm Mon.-Thurs., 8am-2pm and 5pm-10pm Fri., 8am-3pm and 4pm-10pm Sat., 9am-3pm and 4pm-9pm Sun., $12-39), is a longtime SLC favorite featuring fresh seafood, steak, prime rib, chicken, and pasta. Adjacent is an oyster bar.

Vegetarian

Known not just for its healthy, plant-based meals, but also for its innovative cocktails, **Zest Kitchen & Bar** (275 S. 200 W., 801/433-0589, www.zestslc.com, 4pm-9pm Mon, 11am-9pm Tues.-Thurs., 11am-10pm Fri., 10am-10pm Sat., 10am-9pm Sun., $17-19, age 21 and up) is the place to go if you want a touch of vodka in your green smoothie. Besides "farm-to-glass" cocktails, the gluten- and soy-free menu features small plates for sharing, such as a pile of shaved brussels sprouts with spicy almond sauce and entrées like mac and (vegan) cheese or jackfruit pizza.

Brewpubs

The state's oldest brewpub is **Squatters Pub Brewery** (147 W. Broadway, 801/363-2739, www.saltlakebrewingco.com, 11:30am-11pm Mon.-Fri., 10:30am-11pm Sat.-Sun., $12-27). In addition to fine beers and ales, the pub serves sandwiches, burgers, and other American fare in a handsome old warehouse. In summer, there's seating on the back deck.

As for taphouses, the best downtown is the **Beerhive Pub** (128 S. Main St., 801/364-4268, noon-1am Mon.-Sat., noon-10pm Sun.). This handsome old storefront offers more than two dozen regional microbrews on draft and more than 200 in bottles. You'll be able to taste beers from all around the state in one sitting.

Delis and Groceries

Siegfried's Delicatessen (20 W. 200 S., 801/355-3891, www.siegfriedsdelicatessen.com, 11am-5pm Mon.-Wed., 11am-9pm Thurs.-Sat.) has a great selection of charcuterie, cold cuts, breads, pastries, and cheeses. The deli also serves homemade German dishes for both lunch and dinner, with options under $10.

Family-owned **Tony Caputo's Market & Deli** (314 W. 300 S., 801/531-8669, https://

1
2
9" PASSIONFRUIT MOUSSE
$43.95
PETIT CAKES
$28.55
9" WHITE
CHANTILLY
3
4

Spice Kitchen Incubator

With Utah's conservative reputation, it comes as a surprise to some that the state openly welcomes immigrants. This is largely thanks to the fact that the LDS community views itself as descendants of refugees, pushed westward due to religious discrimination.

To help the many refugees and immigrants resettled in Utah establish a livelihood, **Spice Kitchen Incubator** (https://spicekitchenincubator.org)—a program of the International Rescue Committee—provides the tools and training needed to establish a food business. Since 2013, Spice Kitchen has helped over 30 catering companies, food trucks, and restaurants launch, with cuisines running the gamut from Venezuelan and Somalian to Iraqi.

Craving some exciting new eats? Find Spice Kitchen at various farmers markets around town, or order dinner ($10) from a rotating Spice Kitchen business by noon on the Tuesday prior and pick it up to enjoy on Thursday.

caputos.com, 9am-7pm Mon.-Sat., 10am-5pm Sun., sandwiches $12-15) serves Italian deli-style sandwiches you can enjoy in a café-style seating area or take on a day trip. This legendary local spot also stocks a cheese cave, a charcuterie selection, and over 400 chocolate bars.

SOUTH OF DOWNTOWN

Fine Dining

At the aptly named and historic **Log Haven** (6451 E. Mill Creek Canyon Rd., 801/272-8255, www.log-haven.com, 5:30pm-9pm Mon.-Sat., noon-7pm Sun., $32-54), you'll find remarkably good food that leans steak house but also dabbles in New American, with game, fresh seafood, and pasta. Built in the 1920s, the restaurant is splendidly rustic yet upscale, with ample outdoor seating in good weather. Log Haven is 4 miles (6.4 km) east of Salt Lake City in Mill Creek Canyon.

★ **Table X** (1457 E. 3350 S., 385/528-3712, http://tablexrestaurant.com, 5pm-9pm Wed.-Sat., $20-40), with its serious farm-to-table aesthetic, three-chef collaboration, and beautifully reclaimed old building, is a quintessentially modern restaurant. Choose from a five- or seven-course tasting menu ($75-100 pp; a vegetarian tasting menu is available; wine or beverage pairings extra).

1: cocktail at Takashi 2: cakes at Gourmandise
3: the entrance to Log Haven 4: The Bagel Project

Asian

Oh Mai (850 S. State St., 801/575-8888, https://ohmaisandwich.com, 11am-9pm Mon.-Sat., $9-15) specializes in delicious Vietnamese bahn mi sandwiches and pho—try the Vietnamese coffee or Thai iced tea, too.

Breakfast

The Bagel Project (779 S. 500 E., 801/906-0698, https://bagelproject.com, 7:30am-2pm Tues.-Sat.) is the love child of a displaced East Coaster who found a gap in the market for authentic bagels in Utah. Come here for excellent bagels, bialys, sandwiches, and Mandel bread—the shop does sell out, so come early.

French

For classic (though spendy) French cuisine, **La Caille Restaurant** (9565 Wasatch Blvd., near Little Cottonwood Canyon, 801/942-1751, www.lacaille.com, 5pm-9pm Tues.-Sat., 10am-2pm Sun., $48-130) offers superb pastry, crepes, seafood, and meat dishes in an 18th-century rural French atmosphere. Vineyards, gardens, ponds, and manicured lawns surround the re-created French château—it's hard to believe it's in Utah. Dress is semiformal, and reservations are required.

Middle Eastern and Indian

On the edge of downtown, ★ **Laziz Kitchen** (912 Jefferson St. W., 801/441-1228, www.lazizkitchen.com, 11am-9pm Mon.-Thurs.,

11am-10pm Fri., 10am-10pm Sat., 10am-8pm Sun., $12-16) serves food that leans Lebanese, alongside dishes from other Middle Eastern countries. Enjoy traditionally crafted dips, mezze, and other dishes, and put a Lebanese spin on American dishes like burgers.

Vegetarian

Even a meat-loving place like SLC offers a selection of dining options for vegans. **Vertical Diner** (234 W. 900 S., 801/484-8378, https://verticaldiner.com, 9am-10pm daily, $13-18) serves satisfying organic vegetarian cuisine, and a wine list that leans organic.

EAST OF DOWNTOWN

Fine Dining

A top spot for locavore cuisine is ★ **Pago** (878 S. 900 E., 801/532-0777, www.pagoslc.com, 5pm-9pm Mon.-Fri., 10am-2pm and 5pm-9pm Sat.-Sun., $14-21), where the best of local produce, mushrooms, fish, and meat are cooked with Mediterranean flair. Try the roast chicken with figs, baked shallots, and balsamic vinegar.

Breakfast

For one of Salt Lake's favorite breakfasts, drive (or ride your bike) a couple miles east of the city up Emigration Canyon to **Ruth's Diner** (4160 Emigration Canyon Rd., 801/582-5807, https://ruthsdiner.com, 8am-10pm daily summer, operating days and hours vary seasonally, $13-21). The restaurant's namesake was a cabaret singer who opened the restaurant in 1930—Ruth's has been in continuous operation ever since. The diner has a quaint setting that includes a stream, which is a good thing, since you'll almost certainly have to wait for a table.

Indian

Saffron Valley East India Café (26 E St., 801/203-3325, www.saffronvalley.com, 11am-2:30pm and 5pm-10pm Tues.-Fri., 11:30am-3:30pm and 5pm-9pm Sat.-Sun., $15-18) offers a large selection of street-food starters, dosas, salads, and other small plates, including classic Indian and Southeast Asian cuisine as well as unusual dishes like Bombay (vegetarian) sloppy joes and crispy chicken poppers. The food is sophisticated and unusual. Head to the Sugarhouse neighborhood for **Saffron Bistro** (479 E. 2100 S., 801/203-3754, same hours), which combines café, chai house, and market.

Italian and Mediterranean

Although the atmosphere at the Italian-pizzeria spot **Stoneground** (249 E. 400 S.,

a biscuit at Ruth's Diner

801/364-1368, www.stonegroundslc.com, 5pm-9pm Tues.-Thurs., 5pm-10pm Fri.-Sat.) is industrial, windows behold a gorgeous view of the Wasatch Mountains. You can also sit on the mister-cooled patio. The thin-crust pizzas are excellent ($17-20), and pasta dishes and main courses are flavorful and full of character ($26-40).

Vegetarian

Oasis Café (151 S. 500 E., 801/322-0404, www.oasiscafeslc.com, 8am-9pm daily, $16-30) serves an ambitious all-organic menu that borrows tastes and preparations from around the world. While most dishes are vegetarian, fresh fish and some organic meats are also served.

Seafood

Located in a snappily repurposed auto shop just east of city center, ★ **Current Fish and Oyster** (279 E. 300 S., 801/326-3474, www.currentfishandoyster.com, 11am-3pm and 5pm-9pm Mon.-Thurs., 11am-3pm and 5pm-10pm Fri., 5pm-10pm Sat., 5pm-8pm Sun., $21-42) offers innovative preparations of fresh seafood in a stylish dining room or, in good weather, on a gardenlike front patio. Service, setting, and food are all superb and equally matched.

Bars and Nightlife

The best way to check out the club scene is to pick up a copy of *City Weekly*, a free and widely available news and entertainment weekly. If you're just looking for a beer and a spot to meet some locals, try a brewpub. Last call in Utah is 1am, and bars must close by 2am.

★ CRAFT BREWERIES

The craft brewery scene in Salt Lake is young, ever-growing, and tenacious. From German-inspired **TF Brewing** (936 S. 300 W., 385/270-5972, www. tfbrewing.com) and the well-rounded tall boys of **Proper Brewing** (857 S. Main St., 801/953-1707, www.properbrewingco.com) to the inventive ales of **Epic** (825 S. State St., 801/906-0123, www.epicbrewing.com)—which originated in Utah, but switched its headquarters to Denver—there are plenty of fresh perspectives on malt, yeast, and hops in the city.

Keep in mind the local laws before you head out for a beer. Draft beer can be no higher than 5 percent ABV (alcohol by volume). Most breweries will note this on their menu and refer to their full-strength bottled or canned line as "full-strength" or "high point." A brewery is also a great spot to pick up a six-pack, since they can sell refrigerated beer (unlike Utah liquor stores) and are often open on holidays and Sundays, when liquor stores are closed statewide.

BARS

If you're a karaoke person, try out **Twist** (32 Exchange Place, 801/322-3200, www.twistslc.com, nightly), with Tuesday night karaoke and live music Wednesday-Saturday. Another good stop for drinks and good times right downtown is **Bar-X** (155 E. 200 S., 801/355-2287), one of SLC's oldest and most characterful bars, with a focus on cocktails. Right next door, sister establishment **Beer Bar** (161 E. 200 S., 801/355-3618) has a wall full of taps, bottled beer, great sausages, and board games. If you're looking for a quieter setting where you can enjoy a cocktail and some snacks, check out the stylish Western setting at **Whiskey Street Cocktails** (323 S. Main St., 801/433-1371). Take a seat at the 72-foot-long (22-m) cherrywood bar and order a craft cocktail and some Parmesan truffle fries.

If you want to go dancing, you'll find several options, like **Area 51** (451 S. 400 W., 801/534-0819, www.area51slc.com) with theme nights (College Night, Alterna-Mash, Fetish, and more) and three dance floors on two levels. **ECHO** (134 Pierpont Ave., 435/255-8686, www.echokarma.com) bills itself as Utah's nightlife headquarters, and it's one of Salt Lake's most popular spots for cocktails, DJs, theme parties, and events.

If you're into the speakeasy scene, check out the underground bar at **The Rest,** beneath the restaurant **Bodega** (331 S. Main St., 801/532-4452, www.bodegaslc.com). This is a popular (and quite dark) spot for inventive cocktails and good Mexican food, so make a reservation if you don't want to be disappointed.

LIVE MUSIC

The **Tavernacle Social Club** (50 W. Broadway, www.tavernacle.com) is a Salt Lake original with the punniest name in town: a high-energy piano bar with an updated lounge act featuring dueling pianos, sing-alongs, and karaoke Thursday-Tuesday.

To catch the flavor of local and regional bands, check out **Urban Lounge** (241 S. 500 E., www.theurbanloungeslc.com).

Blues jams and jazz bands are featured at **Gracie's Gastropub** (326 S. West Temple St., 801/819-7565, www.graciesslc.com). The food is also good here, so it's worth making an evening of it.

Touring national acts stop at **The Depot** (in the Gateway Center at 400 S. West Temple St., 801/456-2800), a nightclub in the cavernous Union Station—it's also a good spot for meeting friends when there's no live band. Big names often play **The State Room** (638 S. State St., 800/501-2885, www.thestateroom.com), a more intimate venue.

LGBTQ+

Salt Lake City is home to a growing number of LGBTQ-oriented clubs. A good place to start the evening is **Club Try-Angles** (251 W. Harvey Milk Blvd., 801/364-3203, 4pm-1am Mon.-Fri., 6pm-1am Sat., 2pm-1am Sun.), with a pleasant patio for drinks and sunning. The **Sun Trapp** (102 S. 600 W., 385/235-6786, 1pm-1am Mon.-Thurs., 11am-1am Fri.-Sun.) is known for its friendly, welcoming, and laid-back atmosphere.

Accommodations

Salt Lake City offers a modest mix of luxury, boutique, and budget lodging options. If you're looking for world-class, premium hotels, don't stay in Salt Lake—head to Park City, where the crème of the lodging crop lies. If you're willing to settle for run-of-the-mill luxury, look on the bright side: You won't be paying exorbitant prices. The major hotels lie in the downtown area, with a few smaller inns sprinkled around other neighborhoods like the Avenues.

There are several major lodging centers. Downtown Salt Lake City is close to Temple Square, the Salt Palace, and most other attractions. South of downtown near 600 South and West Temple Street is a clutch of hotels and motels, including several business-oriented hotels. While these lodgings are only six blocks from the city center, blocks are very long in SLC (six blocks per mile). Another cluster of hotels and motels lies west along North Temple Street, a quick ride to the airport via the TRAX light rail line. If your trip involves visiting the university, there are a couple good lodging options near campus.

The prices listed below are standard rates. You can frequently beat these prices by checking the hotel's website for specials. Prices can vary by as much as $100 per night within the same week, so the following prices are only guidelines.

1: cocktail at Beer Bar **2:** the underground bar The Rest, located below Bodega **3:** Peery Hotel

1
BODEGA
331
2

3
PEERY
PEERY HOTEL
PEERY HOTEL

TEMPLE SQUARE AND DOWNTOWN

Parking is tight in downtown SLC—expect to pay about $10-15 on top of room costs if you're parking a car at a downtown hotel. Note that pricing at these hotels is particularly dependent on convention traffic. If there's not much going on, it's possible to find a room at SLC's finest for under $200.

$100-150

Overlooking Temple Square is the **Salt Lake Plaza Hotel** (122 W. South Temple St., 801/521-0130 or 800/366-3684, http://plaza-hotel.com, $120-170), which offers a pool and an on-site restaurant in addition to its great location.

$150-200

The ★ **Peery Hotel** (110 W. 300 S., 801/521-4300, www.peeryhotel.com, $150-280) was the first of SLC's historic hotels to be refurbished into an upscale lodging. Its 1910 vintage style is preserved in the comfortable lobby, while the guest rooms are updated and nicely furnished. It's close to the food scene along Pierpont Avenue and there's also a restaurant on the premises.

Some of Salt Lake's grandest heritage homes sit on Capitol Hill, just below the state capitol. One of the most eye-catching is the red sandstone mansion now called the **Inn on the Hill** (225 N. State St., 801/328-1466, http://inn-on-the-hill.com, $175-275). Built in 1906 by a local captain of industry, the inn has 13 guest rooms decorated with period detail, but all with modern amenities such as private baths. Practically every room has broad views over Salt Lake City. Full gourmet breakfasts are included.

One of SLC's most popular convention hotels, the **Hilton Salt Lake City Center** (255 S. West Temple St., 801/328-2000, www.hilton.com, $175-278) is a huge complex with an indoor pool, two fine-dining restaurants, and a bar. When there's no convention in town, it's also a supremely comfortable (and often surprisingly affordable) spot for travelers; when convention crowds are in town, prices can double or triple.

The **Salt Lake City Marriott Downtown at City Creek** (75 S. West Temple St., 801/531-0800 or 800/228-9290, www.marriott.com, $160-320) is directly across from the Salt Palace Convention Center. At this high-quality hotel, there's an indoor-outdoor pool, a sauna, a good restaurant, and a lounge. Weekend rates are often deeply discounted.

One block west of the temple is the **Radisson Salt Lake City Hotel Downtown** (215 W. South Temple St., 801/531-7500 or 888/201-1718, www.radisson.com, $160-200). At this modern 15-story hotel, you'll find a pool and a restaurant, too.

Over $200

The ★ **Hotel Monaco** (15 W. 200 S., 801/595-0000 or 877/294-9710, www.monaco-saltlakecity.com, $260-370) occupies a grandly renovated historic office building in a convenient spot downtown. On the main floor, **Bambara** is one of the most sophisticated restaurants in Utah. Guest rooms are sumptuously furnished—this is no anonymous business hotel in beige and mauve. Expect wild colors and contrasting fabrics, flowers, and excellent service. Pets are welcome and are even invited to the nightly wine reception. If you want to splurge on a hotel in Salt Lake, make it this one.

The ★ **Salt Lake City Marriott City Center** (220 S. State St., 801/961-8700, www.marriott.com, $210-350) sits above Gallivan Center, an urban park and festival space. A luxury-level business hotel, the Marriott has an indoor pool, a recreation area, and a fine-dining restaurant.

SOUTH OF DOWNTOWN

Just south of downtown is a large complex of hotels and motels, mostly large chains, with rooms in almost every traveler's price range. These lodgings aren't very convenient for travelers on foot, but if you have a car or don't mind riding the bus or TRAX, this area has good options and often lower prices.

$50-100

These budget motels won't satisfy finicky travelers, but they're reliable standards. **Motel 6 Downtown** (176 W. 600 S., 801/531-1252, $60-100) has a pool. Pets are allowed at the **Quality Inn Downtown** (616 S. 200 W., 801/534-0808, www.rodewayinn.com, $66-94). The **Metropolitan Inn** (524 S. West Temple St., 801/531-7100, www.metropolitaninn.com, $60-200) has Tempurpedic mattresses in the guest rooms, all with coffeemakers and access to a heated pool and hot tub. Pets are welcome.

$100-150

One hotel with good value in this part of Salt Lake is the **Crystal Inn** (230 W. 500 S., 801/328-4466 or 800/366-4466, www.crystalinnsaltlake.com, $109-210). Guest rooms are very large and nicely furnished. There's an indoor pool, sauna, hot tub, and free hot breakfast buffet for all guests.

One of the best situated of all the south downtown motels is the Marriott-operated **Fairfield Inn & Suites Salt Lake City Downtown** (130 W. 400 S., 801/531-6000, www.marriott.com, $168-260). It's centrally located to all the restaurants and happenings in the city's fast-changing warehouse-loft district. There's a pool, a hot tub, and an airport shuttle.

$150-200

If you're looking for comfortable rooms without breaking the bank, the ★ **Little America Hotel** (500 S. Main St., 801/363-6781 or 800/304-8970, http://saltlake.littleamerica.com, $160-250) is a great place to stay. This large lodging complex, with nearly 850 guest rooms, offers three types of room: Courtside rooms and garden suites, most overlooking a pool or fountain, and executive-level tower suites in a 17-story block with great views. All guests share the hotel's elegant public areas, including two pools and a gym. The restaurant is better than average, and there is free airport transfer.

If you're in Salt Lake for an extended time or are traveling with a family, consider the **DoubleTree Suites by Hilton** (110 W. 600 S., 801/359-7800, http://doubletree3.hilton.com, $194-500). All suites have efficiency kitchens with a coffeemaker, fridge, and microwave along with separate living and sleeping areas; there are two two-bedroom units. Facilities include a pool, sauna, and restaurant.

Over $200

The behemoth ★ **Grand America Hotel and Suites** (555 S. Main St., 801/258-6000 or 800/304-8696, www.grandamerica.com, $214-299) is a full Salt Lake City square block (that's 10 acres/4 ha), with 775 guest rooms, more than half of them suites. Decor is opulent (if not a little gaudy!) with luxury-level amenities. Polish off the fancy experience with afternoon tea or cocktails to the tune of live jazz (7pm-10pm Fri.-Sat.).

Hampton Inn (425 S. 300 W., 801/741-1110, http://hamptoninn.hilton.com, $211-260) offers complimentary breakfast, an indoor pool, a hot tub, and a business center.

Sheraton Salt Lake City Hotel (150 W. 500 S., 801/401-2000 or 888/627-8152, www.sheratonsaltlakecityhotel.com, $243-280) is one of the city's best accommodations for high-quality comfort and service. The lobby areas are very pleasant, and facilities include a great pool and a spa. The rooftop restaurant and lounge are also notable.

EAST OF DOWNTOWN

There aren't many lodging choices in this part of the city, but this is a pleasant residential area without the distinct urban jolt of much of the rest of central Salt Lake City.

Under $50

The Avenues (107 F St. at 2nd Ave., 1 mi/1.6 km east of Temple Square, 801/363-3855, www.avenueshostelsaltlakecity.top, $33-40) offers dorm rooms with use of a kitchen, TV room, and laundry. Although you're likely to meet travelers from all over the world, the hostel is a bit on the shabby side. Beds are available in the dorm (sheets included) or in private rooms, some of which have private baths.

$100-150

Right in the University of Utah's Research Park, the **Marriott University Park Hotel and Suites** (480 Wakara Way, 801/581-1000, www.marriott.com, $130-284) is one of the city's best-kept secrets for high end lodgings in a lovely setting. You can't be disappointed with the views: All guest rooms either overlook the city or look onto the soaring peaks of the Wasatch Range. Guest rooms are nicely appointed—the suites are some of the best in the city. All guest rooms have minibars, fridges, and coffeemakers.

Over $200

The **Anniversary Inn** (460 S. 1000 E., 801/363-4900 or 800/324-4152, www.anniversaryinn.com, $259-279) caters to couples and newlyweds interested in a romantic getaway. All 32 guest rooms are imaginatively decorated according to a theme: Think beds in covered wagons or vintage rail cars, and baths inside a sea cave. Chances are good that your guest room will have its own private waterfall. You get to pick your suite from choices that include The Lighthouse, The Sultan's Palace, and Venice. These guest rooms aren't just filled with kitsch; they are luxury-class accommodations with big-screen TVs, hot tubs, stereos, and private baths. Rates vary widely by room. There's also a second Anniversary Inn (678 E. South Temple St.).

WEST OF DOWNTOWN

Nearly all the following hotels offer transfers to the Salt Lake City Airport. Those with the lowest-numbered addresses on West North Temple Street are closest to downtown; these hotels are about 1 mile (1.6 km) from Temple Square and downtown, and they are inexpensive options if you're looking for a centrally located place to stay.

$50-100

Budget rooms are available at the **Motel 6 Airport** (1990 W. North Temple St., 801/364-1053, www.motel6.com, $67-94), where there's a pool.

Practically next door to the airport terminal is the **Ramada Salt Lake City Airport Hotel** (5575 W. Amelia Earhart Dr., 801/537-7020, www.ramada.com, $59-99), with a pool and a spa.

Grand America Hotel and Suites

$150-200

The **Radisson Hotel Salt Lake City Airport** (2177 W. North Temple St., 801/364-5800, www.radisson.com, $179-205) is a lodge-like building with nicely furnished guest rooms. Guests receive complimentary continental breakfast, and in the evenings, there's a manager's reception with free beverages. Facilities include a pool and spa. Suites come with a loft bedroom area.

CAMPGROUNDS

Of the several commercial campgrounds around the periphery of Salt Lake City, **Camp VIP/Salt Lake City KOA** (1400 W. North Temple, 801/328-0224, www.koa.com, year-round, $89) is the most convenient, located between downtown and the airport. It offers sites for tents and RVs with showers, as well as a swimming pool, game room, playground, store, and laundry.

There are two good US Forest Service campgrounds in Big Cottonwood Canyon (877/444-6777, www.recreation.gov, $28, plus reservation fee of $8 online, $9 phone), about 15 miles (24 km) southeast of downtown Salt Lake City, and another two in Little Cottonwood Canyon, about 19 miles (31 km) southeast of town. All have drinking water, and all prohibit pets because of local watershed regulations.

In Big Cottonwood Canyon, **Spruces Campground** (9.1 mi/14.6 km up the canyon, elev. 7,400 ft/2,256 m) is usually open early June-mid-October. The season at **Redman Campground** (elev. 8,300 ft/2,530 m, first-come, first-served)—between Solitude and Brighton ski areas—is mid-June-early October.

Little Cottonwood Canyon's **Tanners Flat Campground** (4.3 mi/6.9 km up the canyon, elev. 7,200 ft/2,195 m, first-come, first-served) is open mid-May-mid-October. **Albion Basin Campground** (elev. 9,500 ft/2,896 m, first-come, first-served) is high in the mountains a few miles past Alta Ski Area and open early July-late September; go 11 miles (17.7 km) up the canyon (the last 2.5 mi/4 km are gravel).

Information and Services

Salt Lake City's visitor centers are well stocked with information and enthusiastic volunteers. Couple that with excellent public transportation, and you'll find the city and surrounding areas easy to negotiate despite the sprawl.

INFORMATION

Tourism Offices

Volunteers at the **Salt Lake Convention and Visitors Bureau** (downtown in the Salt Palace, 90 S. West Temple St., 801/534-4900, www.visitsaltlake.com, 10am-5pm Mon.-Sat.) will tell you about the sights, facilities, and happenings in town.

The **Utah Travel Council** (300 N. State St., 801/538-1030, www.utah.com, 8am-5pm Mon.-Fri., 10am-5pm Sat.-Sun.) publishes a well-illustrated *Utah Travel Guide,* travel maps, and other helpful publications. The staff at the Travel Council information desk provides advice and literature about Utah's national parks and monuments, national forests, Bureau of Land Management areas, and state parks as well as general travel in the state.

US Forest Service

The **Uinta-Wasatch-Cache National Forest supervisor's office** (857 W. South Jordan Pkwy., South Jordan, UT, 84109, 801/999-2103, www.fs.usda.gov/uwcnf, 8am-4:30pm Mon.-Fri.) has general information and forest maps for all the national forests in Utah, and some forest and wilderness maps of Nevada, Idaho, and Wyoming.

SERVICES

There is a main **post office** (230 W. 200 S., 801/974-2200) downtown. The University of Utah has a post office in the bookstore.

Salt Lake City is a major regional banking center, so you'll have no trouble with most common financial transactions. ATMs are everywhere. If you're depending on foreign currency, consider changing enough for your trip around Utah while you're in Salt Lake City. Exchanging currency is much more difficult in smaller rural towns.

Minor medical emergencies can be treated by **InstaCare Clinics** (389 S. 900 E., 801/282-2400, 9am-9pm daily), with more than 30 outlets in the greater Wasatch Front area. Hospitals with 24-hour emergency care include **Salt Lake Regional Medical Center** (1050 E. South Temple St., 801/350-4111), **LDS Hospital** (8th Ave. and C St., 801/350-4111), **St. Mark's Hospital** (1200 E. 3900 S., 801/268-7111), and **University Hospital** (50 N. Medical Dr./1900 East, 801/581-2121).

For a 24-hour pharmacy, try **Rite Aid** (5540 S. 900 E., 801/262-2981). If you're looking for a drugstore, check the phone book for **Smith's Pharmacy;** there are more than 25 in the Salt Lake metro area.

The **American Automobile Association** (AAA) has offices at 560 E. 500 S. (801/541-9902).

Transportation

AIR

Salt Lake City International Airport (SLC, 776 N. Terminal Dr., 801/575-2400, https://slcairport.com) is conveniently located 7 miles (11.3 km) west of downtown; take I-80 to reach it. Most major US carriers fly into Salt Lake City, and it is the western hub for Delta Airlines, the region's air transportation leader.

Delta Connections (800/325-8224, www.skywest.com) is Delta's commuter partner and flies from SLC to Cedar City and St. George in Utah and to smaller cities in adjacent states.

The recently revamped airport has one terminal, with two concourses. Auto rentals (Hertz, Avis, National, Budget, and Dollar) are in the parking structure immediately across from the terminal. Just follow signs.

Staff at the ground-transportation information desks will know the bus schedules into town and can advise on car services direct to Park City, Sundance, Provo, Ogden, Brigham City, Logan, and other communities. By far the easiest way to get from the airport to downtown is via the TRAX Green line, which runs between the SLC airport and the Salt Lake Central Station. The train stop is located outside door 1A on the ground level. Trains run every 15 minutes on weekdays, and every 30 minutes on weekends; hours are 5:32am-11:06pm Mon.-Fri., 6:25am-11:25pm Sat., and 6:25am-11:37pm Sun. One-way fare is $2.50.

If you're flying in from Phoenix or Los Angeles, consider the Provo airport, which is less than an hour from SLC by car and served by budget airline Allegiant. However, when flying on Allegiant, as with other budget airlines, travelers should expect to pay for "extras" such as carry-on bags and water.

TRAIN

Amtrak (340 S. 600 W., information and reservations 800/872-7245, www.amtrak.com) trains stop at the Salt Lake Central Station (300 S. 600 W.), which also serves as a terminus for local buses, light rail, and commuter trains. The only Amtrak train that currently passes through the city is the ***California Zephyr,*** which runs west to Reno and Oakland and east to Denver and Chicago three times a week. Call for fares, as Amtrak prices tickets as airlines do, with advance-booking discounts, special seasonal prices, and other special rates available. Amtrak office hours, timed to meet the trains, are irregular, so call first.

LONG-DISTANCE BUS

Salt Lake City is at a crossroads of several major interstate highways and has good **Greyhound bus service** (300 S. 600 W., 801/355-9579, www.greyhound.com). Generally speaking, buses go north and south along I-15 and east and west along I-80. In summer, one bus daily leaves from Salt Lake City for Yellowstone National Park.

LOCAL BUS AND LIGHT RAIL

Utah Transit Authority (UTA, 801/287-4636, www.rideuta.com, 6am-7pm Mon.-Sat.) provides inexpensive bus and light rail train service in town and to the airport, the University of Utah, and surrounding communities. Buses go as far north as Ogden, as far south as Provo and Springville, and as far west as Tooele. **TRAX light rail** trains connect the University of Utah, downtown Salt Lake City, the airport, and the southern suburbs. No charge is made for travel downtown within the Free-Fare Square area, generally bounded by North Temple Street, 500 South, 200 East, and 400 West; on TRAX, service is fare-free to Salt Lake Central Station at 600 West.

A TRAX line connects Salt Lake City International Airport with **Salt Lake Central Station.** You can board a light rail train at the airport and ride public transport downtown—or, with a bit of patience, to a ski area in Big or Little Cottonwood Canyons.

During the ski season, you can hop on the **Ski Bus Service** to Solitude, Brighton, Snowbird, and Alta ski areas from downtown, the University of Utah, and other locations. A bus route map and individual schedules are available online (www.rideuta.com) and at the ground transportation information desk at the airport, at the Salt Lake Convention and Visitors Bureau downtown, and at Temple Square visitor centers. Free transfers are provided on request. On Sunday, only the airport, Ogden, Provo, and a few other destinations are served. UTA shuts down on holidays. Fares are $2.50 for 2 hours of travel on both TRAX and the buses; a day pass is $6.25.

BIKE AND SCOOTER SHARING

The nonprofit **GREENbike** (801/333-1110, www.greenbikeutah.org) makes bikes available at over 45 stations in central Salt Lake City. The system is easy to use. Pay a small membership fee online, then download an app to find stations and bike availability. When you're done with your trip, return your bike to any station. The bright green bikes all have a large basket, front and rear LED lights, adjustable seats, and built-in cable locks. You'll also find scooters available throughout the city from Lime (www.li.me) and Bird (www.bird.co); downloading an app is required to ride.

CAR RENTAL

All the major companies and a few local outfits operate in Utah. In winter, opt for a vehicle with 4WD and snow tires—plus ski racks if you need to transport gear. Many agencies have an office or delivery service at the airport: **Avis Rent A Car** (Salt Lake City International Airport, 801/575-2847 or 800/331-1212, www.avis.com), **Budget Rent A Car** (641 N. 3800 W., 801/575-2586 or 800/527-0700, www.budget.com), **Dollar Rent-A-Car** (601 N. 3800 W. and Salt Lake City International Airport, 801/575-2580 or 800/421-9849, www.dollar.com), **Enterprise Rent-A-Car** (151 E. 5600 S., 801/266-3777 or 801/534-1888, www.enterprise.com), **Hertz** (Salt Lake City International Airport, 801/575-2683 or 800/654-3131, www.hertz.com), **National Car Rental** (Salt Lake City International Airport, 801/575-2277 or 800/227-7368, www.nationalcar.com), and **Payless Car Rental** (1974 W. North Temple St., 801/596-2596 or 800/327-3631, www.paylesscar.com).

TAXI AND RIDESHARES

City Cab (801/363-8400), **Ute Cab** (801/359-7788), and **Yellow Cab** (801/521-2100) have 24-hour service. Lyft and Uber are also available.

Big and Little Cottonwood Canyons

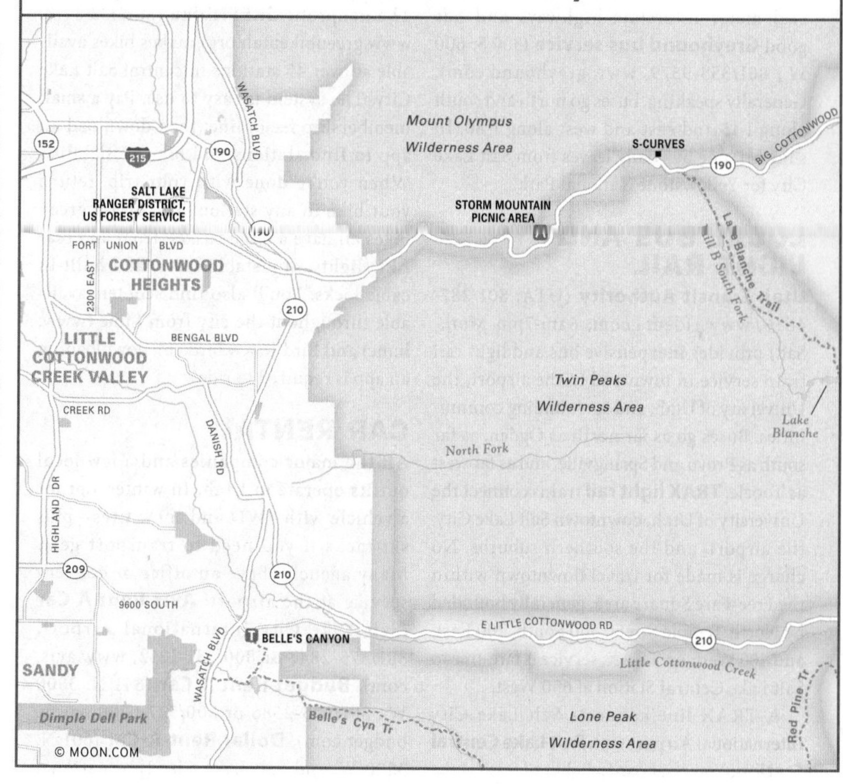

Big Cottonwood Canyon

TOP EXPERIENCE

Formed by an ancient sea's deposits, volcanic activity, and massive ice age glaciers, Big Cottonwood stretches all the way from Salt Lake City to Park City. In the summer, you can drive through Big Cottonwood Canyon until it turns into Guardsman Pass, which leads to the back side of Deer Valley Resort. In the winter, the pass closes, but the canyon's two ski resorts—Solitude and Brighton—drive plenty of traffic from Salt Lake.

Enter the canyon from Wasatch Boulevard and 7000 South, about 15 miles (24 km) southeast of downtown Salt Lake City. The 14-mile (22.5-km) road to Brighton Basin climbs past several picnic areas and sweeping vistas to an elevation of 8,700 feet (2,652 m). Guardsman Pass (open late June-mid-Oct.) turns off just before Brighton and winds up to Guardsman Pass (elev. 9,800 ft/2,987 m) at the crest of the Wasatch Mountains, then drops down into either Park City or Heber City on the other side.

SOLITUDE MOUNTAIN RESORT

The best thing about **Solitude** (801/534-1400 or 800/748-4754, www.solitudemountain.com) is reflected in its name—it's rarely

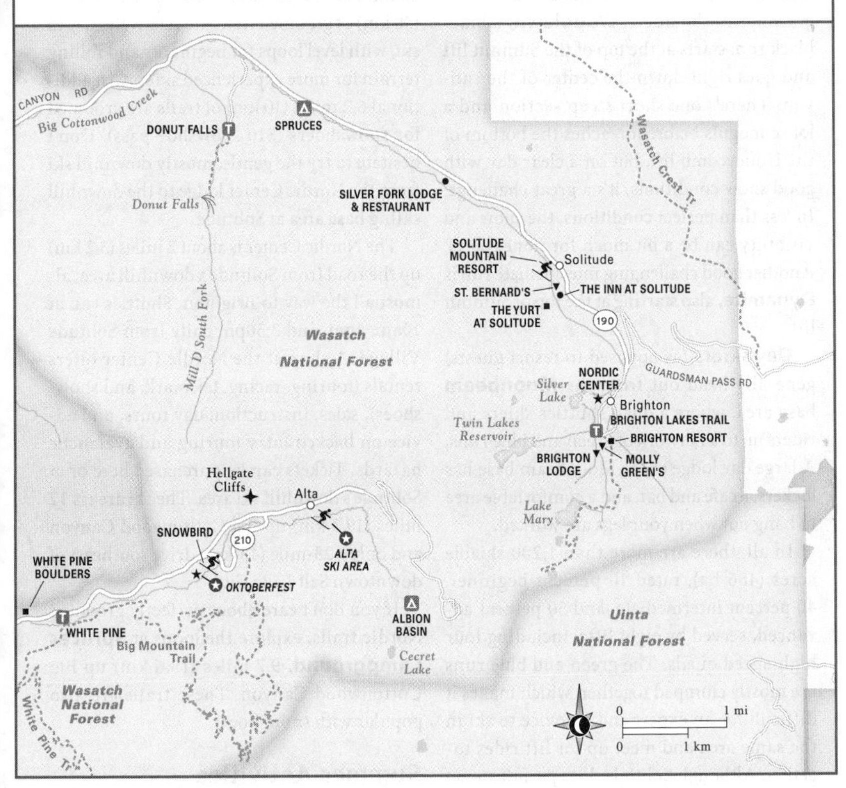

crowded. The other thing that makes this ski area distinctive is the European-style village at the base area. The village square is closed to cars; day visitors park in a paid lot ($10-35 for single occupant vehicle, $5-25 for double occupant vehicle, $0-10 if you carpool in a group of 3 or more; prices vary based on dates) about a 5-minute walk away from the lifts. From the lodging, it's only a short walk to the lifts.

Ski season at Solitude runs from about Thanksgiving until the third week in April, depending on snow.

History

This area was originally called Solitude by silver miners in the early 1900s. It became a ski area served by two chairlifts in 1957, and in 1989, the Emerald Express became Utah's first high-speed quad. Until the Creekside condominiums opened in 1995, Solitude was entirely a day-use area. In 2018, Alterra Mountain Company, the owners of Deer Valley Resort, purchased Solitude.

Terrain and Lifts

Skiers can choose from a wide variety of runs—there are plenty of blue cruisers, and when conditions are good, gates open to expert terrain, including the 400-plus acres (162 ha) of ungroomed powder found at Honeycomb Canyon on the back side of the resort. **Honeycomb lift,** a fixed quad, makes this challenging, largely natural area relatively accessible to experts.

One of the nice things about Honeycomb Canyon is that along with all the steep, double-black tree terrain, there's one run that's accessible to strong intermediate skiers and snowboarders. **Woodlawn,** a blue-black run, starts at the top of the Summit lift and goes right down the center of the canyon. There's one short steep section and a lot of moguls before it reaches the bottom of the Honeycomb lift, but on a clear day with good snow conditions, it's a great challenge. In less than perfect conditions, the snow and visibility can be a bit much for nonexperts. Another good challenging intermediate run is **Dynamite,** also starting at the top of Summit lift.

Day skiers (as opposed to resort guests) generally head out from the **Moonbeam** base area, where a quad shuttles skiers and riders up to a network of green and blue runs. A large day lodge at the Moonbeam base has lockers, a café and bar, and a comfortable area to hang out when your legs are worked.

In all, there are more than 1,200 skiable acres (486 ha), rated 10 percent beginner, 40 percent intermediate, and 50 percent advanced, served by eight lifts, including four high-speed quads. The green and blue runs are mostly clumped together, which makes it difficult for an expert and a novice to ski in the same area and meet up for lift rides together. Although Solitude does permit snowboarding and has a terrain park, most Big Cottonwood boarders head to Brighton.

Lift ticket prices are $115-159 adults, $83-114 seniors 65 and up, and $63-87 ages 5-12. Beginners who stick to the two lowest lifts at the Moonbeam area can buy an $89-99 ticket. It's possible to save a few bucks by purchasing tickets online ahead of time.

Lifts run 9am-4pm daily. Solitude also has a ski school, rentals, and kids' programs.

Solitude Nordic Center

Plenty of snow and nicely groomed tracks make Solitude's **Nordic Center** (Silver Lake Day Lodge, 801/536-5774 or 800/748-4754, ext. 5774, www.solitudemountain.com, 8am-4:30pm daily mid-Nov.-mid-Apr., $24 ages 13-64, $16 seniors and kids ages 5-12) one of the best places in Utah for both traditional cross-country skiers and skate skiers. The 12.4 miles (20 km) of groomed trails are relatively easy to ski, with level loops for beginners and rolling terrain for more experienced skiers. An additional 6.2 miles (10 km) of trails are groomed for snowshoers ($10 snowshoe pass). Don't hesitate to try the gentle, mostly downhill ski from the Nordic Center lodge to the downhill skiing base area at Solitude.

The Nordic Center is about 2 miles (3.2 km) up the road from Solitude's downhill area, almost all the way to Brighton. Shuttles run at 10am, 1pm, and 3:30pm daily from Solitude Village. A shop at the Nordic Center offers rentals (touring, racing, telemark, and snowshoes), sales, instruction, day tours, and advice on backcountry touring and avalanche hazards. Tickets can be purchased here or at Solitude's downhill ski area. The ski area is 12 miles (19.3 km) up Big Cottonwood Canyon and only a 28-mile (45-km) drive southeast of downtown Salt Lake City.

If you don't care about perfectly groomed Nordic trails, explore the loops at **Spruces Campground,** 9.7 miles (15.6 km) up Big Cottonwood Canyon. These trails are also popular with snowshoers.

Summer Activities

During the summer, the **Sunrise lift** (a single round-trip lift ride costs $30 pp) and most summer activities operate 10am-6pm Friday-Sunday.

Twenty miles (32 km) of single-track within the resort area, plus easy access to nearby Wasatch National Forest roads and trails, make Solitude a fun place for **mountain biking.** Bikes are permitted on the Sunrise lift (Fri.-Sun. summer, full-day lift pass $40). Full-suspension mountain bikes ($90 full-day, $75 after 1:30pm) are available for rent.

The 18-hole **disc golf course** is free, although you may want to ride the Sunrise lift to get to the first hole, which is at 9,000 feet

1: Big Cottonwood Canyon 2: Solitude Mountain Resort 3: mountain biking the trails around Solitude 4: Brighton Resort

Getting to the Mountain

A rental car isn't mandatory for a Utah ski trip, even if you want to visit more than one resort. The cheapest way to do this is to stay in Salt Lake City and take the UTA bus to the mountains.

UTA buses (801/743-3882, www.rideuta.com, $5 one-way in winter) run directly between Salt Lake City and Solitude and Brighton resorts, with stops at many hotels and park-and-rides. To reach Snowbird and Alta resorts, take the TRAX Blue Line light rail from downtown south to the Midvale Fort Union station. From the Midvale Fort Union station, bus 972 travels up Big Cottonwood Canyon and bus 994 goes up Little Cottonwood. From the Historic Sandy station (also on TRAX Blue Line), Bus 994 goes up Little Cottonwood. The bus ride from the 7200 South TRAX station to Alta takes a little over an hour. Buses run daily throughout the day in winter.

Even easier than the bus is a shared ride service or shuttle. From the airport, **Canyon Transportation** (801/255-1841, http://canyontransport.com, $49-265 depending on destination and whether you choose shared or private services) runs regular shared shuttles up Big and Little Cottonwood Canyons and to Park City. **Alta Shuttle** (801/274-0225 or 866/274-0225, www.altashuttle.com, any trip $47 one-way) runs back and forth between the airport and Alta and Snowbird resorts in Little Cottonwood Canyon.

Once you get to your destination, don't feel like you're tied to your chosen ski area. UTA runs a shuttle between Solitude and Brighton; regular buses connect Snowbird and Alta. For longer trips, private shuttle buses travel between Big and Little Cottonwood Canyons and the Park City resorts.

(2,743 m) elevation—a pretty good hike up the mountain from the base area.

Food

The Inn at Solitude's restaurant, **St. Bernard's** (801/535-4120, www.solitudemountain.com, 7am-10am daily, hours vary seasonally, $18-24), is the place to go for pre-ski breakfast.

For a quick slice of pizza, an espresso, or good ice cream, stop by the **Stone Haus Pizzeria and Creamery** (801/536-5767, 11am-7pm Sun.-Thurs., 11am-8pm Fri.-Sat. winter, hours may vary seasonally, $12-25), right in the village square. During summer, you'll be able to spot the distinctive grass roof. In winter, it's where cross-country skiers gather for a free shuttle to the Nordic area.

Snowshoe (approximately 0.75 mi/1.2 km, snowshoes provided) to the trailside ★ **Yurt** (801/536-5765, 5:30pm Wed.-Sun. winter) for a five-course dinner ($200). Only 26 people are seated each evening; reservations are required, and it's best to make them well in advance.

Outside the main resort complex, **Silver Fork Lodge** (11 mi/17.7 km up Big Cottonwood Canyon, 801/533-9977, www.silverforklodge.com, 8am-8pm daily in summer, 8am-2pm Mon.-Wed., 8am-8pm Thurs.-Sun. in winter, $18-49) is a favorite destination for a scenic brunch or dinner, followed by a hike or some morning laps at the resort.

Accommodations

Most Solitude lodging lies in the European-style ski village at the base area and is owned and managed by Solitude Mountain Resort (801/534-1400 or 800/748-4754, www.solitudemountain.com). Rates drop by about 50 percent during the summer.

The **Inn at Solitude** ($294-384 winter, $242-262 summer) is a few steps from the base area lifts. As ski resort hotels go, it's rather intimate, with 46 average guest rooms, a fancy restaurant and bar, a spa, and other amenities.

The ski area offers several accommodations with condos, all bookable at www.solitudemountain.com. **Creekside Condos** ($300-500) are right next to the base area lifts. A few steps farther, the condos at **Powderhorn Lodge** are another good option for groups ($100-500). A slightly longer walk to the lifts, **Eagle Springs** ($100-500) has units with easy access to Club Solitude's indoor pool and exercise room. All have fireplaces, full kitchens, TVs, and private decks and come with 1-3 bedrooms. Just outside the main village area, find the **Crossings,** with three-bedroom town houses ($663-795).

About 1 mile (1.6 km) from Solitude, and not part of the resort village, is the **Silver Fork Lodge** (11332 E. Big Cottonwood Canyon, 801/649-9551, www.silverforklodge.com, $130-240, includes breakfast), which has eight rustic B&B rooms without TVs or telephones. The Silver Fork is largely known for its restaurant.

Getting There

From Salt Lake City, take I-80 east to I-215 south to exit 6 (6200 South); follow 6200 South, which becomes Wasatch Boulevard. Follow signs to Big Cottonwood Canyon. Solitude is 14 miles (22.5 km) up Big Cottonwood Canyon.

UTA buses and Canyon Transportation shuttles serve all resorts in Big Cottonwood Canyon.

BRIGHTON RESORT

Brighton (801/532-4731, www.brightonresort.com, 9am-4pm daily mid-Nov.-mid-Apr., night skiing 4pm-9pm Mon.-Sat. mid-Dec.-early Apr.) is a longtime locals' favorite for its excellent skiing and friendly, laid-back atmosphere. There's no Euro-village resort here—it's all about being on the mountain. It's also the least expensive and most snowboard-friendly of the Cottonwood resorts, and is the only place near Salt Lake with a real night-skiing program. The resort is in the Uinta-Wasatch-Cache National Forest and does not have a commercial summer season, but there are plenty of places to hike in the area.

History

This is Utah's oldest ski resort, dating back to 1936, when ski-club members built a "skier tow" from half-inch wire rope and an old elevator drum. Two years later, a T-bar tow was erected, and in 1946, the area's first actual chairlift traveled up Mount Millicent.

Terrain and Lifts

Brighton is the only resort in Utah where every single run is accessible via high-speed quad lifts, which climb as high as 10,500 feet (3,200 m) for a 1,875-foot (572-m) vertical descent to the base. In addition to the 66 runs at Brighton, you can hop on the Sol-Bright run to visit Solitude ski area (a lift there will put you back on a trail to Brighton. Although a lot of the territory is suitable for beginners and intermediates, Brighton does offer some difficult powder-bowl skiing and steep runs.

First-timers can step onto the **Magic Carpet** and be gently carried up to the **Explorer** area, which is also served by a slow-moving (and thus easy to mount and dismount) lift. Beginners with a few runs behind them and cautious intermediate skiers and riders should venture onto the **Majestic lift,** which serves a good network of wide, tree-lined green and blue runs. More advanced skiers will prefer the bowls in the **Millicent** and **Evergreen** areas.

One of the things that make Brighton so popular with snowboarders (besides the fact that they're welcome here) is its lack of long runouts. It also has an open-backcountry policy.

Brighton's terrain parks are among the best in the West. Snowboarders looking for a challenge should head up the **Crest Express** quad and play around the My-O-My and Candyland terrain parks. Just downhill from these areas are two more terrain parks and a half-pipe.

Brighton has a ski and snowboard school, rentals, ski shops, a couple cafeterias, and a sit-down restaurant in the lodge. Many Utah residents learned to ski at Brighton, and its snowboard classes are especially good.

Lift tickets are $89-119 adults, $47-86 seniors 65 and up, $48-70 ages 7-12, free for children under 7 with a paying adult. Rates vary day to day, and tickets must be purchased online.

Food

Slope-side restaurants include the cafeteria and good lunch spot **Alpine Rose** (801/532-4731, ext. 252, 8am-8pm Mon.-Sat., 8am-4pm Sun. mid-Dec.-mid-Mar., 11am-5pm Mon.-Wed., 11am-8pm Thurs.-Fri., 9am-8pm Sat.-Sun. mid-Mar.-mid-Dec., $6-12); the **Milly Chalet** (801/532-4731, ext. 219, 8am-4:30pm Mon.-Thurs., 8am-6pm Fri.-Sun. winter, 8:30am-9pm daily spring-fall, $6-12) at the base of the Millicent quad; and **Molly Green's** (801/532-4731, ext. 206, 11am-10pm daily mid-Dec.-mid-Mar., 11am-9pm Mon.-Sat., 11am-4pm Sun. mid-Mar.-mid-Dec., dinner $10-18, age 21 and over only), a bar and grill with table service.

Accommodations

Adjacent to the slopes is resort-owned **Brighton Lodge** (855/201-7669, $199-289), which offers accommodations with a heated outdoor pool and a spa adjacent to the restaurant. It's much smaller than most ski-resort lodges and very casual.

Getting There

Brighton is at the road's end, 2 miles (3.2 km) past Solitude in Big Cottonwood Canyon. From Salt Lake City, take I-80 east to I-215 south. Take I-215 to exit 6 (6200 South) and follow 6200 South, which becomes Wasatch Boulevard. Follow signs to Big Cottonwood Canyon. Brighton is 16 miles (26 km) up Big Cottonwood Canyon.

UTA buses and Canyon Transportation shuttles serve all resorts in Big Cottonwood Canyon.

HIKING

Hikers in Big Cottonwood Canyon should leave their dogs at home. Because this area is a key part of Salt Lake City's drinking water supply, dogs are prohibited in this watershed. A good map for hikes in the area is the *Trails Illustrated Wasatch Front North,* map 709.

Mineral Fork Trail

This trail (5 mi/8 km one-way) follows an old mining road past abandoned mines, cabins, and rusting equipment to a high glacial cirque. Waterfalls, alpine meadows, wildflowers, and abundant birdlife make the steep climb worthwhile. The signed trailhead is on the south side of the road, 6 miles (9.7 km) up the canyon (0.8 mi/1.3 km past Moss Ledge Picnic Area). You'll climb 2,000 vertical feet (610 m) in 3 miles (4.8 km) to the Wasatch Mine, which has mineralized water that makes up much of the flow of Mineral Fork Creek. Another 2 miles (3.2 km) and 1,400 vertical feet (427 m) of climbing lead to the Regulator Johnson Mine. A loop can be made by climbing the ridge west of Regulator Johnson (no trail) and descending Mill B South Fork Trail to Lake Blanche and the main road, coming out 1.5 miles (2.4 km) west of the Mineral Fork trailhead.

Donut Falls

The easy and popular hike to Donut Falls (0.75 mi/1.2 km one-way) starts just past Jordan Pines Campground and follows a trail that's partly through the woods and partly an old dirt road to the waterfall, which spurts from a "doughnut hole" in a rock inside a small cave. Rockfall and erosion have made the effect a bit less doughnut-like in recent years.

Brighton Lakes Trail

Winding through gorgeous alpine lake country, this easy, family-friendly trail (3 mi/4.8 km one-way) begins behind Brighton Lodge. Silver Lake has a boardwalk giving full access to fishing docks. The first section follows Big Cottonwood Creek through stands of aspen and evergreens. The trail continues south across wildflower-filled meadows, then climbs to Brighton Overlook, 1 mile (1.6 km) from the start. Dog Lake, surrounded by old mine dumps, lies 200 yards (183 m) to the south. Continue on the main trail 0.5 (0.8 km) mile to large and deep Lake Mary, below

1: Donut Falls **2:** aspens along Brighton Lakes Trail

1

2

Mount Millicent. Lake Martha is another 0.5 mile (0.8 km) up the trail. Another mile (1.6 km) of climbing takes you to Lake Catherine, bordered by a pretty meadow on the north and the steep talus slopes of Sunset and Pioneer Peaks on the south. Total elevation gain for the 3-mile (4.8-km) hike to Lake Catherine is 1,200 feet (366 m). Hikers can also go another 0.5 mile (0.8 km) to Catherine Pass and descend 1.5 miles (2.4 km) to Albion Basin in Little Cottonwood Canyon. Sunset Peak (10,648 ft/3,246 m) can be climbed by following a 0.5-mile (0.8-km) trail from the pass.

CLIMBING

While both Cottonwood Canyons have extensive rock climbing, Big Cottonwood is the less popular of the two. But from end to end, crags of quartzite beckon, with sport and trad climbs aplenty. Big Cottonwood also has some bouldering as well as a few ice climbs and alpine-style climbs.

S-Curves

In the northern part of Big Cottonwood, the road traces the shape of an "S." Here you'll find four big crags, largely composed of steep sport routes in a variety of grades. This area does tend to draw crowds, due to a short approach and ample protection. But you can elude them if you seek out a hidden gem like **Skyscraper** (5.8+, 170 ft/52 m) on the upper wall, 4.25 miles (6.8 km) up the canyon across the road via Mill B North Fork trail. Skyscraper is a long, exposed climb requiring a 70-meter rope, nine quickdraws, and material to build a tree anchor at the top, where you'll find panoramic views of Big Cottonwood Canyon.

Storm Mountain Picnic Area

The **Storm Mountain Picnic Area** ($10 entrance fee) is the unofficial hub of climbing in Big Cottonwood, with over 70 climbs running the gamut from bouldering and trad to ice in winter. It's also easy to find since—as its name suggests—Storm Mountain doubles as a picnic area with bathrooms. The area can be found 2.85 miles (4.6 km) up the canyon on the left; just look for signs and park in the designated lot. If you park alongside the road, the day-use fee is waived.

One of the classics here is **Goodro's Wall** (5.10c, trad, one pitch), which some say was the first 5.10 in the United States. Local climber and climbing instructor Harold Goodro—also former Alta ski patroller—bagged the first ascent in 1949. Find this climb in the sub-area dubbed Storm Mountain Island. Bring nuts and cams 2 inches (5 cm) and smaller for protection and enjoy the hand crack and roof moves.

CAMPGROUNDS

All Uinta-Wasatch-Cache National Forest campgrounds have water in summer. Reserve sites at 877/444-6777 or www.recreation.gov ($8 reservation fee). To protect the Salt Lake City watershed, dogs are not permitted at these campgrounds, and this is strictly enforced.

At an elevation of 7,500 feet (2,286 m), **Spruces Campground** (9.7 mi/15.6 km up the canyon, late May-mid-Oct., $28) is the largest campground in the area. Between Solitude and Brighton, **Redman Campground** (13 mi/20.9 km up the canyon, mid-June-early Oct., $28) sits at an elevation of 8,300 feet (2,530 m).

Little Cottonwood Canyon

TOP EXPERIENCE

The road through this nearly straight glacial valley ascends 5,500 vertical feet (1,676 m) in 11 miles (17.7 km). Splendid peaks rise to more than 11,000 feet (3,353 m) on both sides of the canyon. In winter and spring, challenging terrain attracts skiers to the Snowbird and Alta ski areas. Enter Little Cottonwood Canyon from the junction of Highway 209 and Highway 210, 4 miles (6.4 km) south of the entrance to Big Cottonwood Canyon.

The discovery of silver first attracted people to Little Cottonwood in 1865. Around 400 folks still call the town of Alta home, but thousands of people once lived up this canyon during the mining boom, which led to significant deforestation. Granite for the Salt Lake Temple came from quarries 1 mile (1.6 km) up the canyon on the left. The canyon is also the site of the Granite Mountain Record Vaults, containing genealogical and historical records of the LDS Church stored on millions of rolls of microfilm. Neither site is open to the public.

SNOWBIRD

When you drive up Little Cottonwood Canyon, **Snowbird** (801/933-2222 or 800/232-9542, road and snow report 801/933-2100, www.snowbird.com) is the first resort you approach. It's about a 40-minute drive from the heart of downtown Salt Lake City when ski traffic isn't an issue. Aside from sheer convenience, Snowbird is known for its great snow—an average of 500 inches (12.7 m) a year, and much of that classified as light champagne powder. It's a sweeping, adventurous place to ski or ride, with lots of varied terrain.

History

Snowbird's cofounder and developer, Dick Bass, was well known in mountaineering circles as the author of *Seven Summits*, his account of climbing the highest peak on every continent. He reportedly had the vision for this resort, including the deluxe Cliff Lodge, while he was holed up in a tent on Mount Everest. The soaring 11-story, windowed atrium at the sturdy concrete Cliff imparts a sense of openness that was lacking in that Everest tent. Along with open space and light, Bass also had a vision of a spa.

It was important to Bass to build an environmentally friendly resort, and much effort was taken to preserve trees and improve the quality of the watershed, which mining had degraded. Mine tailings were removed and lodges built in their place to avoid harming existing trees and vegetation.

Terrain and Lifts

Snowbird is on the west side of the Wasatch Range, with ski runs mostly on the north face of the mountains. There are three distinct areas: **Peruvian Gulch, Gad,** and **Mineral Basin** on the back side. If 2,500 skiable acres (1,012 ha) aren't enough to keep you busy, you can buy a lift ticket that lets you ski between Snowbird and neighboring Alta.

Plenty of lifts serve Snowbird, including six high-speed quads and a tram that can ferry up to 125 skiers at a time to the top of Peruvian Gulch. The runs here are also long (Chip's Run, from the top of the tram, is 2.5 mi/4 km), meaning that you don't have to hop a lift every few minutes. Unless it's a powder day, when locals call in sick and head for the mountains, lines aren't usually a problem, especially midweek. The one place that does get crowded is the tram; lines can be quite long, especially first thing in the morning and just after lunchtime. But the tram is a great way to get up the mountain quickly, with access to the best territory.

Twenty-seven percent of runs are classed as beginner, 38 percent intermediate, and 35 percent advanced, with the longest run

Peruvian Tunnel/ Cottonwood Heritage Center
SLOW DOWN

Multi-Resort Passes

The **IKON Pass** (www.ikonpass.com) provides access to up to 44 destinations, including Utah's Deer Valley, Alta, Snowbird, Solitude, and Brighton. An $829 season pass has blackout dates around holidays, unlimited access to Solitude, and 5 days at the other included Utah resorts. One caveat: Alta and Snowbird are lumped together, so you'll get 5 days total to both, rather than each. For $1,159, blackout days are eliminated. It might sound like a lot, but lift tickets to individual resorts quickly add up. Other participating resorts include Big Sky, Jackson Hole, and Steamboat.

If you plan to visit mostly areas owned by Vail Resorts (and there are many), check out the **Epic Pass** (www.epicpass.com). The only Utah resorts covered by this $909 pass are Park City Mountain Resort and Snowbasin.

The **Mountain Collective Pass** (https://mountaincollective.com) includes 2 days of access at 16 resorts, including Alta and Snowbird. An adult pass costs $489; kids 12 and under can get a pass for $149. Other western US ski areas included are Big Sky and Jackson Hole. An additional benefit of this pass is that it may give you a discount at some Alta-area lodgings.

If you prefer smaller, independently owned resorts, check out the Indy Pass (www.indyskipass.com), which gets you two free lift tickets and an additional discounted ticket at ski areas in the United States, Canada, and Japan. Beaver Mountain in Logan, Eagle Point in Beaver, and Powder Mountain in the Ogden area are the participating Utah resorts. Adult passes start at $319 and kids' passes start at $189. Blackout dates apply.

Note that rates and included resorts for these passes do vary from season to season.

descending 3,200 feet (975 m) across 3.5 miles (5.6 km). There's also plenty of ungroomed terrain. You'll find a terrain park on the Big Emma run, under the Mid-Gad lift. Snowbird's ski and snowboard schools and separate bunny hill make it a good place to learn. Guided ski tours of mostly blue runs last about 2 hours (free with lift ticket purchase) and leave from the Snowbird Plaza deck at 9:30am and 10:30am daily.

Skiers and snowboarders alike should check out the Mineral Basin area, where two high-speed quads serve a great network of runs. Reach it by taking the tram to the top of Hidden Peak (11,000 ft/3,353 m), then following signs to the back side of the mountain, or by riding the Peruvian Express lift to a "magic carpet" through a 600-foot-long (183-m) tunnel displaying historic Snowbird exhibits to Mineral Basin (an experience in and of itself).

Ski instruction and programs are available for children and adults. Snowbird also offers a number of adaptive ski programs (801/834-0476, http://wasatchadaptivesports.org) using sit-skis, mono-skis, and outriggers.

Lift tickets for adults cost $167-196; add access to Alta's lifts and you'll pay $199-219. Seniors pay $142-167, youth (ages 7-12) tickets are $100-118. Half-day and multiday passes are also available. The exceptionally long season at Snowbird runs mid-November-May, and sometimes as late as early July, though only a couple lifts remain open past May.

Wasatch Powderbird Guides (801/436-6917, www.powderbird.com) offers heli-skiing in the peaks above the regular runs. Rates start at $1,810 for a day (six or seven runs).

Summer Activities

Snowbird offers a loaded array of family recreation and resort facilities in summer, along with hiking, biking, and scenic lift rides. In fact, the base area can take on an amusement park-like atmosphere with all the kids' activities. All lodging, spa, and recreational facilities remain open year-round, as do many restaurants and stores.

Get away from the hubbub at the base with a tram ride to 11,000-foot (3,353-m) **Hidden**

1: Little Cottonwood Canyon 2: Snowbird aerial tram 3: the Peruvian Express lift

The Greatest Snow on Earth

What makes Utah's snow so great? In a word, geography. Storms come in from the Pacific, pushed by a cold jet stream across the Great Basin. When these storm clouds encounter the Wasatch peaks, the jet stream forces them upward into even colder air, where they release moisture. Very cold temperatures ensure this moisture falls as light, dry snow.

Storm fronts often become trapped in the Salt Lake Valley, laden with moisture and too heavy to rise out of the Great Basin. These heavy clouds make it partway out of the basin, dump snow on the nearby mountains, then drop back to the Great Salt Lake, where they pick up more moisture. This cycle continues until the storm weakens and the clouds release enough moisture to float over the tops of the mountains and continue eastward.

Peak (11am-8pm daily) for a fantastic panorama of the Wasatch Range, the surrounding valleys, and the distant Uinta Mountains. Round-trip one-ride tickets are $28 adults, $22 ages 7-16 and seniors, and free for children under 7. The Peruvian chairlift also runs in the summer; jeep trails connect the two lifts, and a pass is good on either one. Mountain bikers can ride the jaunty 7.5-mile (12.1-km) **Big Mountain Trail** downhill from the top of the tram to the base.

Big kids and kids at heart will love the **mountain coaster** (kind of like a personal roller coaster, $25 adults, $20 children per ride). An all-day pass for activities, including the coaster, jumping alpine slide, climbing wall, and more, goes for $49 or $36 for children under 48 inches tall.

The **Activity Center** (in the Snowbird Center, 801/933-2147) is the hub for summer activities. It also rents mountain bikes and can arrange horseback rides in Mineral Basin. Ask for a free map of local trails. Guided hikes are available, and there's a nature trail adapted for guests with disabilities. If you're looking to relax, the Cliff Spa and Salon offers beauty and massage treatments. Snowbird is also the site of frequent summertime musical and arts events.

★ Oktoberfest

Since 1973—just a couple years after Snowbird's founding—an annual Bavarian celebration of beer has taken over the far end of Little Cottonwood Canyon. On weekends during 2 months in late summer and early fall, Snowbird hosts **Oktoberfest** (www.snowbird.com/oktoberfest, noon-6pm Sat.-Sun. mid-Aug.-mid-Oct., admission free, $10 parking). The festival takes over Snowbird's entire base area with a biergarten, a marktplatz of crafts, polka, and a German food tent. Best of all, admission is free and beer and food are reasonably priced.

Between the alpine backdrop with glittering foliage and the many festivities, this is a magical time to be at Snowbird. Find crafts and tchotchkes as you stroll through Der Marktplatz, and fill your souvenir stein with local beers from Uinta, Bohemian, and other local breweries. Next, head to the food tent where you can watch traditional polka dancing while eating schnitzel, bratwurst, apple strudel, and other Bavarian favorites. Food tents are also available. At 3pm, alphorns bellow into the mountains on the central deck or at the top of the tram.

Spa

The Cliff Spa (801/933-2225) offers all sorts of massage therapies, facials, manicures, yoga and Pilates classes, a weight room, cardio equipment, and its own rooftop outdoor pool. It's much nicer and more complete than most hotel spas. A **day pass** ($35 hotel guests, $50 visitors) permits access to yoga classes and workout facilities. Nonguests are welcome. It's best to make an appointment for massages and other treatments at least a day or two in advance.

Food

Refuel after those pow turns with burgers or chili at **Mid-Gad Restaurant** (801/933-2245, 11am-8pm, hours may vary with season and weather, $12-17) or at the **Forklift** (801/933-2440, 7am-3pm and 3pm-5pm daily, $15-30), a sandwich-and-burger joint near the base of the tram. At the top of Hidden Peak tram, **Summit Restaurant** (801/933-2222, 9am-3pm daily, $10-25) houses an upscale cafeteria-style restaurant.

The ★ **Aerie** (801/933-2160 or ext. 5500, 5pm-9pm daily, $26-52) is the Cliff Lodge's high-end, 10th-floor restaurant, offering excellent steaks and pasta paired with sunset mountain views. If you'd like to partake of the Aerie's scenery but aren't up for the splurge, check out the sandwiches and small-plates menu in the Aerie's lounge.

Another relatively elegant spot for dinner is the **Lodge Bistro** (807/933-2145 or ext. 3042, 5pm-9pm Wed.-Sun., $22-49), located in the Lodge at Snowbird. The menu has a French influence, with a tasty croque-monsieur.

The grab-and-go espresso bar in the Cliff's **Atrium** (801/933-2140, 7am-3pm daily winter, 7am-11am daily summer, $5-10) serves granola, pastries, and breakfast sandwiches. It's quick and has a splendid view of the mountain.

In the Iron Blosam Lodge, the casual **Wildflower Restaurant** (807/933-2230 or ext. 1042, 4pm-9pm daily winter, $17-28) serves up Italian dinners as good as the views.

Snowbird throws it back to the 1970s at its newest restaurant, ★ **SeventyOne** (801/933-2222, www.snowbird.com/seventyone, 7am-10pm daily, $13-36), named for the year Snowbird opened. The restaurant's decor includes colorful booths, funky light fixtures, and a gold-plated bar. The open kitchen plates up updated '70s Americana like brisket baked ziti, chicken cordon bleu, and vegan meatloaf. Breakfast is buffet style ($27 pp).

Accommodations

All Snowbird's accommodations are run by the resort, and the best way to find out about the many options is to call the **reservation line** (800/232-9542) or check online (www.snowbird.com). Rates vary wildly according to season, day of week, and view, but are generally quite high during the winter and drop by more than half in summer.

The most upscale place to stay at Snowbird is the ski-in/ski-out ★ **Cliff Lodge,** with

mountain biking at Snowbird

over 500 rooms, four restaurants, conference facilities, shops, a year-round outdoor pool, and a top-notch spa. One nice practical detail is the ground-floor locker (complete with boot dryer) assigned to each guest. The Cliff is swanky without being snobbish or stuffy, although in parts of the lodge, the brutalist architecture and limited windows feel a little suffocating. Standard winter room rates start at around $550 (even the most basic rooms can sleep four), with many package deals available, including better rates on multiday packages that include lift tickets. During the summer, it's common to find rates around $200. The west wing of the Cliff has been remodeled into studio condos with kitchens and hot tubs.

The **Lodge at Snowbird,** the **Inn at Snowbird,** and the **Iron Blosam Lodge,** which has timeshare units and requires a Saturday-Saturday stay, are the resort's three condominium complexes. All offer guest laundry, pools, steam and sauna areas, restaurants, and many units with kitchens, and are just a short walk from the tram loading area. Most are one-bedroom units with rates starting at $385.

More condos are available through **Canyon Services** (800/562-2888, www.canyonservices.com) between Snowbird and Alta. These upscale accommodations are available in several different complexes and in units with 2-7 bedrooms; winter rates are around $630-1,500 per night (booking early may save you $100 or more a night), with a four-night minimum.

If these prices seem prohibitive, remember that Salt Lake City is just down the hill, and city buses run up the canyon several times a day.

Getting There

The resort at Snowbird is 6 miles (9.7 km) up Little Cottonwood Canyon and 25 miles (40 km) southeast of downtown Salt Lake City. Snow tires are required November 1-May 1. During heavy snowstorms, the canyon may be temporarily restricted to vehicles with 4WD or chains, or close entirely for avalanche mitigation measures.

UTA buses and Canyon Transportation shuttles serve all resorts in Little Cottonwood Canyon. Snowbird provides free shuttle service between the different areas of the resort during the ski day.

★ ALTA SKI AREA

Alta (801/359-1078, snow report 801/572-3939, www.alta.com) has a special mystique among skiers. Chalk this up to a combination of deep powder, wide-open terrain, charming accommodations, and an authentically rustic, old-fashioned vibe amid a sea of Disney World-esque, corporate resorts. Many Alta skiers have been coming here for decades—it's not uncommon to share a lift with a friendly 70-year-old who's headed straight for the steepest run. Like Deer Valley, Alta doesn't allow snowboarders.

If you're in it more for the ski lifestyle than the actual skiing, Alta's not the best resort for you. There's no shopping, nightlife, or après scene to speak of. Unlike Park City's resorts, there are no housing developments surrounding and amid the runs at Alta or Snowbird, which creates a much more natural, peaceful feeling. The lack of development is largely thanks to the late Bill Levitt, former owner of Alta Lodge and mayor of Alta for 34 years, who fought developers all the way to the US Supreme Court.

Dogs are not permitted in the town of Alta, unless they receive a special permit. Appeal to the powers-that-be at the town offices, if you're so motivated.

History

The little town of Alta owes its original reputation to rich silver veins and the mining camp's rip-roaring saloon life. Mining started in 1865 with the opening of the Emma Mine and peaked in 1872, when Alta had a population of 5,000 served by 26 saloons and six

1: a skier catching some air at Alta Ski Area 2: Alta Ski Area

1
2
OPEN

breweries. Crashing silver prices the following year and a succession of deadly avalanches ended the boom. Little remains from the old days except abandoned mine shafts, a few shacks, and the cemetery.

By the 1930s, only one resident was left, George Watson, who elected himself mayor. In 1938, he deeded 1,800 acres to the US Forest Service. There is some present-day speculation that Watson didn't ever really own the deeded land, but he did take advantage of the tax breaks he got by handing it over to the government.

Ski enthusiasts brought Alta back to life. The Forest Service hired famous skier Alf Engen to determine Alta's potential as a site for a future ski area. In 1939, Alta's Collins chairlift became the second lift in the United States—though some complained that the $1.50 per day lift tickets reserved the sport for the rich. Some of the original Collins single chairs are still around. Look for them in the Wildcat Base parking lot near the Goldminer's Daughter Lodge.

Terrain and Lifts

The first thing to know about Alta is that it's for skiers—snowboards aren't allowed. Even though it's right next door to Snowbird, the vibe is totally different. Whereas Snowbird feels modern and massive, Alta has an almost rustic European quality. To keep the slopes from becoming too crowded, Alta limits the number of skiers allowed, mostly during holidays and powder-filled weekends.

Alta's season usually runs mid-November-April. Average total snowfall is about 500 inches (12.7 m) per year, and snow levels usually peak in March, with depths of about 120 inches (3 m). Lifts include three high-speed quads, a high-speed triple, four slower chairlifts, and several tow ropes.

Even though Alta has the reputation of being an experts' ski area, there's a fair amount of nice beginner and intermediate territory. Of the 119 runs, 15 percent are rated beginner, 30 percent intermediate, and 55 percent advanced. The longest run is 3.5 miles (5.6 km) and drops 2,500 vertical feet (762 m). Skiers should keep their eyes open as they ride the lifts—porcupines are a common sight in the treetops.

A good strategy for skiing Alta's 2,200 acres (890 ha) is to begin the day warming up around the Albion Base on the east side of the resort, before heading up the Supreme lift to the top of Albion Basin, with steep blue runs and some of Alta's famously "steep and deep" black runs. Later in the day, head to the Wildcat side, after the sun has had a chance to soften the snow there.

Holders of the Alta-Snowbird pass can cut over to Snowbird's Mineral Basin area from the top of Alta's Sugarloaf lift. The cut-across is not difficult, and Mineral Basin is a fun place to ski.

Alta's **Alf Engen Ski School** (801/799-2271) offers a wide variety of lessons; rentals and child-care services are also available. Guided snowcat skiing and snowboarding in the Grizzly Gulch backcountry are available for expert skiers and riders with solid off-piste experience. A 2-hour beginner group class costs $150 for adults and $108 for kids; multi-week programs for expert skiers are also available. Call the ski school to reserve a spot.

Lift ticket prices are $159-179 adults, $80-90 under age 12. **Alta-Snowbird combo-ticket** costs are $199-219 adults, $125-135 children.

Cross-Country Skiing

Cross-country skiers can follow a 1.9-mile (3-km) loop groomed for both classic and skate skiing (free). It's not the world's most exciting trail—it essentially parallels the tow rope that runs between the Wildcat and Albion lifts—but it's a good place to learn cross-country techniques or get your legs in shape at the beginning of the season.

More ambitious Nordic skiers can head up the unplowed summer road to Albion Basin. Snowcats often pack the snow. The road begins at the upper end of the Albion parking lot, then climbs gently to the top of the Albion lift, where skiers can continue to

Dealing with High Altitude

If you live at sea level and leave home at 5pm on Thursday, fly to Salt Lake City, and get the first tram up from the Snowbird base area at 9am on Friday, you'll have gained 11,000 feet (3,353 m) in less than 24 hours.

It's hard to predict who will be immobilized by the altitude. Men seem to have more problems than women, and athletes often feel worse than more-sedentary people. But the altitude (and the dry air that goes along with it) can have a host of effects.

SOME EFFECTS OF HIGH ALTITUDE

- Fatigue and sleeplessness
- Dizziness
- Shortness of breath
- Loss of appetite and eventually nausea
- Increased drug potency, especially with tranquilizers and sedatives
- Increased UV radiation: People taking tetracycline are especially sensitive to the sun.
- Stuffy nose: The dry air can make your sinus tissues swell and feel stuffy.

TIPS

- Don't expect to go full steam all at once. If possible, spend a day in Salt Lake City before you go up to Park City or into the Cottonwood Canyons. For some, day two can be particularly rough, so don't feel bad about knocking off early and taking a nap. Rest is good, even when sleep is difficult.
- Don't take it too easy. It's best to get some light exercise.
- Drink lots of water (more than you think you need) and avoid alcohol for the first 2 or 3 days (or at least reduce your intake).
- Decrease salt intake to prevent fluid retention.
- Breathe deeply.
- Use nasal saline spray and a vaporizer at night. Some ski resorts have them in guest rooms.
- Try not to arrive with a cold if you can help it!
- If you're seriously prone to high altitude's ill effects, consult your doctor before your trip. Diamox, a prescription drug, stimulates the respiratory system and decreases fluid retention, easing the effects of high altitude.

Albion Basin. Intermediate and advanced skiers can also ski to Catherine Pass and Twin Lakes Pass. Cross-country skiers may ski the beginner (green) Alta trails.

Food

Since almost all of Alta's lodges include breakfast and dinner for guests, Alta does not have a highly developed restaurant scene. All lodge dining rooms are open to the public, and Rustler and Alta Lodge are particularly good places for dinner.

Stop for lunch on the mountain at **Watson Café** (801/799-2296, 10:30am-3:30pm daily winter, $10-15), midmountain beneath the top of Wildcat lift. Upstairs, at **Collins Grill** (801/799-2297, 11:30am-2:30pm daily winter, $16-25), you can pull off your ski boots and wear restaurant-provided slippers for a sit-down lunch.

The Snowpine Lodge has a stylish restaurant, **Swen's** (801/742-2000, www.snowpine.com, 7am-10am and 5pm-9pm daily, $24-210), with a big open kitchen, communal table, expansive views, and a menu ranging from inventive pastas and seafood to an epic Wagyu tomahawk.

Accommodations

Alta's accommodations are excellent, though pricey: Even bunk beds in a dorm room cost well over $100. There's an additional room tax of more than 12 percent, and most lodges tack on a 15 percent service charge in lieu of tipping. Room rates at all lodges listed here, however, do include breakfast and dinner. In summer, room rates drop by nearly half.

The easiest way to find a room is go to the lodging page on Alta's website, where you can enter your dates of travel and link to available lodges and condos. The local visitor's bureau website (www.discoveralta.com) has a similar feature.

In Alta, one of the most charming and central places to stay is the **Alta Lodge** (801/742-3500 or 800/707-2582, www.altalodge.com, dorm bed $198-387 pp, standard room $333-800 includes breakfast, afternoon tea, and dinner), an old-fashioned ski lodge. Built in 1939, Alta Lodge has a relaxed atmosphere and a lively bar, the Sitzmark Club. There are no TVs in the guest rooms (but there is Wi-Fi), but a game room off the lobby has a big TV. The lodge also has a good ski-and-play program for kids.

The **Alta Peruvian Lodge** (801/742-3000 or 800/453-8488, www.altaperuvian.com, dorm bed $199 pp, standard room $539-609 includes breakfast, lunch, and dinner) also has a low-key vibe, despite its large heated outdoor pool and grand lobby. The Peruvian has a colorful history. In 1947, its owner acquired two hospital barracks from Brigham City, over 100 miles (161 km) to the north, hauled them to Alta, and hooked them together. Although that original structure still stands in a convenient location near the Wildcat Base, the lodge has been considerably updated and modernized.

Laden with amenities yet still laid-back, ★ **Alta's Rustler Lodge** (801/742-4200, www.rustlerlodge.com, dorm bed $196 pp, standard room $482-652 d includes breakfast and dinner) has a heated outdoor pool, a fine-dining restaurant, and spacious guest rooms. Après-ski, it's common to see guests wandering around the lobby swathed in their thick hotel bathrobes. The Rustler spa offers massage, facials, and full-body skin care; call the lodge to book an appointment.

Alta's oldest place to stay is **Snowpine Lodge** (801/742-2000, www.snowpine.com, standard room $499-599 includes breakfast and dinner). Though it was built in 1938, an extensive remodel and expansion has made it newly luxurious, fully Instagrammable, and rustic no more. It now has six floors, a spa, an outdoor pool, and a game room.

The **Goldminer's Daughter Lodge** (801/742-2300, www.goldminersdaughterlodge.com, dorm bunk usually for men $185 pp, standard room $320-669 includes breakfast and dinner) is close to the base of the Wildcat lift, near the large parking area, with easy ski-in/ski-out access. While the Goldminer's Daughter doesn't have quite the history or ambience of its neighboring lodges, it's plenty comfortable.

In addition to the traditional ski lodges, there are condos available for rent, including a wide range of properties through **Alta Chalets** (801/424-2426, www.altachalets.com). Be sure to pick up groceries in Salt Lake City, since there are no food stores up here.

Getting There and Around

Alta is 8 miles (12.9 km) up Little Cottonwood Canyon. Snow tires are required in the canyon November 1-May 1. During extremely heavy snowstorms, the canyon may be temporarily restricted to vehicles with 4WD or chains, or shut down entirely.

Parking can be difficult in Alta. Pay attention to the No Parking signs, as parking regulations are enforced. Friday-Sunday and on holidays, advance parking reservations are required (www.altaparking.com, $25).

UTA buses and Canyon Transportation shuttles serve all resorts in Little Cottonwood Canyon. **Alta Shuttle** (801/274-0225 or 866/274-0225, www.altashuttle.com, $47 one-way) runs between the airport and Alta.

It's easy to get around Alta without a car, thanks to the **Alta Resort Shuttle** (801/301-0122, 7am-6pm daily winter, on-demand in the evening, free), which swings by most of the local condos and the Wildcat Base on its continuous loop.

HIKING

Because this canyon is part of the Salt Lake City watershed, environmental regulations prohibit pets, even in the car, so leave your dog or adventure cat at home.

White Pine, Red Pine, and Maybird Gulch

These three popular trails lead to pretty alpine lakes and wildflowers. Red Pine and Maybird Gulch are in the Lone Peak Wilderness (www.fs.usda.gov/uwcnf). All three trails begin from the same trailhead, then diverge into separate valleys.

Start from the White Pine trailhead (elev. 7,700 ft/2,347 m), 5.3 miles (8.5 km) up the canyon and 1 mile (1.6 km) beyond Tanners Flat Campground. The trails divide after 1 mile (1.6 km): Turn sharply left for White Pine Lake or continue straight across the stream for Red Pine Lake and Maybird Gulch. Red Pine Trail contours around a ridge, then parallels Red Pine Fork to the lake (elev. 9,680 ft/2,950 m)—a beautiful deep pool ringed by conifers and meadows. Maybird Gulch Trail begins 2 miles (3.2 km) up Red Pine Trail from White Pine Fork and leads to tiny Maybird Lakes. From the trailhead, White Pine Lake is 3.5 miles (5.6 km) with 2,300 feet (701 m) of elevation gain, Red Pine Lake is 3.5 miles (5.6 km) with 1,920 feet (585 m) of elevation gain, and Maybird Lakes are 4.5 miles (7.2 km) with 2,060 feet (628 m) of elevation gain.

Peruvian Gulch-Hidden Peak Trail

These Snowbird area trails give you the advantage of hiking just one way (either up or down) by using the Snowbird tram ($28). From the top of Hidden Peak (elev. 11,000 ft/3,353 m), the trail crosses open rocky country on the upper slopes and tree-filled ridges lower down, then follows an old mining road down Peruvian Gulch. Elevation change along the 3.5-mile (5.6-mile) trail is 2,900 feet (884 m).

Catherine Pass

It's a lovely 1.5-mile (2.4-km) hike to Catherine Pass (with 900 ft/274 m of elevation gain) and just under 5 miles (8 km) to Brighton. After the big parking area just past Snowpine Lodge, the road turns to dirt; follow it another 2 miles (3.2 km) to a trailhead for Catherine Pass.

Cecret Lake Trail

At the end of the road past Snowpine Lodge is the Albion Basin Campground and Cecret Lake trailhead, which climbs glacier-scarred granite slopes to a pretty alpine lake (elev. 9,880 ft/3,011 m) below Sugarloaf Mountain. Wildflowers put on colorful summer displays along the way. The trail is just 1 mile (1.6 km) long with 360 feet (110 m) of elevation gain, making for a good family hike. Continue another mile for views of Mount Timpanogos from Germania Pass.

CLIMBING

Little Cottonwood is known for pearl-white granite walls, slab climbing, and steep cracks that will wear you out in a good way.

Hellgate Cliffs

Unlike the majority of rock in Little Cottonwood, Hellgate offers hard climbing on limestone cliffs. This area is not very "clean," meaning you'll find loose rock, making helmets nonnegotiable. The short yet steep approach trail starts 9 miles (14.5 km) up the canyon on the left side of the road across from the Alta Peruvian Lodge. **Hellraiser** (5.10b, mixed, 500 ft/152 m, 5 pitches) is a fun route involving an arête, cracks, and slabs. The canyon views from the top of any of Hellgate's climbs are spectacular.

White Pine Boulders

Boulderers of all stripes can find fun problems in this area. Just under 5 miles (8 km) up the canyon, there's a pullout by a rock wall on the left side of the road. From this pullout, you can access several different subsets of boulders by heading north or south. A classic area is the **Party Pit,** which can be found south of the pullout after crossing the logs over Little Cottonwood Creek. Among the southern White Pine Boulders, the Party Pit cluster sits in the middle. Mom Boulder—distinguishable by hash marks across its surface—has a few classics at various grades. Beginners can boogie up Deserter (V1), while more advanced climbers can test their nerve on the crimpy After Party (V7).

CAMPGROUNDS

Tanners Flat Campground (with water, mid-May-mid-Oct., $28) is 4.3 miles (6.9 km) up Little Cottonwood Canyon at an elevation of 7,200 feet (2,195 m). **Albion Basin Campground** (with water, late June-mid-Sept., $28) is 11 miles (17.7 km) up the road, near the head of the canyon, at an elevation of 9,500 feet (2,896 m); the last 2.5 miles (4 km) are gravel road. Both campgrounds accept reservations (877/444-6777, www.recreation.gov, $8 reservation fee).

Northern Utah

Travelers may think northern Utah is dominated by sprawling suburbs, but there are plenty of noteworthy destinations in the area. Great Salt Lake, one of Utah's signature features, is a remnant of a network of ice age lakes that once covered the West.

If you're attuned to the news, you may have heard this lake is rapidly disappearing due to a drought exacerbated by climate change and water overuse. Hopefully, recent initiatives will protect the lake, but it's worth making a stop to this one-of-a-kind, endangered water body during your trip. The best areas to visit are its southern shores in Great Salt Lake State Park, or its largest island. At Antelope Island, you can see hundreds of bird species, plus bison grazing alongside the island's namesake pronghorn.

The region also has a rich railroad history. Ogden was born of the railroads, and the city's historic downtown is dominated by Union Station, now home to multiple museums. The first transcontinental railway joined the Atlantic and Pacific coasts near here in 1869, at Promontory Summit, which is now preserved as the Golden Spike National Historic Site, with a visitor center and exhibits. Nearby, the iconic land art Spiral Jetty and its population of wild horses beckons.

The Wasatch Mountains east of Ogden are filled with the promise of adventure. Ogden Canyon, just east of town, has good hiking trails and leads to some of the state's best skiing at Snowbasin and Powder Mountain. Logan Canyon offers trails to lakes and wildflower meadows.

GREAT SALT LAKE STATE PARK

Popular for sailing, kayaking, and boating, **Great Salt Lake State Park** (14 mi/22.5 km west of Salt Lake City, take I-80 exit 104, 801/828-0787, sunrise-sunset, $5 per vehicle, paved launches available) is the primary marina along the southern shores. A small (five-site) campground ($35, www.reserveamerica.

The Ghost of Saltair

the Saltair Resort on the banks of the Great Salt Lake

Bathers have enjoyed hopping into Great Salt Lake ever since the 1847 arrival of LDS pioneers. Extreme buoyancy in the dense water makes it impossible to sink—no swimming ability needed! But if you put your head underwater, the salty water will seriously irritate your eyes, throat, and nose. Algae blooms during summer, there's a rowdy brine fly population, and the water's odor is unpleasant.

Beginning in the 1880s, several resorts popped up along the lake's east and south shores. Besides bathing, guests could enjoy lake cruises, dances, bowling, arcade games, and roller-coaster rides. Saltair Resort was the grandest of the old resorts. Completed in 1893, the Moorish structure rose five stories and contained a huge dance floor that could fit as many as 1,000 couples. After 1930, low water levels, the Great Depression, fires, and fewer visitors gradually brought an end to Saltair. Its buildings burned for the second time in 1970.

In the 1980s, a developer built a smaller replica of the **Saltair Resort** (13 mi/20.9 km west of Salt Lake City, near I-80 exit 104, www.thesaltair.com) on Great Salt Lake's southern shore. The building is now mostly used as a concert venue. From the Saltair parking, visitors can cross the beach for a swim in the lake.

com) right on the lake is really just a parking lot and best for RVs. In addition, there's a visitor center, gift shop, picnic area, and restrooms. Adjacent to the marina is a beach, and when the lake waters are high enough, you can swim or float in the saline water. Because of the salty residue the water can leave on your skin, you'll also be glad that the park offers freshwater showers.

★ ANTELOPE ISLAND STATE PARK

Just a short distance offshore in the Great Salt Lake, **Antelope Island State Park** (office 4528 W. 1700 S., Syracuse, 801/773-2941, https://stateparks.utah.gov, $15 per car, $3 bicycles and pedestrians) seems a world away. Since it's accessed from its north end, it is closer by road to Ogden than SLC. Its rocky slopes, rolling grasslands, marshes, and sand dunes instill a sense of remoteness and rugged beauty. An extension of the Oquirrh Mountains, Antelope Island is the largest of the lake's 10 islands, measuring 15 miles (24 km) long and 5 miles (8 km) wide. Frary Peak (elev. 6,596 ft/2,010 m) rises in the center.

The entire island is a state park, through which runs a 7-mile (11.3-km) paved causeway that accesses trails for mountain biking, hiking, and horseback riding. There's also a marina for sailboats and kayaks. History buffs will also enjoy a tour of Fielding Garr Ranch, which is home to the oldest settler building in Utah (constructed in 1848).

The visitor center offers exhibits on the island's natural and human history. Rates for **campsites** (reservations 800/322-3770, http://utahstateparks.reserveamerica.com, $18 tents, $38-76 RVs with hookups) include the park's day-use fee. Showers and restrooms are available in the swimming area in the northwest corner of the island. Take I-15 exit 332, near Layton, and then drive 9 miles (14.5 km) west to the start of the causeway and the entrance booth.

Archaeologists have found prehistoric sites showing that Native Americans came here long ago, perhaps on a land bridge during times of low water levels. In 1843, explorers John Frémont and Kit Carson rode their horses across a sandbar to the island and named it after the antelope (pronghorn) herds that they hunted for food.

Antelope Island is now home to somewhere between 550 and 700 bison, as well as deer, bighorn sheep, pronghorn, and other wildlife. The best place to see bison is usually along the road on the east side of the island near the ranch. The yearly bison roundup (late Oct.) is a big event for both cowboys and visitors: The bison are driven to corrals on the north end of the island and given veterinary checkups.

Largely due to its brine fly and shrimp population, Great Salt Lake is an important migratory stop for hundreds of bird species. Antelope Island is a good place to look for eared grebes, avocets, black-necked stilts, willets, sanderlings, long-billed curlews, burrowing owls, chukars, and all sorts of raptors. The same insect life that attracts birds can attack visitors, especially during May-June—it might be worth avoiding the island during these months, but you can always call ahead for current conditions.

Antelope Island State Park

Great Salt Lake

cairns on the shores of the Great Salt Lake

Since fur trappers came upon it in the 1820s, this lake has both mystified and entranced visitors. Early Euro-American explorers guessed that it must be connected to the ocean, not realizing that they had come across a body of water far saltier. Only the Dead Sea has a higher salt content. When LDS pioneers first tried evaporating the lake water, they found the residue bitter tasting: The resulting salt is only 84 percent sodium chloride (table salt), and the remaining 16 percent is a mix of sulfates and chlorides of magnesium, calcium, and potassium.

The lake's northern arm, isolated by a railroad causeway, contains the highest mineral concentrations—about twice those of the southern arm. Bacteria and algae grow in such numbers that they sometimes tint the water orange-red or blue-green. A tiny brine shrimp (*Artemia salina*) and two species of brine fly (*Ephydra* spp.) are about all that can live in the lake. The lake attracts more than 257 species of birds, depending on the season, and is a major stop for millions of migratory birds.

The lake is always changing, rising with spring snowmelt, then falling due to evaporation in late summer and autumn. But the more permanent changes to the lake—namely its rapid decline—have drawn national attention. Due to climate change and diversion projects, the lake is in critical condition, threatening everything from the already compromised air quality of Salt Lake to snowfall and the ski industry (hello, lake effect) to bird populations. You can learn more about this grave environmental issue and how you might help through the Save Our Great Salt Lake group (www.saveourgreatsaltlake.org).

For those who just want to see and perhaps swim in the lake, the easiest access is along I-80, which skirts the southern shores of the lake past the Great Salt Lake State Park and the Saltair event space. At Antelope Island State Park, near Ogden in northern Utah, a causeway links the island to the mainland.

GREAT SALT LAKE DESERT

Ancient Lake Bonneville once covered 20,000 square miles (51,800 sq km) of what is now Utah, Idaho, and Nevada. When the lake broke through the Sawtooth Mountains, its level declined precipitously, leaving the 2,500-square-mile (6,475-sq-km) Great Salt Lake and huge expanses of salt flats to the south and west. These salt flat remnants of Lake Bonneville west of Salt Lake City are almost completely white and level, and they

Out in the Desert

Two military installations, the Utah Training and Test Range and the Dugway Proving Ground, along with the Tooele Army Depot, a chemical and biological weapons storage area, occupy much of the land in the Great Salt Lake Desert. They are all extremely high-security areas.

UTAH TRAINING AND TEST RANGE (UTTR)

Created in 1979 for cruise-missile testing, the UTTR provides the huge amount of land necessary to train military air crews and test weapons. Fighter pilots and crews use mock targets for practice, and the military tests smart munitions, long-range standoff weapons, remote-controlled air vehicles, boost-glide precision-guided munitions, air-to-air missiles, and autonomous loitering anti-radiation missiles, as well as to dispose of explosives. The UTTR also has the largest overland contiguous block of supersonic authorized restricted air space in the continental United States—over 2,675 square miles (6,928 sq km).

Although the UTTR quite obviously does not allow visitors, the Hill Aerospace Museum, located at the Hill Air Force Base just south of Ogden in the town of Roy, is open to the public and displays military aircraft.

DUGWAY PROVING GROUND

Spanning about 800,000 acres (323,750 ha), Dugway Proving Ground helps evaluate, test, and develop chemical and biological defenses, as well as conduct environmental technology testing. Dugway is also the Defense Department's leader in testing battlefield smokes and obscurants.

Stranger still, Dugway has developed a following among ufologists (those who study UFOs), who suspect that the base's secret status, underground facilities, and low profile make it the perfect place for sequestering alien artifacts and other items of extraterrestrial origin.

TOOELE ARMY DEPOT

In the summer of 1996, the army began burning part of the nation's store of chemical weapons at the Tooele Army Depot, 10 miles (16.1 km) south of the town of Tooele and 55 miles (89 km) from Salt Lake City. The depot held the nation's single largest cache of chemical weapons, with 44 percent of the arsenal stored in underground bunkers called igloos. Part of the reason for incineration—besides treaty requirements with the former USSR—was the far greater risk of leakage and environmental damage from storing chemical agents in bunkers. The chemicals destroyed include sarin, mustard gas, nerve gas, and lewisite, a skin-blistering agent. The last of Tooele Army Depot's chemical weapons were destroyed in 2007. The depot now tests and stores weapons.

go on for more than 100 miles (161 km). It is commonly said that one can see the earth's curvature at the horizon, although this apparently takes a very discerning eye.

For most, the draw of the salt flats is to explore the moon-like, mind-bending terrain—and take some photos that lend themselves to optical illusion. Some come to see how high they can push the miles per hour on this limitless landscape, but keep in mind that it's easy to get stuck in the salt post-rain, or worse, crash. The pros, however, do it every summer during Speed Week. One more curiosity found here? Scuba diving and snorkeling at the Bonneville Seabase, home to a 62-foot-deep (19-m) abyss (www.seabase.net).

The easiest access to the Great Salt Lake Desert lies along I-80 between Salt Lake City and the Nevada border. Wendover offers the closest lodging and dining.

TOP EXPERIENCE

★ Bonneville Salt Flats International Speedway

A brilliant white layer of salt left behind by prehistoric Lake Bonneville spans over 44,000 acres (17,806 ha) of the Great Salt Lake Desert.

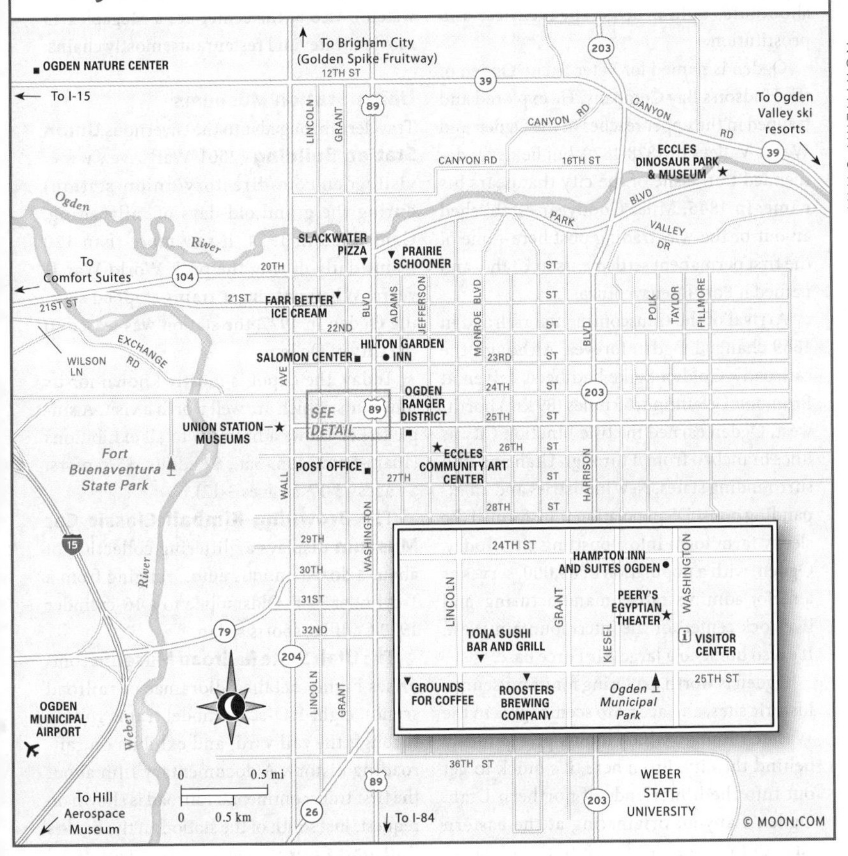

For much of the year, a shallow layer of water sits atop the salt flats. The hot sun usually dries out the flats enough for speed runs in summer and early fall.

Cars began running across the salt in 1914 and continue to set faster and faster times. Rocket-powered vehicles have exceeded 750 miles (1,207 km) per hour. The main speedway is 10 miles (16.1 km) long and 80 feet (24.4 m) wide. A small tent city goes up near the course during the annual **Speed Week** in August; vehicles of an amazing variety of styles and ages take off individually to set new records in their classes. The salt flats, just east of Wendover, are easy to access: Take I-80 exit 4 and follow the paved road 5 miles (8 km) north, then east. Signs and markers indicate if and where you can drive on the salt. Soft spots underlaid by mud can trap vehicles venturing off the safe areas. Take care not to be on the track when racing events are being held.

OGDEN

Located at the northern edge of the Wasatch Front urban area off I-15, 35 miles (56 km) north of Salt Lake City, charming Ogden was one of the West's most important rail hubs at the beginning of the 20th century. Downtown, vestiges of the city's affluence remain in the grand architecture, the impressive Union

Pacific Depot, and its colorful Historic 25th Street—once a sordid hot spot of Wild West shootouts, opium dens, speakeasies, and prostitution.

Ogden is named for Peter Skene Ogden of the Hudson's Bay Company. He explored and trapped in the upper reaches of the Ogden and Weber Valleys in 1828-1829, but he never descended to the site of the city that bears his name. In 1846, Miles Goodyear established an out-of-the-way trading post here—one of the first permanent settlements in Utah—and named it Fort Buenaventura.

Arrival of the transcontinental railroad in 1869 changed Ogden forever. Although the railroad's Golden Spike had been driven at Promontory Summit, 55 miles (89 km) northwest, Ogden earned the title Junction City as lines branched from it through Utah and into surrounding states. New industries and an expanding non-LDS population transformed the sleepy farm town into a bustling city. Today, Ogden, with a population of 84,000, serves as a major administrative, manufacturing, and livestock center for the intermountain West. It's also home to a large Air Force base.

Ogden is worth exploring for its museums, historic sites, and access to scenic spots in the Wasatch Range, which looms precipitously behind the city. From here, it's quick to get out into the hinterlands of northern Utah. Ogden Canyon, originating at the eastern edge of town and leading into the Wasatch, tours lakes, campgrounds, hiking trails, and three downhill ski areas. Several 2002 Winter Olympic events took place in the Ogden area, including the downhill and super-G ski races and the men's and women's curling competition.

Sights

The **Salomon Center,** at 23rd and Keisel Streets, is a sports, recreation, and fitness center complete with Gold's Gym, a wave pool for surfing practice, a climbing wall, and **iFLY Indoor Skydiving** (801/528-5348, www.iflyutah.com, 11am-9pm Mon.-Sat., 11am-5pm Sun., $69 and up), a vertical wind tunnel that re-creates the experience of skydiving. (If skydiving lessons are going on, it's fun just to watch.) Also at the center are a Megaplex 13 movie theater and restaurants, mostly chains.

Union Station Museums

Travelers thronged into the cavernous **Union Station Building** (2501 Wall Ave., www.visitogden.com/directory/union-station) during the grand old days of railroading. Completed in 1924, it saw more than 120 trains daily during the peak World War II years. When passenger trains stopped serving Ogden in 1977, the station was leased to the City of Ogden.

Today, the depot is mostly known for its museums, which are well worth a visit. A single ticket allows admission to all exhibitions (10am-5pm Mon.-Sat., $7 adults, $5 seniors, $4 ages 13-17, $3 ages 3-12).

The **Browning-Kimball Classic Car Museum** displays a glittering collection of about a dozen antique autos, ranging from a 1-cylinder 1901 Oldsmobile to a 16-cylinder 1930 Cadillac sports sedan.

The **Utah State Railroad Museum** comprises highly detailed dioramas of railroad scenes, eight HO-scale model trains rolling through the rail yard, and exhibits on railroading history. A documentary film about the first transcontinental railroad is shown on request. Just south of the station, at the **Eccles Railroad Center,** you can visit giant diesel locomotives and some cabooses.

Browning Firearms Museum (upstairs) contains the gun shop and many examples of firearms invented by the Browning family. John M. Browning (1855-1926), a genius in his field, held 75 major gun patents. He developed the world's first successful automatic firearms, which used gases from the bullet to expel the old shell, load a new one, and cock the mechanism. Exhibitions display both military and civilian handguns, automatic weapons, rifles, and shotguns.

1: the Bonneville Salt Flats **2:** racing on the Bonneville Salt Flats International Speedway

1
WELCOME TO THE
BONNEVILLE SALT FLATS
AND UTAH'S FAMED MEASURED MILE–
SITE OF WORLD LAND–SPEED RECORD RUNS
2
Model "A"
494
Driver...Scott Goetz
CXRACING

The **Utah Cowboy and Western Heritage Museum** commemorates Utah's frontier past, honoring cowboys and the other men and women who settled Utah—and those who continue to champion the Western way of life.

Myra Powell Gallery displays paintings, sculpture, and photography in a former pigeon roost. Exhibitions rotate monthly.

Historic 25th Street

Also known as Two-Bit Street, **Historic 25th Street** runs through Ogden's downtown and has one of the most colorful histories of any street in the state. It's survived booms and busts and borne witness to the outrageous and the violent alike. When Ogden was the railroad's main transport hub, this was the city's main thoroughfare. Running between Washington Boulevard and the Union Pacific Depot, the street boasted the city's first grocery stores, blacksmith shops, livery stables, hotels, and restaurants, many of which were run by immigrants attracted by the railroads.

Take a stroll to discover the street's history through plaques on landmark buildings. Victorian buildings, views of the Wasatch, and a quirky cast of locally owned businesses, restaurants, and galleries—it's easy to spend an afternoon discovering 25th. This historic thoroughfare also hosts many of Ogden's festivals, including the annual Harvest Moon Celebration and summer farmers markets.

On summer Saturdays, the **25th Street Farmers and Art Market** (25th St. and Grant Ave.) takes over Ogden Municipal Park. Also in the park is the **Ogden Amphitheater,** which hosts free events early June-mid-August, including movies and classical music concerts (www.ogdenamphitheater.com).

Peery's Egyptian Theater

You can't miss the unusual facade of the venerable **Peery's Egyptian Theater** (2415 Washington Blvd., 801/689-8700 or 866/472-4627, www.egyptiantheaterogden.com). Looking suspiciously like an Egyptian sun temple, this old-time movie palace and vaudeville theater was built in 1924 during the period of Egyptomania that followed the discovery of King Tut's tomb. After falling into disrepair, the old theater was completely refurbished and now serves as Ogden's performing arts center. The interior of the hall is equally astonishing, with a sun that moves across the ceiling and glittering stars. The Egyptian keeps busy with a series of top-notch

Historic 25th Street

musical performances and regional theater productions.

Adjacent to the Egyptian is the **David Eccles Conference Center** (801/689-8600), a handsome building designed to harmonize architecturally with the theater. Together, the conference center and the theater form the core of Ogden's convention facility.

Fort Buenaventura State Park

Miles Goodyear built the original **Fort Buenaventura** (office 2450 S. A Ave., 801/399-8099, www.wcparksrec.com/fort buenaventura, 9am-dusk daily spring-fall, $2) in 1846 to serve as a trading post and way station for travelers crossing the remote Great Basin region. Now a replica of the tiny fort provides a link with Utah's mountain-man past. The location, dimensions, and materials used for the stockade and three cabins closely follow the originals. The 32-acre (13 ha) park has a campground, an 18-hole disc golf course, and a pond popular for canoeing in summer (rentals are available). From downtown Ogden, take 24th Street west across the rail yard and the Weber River, turn left onto A Avenue, and follow signs.

Eccles Community Art Center

A series of monthly changing exhibitions at the **Eccles Community Art Center** (2580 Jefferson Ave., 801/392-6935, www.ogden4arts.org, 9am-5pm Mon.-Fri., 9am-3pm Sat., free), in a historic mansion, displays the best of regional paintings, sculpture, photography, and mixed media. The ornate mansion, once owned by the philanthropic Eccles family, whose name is attached to many arts centers in northern Utah, is an attraction in itself. Turrets, cut glass, and carved woodwork decorate the brick and sandstone structure, built in 1893 in a Richardsonian-Romanesque style.

Ogden Nature Center

The **Ogden Nature Center** (966 W. 12th St., 801/621-7595, www.ogdennaturecenter.org, 9am-5pm Mon.-Fri., 9am-4pm Sat., $5 ages 12-65, $4 age 65 and up, $3 ages 2-11) is a 127-acre (51-ha) wildlife sanctuary on the outskirts of Ogden. It's a popular spot for school field trips and summer camps, and it's also fun just to visit on your own. Hiking trails lead through woods, wetlands, and open fields. Deer, porcupines, muskrats, rabbits, snakes, and about 130 species of birds have been spotted here. The visitor center offers classes, workshops, displays, picnic facilities, and activities year-round. To get here, follow West 12th Street northwest from downtown.

Eccles Dinosaur Park and Museum

Paths at the leafy **Eccles Dinosaur Park** (1544 E. Park Blvd., 801/393-3466, www.dinosaurpark.org, 10am-5pm Mon.-Sat., noon-5pm Sun. Labor Day-Memorial Day, 10am-6pm daily Memorial Day-Labor Day, $7 adults, $6 seniors and students 13-17, $5 ages 2-12) lead to more than 100 realistic life-size replicas of dinosaurs, complete with robotics, making this a favorite with children. Exhibitions are based on the most up-to-date studies of paleontologists, and the replicas were created by the same folks who build "dino-stars" for Hollywood films. A large museum includes some impressively large skeletons and an area to watch technicians work on recently excavated bones.

Events

In summer, the amphitheater in downtown **Ogden Park** (25th St. and Washington Ave.) is the site of the **Ogden Twilight concert series** (www.ogdentwilight.com). Although they're not free, tickets are inexpensive ($15-20), and acts are fairly well-known (think Beck or Flaming Lips).

On Saturday mornings during the summer, the entire downtown stretch of 25th Street is taken over by a **farmers market** and **craft booths.**

Food

Quite a few good restaurants line 25th Street, the main drag through Ogden. In addition to the dining options below, there are bakery cafés, a Greek restaurant, sushi joints, taverns with burgers, and home-style Mexican food. If you've got time, just saunter along 25th Street, and you'll be sure to find a good spot.

Breakfast and Cafés

If your idea of breakfast is strong coffee, fresh pastries, and a croissant breakfast sandwich, head to **Grounds for Coffee** (111 25th St., 801/392-7370, www.groundsforcoffee.com, 7am-8pm Sun.-Thurs., 7am-10pm Fri.-Sat., $3-5), the city's best coffee shop, located in a beautifully preserved 19th-century storefront along historic 25th Street.

Casual Dining

One of the liveliest places along 25th Street is ★ **Roosters Brewing Company** (253 25th St., 801/627-6171, http://roostersbrewingco.com, 11:30am-10pm Mon.-Fri., 10am-10pm Sat., 10am-9pm Sun., $13-25), a brewpub with good food (burgers, pizzas, ribs, sandwiches, etc.) and good microbrews. It's a popular weekend brunch spot, and in summer there's a pleasant shady deck.

If you're looking for unusual pizza and craft beers, head to **Slackwater Pizza** (1895 Washington Blvd., 801/399-0637, http://slackwaterpizzeria.com, 11am-10pm Mon.-Thurs., 11am-11pm Fri.-Sat., 10am-9pm Sun., pizzas $13-15), where you'll find traditional margherita as well as tikka masala and barbecued pork pies, alongside a wide selection of local beers. Slackwater is not the best choice if you're looking for an intimate or quiet place to dine.

The sushi is fresh and lovely at ★ **Tona Sushi Bar and Grill** (210 25th St., 801/622-8662, http://tonarestaurant.com, 11:30am-2:30pm and 5pm-9:30pm Tues.-Thurs., 11:30am-2:30pm and 5pm-10pm Fri.-Sat., rolls $8-19), with a wide range of Japanese dishes besides the sushi and sashimi; enjoy a bento box or rice bowl at lunchtime.

Satisfy a craving for ice cream at **Farr Better Ice Cream** (274 21st St., 801/393-8629, 10am-10pm Mon.-Sat.), a longtime Ogden favorite.

Fine Dining

Dine in a covered wagon circled around "camp" at **Prairie Schooner** (445 Park Blvd., 801/392-2712, http://prairieschoonerrestaurant.com, 11am-9pm Mon.-Thurs., 11am-10pm Fri., 3pm-10pm Sat., $14-59). The menu includes everything from burgers to big surf-and-turf combos, with a focus on steaks. Kids love this place.

Accommodations

$50-100

At I-15 exit 347, the pet-friendly **Comfort Suites of Ogden** (2250 S. 1200 W., 801/621-2545, www.comfortsuites.com, $83-184) has an indoor pool; all guest rooms have efficiency kitchens and rates include continental breakfast.

$100-150

The **Hampton Inn and Suites Ogden** (2401 Washington Blvd., 866/394-9400, http://hamptoninnogden.com, $104-169) is a grand art deco souvenir of the early 20th century. In addition to comfortable guest rooms and a gracious formal lobby, guests are offered a business center and a fine-dining restaurant. The Hampton Inn has been completely renovated and refurbished, and it's a charming place to stay, with frequent rate specials on the hotel's website.

$150-200

For a unique lodging experience in a pretty setting, consider the ★ **Alaskan Inn and Spa** (435 Ogden Canyon, 801/621-8600, www.alaskaninn.com, $169-259), 6 miles (9.7 km) east of Ogden. A 26-unit log lodge and cabin complex, the Alaskan Inn sits along the banks of a mountain stream. Book a suite in the central lodge building or reserve an individual log cabin. The rustic decor includes hand-hewn pine furniture, brass lamps, and Western art. Breakfast is included.

One of Ogden's newest hotels is the ★ **Hilton Garden Inn** (2271 S. Washington Blvd., 801/399-2000, http://hiltongardeninn3.hilton.com, $159-216), a striking hotel right next to the Salomon Center with amenities such as HDTVs, a business center, and an indoor pool. Although breakfast is not included, it's available for about $10 extra per couple, and there's a good restaurant in the hotel.

Information and Services

The helpful **Ogden Convention and Visitors Bureau Information Center** (2411 Kiesel Ave., 801/778-6250 or 800/255-8824, www.visitogden.com, 9am-5pm Mon.-Fri.) can tell you about the sights, facilities, and goings-on for Ogden and surrounding communities, including Davis, Morgan, and Box Elder Counties.

Visit the **Ogden Ranger District Office** (507 25th St., 801/625-5112, 8am-4:30pm Mon.-Fri.) to find out about local road conditions, camping, hiking, horseback riding, ski touring, snowshoeing, and snowmobiling.

Hospital care and physician referrals are provided by **McKay-Dee Hospital Center** (4401 Harrison Blvd., 801/387-2800) and **Ogden Regional Medical Center** (5475 S. 500 E., 801/479-2111). There is a **post office** (2641 Washington Blvd., 801/627-4184) downtown.

Getting There

Utah Transit Authority (UTA, 2393 Wall Ave., 877/621-4636, www.rideuta.com, 7am-6pm Mon.-Fri.) buses serve many areas of Ogden and head south to Salt Lake City and Provo. Buses operate Monday-Saturday and offer some late-night runs. The UTA's Front Runner commuter train also travels between Salt Lake City and Ogden. **Greyhound** (801/394-5573, www.greyhound.com) provides long-distance service from the bus terminal (2393 Wall Ave.).

Most air travelers use **Salt Lake City International Airport** (SLC, 776 N. Terminal Dr., 801/575-2400, www.slcairport.com), just 35 miles (56 km) away. Budget airline Allegiant provides service from Phoenix to **Ogden-Hinckley Airport** (3909 Airport Rd., 801/629-8262, http://flyogden.com).

Yellow Cab (801/394-9411) provides 24-hour taxi service. Lyft and Uber are also available.

OGDEN VALLEY

Cliffs rise thousands of feet above narrow Ogden Canyon, just barely allowing Highway 39 and the Ogden River to squeeze through. In autumn, the fiery reds of maples and the golden hues of oaks add color to this scenic drive deep within the Wasatch Range. Ogden Canyon begins on the eastern edge of Ogden and emerges about 6 miles (9.7 km) later at Pineview Reservoir in the broad Ogden Valley.

This fertile agricultural basin is a crossroads for recreationalists. In winter, skiers turn south from the reservoir to Snowbasin ski area and north to the Nordic Valley and Powder Mountain ski areas. Summer visitors have a choice of staying at swimming beaches and campgrounds on the shore of Pineview Reservoir or heading to canyons and mountain peaks in the Wasatch Range.

★ Snowbasin

Owned by Sun Valley, **Snowbasin** (3925 E. Snowbasin Rd., Huntsville, 801/620-1000 or 888/437-5488, snow report 801/620-1100, www.snowbasin.com) is now one of Utah's largest ski areas, with an excellent lift system, great panoramic views, and few crowds. Although it gets a bit less snow than the Cottonwood resorts, Snowbasin is well equipped with snow-making machines.

UTA ski buses run to the resort from Ogden and Layton.

Terrain and Lifts

With more than 3,200 acres (1,295 ha) of terrain and relatively few other skiers and snowboarders, there's almost always room to roam here. The area is well covered with speedy lifts, meaning that you can spend more time skiing and less time standing in line or sitting on chairlifts. Three triple chairlifts, two high-speed quads, two gondolas, and a short 15-person tram serve 107 runs, of which 20 percent are rated beginner, 50 percent intermediate, and 30 percent expert; snowboarding

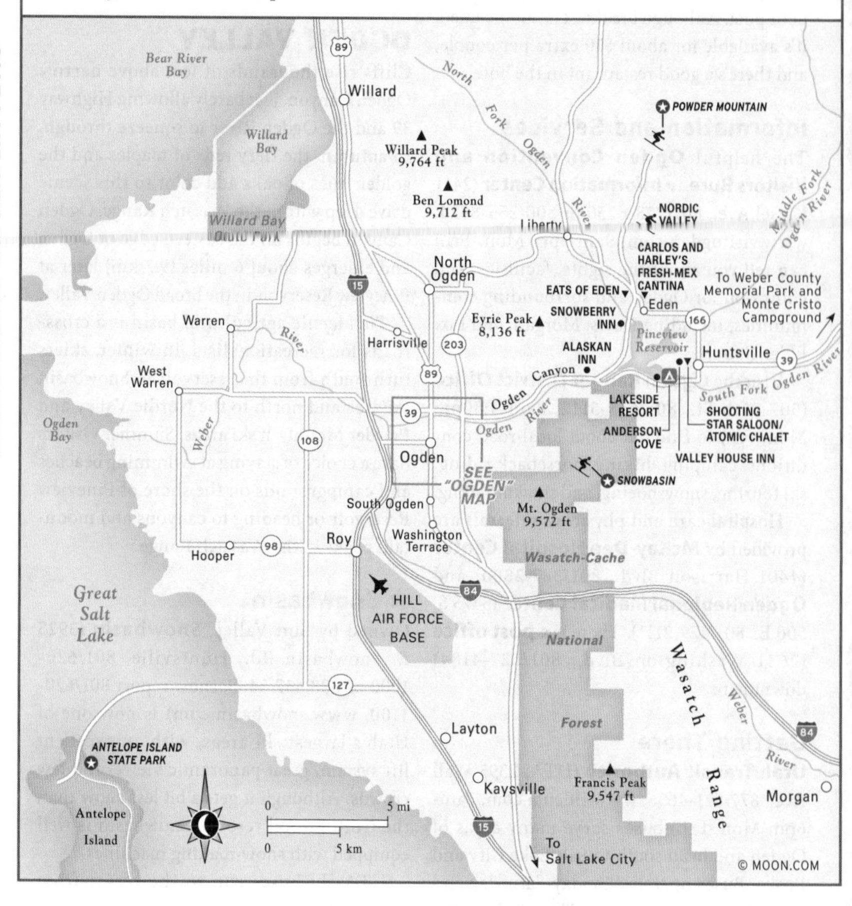

is allowed. The longest run is 3 miles (4.8 km) and drops 2,400 feet (732 m) in elevation.

Snowbasin is a double-black skier's dream. The north side of the mountain (the John Paul area) has incredible expert terrain. There are also steep chutes off the top of the Strawberry Express gondola. But intermediate skiers will have a good time at the Strawberry area, with nicely groomed, long blue cruisers. Beginners will find limited territory but a couple of nice long runs.

The five terrain parks include 65 rails, a large pipe, and many other features.

Ski season at Snowbasin normally runs Thanksgiving-mid-April. Adult **lift tickets** are $135-195 full-day, $105-135 half-day (sold starting at 12:30pm); youth rates are $85-145 full-day, $60-85 half-day; seniors (65 and older) pay $105-165 full-day, $85-106 half-day, and people over age 75 pay $59-79 full-day, $39-45 half-day.

Near parking area 2, find a 16-mile (26-km)

1: lift at Snowbasin **2:** spring skiing at Snowbasin **3:** Powder Mountain **4:** Shooting Star Saloon

1
2
3
4
SINCE~1879
SHOOTING STAR
SALOON
Open Daily
NO
PERSONS
UNDER
21

Nordic area groomed for classic and skate cross-country skiing (free).

Snowbasin offers a ski school, a ski shop, rentals, and weekend lodges.

Summer Activities

The lifts at Snowbasin remain open in summer for hikers ($25) and bikers ($35), making it easy to reach the high country. Hikers can pull off the ski area access road to hike the **Green Pond Trail,** which heads a relatively gentle 2.5 miles (4 km) up to a picnic area and pond. Kid-friendly summertime activities include a climbing wall and spider (bungee) jump as well as Sunday-afternoon nature adventures, which coincide with the Sunday Brews, Blues and BBQ.

Lodging

Snowbasin doesn't offer slope-side accommodations, but the ski area is affiliated with **Lakeside Resort** on Pineview Reservoir (6486 E. Hwy. 39, Huntsville, 801/745-3194, $179-459 for two-bed condos), a high-end resort a 10-minute drive away.

Dining

Dining options are relatively limited at Snowbasin and include **Earl's Lodge** (801/621-1000, 8am-4pm daily in ski season, $15-45), the mountaintop **Needles Lodge** (801/620-1021, 9am-4pm Sun.-Fri., 9am-8pm Sat. in ski season, $13-20), and **John Paul Lodge** (801/620-1021, 9am-3pm daily in ski season, $15-45).

Nordic Valley

The recently expanded **Nordic Valley** (Eden, 385/298-0155, www.nordicvalley.ski) is the closest ski area to Ogden and especially popular with families. Don't get its name wrong—this is downhill skiing, and it's an unintimidating place to learn to ski. Three chairlifts and a magic carpet serve 19 runs and a terrain park. About 35 percent of the territory is beginner level, 45 percent intermediate, and 20 percent expert. Elevation drop is 1,000 feet (305 m). You can ski at night, too—all runs are under lights Monday-Saturday. The season runs daily early December-late March. Adult **lift tickets** cost $45-50 full-day, $35-45 half-day, $45 night; children's rates are $35 full-day, $35 half-day or night. The resort has a ski school, a ski shop, and a day lodge.

During the summer, a lift ride is $12, and $15 with a bike. Summer activities include a very long slip 'n' slide and disc golf.

Nordic Valley is 15 miles (24 km) northeast of Ogden; go through Ogden Canyon, turn left at Pineview Dam, and follow the signs.

★ Powder Mountain

Powder Mountain (801/745-3772, www.powdermountain.com) has long been an under-the-radar destination for skiers and riders in search of great terrain without the crowds. The ski area only sells 1,500 tickets a day to keep traffic at bay and also provides access to incredible backcountry terrain.

One triple chairlift and five quads (four fixed and one detachable) reach two different peaks and serve 154 runs (25 percent beginner, 40 percent intermediate, and 35 percent expert). Three surface tows supplement the chairlifts for beginners; for expert skiers, there is a huge skiable area that's not lift-served (snowcats are often used to access more remote areas). Plentiful powder can be found at elevations of 6,895-8,900 feet (2,102-2,713 m). There are also two terrain parks.

In total, Powder Mountain offers 8,464 skiable acres (3,425 ha). You can ski at night from the Sundown lift until 9pm. Powder Mountain's season lasts mid-November-mid-April. Adult day **lift tickets** cost $119-159, $39 night; ages 7-18 $69-89 day, $35 night; ages 65-74 $89-109 day, $35 night; military $79-109; 75 and older free. Facilities include a ski school, ski shops, rentals, and weekend lodges.

Powder Mountain is 19 miles (31 km) northeast of Ogden; drive through Ogden Canyon, turn left at Pineview Dam, and follow the signs. During the winter, UTA runs a ski bus from Ogden. A shuttle also runs from Eden, and it's well worth taking to avoid the steep, narrow road to the lifts. In summer, mountain bikers are free to use the trails, but there is no lift-assisted hiking or biking.

Food and Accommodations

With ski-in/ski-out access, **Columbine Inn** (801/745-1414, www.columbineinnutah.com) has simple hotel-style guest rooms ($125-210), as well as condos, suites, and cabins with full kitchens and fireplaces ($350-485). Rates are much lower in summer. Upscale condo rentals adjacent to the resort are also available from Powder Mountain Getaways (www.powdermountain.com/resort/lodging/powder-mountain-getaways).

Powder Mountain also offers a few dining options, including **Hidden Lake Cantina** (10:30am-3pm daily) with Mexican grab-and-go options and some limited seating and **Powder Keg Pub** (510/724-7300, www.powderkegpub.com, noon-7pm Mon.-Thurs. and Sat., noon-8pm Fri., brunch Sun. 10am-4pm, closed major holidays), serving ramen, rice bowls, and beers on tap with live music.

Most skiers and riders drive up from Salt Lake City or Ogden; the Ogden Valley lodgings are also lovely and convenient, with a number of B&Bs and condos catering to skiers.

Pineview Reservoir

This many-armed lake on the Ogden River provides excellent boating, fishing, waterskiing, and swimming (elev. 4,900 ft/1,494 m). Off Highway 162, **North Arm Wildlife Viewing Trail** makes a 0.4-mile (0.6-km) loop at the north end of the reservoir, where the North Fork of the Ogden River joins the reservoir. Day-use, including boat launch, is $18 at Anderson Cove. Rent a kayak, canoe, or paddleboard at **Detours** (237 S. 7400 E., Huntsville, 801/247-0561, www.detoursutah.com, 10am-7pm Thurs.-Sun.).

Food

The bucolic Ogden Valley, just minutes from downtown Ogden, is a fine place to enjoy a meal. The little town of Huntsville offers a couple of places to eat, including Utah's oldest bar, the ★ **Shooting Star Saloon** (7345 E. 200 S., 801/745-2002, 11am-9pm Mon.-Sat., 11am-8pm Sun., sandwiches $5-9), which has been in business since 1879. This is a favorite place to come for no-frills, non-customizable burgers. The bar boasts the stuffed head of an enormous St. Bernard dog rumored to be the subject of Jack London's *Call of the Wild.*

Near Eden, **Eats of Eden** (2529 N. Hwy. 162, 801/745-8618, www.eatsofedenutah.com, 4:30pm-9pm Tues.-Fri., 11:30am-9pm Sat., $8-11) is a lively restaurant that serves good sandwiches on homemade bread. The deep-dish pizza hits the spot after a day of skiing.

An old general store houses **Carlos and Harley's Fresh-Mex Cantina** (5510 E. 2200 N., Eden, 801/745-8226, http://carlosandharleys.com, 11am-8pm Sun.-Thurs., 11am-9pm Fri.-Sat., $14-25). During the summer, you can eat your Tex-Mex on a sprawling patio.

Accommodations

A fun place to stay is the ★ **Atomic Chalet** (5917 E. 100 S., Huntsville, 801/425-2813, www.atomicchalet.com, $150-165), a B&B right on Pineview Reservoir 10 miles (16.1 km) from Snowbasin. It's a lodge-like building with a casual and relaxed vibe, and it's a favorite of skiers in winter, when a two-night minimum stay is required. All three guest rooms have a private bath, fridge, TV, and free Wi-Fi.

At the **Valley House Inn** (7138 E. 200 S., Huntsville, 801/745-8259, http://valleyhouseinn.com, $250-295), a sweet B&B in a historic house, guests can stay in an upscale-rustic room with log walls, with breakfast delivered to a dining nook. This is a favorite spot for romantic getaways.

On the northern arm of Pineview Reservoir is a charming log B&B, the **Snowberry Inn** (1315 N. Hwy. 158, Eden, 801/745-2634, www.snowberryinn.com, $183-206). The inn overlooks the reservoir and provides access for water sports and swimming, while Ogden-area ski resorts are only 15 minutes away. All eight guest rooms come with private baths;

guests share a hot tub, a billiard table, and a TV room.

A number of condo developments have sprung up in the Ogden Valley to serve the needs of skiers at the local ski areas. For a selection of condo options, check out http://lakesideresortproperties.com.

Campgrounds

Camp on the south shore of Pineview Reservoir (and close to the highway) at **Anderson Cove** (801/625-5306, www.recreation.gov, May-late Sept., $22-24 tent, $30-32 RV, plus $8 reservation fee).

Several smaller campgrounds (Magpie, Botts, South Fork, Perception Park, Upper and Lower Meadows, and Willows, $24-52, $8 reservation fee) on Highway 39 about 5-10 miles (8-16 km) east of Huntsville are on the South Fork of the Ogden River.

Weber County Memorial Park (801/399-8230, first-come, first-served, $30) is 1 mile (1.6 km) down the paved road from Causey Reservoir, a narrow crescent-shaped lake in the upper South Fork of the Ogden River. A paved road crosses the river to individual sites; three group sites can be reserved. Water is available late May-mid October. The turnoff for Causey Reservoir is on Highway 39, 1 mile (1.6 km) east of Willows Campground.

Monte Cristo Campground (Hwy. 39, between mileposts 48 and 49, 30 miles (48 km) east of Huntsville, 21 miles (34 km) west of Woodruff, July-Nov., $34) sits at 8,400 feet (2,560 m) elevation in mountain forests of spruce, fir, and aspen.

Getting There

Ogden Canyon begins on the eastern edge of Ogden and extends 6 miles (9.7 km) to Pineview Reservoir in the broad Ogden Valley. Reach the canyon from Ogden by heading east on 12th Street (take I-15 exit 347).

★ GOLDEN SPIKE AND SPIRAL JETTY

At 12:47pm on May 10, 1869, rails from the East Coast and the West Coast met for the first time. People across the country closely followed telegraph reports as dignitaries and railroad officials made their speeches and drove the last spikes, then everyone broke out in celebration. The joining of the Central Pacific and Union Pacific rails at this 4,905-foot-high (1,495-m) windswept pass in Utah's Promontory Mountains marked a new chapter, at last linking both sides of the nation.

During the construction, a hastily built town of tents, boxcars, and wooden shacks sprang up along a single muddy street. Outlaws and crooked gambling houses earned Promontory Summit a reputation as a diabolic little town. The party ended 6 months later when the railroads moved the terminal operations to Ogden. Soon, only a depot, roundhouse, helper engines, and other rail facilities remained. In 1904, the Lucin Cutoff across Great Salt Lake bypassed the long, twisting grades of Promontory Summit, dramatically reducing traffic along the old route. The final blow came in 1942, when the rails were torn up for wartime industries.

These days, Promontory Summit is more or less in the middle of nowhere. Much of the drive is along rural, quiet roads, so stock up on food and supplies before you head out.

Golden Spike Visitor Center

The Golden Spike National Historic Site, authorized by Congress in 1965, re-creates this momentous episode of railroad history. The **Golden Spike Visitor Center** (32 mi/52 km west of Brigham City, 435/471-2209, www.nps.gov/gosp, 9am-5pm daily except Thanksgiving, Christmas, and New Year's Day, motor vehicles $20, cyclists $10) offers exhibits on the challenges of building the railroad and those who made it possible. The 20-minute film, *The Golden Spike,* presents a detailed account of building the transcontinental railroad. Rangers give talks several times a day in summer. Historical markers

1: a replica of a steam train at Golden Spike **2:** Spiral Jetty

1
60
2

behind the visitor center indicate the spot where the last spike was driven.

The two locomotives that met here in 1869, Central Pacific's *Jupiter* and Union Pacific's *119*, succumbed to scrap yards around the turn of the 20th century. However, they have been born again in authentic replicas. Every day in summer (10am, 10:30am, 1pm, 4pm, 4:30pm), one or both trains steam along a short section of track from the engine house to the historic spot (you can't ride these engines though). In winter, the locomotives are stored in the engine house; tours are usually available by contacting the visitor center.

The annual **Last Spike Ceremony** (May 10) reenacts the original celebration with great fanfare. The **Railroaders Festival** on the second Saturday of August has special exhibits, a spike-driving contest, reenactments, handcar races, and entertainment. Reenactments of the ceremony are also held at 11am and 1:30pm on Saturdays and holidays May-Labor Day at trackside in front of the locomotives, where the original ceremony was held over 150 years ago on May 10, 1869.

From I-15, exit 368 for Brigham City, head west on Highway 13 and Highway 83 and follow the signs for 29 miles (47 km). If you're coming from the north, it's about 29 miles (47 km) from I-84's exit 40; follow signs to Highway 83 and the Golden Spike.

Orbital ATK Flight Systems Facility

Many buildings of this giant aerospace corporation are scattered across the countryside about 6 miles (9.7 km) northeast of the Golden Spike National Historic Site. If you drive this route on the way to or from the Golden Spike site, you can't miss it. You can't tour the facility, but you can visit a display of missiles, rocket engines, and a space shuttle booster casing in front of the administrative offices. Turn north and go 2 miles (3.2 km) on Highway 83 at the junction with the Golden Spike National Historic Site road, 8 miles (12.9 km) east of the visitor center.

TOP EXPERIENCE

Spiral Jetty

Art lovers may be more interested in the land art near Promontory Summit than the historic railroad site. Robert Smithson built his massive spiral from mud, salt crystals, and basalt on the northeastern shore of Great Salt Lake in 1970. The 1,500-foot-long (457-m), 15-foot-wide (4.6-m) jetty is in a remote area about 16 miles (26 km) southwest of the Golden Spike Visitor Center. Although the gravel roads are generally well graded, it's best to make the drive in a vehicle with decent clearance; don't attempt the trip in wet weather when things can get mucky. While this artwork used to be inundated by the Great Salt Lake at times, that's almost never the case anymore with Utah's drought. Find driving directions at www.diaart.org/visit/visit/robert-smithson-spiral-jetty, or stop in at the Golden Spike Visitor Center for a map.

LOGAN CANYON

From its mouth on the east edge of Logan, Logan Canyon, with its steep limestone cliffs, winds more than 20 miles (32 km) into the Bear River Range, a northern extension of the Wasatch Mountains. Paved US 89 follows the canyon and is a designated scenic byway. If you're looking for a day trip out of Logan, just head up the canyon—you'll pass lots of picnic areas, campgrounds, fishing spots, and hiking trails, where you can easily spend a few blissful hours.

Steep slopes on the west rise to rolling plateau country across the top of the range, and moderate slopes descend to Bear Lake on the east. The route climbs to an elevation of 7,800 feet (2,377 m) at Bear Lake Summit, which offers a good view of the lofty Uintas of northeastern Utah. In autumn, maples of the lower canyon turn a brilliant crimson, while aspens in the higher country glow gold. Roadside geological signs explain features in Logan Canyon. Picnic areas are free, but you have to pay to picnic at some campgrounds.

A mile-by-mile guide to the canyon is

available from the **Cache Valley Visitors Bureau** (199 N. Main St., 435/755-1890, www.explorelogan.com, 8am-5pm Mon.-Fri.) in Logan.

Hiking

Several easy to moderate hikes make Logan Canyon a lovely and convenient destination for a little exercise and an eyeful of nature. Four miles (6.4 km) up the canyon, **Riverside Nature Trail** winds along the Logan River between Spring Hollow and Guinavah Campground, a 1.5-mile (2.4-km) one-way stroll with good bird-watching. From Guinavah, you can loop back to Spring Hollow via the **Crimson Trail,** named for the foliage visible in fall. This more strenuous trail takes you up limestone cliffs and down in another 2 miles (3.2 km). Five miles (8 km) up, find the trailhead for **Wind Cave,** a 1-mile (1.6-km), 1,100-foot (335-m) climb to eroded caverns and arches.

Jardine Juniper Trail begins at Wood Camp Campground, 10 miles (16.1 km) up the canyon. The trail climbs 1,900 vertical feet (579 m) in 4.4 miles (7 km) to Old Jardine, a venerable Rocky Mountain juniper tree. Still alive after 1,500 years, it measures about 27 feet (8.2 m) in circumference and 45 feet (13.7 m) high. A mile (1.6 km) farther is **Logan Cave,** a 2,000-foot-long (610-m) cavern where a gate protects the endangered Townsend's big-eared bats that nest and hibernate here.

Forest Road 174 heads north about 20 miles (32 km) from Logan and provides access to **Tony Grove Lake,** an exceptionally pretty alpine lake (elev. 8,050 ft/2,454 m) with a nature trail, a campground, and trails into the Mount Naomi Wilderness. The 8-mile (12.9-km) round-trip hike to Naomi Peak is known for its wildflowers.

At **Bear Lake Summit,** 30 miles (48 km) from Logan, the **Limber Pine Nature Trail** originates at the parking area on the right and terminates at a massive limber pine 25 feet (7.6 m) in circumference and 44 feet (13.4 m) high. This tree was once thought to be the world's oldest and largest limber pine, but a forestry professor discovered that it's really five trees grown together and "only" about 560 years old. The easy, self-guided walk takes about an hour; Bear Lake can be seen to the east.

Skiing

Beaver Mountain Ski Area (Garden City, 435/753-0921, www.skithebeav.com, 9am-4pm daily early Dec.-late Mar., $60 adults, $45 over age 70 and under age 11) operates six chairlifts serving 48 runs, the longest of which is 2.25 miles (3.6 km) and drops 1,600 vertical feet (488 m). A cafeteria, ski shop, rentals, and lessons are available at the day lodge. Half-day passes are available for about $10 less. Go northeast 28 miles (45 km) on US 89, then north 1.5 miles (2.4 km) on Highway 243.

Accommodations

A handsome timber-and-stone lodge, **Beaver Creek Lodge** (435/946-3400 or 800/946-4485, www.beavercreeklodge.com, starting at $189) not only offers guest rooms, but also has horseback rides, snowmobile or four-wheeling rentals, and cross-country ski trails in winter. The layout and modest size of the lodge make it a good place for group get-togethers. The lodge is about 28 miles (45 km) northeast of Logan on US 89, just past the turnoff for Beaver Mountain Ski Area.

Campgrounds

There are 10 Forest Service campgrounds along US 89 in Logan Canyon, so finding a place to pitch a tent is usually pretty easy. The closest ones to Logan are **Bridger** (no reservations, mid-May-early Sept., $22) and **Spring Hollow** (877/444-6777, www.recreation.gov, mid-May-mid-Oct., $24, $8 reservation fee) Campgrounds, 3 and 4 miles (4.8 and 6.4 km) from town, respectively. **Guinavah-Malibu Campground** ($22, reservations accepted) is just a few miles farther, and **Wood Camp Campground** (US 89, 435/755-3620, no reservations, mid-May-mid-Oct., $20) is 10 miles (16.1 km) up Logan Canyon. **Tony Grove Lake Campground** (877/444-6777, www.recreation.gov, mid-June-Sept., $24,

$8 reservation fee) is 19 miles (31 km) east of Logan at 8,100-feet (2,469-m) in elevation. Expect cool temps and possibly snow in summer. The 7,000-foot-high (2,134-m) **Sunrise Campground** (877/444-6777, www.recreation.gov, late May-Sept., $22, $8 reservation fee), about 30 miles (48 km) from Logan, has good views of Bear Lake.

Getting There

From Salt Lake City, it's a 1.5-hour drive (84 mi/135 km) to Logan Canyon via I-15 North and US 91 North, which turns into US 89 and eventually into the Main Street through the town of Logan. From here, East Center Street and Canyon Road lead east to Logan Canyon.

★ BEAR LAKE

The Caribbean in Utah? It sort of feels like it at this natural freshwater lake, about half of which is in northern Utah and a little more than half in southern Idaho. The reason for the rich blue hue is calcium carbonate. Bear Lake is as fun as it is pretty, with boating, fishing, beach activities, hiking, and camping.

There are three distinct areas: **the marina,** where you can launch your own boat or a rented one; popular **Rendezvous Beach,** which closely simulates a coastal experience, sand and all; and the lovely campgrounds and quieter shores of the **Eastside.** At Eastside, the Cisco Beach area offers inland scuba diving. There's also great fishing—including ice fishing in winter—for Bonneville cisco, Bonneville whitefish, Bear Lake whitefish, Bonneville cutthroat trout, and several other fish.

In both Utah and Idaho, the lake is managed as a state park and open year-round. In Utah, day-use fees vary throughout the year ($10 Nov.-Apr., $15 May and Sept.-Oct., $20 Memorial Day weekend-Labor Day). Fees are lower for seniors, but higher for non-Utah residents. You can also enter the park with a Utah state parks pass, available for purchase at the park. A number of developed campgrounds can be found across the Rendezvous Beach area and the Eastside area, with tent sites, full hookups for RVs, boat sites, and group sites. Fees vary considerably by season and site; reserve online Memorial Day weekend-Labor Day at www.utahstateparks.reserveamerica.com; campgrounds are first-come, first-served the rest of the year.

This massive 20-mile-long (32-km), 8-mile-wide (12.9-km), 208-feet-deep (63-m) lake was formed nearly 30,000 years ago by earthquakes. There are indeed black bears in

Bear Lake

the area, but you're more likely to find them among the trees near the lake than around its shores. There are also several caves in the area worth exploring, including Minnetonka Cave.

The two towns closest to the lake are Fish Haven in Idaho, and Garden City in Utah, both of which offer accommodations, dining, and amenities. The area is famous for its flavorful raspberries, and you'll find many specialties featuring this locally grown ingredient, including an outstanding raspberry milkshake at **Crepes and Coffee** (235 N. Bear Lake Blvd., Garden City, 435/946-2696, www.crepesandcoffeebearlake.com, 7am-2pm Mon.-Sat., 7am-1pm Sun., closed seasonally, $7-10).

Getting There

From Salt Lake City, the route to Bear Lake is the same as it is to Logan Canyon, except continue on US 89 northeast through the town of Logan, which leads directly to the lake. Total drive time is about 2 hours, 15 minutes.

Park City and the Wasatch Back

Among ski towns, Park City manages to strike a balance between convenience and adventure. Many of the best ski towns out West tend to lie hours from a major airport, while Park City sits about 30 minutes from Salt Lake City International Airport and the state capital.

Like many places with properties on the National Historic Register, the town celebrates its history, which accelerated with the discovery of silver in 1868. The first mine in Park City was established soon after, and as more mines opened, people poured into the area to find work and homestead. In 1872, the town was officially dubbed "Parley's Park City," after Parley P. Pratt, an early LDS leader and explorer. In 1898, the population peaked at nearly 10,000 people; today, there are some

Highlights

Look for ★ to find recommended sights, activities, dining, and lodging.

★ **Deer Valley:** This resort of the rich and famous has crisp groomers, extravagant Bloody Marys, and lavish lunch options (page 134).

★ **Backcountry Skiing:** If you want to escape resort crowds, earn your turns—or book a cat or helicopter. If you don't have the gear or knowledge, find a guide service to get you out there safely (page 137).

★ **Mountain Biking:** An International Mountain Bike Association Gold-rated ride center, Park City is home to hundreds of miles of single-track that rival its snow (page 140).

★ **High West Saloon:** At Park City—the largest ski resort in North America—you can ski right into Old Town to warm up with a toddy at High West (page 149).

★ **Utah's Little Switzerland:** Verdant and mountainous, Midway is home to charming Swiss vibes, the trails of Wasatch Mountain State Park, and a hot spring in a deep crater (page 154).

★ **Sundance Resort:** Not the festival, but the resort established by Robert Redford between Heber and Provo. Low-key skiing, beautiful hiking, an art studio, and fine dining make Sundance a fabulous place to while away a weekend (page 160).

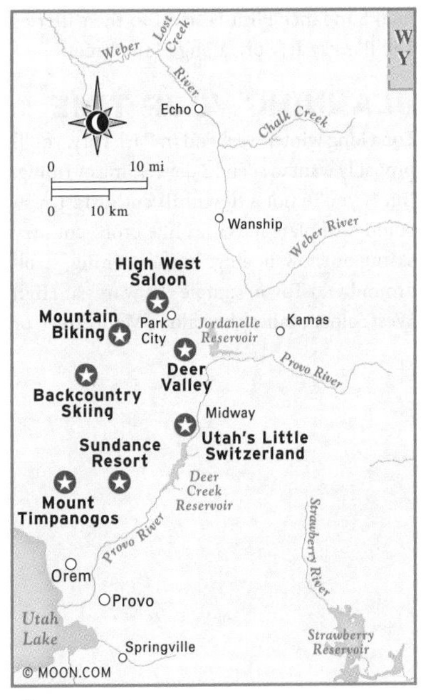

★ **Mount Timpanogos:** At 11,753 feet (3,582 m), Mount Timpanogos may not be Utah's tallest peak, but its lore and beauty make it the state's most popular summit (page 162).

8,400 residents in the area. Around the turn of the century, the town shortened its name to "Park City."

While a few buildings in Park City's historic Old Town stretch back to its earliest days, the Great Fire of 1898 destroyed most of its buildings. But within two years, the town had rebuilt, swapping flammable wood for brick. As a result, most of the historic buildings on Main Street date back to the turn of the 20th century.

After the mines began to close, a mining company established the first ski area in 1963: Treasure Mountain, now part of Park City Mountain Resort. Today, it's a world-class skiing destination that even hosted the 2002 Olympics.

While by day, Park City is a ski town—and in summer, a town ruled by trails for hiking and mountain biking—the community moonlights as a hub for the arts, from the annual Sundance Film Festival to the galleries and Banksy artwork along Main Street.

PLANNING YOUR TIME

For a long winter weekend in Park City, you'll probably want to spend 2 days skiing or riding. But if you're not a downhill enthusiast, you could also plan activities like cross-country skiing or snowshoeing. In the evening, stroll around Old Town, sample the wares at High West Saloon, gallery hop along Main Street, or treat yourself to a massage at one of the many high-end spas in the area. With more time, take a day off skiing for a snowshoe tour or even a dogsledding ride.

If you're visiting in summer, clock some miles on Park City's gold-rated mountain bike trail system. If you don't have much mountain biking experience, hire a guide and rental, or just enjoy the trails on foot. In between adventures, visit the Utah Olympic Park or explore the area through hiking, scenic lift rides, and perhaps a day on the Jordanelle Reservoir. Long weekend trips might be dominated by one big hike or bike ride, complemented by another outdoor excursion on the water, for example.

Summer or winter, if you have longer than a weekend, add on a trip to one of Park City's neighboring towns, like Midway for a hot spring soak and Swiss charm or Sundance for a one-night stay and splurge-y dinner.

If you're planning a Park City trip during peak season (June-August, December-March) or during a holiday or festival weekend, you may find yourself sitting in the traffic you sought to escape or unable to secure a dinner reservation. If the crowds sound far less than appealing, consider planning your visit strategically around these busy times, or over weekdays versus weekends. If your travel dates aren't negotiable, book accommodations, ski tickets, and restaurant reservations as far in advance as possible.

Previous: wetlands meet mountains in Park City; Park City's Mid-Mountain Trail; ski lift at Deer Valley.

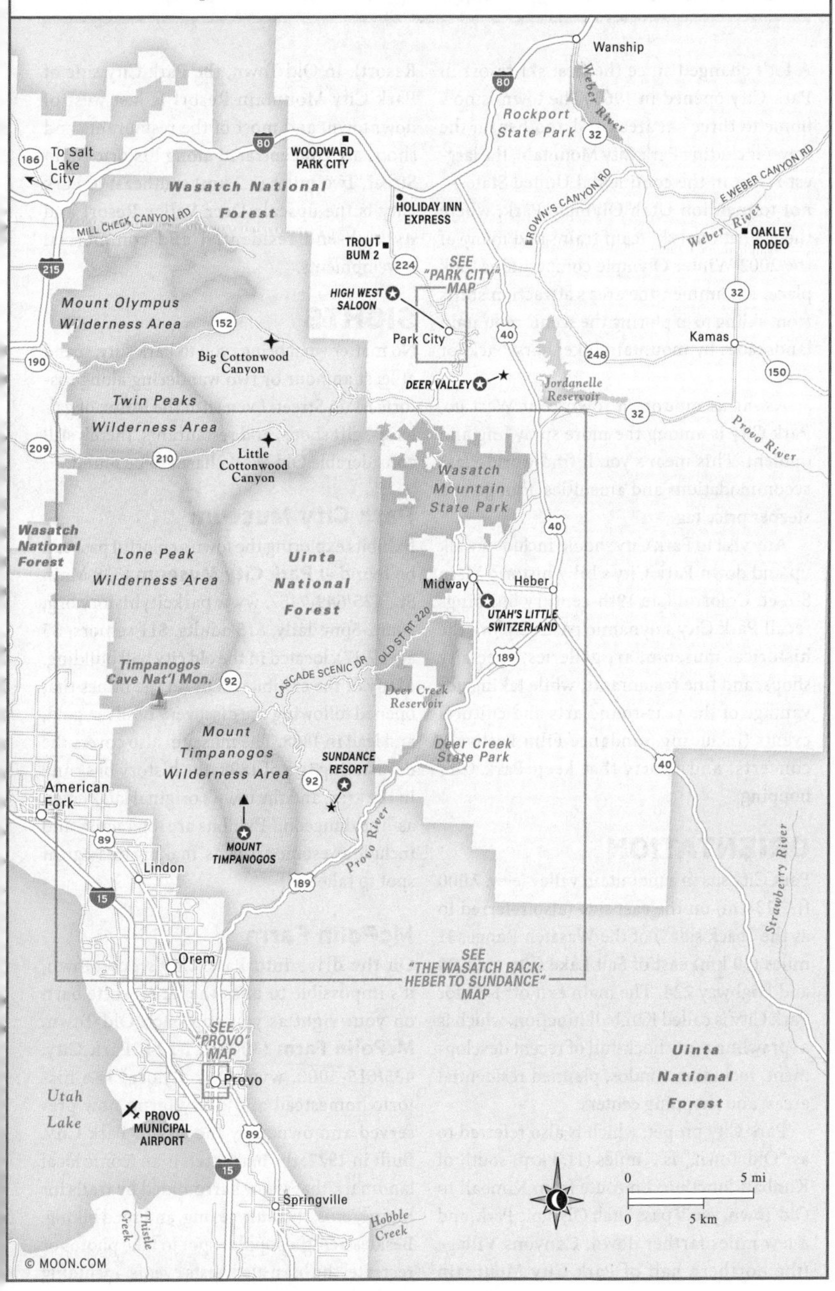

Park City and the Wasatch Back
Wanship
Rockport State Park
Weber River
To Salt Lake City
WOODWARD PARK CITY
Wasatch National Forest
HOLIDAY INN EXPRESS
MILL CREEK CANYON RD
BROWN'S CANYON RD
E WEBER CANYON RD
OAKLEY RODEO
TROUT BUM 2
SEE "PARK CITY" MAP
HIGH WEST SALOON
Mount Olympus Wilderness Area
Park City
Kamas
Big Cottonwood Canyon
DEER VALLEY
Jordanelle Reservoir
Twin Peaks Wilderness Area
Provo River
Little Cottonwood Canyon
Wasatch Mountain State Park
Wasatch National Forest
Lone Peak Wilderness Area
Uinta National Forest
Midway
Heber
UTAH'S LITTLE SWITZERLAND
OLD ST RT 220
CASCADE SCENIC DR
Timpanogos Cave Nat'l Mon.
Deer Creek Reservoir
Mount Timpanogos Wilderness Area
SUNDANCE RESORT
Deer Creek State Park
American Fork
MOUNT TIMPANOGOS
Lindon
Strawberry River
Orem
SEE "THE WASATCH BACK: HEBER TO SUNDANCE" MAP
SEE "PROVO" MAP
Provo
Utah Lake
PROVO MUNICIPAL AIRPORT
Uinta National Forest
Springville
Hobble Creek
Thistle Creek
0 5 mi
0 5 km
© MOON.COM

Park City

A lot's changed since the first ski resort in Park City opened in 1963. The town is now home to three ski areas and another on the way—including Park City Mountain, the largest resort in the continental United States—not to mention Utah Olympic Park, where the US national ski team trains and many of the 2002 Winter Olympic competitions took place. In summer, the area's attraction shifts from skiing to exploring the scenic mountain landscapes by mountain bike, horseback, or foot.

As far as mountain towns out West go, Park City is among the more sprawling and opulent. This means you'll find world-class accommodations and amenities, though at a steeper price tag.

Any visit to Park City should include a walk up and down Park City's hilly historic Main Street. Colorful late 19th-century buildings recall Park City's dynamic past. Explore the historical museum, art galleries, specialty shops, and fine restaurants, while taking advantage of the year-round arts and cultural events (including Sundance Film Festival), concerts, and sports that keep Park City hopping.

ORIENTATION

Park City sits in a mountain valley (elev. 7,000 ft/2,134 m) on the east side (also referred to as the "back side") of the Wasatch Range, 31 miles (50 km) east of Salt Lake City via I-80 and Highway 224. The main exit off I-80 for Park City is called Kimball Junction, which is a sprawling area chock-full of recent development, including condos, planned residential areas, and shopping centers.

Park City proper, which is also referred to as "Old Town," is 7 miles (11.3 km) south of Kimball Junction. En route from Kimball to Old Town, you'll pass Utah Olympic Park, and a few miles farther down, Canyons Village (the northern half of Park City Mountain Resort). In Old Town, the Park City side of Park City Mountain Resort is just west of downtown, and most of the restaurants and shops are concentrated along historic Main Street. Two miles (3.2 km) southeast of Park City is the upscale Deer Valley Resort and its high-end residential and commercial developments.

SIGHTS

No matter what brings you to Park City, spend at least an hour or two wandering along historic Main Street. Even with the influx of galleries, gift shops, and restaurants, there's still considerable Old West charm to be found.

Park City Museum

Exhibits exploring the town's colorful past can be found at **Park City Museum** (528 Main St., 435/649-7457, www.parkcityhistory.org, 10am-5pm daily, $15 adults, $11 seniors, $5 ages 7-17), located in the old city hall building. Many of the exhibits focus on the mines that opened following the discovery of silver, gold, and lead in 1868. The museum also covers the devastating fire of 1898, the history of skiing in the area, and the town's original jail known as "the dungeon." Exhibits are interactive and include awesome artifacts, making this a great spot to take kids.

McPolin Farm

On the drive into Park City's downtown, it's impossible to miss the large white barn on your right as you approach Old Town. **McPolin Farm** (3000 UT-224, Park City, 435/615-5000, www.parkcity.org) is a historic homestead and dairy farm, now preserved and owned by the city of Park City. Built in 1922, the barn itself is an iconic local landmark that's now surrounded by trails for hiking, cross-country skiing, and road biking. Besides being a popular spot to take photos or recreate, the barn also hosts events, including

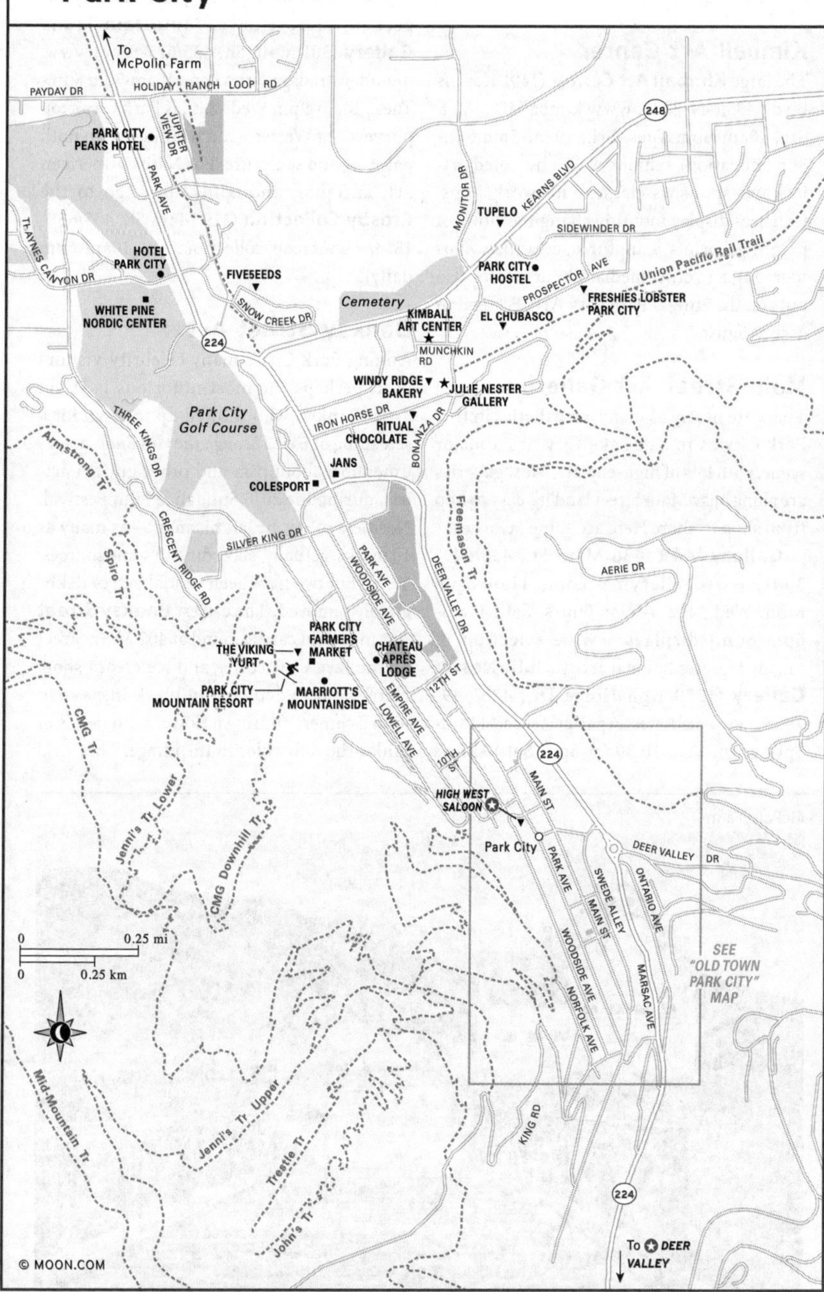

Park City
To McPolin Farm
PAYDAY DR
HOLIDAY RANCH LOOP RD
JUPITER VIEW DR
PARK CITY PEAKS HOTEL
PARK AVE
248
MONITOR DR
KEARNS BLVD
TUPELO
SIDEWINDER DR
THAYNES CANYON DR
HOTEL PARK CITY
FIVE5EEDS
PARK CITY HOSTEL
PROSPECTOR AVE
Union Pacific Rail Trail
WHITE PINE NORDIC CENTER
SNOW CREEK DR
Cemetery
FRESHIES LOBSTER PARK CITY
KIMBALL ART CENTER
EL CHUBASCO
224
MUNCHKIN RD
WINDY RIDGE BAKERY
JULIE NESTER GALLERY
THREE KINGS DR
Park City Golf Course
IRON HORSE DR
RITUAL CHOCOLATE
BONANZA DR
Armstrong Tr
JANS
COLESPORT
Freemason Tr
CRESCENT RIDGE RD
SILVER KING DR
PARK AVE
WOODSIDE AVE
DEER VALLEY DR
AERIE DR
Spiro Tr
PARK CITY FARMERS MARKET
THE VIKING YURT
CHATEAU APRÈS LODGE
PARK CITY MOUNTAIN RESORT
MARRIOTT'S MOUNTAINSIDE
EMPIRE AVE
12TH ST
LOWELL AVE
CMG Tr
10TH ST
224
MAIN ST
HIGH WEST SALOON
Park City
DEER VALLEY DR
Jenni's Tr Lower
CMG Downhill Tr
PARK AVE
SWEDE ALLEY
MAIN ST
ONTARIO AVE
WOODSIDE AVE
0
0.25 mi
0
0.25 km
SEE "OLD TOWN PARK CITY" MAP
NORFOLK AVE
MARSAC AVE
Mid-Mountain Tr
Jenni's Tr Upper
Trestle Tr
KING RD
224
John's Tr
To DEER VALLEY
© MOON.COM

full-moon snowshoeing, tours, and a scarecrow festival.

Kimball Art Center

The large **Kimball Art Center** (1401 Kearns Blvd., 435/649-8882, www.kimballartcenter.org, 10am-6pm Tues.-Fri., 10am-5pm Sat.-Sun., donation) exhibits works by noted artists and sponsors classes and workshops. Galleries display monthly changing shows of paintings, prints, sculptures, ceramics, photography, and other media. The art center also puts on the annual Park City Arts Festival in early August.

Main Street Art Galleries

There are nearly as many art galleries in tiny Park City as in Salt Lake City; it's a major scene, with lots of high-end art. Most galleries are along busy Main Street, and it's easy to hop from shop to shop. Here are some favorites.

Gallery MAR (436 Main St., 435/649-3001, www.gallerymar.com, 11am-7pm Mon.-Wed., 10am-9pm Thurs.-Sat., 11am-6pm Sun.) displays a wide selection of mostly representational artists. **Julie Nester Gallery** (1280 Iron Horse Dr., 435/649-7855, www.julienestergallery.com, 11am-5pm Mon.-Fri., 10:30am-5pm Sat.) shows national contemporary artists, with more sophisticated works than you'd usually expect in a resort town. **Mountain Trails Gallery** (301 Main St., 435/615-8748, www.mountaintrailsgalleries.com, 10am-7pm Sun.-Tues., 10am-9pm Wed.-Sat.) is Park City's top purveyor of Western and wildlife art, in both painting and sculpture. For Native American art, antiques, and collectibles, go to the **Crosby Collection** (419 Main St., 435/658-1813, www.crosbycollection.com, 10am-6pm daily).

Banksy Street Art

Among Park City's many celebrity visitors past, perhaps the most notorious is street artist Banksy, who showed up in town for a screening of *Exit Through the Gift Shop*, a documentary about him and other graffiti artists, during the 2010 Sundance Film Festival. Needless to say, he left his mark—as many as 10 marks, actually, according to some sources. Yet all but two have been vandalized or deliberately removed. The easiest **Banksy Street Art** to behold can be found at 402 Main Street by the Java Cow coffee and ice cream shop. Here, Banksy depicted in black ink a man with a camera filming a flower with petals of pink—the only color in the image. This local

McPolin Farm

artistic asset has been framed in wood and covered in glass for protection, so it's relatively easy to spot as you walk along Main Street.

SKIING AND SNOWBOARDING

TOP EXPERIENCE

Park City Mountain Resort

Vail-owned **Park City Mountain Resort** (435/649-8111, www.parkcitymountain.com) is the largest ski and snowboard resort in the United States (though nearby Powder Mountain in the Ogden area technically has more acres, much of its skiable terrain is actually in-bounds backcountry versus lift-accessed). Park City Mountain (PCMR) was originally two different resorts: Park City and Canyons. Though now conjoined via a gondola, these two areas still have separate base areas: the Park City base by Old Town and Canyons Village, closer to Kimball Junction.

Terrain and Lifts

Quicksilver Gondola links the Park City and Canyons sides of the mountain. The gondola runs both ways, linking the two formerly separate resorts; trails have been cut to take advantage of some of the territory in between.

Unlike most ski areas, where beginners are confined to lower-elevation slopes, PCMR's High Meadow area by Red Pine Lodge at the top of the gondola is a great hub for families and newer skiers. Wide-open blues can be found in the Dreamcatcher/Dreamscape area on the Canyons side, and off the Payday lift on the Park City side. The tree skiing is lovely under the Peak 5 lift, where you may find powder stashes after other areas get skied off. Advanced skiers should book it up the 9990 lift; test your legs on the moguls of 94 turns or turn right at the top of the lift and traverse all the way to the steep Red Pine Chutes. On the Park City side, McConkey's and Jupiter Bowls offer the most challenging terrain.

In total, the combined resort has nine hotels, more than two dozen restaurants, and 7,300 skiable acres (2,954 ha) encompassing a 22-mile (35-km) network of nearly 330 trails on 17 mountain peaks linked by 41 lifts, seven terrain parks, 13 bowls, one superpipe, and one minipipe. Ski season usually runs mid-November-mid-April. Lifts operate 9am-4pm daily.

PCMR has dynamic pricing for **lift tickets,** which means prices change from day to day based on demand. Instead of buying a ticket, you'll be buying an **Epic Pass,** which provides access to Park City in addition to several other mountains around the country and world. There are many passes to choose from, including 1-day, 3-day, 7-day, or a full pass with no blackout dates. Base rates for a 1-day pass that includes PCMR start at $101 adults, $52 ages 5-12. Buying in advance (www.epicpass.com) will save you money and time waiting in lines.

Summer Activities

Although Park City shuts down most of its lifts for the summer, the resort remains open and maintains some 30 miles (48 km) of trails for **mountain biking, hiking,** and **horseback riding.** You can ride up the **Crescent or Payday lifts** ($27 adult day pass, $23 ages 5-12, $37 bike haul) with a bike or cooler backpack filled with lunch. A free map of designated mountain biking trails is available from the resort and local bike shops.

The **Adventure Park** (late May-early Oct., 10am-7pm daily in summer, reduced hours in late spring and early fall) offers mini golf, disc golf, a rock climbing wall, and several other thrills. Kids and kids at heart will enjoy the **Mountain Coaster** ($33 driver, $17 passenger 38-53 inches tall), which winds through aspen glades on an elevated mile-long (1.6-km) track.

The **Alpine Slide** ($28 adults per ride, $17 under 35-47 inches tall and older than age 2) is like a beginner-friendly toboggan on a giant curving slide.

You'll also find two **ziplines** ($18-36), the longest of which, **ZipRider,** makes a 60-second, 500-foot (152-m) plunge. At its highest point, the rider is suspended 110 feet (33.5 m) off the ground. Riders must weigh 75-275 pounds (34-125 kg). A second zipline, called **Flying Eagle,** is a two-person ride with no weight minimum.

Golf (435/615-4728, $115) is the main summer activity on the Canyons side, though you'll find plenty of hiking and mountain biking trails here as well.

Food

Midmountain, at the top of Red Pine gondola, **Red Pine Lodge** (435/615-4828, 9am-4pm daily, $9-22) is a good place to grab a breakfast burrito or pizza, burgers, soup, and salad for lunch. Far better food—and spirited cocktails, versus only beer and wine—is served at **Lookout Cabin** (435/615-2892, 11:30am-2:15pm daily, $28-32, reservations suggested), a sit-down restaurant at the midway point of the Orange Bubble lift. Also on the Canyons side, ★ **Cloud Dine** (435/615-2892, 10am-3:30pm daily, $15-30), at the top of the Dreamcatcher and Dreamscape lifts, serves sandwiches, pizza, and, in the morning, fresh doughnuts.

On the Park City side, **The Viking Yurt** (435/615-9878, www.vikingyurt.com, lunch 11am-2:30pm, dinner 6pm-10pm, lunch $11-13, dinner $280 pp including tax and tip) is owned by a native Norwegian and his wife (a local) who pay homage to Norwegian/Scandinavian cuisine. By day, the yurt serves lunch items like soup alongside giant cookies, glogg, and other cocktails. At night, a sled transports diners to the yurt, where a multicourse dinner awaits with live piano. It's a splurge, but worth it. You can also ski straight from the Park City side into Old Town; **High West Saloon** (page 149) is a popular ski lunch destination.

In the Grand Summit Hotel at the Canyons base, **The Farm** (435/615-8080, 11:30am-10pm daily, $28-52) uses locally sourced ingredients in dishes ranging from a really good burger to steelhead trout with pasta, wild mushrooms, and truffled leek cream.

Accommodations

By far the easiest way to navigate the nearly endless lodging options at Canyons Village and other Park City Mountain Resort hotels is to contact **Park City Mountain Central Reservations** (435/602-4099 or 800/331-3178, www.parkcitymountain.com) or use the website's search engine. Except for off-season reservations, it's important to book early since these conveniently located resort hotels fill up quickly.

At the Canyons Village base within walking distance to chairlifts, Grand Summit Hotel, Sundial Lodge, and Silverado Lodge are all resort-owned lodging options with a mix of rooms and condos. Across from the Orange Bubble lift, **Grand Summit** has a full-service health club and spa, an indoor-outdoor pool, three restaurants, a bar, and a brewpub. About 100 yards from the gondola, **Sundial Lodge** has an outdoor heated pool, a hot tub, and gym. A more budget-friendly option, **Silverado** is a few steps farther downhill. Expect to pay $500-1,100 for most guest rooms near the base area during ski season. If you book far in advance, it's possible to find rooms in the $300-400 range. Condos can top out at well over $1,000 per night.

There are also a couple other non-resort-owned, ski-in/ski-out lodging options. **Hyatt Centric Park City Lodges** (3551 N. Escala Ct., 435/940-1234, www.hyatt.com/hyatt-centric, $740-900) are near the base of the Sunrise lift. **Pendry** (2417 W. High Mountain Rd., 435/800-1990, www.pendry.com/park-city, $900-1,200) is a newer five-star hotel with crisp rooms and suites, a gorgeous outdoor pool, a spa, a Japanese-style grill, and a funky pizza parlor. One of the least expensive options within walking distance to the lifts, the newer **YotelPAD** (2670 Canyons Resort Dr., 435/731-5090, www.yotelpadparkcity.com, $350-450) offers studios and rooms with a pool, gym, and game room.

Just a little way downslope, and served by

1: fresh lines in the backcountry near Park City **2:** High West Saloon **3:** fresh doughnuts at Cloud Dine **4:** skiing on Park City Mountain

1
2
21+
OPEN 7 DAYS A WEEK
11Am-10Pm
PHYSICAL ID REQUIRED
3
4

the Waldorf gondola, the **Waldorf Astoria Park City** (2100 W. Frostwood Blvd., 435/647-5500, www.parkcitywaldorfastoria.com, $1,000 and up during ski season, $400 and up in summer, mandatory $45 resort fee) is another great option set off a bit from the hubbub of the base.

Although resort lodgings are prohibitively expensive for many travelers, two of Park City's least expensive hotels, the **Best Western Plus Landmark** (6560 N. Landmark Dr., 435/649-7300, www.bwlandmarkinn.com, $120-300) and the **Holiday Inn Express** (1501 W. Ute Blvd., 435/658-1600, www.holidayinn.com, $175-200) are near Kimball Junction, about 1 mile (1.6 km) from the Canyons.

TOP EXPERIENCE

★ Deer Valley Resort

Deer Valley Resort (435/649-1000 or 800/424-3337, www.deervalley.com) is the crème de la crème of Utah ski areas. You'll find good, uncrowded skiing on immaculately groomed trails alongside the most premium accommodations, gourmet dining, attentive service, and polished brass everywhere. But snowboarders beware: This is a skier-only resort. Despite its reputation as a glitzy resort for the 1 percent, the skiing here can be great, and the people riding the lifts are usually friendly and interesting—think longtime locals with impeccable ski form.

The ski area is 1.5 miles (2.4 km) south of downtown Park City (33 mi/53 km east of Salt Lake City), and free shuttle buses connect the resort and town.

Although a small ski operation called Snow Park operated here 1947-1965, Deer Valley did not open until 1981. The original owners, Edgar and Polly Stern, wanted to create a resort as accessible as it was luxurious. Their formula worked, and you'll frequently end up skiing past massive mansions. In 2002, the Olympic slalom, mogul, and aerial events were held at Deer Valley. And in 2017, Deer Valley was acquired by Alterra Mountain Company, which also owns Solitude, Steamboat, and about a dozen other ski resorts.

Terrain and Lifts

Deer Valley spans six mountains: Bald Eagle, Bald Mountain, Little Baldy, Empire Canyon, Lady Morgan, and Flagstaff. The main base area and parking is at Snow Park, but the mid-mountain Silver Lake area is much more of a hub. The Homestake lift connects Snow Park and Silver Lake. If you're not staying in the Deer Valley area, avoid parking challenges by hopping the free bus, which stops at both Snow Park and Silver Lake.

Twenty-one lifts (9am-4:15pm daily), including one high-speed four-passenger gondola and 12 high-speed quads, serve 101 runs, six bowls, and a vertical drop of 3,000 feet (914 m). The longest run is 2.8 miles (4.5 km). Twenty-seven percent of the skiing is rated easier, 41 percent more difficult, and 32 percent most difficult. Deer Valley has a reputation for mellow terrain (and it's true that there's a green or blue down from the top of every lift), but there's plenty of challenging territory for advanced skiers, especially in Empire Canyon via the Lady Morgan lift.

Deer Valley is famous for its meticulously groomed trails. To find out what has been groomed, check the boards at the top of every mountain. Mountain hosts can also steer you to freshly groomed trails or onto ungroomed powder.

The majestic **Snow Park Lodge** (elev. 7,200 ft/2,195 m) contains the main ticket office, a ski school, rentals, a ski shop, childcare service, a gift shop, and a restaurant. You can drive 3 miles (4.8 km) and 1,000 feet (305 m) higher to **Silver Lake Lodge** (parking is more limited), a major hub of activity with more restaurants and luxury hotels.

Bald Eagle Mountain, near the Snow Park base, contains the main beginners' area and served as a site for the 2002 Olympics. Aspiring slalom skiers can take a run on the

1: chairlift at Deer Valley Resort **2:** pho at Deer Valley's Silver Lake Lodge **3:** skiing at Deer Valley

1
2

3

Know You Don't course; the Champion mogul course is also open to the public. At 9,400 feet (2,865 m), Bald Mountain is steeper and more exposed, with intermediate and advanced runs that take in spectacular views, but often get skied out by afternoon. Find steep, ungroomed trails in the Sultan and Mayflower areas.

On the right (west) side of Flagstaff Mountain (elev. 9,100 ft/2,774 m), the snow often holds up well, making its intermediate and beginner trails good bets for skiing later in the day. Empire Canyon (elev. 9,570 ft/2,917 m) has skiing for all abilities, including a family ski area off the Little Chief lift, challenging intermediate terrain, and some of Deer Valley's most advanced skiing, including eight chutes and three bowls. The classic last run of the day is Last Chance, which passes stunning homes and their amazing yard art. Tired skiers can also ride the Silver Lake Express bus back to the Snow Park base.

To prevent overcrowded trails, Deer Valley restricts the number of skiers on the mountain and often restricts ticket sales during Christmas, New Year's, and Presidents Day weeks. If you're planning on skiing during the holidays, reserve lift tickets at least a few days in advance.

Depending on month and day, **lift ticket** costs are $189-259 adults, $142-194 seniors 65 and over, $117-161 ages 5-12, $45 kids under 5.

Summer Activities

Hikers and sightseers can catch the Sterling, Silver Lake, and Ruby Express lifts (10am-5pm daily mid-June-Labor Day, full-day pass all lifts $26, single ride $16) to explore more than 50 miles (81 km) of trails running from the peak.

Mountain bikers pay $58 for a day pass ($5 less Mon.-Thurs.); helmets are required. Mountain biking instruction, rentals, and tours are available; call the resort (888/754-8477) for more information. The downhill mountain bike trails at Deer Valley are by far considered the best and most challenging in Utah, though there are some beginner-friendly options as well as some uphill single-track to explore.

Summer is also the season for off-road cycling events, Utah Symphony concerts, and music festivals. For horseback rides, call Deer Valley's Boulder Mountain Ranch (866/783-5819).

Food

Several cafeteria-style restaurants make Silver Lake Lodge a good spot for a quick lunch. On a sunny day, enjoy a picnic lunch in the lawn chairs on McHenry's Beach in front of the lodge, or warm up inside with a bowl of pho from **Silver Lake Restaurant** (435/649-1100, 11am-3pm daily winter, $17). A couple small coffee shops on the mountain serve Deer Valley's trademark turkey chili ($17) and good cookies. At any of Deer Valley's restaurants, look for dishes featuring cheese from **Deer Valley Artisan Cheese,** made using cow and goat milk from nearby Heber Valley.

For a sit-down lunch, après-ski, or dinner, **Royal Street Café** (435/645-6724, 11:30am-8pm daily winter, 11:30am-3pm daily summer, $16-36) in Silver Lake Lodge is a good bet. At dinnertime, the award-winning **Mariposa** (435/649-6632, 5:30pm-9pm Wed.-Sun. in ski season, $28-60, reservations recommended) is a wonderful splurge, with six- and eight-course inventive tasting menus featuring ingredients like Wagyu beef, Norway trout, and butternut squash.

In Silver Lake Village at **Goldener Hirsch Inn** (435/655-2563, 11:30am-9pm daily, $28-69, reservations recommended), dishes reflect both Austrian heritage and North American pizzazz: Wiener schnitzel ($49) is the house specialty, and fondue ($46) is a popular après option.

It's a treat to visit the old-world inspired Stein Eriksen Lodge, and a meal at its elegant **Glitretind Restaurant** (435/645-6455, www.steinlodge.com, 11:30am-9pm daily, $32-61, reservations recommended) provides a good reason to do so. The Glitretind serves contemporary cuisine and one of the state's largest wine lists.

If you take an informal survey of skiers here, the most popular meal in Deer Valley seems to be the **Seafood Buffet** at the **Snow Park Lodge** (435/645-6632, 6:15pm-9pm Thurs.-Mon. in ski season, $80 adults, $30 children). Both quality and quantity are unstinting.

Accommodations

Abundant condominium lodgings surround the slopes. The best way to book is through **Deer Valley Central Reservations** (435/645-6528 or 800/558-3337, www.deervalley.com). The website has an interactive map with an overview of accommodations and prices. Package deals are available, but rates are still high—it's hard to find a condo under $1,000 or a room less than $500 per night, and the least expensive rooms book up fast.

Accommodations are in three main areas: **Snow Park,** the Deer Valley base area, which is about 1 mile (1.6 km) from downtown Park City; the **Silver Lake** area, located midmountain approximately 3.2 miles (5.1 km) from the Snow Park base area; and the **Empire Pass** area, which has a few condos and the extravagant **Montage** hotel, located a short distance past Silver Lake.

Budget-minded Deer Valley skiers might also consider staying in Park City (a couple miles away), in Salt Lake City (about an hour away), or in the town of **Heber** (about a half hour away, with several no-frills motels).

If money is no object, book a room at the luxurious **Stein Eriksen Lodge** (7700 Stein Way, 435/649-3700 or 800/453-1302, www.steinlodge.com, roughly $1,000-4,500), a midmountain ski-in/ski-out hotel in the Silver Lake area. The lodge is like a Norwegian fantasy castle built of log and stone. Guest rooms are exquisitely appointed, and there's a day spa with a pool and fitness room. The restaurant here is one of the best rated in the area. You can book through the lodge or through Deer Valley Central Reservations.

In Silver Lake Village, **Goldener Hirsch Inn** (7570 Royal St. E., 435/645-6528 or 800/558-3373, www.goldenerhirschinn.com, $1,400-1,600) is a small Austrian-style ski-in/ski-out inn with beautifully furnished rooms (the gorgeous hand-carved beds were imported from Austria), hot tubs, a sauna, a lounge, and underground parking. The restaurant is also incredible, and shoulder-season rates can drop to about $370.

At the Snow Park base, **The Lodges at Deer Valley** (435/615-2600 or 800/558 3337, www.deervalley.com, rooms $445-495, condos $675-3,000+) has hotel rooms with mini-fridges and toasters, as well as full-kitchen condos, plus a year-round outdoor pool and hot tub. Although these accommodations aren't ski-in/ski-out, a shuttle ferries skiers to the lifts.

Another premium spot near the base of the lifts is **The St. Regis Deer Valley** (2300 Deer Valley Dr. E., 435/940-5700, www.stregisdeervalley.com, $2,000-3,000) with beautifully outfitted rooms that mix rustic and contemporary decor. The St. Regis sits on a bluff above the Snow Park lifts, and primary access to the lifts is via a funicular.

High above Deer Valley, at an elevation of 8,300 feet (2,530 m), is **Montage Deer Valley** (9100 Marsac Ave., 435/604-1300, www.montagehotels.com/deervalley, $2,270-5,000+), a premium resort hotel with the monumentality of a grand mountain lodge and the finesse of a luxury hotel. In addition to fine dining (five dining options) and a 35,000-square-foot (3,252-sq-m) spa, the Montage offers ski-in/ski-out access out your backdoor via the Empire and Ruby Express lifts.

★ Backcountry Skiing

If you'd rather swap lift lines for backcountry powder, there's great terrain to be found, both resort-accessed and further afield. However, unless you're an advanced skier with avalanche safety gear and knowledge, don't head into the backcountry without a guide. And always take the current avalanche forecast from the **Utah Avalanche Center** (www.utahavalanchecenter.org) into consideration before heading into the backcountry.

Resort-Accessed Backcountry

Park City Mountain offers numerous access gates, mostly on the Canyons side. One of the best options is accessible from the top of the Peak 5 chairlift. When you dismount the lift, head up a short hill to the right, at the top of which is an access gate. Follow the established skintrack, and at the top of the ridge, you can head looker's left or right to find a good line. Remember that just because this backcountry terrain is accessed via the resort, it's not controlled for avalanches, and you should have a shovel, beacon, and probe, along with a trusted partner and safety knowledge to enter.

Park City Powder Cats

The best catskiing in the area can be found at **Park City Powder Cats** (8340 E. Weber Canyon Rd., Oakley, 435/649-6596, https://pccats.com, $799 pp), which provides exclusive access to 43,000 acres (17,401 ha) in the High Uintas Wilderness area—that also served as a recurring film set for the show *Yellowstone*. All the elevation gain is achieved via snowcats during full-day excursions that cover intermediate to advanced terrain across four consecutive bowls: M&M, No Name, 4 Eagle, and Giant Steps.

Inspired Summit Adventures

If the idea of "earning your turns" is actually appealing, but you lack avalanche knowledge and safety gear, book a private backcountry tour with **Inspired Summit Adventures** (435/640-4421, www.inspiredsummit.com, starting at $485 pp for human-powered backcountry ski trips). Tours can be customized to your fitness and skiing ability level. Inspired Summit Adventures also guides hut trips (skiing from hut to hut with overnight stays), mountain biking, rock climbing, backpacking, and more, so consider them for year-round recreation needs.

OTHER WINTER RECREATION

Utah Olympic Park

Built for the 2002 Olympics, **Utah Olympic Park** (3419 Olympic Pkwy., 435/658-4200, www.utaholympiclegacy.org, 10am-5pm daily, basic admission is free and includes two museums devoted to winter sports) was the site of the bobsled, luge, and ski-jump competitions.

The mission of the park now is to train aspiring athletes, and visitors can often watch them. During the summer, freestyle skiers do acrobatic jumps into a huge swimming pool. On Saturday afternoons in summer, there's a freestyle aerial show. There's also a museum dedicated to the '02 Games and local skiing history on-site.

White Pine Touring

Park City's cross-country ski center, **White Pine Touring Nordic Center** (1541 Thaynes Canyon Dr., 435/649-6249, www.whitepinetouring.com, 9am-6pm daily mid-Nov.-early Apr., $24 adults, $12 ages 6-12 and seniors 65-74) offers rentals, instruction, and guided snowshoe tours. It has a touring center and about 12.4 miles (20 km) of groomed trails right in town. White Pine also has a yurt ($750) in the Uinta Mountains that's available year-round. There is a year-round office and shop (1790 Bonanza Dr., 435/649-8710, 9am-5pm daily).

Sleigh Rides and Dogsledding

Riding through the snow to a restaurant is a great way to turn dinner into an adventure. **Snowed Inn Sleigh Company** (435/647-3310, www.snowedinnsleigh.com, $115 adults, $80 children, reservations required) takes guests on a sleigh ride to a lodge where dinner is served; short rides without dinner are also available ($25). A heated snow-cat ride heads to **The Viking Yurt** (435/615-9878, www.vikingyurt.com, $280 pp) for a six-course dinner. For a daytime dogsledding

1: The best views are in the backcountry on skis. **2:** catskiing with Park City Powder Cats **3:** green ski jumps of Utah Olympic Park **4:** fall in Park City

1
2
3
4

romp, **Luna Lobos** (4733 Browns Canyon Rd., Peoa, 435/783-3473, www.lunalobos.com, $225 pp) is a family-owned operation less than a 30-minute drive from Park City.

SUMMER RECREATION

Hiking

The ski areas open their trails to hikers in summer. **Deer Valley** (435/649-1000 or 800/424-3337, www.deervalley.com) and **Park City** (435/649-8111, www.parkcitymountain.com) both offer lift-assisted hiking, or you can hike up the trails for free. From downtown Park City, follow trail signs to the mountain; well-marked trails start just on the edge of town and head uphill. **Mountain Trails Foundation** (https://mountaintrails.org) has good interactive maps on its website.

When hiking around Park City, stay clear of relics of the mining past that lie scattered about. You're likely to come across miners' cabins in all states of decay, aerial tramway towers, rusting machinery, and piles of tailings. Unlike other parts of the Wasatch Range, most of the land here belongs to mining companies and other private owners. Visitors should keep a distance from mine shafts—which can be hundreds of feet deep—and respect No Trespassing signs.

TOP EXPERIENCE

★ Mountain Biking

Park City is home to a mountain biking trail system rated gold by the International Mountain Bike Association—there are only four of these in the country! While Park City might not offer the most technical riding around, it does have over 350 miles (565 km) of impeccably marked single-track for all ability levels. Few rides require toughing it out on ranch roads or asphalt to meet riding objectives, and almost all include stop-worthy views. For detailed, downloadable maps of most of these trails, check out the **Mountain Trails Foundation** (https://mountaintrails.org) or visit a local bike shop.

Both Park City resorts keep at least one lift open for bikers and hikers during the summer. **Deer Valley** (435/649-1000 or 800/424-3337, www.deervalley.com) has 55 stunning miles (89 km) of single- and double-track trails and is much more downhill oriented, with some of the most technical descents in the area. **Park City** (435/649-8111, www.parkcitymountain.com) has 35 miles (56 km) of trails.

A couple classic rides include **Wasatch Crest Trail** (12.5 mi/20.1 km one-way, 2-3 hours depending on pace, about 1,080 ft/329 m elevation gain), which is often ridden as a shuttle, and tours spectacular scenery along the Wasatch ridge, as well as **Mid-Mountain Trail** (21.9 mi/35 km one-way, 3-5 hours depending on pace, about 1,800 ft/549 m elevation gain, moderate), which runs from Deer Valley to Pinebrook, just west of Park City. Many Park City loops involve a stretch on Mid-Mountain, but the trail can also be ridden end-to-end with a shuttle.

Gravel and Road Riding

The **Historic Union Pacific Rail Trail State Park** (435/649-6839, https://stateparks.utah.gov, dawn-dusk daily year-round, free) is a multiuse nonmotorized trail built for hikers, bicyclists, horseback riders, and cross-country skiers. The trail parallels I-80 and runs about 30 miles (48 km) from Deer Valley through Park City and the town of Coalville north to Echo Canyon. In Park City, from Park Avenue, turn onto Kearns Boulevard, then right onto Bonanza Drive. After about 200 yards, turn left onto Prospector Avenue, where you can catch the trail behind the Park City Plaza; the parking area is on the right. Rent a bike from **White Pine Touring** (1790 Bonanza Dr., 435/649-8710, 9am-5pm daily), which also has easy access to the trail.

Hot-Air Ballooning

A flight above Park City on a hot-air balloon is an exhilarating experience. Balloons

1: hot-air ballooning **2:** fishing for trout on the Provo River **3:** mountain biking in Park City

1
2

3

Kid-Friendly Year-Round

Enjoy winter skiing or snowboarding, tubing, summer mountain biking, indoor or outdoor skateboarding, BMX, scooter riding, or even parkour at the sprawling **Woodward Park City** (3863 W. Kilby Rd., 435/658-2648, www.woodwardparkcity.com, noon-8pm Mon.-Thurs., 10am-8pm Fri., 9am-8pm Sat.-Sun., all-access tickets $99-159). The terrain isn't particularly steep (vertical drop is just 349 ft/106 m), but it's a good place for kids to have fun and pick up some skills. Ski runs are 36 percent beginner, 45 percent intermediate, and 18 percent advanced over 11 trails served by one quad lift and three surface lifts. There's also a great indoor kids' area.

take off in the early morning year-round, weather permitting, and trips typically include a continental breakfast and post-flight champagne toast. The cost is $280-300 for 1 hour with either **Bigfoot Balloons** (385/285-5899, www.bigfootballoons.com) or **Skywalker Balloon Company** (801/824-3934, www.utahballoonrides.com). If you're content to watch from the ground, visit during September, when the Autumn Aloft festival fills the sky with balloons.

Fishing

Fly fishing is a favorite pastime in the mountain streams and lakes of the Wasatch Mountains. The Weber and Provo Rivers are well known for their wily native cutthroat, wild brown, and rainbow trout as well as Rocky Mountain whitefish. Get your fishing license, supplies, and a guide at **Trout Bum 2** (4343 N. Hwy. 224, Ste. 101, 435/658-1166 or 877/878-2862, www.troutbum2.com, 9am-5pm Mon.-Sat.).

Golf

The Park City area has several 18-hole courses, including the city-owned **Park City Golf Course** (1541 Thaynes Canyon Dr., 435/615-5800, www.parkcitygolfclub.org, nonresidents $55). Owned by Park City Mountain Resort, **Canyons Golf Course** (4000 Canyons Resort Dr., 435/615-4728, www.parkcitymountain.com, $115) is a 6,256-yard, par-70 course, designed by Gene and Casey Bates. A short distance away in Midway, **Wasatch Mountain State Park** (435/654-0532, https://stateparks.utah.gov/golf/wasatch/, $75) has two outstanding public courses.

Horseback Riding

Red Pine Adventures (2050 White Pine Canyon, 435/649-9445 or 800/417-7669, www.redpinetours.com, from $150) offers trail rides of varying lengths; 1.5-hour rides start several times a day.

Water Sports

Hone your stand-up paddling skills with **PCSUP** (1375 Deer Valley Rd. S., 801/558-9878, www.parkcitysup.com); board rentals are available. **Boating, waterskiing,** and **stand-up paddling** are popular activities at the Jordanelle, Rockport, and Echo Reservoirs.

ENTERTAINMENT AND EVENTS

Nightlife

As you'd expect in a ski resort, nightlife centers on bars and dance clubs, mostly around Park City's Main Street, although many of the lodges and larger hotels have bars and clubs of their own. The **Marquis** (427 Main St., 435/310-5594, www.themarquispc.com) is the largest music venue in town, with long lines at the door, a usually packed dance floor, and VIP tables.

A favorite local haunt, **No Name Saloon** (447 Main St., 435/649-6667, www.nonamesaloon.com, 11am-1am Mon.-Fri., 10am-1am Sat.-Sun.) is a sports bar with food, including what's often called the town's best burger—head up to the rooftop for open-air vibes and views. Duck into **The Spur** (352 Main St., 435/615-1618, www.thespurbarandgrill.com, 11am-1am daily) for rock, acoustic folk, or bluegrass and a convivial atmosphere. Right next to Park City Live, **The Cabin** (427 Main St., 435/565-2337, www.thecabinparkcity.com, 11am-1am Wed.-Sun.) has music every night, a good list of beers, and cocktails (including the $30 Elkupine).

For the best cocktails in town, head to **High West Saloon** (703 Park Ave., 435/649-8300, www.highwest.com, 11am-9pm daily), located at the bottom of Park City Mountain's Quittin' Time run inside a collection of historic buildings one block off Main Street. You can also drive 30 minutes northeast to Wanship to tour **High West Distillery** (435/649-8300, 11am-3pm Wed.-Sun., reservations required), located by the posh Lodge at Blue Sky. Another great spot for cocktails is **Alpine Distilling's Social Aid & Pleasure Club** (364 Main St., 435/200-9537, www.alpineparkcity.com, 3pm-10pm Tues.-Sun.), with an under-the-radar, hip vibe and crafty drinks featuring the distillery's gin and other spirits about a block off Main Street. Find good craft brews at **Top of Main Brew Pub** (250 Main St., 435/649-0900, www.wasatchbeers.com, 11:30am-9pm Mon.-Fri., 10:30am-9pm Sat.-Sun.).

Events

One of the state's biggest—and glitziest—events takes over Park City every January: **Sundance Film Festival** (435/658-3456, www.sundance.org; see page 145). Also in January, the **FIS Freestyle World Cup** brings big mountain skiers to the slopes at Deer Valley. Not surprisingly, **Fourth of July** weekend is a busy time with a parade, nearby rodeo, and concert.

In early August, some 200 artists exhibit their work on Main Street for the **Kimball Arts Festival** (435/649-8882, www.kimballartcenter.org), along with live music, food vendors, and more. Contact the **Park City Visitor Information Center** (1794 Olympic Pkwy., 435/658-9616, www.visitparkcity.com) for the latest news on other happenings around town.

The Arts

Concerts

Summer is music festival time in Park City. The **Utah Symphony** and other classical performers, including the **Utah Opera,** take the stage at Deer Valley's **Snow Park Outdoor Amphitheater** (2250 Deer Valley Dr. S., 435/649-1000, www.deervalleymusicfestival.org) early July-early September for a summer concert series. The **Park City Beethoven Festival** (435/649-5309, www.pcmusicfestival.com) offers chamber music at various locations around town spring-fall.

Theater

In the heart of Old Town, the **Egyptian Theatre** (www.egyptiantheatrecompany.org) stages dramas, concerts, comedies, musicals, and children's shows year-round in the historic Egyptian Theatre (328 Main St., 855/745-7469).

SHOPPING

Park City's primary shopping venue is historic **Main Street,** which is lined with upscale boutiques, gift shops, galleries, and outdoor goods stores.

Markets

The open-air **Park Silly Market** (435/714-4036, http://parksillysundaymarket.com, 10am-5pm Sun. early June-late Sept.) takes over the lower stretch of Main Street during Sundays in summer. You'll find lots of crafts, handmade clothing and hats, and at the bottom of the street, food and beer carts and live music. It makes for agreeable shopping and fascinating people-watching. The **Park City Farmers Market** (1315 Lowell Ave., noon-6pm Wed. early June-Oct.) is held in a parking lot by the Canyons Village base of Park City Mountain Resort.

July Oakley Rodeo

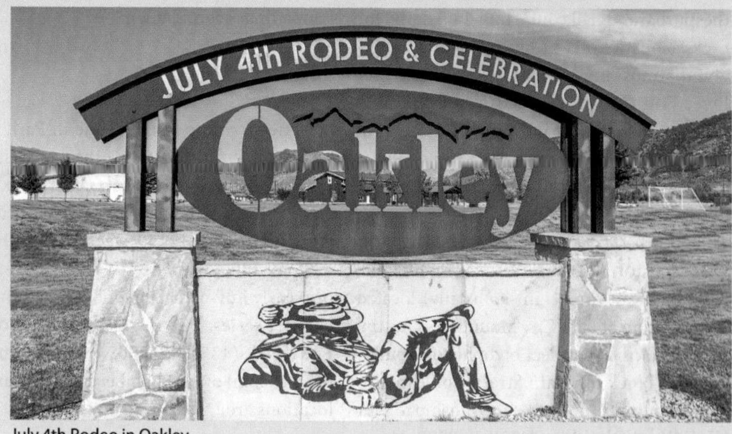

July 4th Rodeo in Oakley

Since 1935, the **Oakley Rodeo** (4300 UT 32, 435/783-5734, www.oakleycity.com, 4 days in early July at 8pm, tickets start at $15) has been staged in Oakley. This annual summer event spans several days and sells out months in advance, so buy tickets well ahead of time. Catch classic competitions like barrel racing and bull riding, a rodeo clown, and a different lineup of competitions every night. All seating is outside under the sun, so bring a hat and layers depending on the forecast. While you can buy or bring your own food, alcohol is strictly prohibited.

Books and Cards

Dolly's Bookstore (510 Main St., 435/649-8062, http://dollysbookstore.com, 10am-10pm daily) has a good selection of books for all ages and interests. **Atticus** (738 Main St., 435/214-7241, www.atticustea.com, 7am-6:30pm daily) combines the virtues of a bookstore, selling used and new reads, and a tea and sandwich shop.

Clothing

Panache (738 Main St., 435/649-7037, 10am-6pm daily) sells stylish high-end women's clothing and jewelry. **Olive & Tweed** (608 Main St., 435/649-9392, 10am-6pm daily) is an artisans co-op featuring women's clothing, jewelry, and lots of gifts. **Cake Boutique** (577 Main St., 435/649-1256, https://cakeparkcity.com, 10am-7pm Mon.-Thurs., 10am-9pm Fri.-Sat., 11am-6pm Sun.) is a fashion-forward clothing store that veers toward designer hipster wear with lots of denim.

For high-end Western goods, head to **Burns Cowboy Shop** (363 Main St., 435/649-6300, 11am-6pm Mon.-Sat.).

If your budget doesn't allow for shopping in Park City's high-end boutiques, check the good selection of pre-owned clothing at **Exchange Consignment** (605 Main St. #202, 435/649-3726, www.exchangeconsignmentparkcity.com, 11am-5pm Mon.-Sat.).

Native American Artwork

At **Tanner Trading** (550 Main St., 435/645-9177, www.tannertrading.com, 10am-6pm Mon.-Thurs., 10am-8pm Fri.-Sat.), you'll find a large collection of Native American artwork, including pottery, sculptures, Zuni and Hopi jewelry, and Navajo rugs. Some Western goods are also stocked here.

Sundance Film Festival

Park City during the Sundance Film Festival

Robert Redford started Sundance in 1981 as a venue for independent films. Since then, the **Sundance Film Festival** (435/658-3456, www.sundance.org) has become the nation's foremost venue for new and innovative cinema. The festival is held in the second half of January at the height of the ski season, so Park City is absolutely packed and then some during that time. As the festival has grown, some films are now shown in Salt Lake City theaters, as well as in Peery's Egyptian Theater in Ogden. Make plans well in advance if you want to attend any of the screenings or festival activities.

If you can't get tickets, put your name on waiting lists or join the lines at the theaters for canceled tickets and you'll probably be able to get into something. However, tickets to less well-known films are usually available at the last minute. If you are coming to Park City expressly to see the films, inquire about package tours that include tickets.

Park City is exciting during the festival, as the glitterati of New York and Hollywood descend on the town. You'll probably spy celebrities, some wild clothing, and lots of deal making.

Outdoor Equipment and Rentals

Old Town—and Park City in general—is a veritable hub of outdoor gear and apparel shops. You can find sustainability-centric supplies at **Patagonia** (632 Main St., 435/659-2280, www.patagonia.com, 10am-7pm daily), premium Swedish apparel for the alpine at **Fjällräven** (440 Main St., 435/565-6389, www.stores.fjallraven.com, 11am-6pm Mon.-Sat., 11am-5pm Sun.), colorful packs and styles made from responsibly sourced materials at **Cotopaxi** (333 Main St., 435/699-3201, www.cotopaxi.com, 10am-6pm Sun.-Thurs., 10am-7pm Fri.-Sat.), and the priciest, most Aspen-tastic skiwear at **Gorsuch** (333 Main St., 435/731-8053, www.gorsuch.com, 8am-7pm daily). Check out **Storm Cycles** (1153 Center Dr., 435/200-9120, www.stormcycles.net, 10am-6pm Mon.-Fri., 10am-5pm Sat.) over in Kimball Junction for all things bike, including rentals and demos.

At both of Park City Mountain Resort's base areas and at Deer Valley's Snow Park base, you'll find several gear rental shops to pick up the equipment you need for adventure. Beyond the base areas in Park City, there are a couple of great locally owned shops for ski rentals, bike rentals, and much more in the way of outdoor gear, including **Cole Sport** (1615 Park Ave., 435/649-4806, www.colesport.com, 10am-6pm daily) and **JANS Mountain Outfitters** (1600 Park Ave., 435/649-4949, www.jans.com, 9am-5pm daily), which also operates a fly-fishing shop.

FOOD

Park City is home to some great restaurants, though almost all are pretty spendy. Generally, the closer to Old Town or Deer Valley you get, the higher the tab at the evening's end. The listings below are just a smattering of what you'll find in a very small area. The five blocks of historic Main Street alone offer many fine places to eat, and each of the resorts, hotels, and lodges offers more good options. Note that some restaurants close or reduce hours in May and November—the so-called mud season. During ski-season weekends, dinner reservations are strongly advised for all but the most casual restaurants.

Old Town

Named for the robust clear brandy that Italians tend to present after a meal, **Grappa** (151 Main St., 435/645-0636, www.grapparestaurant.com, 5pm-9pm Sun.-Thurs., 5pm-10pm Fri.-Sat., $38-66) was the first restaurant in the local Bill White Restaurant Group, which has grown to include eight locally beloved concepts plus a farm that supplies many of the restaurants' ingredients. Established in 1992 inside a century-plus-old building, Grappa has a time-weathered Italian vibe. Try the osso bucco with polenta and kale, and if you're a spirited drinker, end dinner with a few sips of grappa.

No Name Saloon & Grill (447 Main St., 435/649-6667, www.nonamesaloon.com, 11am-1am Mon.-Fri., 10am-1am Sat.-Sun., $16-20, age 21 and up only) is a veritable museum inside an old firehouse. In this favorite local haunt, vintage skis, a motorcycle, a taxidermy buffalo head, and firefighting paraphernalia comprise the decor. Most of the food is standard bar fare, but the signature buffalo burger is the bomb. Head up to the rooftop patio for graffiti-laden toilets à la Marcel Duchamp and great views of Main Street.

Just about every dish at ★ **Handle** (136 Heber Ave., 435/602-1155, https://handleparkcity.com, 5pm-close daily, $20-92) will blow you away with its impeccable balance of flavor and texture. With mood lighting and a buzzy vibe, the restaurant is a fun spot to share several dishes among the table. Local and seasonal ingredients shine in dishes like toast with pork belly, taleggio, cherries, and beet or fried chicken with red pepper cream. Don't skip the dessert menu either.

Oishi Sushi Bar (710 Main St., 435/640-2997, www.oishisushiparkcity.com, 5pm-9pm daily, rolls $11-25) is an authentic spot, from the menu to the dimly lit space with an outdoor fire pit. Don't miss the unique house Oishi Roll with salmon, lemon, and steamed asparagus topped with tuna and spicy mayo.

Since 1979, family-owned **Davanza's** (690 Park Ave., 435/649-2222, www.davanzas.com, 11am-9pm daily, large pizzas start at $15) has been whistling the same tune: good pizza and good beer at a good price—all accessible from Park City Mountain's Town Lift. The pizza may not blow you away, but it gets the job done, with a satisfying cracker-thin crust.

A local's favorite on the outskirts of Old Town on the way to Deer Valley Resort, **Deer Valley Grocery Café** (Deer Valley Plaza, 1375 Deer Valley Dr., 435/615-2400, www.deervalley.com, 8am-3:30pm daily, $10-16) offers a low-key setting with plenty of to-go options. You'll find a typical café menu of espresso drinks, soups, salads, and sandwiches for breakfast and lunch, along with vegan options. The standout order is the turkey chili, which is also available as a take-home chili kit so you can re-create the experience back home or gift it to a friend. Deer Valley Grocery Café also operates a bakery with fresh bread, pastries, and desserts.

Old Town Park City

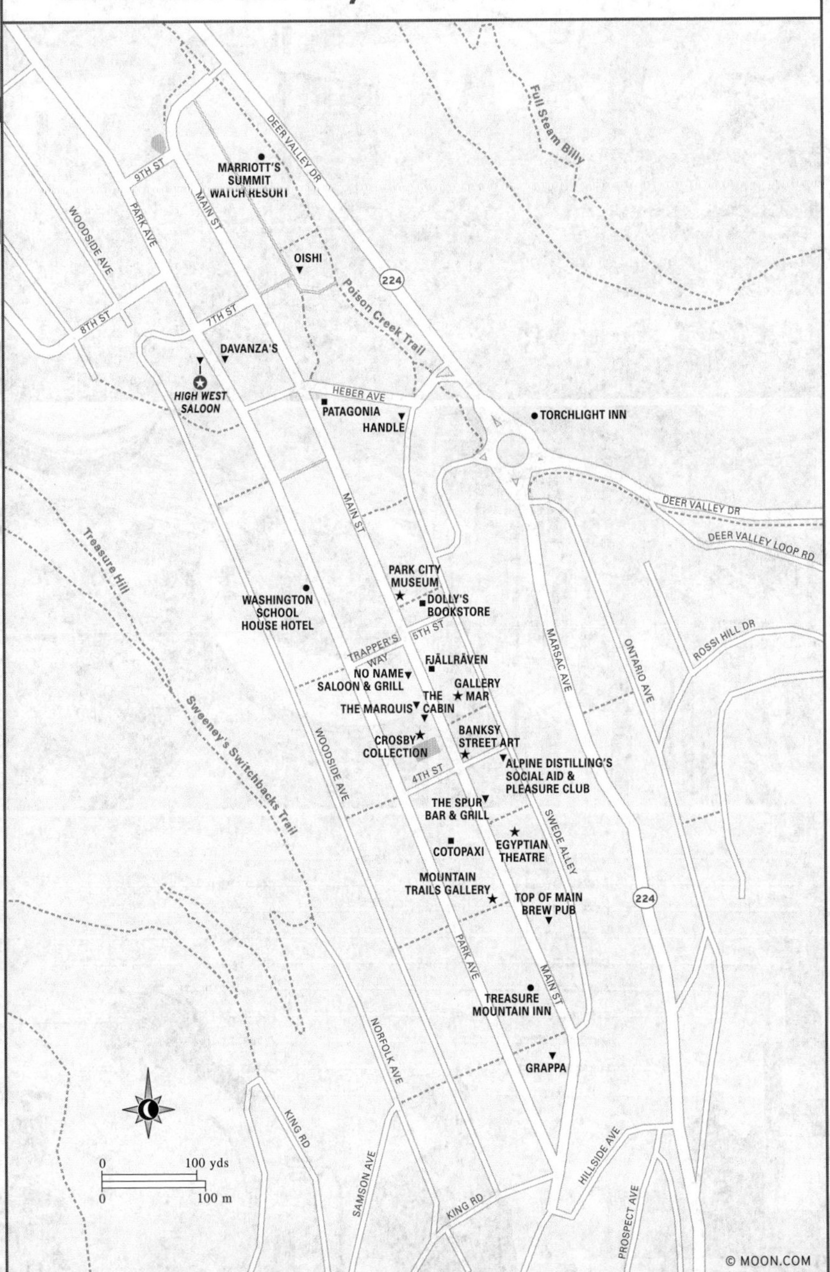

SHRED
FB
1
2
Pizza & More...
3
4
COFFEE MENU 8 OZ 12 OZ 16 OZ
ESPRESSO 3.5
CAFE LATTE 3.75 4.25 5.0
FLAT WHITE 4.25 5.0
CAPPUCCINO 4.25 5.0
AMERICANO 3.75
BEETLATTE 4.5
MATCHA LATTE 4.5
TURMERIC LATTE 4.5
CHA LATTE
COLD BREW
NITRO
AUSSIESTYLE 6.0
ICED TEA 3.5
HOT CHOCOLATE

★ High West Saloon

If you've got a few nights in Park City, be sure to dedicate one to ★ **High West Distillery & Saloon** (703 Park Ave., 435/649-8300, www.highwest.com/saloon, 11am-9pm daily, $20-56, age 21 and up only, no reservations accepted). Seared shishitos, pickle-brined chicken wings, and a burger with a sweet-savory onion-bacon jam are all great bets. The decor is upscale Wild West, with beautiful wood walls and flooring, a reclaimed wood bar, and dozens of candles lining the walls. Start with a High West sampler or a whiskey cocktail. High West is also the only ski-in/ski-out distillery in the world—zip down from the mountain for lunch and a hot toddy.

Prospector Square and Vicinity

Tupelo (1500 Kearns Blvd., 435/292-0888, https://tupeloparkcity.com, 5pm-10pm daily, $32-50) serves real-deal Southern cuisine—that won't weigh you down. Be sure to order biscuits for the table to mop up the beautiful sauces that come with your dish.

"World's Best Lobster Roll" in Park City? **Freshie's Lobster Co.** (1915 Prospector Ave., 435/631-9861, www.freshieslobsterco.com, 11am-8pm daily, $8-32) is owned by New England natives, who managed to secure Maine's inaugural 2017 lobster roll festival win. Originally a food truck, Freshies now has locations in Park City and Salt Lake. Imagine big, mayo-tossed chunks of fresh lobster, imported within 24 hours from Maine, tucked into a buttered hot dog bun. Rolls are $12-26, depending on size—spendy, but worth it.

Eating on a budget in Park City isn't always easy. That's one reason to head to **El Chubasco** (1890 Bonanza Dr., Ste. 115, 435/645-9114, www.elchubascomexicangrill.com, 11am-9pm daily, $7-16), but others include the laid-back vibe and extensive salsa bar. El Chubasco sweeps the award for Park City's Best Mexican Restaurant just about every year. Tacos come in the traditions of Mexico's Michoacán area. Savor the chiles rellenos or a gigantic burrito, adorned with a few of the 20-plus salsas available.

Tucked into the corner of a shopping mall, **Este Pizza** (1781 Sidewinder Dr., 435/731-8970, www.estepizzaparkcity.com, 11am-9pm Mon.-Thurs., 11am-10pm Fri.-Sat., 4pm-9pm Sun., $17-20 for a cheese pizza plus more for toppings) is the best place for a good, New York-style pie in Park City.

Australian café culture thrives at ★ **Five5eeds** (1600 Snow Creek Dr., 435/901-8242, www.five5eeds.com, 7:30am-3pm daily, $16-22), a breakfast and lunch spot easily overlooked in the Snow Creek shopping center. The menu leans healthy, but not ascetically so. Go full wholesome with the PC Superfood Grain Salad, or strike a balance with the pulled pork Benedict with apple cider hollandaise and Granny Smith apples. Try the "Aussie-style" cold brew on nitro.

The pastry case at ★ **Windy Ridge Bakery** (1755 Bonanza Dr., 435/647-2906, www.windyridgebakery.com, 8am-4pm Tues.-Thurs., 8am-6pm Fri.-Sat., 8am-2pm Sun.) is hard to resist, with colorful pastries, towering pies, and tempting petit four. The bakery is strictly to-go, but is not strictly sweets, with fabulous quiches, lasagna, and more.

Ritual Chocolate Cafe (1105 Iron Horse Dr., 435/200-8475, www.ritualchocolate.com, 8am-5pm Tues.-Sun.) is a lovely café that also sells the local, award-winning Ritual chocolate. Order one of the luscious sipping chocolates, made with ethically sourced cacao. Ritual Chocolate bars also make great gifts; try the Mid-Mountain (named for the local trail) and the minty Ski Dreams.

Kimball Junction

Despite its location in a strip mall, ★ **Cortona** (1612 W. Ute Blvd. #112, 435/608-1373, www.cortonaparkcity.com, 5pm-9pm Tues.-Sat., $25-32, reservations required) serves the best Italian food in Park City. Locals flock to the warm, trattoria-esque

1: rooftop patio of No Name Saloon & Grill **2:** skis and slices of pizza at Davanza's **3:** colorful salads at Handle **4:** Australian café culture thrives at Five5eeds.

space decorated with paintings of pastoral Italy brushed right onto the flaxen walls in true Tuscan style. If lasagna is your thing, you also need to state that you'd like an order of it when making your reservation. The posted menu changes frequently since all pastas are made fresh every day, and there's always a pasta del giorno.

With its open-air interior, lively bar, and live music by evening, **Hearth and Hill** (1153 Center Dr., 435/200-8840, www.hearth-hill.com, 11:30am-9pm Mon.-Sat., 10am-9pm Sun., $12-38) is a great spot for gathering. The menu is a bit all over the place, from new American to Asian fusion—mostly hits, a few misses. Just a few storefronts down, check out the restaurant's other concept, **Hill's Kitchen** (1153 Center Dr., Ste. G160, 435/800-2870, www.hills-kitchen.com, 7:30am-3:30pm daily), for excellent coffee, eye-catching pastries and treats, and healthy takeout lunch and dinner fare.

With a Mediterranean-leaning menu focused on roasted proteins and veggies, the fast-casual ★ **Vessel Kitchen** (1784 Uinta Way, Ste. 1E, 435/200-8864, www.vesselkitchen.com, 11am-9pm daily, $6-17) is an awesome spot for lunch or takeout dinner. Don't miss the hummus, roasted cauliflower, or citrus beets in bowl, salad, or plate formation.

Inspired by her grandma Florence's recipes, Sheron Grant opened **11Hauz** (1241 Center Dr., 435/200-8972, www.11hauz.com, 3pm-8pm Mon.-Wed., 11:30am-8pm Thurs., 11:30am-8:30pm Fri.-Sat., $13-43) with her family to bring Jamaican fare to the area. Inside, find colorful walls, rustic wood tables, and reggae on the stereo. As enjoyable as the food are the menu subheadings: Finga Tings, Green Tings, and Full Yuh Belly. Don't miss the jerk wings with a mango-pineapple chutney, the coconut-cream Rasta Pasta, or the weekend special: goat, made with an Indo-Jamaican spice mix.

Everything you could want in a coffee shop exists at ★ **Park City Coffee Roasters** (1764 Uinta Way, 435/647-9097, www.pcroaster.com, 7am-6pm daily), in a lively corner of Kimball Junction. The house-roasted coffee makes for tasty lattes, and the scones and cinnamon buns are hard to resist. With various different seating areas and a great patio, this is also a good spot for getting some work done.

ACCOMMODATIONS

Park City is awash in condos, hotels, and B&Bs—guest capacity far exceeds the town's permanent population. Rates peak dramatically during ski season, when accommodations may also be hard to find. Most hotels have four different winter rates, which peak around Christmas, during Sundance Film Festival, and in February-March. You'll find different rates for weekends and weekdays as well.

Many properties have rooms at a wide range of prices, from bunk rooms to basic hotel rooms to multiroom suites. The following price categories are for a standard double room in the winter high season (but not during the peak of the peak). Summer rates are usually about half those given below, and even lower in spring and fall. During ski season, minimum stay requirements may apply—sometimes a weekend, sometimes a full week. Park City's hotel tax is nearly 13 percent on top of whatever you're quoted.

The following accommodations are in addition to the lodges and hotels operated by or located at **Deer Valley** (435/645-6528 or 800/558-3337, www.deervalley.com) and **Park City Mountain Resort** (lodging 435/602-4099 or 800/331-3178, www.parkcitymountain.com).

Reservation Services

The easiest way to find a room or condo in Park City is to contact one of the following reservation services, many of which also offer ski, golf, or other recreational packages: **Park City Lodging** (855/348-6759, www.parkcitylodging.com), **Stay Park City** (888/754-3279, www.stayparkcity.com), and **Resort Property Management** (435/655-6529 or 800/645-4762, www.resort

propertymanagement.com). **All Seasons Resort Lodging** (888/575-2775, www.allseasonsresortlodging.com) handles a vast number of condo units throughout the valley. The **Park City Area Chamber of Commerce** (www.visitparkcity.com) also has an online lodging search engine.

$50-100

By far the most budget-friendly option in Park City, **Park City Hostel** (1781 Sidewinder Dr., 435/731-8811, www.parkcityhostel.com, dorm bed $45, private room $71-80) offers bunk beds and a few private rooms in a newer, well-kept space in Prospector Square.

Park City's classic budget option, **Chateau Après Lodge** (1299 Norfolk Ave., 435/649-9372, www.chateauapres.com, men's dorm bed $60, private room $175-250; open for groups only in summer), is a short walk from the Park City Mountain Resort base. The lodge has a dedicated following among serious skiers, and although even the men's dorm is a barracks and regular guest rooms are far from elegant, this family-run lodge is a great deal. It's also a good spot to meet skiers from all over the world at the breakfast buffet.

It's also possible to find high-quality lodging in this price range in Heber City, about 20 minutes from Park City, or in Salt Lake City, less than 35 miles (56 km) away.

$100-200

Near Kimball Junction, **Holiday Inn Express** (1501 W. Ute Blvd., 435/658-1600, www.holidayinn.com, $170-200) is only about 1 mile (1.6 km) from the Canyons Village area and a bargain for the area. A few other chain hotels are located near the freeway, not far from Park City's Canyons Village.

$200-300

A little ways from downtown, **Park City Peaks Hotel** (2346 Park Ave., 435/649-5000 or 800/649-5012, www.parkcitypeaks.com, $288-400) is a great option with modern decor, a great Italian restaurant with wood-fired pizza called Versante, and low rates in summer.

Not surprisingly, downtown Park City is peppered with chain hotels, where you can usually find a room for about $300-400 in winter, a bit less in summer, and substantially less in spring and fall.

Over $300

Right downtown, the ★ **Treasure Mountain Inn** (255 Main St., 435/655-4501 or 800/344-2460, www.treasuremountaininn.com, $300-525) is a large complex of three buildings with several beautifully furnished room types, all with kitchens. If you want a quiet room in this central locale, ask for one that faces the back pool and garden.

Despite its pedestrian name, the Marriott-owned **Hotel Park City** (2001 Park Ave., 435/940-5000, www.hotelparkcity.com, $800-2,900) is sumptuous, even by Park City standards. This all-suite hotel has comfy leather sofas, luxurious baths, a heated outdoor pool, a spa and fitness center, and a Ruth's Chris Steakhouse. It is a little too far to walk from the hotel to Main Street. In spring and fall, rates can drop to about $250.

Built in 1889 as the town's elementary school, the ★ **Washington School House Hotel** (543 Park Ave., 435/649-3800 or 800/824-1672, www.washingtonschoolhouse.com, $950-1,150) is now one of the best boutique accommodations in town. There are four large standard guest rooms and four suites, each curated with antiques and art. The hotel also has an outdoor heated pool, hot tub, sauna, and ski lockers. During the summer, it's possible to get a room for about $550.

A less vaunted but still luxurious and friendly B&B, the **Torchlight Inn** (255 Deer Valley Dr., 435/612-0345, $389-560) is on the edge of downtown Park City.

Marriott's Summit Watch Resort (780 Main St., 435/647-4100, www.marriott.com, hotel room with kitchenette $569-1,000) is a cluster of condo hotels right at the base of Main Street near Town Lift, with options ranging from studios to two-room villas. All guest rooms have kitchens and there's a central pool.

Right at the main base of the Park City Mountain Resort, **Marriott's MountainSide** (1305 Lowell Ave., 435/940-2000 or 800/940-2000, www.marriott.com, hotel room with kitchenette $569-1,200) is a top-notch ski-in/ski-out choice. Although you can walk to town from here, it's a bit of a schlep in winter.

For one of the most unique luxury options in the area, drive 30 minutes northeast to Wanship and the **Lodge at Blue Sky** (27649 Old Lincoln Hwy., Wanship, 866/296-8998, www.aubergeresorts.com/bluesky, hotel room with kitchenette $1,500-2,900), co-located with High West Distillery. "Adventures" are part of the attraction—everything from snowshoeing to heli-mountain biking. The rooms, the infinity pool, and the acclaimed restaurant Yuta ($38-85) are all lovely. If you're coming to Park City to ski, Blue Sky is a bit too remote to be convenient, but it's an awesome choice if you're not a skier or are visiting in summer.

Campgrounds

Park City RV Resort (2200 W. Rasmussen Rd., 435/260-4267, www.parkcityrvresort.com, RVs $77) offers seasonal tent and year-round RV sites with showers and laundry. From I-80, take exit 145 for Park City and travel west 1 mile (1.6 km) on the north frontage road. The campground is about 6 miles (9.7 km) from Park City.

INFORMATION AND SERVICES

A few Main Street storefronts advertise "visitors information"; these places are almost invariably real estate offices, although they do have racks of brochures. For the best selection of info and genuinely helpful staff, visit the **Park City Visitor Information Center** (1794 Olympic Pkwy., 435/658-9616, www.visitparkcity.com, 9am-5pm daily) near Kimball Junction at the turnoff to Utah Olympic Park. There's a branch office in the Park City Museum (528 Main St.).

GETTING THERE AND AROUND

The 32-mile (52-km) drive from Salt Lake City to Park City takes about 40 minutes (allow more time in the winter). From SLC, take I-15 to I-80 East; follow I-80 for about 24 miles (39 km) to exit 145 (UT 224), which eventually flows into downtown Park City. It's well signed and hard to lose your way.

If you'd rather skip the hassle of driving, **Peak Transportation** (888/850-8333, www.peaktransportation.com, $180 one-way depending on number of passengers) and **Canyon Transportation** (801/255-1841, www.canyontransport.com, $49 one-way) both make regular runs between Park City and Salt Lake City International Airport or downtown. Resorts also offer car rentals in Park City.

Park City Transit (435/615-5000) operates a trolley bus up and down Main Street (about every 10 minutes daily) and has several bus routes to other parts of town, including the Park City, Canyons Village, and Deer Valley ski areas (every 10-20 minutes daily). All buses are free; pick up a transit guide from the visitor center in Kimball Junction (1794 Olympic Pkwy., 435/658-9616), in the Park City Museum (528 Main St., 435/649-7457), on any of the buses, or on the https://parkcity.org website. Parking can be extremely difficult in downtown Park City, so it's a good idea to hop a bus. Uber and Lyft also serve Park City.

The Wasatch Back

The Wasatch Back consists of the eastern, less urban side of the Wasatch Mountains. Topographically, this region lies on the "back" side of the nearly 12,000-foot (3,658-m) mountain range. While Park City is the most prominent place in the region, several other towns, sights, and Wasatch peaks accessible from this area deserve the visitor's attention—this is the Greater Wasatch Back.

The largest of these towns is Heber, which got a tad tempted by the development opportunities that come with being a bedroom community of Park City in a picturesque valley. But look past the big box stores and chain restaurants, and you'll find many unique attractions and restaurants. The verdant Heber Valley, which stays a little warmer than Park City, is also a golfer's paradise, with a choice of three scenic golf courses open to the public, all with alpine backdrops.

The Heber Valley also includes the town of Midway, just a 5-minute drive to the west of Heber. In addition to golf, Midway is also known for its proud Swiss heritage, hot springs, and artistic streak. It's also quieter and quainter than Heber, and is by far the better of the two towns to spend a night or two.

Midway is also the gateway to Wasatch Mountain State Park, which consists of 23,000 acres (9,308 ha) of state-preserved land. The park offers hiking, mountain biking, golfing, and camping in the summer, and Nordic skiing, tubing, and snowshoeing in the winter. Soldier Hollow Nordic Center, located within the park, even served as a venue for the 2002 Winter Olympics.

Just south of Heber past Deer Creek Reservoir lies Provo Canyon and the town of Sundance, which will take you by surprise in a good way. Dominated by the Sundance Resort—owned by Robert Redford—Sundance is a delightful getaway with skiing, mountain biking, and some of the best food in the state.

Just a couple miles south of Sundance lies Mount Timpanogos, perhaps the most glorious peak in the Wasatch Range, and the second tallest, too. Visitors flock to Mount Timp, as it's locally referred to, to explore its caves, hike in the mountain's foothills, or put in a full day to reach its 11,753-foot (3,582-m) summit. Running southeast of Mount Timpanogos, with access just minutes from Sundance, the Provo River is a popular spot for tubing and river sports on hot summer days.

HEBER CITY AND MIDWAY

Sights

Heber Valley Historic Railroad

Ride a turn-of-the-20th-century train pulled by steam locomotive number 618 past Deer Creek Lake into scenic Provo Canyon. **Heber Valley Railroad** (450 S. 600 W., 435/654-5601, http://hebervalleyrr.org, year-round, $25-30 adults, $15 ages 2-11) offers scenic tours, plus a variety of dinner and adventure options as well, including various holiday-themed rides that book out well in advance.

Soldier Hollow

Site of the 2002 Olympic and Paralympic cross-country skiing and biathlon events, **Soldier Hollow** (435/654-2002, https://utaholympiclegacy.org, trail pass $10) offers roughly 20 miles (32 km) of trails (including some easy ones) for cross-country skiing, snowshoeing, biathlon, and mountain biking. There's also a tubing hill ($27-30 for 2 hours ages 13 and up, $28 ages 6-12, $20 ages 3-5). Rentals are available at the lodge. From Heber City, head west on 100 South to Midway. Take a left on Center Street (Hwy.

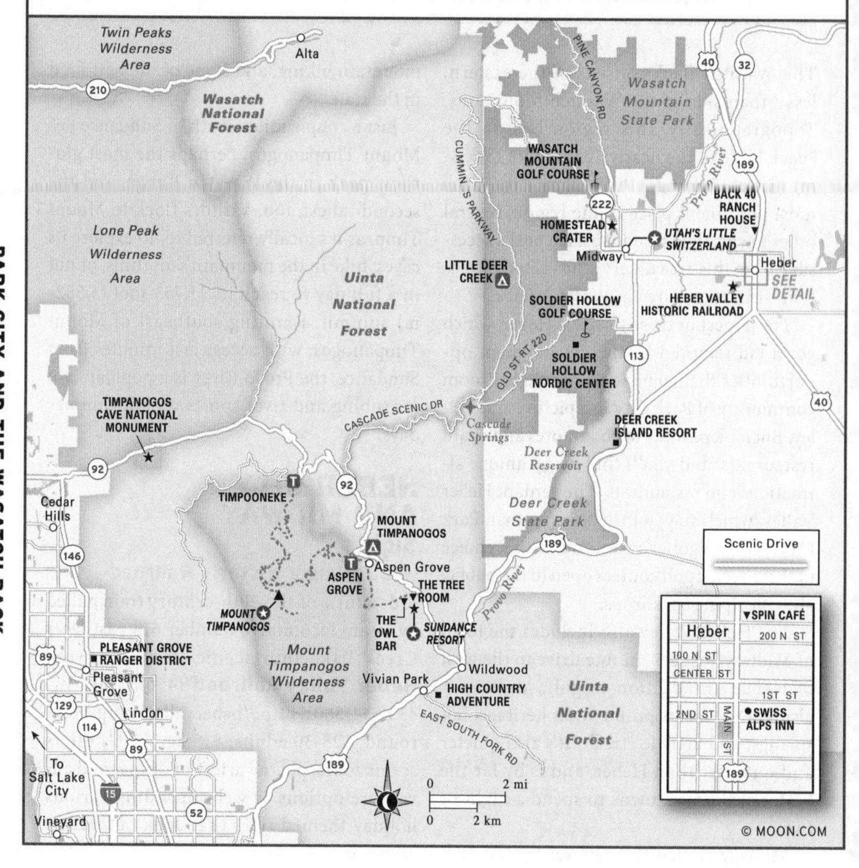

113) in Midway and head south for 3.5 miles (5.6 km) to Soldier Hollow.

Homestead Crater

Just northwest of Midway, on the grounds of the Homestead Resort, is a large, 10,000-year-old volcanic-like cone called the Crater. This geological curiosity is actually composed of travertine limestone deposited by the local hot springs. Water once flowed out of the top, but since the crater's discovery in the late 19th century, it's piped to a 65-foot-deep (105-m), 95°F (35°C) pool deep in the Crater's belly. **Homestead Crater** (435/657-3840, www.homesteadresort.com, noon-8pm Mon.-Thurs., 10am-8pm Fri.-Sat., 10am-4pm Sun., $18 adults, $15 kids, reservations required) is accessible for swimming, scuba diving ($27), snorkeling ($26), and even yoga via **Park City Yoga Adventures** (www.parkcityyogaadventures.com, $100-150 pp).

★ Utah's Little Switzerland

In the late 19th century, Swiss families began to arrive in Midway and the Heber Valley. These immigrants gave the town its Swiss

1: Midway **2:** a historic train on display at the Heber Valley Railroad **3:** Midway Mercantile **4:** a "scone" at Swiss Days in Midway

1
2
3
4

character, which is apparent naturally in the verdant, alpine landscape, and culturally in everything from the architecture to the local dairy industry. The local favorite is **Heber Valley Artisan Cheese** (920 River Rd., Midway, 435/654-0291, www.hebervalleyartisancheese.com, 10am-6pm Mon.-Sat.), which has been family-run since 1929 and produces award-winning artisan cheese, including an Emmental swiss. The dairy has a small farm store and regularly hosts tours and events.

The Swiss influence is also apparent in several of the accommodations in the area, from the Swiss Alps Inn in Heber to Zermatt Resort in Midway.

The best display of the area's Swiss heritage occurs during its annual **Swiss Days** (Midway Town Hall, 140 W. Main St., https://midwayswissdays.org, free), which includes music, crafts, and, of course, cheese. Specific dates vary, but Swiss Days is typically held the Friday and Saturday before Labor Day. The festival has been taking place since the 1940s and gathers some 200 vendors in Midway Town Square, offering Swiss-themed wares, from dirndls and hats to swiss cheese sandwiches.

Entertainment and Events

Horse shows and rodeos take place throughout the summer in the Heber City area (www.gohebervalley.com). The **Utah High School Rodeo Finals** are held in early June. **Wasatch County Fair Days** features a parade, a rodeo, exhibits, and a demolition derby in early August. Labor Day weekend brings **Swiss Days** (https://midwayswissdays.org) to Midway as well as a huge gathering of border collies and their fans to Soldier Hollow for the **Soldier Hollow Classic Sheepdog Championship** (http://soldierhollowclassic.com).

Food

Heber City

American-style cafés line Main Street, along with plenty of fast food. A fun, casual spot with good food, **Spin Café** (220 N. Main St., 435/654-0251, www.spincafe.net, 11:30am-8pm Sun.-Mon. and Thurs., 11:30am-8:30pm Fri.-Sat., $16-21) serves barbecue, burgers, and gelato. There are also good vegetarian and gluten-free menus.

On the outskirts of Heber, **Back 40 Ranch House Grill** (1223 N. Hwy. 40, 435/654-3070, www.back40utah.com, 11am-3:30pm and 4:30pm-10pm Mon.-Sat., 10am-10pm Sun., $15-36) takes food and its origins seriously: witness the house-made potato chips. The farm-to-table menu covers all the comfort food bases, and the patio is where it's at come summer.

Take a drive over to the tiny town of Woodland for a weekend breakfast biscuit sandwich or lunchtime burger at the **Woodland Biscuit Company** (2734 E. UT 35, Woodland, 435/783-4202, www.woodlandbiscuitcompany.com, 9am-12:30pm Sat.-Sun., 5pm-9pm Wed., $14-19).

Midway

The dining room at the **Blue Boar Inn** (1235 Warm Springs Rd., 435/654-1400, www.theblueboarinn.com, 8am-9pm daily, $30-42), which puts out elegant takes on European classic dishes, is also highly regarded.

Arguably the most inventive food in Heber Valley can be found at ★ **Midway Mercantile** (99 E. Main St., 435/222-8003, www.midwaymercantile.com, 11:30am-10pm Mon.-Sat., 4pm-10pm Sun., $17-38), which is located in an 1874-built general store. You'll find artfully prepared surf and turf, handmade pastas, stone hearth-fired pizza, and a lively cocktail list.

Accommodations

Heber City motels are generally well maintained and reasonably priced. A few miles west, Midway has several more expensive and luxurious resorts.

Heber City

The **Swiss Alps Inn** (167 S. Main St., 435/654-0722, www.swissalpsinn.com, $90-130) is a budget motel with an outdoor pool, a playground, and two suites with full kitchens.

On the southern edge of town, the **Holiday Inn Express** (1268 S. Main St., 435/654-9990 or 888/465-4329, www.hiexpress.com, $175-180) is a good choice for those who don't appreciate the quirks of small-town budget motels.

Midway

The most unique place to stay in the Heber Valley is **Homestead Resort** (700 N. Homestead Dr., 435/654-1102 or 800/327-7220, www.homesteadresort.com, $199-249), which is centered upon the hot spring-filled Homestead Crater. In addition to this giant hole in the ground, there's an indoor and outdoor pool. The rooms themselves are country-style, but comfortable. The resort also offers an 18-hole golf course ($54), but you'll find better courses down the road at Wasatch Mountain State Park. Stables offer horseback riding, hayrides (sleigh rides in winter), and bicycle rentals.

The **Blue Boar Inn** (1235 Warm Springs Rd., 435/654-1400 or 888/650-1400, www.theblueboarinn.com, $240-330) is near an entrance to Wasatch Mountain State Park and the park's popular golf course. Each of the inn's 12 meticulously decorated guest rooms is devoted to a different poet or author; there's also a very good restaurant and a cozy pub on-site.

The **Zermatt Resort** (784 W. Resort Dr., 435/657-0180 or 866/937-6288, www.zermattresort.com, $240-379) is a giant Swiss-style lodge with restaurants, a bakery, swimming pools, and a spa.

Information and Services

The **Heber Valley Chamber of Commerce** (475 N. Main St., 435/654-3666, www.gohebervalley.com, 9am-5pm Mon.-Fri.) has info on Heber City and Midway businesses. The **Heber Ranger District Office** (2460 S. US 40, 435/654-0470, 9am-5pm Mon.-Fri.) manages the Uinta National Forest lands east and southeast of Heber City.

The **Heber Valley Hospital** (1485 S. US 40, 435/654-2500) has 24-hour emergency care.

Getting There

To reach Heber City, take I-80 (from about 25 mi/40 km east of Salt Lake City) to exit 146 and head 17 miles (27 km) south on US 40. No public transportation serves this area.

WASATCH MOUNTAIN STATE PARK

Utah's second-largest state park, **Wasatch Mountain State Park** (435/654-1791, tee times 435/654-0532, https://stateparks.utah.gov, day-use $10, 18 holes of golf $75) spans 22,000 acres (8,903 ha) of valleys and mountains on the east side of the Wasatch Range. Unpaved scenic drives lead north through Pine Creek Canyon to Guardsman Pass Road (turn right for Park City or left over the pass for Brighton), northwest through Snake Creek Canyon to Pole Line Pass and American Fork Canyon, and southwest over Decker Pass to Cascade Springs.

Recreation

The 1.5-mile (2.4-km) **Pine Creek Nature Trail** begins near site 21 in the Oak Hollow Campground. The vast park is also a popular place for off-roading. In fall, join a guided OHV leaf-peeping tour.

The excellent **Lake** and **Mountain Golf Courses** (975 W. Golf Course Dr., 435/654-0532) are in the main part of the park. The newer Gold and Silver courses are at **Soldier Hollow Golf Course** (1370 W. Soldier Hollow Ln., 435/654-7442), which occupies a corner of the park. A clubhouse includes a pro shop and a café.

Winter brings snow depths of 3-6 feet (1-2 m) mid-December-mid-March. Separate **cross-country ski** and **snowmobile** trails begin near Soldier Hollow. **Homestead Adventure Center** (Homestead Resort, 700 N. Homestead Dr., Midway, 435/654-1102) provides equipment for both sports.

The park also has a growing network of

1
2

hiking and mountain biking trails. A standout option is the **Wasatch Over Wasatch (WOW) Trail** (9.4 mi/15.1 km one-way, 5-6 hours depending on pace, 2,400 ft/732 m elevation gain, strenuous), which for mountain bikers is best ridden downhill with a shuttle. The trail tours diverse and spectacular scenery, from wildflower fields to aspen groves.

Campgrounds

Wasatch Mountain State Park has three campgrounds (435/654-1791, https://stateparks.utah.gov, reservations 800/322-3770 or www.reserveamerica.com, day-use $10, campsites $35-90, cabins $70-85). The large **Oak Hollow Campground** (tents) and **Mahogany Campground** (RVs) both have showers and hookups available late April/early May-late October. **Little Deer Creek Campground** (water June-mid-Sept.) is in a more secluded aspen forest. Groups often reserve all the sites.

Getting There

To reach the main entrance of Wasatch Mountain State Park, drive west 3 miles (4.8 km) from Heber City to Midway, then follow signs north 2 miles (3.2 km).

JORDANELLE STATE PARK

Upstream of Heber on the Provo River, the **Jordanelle State Park** (435/649-9540, https://stateparks.utah.gov) reservoir is a popular spot for boaters and anglers. There are three main recreation areas. The most developed, **Hailstone Recreation Area** (435/649-9540 or 800/322-3770, day-use $20) has a large campground, restrooms and showers, day-use shaded pavilions, a marina with 80 boat slips, a general store, and a small restaurant. At the upper end of the reservoir's east arm, **Rock Cliff Recreation Area** (435/782-3030, day-use $10) has restrooms, a nature center, boardwalks with interpretive displays, and day-use pavilions. At **Ross Creek** (day-use $15) visitors can catch a trail that runs the perimeter of the lake and launch nonmotorized boats from a ramp.

Jordanelle State Park offers walk-in camping at the **Rock Cliff Recreation Area** (435/782-3030, day-use $10, camping $30, restrooms with hot showers available). **Hailstone Recreation Area** (435/649-9540 or 800/322-3770, www.reserveamerica.com, day-use $20, campsites $30-35, RVs $45, cabins $125-150, restrooms and shows available) has more amenities, including a general store, laundry, and small restaurant. Facilities include wheelchair access with raised tent platforms.

DEER CREEK STATE PARK

The 7-mile-long (11.3-km) Deer Creek Reservoir in **Deer Creek State Park** (Midway, 435/654-0171, https://stateparks.utah.gov, day-use $15-20) lies in an idyllic setting below Mount Timpanogos and other peaks of the Wasatch Range. A developed area near the lower end of the lake has a campground with showers, a picnic area, a paved boat ramp, a dock, and a fish-cleaning station. **Island Beach Area,** 4.5 miles (7.2 km) to the northeast, has a gravel swimming beach, marina, snack bar, boat ramp, and rentals of fishing boats, ski boats, and personal watercraft. Rainbow trout, perch, largemouth bass, and walleye swim here. Good winds for sailing blow most afternoons. You'll often see a lineup of catamarans at the sailboat beach near the campground and crowds of sailboarders at the Island Beach Area. **Deer Creek Island Resort** (Island Beach Area, 435/654-2155, www.deercreekislandresort.com) has paddleboard, kayak, and canoe rentals.

ALPINE SCENIC LOOP

This very narrow paved highway winds through some of the most beautiful alpine terrain in Utah. Mount Timpanogos rises to 11,753 feet (3,582 m) in the center of the loop, with sheer cliff faces and jagged ridges

1: biking the Wasatch Over Wasatch (WOW) Trail in the Heber Valley **2:** paddleboarding on the Jordanelle State Park reservoir

in every direction. More than a dozen campgrounds and several picnic areas line the way. You don't need to pay to just do the drive, but if you're going to stop to hike, fish, picnic, or camp, you need a recreation pass for the area ($6 per vehicle for 3 days; buy pass at entrance to American Fork Canyon or at self-service locations along the route).

Anglers can try for trout in swift, clear streams. Autumn brings brilliant gold to the aspens and scarlet to the maples. Winter snow closes the loop at higher elevations and attract skiers to Sundance Resort. A drive on US 89 or I-15 completes the approximately 40-mile (64-km) loop. With a few stops, a full day can easily be spent on the drive. If you'd like to see Timpanogos Cave en route, begin the loop from the north to avoid waiting in ticket lines in the afternoon.

Most of the picnic areas and campgrounds (801/785-3563 or 877/444-6777, www.recreation.gov, $26-33, all have water) are along American Fork Canyon at elevations of 5,400-6,200 feet (1,646-1,890 m). Higher recreation areas are **Granite Flat Campground** (elev. 6,800 ft/2,073 m, June-Sept.), **Timpooneke Campground** (elev. 7,400 ft/2,256 m, June-Oct.), **Mount Timpanogos Campground** (elev. 6,800 ft/2,073 m, June-Oct.), and **Theater in the Pines Picnic Area** (elev. 6,800 ft/2,073 m). The **Pleasant Grove Ranger District Office** (390 N. 100 E., Pleasant Grove, 801/785-3563) of the Uinta-Wasatch-Cache National Forest has information and maps for recreation areas along the Alpine Scenic Loop and for the Lone Peak and Mount Timpanogos Wildernesses. (You'll pass the office if you take US 89 and Highway 146 between Provo or Orem and the mouth of American Fork Canyon.)

CASCADE SPRINGS

Crystal clear water flows down a series of travertine-specked terraces amid lush vegetation at this beautiful spot. The springs produce more than 7 million gallons (26.5 million liters) of water daily. Boardwalks (some accessible for people with disabilities) and short trails with interpretive signs allow a close look at the stream and pools. Trout can be seen darting through the water (fishing is prohibited).

The drive here is also very pretty, either from the Alpine Scenic Loop or from Heber Valley. A paved road (Forest Rd. 114) branches off the Alpine Scenic Loop near its summit (between mileposts 18 and 19) and winds northeast 7 miles (11.3 km) to the springs. An unpaved road, passable by car if the road is dry, begins on the west edge of Heber Valley and climbs high above the valley, offering good views, then drops down to the springs. Turn west and go 7 miles (11.3 km) on Highway 220 from Highway 113 (between Midway and Charleston) and follow signs.

TOP EXPERIENCE

★ SUNDANCE RESORT

Since Robert Redford purchased this land in 1969, he has worked toward striking an ideal blend of recreation, the arts, and natural beauty. Today, **Sundance** (8841 N. Alpine Loop Rd., 801/224-4107, lodging reservations 800/892-1600, www.sundanceresort.com, $469-699) is now a ski resort by winter, a hiking and mountain biking destination by summer, a purveyor of the arts year-round, and one of the most unique lodges in Utah, with some noteworthy dining options. In 1980, Redford also founded the **Sundance Institute** to support independent filmmakers and host the annual Sundance Film Festival, which is centered in Park City but also hosts screenings at the resort. While Redford sold Sundance in 2020, the resort retains the same unique charm that "the Sundance Kid" worked so hard to build.

Downhill Skiing

Downhill skiing (801/223-4849, mid-Dec.-Apr.) is pretty relaxed at Sundance. The resort's four lifts take skiers high on the

1: a panorama from the summit of Alpine Scenic Loop **2:** Sundance Resort

1
2
OUTLAW EXPRESS

southeast slopes of Mount Timpanogos. The 45 runs on 5,000 acres (2,023 ha) provide challenges for people of all abilities, with 2,150 feet (655 m) of total vert. Ski instruction, rentals, accommodations, restaurants, and packages are available. **Lift tickets** cost $129 full day, $59 night adults; $89 full-day, $49 night under age 13; $65 day, $50 night seniors. Night skiing runs 4:30pm-9pm Monday, Wednesday, and Friday-Saturday. Prices jump by about $10 during winter holidays.

Sundance Nordic Center (801/223-4170, $20 adults, $9 ages 7-12, free seniors 65 and up) offers more than 10 miles (16.1 km) of Nordic track, lessons, and rentals. About once a month, guides lead a "night-owling" snowshoe hike ($60, reservations required), which begins at 6:30pm and offers a chance to call owls. Full moon tours are also available.

Summer Recreation

Sundance is at least as busy in the summer as in the winter, with activities ranging from the mellow (scenic lift rides $26 adults, $24 children and seniors) to the vigorous (mountain biking $50 for lift access). The Provo River is a great fly-fishing destination, and the resort can set you up with a guide. Horseback rides, river rafting, and hiking are also easy to arrange.

The Arts

Sundance's art programs are what make the resort really stand out. The **Art Studio** hosts workshops in drawing, painting, pottery, jewelry making, printmaking, and photography ($150 per class, $80 for kids' classes). A glassblower's studio offers visitors a chance to watch (and buy) but not do. Sundance also hosts artists-in-residence, and every Saturday (noon-5pm), these artists open their studios to guests.

Music and theater also thrive at Sundance. In summer, the resort hosts free outdoor concerts, a Bluebird Café concert series with Nashville musicians, and plays. You'll also find free live music on most Friday and Saturday nights at the Owl Bar.

Food and Accommodations

Guest rooms are beautifully decorated. If you've ever received the Sundance catalog, you'll know the sort of high-Western romantic furnishings to expect. Standard guest rooms run $293-498; also available are studios, suites, and multi-bedroom houses. The resort's on-site spa books appointments 11am-7pm Sunday-Thursday, 10am-8pm Friday-Saturday.

Sundance has several restaurants in the main compound, including an excellent deli, the **Foundry Grill** (866/932-2295, 7:30am-10am, 11:30am-3pm, and 5pm-9pm Mon.-Thurs.; 7:30am-10am, 11:30am-3pm, and 5pm-9:30pm Fri.-Sat., dinner entrées $28-95), and the elegant and highly recommended ★ **Tree Room** (866/627-8313, 5pm-9pm Wed.-Sat., $36-60), which features a literal tree around which the dining room was built. The actual restaurant-bar at the **Owl Bar** (801/223-4222, 4pm-11pm Mon.-Thurs., 4pm-1am Fri., noon-1am Sat., noon-11pm Sun.) was moved from Thermopolis, Wyoming; it's from the Rosewood Bar, once frequented by the Hole-in-the-Wall Gang.

Getting There

Sundance Resort can easily be reached by taking US 189 from Provo, Orem, or Heber City. Turn northwest and go 2.5 miles (4 km) on Highway 92 (Alpine Scenic Loop).

TOP EXPERIENCE

★ MOUNT TIMPANOGOS

Mount Timpanogos is the undisputed glory of the Wasatch. At 11,753 feet (3,582 m), it's the second-highest peak in the range, runner-up to Mount Nebo to the south by some 200 feet (61 m). Yet a unique silhouette, rich mythology, and a breathtaking path to the summit make Timpanogos Utah's most iconic

1: Emerald Lake on Mount Timpanogos **2:** snowfields in midsummer on the hike to Mount Timpanogos' summit **3:** view of Utah Lake from the top of Mount Timpanogos **4:** hiking the trail to Timpanogos Cave

1
2
3
4

mountain. Encompassing the mountain and its foothills is a 10,518-acre (4,256-ha) designated wilderness area, where people come to chase waterfalls, camp in the foothills, explore caves, and summit Timp.

The mountain takes its name from the Timpanogos Nation (www.timpanogostribe.com), part of the Shoshone tribe. In the mid-19th century, after a series of wars with and massacres by the LDS pioneers, the Timpanogos moved to the Uinta Valley Reservation, over 100 miles (161 km) away from the mountain they hold sacred. The name "Timpanogos" translates to "rock canyon of water": tumpi (rock) plus panogos (canyon of water).

This is also a mountain with a myth: Millennia ago, during a severe drought—a drought supported by the historical record—the Timpanogos people called upon a princess named Utahna to sacrifice herself to bring rain. As she was about to jump off the mountain to her death, a warrior named Red Eagle stopped her in her tracks. Perhaps caught up in the wild emotions of the moment, Utahna mistook Red Eagle for the great god of Mount Timpanogos. Together, they decamped to the caves, where they fell in love.

Soon after, an animal attacked Red Eagle. Seeing his mortal wounds, Utahna realized that Red Eagle was not a god and sealed her fate as a sacrifice. Red Eagle retrieved her body and carried her back to the caves, where their hearts become entwined in a massive, 4,000-pound (1,814-kg) stalactite: the Great Heart of Timpanogos, which you can see at the Timpanogos Cave National Monument today. From afar, the profile of Mount Timpanogos itself shows Utahna, lying on her back in the Wasatch for all eternity.

Hiking and Biking

There are two trails to the summit of Mount Timpanogos: **Timpooneke Trail** from Timpooneke Campground, and **Aspen Grove Trail** from Theater in the Pines Picnic Area. Both trailheads are just off the Alpine Scenic Loop. One-way distances to the summit are 9.1 miles (14.6 km) on Timpooneke Trail (4,350 ft/1,326 m of elevation gain) and 8.3 miles (13.3 km) on Aspen Grove Trail (4,900 ft/1,494 m of elevation gain); mileage records vary, perhaps due to trail work over the years and the scree scramble to the top. A loop hike connecting both trails (highly recommended for ambitious hikers) can be done with a shuttle between the two trailheads.

If a trip to the summit sounds too ambitious, hike the first paved mile along Aspen Grove Trail to a waterfall. Keep going for a little less than 5 miles (8 km) to see mountain lakes, including **Emerald Lake.** The **Summit Trail** branches off west of Emerald Lake, climbs a steep slope, and follows a jagged ridge southeast to the top. The deep blue waters of Emerald Lake are directly below.

Mountain bikers can also grunt uphill on Aspen Grove Trail, though some bikers prefer to stick to the road, which is often lightly traveled. Just north of the turnoff for Cascade Springs, the Alpine Loop Summit Trailhead provides access to a network of mountain bike trails.

Hiking season is mid-July-mid-October. In winter and spring, summiting Mount Timpanogos becomes a semi-technical mountaineering ascent requiring specialized equipment and knowledge. The **Pleasant Grove Ranger District Office** (390 N. 100 E., Pleasant Grove, 801/785-3563) can provide advice on hiking conditions.

TIMPANOGOS CAVE NATIONAL MONUMENT

Beautiful cave formations reward those who hike the trail to the entrance of **Timpanogos Cave** (801/756-5239, www.nps.gov/tica, 6:45am-3:30pm daily mid-May-Labor Day, cave tours $12 adults, $7 ages 2-11, $2 under 2) on the north side of Mount Timpanogos. Tunnels connect three separate limestone caves, each of which has a different character. The first cave was discovered by Martin Hansen in 1887 while he was tracking a mountain lion.

Stop at the visitor center to learn about the caves' formation, history, and ecology. You can obtain tickets at the visitor center for **ranger-led tours,** or purchase in advance online (877/444-6777, www.recreation.gov, up to 30 days in advance, mid-May-Labor Day)—tours do sell out on weekends in peak season, so it's ideal to book ahead. Allow about 3-4 hours total, including 45-60 minutes for the tour. Even though the trail is paved, the 3-mile (4.8-km) round-trip hike from the visitor center to the caves is moderately difficult, with 1,065 feet (325 m) of elevation gain. Wheeled vehicles (including strollers) and pets aren't allowed. The 0.3-mile (0.5-km) tours start at the end of the trail. The underground temperature is about 45°F (7°C) all year, so bring a layer.

Aspiring spelunkers can sign up for an **Introduction to Caving tour** (877/444-6777, www.recreation.gov, 9:30am daily, $22 over age 14, reservations required), which involves scrambling and crawling. Wear hiking clothes and closed-toed hiking boots and bring smooth-leather gloves. Although the tour lasts 1.5 hours, plan to spend about 4 hours to complete both the tour and hike to the starting point.

A snack bar at the visitor center is open in summer. Picnickers can use tables across the road from the visitor center and at a site 0.25 mile (0.4 km) west. The **visitor center** is 2 miles (3.2 km) up American Fork Canyon on the Alpine Scenic Loop (Hwy. 92); to continue along this route up American Fork Canyon requires a $6 pass (for 3 days), but if you're only going to Timpanogos Cave, you don't need a pass.

You can take I-15 exit 279 for American Fork if you're coming north from Provo or I-15 exit 287 for Alpine if you're coming south from Salt Lake City.

Provo

Provo (pop. 117,000) has a striking setting on the shore of Utah Lake beneath the west face of the Wasatch Range. The city is best known as the home of Brigham Young University (BYU), a large school sponsored by the Church of Jesus Christ of Latter-day Saints.

The city also contains rich architectural heritage. At the turn of the 20th century, this hardworking young city constructed its civic buildings with style and substance, including Victorian mansions and vernacular worker homes. The visitor center (www.utahvalley.com) provides self-guided tour brochures that describe the city's historic architecture.

SIGHTS

Provo Temples

The modern **Provo Utah Temple** (2200 N. Temple Hill Dr.) of white cast stone incorporates floral elements and a central golden spire. Visitors can't go inside but are welcome to visit the landscaped grounds.

Provo City Center Temple (100 S. University Ave.) stands at the corner of 100 South and University Avenue in downtown Provo, where the city's tabernacle stood until it was destroyed by fire in 2010. The new temple, completed in 2015, is much more traditional looking than the modern building near the university.

Utah Lake State Park

The largest natural body of freshwater in the state, Utah Lake is 24 miles (39 km) long and 11 miles (17.7 km) wide; its average depth is only 9.4 feet (2.9 m). It drains north into the Great Salt Lake. Mountains form the skyline in all directions. Swans, geese, pelicans, ducks, and other migratory birds stop here. For the best bird-watching, head to the south end of the lake near the Provo Airport. **Utah Lake State Park** (4400 W. Center St., 801/375-0731, https://stateparks.utah.gov, day-use $20 Apr.-Oct., $10 Nov.-Mar., camping with

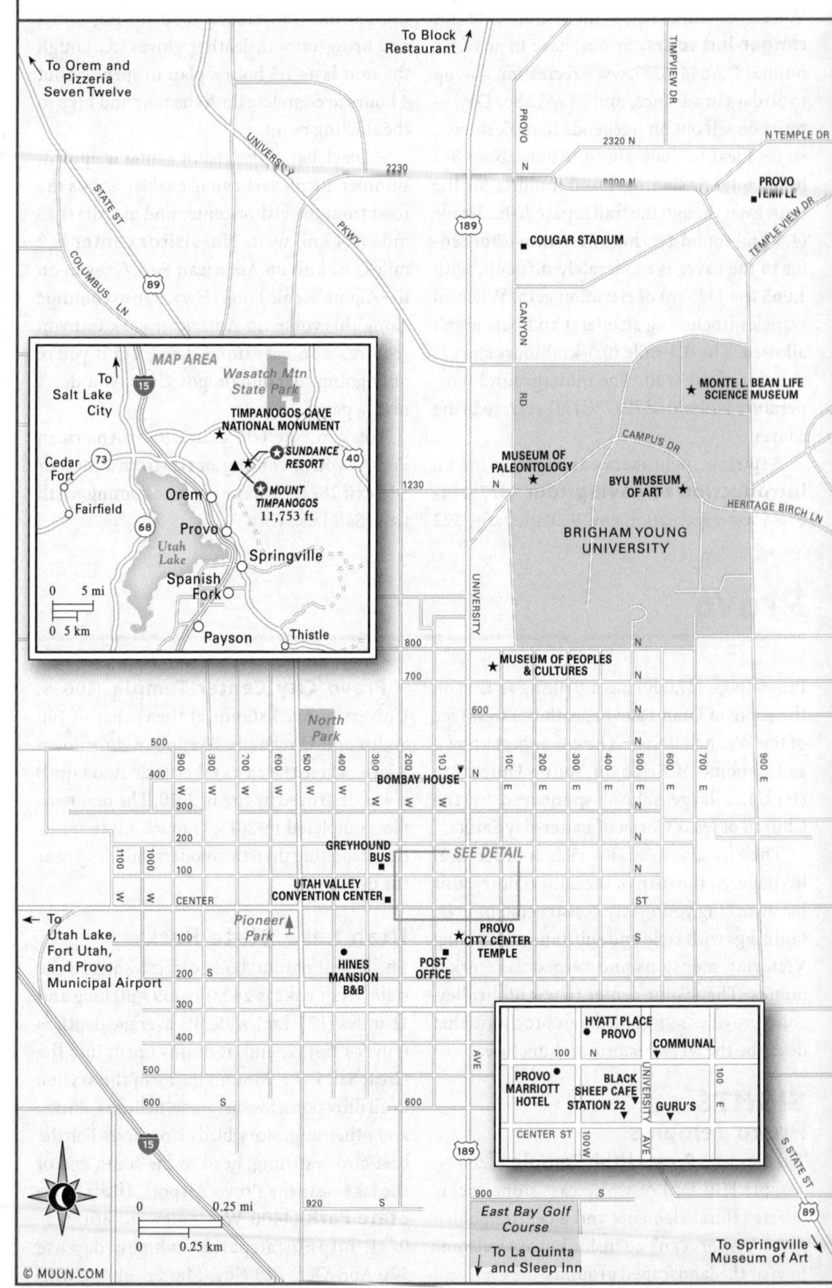
Provo
To Block Restaurant
To Orem and Pizzeria Seven Twelve
TIMPVIEW DR
PROVO
2320 N
N TEMPLE DR
UNIVERSITY
2230
STATE ST
PROVO TEMPLE
TEMPLE VIEW DR
189
COUGAR STADIUM
PKWY
COLUMBUS LN
89
CANYON
RD
MAP AREA
To Salt Lake City
15
Wasatch Mtn State Park
TIMPANOGOS CAVE NATIONAL MONUMENT
SUNDANCE RESORT
40
Cedar Fort
73
MOUNT TIMPANOGOS 11,753 ft
Orem
Fairfield
68
Provo
Utah Lake
Springville
Spanish Fork
Payson
Thistle
0 5 mi
0 5 km
MONTE L. BEAN LIFE SCIENCE MUSEUM
CAMPUS DR
MUSEUM OF PALEONTOLOGY
BYU MUSEUM OF ART
1230
HERITAGE BIRCH LN
BRIGHAM YOUNG UNIVERSITY
800
MUSEUM OF PEOPLES & CULTURES
700
North Park
600
500
400
300
200
100
CENTER
BOMBAY HOUSE
GREYHOUND BUS
SEE DETAIL
UTAH VALLEY CONVENTION CENTER
To Utah Lake, Fort Utah, and Provo Municipal Airport
Pioneer Park
PROVO CITY CENTER TEMPLE
HINES MANSION B&B
POST OFFICE
HYATT PLACE PROVO
COMMUNAL
PROVO MARRIOTT HOTEL
BLACK SHEEP CAFE
STATION 22
GURU'S
CENTER ST
100W
AVE
S STATE ST
900
920
East Bay Golf Course
To La Quinta and Sleep Inn
To Springville Museum of Art
0 0.25 mi
0 0.25 km
© MOON.COM

water and electric hookups about mid-Mar.-Oct., $40) provides recreational facilities on the east shore, just a short drive from downtown Provo. Visitors come for waterskiing, sailboarding, paddleboarding, and fishing; four paved boat ramps, docks, and slips are available.

Head west 4 miles (6.4 km) on Center Street from downtown Provo or take the I-15 exit for West Center Street and go west 3 miles (4.8 km).

Bridal Veil Falls

The two-tiered, 607-foot-tall (185-m) Bridal Veil Falls is at the southern end of Provo Canyon, about 10 miles (16.1 km) from downtown Provo. Although you can see the falls from the pullout along US 189, it's best to take the exit into the parking area and hike up a short, paved path to the pool of water at the base. During the winter, this is a popular spot for ice climbing.

Springville Museum of Art

The **Springville Museum of Art** (126 E. 400 S., Springville, 801/489-2727, http://smofa.org, 10am-5pm Tues. and Thurs.-Sat., 10am-8pm Wed., free) started in the early 1900s as the collection of Springville High School, but when it began to receive gifts of major works from artists Cyrus Dallin and John Hafen, townspeople decided a dedicated building was needed. They built this fine Spanish-style structure during the Depression with federal and LDS Church assistance. You'll find a permanent collection of some 2,000 works from Native Americans, early pioneers, and modern local artists; about 15 exhibits a year; and a sculpture garden.

Brigham Young University

Brigham Young University (north of 800 North, between University Ave. and 900 East, 801/422-4636, www.byu.edu) had a modest beginning in 1875 as Brigham Young Academy, established under the direction of LDS Church president Brigham Young. Like the rest of Provo, BYU's population and size have grown dramatically in recent decades. BYU is one of the largest church-affiliated schools in the world. Students aren't required to be LDS, but about 98 percent of the 30,000-strong student body does belong to the LDS Church. Everyone attending the school must follow a dress and grooming code. Almost all activities shut down for about an hour at 11am Tuesday for a university-wide devotional hour.

Anyone can visit BYU's 600-acre (243-ha) vast and pretty campus. The expansive **Hinckley Alumni and Visitor Center** (801/422-4663, http://hinckleycenter.byu.edu, 8am-5pm Mon.-Fri.) provides literature and advice about sights, events, and facilities open to the public.

Museum of Art

BYU is home to one of the largest university art museums in the West, the **BYU Museum of Art** (North Campus Dr., 801/422-8287, http://moa.byu.edu, 10am-6pm Mon.-Wed., 10am-9pm Thurs.-Fri., free except occasional special exhibits), with a collection of more than 17,000 works. On display are famous pieces, including Rembrandt's *Raising of Lazarus,* Gifford's *Lake Scene,* and Warhol's *Marilyn.* The building itself is a work of art, with a polished granite exterior, hardwood floors, and high-ceilinged galleries bathed in natural light.

Monte L. Bean Life Science Museum

Mounted animals and dioramas depict wildlife of Utah and distant lands at the **Life Science Museum** (645 E. 1430 N., 801/422-5050, http://mlbean.byu.edu, 10am-9pm Mon.-Fri., 10am-5pm Sat., free). The exhibits not only identify the many species on display, but also show how they interact within their environments. The museum hosts movies, talks, workshops, and live animal demonstrations.

Museum of Paleontology

The **Museum of Paleontology** (1683 N. Canyon Rd., 801/422-3680, http://geology.

1

2
BYU
BRIGHAM YOUNG UNIVERSITY

byu.edu/museum, 9am-5pm Mon.-Fri., free), across from **Cougar Stadium,** features excellent exhibits of dinosaurs and early mammals. BYU has a good program in paleontology, and students excavate bones from Utah and other western states. A viewing window lets you observe researchers cleaning and preparing bones.

Museum of Peoples and Cultures

Originally a place for the Department of Anthropology to stash its collections, the **Museum of Peoples and Cultures** (2201 N. Canyon Rd., 801/422-0020, http://mpc.byu.edu, 9am-5pm Mon.-Fri., free) now has a broader collection that communicates knowledge about both modern and ancient peoples of the world. Exhibits reflect research in the Great Basin of Utah, the American Southwest, Mesoamerica, South America, the Near East, and Polynesia; one recent exhibit explored the textiles of the ancient Andes.

RECREATION

Most of Provo's recreation hot spots are northeast of town in the mountains. In town, you can hike to the big Y on the side of (naturally) Y Mountain. The steep but not too difficult 2.4-mile (3.9-km) one-way trip will reward hikers with good views of the valley and town. The trailhead is east of the BYU campus. Take 900 East north and turn right onto 820 North, which becomes Oakmont Lane; turn right onto Oakcliff Drive, and right again onto Terrace Drive, which will take you to Y Mountain Trailhead Road.

Take a 2-hour **rafting trip** down the Provo River Canyon ($59 adults, $49 under age 13) or a 3-hour trip down the Weber River ($85 adults, $70 under age 13) with **High Country Adventure** (801/224-2500, www.highcountryadventure.com, June-Labor Day). It also offers river tubing and paddleboarding.

1: downtown Provo **2:** BYU stadium in Provo

FOOD

Downtown Provo has a pretty good restaurant row along Center Street, on both sides of University Avenue. This is an attractive part of town, with turn-of-the-20th-century storefronts and a shady median that makes the area parklike. There are quite a number of international eateries, thanks to the university crowd. Within a few blocks, you'll find Italian, Chinese, Peruvian, Salvadoran, and Brazilian restaurants, as well as a vegan cafe.

Near the busy intersection of Center Street and University Avenue, find the casual and almost-hip (in a yoga sort of way) **Guru's** (45 E. Center St., 801/375-4878, http://guruscafe.com, 8am-9pm Mon.-Thurs., 8am-10pm Fri.-Sat., 9am-2pm Sun., $10-20), which serves good pasta, rice bowls, wraps, pizzas, and salads. It's also a reliable place for breakfast.

★ **Black Sheep Cafe** (19 N. University Ave., 801/607-2485, 11:30am-2:30pm and 5pm-9pm Mon.-Thurs., 11:30am-2:30pm and 5pm-9:30pm Fri., noon-3pm and 5pm-9:30pm Sat., $15-30) serves creative takes on Native American dishes such as Navajo tacos and Southwestern specialties like posole in a tidy modern dining room.

On the west side of Center Street, **Station 22** (22 W. Center St., 801/607-1803, http://station22cafe.com, 8am-3pm and 5pm-9pm Mon.-Thurs., 8am-3pm and 5pm-10pm Fri.-Sat., $15-20) cooks up Southern comfort food. No alcohol, but a large "craft soda" menu features good homemade root beer as well as birch beer, sarsaparilla, and cream sodas.

North of Center Street on University Avenue is **Bombay House** (463 N. University Ave., 801/373-6677, www.bombayhouse.com, 4pm-9pm Mon.-Sat., $14-20), the city's top choice for Indian food, with excellent tandoori specialties.

A particularly stylish and delicious downtown restaurant is ★ **Communal** (102 N. University Ave., 801/373-8000, www.communalrestaurant.com, 9am-2pm and 5pm-10pm Mon.-Sat., $28-55), where food is locally sourced (farmers share the spotlight with the chefs) and diners have the option of sharing a large central table (there are also a few smaller tables). Settle in, get to know your neighbors, and enjoy an order of pork loin with mustard sauce and pickled mustard seeds. Sides ($8-13) are extra, but you can easily share a main dish and add a couple sides.

For more farm-to-table food, head north to Orem, where **Pizzeria Seven Twelve** (320 S. State St., Orem, 801/623-6712, 11:30am-9:30pm Mon.-Sat., $15-17) pulls delicious, seasonally inspired pizzas from a wood-fired oven heated to 712°F (378°C). Round out the meal with a lime-tossed watermelon salad.

Although Sunday brunch can be hard to come by in Provo, **Block Restaurant** (3330 N. University Ave., 801/885-7558, www.blockrestaurantgroup.com, 5pm-9pm Tues.-Fri., 10am-1:30pm and 5pm-9pm Sat., 10am-2pm Sun., brunch $14-22, dinner $30-55) has it covered with a tasty (and quite rich) avocado Benedict. Dinners, such as gnocchi with short ribs and pickled shallots, are similarly well prepared with lots of local ingredients. You can even get an alcoholic beverage with your brunch (or dinner) here.

ACCOMMODATIONS

Most of Provo's accommodations are chain motels along South University Avenue, the long commercial strip that runs from I-15 exit 266 to downtown. The downtown area offers older but well-maintained properties. If you're concerned more with price than amenities, look for a string of budget motels at the south end of town.

Tucked just off University Avenue, the **Sleep Inn** (1505 S. 40 E., 385-207/2676, www.sleepinnprovo.com, $138-162) is a good bet and convenient to downtown. Pets are permitted, and there's a small pool and an exercise room.

Just a few miles north of Provo, a pet-friendly **La Quinta** (521 W. University Pkwy., Orem, 801/226-0440, www.wyndhamhotels.com/laquinta, $115-149) is right off I-15 and makes a good jumping-off point for trips up Provo Canyon.

The **Provo Marriott Hotel & Conference Center** (101 W. 100 N., 801/377-4700, www.marriott.com, $322-673), in the heart of downtown, is an upscale business and conference hotel. Guest rooms are nicely appointed, and facilities include a pool, spa, and weight room. Another good downtown choice is the relatively new and swanky (for Provo) **Hyatt Place Provo** (180 W. 100 N., 801/609-2060, www.hyatt.com, $185-499); it has an outdoor pool and allows pets.

Although Provo's hotels are fine places to stay, if you want to get away from the chains, consider booking at **Hines Mansion B&B** (383 W. 100 S., 801/374-8400, www.hinesmansion.com, $179-240). The decor of the nine guest rooms ranges from a sweet Victorian theme to a Western lodge style—the "Library" room even has a secret passage. Although the B&B is within walking distance of downtown restaurants, it's not in a particularly charming neighborhood.

Campgrounds

Lakeside RV Campground (4000 W. Center St., 801/373-5267, www.lakesidervcampground.com, year-round, tents $39, RVs $57-60), just before Utah Lake State Park, has showers, a pool, laundry, and a store; tent campers can't have dogs.

INFORMATION AND SERVICES

Utah Valley Convention Center (220 W. Center St., 801/851-2100 or 800/222-8824, www.utahvalley.com, 9am-5pm Mon.-Fri.) offers advice on sights and services in Provo and the Utah Valley.

There is a **post office** (95 W. 100 S., 801/275-8777), and medical treatment is available at **Utah Valley Regional Medical Center** (1034 N. 500 W., 801/373-7850).

GETTING THERE

Allegiant Airlines (702/505-8888, www.allegiantair.com) offers flights between the Provo airport (PVU, 5 mi/8 km west of downtown) and Los Angeles and Phoenix. **Enterprise** (801/377-7100) and **Hertz** (385/237-8970) rent cars at the airport.

Utah Transit Authority (UTA) (801/375-4636, www.rideuta.com) provides local bus service in Provo and connects with Springville, Salt Lake City, Ogden, and other towns; buses don't run on Sunday in Provo. **Greyhound** (70 W. 750 S., 801/231-2222, www.greyhound.com) has two northbound and two southbound bus departures daily. **Amtrak** (300 W. 600 S., 800/872-7245, www.amtrak.com) runs the Chicago-Oakland *California Zephyr* train via Provo once daily in each direction.

Zion and Bryce

In southwestern Utah, the Mojave Desert, the Great Basin, and the lofty cliffs of the Colorado Plateau join, forming some of the most spectacular scenery on earth. It's in this geologically riveting landscape where you'll find two of the nation's most popular parks: Zion and Bryce. But it's not all rocks and desert—these lands are also home to flower-filled meadows, skiing, and tranquil lakes.

When people imagine Zion, they usually think of Zion Canyon and its steep walls laced with hanging gardens that manage to eke out an existence in the vertical. The dicey path to the celestial views of Angels Landing also come to mind, along with the Virgin River rising as the canyon's walls narrow. But there's more to Zion than meets the eye, from the Kolob Canyons section and the park's back roads to

Highlights

Look for ★ to find recommended sights, activities, dining, and lodging.

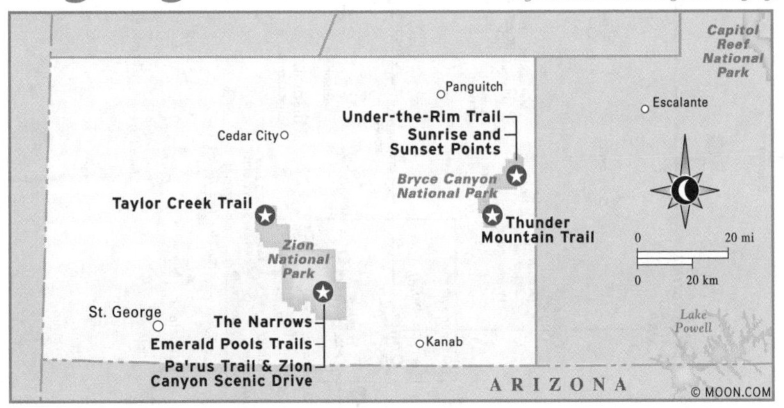

★ **Emerald Pools Trails:** No Angels Landing permit? No problem—hike Zion's Kayenta Trail to see a series of pools, each majestic in its own way (page 186).

★ **The Narrows:** Hike Zion Canyon's narrowest point by wading or swimming (depending on precipitation levels and season) through the Virgin River between steep walls rife with hanging gardens (page 188).

★ **Taylor Creek Trail:** In Kolob Canyons, a quieter section of Zion, follow Taylor Creek Trail past two historic cabins and wildflowers to a brooding, glorious alcove (page 191).

★ **Pa'rus Trail and Zion Canyon Scenic Drive:** Skip the Disney World vibes of Zion's crowded shuttles by cycling from viewpoint to viewpoint on a bike or e-bike (page 193).

★ **Sunrise and Sunset Points:** Linked by a stretch of the Rim Trail, these two viewpoints in Bryce Canyon National Park offer particularly stunning views as the sun rises and falls (page 206).

★ **Under-the-Rim Trail:** Hike 23 miles (37 km) through vanilla-scented ponderosa pine trees and hoodoos on Bryce's longest trail (page 212).

★ **Thunder Mountain Trail:** This epic, hoodoo-filled mountain bike trail can be ridden as a shuttle or by parking at the trailhead and biking up the paved Red Canyon path (page 221).

Zion and Bryce

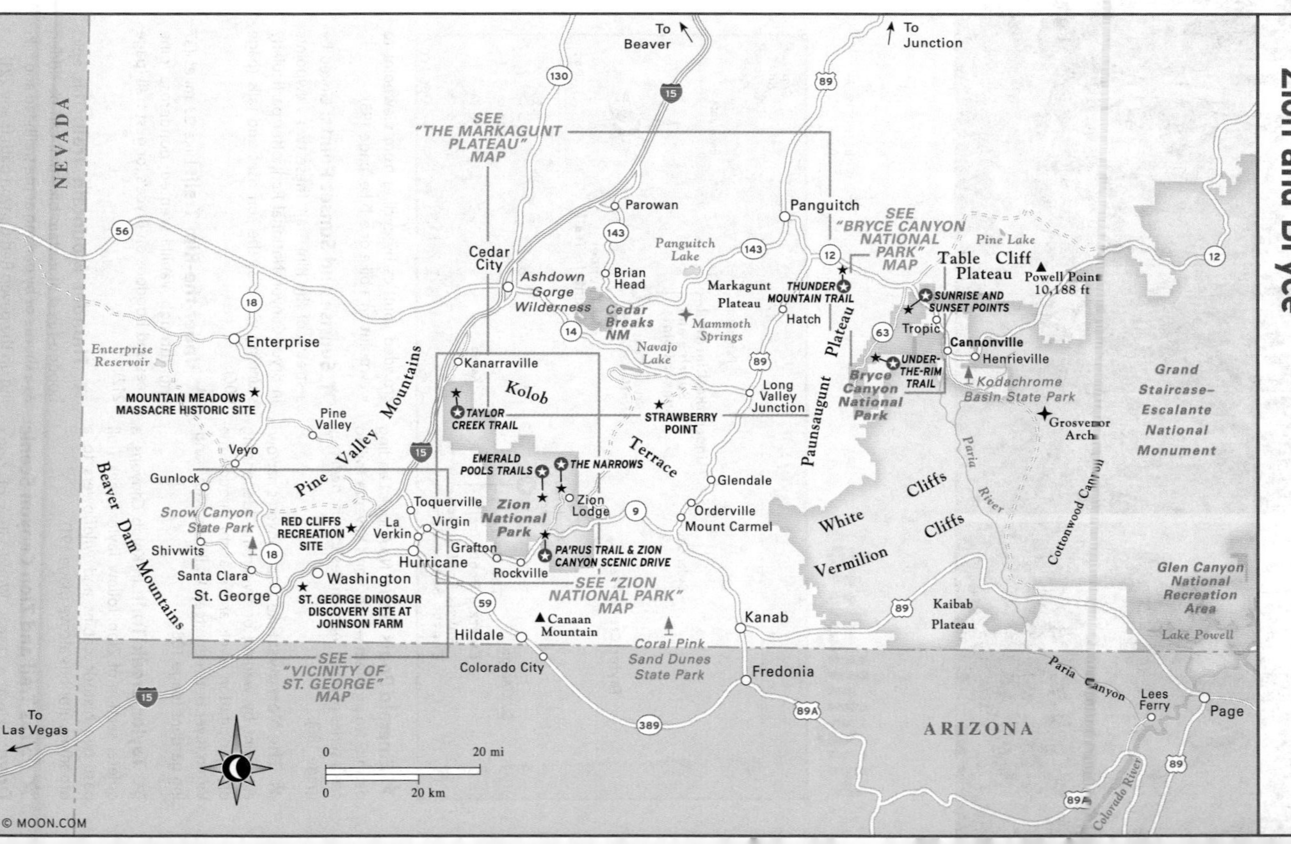

Avoid the Crowds

Many areas outside Zion and Bryce are often less crowded but equally compelling.

- **Cedar Breaks National Monument** (page 250) preserves a hoodoo-filled amphitheater similar to Bryce Canyon, but without the crowds.
- **Red Canyon** (page 219) is immediately west of Bryce and shares its geology, but because it's not a national park, you can mountain bike amid the red-rock formations. Dogs are allowed on trails here, too.
- **Kodachrome Basin State Park** (page 260), between Bryce Canyon and Grand Staircase-Escalante, is ringed by remarkable pink cliffs plus odd rock pillars called sand pipes.
- **Snow Canyon State Park** (page 238) just outside St. George offers great hiking, mountain biking, rock climbing, and camping across a red-rock landscape.

dynamic canyoneering routes for the intrepid. While St. George is the nearest bustling city, the town of Springdale makes the most pleasant base for a Zion trip.

Up in latitude and elevation, Bryce is the land of hoodoos, and there's nowhere like it anywhere in the world. In many ways, it actually makes sense to stick to the tourist circuit and vie with the crowds here in order to see the unequivocal geologic marvels that are so popular for good reason.

Yet for every viewpoint along the scenic drives of Bryce and Zion, there's another destination worth checking out in this stretch of southwestern Utah, from national monuments with sparser crowds to national forest lands filled with trails and views.

PLANNING YOUR TIME

If you have a **week** to enjoy this corner of Utah, spend a couple days exploring Zion and another day or two at Bryce. An ideal week would begin near **St. George,** either camping at Snow Canyon State Park or finding the perfect balance of exertion and relaxation at a local spa resort, then heading to **Zion** for a couple days of hiking. From Zion, head northeast to **Bryce** for two hoodoo-filled days. Don't forget to venture outside Bryce's borders to check out the great scenery and trails at nearby **Kodachrome Basin State Park** and **Red Canyon.** From the Bryce area, head west across the Markagunt Plateau (spend a summer night at Cedar Breaks or a winter day skiing at Brian Head) to **Cedar City,** where the summertime Shakespeare Festival makes a good end to the trip.

Guided bus and van tours of many of southwestern Utah's grandest sights are available from **Southern Utah Scenic Tours** (435/656-1504 or 888/404-8687, www.utahscenictours.com).

Previous: the spectacular hoodoos of Bryce Amphitheater; Lower Emerald Pool; The Narrows.

Zion National Park

TOP EXPERIENCE

Zion National Park (435/772-3256, www.nps.gov/zion, $35 per vehicle, $30 motorcyclists, $20 pedestrians or bicyclists) is a magnificent park with soaring scenery. When you visit Zion, the first thing to catch your attention will be the sheer cliffs and great monoliths of Zion Canyon. Energetic streams and other forces of erosion sculpted this rock. Little trickles of water percolating through massive chunks of sandstone have created both dramatic canyons and markedly undesertlike habitats, enabling an incredible variety of plants to find niches. The large park spreads across 147,000 acres (59,489 ha), eight geologic formations, and four major vegetation zones. Elevations range from 3,666 feet (1,117 m) in lower Coalpits Wash to 8,726 feet (2,660 m) atop Horse Ranch Mountain.

The canyon's name is credited to Isaac Behunin, a Latter-day Saints pioneer who believed this spot to be a refuge from religious persecution. When Brigham Young later visited the canyon, however, he found tobacco and wine in use and declared the place "not Zion," which some dutiful followers then began calling it. An 1872 scientific expedition led by John Wesley Powell helped make the area's wonders known to the outside world. Efforts by the National Park Service's first director and others led to the designation of Mukuntuweap (Straight Canyon) National Monument in 1909, followed by the establishment of Zion National Park in 1919.

Zion's grandeur prevails year-round. Even rainy days—when waterfalls plunge from nearly every crevice in the cliffs—are memorable as long as you heed flash-flood warnings. Summer can be uncomfortably hot, with highs hovering above 100°F (38°C). Though summer may be the most unpleasant time to visit due to the heat, crowds still predictably peak, making it the least optimal season to be in Zion.

In terms of enjoyable temperatures, spring and fall are the best times to visit. These shoulder seasons also offer the best chance of seeing wildlife and wildflowers. Around mid-October-early November, cottonwood trees and other plants blaze with color.

Winter may be the most underrated time to plan a Zion trip. Nighttime temperatures drop to near freezing, and the weather tends to be unpredictable, with bright sunshine one day and freezing rain the next. If you can tolerate the cold, you'll find snow-covered slopes contrasting with colorful rocks. Snow may block some of the high-country trails and the road to Lava Point, but the rest of the park is open and accessible year-round.

EXPLORING THE PARK

Zion National Park has four main sections: **Zion Canyon, East Zion**—a higher-elevation area east of Zion Canyon—the **Kolob Terrace,** and **Kolob Canyons.** The highlight for most visitors is 2,400-foot-deep (732-m) Zion Canyon. **Zion Canyon Scenic Drive** winds through the canyon floor along the North Fork of the Virgin River, past some of the most spectacular scenery in the park. A **shuttle bus** ferries visitors along this route spring-fall, when it's closed to private vehicles. Hiking trails branch off to lofty viewpoints and narrow side canyons. At the end of the drive, water-based adventures await with the canyoneering route through the Virgin River at the **Narrows.**

The spectacular **Zion-Mount Carmel Highway,** with its switchbacks and tunnels, provides access to the canyons and high plateaus east of Zion Canyon. Two other roads enter the rugged Kolob section northwest of Zion Canyon. Kolob is a Latter-day Saints name meaning "the brightest star, next to the seat of God." The Kolob section includes rarely visited wilderness areas. **Kolob Canyons Road,** in the extreme northwestern section of the park, begins just off I-15 exit 40

Zion National Park

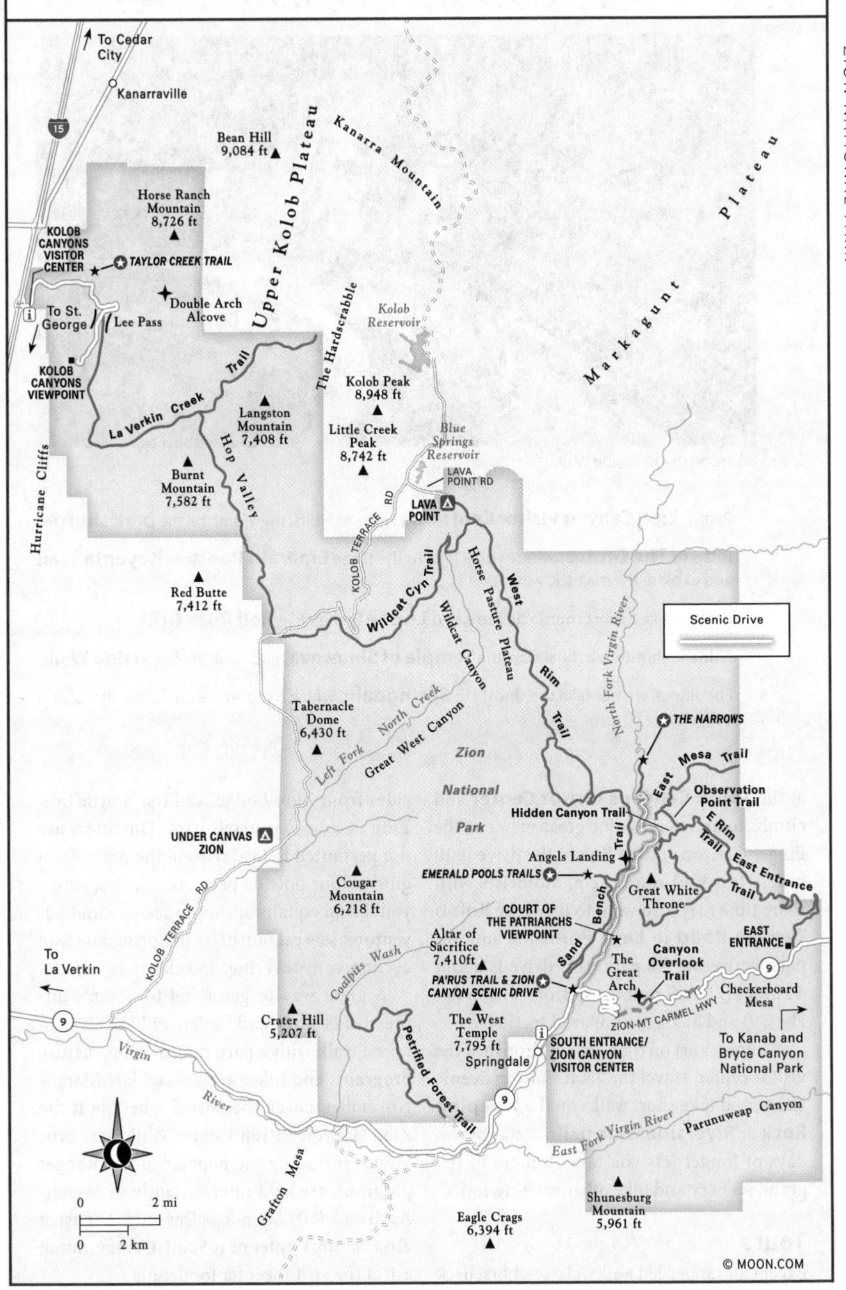

Zion in One Day

hikers on the Riverside Walk

- Park at **Zion Canyon Visitor Center.** Enjoy the exhibits, then jump on the **park shuttle.**
- Head to **The Grotto,** where you'll hike to the three **Emerald Pools** via **Kayenta Trail** and explore the majestic waters.
- Walk or take a short shuttle ride to **Zion Lodge** for lunch at **Red Rock Grill.**
- Ride the shuttle to its final stop, the **Temple of Sinawava,** and stroll the **Riverside Walk.**
- For dinner, walk or take the shuttle to **Springdale,** which has good restaurants, shops, and galleries.

at the **Kolob Canyons Visitor Center** and climbs to an overlook for great views of the Finger Canyons of the Kolob; the drive is 10 miles (16.1 km) round-trip. Motorists with more time may also want to drive the **Kolob Terrace Road** to **Lava Point** for another perspective on the park; this drive is about 44 miles (71 km) round-trip from Virgin (on Hwy. 9) and has some unpaved sections.

Visitors short on time usually drop in at the visitor center, travel the Zion Canyon Scenic Drive, and take short walks on the **Weeping Rock** or **Riverside Walk** trails. A stay of two days or longer lets you take in more of the grand scenery and hike other inviting trails.

Tours

Except for ranger-led walks, classes, horseback rides from Zion Lodge, and the shuttle bus, Zion is a do-it-yourself park. Outfitters are not permitted to lead trips in the park. For a guided tour outside park boundaries, where you'll find equally stunning scenery and adventure, several outfitters in Springdale lead cycling, canyoneering, and climbing trips.

A great way to get a feel for Zion's impressive geology and variety of habitats is to take a walk with a park ranger. Many nature programs and hikes are offered late March-November; check the posted schedule at the Zion Canyon Visitor Center. Children's programs, including the popular Junior Ranger program, are held intermittently in March-April and daily Memorial Day-mid-August at Zion Nature Center near South Campground; ask at the visitor center for details.

The Rocks of Zion

The rock layers at Zion began as sediments of oceans, rivers, lakes, or sand dunes deposited 65-240 million years ago. The soaring Navajo sandstone cliffs that form distinctive features like the Great White Throne and the Three Patriarchs were originally immense sand dunes. Look for the slanting lines in these rock walls, which result from shifting winds as the sand dunes formed. Calcium carbonate in the sand piles acted as a glue to turn the dunes into rock, and it's also responsible for the white color of many of the rocks. The reddish rocks are also Navajo sandstone, but they've been stained by iron oxides—essentially rust.

Kayenta shale is the other main rock you'll see in Zion. The rippled gray rock is Kayenta shale. This shale, which lies beneath Navajo sandstone, is much less permeable than the sandstone. Water can easily trickle through the relatively porous sandstone, but when it hits the impermeable Kayenta shale, it runs along the top surface of the rock and seeps out on the side of the nearest rock face. Weeping Rock, with its lush cliffside springs, is a good place to see the junction between Navajo sandstone and Kayenta shale.

A gradual uplift of the Colorado Plateau, which continues today, has caused the formerly lazy rivers on its surface to pick up speed and knife through the rock layers. You can really appreciate these erosive powers during flash floods, when the North Fork of the Virgin River or other streams roar through their canyons. Erosion of some of the Virgin River's tributaries couldn't keep up with the main channel, and they were left as "hanging valleys" on the canyon walls. A good example is Hidden Canyon, which is reached by trail in Zion Canyon.

Faulting has broken the Colorado Plateau into a series of smaller plateaus. At Zion you are on the Kolob Terrace of the Markagunt Plateau, whose rock layers are younger than those of the Kaibab Plateau at Grand Canyon National Park and older than those exposed on the Paunsaugunt Plateau at Bryce Canyon National Park.

Although some erosive forces, like flash floods, are dramatic, the subtle freezing and thawing of water and the slow action of tree roots are responsible for most of the changes. Water seeps into the Navajo sandstone, accumulating especially in the long vertical cracks in the cliffs. The dramatic temperature changes, especially in the spring and fall, cause regular freezing and thawing, slowly enlarging the cracks and setting the stage for more dramatic rockfall. Erosion and rockfall continue to shape Zion Canyon. In 2019, a huge rockslide crashed down at Weeping Rock, leaving many trails closed awaiting repair. Check the park website or ask at the visitor center about the current status.

The **Zion National Park Forever Project** (435/772-3264, www.zionpark.org) is authorized to run educational programs in the park, which include animal tracking, photography, and archaeology; fees vary.

ZION CANYON

During the busy spring, summer, and fall seasons, you'll be traveling up and down Zion Canyon in a shuttle bus. Most visitors find this to be an easy and enjoyable way to visit the following sites. Buses are scheduled to run every 6-10 minutes.

Zion Canyon Visitor Center

The park's sprawling **Zion Canyon Visitor Center** (435/772-3256, 8am-6pm daily mid-Apr.-late May and Sept.-mid-Oct., 8am-7pm daily late May-Aug., 8am-5pm daily mid-Oct.-mid-Apr., hours vary year to year, see www.nps.gov/zion for up-to-date information), between Watchman and South Campgrounds, is a hub of activity. The plaza outside the building features good interpretive plaques with enough info to get you going on a hike. Inside, a large area is devoted to backcountry information; staff members can answer your questions about various trails, give you updates on the weather, and help you arrange a shuttle to remote trailheads. The wilderness desk (435/772-0170) opens at 7am daily late April-late November, an hour earlier than the rest of the visitor center. A Backcountry Shuttle Board allows hikers to coordinate transportation between trailheads.

The busiest part of the visitor center is the bookstore, stocked with an excellent selection of books covering natural history, human history, and regional travel. Topographic and geologic maps, posters, and postcards are also sold here.

Zion Nature Center

At the northern end of South Campground, the **Zion Nature Center** (2pm-6pm daily Memorial Day-Labor Day) offers programs for kids, including Junior Ranger activities for ages 6-12. Although there's no shuttle stop for the Nature Center, it's an easy walk along the **Pa'rus Trail** from the Zion Canyon Visitor Center. Programs focus on natural history topics like insects and bats. Many Junior Ranger activities can be done on your own—pick up a booklet ($1) at the visitor center bookstore.

Zion Human History Museum

The **Zion Human History Museum** (9am-6pm daily mid-Apr.-late May and early Sept.-early Oct., 9am-7pm daily late May-early Sept., 10am-5pm Sat.-Sun. early Oct.-mid-Apr., entry included in park admission) takes you on a tour through southern Utah's cultural history with a film introducing the park and exhibits about Native American and Latter-day Saints history. It's at the first shuttle stop after the visitor center. This is a good place to stop when you're maxed out on hiking or if the weather forces you inside. The museum's back patio is an ideal place to watch the sun rise over the tall peaks of the West Temple and Altar of Sacrifice, so named because of the red streaks of iron on its face.

Court of the Patriarchs Viewpoint

A very short trail from the shuttle stop leads to the view of the Patriarchs, a trio of peaks named, from left to right, Abraham, Isaac, and Jacob. Mount Moroni, the reddish peak on the far right, partially blocks the view of Jacob. Although the official viewpoint is a fine place to behold these peaks, you'll get an even better view if you cross the road and head about 0.5 mile (0.8 km) up **Sand Bench Trail.**

The Grotto

Positioned right along the riverbank with plenty of shade, **the Grotto** is a popular place for a picnic. From here, the **Grotto Trail** leads back to the lodge; across the road, the **Kayenta Trail** links to the **Upper Emerald Pool Trail** and the **West Rim Trail,** which leads to Angels Landing and, eventually, to the Kolob Terrace section of the park.

Visible from several points along Zion Canyon Drive is the **Great White Throne.** Topping out at 6,744 feet (2,056 m), this bulky chunk of Navajo sandstone has become, along with the Three Patriarchs, emblematic of the park. Ride the shuttle in the evening to watch the rock change color in the light of the setting sun.

Weeping Rock

Several hikes start at Weeping Rock, including **Weeping Rock Trail,** which was closed at the time of writing due to rockfall. The slab of Navajo sandstone that dropped 3,000 feet (914 m) from the side of Cable Mountain injured several visitors (all survived). A Utah Geological Survey report has found the area to be susceptible to large rockfalls, and partial closures persist.

Weeping Rock is home to hanging gardens and many moisture-loving plants, including the striking Zion shooting star, which you can still peer at from behind the closure gate off the road. The rock "weeps" because this is a boundary between porous Navajo sandstone and denser Kayenta shale. Water trickles down through the sandstone, and when it can't penetrate the shale, it moves laterally to the face of the cliff. You can also see cables and rigging used by pioneers at this site in the early 1900s.

Big Bend

Look up: This is where you're likely to see rock

Flora and Fauna of Zion

Many different plant and animal communities live in the rugged terrain of deep canyons and high plateaus. Because the park is near the meeting place of the Colorado Plateau, the Great Basin, and the Mojave Desert, species representative of all three regions can be found here.

Only desert plants can endure the long dry spells and high temperatures found at Zion's lower elevations; these include cacti (prickly pear, cholla, and hedgehog), blackbrush, creosote bush, honey mesquite, and purple sage. Cacti and yuccas are common throughout the park. Pygmy forests of piñon pine, Utah juniper, live oak, mountain mahogany, and cliffrose grow between about 3,900 and 5,600 feet (1,189 and 1,707 m).

prickly pear in Kolob Canyons

Once you get above the canyon floor, trees such as ponderosa pine and Douglas fir can thrive thanks to the moisture they draw from the Navajo sandstone. White firs and aspens are also common on high cool plateaus. Permanent springs and streams support a profusion of greenery such as cottonwoods, box elders, willows, red birches, horsetails, and ferns. Watch out for poison ivy in moist, shady areas.

Colorful wildflowers pop out of the ground—indeed, even out of the rocks—at all elevations from spring through autumn. In early spring, look for the Zion shooting star, a plant in the primrose family found only in Zion. Its nodding pink flowers are easily spotted along the Emerald Pools trails and at Weeping Rock. You're also likely to see desert phlox, a low plant covered with pink flowers, and by mid-May, golden columbine.

Mule deer are common throughout the park. Also common is a type of beaver called a bank beaver, which lives along the banks of the Virgin River rather than in log lodges, which would be too frequently swept away by flash floods. Even though these beavers don't build log lodges, they still gnaw like crazy on trees—look near the base of riverside trees near Zion Lodge for their work. Other wildlife include elk, mountain lions, bobcats, black bears, reintroduced bighorn sheep, coyotes, gray foxes, porcupines, ringtail cats, black-tailed jackrabbits, rock squirrels, cliff chipmunks, beavers, and many species of mice and bats.

Birders have spotted more than 270 species in and near the park, but most common are red-tailed hawks, turkey vultures, quails, mallards, great horned owls, hairy woodpeckers, ravens, scrub jays, black-headed grosbeaks, blue-gray gnatcatchers, canyon wrens, Virginia's warblers, white-throated swifts, and broad-tailed hummingbirds. Zion's high cliffs are good places to look for peregrine falcons; try spotting them from the cliffs at the Angels Landing trail.

Hikers and campers will undoubtedly see northern sagebrush lizards, and hikers need to watch for western rattlesnakes, although these relatively rare reptiles are unlikely to attack unless provoked.

climbers on the towering walls or hikers on Angels Landing.

Temple of Sinawava

The last shuttle stop is at this red-rock amphitheater—named for a Paiute coyote spirit—that precedes the most drastic narrowing of these 2,000-foot (610-m) canyon walls. Riverside Walk (1 mi/1.6 km one-way), a paved wheelchair-accessible path, hugs the eastern side of the Virgin River up the canyon alongside hanging gardens and birds nesting in holes in the cliffs. This path terminates at the Narrows, where you have to wade (and sometimes swim, depending on the water level) the Virgin River to continue. Don't continue without proper footwear and gear.

EAST OF ZION CANYON

The east section of the park is a land of sandstone slickrock, hoodoos, and narrow canyons. You can see much of the dramatic scenery along the Zion-Mount Carmel Highway (Hwy. 9) between the East Entrance Station and Zion Canyon. If you want to pull off the road and explore, try hiking a canyon or heading up a slickrock slope (the pass between Crazy Quilt and Checkerboard Mesa is one possibility).

Highlights on the plateau include views of the White Cliffs and Checkerboard Mesa (both near the East Entrance Station) and a hike on the Canyon Overlook Trail (it begins just east of the long tunnel). Checkerboard Mesa's distinctive pattern is caused by a combination of vertical fractures and horizontal bedding planes, both accentuated by weathering. The highway's spectacular descent into Zion Canyon goes first through a 530-foot (162-m) tunnel, then a 1.1-mile (1.8-km) tunnel, followed by a series of six switchbacks to the canyon floor.

KOLOB TERRACE

The Kolob Terrace section of the park is a high plateau roughly parallel to and west of Zion Canyon. From the town of Virgin (15 mi/24 km west of the South Entrance Station on Hwy. 9), the steep Kolob Terrace Road—paved, though unsuitable for trailers—runs north through ranch land and up a narrow stretch of land with drop-offs on either side before widening onto a high plateau. The Hurricane Cliffs rise from the west, while the back of Zion Canyon's walls lie to the east. The road passes in and out of the park, terminating at Kolob Reservoir, a popular boating and fishing destination outside the park. Snow usually blocks driving through the Kolob Terrace section in winter.

Lava Point

The panorama from **Lava Point** (elev. 7,890 ft/2,405 m) takes in the Cedar Breaks hoodoos to the north, the Pink Cliffs to the northeast, Zion Canyon Narrows to the east, the monoliths of Zion Canyon to the southeast, and Arizona's Mount Trumbull to the south. Sitting atop a lava flow, Lava Point is a good place to cool off—temperatures are about 20 degrees Fahrenheit (11 degrees C) cooler than in Zion Canyon—and is filled with aspens, ponderosa pines, Gambel oaks, and white firs. A small primitive campground near the point offers free sites during the warmer months. From Virgin, take Kolob Terrace Road about 21 miles (34 km) north to the Lava Point turnoff; the viewpoint is 1.8 miles (2.9 km) farther on a well-marked, unpaved spur road. Vehicles longer than 19 feet (5.8 m) are prohibited on the Lava Point road. The trip from Virgin to Lava Point takes about an hour.

Kolob Reservoir

This high-country lake north of Lava Point has good fishing for rainbow trout. An unpaved boat ramp is at the south end near the dam. You can camp along the shore, although there are no facilities. To reach the reservoir, continue north 3.5 miles (5.6 km) on Kolob Terrace Road from Lava Point turnoff. The fair-weather road can be followed past the reservoir to Cedar City. Blue Springs Reservoir, near the Lava Point turnoff, is closed to the public.

KOLOB CANYONS

Northwest of Zion Canyon is the Kolob Canyons area, originally a national monument that was added to the park in 1956 and includes remote backcountry.

Kolob Canyons Visitor Center

Although it's small and has just a handful of

1: A lizard bathes in the desert sun in Kolob Canyons. **2:** penstemon in Kolob Canyons **3:** Kolob Canyons

exhibits, the **Kolob Canyons Visitor Center** (435/772-3256, 8am-5pm daily mid-Mar.-mid-Oct., 8am-4:30pm daily mid-Oct.-mid-Mar.) is a good place to stop for information on exploring the Kolob region. Hikers can learn about current trail conditions and obtain the permits required for overnight trips and Zion Narrows day trips. The visitor center and the start of Kolob Canyons Road are just off I-15 exit 40.

Kolob Canyons Road

This paved 5-mile (8-km) scenic drive begins at the **Kolob Canyons Visitor Center** (3752 E. Kolob Canyons Rd., New Harmony, 435/772-3256, 8am-5pm daily mid-Mar.-mid-Oct., 8am-4:30pm daily mid-Oct.-mid-Mar.) just off I-15. It winds past the Kolob's dramatic Finger Canyons to the Timber Creek Overlook Trail. The first part of the drive follows the 200-mile-long (320-km) Hurricane Fault, which forms the west edge of the Markagunt Plateau. Look for the tilted rock layers deformed by friction as the plateau rose nearly 1 mile (1.6 km). The **Taylor Creek Trail,** which begins 2 miles (3.2 km) past the visitor center, provides a close look at the canyons. At the Lee Pass trailhead, 4 miles (6.4 km) beyond the visitor center, **La Verkin Creek Trail** takes you to Kolob Arch and beyond. Signs at the end of the road identify the buttes, mesas, and mountains.

Lee Pass is named for John D. Lee, who was the only person ever convicted in the Mountain Meadows Massacre; he's believed to have lived nearby for a spell after the 1857 incident, in which an alliance of Latter-day Saints and Native Americans attacked a California-bound wagon train, killing about 120 people. Only children too young to tell the story were spared. The Latter-day Saints community tried to cover up the incident and hindered federal attempts to apprehend the killers. Only Lee, who oversaw Native American affairs in southern Utah at the time, was ever brought to justice; he was later executed.

HIKING

Zion Canyon

The trails in Zion Canyon provide perspectives of the park not available from the road. Many trails require long ascents but aren't too difficult if taken at a leisurely pace. Carry water on all hikes, even the shortest walks. **Trails are sometimes closed due to rockfall;** always check the park website (www.nps.gov/zion) or the visitor center for the latest trail conditions. Descriptions of the following trails are given in order from the mouth of Zion Canyon to the Virgin River Narrows.

Experienced hikers can do countless off-trail routes in the canyons and plateaus surrounding Zion Canyon. Rangers can suggest the best areas for this. Rappelling and other climbing skills may be needed to negotiate drops in more remote canyons. Groups cannot exceed 12 hikers per trail or drainage. Overnight hikers must obtain **backcountry permits** from the Zion Canyon or Kolob Canyons Visitor Centers or from https://zionpermits.nps.gov (online reservations $5, nonrefundable). Permit fees are based on group size: $15 for 1-2 people, $20 for 3-7, and $25 for 8-12. Some areas of the park—mainly near roads and major trails—are closed to overnight use. Ask about shuttles to and from backcountry trailheads outside Zion Canyon at the visitor center's Wilderness Desk (435/772-0170). Shuttles are also available from **Zion Rock and Mountain Guides** (1458 Zion Park Blvd., Springdale, 435/772-3303, www.zionrockguides.com) and **Zion Guru** (792 Zion Park Blvd., Springdale, 435/632-0432, www.zionguru.com).

Archeology Trail

Distance: *0.8 mile (1.3 km) round-trip*
Duration: *30 minutes*
Elevation gain: *80 feet (24 m)*
Effort: *easy-moderate*
Trailhead: *just north of Watchman Campground*
Shuttle stop: *Zion Canyon Visitor Center*

This short uphill walk with interpretive signage leads to an Ancestral Puebloan food

Navajo Sandstone

Take a look anywhere along **Zion Canyon** and you'll see 1,600- to 2,200-foot (488- to 671-m) cliffs of Navajo sandstone. According to researchers at the University of Nebraska-Lincoln, these big walls were formed from immense sand dunes deposited during a hot dry period about 200 million years ago, when the landmass on which they sit was located about 15 degrees north of the equator (about the same location as Honduras is today). Shifting winds blew the sand in one direction, then another—a careful inspection of the sandstone layer reveals the diagonal lines resulting from this "cross-bedding." The shift patterns in the sandstone—the slanting striations easily seen in the cliff faces—were caused in part by intense monsoon rains, which compacted and moved the dunes.

striations of rock east of Zion Canyon

Eventually, a shallow sea washed over the dunes, leaving shells behind. As the shells dissolved, their lime seeped down into the sand, cementing it into sandstone. After the Colorado Plateau formed, rivers cut deeply through the sandstone layer. As a result, the cliff's lower layers are stained red from iron oxides.

The east side of Zion is a particularly good place to view the warps and striations in the sandstone. Get up close and personal with **Checkerboard Mesa** to see the intricate patterns, or check out the **Great White Throne,** which is largely white Navajo sandstone. But really, with the right light and a pair of binoculars, examination along any part of Zion Canyon's big walls will reveal the cross-bedding.

storage site. The trail starts across the road from the visitor center parking lot, at the entrance to Watchman Campground; look for the colorful sign and follow the trail. From the top of the hill, take in views of the lower canyon. Although it's not the park's most spectacular hike, it's worth exploring to get an idea of Ancestral Puebloan life. Artifacts from the site are exhibited at the Zion Human History Museum.

Watchman Trail

Distance: *3.3 miles (5.3 km) round-trip*
Duration: *2 hours*
Elevation gain: *370 feet (113 m)*
Effort: *easy-moderate*
Trailhead: *just north of Watchman Campground*
Shuttle stop: *Zion Canyon Visitor Center*

This hike doesn't summit 6,555-foot (1,998-m) Watchman Peak, but it does lead to a mesa with a good view of this prominent mountain. The hike starts off unspectacularly, but gets more interesting as it gains elevation. At the top of the mesa, the Watchman pops into view. The short mesa-top loop trail is worth taking for views of Springdale and wildflowers, including those of barrel cacti.

During the middle of the day, this trail can bake in the sun. Try to hike it on a cool day or at dawn or dusk. It's a good shakedown hike to do on the evening you arrive at Zion. As soon as the sun drops behind the canyon walls, set out—on long summer evenings, you'll have plenty of time to complete it before dark.

Sand Bench Trail

Distance: *4.5 miles (7.2 km) round-trip*
Duration: *3 hours*
Elevation gain: *500 feet (152 m)*
Effort: *easy*

Trailhead: *Zion Lodge*
Shuttle stops: *Court of the Patriarchs or Zion Lodge*

This loop trail has good views of the Three Patriarchs, the Streaked Wall, and other monuments of lower Zion Canyon. March-October, outfitters across the road from Zion Lodge offer horseback rides here, which churn up dust and leave an uneven surface (among other things), so hikers usually prefer to go elsewhere during those months. From the riparian forest along Birch Creek, the trail climbs onto dry benchland. Piñon pines, junipers, sand sage, yuccas, prickly pear cacti, and other high desert plants live here. From the Court of the Patriarchs Viewpoint, walk across the scenic drive, then follow a service road to the trailhead. A 1.2-mile (1.9-km) trail extension runs north along the river, connecting the trailhead with Zion Lodge.

★ Emerald Pools via Kayenta Trail

Distance: *4 miles (6.4 km) round-trip*
Duration: *2 hours*
Elevation gain: *350 feet (107 m)*
Effort: *moderate*
Trailhead: *across the footbridge from the Grotto*
Shuttle stop: *The Grotto*

Pools, small waterfalls, and views of Zion Canyon make this hike a favorite. The trail begins at the Grotto, crosses a footbridge, and turns left onto Kayenta Trail, which you'll climb for 1 mile (1.6 km), gaining views of Zion Canyon below. At the end of Kayenta Trail is the Middle Emerald Pool, where you can access well-marked short trails to the Upper Pool (0.5 mi/0.8 km) and the Lower Pool (0.6 mi/1 km). Visit them in any order. The 4-mile (6.4-km) round-trip distance for this hike includes hiking to all three pools via Kayenta Trail.

Upper Emerald Pool resembles a mini beach scene, with folks wading in the shallow water and picnicking in the sand. Lower Emerald Pool offers the most visually unique experience—a trail passes under an overhanging rock with water dripping or spraying down it, depending on how wet the year has been. Below, you'll be able to spot the pool. True to their name, all three pools have a greenish tint, some more than others, thanks to the algae inhabiting them.

Although the Emerald Pools trails are relatively easy, there are steep rocky steps, and parts of the trail can get icy and slippery any time of year. Several people have died in falls on the Emerald Pools trails, so hike with caution.

West Rim Trail to Angels Landing

Distance: *5.4 miles (8.7 km) round-trip*
Duration: *4 hours*
Elevation gain: *1,488 feet (454 m)*
Effort: *strenuous*
Trailhead: *across the road from the Grotto picnic area*
Shuttle stop: *The Grotto*
Permit required

This strenuous trail leads to some of the best views of Zion Canyon. From the Grotto (elev. 4,300 ft/1,311 m), cross the footbridge, then turn right along the river. The trail, which was blasted out of the cliff side by the Civilian Conservation Corps in the 1930s, climbs up into the shady depths of the aptly named Refrigerator Canyon. Walter's Wiggles, 21 closely spaced switchbacks, wind up to a trail junction and Scout Lookout, with excellent canyon views. If you turn around here, your hike will be 4 miles (6.4 km) round-trip and gain 1,050 feet (320 m) in elevation. If you continue, it's a daunting 0.5 mile (0.8 km) to the summit of Angels Landing.

Angels Landing itself is a sheer-walled monolith 1,500 feet (457 m) above the North Fork of the Virgin River. Although the trail to the summit is rough and very narrow, chains provide security on the sections with high exposure. Hike this final approach to Angels Landing carefully and only in good weather; don't go if the trail is covered with snow or ice or if thunderstorms threaten.

1: Kayenta Trail **2:** en route to Angels Landing **3:** lush scenery along the Riverside Trail **4:** hikers wading in The Narrows

1
2
3
4

Children must be closely supervised, and anyone afraid of heights should skip this trail. Once on top, the panorama makes the effort worthwhile. Not surprisingly, it's best to do this steep hike during the cooler morning hours. Start extra-early to avoid the crowds, which can make the final stretch all the more frightening.

Energetic hikers can continue 4.8 miles (7.7 km) on the main trail from Scout Lookout to **West Rim Viewpoint,** which overlooks the Right Fork of North Creek. This strenuous 12.8-mile (20.6-km) round-trip hike includes 3,070 feet (936 m) of elevation gain. West Rim Trail continues through Zion's backcountry to Lava Point (elev. 7,890 ft/2,405 m), where there's a primitive campground. Unless you plan to backpack in and return the way you came the next day, a car shuttle is needed to hike the 13.3 miles (21.4 km) one-way from the Grotto to Lava Point. Make the hike easier by starting at Lava Point and hiking down to the picnic area—although this still constitutes a long day hike with little or no water available most of the year.

Note that the park is piloting a **permit** program (my best guess is that this will become permanent), so anyone who wishes to reach Angels Landing must obtain a permit. There's a seasonal lottery system ($3 pp, apply 1-3 months in advance, specific seasonal lottery windows listed at www.nps.gov/zion). You can also try your luck at getting a next-day permit ($6 pp); apply by 3pm the day before you want the permit. Both permit types are available at www.recreation.gov.

Weeping Rock Trail

Distance: *0.5 mile (0.8 km) round-trip*
Duration: *30 minutes*
Elevation gain: *100 feet (30 m)*
Effort: *easy*
Trailhead: *Weeping Rock parking area*
Shuttle stop: *Weeping Rock*

This easy trail winds past lush vegetation and wildflowers to a series of cliff-side springs above an overhang. The springs emerge where water seeping through more than 2,000 feet (610 m) of Navajo sandstone meets a layer of impervious shale. Note: At the time of writing, the Weeping Rock Trail was closed due to rockfall; check www.nps.gov/zion for current information.

Riverside Walk

Distance: *2.2 miles (3.5 km) round-trip*
Duration: *1-2 hours*
Elevation gain: *57 feet (17 m)*
Effort: *easy*
Trailhead: *Temple of Sinawava parking area*
Shuttle stop: *Temple of Sinawava*

One of the most popular and easiest hikes in the park, this nearly level paved trail begins at the end of Zion Canyon Scenic Drive and heads upstream along the Virgin River to the Narrows. While you can complete the walk quickly, allow a little more time to take in the hanging gardens, explore the riverbank in accessible spots, and cool off in the shallow water. Countless springs and seeps on the canyon walls support plants and swamps, attracting wildlife like squirrels and deer. Most springs occur at the boundary between the porous Navajo sandstone and the less permeable Kayenta Formation below. At trail's end, the canyon is wide enough only for the river. To continue, you must wade with waterproof, high-traction footwear—and sometimes even swim. Riverside Walk is wheelchair accessible, though there can be a few spots with slick, uneven terrain.

TOP EXPERIENCE

★ The Narrows (Bottom Up)

Distance: *9.4 miles (15.1 km) round-trip*
Duration: *8 hours*
Elevation gain: *200 feet (61 m)*
Effort: *strenuous*
Trailheads: *end of Riverside Walk*
Shuttle stop: *Temple of Sinawava*

Upper Zion Canyon is the most famous backcountry area in the park, and among the most strenuous. There's no trail, and significant wading or swimming is required, sometimes knee- to chest-deep. At the canyon's narrowest, the high fluted walls are only 20 feet (6 m) apart, and little sunlight penetrates the depths. Mysterious side canyons beckon. The haunting lighting, the sense of adventure required to navigate the canyon, and otherworldly hanging gardens make this hike worth the hype.

To hike the Narrows bottom up, hikers should be well outfitted and in good shape—river hiking is more tiring than land hiking. Hazards include flash floods and hypothermia; even in summer, expect water temperatures of about 68°F (20°C) and around 38°F (3°C) in winter. Finding the best time to go can be tricky. In spring, runoff is usually too high. Summer thunderstorms bring toxic cyanobacteria blooms (which means keeping water away from your face, or avoiding contact altogether if toxicity is too high) and flash-flood risks that can temporarily close the hike altogether. In winter, the water is too cold, unless you're in a dry suit. Early summer (mid-June-mid-July) and early autumn (mid-Sept.-mid-Oct.) are the best windows.

What exactly does "bottom up" mean? Hiking the Narrows this way means navigating it south to north, starting from the main Zion Canyon. The benefits of doing so are easy access, no permit required, few technical challenges, and a length that can be knocked out in a day. The downside is that most people hike the Narrows this way, so you'll deal with more crowds, especially toward the beginning. Hiking the Narrows from the top down is a 2-day adventure requiring an overnight permit. Top-down access is via a remote road, and you may need to book a guide if you lack the navigation skills to confidently execute this adventure independently.

Don't be tempted to wear river sandals or sneakers up the Narrows; it's easy to twist an ankle on the slippery rocks. You can use hiking boots you don't mind drenching, but the ideal solution is available from **Zion Adventures** (36 Lion Blvd., Springdale, 435/772-1001, www.zionadventures.com) and other Springdale outfitters. They rent specialized river-hiking boots, along with neoprene socks, hiking poles, and, in cool weather, dry pants and dry suits. Boots, socks, and sticks rent for $29; with a dry suit, the package costs $59. They also offer guidance on hiking the Narrows and lead tours of the section below Orderville Canyon ($279-309 pp, varies by season). **Zion Outfitter** (7 Zion Park Blvd., Springdale, 435/772-5090, https://zionoutfitter.com), located just outside the park entrance, and **Zion Guru** (795 Zion Park Blvd., Springdale, 435/632-0432, www.zionguru.com) provide similar services at comparable prices.

Before your hike, check conditions and the forecast with rangers at the Zion Canyon Visitor Center—they can also provide pointers and a handout with useful information. No permit is needed if you're not going farther than Big Springs.

For a half-day trip, follow the Narrows 1.5 miles (2.4 km, about 2 hours) upstream from the end of the Riverside Walk to Orderville Canyon, then back the same way. Orderville Canyon makes a good destination itself since it attracts less hoopla than Zion Canyon, isn't very difficult to canyoneer, and is arguably just as beautiful. This canyon can be accessed via a side road off Kolob Terrace Road. A permit is required to explore this area beyond the first 0.25 mile (0.4 km). In the main canyon of the Narrows, day hikers without permits must turn around at Big Springs, about 2.5 miles (4 km) past Orderville.

The Narrows (Top Down)

Distance: *32 miles (52 km) round-trip*
Duration: *36-48 hours (overnight backpacking permit required)*
Elevation gain: *668 feet (204 m)*
Effort: *strenuous*
Trailheads: *Chamberlain's Ranch*
Camping: *Designated campsites included in permit*
Water sources: *Big Springs*

Given its length, this trek must be done as an overnight backpacking trip. While this journey takes you into Zion Canyon and back, it actually begins a 1.5-hour drive away on Bureau of Land Management (BLM) land, taking you through wilderness and eventually into the national park via the canyon. To reach the trailhead, take Highway 9 east from the park, and head north for 18 miles (29 km) on a dirt road.

Hiking the Narrows top down involves starting at Chamberlain's Ranch in the Big Springs area and hiking the Virgin River downstream. While much more difficult to access and navigate, the top-down Narrows route offers a more adventurous, less crowded experience than the more popular bottom-up hike. There's something about starting in the backcountry and spending a night in a canyon that feels more magical than beginning amid crowds at the end of Zion's Scenic Drive—although this immersive experience isn't for everyone.

A **wilderness permit** (https://zionpermits.nps.gov) obtained a month in advance is required for overnight hikes starting at Chamberlain's Ranch. This permit will give you access to the 2-day hike as well as to a one-night stay at a designated campsite. You will also be issued a plastic bag designed to collect human waste. No camping is permitted below Big Springs. Group size for hiking and camping is limited to 12 people along the entire route.

You can also hike the Narrows from Chamberlain's Ranch as a 1-day trip, either by arranging for a shuttle at either end of the hike, or by hiking only partway up the canyon, then turning around. During the summer, **Zion Adventures** (36 Lion Blvd., Springdale, 435/772-1001, www.zionadventures.com, 6:15am and 9:45am daily, reservations required, $55 pp) offers a shuttle to Chamberlain's Ranch. There is a small discount if you also rent gear from them. **Zion Rock & Mountain Guides** (1458 Zion Park Blvd., Springdale, 435/772-3303, www.zionrockguides.com) has a similar service.

East of Zion Canyon

The shuttle bus doesn't access the trailheads east of Zion Canyon, but there are numerous pullouts and small parking lots along this stretch of Highway 9. While formal trails are limited here, you can pull over and scramble around the enticing slickrock features, like Checkerboard Mesa, near the road. Longer excursions should only be taken with a map and navigation skills.

The fun **Canyon Overlook Trail** starts on the road east of Zion Canyon and features great views without the stiff climbs found on many Zion trails. The trail winds along the ledges of Pine Creek Canyon, which opens into a valley. Panoramas at trail's end take in lower Zion Canyon in the distance, including the 580-foot-high (177-m) Great Arch of Zion—termed a "blind arch" because it's open only on one side. On a busy day, finding parking in the lot can be more challenging than the hike itself.

Highway 9

Trails in this area head north from Highway 9 west of the town of Springdale and are accessible without paying the park entrance fee.

From the parking area on Highway 9 just west of Rockville, a trail heads 2.5 miles (4 km) up **Huber Wash,** through painted desert and canyons. One of the highlights of this hike is all the petrified wood you'll encounter. Where the trail ends in a box canyon decked with a hanging garden—at the 2.5-mile (4-km) mark—there's even a petrified-wood logjam. You can try to clamber up it and catch the Chinle Trail (5 mi/8.1 km); take it back to Highway 9, where you'll exit about 2.5 miles (4 km) east of the Huber Wash trailhead. This trail is too hot to hike in summer, but it's a good cool-weather destination. Even then, bring plenty of water.

The Huber Wash trailhead is about 6 miles (9.7 km) west of the park entrance on Highway 9, near a power substation.

Kolob Terrace

Two trails—West Rim and Wildcat Canyon—begin from Lava Point trailhead in the remote West Rim area of the park. You can reach the trailhead via the Kolob Terrace Road or by hiking the 1-mile (1.6-km) **Barney's Trail** from site 2 in the Lava Point Campground.

The **West Rim Trail** drops 3,600 feet (1,097

m) southeast into Zion Canyon; the majority of that descent occurs in the last 6 mi (9.7 km). This is the western end of the same trail that takes hikers from Zion Canyon to Angels Landing.

From its start on the edge of the Kolob Plateau to its end in Zion Canyon, the West Rim Trail passes through a wide range of ecosystems, including sandstone domes and an unexpected pond at Potato Hollow (water can also be found at Sawmill and Cabin Springs). The trail is most often done as a 2-day backpacking trip; there are several campsites available along the trail with access to water.

Wildcat Canyon Trail heads southwest from Lava Point to a trailhead on **Kolob Terrace Road** (16 mi/26 km north of Virgin), so if it's possible to arrange a shuttle, you can do this as a one-way hike in about three hours. The trail, which runs over slickrock, through forest, and past cliffs, includes views of the Virgin River's Left Fork drainage, but it lacks a reliable water source. You can continue north and west toward Kolob Arch by taking the 4-mile (6.4-km) **Connector Trail** to the **Hop Valley Trail.**

Snow blocks the road to Lava Point for much of the year; the usual season is May or June until early November. Check road conditions with the Zion Canyon or Kolob Canyons Visitor Centers. From the South Entrance Station in Zion Canyon, drive west 15 miles (24 km) on Highway 9 to Virgin, turn north and go 21 miles (34 km) on Kolob Terrace Road (signed Kolob Reservoir), then turn right and go 1.8 miles (2.9 km) to Lava Point.

A special hike for strong swimmers is the **Left Fork of North Creek,** aka the Subway. This challenging 9-mile (14.5-km) day hike involves, at the very least, lots of route-finding and many stream crossings.

Like the Narrows, the Left Fork can be hiked either partway up, then back down (starting and ending at the Left Fork trailhead), or with a shuttle, from an upper trailhead at the Wildcat Canyon trailhead downstream to the Left Fork trailhead. The top-to-bottom route requires rappelling skills and at least 60 feet (18 m) of climbing rope or webbing. It also involves swimming through several deep sections of very cold water.

Even though the hike is in a day-use-only zone, the National Park Service requires a special permit, which, unlike other Zion backcountry permits, is available ahead of time through a somewhat convoluted lottery process. Prospective hikers should visit the park's permitting website (https://zionpermits.nps.gov) to be introduced to the complicated lottery system of applying for a permit to hike the Subway. Lotteries are run monthly for hiking dates 3 months in the future. Each lottery entry costs $5, and each individual hiker can apply only once per month. There's also a last-minute lottery, held two days in advance of the hike. Finally, if there are any remaining permits available, they are dispensed the day before the hike at the visitor center.

The Left Fork trailhead is on Kolob Terrace Road, 8.1 miles (13 km) north of Virgin.

Kolob Canyons

You're more likely to have the trails to yourself in this section of the park.

★ Taylor Creek Trail

Distance: *5 miles (8 km) round-trip*
Duration: *4 hours*
Elevation gain: *450 feet (137 m)*
Effort: *easy-moderate*
Trailhead: *2 miles (3.2 km) east of Kolob Canyons Visitor Center, left side of the road*

This excellent day hike from Kolob Canyons Road heads upstream along the Middle Fork of Taylor Creek. Double Arch Alcove is 2.7 miles (4.3 km) from the trailhead; you could continue on, but 350 yards (320 m) past the arch, a giant rockfall that occurred in 1990 blocks the route. Along the way, you'll enjoy easy creek crossings, decent shade, smatterings of wildflowers, and two historic cabins. From this trail, you can also explore the North Fork of Taylor Creek.

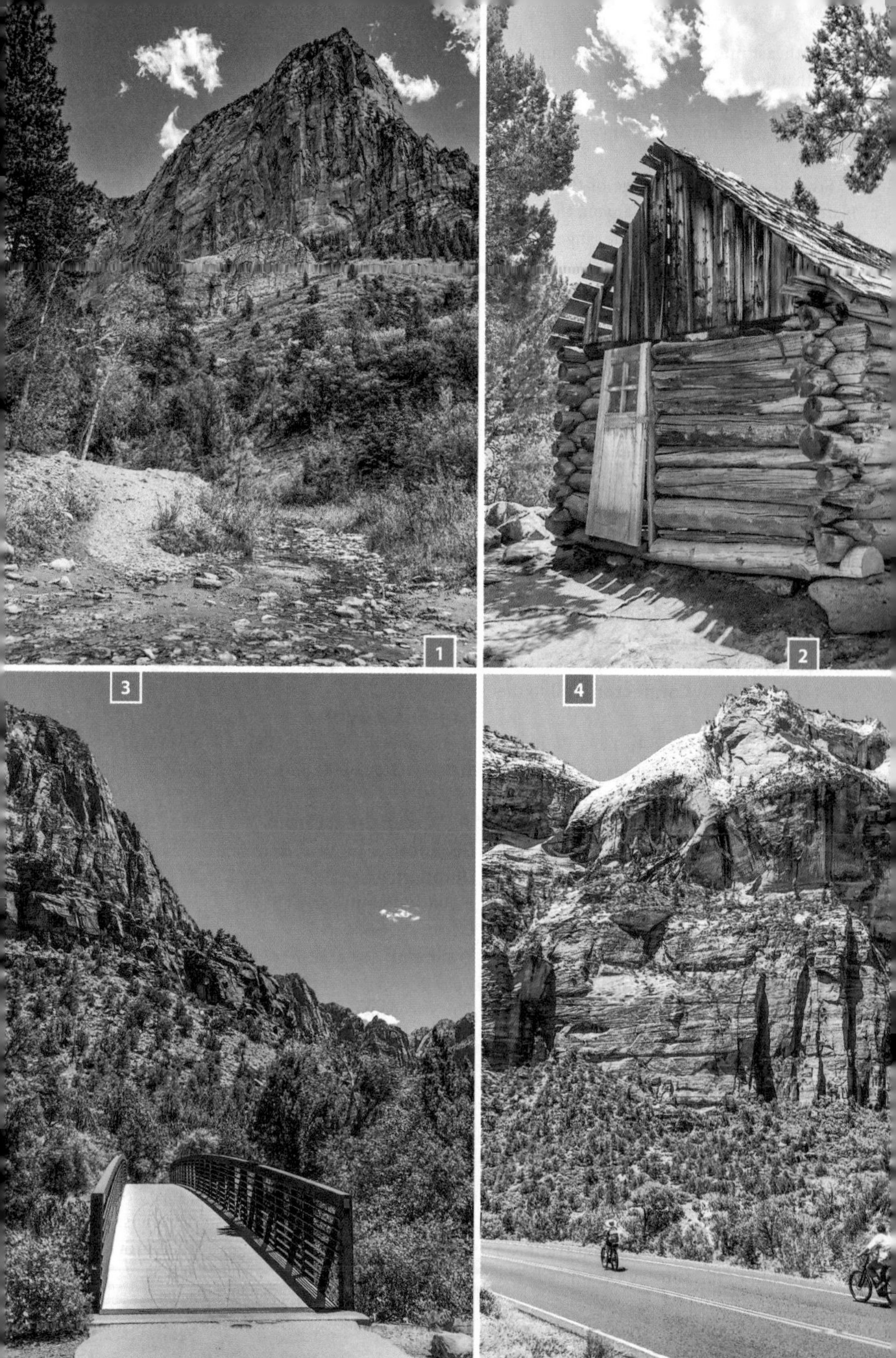
1
2
3
4

BIKING

One of the fringe benefits of the Zion Canyon Shuttle is the great biking resulting from the lack of car traffic. It used to be too scary to pedal along narrow, traffic-choked Zion Canyon Scenic Drive, but now it's a joy. When the shuttle buses get crowded (and they do), biking is a great way to get to the sights up the canyon.

If you decide you've had enough cycling, every shuttle bus has a rack that can hold two bicycles. Bike parking is plentiful at the visitor center and every shuttle stop.

Outside the Zion Canyon area, **Kolob Terrace Road** is a good place to stretch your legs on a ride; it's 22 miles (35 km) to Kolob Reservoir.

★ Pa'rus Trail and Zion Canyon Scenic Drive

Quiet stretches of pedaling with Zion Canyon momentarily all to yourself. The freedom to hop on or off easily to check out sights or trails. No car traffic to vie with. There are many reasons to explore bustling Zion Canyon by bike. To ride from the visitor center to the road's end at the Temple of Sinawava and back, this easy ride is just under 16 miles (26 km) with less than 500 feet (152 m) of elevation gain.

Begin your Zion Canyon bike journey on the 2-mile (3.2-km) paved and relatively flat Pa'rus Trail, which is open to cyclists, pets, and pedestrians alike. When this trail ends, join **Zion Canyon Scenic Drive** and pedal along the shoulder. Shuttle buses won't pass you until you pull over to the side of the road, so let the bus pass as soon as you safely can. Bring a lock to secure your bike at shuttle stops if you plan to do any hiking or sightseeing, and be sure to carry extra water (a hydration pack is a good idea). More and more people are doing this ride by e-bike to enjoy the perks of biking, without the effort—or to tow along young kids.

Bicycle Rentals

While there are no bike rentals available within the park, plenty of rentals can be found in nearby Springdale. Three-speed cruiser bikes are available at **Zion Outfitter** (7 Zion Park Blvd., Springdale, 435/772-5090, https://zionoutfitter.com, 7am-9pm daily). **Zion Adventures** (36 Lion Blvd., Springdale, 435/772-1001, www.zionadventures.com, 8am-7pm daily Mar.-Oct., 8am-7pm daily Nov., 9am-7pm daily Dec.-Feb.) rents road bikes ($49 per day) and e-bikes ($95 per day), both of which are good for park roads. **Zion Cycles** (868 Zion Park Blvd., Springdale, 435/772-0400, www.zioncycles.com, 9am-5pm daily), tucked behind Zion Pizza Noodle, has similar rentals.

ROCK CLIMBING

In early spring and fall (summer is too hot), climbers come to ascend the nearly 400 routes found across Zion's Navajo sandstone walls and navigate the dozens of routes through the park's canyons. As far as big-wall climbing areas go, Zion's sandstone is far more fragile than Yosemite's granite. It crumbles and flakes, especially when wet. To protect the rock and yourself, stay off sandstone during and following rain (if the ground is wet, the rock may be too).

The majority of the climbing in Zion is trad (using traditional gear protection) and multi-pitch. Note that if you're attempting a long multi-pitch route that involves sleeping in a portaledge along the wall, you need to obtain a permit (https://zionpermits.nps.gov, 1-2 people $15 plus $5 reservation fee). Kolob Canyons also has 50-some routes and more sport climbing than you'll find up Zion Canyon. Many of the climbs are multi-pitch, from 2 pitches to 10 or more. A few of the classics of the area include Moonlight Buttress (5.8 C1, trad/aid, 10 pitches), Led by Sheep (5.6, trad, 4 pitches), and The Headache (5.10, trad, 4 pitches).

1: Taylor Creek Trail **2:** historic cabin along Taylor Creek Trail **3:** Pa'rus Trail **4:** cyclists riding along Zion Canyon Scenic Drive

For route descriptions, visit www.mountainproject.com or pick up a copy of *Desert Rock* by Eric Bjørnstad or *Rock Climbing Utah* by Stewart M. Green. Both books are sold at the Zion Canyon Visitor Center. The backcountry desk in the visitor center also has a notebook full of route descriptions from past climbers. Check here to make sure your climbing area is open—some close to protect nesting peregrine falcons—and bring binoculars to scout routes from the canyon floor.

If you aren't prepared to tackle the 2,000-foot-high (610-m) canyon walls, you can check out a growing number of bouldering areas, some close to the park's south entrance. One huge boulder lies 40 yards (37 m) west of the park entrance; the other is a large slab with a crack, located 0.5 mile (0.8 km) north of the entrance.

If watching Zion's climbers inspires you to rope up, **Zion Adventures** (36 Lion Blvd., Springdale, 435/772-1001, www.zionadventures.com) runs half-day and daylong climbing clinics for beginner and experienced climbers. Similar offerings are provided by **Zion Rock and Mountain Guides** (1458 Zion Park Blvd., Springdale, 435/772-3303, www.zionrockguides.com), **Red Desert Adventure** (435/668-2888, www.reddesertadventure.com), and **Zion Mountaineering School** (1458 Zion Park Blvd., Springdale, 435/772-3303, www.guidesinzion.com). Outfitters are not permitted to lead climbs inside the park, so these activities are held outside park boundaries.

HORSEBACK RIDING

Trail rides on horses and mules leave from the **corral near Zion Lodge** (435/679-8665, www.canyonrides.com, Mar.-Oct.) and head down the Virgin River. A 1-hour trip ($50) goes to the Court of the Patriarchs, and a half-day ride ($100) follows the Sand Bench Trail. Riders must be at least age 7 for the short ride and age 10 for the half-day ride, and riders can weigh no more than 220 pounds.

FOOD AND ACCOMMODATIONS

Within the park, lodging is limited to Zion Lodge and three campgrounds. Look to Springdale or the east entrance of the park for more options.

Zion Lodge

The rustic **Zion Lodge** (435/772-7700 or 888/297-2757, www.zionlodge.com, $189-284)

Zion Lodge

is in the heart of Zion Canyon, 3 miles (4.8 km) up Zion Canyon Scenic Drive. Zion Lodge provides the only accommodations and food options within the park. It's open year-round; reservations can be made up to 13 months in advance, and for spring through fall stays, it's typically booked out many months in advance. There are four accessible hotel rooms (two with grab bars, two with roll-in showers), and a wheelchair is available for loan. Motel rooms and cabins (gas fireplaces, no TVs) near the main lodge are a little less expensive.

Dine inside the lodge at the **Red Rock Grill** (435/772-7760, 6:30am-9pm daily, dinner entrées $16-30, dinner reservations required), featuring a Southwestern and Mexican-influenced menu for breakfast (6:30am-11:30am), lunch (11:30am-5pm), and dinner (5pm-9pm) daily. There's also snack bar called the **Castle Dome Café** (breakfast, lunch, and dinner daily spring-fall) with fast food and a patio beer garden cart.

The lodge also has evening programs, a gift shop, Wi-Fi in the lobby (not high-speed), and accessible public restrooms.

Campgrounds

Zion Canyon Campgrounds

Campgrounds in the park often fill up quickly during peak season and major holidays, so advance reservations are recommended. Water is available, but no shower (for just $4, you can shower at Zion Outfitter). **Watchman Campground** (reservations up to 6 months in advance, 877/444-6777, information 435/772-3256, www.recreation.gov, tents $20, RVs $30) has 197 sites open year-round, including 65 that can accommodate RVs with electrical hookups ($30). There are seven accessible sites with paved pads. There are also other flat sites and six accessible restrooms. Prime riverside spots are available. **South Campground** (reservations up to 2 weeks in advance, 877/444-6777, information 435/772-3256, www.recreation.gov, Mar.-Oct., $20) has 128 sites, including a few choice walk-in sites and easy access to the Pa'rus Trail.

Securing a site at either of these campgrounds gives you easy access to the park and the shuttle system, as well as to good restaurants and amenities within walking distance in Springdale. Some of the fruit trees planted in the campgrounds by early pioneers are still producing; you can pick your own. Sometimes, during April-May, these campgrounds see an influx of western tent caterpillars that defoliate the trees.

Private campgrounds can be found nearby in Springdale and east of the park's east entrance. Camping supplies, sack lunches, and groceries are available just outside the park entrance at **Happy Camper Market** (Springdale shuttle stop, 95 Zion Park Blvd., 435/772-7805, 7am-10pm daily).

Kolob Campgrounds

Up Kolob Terrace Road are six first-come, first-served sites at **Lava Point Campground** (no water, May-Sept., $20), a small primitive campground. With 22 full hookup campsites open to both tents and RVs, the **Red Ledge RV Park** (Kanarraville, 435/586-9150, www.redledgervandcampground.com, Apr.-Nov., tents $23, RVs $30-34) is the closest commercial campground to the Kolob Canyons area; go 2 miles (3.2 km) north on I-15, take exit 42, and continue 4.5 miles (7.2 km) into the center of Kanarraville, a tiny agricultural community named after a local Paiute chief. The campground is primarily geared toward RVs, but has some tent sites, a store, showers, and laundry.

GETTING THERE AND AROUND

Zion National Park is 43 miles (69 km) northeast of St. George, 60 miles (97 km) south of Cedar City, 41 miles (66 km) northwest of Kanab, and 86 miles (138 km) southwest of Bryce Canyon National Park. There are **two entrances** to the **main section** of the park: From Springdale, you enter the south end of Zion Canyon, near the visitor center and the Zion Canyon shuttle buses. From the east, you enter via the Zion-Mount Carmel Highway (Hwy. 9) and pass through a long tunnel before popping into Zion Canyon a few miles north of the visitor center. From Las Vegas, it's a 160-mile (257-km) drive to the entrance of Zion. The majority of the drive is on I-15; just past St. George, you'll exit onto Highway 9 and take it for a little over 30 miles (48 km) through Springdale to the park's south entrance.

There's a separate entrance for the **Kolob Canyons** area, in the park's northwest corner. Reach this area via Kolob Canyons Road, which begins just off I-15 exit 40 at the Kolob Canyons Visitor Center and climbs to an overlook; the drive is 10 miles (16.1 km) round-trip.

The less traveled Kolob Terrace part of the park is accessed by Kolob Terrace Road, which runs north from Highway 9 from the tiny town of Virgin and accesses backcountry sites. There's no entrance station or visitor center on Kolob Terrace Road.

If you visit Zion off-season or before 9am or after 3pm, there may be **parking** spaces available in the visitor center lot. Otherwise, just park in Springdale (most lots charge a fee) and catch a shuttle bus, walk, or bike to the park entrance.

Zion Lodge guests may obtain a pass authorizing them to drive to the lodge, but in general, private vehicles are not allowed to drive up Zion Canyon Road. It's fine to drive to the campgrounds; the road between the park entrance and the Zion-Mount Carmel Highway junction is open to all vehicles. In the off-season (Nov.-Feb.), private vehicles are allowed on all roads.

Zion Shuttles

The road through Zion Canyon is narrow, with few pullouts, so to keep the road from becoming a parking lot, a wheelchair-accessible **shuttle bus** (www.nps.gov/zion, every 7-10 minutes from 6am daily Mar.-late-Nov.) provides regular service through the canyon in peak season. The route starts just inside the park entrance, at the Zion Canyon Visitor Center, and runs the length of Zion Canyon Road, stopping at scenic overlooks, trailheads, and Zion Lodge. The last shuttle of the day leaves the Temple of Sinawava at 8:15pm. The shuttle service is unavailable during the off-season (late Nov.-early Mar., except during the last two weeks of Dec.), and private vehicles are allowed on all roads during this time. Pets are not allowed on the shuttle; only service animals are permitted.

For much of the year, the **Springdale Shuttle** (www.nps.gov/zion, every 10-15 minutes daily Mar.-late-Nov. and last two weeks of Dec., free) runs between Springdale and Zion Canyon Village, a commercial district on the edge of Springdale by the park's main south entrance. In Springdale, this shuttle stops within a short walk of every Springdale hotel and near several visitor parking lots at the edge of town. Zion Canyon Village is less than 0.5 mile (0.8 km) to the visitor center, where you can pick up the Zion Canyon Shuttle. In peak season, the last park shuttle of the day leaves the Temple of Sinawava at 8:15pm, and the last Springdale shuttle of the day leaves Zion Canyon Village at 9pm.

The park adjusts hours of operation from year to year for both shuttles, so check online for the most up-to-date info (www.nps.gov/zion). The Springdale shuttle bus is wheelchair accessible. Pets are not allowed on the shuttle, but service animals are permitted.

The Zion-Mount Carmel Tunnel

If your vehicle is 7 feet, 10 inches (2.4 m) wide, 11 feet, 4 inches (3.5 m) high, or 40 feet (12.2 m) long (50 ft/15.2 m with a trailer) or larger, you will need a **traffic-control escort** through the narrow 1-mile-long (1.6-km) **Zion-Mount Carmel Tunnel.** Vehicles of this size are too large to stay in one lane while traveling through the tunnel, which was built in the 1920s. Most **RVs, buses, trailers,** and **fifth-wheels,** and some **camper shells,** will require an escort—which basically means staff will stop oncoming traffic so you can drive down the middle of the tunnel. Expect to pay a $15 fee per vehicle in addition to the park entrance fee (payable at the park entrance station before entering the tunnel). The fee is good for two trips through the tunnel for the same vehicle over a 7-day period. Traffic-control staff are present at the tunnel 8am-8pm daily late April-late August. The rest of the year, hours vary; see www.nps.gov/zion or the visitor center. Oversized vehicle passage must be arranged at the entrance station at Zion Canyon Visitor Center, at Zion Lodge, or by calling 435/772-3256. Bicycles and pedestrians are not allowed in the tunnel.

Vicinity of Zion

Just past the mouth of Zion Canyon near the park's south entrance are several small towns with good—even appealing—services for travelers. Springdale has the widest range of services, including excellent lodgings and restaurants. Rockville has a few B&Bs. Hurricane is a hub for less expensive chain motels.

SPRINGDALE AND VICINITY

Latter-day Saints settled tiny Springdale (pop. 489) in 1862; however, with its location just outside the park's south entrance, the town is geared toward serving park visitors. High-quality hotels and B&Bs, charming restaurants, and frequent shuttle bus service to the park's entrance make Springdale an appealing base for a visit to Zion. Springdale is oriented vertically along a 2-mile (3.2-km) stretch of Highway 9 called Zion Park Boulevard and the Virgin River. Most of the accommodations and restaurants are right off Zion Park Boulevard, and it's feasible to walk pretty much anywhere within town. Farther down the road are the smaller towns of Rockville, Virgin, and Hurricane, where you'll find a few accommodations and restaurants. Springdale is just over 1 mile (1.6 km) from the Zion Canyon Visitor Center, so it's easy to walk, bike, or ride the shuttle into the park if you're staying there.

O. C. Tanner Amphitheater

The highlight at the open-air **O. C. Tanner Amphitheater** (144 Lion Blvd., Springdale, 435/652-7994, admission varies) is a series of musical concerts held Friday or Saturday evening throughout summer.

Outfitters

Here you can buy gear, pick up canyoneering skills, take a guided mountain bike ride (outside the park), or learn to climb big sandstone walls.

Campers who left that crucial piece of equipment at home should visit **Zion Outdoor** (868 Zion Park Blvd., Springdale, 435/772-0630, www.zionoutdoor.com, 9am-9pm daily), as should anybody who needs to spruce up their wardrobe with some stylish outdoor clothing.

Rent a bike or equipment to hike the Narrows at **Zion Outfitter** (7 Zion Park Blvd., Springdale, 435/772-5090, https://zionoutfitter.com, 7am-9pm daily).

Canyoneering supplies, including gear to hike the Narrows or the Subway, are available from **Zion Adventures** (36 Lion Blvd., Springdale, 435/772-1001, www.zionadventures.com, 8am-8pm daily Mar.-Oct., 8am-7pm daily Nov., 9am-7pm daily Dec.-Feb.), **Zion Guru** (795 Zion Park Blvd., Springdale, 435/632-0432, www.zionguru.com), and **Zion Rock and Mountain Guides** (1458 Zion Park Blvd., Springdale, 435/772-3303, www.zionrockguides.com).

Food

Breakfast

A short walk from the park entrance, **Café Soleil** (205 Zion Park Blvd., Springdale, 435/772-0505, 6:30am-4pm daily spring-fall, 8am-4pm Wed.-Mon. winter, $8-12) is a bright friendly place for breakfast or a lunch-time sandwich.

★ **Deep Creek Coffee** (932 Zion Park Blvd., Springdale, 435/669-8849, https://deepcreekcoffee.com, 6am-2pm Mon.-Wed., 6am-6pm Thurs.-Sun.) is the place to hang out in the morning. Besides excellent coffee drinks and made-from-scratch chai, they serve tasty smoothies, quinoa bowls, and sandwiches ($8-12).

Lunch

You can get a good burger or a Mexican-inspired meal at **Oscar's Café** (948 Zion Park Blvd., Springdale, 435/772-3232, www.cafeoscars.com, 7am-9pm daily, $16-30), which has a pleasant patio set off the main road.

Springdale's sole brewpub is the **Zion Canyon Brew Pub** (95 Zion Park Blvd., Springdale, 435/772-0336, www.zionbrewery.com, 11:30am-10pm daily, $15-29), right at the pedestrian gate to the park. The pub offers six flagship brews and many seasonal options, and its upscale pub grub is made from scratch. Pair an elk burger with a chocolaty Conviction Stout.

The town's only full-fledged supermarket, **Sol Foods** (995 Zion Park Blvd., Springdale, 435/772-3100, www.solfoods.com, 7am-11pm daily), stocks groceries, deli items, hardware, and camping supplies. Here you can procure homemade soups and a variety of delicious breakfast and lunch sandwiches.

Dinner

An old gas station has become the ★ **Whiptail Grill** (445 Zion Park Blvd., Springdale, 435/772-0283, www.whiptailgrillzion.com, 2pm-9:30pm Mon.-Fri., noon-9:30pm Sat.-Sun., $16-30), a casual spot serving innovative homemade Mexican-style food, like spaghetti squash enchiladas or fish tacos jazzed up with grape salsa. There's very little seating inside, so plan to eat at the outdoor tables (warmed and lit by gas torches by evening) or take your meal to go.

A good, reasonably priced place to bring a family with picky eaters is **Zion Pizza and Noodle** (868 Zion Park Blvd., Springdale, 435/772-3815, www.zionpizzanoodle.com, 4pm-10pm daily spring-fall, hours vary in winter, $16-19), which is housed in an old church and features a beer garden. The wide-ranging menu at this busy restaurant includes stone-fired pizzas, pasta dishes, calzones, and salads.

The **Spotted Dog Café** (Flanigan's Resort & Spa, 428 Zion Park Blvd., Springdale, 435/772-0700, www.flanigans.com, breakfast buffet 7am-10am daily spring-fall, dinner 5pm-9pm daily spring-fall, 5pm-8pm Thurs.-Sun. winter, dinner $15-28) inside Flanigan's Resort & Spa is one of Springdale's top restaurants. It has a good wine list and a full bar and uses high-quality ingredients for its American bistro cuisine, like pepita-crusted grilled trout and game meatloaf (made with bacon, elk, buffalo, and beef). Be sure to order a salad with your dinner—the house salad is superb. If you want to eat outside, try to get a table on the back patio, which is quieter and more intimate than the dining area out front.

A longtime Springdale favorite is the **Bit & Spur Restaurant** (1212 Zion Park Blvd., Springdale, 435/772-3498, www.bitandspur.com, reservations advised spring-fall, 4pm-9pm daily spring-fall, 5pm-9pm Thurs.-Sun. winter, closed mid-Dec.-mid-Jan., $18-38), a lively Mexican-influenced place. The menu expands on typical south-of-the-border concoctions with dishes like sweet-potato tamales, while the cocktail menu takes playful jabs at local culture with drinks like the Mint Rumney.

★ **King's Landing Bistro** (1515 Zion Park Blvd., Springdale, 435/772-7422, www.klbzion.com, 5pm-9pm Tues.-Sat., $23-35), located at the Driftwood Lodge, serves some of Springdale's most innovative dinners. Start off with bison carpaccio, then move on to a pork steak topped with bacon lardons or king salmon served with gnocchi. Sit outside and enjoy the views.

Accommodations

Springdale offers a wide range of great accommodations. Rockville has several B&Bs, and Hurricane, the next town west of the park, has standard chain motels and the least expensive rooms in the area. During the off-season (late fall-early spring), rates drop substantially.

$100-150

The least expensive lodgings in Springdale are the motel rooms at **Zion Park Motel** (865 Zion Park Blvd., Springdale, 435/772-3251, www.zionparkmotel.com, $94-204), an older, well-kept motel with a small pool, located about 1 mile (1.6 km) from the park entrance.

The hosts at the **Bunk House Inn at Zion** (149 E. Main St., Rockville, 435/772-3393, www.bunkhouseatzion.com, 2-night minimum, $125) are dedicated to living sustainably, and they bring this ethic into their simple two-room B&B. The views are remarkable from this quiet spot in Rockville.

Also in quiet Rockville, just a short drive from the park, is **2 Cranes Inn** (125 E. Main St., Rockville, 435/216-7700, www.2cranes zion.com, $110-155). Here you'll find a Zen-meets-Southwest atmosphere, four rooms with private baths, great outdoor spaces (including a labyrinth), and a communal kitchen stocked with coffee, tea, and a few breakfast basics.

Under the Eaves B&B (980 Zion Park Blvd., Springdale, 435/772-3457, www.undertheeaves.com, $139-289) features six homey guest rooms and a spacious suite, all in a vintage home and a garden cottage. Children over age eight are welcome, and all guests get breakfast included, served at a nearby restaurant.

Over $150

★ **Flanigan's Resort & Spa** (450 Zion Park Blvd., Springdale, 435/772-3244, www.flanigans.com, $100-400) is a quiet and convenient place to stay. Guest rooms and a handful of unique suites are set back off the main drag and face a pretty courtyard. Up on the hill behind the inn, a labyrinth provides an opportunity to take a meditative walk in a stunning setting. An excellent restaurant (the Spotted Dog Café), a pool, and spa services make this an inviting place to spend several days. Two villas, essentially full-size houses, are also available.

Probably the most elegant place to stay is the ★ **Desert Pearl Inn** (707 Zion Park Blvd., Springdale, 435/772-8888 or 888/828-0898, www.desertpearl.com, 2-night minimum, $190-360), a very handsome lodge-like hotel perched above the Virgin River, complete with a pool and a hot tub. Some guest rooms have river views. Much of the wood used for the beams and the finish moldings was salvaged from a railroad trestle made of century-old Oregon fir and redwood that once spanned the north end of the Great Salt Lake. The guest rooms are all large and beautifully furnished.

The closest lodging to the park is **Cable Mountain Lodge** (147 Zion Park Blvd., Springdale, 435/772-3366 or 877/712-3366, www.cablemountainlodge.com, $120-600). Along with being extremely convenient, it's very nicely fitted out, with a pool and guest rooms with microwaves and fridges or small kitchens; two ADA-accessible rooms are also available. Modern architecture and decor are a nice complement to the spectacular views. Regular hotel rooms are referred to as studios; a number of suite options are also available.

Just outside the south gates to Zion, the ★ **Cliffrose Lodge** (281 Zion Park Blvd., Springdale, 435/772-3234 or 800/243-8824, www.cliffroselodge.com, $215-860) sits on 5 acres (2 ha) of well-landscaped gardens with riverfront access. A Hilton hotel, the Cliffrose offers lovely guest rooms (some riverside), suites, and villas (essentially three-bedroom condos). There's also a pool and a laundry room. The Cliffrose is favored by many long-time Zion fans.

The **Driftwood Lodge** (1515 Zion Park Blvd., Springdale, 435/772-3262, www.driftwoodlodge.net, $120-280) is a six-building complex with a good restaurant, a pool, and a spa on spacious grounds. There are also a few pet-friendly rooms with fridges and microwaves. It also offers electrical vehicle charging and a shuttle to the park entrance.

For a place with personality, try the **Novel House Inn** (73 Paradise Rd., Springdale, 435/772-3650 or 800/711-8400, www.novelhouse.com, $376-591), a small family-run inn off the main drag with 10 guest rooms, each decorated with a literary theme and named after an author, including Mark Twain, Rudyard Kipling, and Louis L'Amour. All rooms come with private baths, TVs, great views, and a voucher for breakfast at Oscar's Café, just around the corner.

Expect a very friendly welcome at the **Harvest House B&B** (29 Canyon View Dr., Springdale, 435/772-3880, www.harvesthouse.net, $167-229), which has four guest rooms at the center of Springdale within easy walking distance of the park entrance. All rooms have private baths, and you'll enjoy the garden setting and the outdoor hot tub.

Red Rock Inn (998 Zion Park Blvd., Springdale, 435/669-0646, www.redrockinn.com, $174-349) offers accommodations in individual cabins and a cottage suite amid gardens and patios, all with canyon views. Breakfast vouchers for Oscar's Café, a 2-minute walk away, are included in the room rates.

Even though it's a chain motel, the **Holiday Inn Express** (1215 Zion Park Blvd., Springdale, 435/772-3200, www.hiexpress.com, $100-306) is an attractive option; it's part of a complex with a restaurant, a swimming pool, and standard hotel rooms, along with various suites and kitchen units.

Campgrounds

If you aren't able to camp in the park, the **Zion Canyon Campground** (479 Zion Park Blvd., Springdale, 435/772-3237, www.zioncamp.com) is a short walk from the park entrance. Along with 15 tent sites (no dogs allowed, $49) and 131 RV sites ($59-89), there are motel rooms ($140-170). The sites are crammed pretty close together, but a few are right on the bank of the Virgin River. Facilities at this busy place include a store, a pizza parlor, a game room, a laundry room, and showers.

For the ultimate glamping experience, **Under Canvas Zion** (3955 Kolob Terrace Rd., Virgin, 888/496-1148, www.undercanvas.com/zion, early Mar.-early Nov., $359-559) offers luxury safari tents on 196 acres bordering the park's west side. Choose from a variety of large wall tents or tepees, some with private en suite baths, and all fitted with fine bedding and furniture. In other words, this isn't exactly roughing it, and the nightly rates reflect that. Adventure packages are also available with customizable outdoor activities, and include three camp-cooked meals a day.

At the other end of the luxe spectrum, go off grid at the **Zion Wright Family Ranch** (12120 W. Hwy. 9, 435/231-2008, www.zionwrightfamilyranch.com, $35). This private, no-frills, family-owned campground has dispersed sites in a beautiful and quiet spot several miles up the Kolob Terrace Road from Virgin. For slightly upgraded accommodations, the ranch also has a yurt ($100) and an RV ($400) for rent. The hosts also offer horseback rides.

Information and Services

People traveling with their dogs have a bit of a dilemma when it comes to visiting Zion. No pets are allowed on trails (except the Pa'rus Trail) or in shuttle buses, and it's unconscionable to leave a dog inside a car here in the warmer months. The closest options for dog day care are over in Hurricane and include **On the Spot Play and Stay** (1545 W. State St., Hurricane, 435/680-6666, www.onthespotplayandstay.com, $6 per hour, $40 per night) and **Zion Canyon Canine Recreation Center & Spa** (90 E. State St., Hurricane, 435/772-9029, www.zioncanyoncanine.com, day care $30 per day weekday, $50 weekend, $40-45 per night).

The **Zion Canyon Medical Clinic** (120 Lion Blvd., Springdale, 435/772-3226) provides urgent-care services.

Getting There

Springdale is located at the mouth of Zion Canyon, just outside the park's main (south) entrance. It's about 40 miles (64 km) from St. George to Springdale. From I-15 just north of St. George, take exit 16 and head east on Highway 9. If you're coming from the north, take I-15 exit 22, head southeast through Toquerville, and meet Highway 9 at the town of La Verkin. From Toquerville to Springdale is about 22 miles (35 km).

GRAFTON

Grafton is one of the best-preserved and most picturesque ghost towns in Utah. LDS families founded Grafton in 1859, though the original site was 1 mile (1.6 km) away and relocated after a big flood. Hostilities with the Paiutes during the Black Hawk War forced residents to depart again for safer areas from 1866 to 1868. Floods and irrigation difficulties made life hard even in the best of times, and the population declined in the early 1900s until only ghosts remained.

Filmmakers discovered Grafton and used it for *Butch Cassidy and the Sundance Kid,* among other films. A schoolhouse, a store, houses, and cabins still stand. Grafton's cemetery is worth a visit; it's on the left at a turn 0.3 mile (0.5 km) before the town site. From Springdale, follow Highway 9 southwest 2 miles (3.2 km) to Rockville; turn south and go 3.5 miles (5.6 km) on Bridge Road (200 East). The last 2.6 miles (4.2 km) are unpaved but should be passable by cars in dry weather. Keep right at a road junction 1.6 miles (2.6 km) past Rockville.

Bryce Canyon National Park

TOP EXPERIENCE

In **Bryce Canyon National Park** (435/834-5322, www.nps.gov/brca, $35 per vehicle, $30 motorcycles, $20 pp pedestrians or cyclists, entry good for 7 days and unlimited shuttle use), a geologic fairyland of rock spires rises beneath the high cliffs of the Paunsaugunt Plateau. This intricate maze, eroded from a soft limestone, now glows red, orange, pink, yellow, and cream, depending on the view and time of day. The rocks provide a continuous show of changing color as the sun's rays and cloud shadows move across the landscape.

Looking at these rock formations is like looking at puffy clouds in the sky; it's easy to find images in the shapes of the rocks. Some see the natural rock sculptures as Gothic castles, others as Egyptian temples, subterranean worlds inhabited by dragons, or vast armies of a lost empire. The Paiute people have a tale of the Legend People that relates how various animals and birds once lived in a beautiful city built for them by Coyote; when the Legend People began behaving badly toward Coyote, he transformed them all into stone.

Bryce Canyon actually isn't a canyon at all, but rather the largest of a series of massive amphitheaters cut into the Pink Cliffs. In Bryce Canyon National Park, you can gaze into the depths from viewpoints and trails on the plateau rim or hike down moderately steep trails and wind your way among the spires. A 17-mile (27-km) scenic drive traces the length of the park, passing many overlooks and trailheads. Beyond the road, you can explore the park's nearly 36,000 acres (14,570 ha) of spectacular rock features, dense forests, and expansive meadows.

The park's elevation ranges 6,600-9,100 feet (2,012-2,774 m), so it's usually much cooler here than at Utah's other national parks. Expect tolerably hot days in summer, frosty nights in spring and fall, and snow October-April. The visitor center, the scenic drive, and one campground stay open year-round.

THE HOODOOS

The park's landscape originated about 60 million years ago as sediments in a large body of water, named Lake Flagstaff by geologists. Silt,

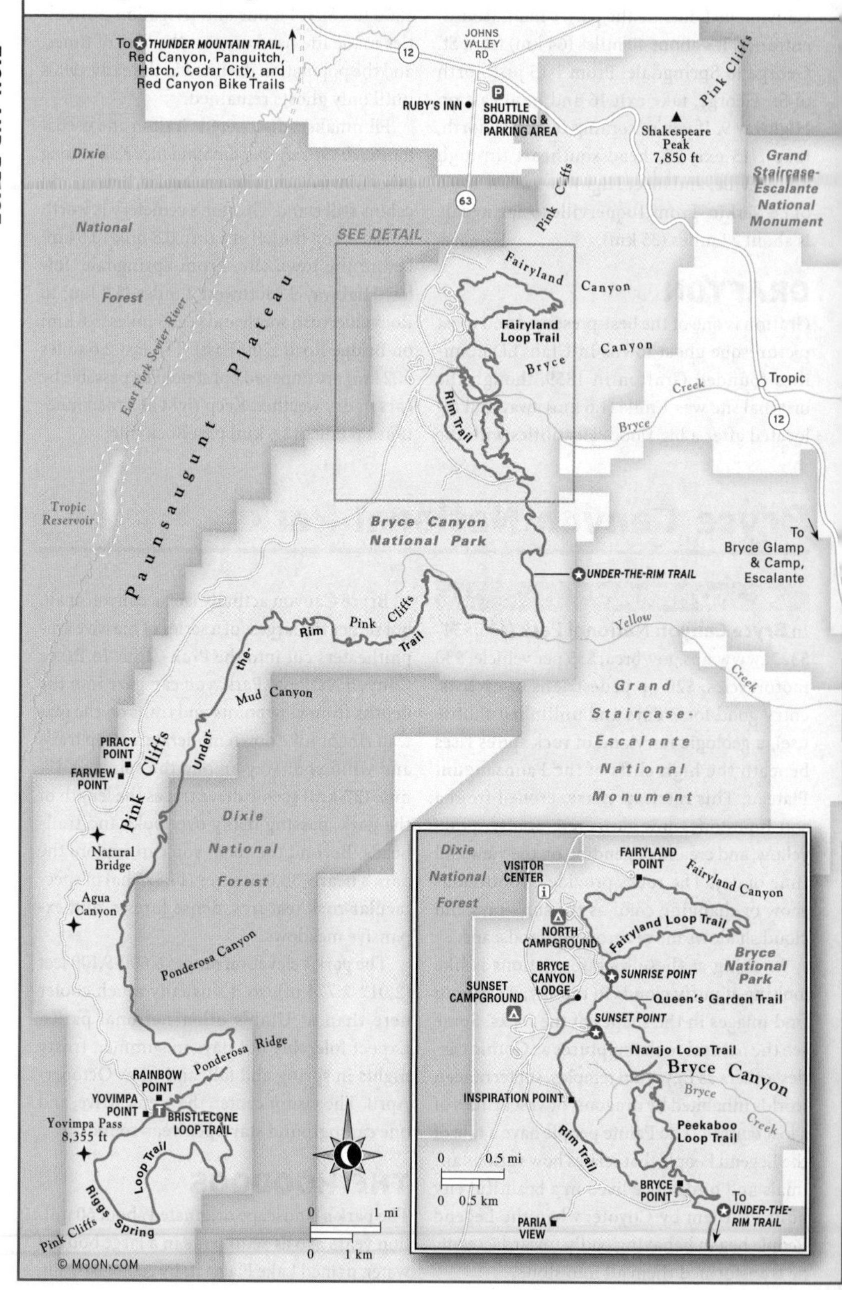
Bryce Canyon National Park
To THUNDER MOUNTAIN TRAIL, Red Canyon, Panguitch, Hatch, Cedar City, and Red Canyon Bike Trails
12
JOHNS VALLEY RD
RUBY'S INN
SHUTTLE BOARDING & PARKING AREA
Pink Cliffs
Shakespeare Peak 7,850 ft
Grand Staircase-Escalante National Monument
Dixie
National
Forest
63
SEE DETAIL
Fairyland Canyon
Fairyland Loop Trail
Bryce Canyon
Rim Trail
Tropic
Creek
Bryce
East Fork Sevier River
Paunsaugunt Plateau
Tropic Reservoir
Bryce Canyon National Park
To Bryce Glamp & Camp, Escalante
UNDER-THE-RIM TRAIL
Yellow Creek
Rim Pink Cliffs Trail
Under-the-
Mud Canyon
Grand Staircase-Escalante National Monument
PIRACY POINT
FARVIEW POINT
Pink Cliffs
Natural Bridge
Agua Canyon
Dixie National Forest
Ponderosa Canyon
Ponderosa Ridge
RAINBOW POINT
YOVIMPA POINT
BRISTLECONE LOOP TRAIL
Yovimpa Pass 8,355 ft
Loop Trail
Riggs Spring
Pink Cliffs
0 1 mi
0 1 km
© MOON.COM
Dixie National Forest
VISITOR CENTER
FAIRYLAND POINT
Fairyland Canyon
NORTH CAMPGROUND
Fairyland Loop Trail
Bryce National Park
BRYCE CANYON LODGE
SUNRISE POINT
SUNSET CAMPGROUND
Queen's Garden Trail
SUNSET POINT
Navajo Loop Trail
Bryce Canyon
INSPIRATION POINT
Bryce Creek
Rim Trail
Peekaboo Loop Trail
0 0.5 mi
0 0.5 km
BRYCE POINT
To UNDER-THE-RIM TRAIL
PARIA VIEW

Bryce in One Day

Sunrise Point

- Wake up early to catch the morning light at **Sunrise Point.** Then drive on to Rainbow Point.
- If you sleep in, drive straight to **Rainbow Point** at the road's end, with sweeping views of southern Utah.
- Drive to **Sunset Point,** where you can descend from the rim on the **Navajo Loop Trail.** At the bottom of the loop, take **Queen's Garden Trail** back up to Sunrise Point, where a short paved section of the Rim Trail connects the two trailheads. This hike is about 3 miles (4.8 km) and takes a little over an hour.
- Get lunch and snacks at the **General Store.**
- Spend the afternoon walking along the **Rim Trail.** Head to the **Lodge at Bryce Canyon** for dinner; it's the best food for miles.

calcium carbonate, and other minerals settled on the lake bottom. These sediments consolidated and became the Claron Formation, a soft, silty limestone with some shale and sandstone. Lake Flagstaff had long since disappeared when the land began to rise as part of the Colorado Plateau uplift about 16 million years ago. Uneven pressures beneath the plateau caused it to break along fault lines into a series of smaller plateaus at different levels, known as the Grand Staircase. Bryce Canyon National Park occupies part of one of these plateaus—the Paunsaugunt.

The spectacular Pink Cliffs on the east edge contain the famous erosional features known as hoodoos, carved in the Claron Formation. Variations in hardness of the rock layers result in these strange features, which seem almost alive. Water flows through cracks, wearing away softer rock around hard erosion-resistant caps. Finally, a cap becomes so undercut that the overhang allows water to drip down, leaving a "neck" of rock below the harder cap. Traces of iron and manganese provide the distinctive coloring.

The hoodoos continue to change—new ones form and old ones fade away. Despite appearances, wind plays little role in creating the landscape; it's the freezing and thawing, snowmelt, and rainwater that dissolve weak layers, pry open cracks, and carve out the forms. The plateau cliffs, meanwhile, recede at a rate of about 1 foot (0.3 m) every 50-65 years; look for trees on the rim that now overhang the abyss. Listen, and you might hear the sounds of pebbles falling away and rolling down the steep slopes.

Bryce Point is a good spot for a huge panoramic view filled with hoodoos. To pack the most hoodoos into a short visit, hike the 1-mile (1.6-km) section of the **Rim Trail** between Sunrise and Sunset Points. This area of the **Bryce Amphitheatre** has the highest concentration of hoodoos and offers the most up-close and personal views. To further immerse yourself in their geology, hike the **Queen's Garden** or **Navajo Trails** (or connect the two to form a loop).

EXPLORING THE PARK

Allow at least half a day to see the visitor center exhibits, enjoy the viewpoints along the scenic drive, and take a few short walks. Another half day can be spent on a longer hike in Bryce, whether on one of the trails on the main circuit like Navajo Loop, or a less traveled trail like Fairyland Loop or Tropic Trail.

Visitor Center

From the turnoff on Highway 12, follow signs past Ruby's Inn for 4.5 miles (7.2 km) south to the park entrance; the **Bryce Canyon Visitor Center** (435/834-5322, 8am-8pm daily May-Sept., 8am-6pm daily mid-Mar.-Apr. and Oct., 8am-4:30pm daily Nov.-mid-Mar., hours vary year to year, see www.nps.gov/brca for up-to-date information) is a short distance farther, on the right. A 20-minute video, shown every half hour, introduces the park. Geologic exhibits illustrate how the land was formed and how it has changed. Historical displays cover the Paiute people, early nonnative explorers, trees, flowers, and wildlife. Rangers present a variety of naturalist programs, including short hikes, mid-May-early September; see the posted schedule.

Tours

The most basic tour of the park, which comes with the price of admission, is a ride on the wheelchair-accessible park shuttle bus. Buses run every 15 minutes or so during the peak part of the day, and the trip from Ruby's Inn (the closest lodging to the park) to Rainbow Point takes 50 minutes. You can get off at any stop to hike or sightsee, then catch another bus. Shuttle season is early April-mid-October; shuttle use is voluntary, but rigs longer than 20 feet (6 m) aren't allowed on the main park road during times that the shuttle is running.

Best Western Plus Ruby's Inn (26 S. Main St., 877/758-6991, www.rubysinn.com), a hotel, restaurant, and recreation complex at the park entrance, is a good place to survey opportunities for guided trips around Bryce. The lobby is filled with recreational outfitters, along with vendors who organize horseback rides ($75-145), hayrides, barn dances, chuck wagon dinners, and even virtual reality tours of southern Utah. During the summer, Ruby's also sponsors a **rodeo** (866/782-0002, 7pm Wed.-Sat., $15 adults, $10 ages 5-11) across from the inn.

While horseback rides are a long-standing enjoyable way to experience Bryce, you can also explore the terrain on a noisier steed: Guided all-terrain vehicle (ATV) tours of Red Canyon are offered by **Ruby's ATV Tours** (435/834-8032, 1-hour trip $85-165, depending on vehicle).

If you'd like to get a look at Bryce and the surrounding area from the air, take a tour with **Bryce Canyon Airlines** (Ruby's Inn, 435/834-8060), which offers both plane and helicopter tours. There's quite a range of options, but a 35-minute airplane tour (2-person minimum, $175 pp) provides a good look at the surroundings.

SCENIC DRIVE

From elevations of about 8,000 feet (2,440 m) near the visitor center, the park's scenic drive

---

1: hoodoos in Bryce Canyon **2:** Bryce Amphitheater

1

2

"A Hell of a Place to Lose a Cow"

LDS pioneer Ebenezer Bryce homesteaded near the town site of Tropic in 1875, but the work of scratching a living from the rugged land became too hard. He left five years later for more promising areas in Arizona. The name of the park commemorates his efforts. He is remembered as saying of the area, "Well, it's a hell of a place to lose a cow."

A later settler, Ruben "Ruby" Syrett, recognized the tourism potential of the area and opened the first small lodge near Sunset Point in 1919, then Ruby's Inn in 1924. Enthusiasm for the scenic beauty led to the creation of Bryce Canyon National Monument in 1923. The name changed to Utah National Park in the following year, and then it took its current name in 1928. Tours organized by the Union Pacific Railroad, beginning in the late 1920s, made Bryce well known and easily visited.

gradually winds 1,100 feet (335 m) higher to Rainbow Point. About midway, ponderosa pines give way to spruce, fir, and aspen trees. On a clear day, you can enjoy vistas of more than 100 miles (161 km) from many viewpoints. Because of limited parking along the drive, trailers and RVs longer than 20 feet (6 m) must be left at the visitor center or your campsite. Visitors wishing to see all the viewpoints from Fairyland Point to Bryce Point can walk on the Rim Trail, 5.5 miles (8.9 km) one-way.

Note that even though viewpoints are described here in north-to-south order, the stops are all on the east side of the drive, so rangers recommend driving all the way up to Rainbow Point, then visiting viewpoints on your way back down to avoid numerous lefthand turns across oncoming traffic.

Fairyland Point

The turnoff for Fairyland Point is just inside the park boundary, right before you get to the booth where payment is required; go north 0.8 mile (1.3 km) from the visitor center, then east 1 mile (1.6 km). Whimsical rock formations line Fairyland Canyon a short distance below. You can descend into the area on the **Fairyland Loop Trail** or follow the **Rim Trail** for more views.

★ Sunrise and Sunset Points

These overlooks are off to the left about 1 mile (1.6 km) south of the visitor center, and they're connected by a 0.5-mile (0.8-km) paved section of the **Rim Trail.** Panoramas from each point take in swaths of Bryce Amphitheater and beyond, including the Aquarius and Table Cliff Plateaus to the northeast, and the colorful cliffs rising 2,000 feet (610 m) or higher.

If you can, come early to Sunrise Point for a peaceful dawn viewing, or linger late at Sunset Point for a golden hour hoodoo encounter. A short walk down either the **Queen's Garden Trail,** which begins at Sunrise Point, or the **Navajo Loop Trail,** which starts at Sunset Point, will bring you closer to the **hoodoos,** making for a totally different experience than that found atop the rim.

Inspiration Point

It's well worth the 0.75-mile (1.2-km) walk from Sunset Point south along the **Rim Trail** to see a fantastic maze of hoodoos in the "Silent City" from Inspiration Point, which actually consists of three viewpoint levels. The Lower and Mid viewpoints are also accessible by car via a spur road near the Bryce Point turnoff. Weathering along vertical joints has cut rows of narrow gullies, some more than 200 feet (61 m) deep. It's a short but steep 0.2-mile (0.3-km) walk to Upper Inspiration Point.

1: Zion Scenic Drive **2:** Sunrise and Sunset Points are a short distance from one another on the Rim Trail.

1
2
SUNRISE POINT
SUNSET POINT

Bryce Canyon in Winter

Bryce in winter

Although Bryce is most popular during the summer months, it is especially beautiful and otherworldly during the winter, when the rock formations are topped with snow. Because of the high elevation (8,000-9,000 ft/2,438-2,743 m), winter lasts a long time, often into April.

The main park roads and most viewpoints are plowed. The **Rim Trail** makes an excellent, easy snowshoe or cross-country ski route. The unplowed **Paria Ski Trail** (a 5-mi/8-km loop) and **Fairyland Ski Trail** (a 2.5-mi/4-km loop) are also good routes. Rent cross-country ski equipment just outside the park at Ruby's Inn.

At the visitor center, the **Bryce Canyon Snowshoe Program** (435/834-4747, www.nps.gov/brca, 1pm daily when possible, free) offers free snowshoes and poles when you join a guided hike with a snowshoe ranger. These 1-mile (1.6-km) outings are designed for beginners and depend on snow depth and ranger availability. On full-moon nights November-March, rangers add a moonlit snowshoe hike.

Although **trail closures** are relatively common due to rockfall or slick conditions, winter can be a fabulous time to explore the hoodoos. Crampons or simpler traction devices (such as Yaktrax) are often far safer than snowshoes for hiking steep trails with packed snow or ice.

During the winter, most of the businesses around the park entrance shut down. The notable exception is **Ruby's Inn** (26 S. Main St., 435/834-5341 or 866/866-6616, www.rubysinn.com), which is a wintertime hub of activity. Rates are considerably lower this time of year: January-March, most guest rooms go for about $70. The inn hosts the **Bryce Canyon Winter Festival** during Presidents Day weekend in February. The 3-day festival includes cross-country skiing and snowshoeing clinics, demos, and tours. This is also the time and place to pick up tips on ski archery and winter photography.

Bryce Point

This overlook at the south end of Bryce Amphitheater takes in expansive views to the north and east. It's also the start for the **Rim, Peekaboo Loop,** and **Under-the-Rim Trails.** From the turnoff 2 miles (3.2 km) south of the visitor center, follow signs 2.1 miles (3.4 km) in.

Paria View

Cliffs drop precipitously into the headwaters of Yellow Creek, a tributary of the Paria

River. Distant views take in the Paria River Canyon, White Cliffs (of Navajo sandstone), and Navajo Mountain. The rim of the park's plateau forms a drainage divide. Precipitation falling west of the rim flows gently into the East Fork of the Sevier River and the Great Basin; precipitation landing east of the rim rushes through deep canyons in the Pink Cliffs to the Paria River, then on to the Colorado River and the Grand Canyon. Take the turnoff for Bryce Point, then keep right at the fork.

Farview Point

This sweeping panorama takes in a lot of geology. You'll see levels of the Grand Staircase that include the Aquarius and Table Cliff Plateaus to the northeast, Kaiparowits Plateau to the east, and White Cliffs to the southeast. Look beyond the White Cliffs to see a section of the Kaibab Plateau that forms the North Rim of the Grand Canyon. The overlook is to the west, 9 miles (14.5 km) south of the visitor center.

Piracy Point

At this quieter overlook, you'll feel like you're in an airplane flying low over a busy shipyard. The buttes and hoodoos below strikingly resemble wooden pirate ships afloat in a sea of pines, especially if you squint your eyes. Interestingly enough, this point overlooks a process called "stream piracy," where one stream of a river diverts water from another. The streams in question are Willis Creek, which is starting to divert water from Sheep Creek—both tributaries of the Paria River. From Farview Point, head north on a very short, shaded trail to get here.

Natural Bridge

This large feature lies just off the road to the east, 1.7 miles (2.7 km) past Farview Point. The span is 54 feet (16 m) wide and 95 feet (29 m) high. Despite its name, this is an arch formed by weathering from rain and freezing, not by stream erosion, as with a true natural bridge. Once the opening reached ground level, runoff began to enlarge the hole and dig a gully through it.

Agua and Ponderosa Canyons

You can admire sheer cliffs and hoodoos from the Agua Canyon overlook to the east, 1.4 miles (2.3 km) past Natural Bridge. With a little imagination, you may be able to pick out two disparately sized hoodoos known as the Hunter and the Rabbit (or Backpacker) below. The Ponderosa Canyon overlook, 1.8 miles (2.9 km) farther east, offers a panorama similar to that at Farview Point.

Yovimpa and Rainbow Points

The land drops away in rugged canyons and fine views at the end of the scenic drive, 17 miles (27 km) south of the visitor center. At an elevation of 9,115 feet (2,778 m), this is the highest area of the park. Yovimpa and Rainbow Points are only a short walk apart yet offer different vistas. The **Bristlecone Loop Trail** is an easy 1-mile (1.6-km) loop from Rainbow Point to ancient bristlecone pines along the rim. The **Riggs Spring Loop Trail** makes a good day hike; you can begin from either Yovimpa Point or Rainbow Point and descend into canyons in the southern area of the park. The **Under-the-Rim Trail** starts from Rainbow Point and winds 23 miles (37 km) to Bryce Point; day hikers can make a 7.5-mile (12.1-km) trip by using the Agua Canyon Connecting Trail and a car shuttle.

HIKING AND BACKPACKING

Hikers get to take their Bryce experience beyond the overlook panoramas and get up close to the hoodoos, along with the local flora and fauna. Because almost all the trails head down off the canyon's rim, they're moderately difficult, with many ups and downs, but the paths are well graded and signed. Hikers not accustomed to the 7,000- to 9,000-foot (2,134- to 2,743-m) elevation will find the trails strenuous and should allow extra time.

Many of the trails at Bryce meander below the rim and can easily be connected to form

loops of varying mileage. Check out a map to design the type of hike you want, or talk to a ranger, who can suggest a multiple-trail loop. Pets must stay above the rim; they're allowed on a 0.5-mile (0.8-km) stretch of the Rim Trail between Sunset and Sunrise Points. Ask at the visitor center for current trail conditions and water sources; you can also pick up a free hiking map. Given Bryce's high altitude, snow may block some trail sections in winter and early spring.

Rim Trail

Distance: *11 miles (17.7 km) round-trip*
Duration: *5-7 hours*
Elevation gain: *540 feet (165 m)*
Effort: *easy-moderate*
Trailheads: *Fairyland Point, Bryce Point*
Shuttle Stops: *Fairyland Point, Bryce Point*

Following the edge of Bryce Amphitheater, this trail involves minimal elevation change or technical terrain, but due to its length, falls somewhere between easy and moderate. Most people walk short sections of the rim in leisurely strolls or use the trail to connect with one of the five other trails that head down beneath the rim. Near the lodge, there's a 0.5-mile (0.8-km) stretch of trail between Sunrise and Sunset Points that is paved, nearly level, and wheelchair accessible; other parts are gently rolling.

Fairyland Loop Trail

Distance: *8 miles (13 km) round-trip*
Duration: *4-5 hours*
Elevation gain: *2,300 feet (701 m)*
Effort: *strenuous*
Trailheads: *Fairyland Point, Sunrise Point*
Shuttle Stops: *Fairyland Point, Sunrise Point*

This trail winds in and out of colorful rock spires in the northern part of Bryce Amphitheater, a somewhat less visited area 1 mile (1.6 km) off the main park road. The most common trailhead is Fairyland Point, and you can hike the loop in either direction, but counterclockwise is considered the easier option. You can also begin this loop hike at Sunrise Point, where you'll have to vie with more crowds in the first mile. Although the trail is well graded, remember that no matter which direction you hike this loop, there's a steep, unrelenting climb at the end to return to the rim. You can take a loop hike of 8 miles (13 km) from either Fairyland Point or Sunrise Point by using a section of the **Rim Trail;** a car shuttle between the two points saves 3 hiking miles (4.8 km). The whole loop is too long for many visitors, who enjoy short trips down and back to see this enchanting and quieter rock "fairyland."

1: Natural Bridge 2: Ponderosa Canyon

Queen's Garden Trail

Distance: *1.8 miles (2.9 km) round-trip*
Duration: *1.5 hours*
Elevation gain: *320 feet (98 m)*
Effort: *easy-moderate*
Trailhead: *Sunrise Point*
Shuttle Stop: *Sunrise Point*

This popular trail drops from Sunrise Point through impressive features in the middle of Bryce Amphitheater to a **hoodoo** resembling a portly Queen Victoria. The easiest excursion below the rim, Queen's Garden also makes a good loop with **Navajo Loop** and **Rim Trails;** most people who do the loop prefer to descend the steeper Navajo Loop and climb out on Queen's Garden Trail for a 3.5-mile (5.6-km) hike.

Navajo Loop Trail

Distance: *1.3 miles (2.1 km) round-trip*
Duration: *1.5 hours*
Elevation gain: *520 feet (158 m)*
Effort: *moderate*
Trailhead: *Sunset Point*
Shuttle Stop: *Sunset Point*

From Sunset Point, this trail tours stunning hoodoo scenery as it drops 520 vertical feet (158 m) in 0.7 mile (1.2 km) through a narrow canyon. At the bottom, the loop leads into deep, dark **Wall Street**—an even narrower canyon 0.5 mile (0.8 km) long—before returning to the rim. Of all the trails in the park, this is the most prone to rockfall, so watch for slides or the sounds of falling rocks; it's not uncommon for at least part of the trail to be closed for rockfall. Other destinations from the bottom of Navajo Loop are **Twin Bridges, Queen's Garden Trail, Peekaboo Loop Trail,** and **Tropic Trail.**

Peekaboo Loop Trail

Distance: *5.5 miles (8.9 km) round-trip*
Duration: *3-4 hours*
Elevation gain: *1,500 feet (457 m)*
Effort: *moderate-strenuous*
Trailhead: *Bryce Point*
Shuttle Stop: *Bryce Point*

This enchanting walk is full of surprises at every turn—and there are lots of turns. The trail is in the southern part of Bryce Amphitheater, where many striking rock features await. The loop itself involves many ups and downs and a few tunnels. You can extend your hike by adding on **Navajo Loop** and **Queen's Garden Trail,** which connect with Peekaboo. This is the only trail in the park allowing equestrian use, and horseback riders have the right-of-way; if possible, step to higher ground when you allow them to pass.

★ Under-the-Rim Trail

Distance: *23 miles (37 km) one-way*
Duration: *2 days or longer*
Elevation gain: *1,500 feet (457 m)*
Effort: *strenuous*
Trailheads: *Bryce Point, Rainbow Point*
Shuttle Stops: *Bryce Point, Rainbow Point*

The longest trail in the park winds 23 miles (37 km) below the Pink Cliffs. The most common way to follow this route is from Bryce Point up to Rainbow Point. The trail takes you through stunning hoodoo scenery, canyons, and ponderosa groves. Allow two days to hike the entire trail; arrange a shuttle or parked car unless you plan to hike back for a total of 46 miles (74 km). While parts of the trail can be busy, by venturing into Bryce's backcountry, you'll enjoy a more peaceful journey through the park.

There are seven designated campsites; the Swamp Canyon site is more or less at the halfway point. Water on this trek is unreliable, so pack in your own and check with a ranger on the status of sources. Four connecting trails along the scenic drive also make it easy to cover sections of Under-the-Rim Trail on day hikes. Another option is to combine Under-the-Rim and **Riggs Spring Loop** for a total of 31.5 miles (51 km).

Bristlecone Loop Trail

Distance: *1 mile (1.6 km) round-trip*
Duration: *30 minutes-1 hour*
Elevation gain: *195 feet (59 m)*
Effort: *easy*
Trailheads: *Rainbow Point, Yovimpa Point*
Shuttle Stop: *Rainbow Point*

This easy 1-mile (1.6-km) loop begins from either Rainbow or Yovimpa Point and explores viewpoints and ancient bristlecone pines along the rim. These hardy trees survive fierce storms and extremes of hot and cold that no other tree can. Some of the bristlecone pines here are 1,700 years old.

Riggs Spring Loop

Distance: *8.5 miles (13.7 km) round-trip*
Duration: *5-6 hours*
Elevation gain: *1,625 feet (495 m)*
Effort: *strenuous*
Trailhead: *Rainbow Point*
Shuttle Stop: *Rainbow Point*

One of the park's more challenging day hikes or a leisurely overnighter, this trail begins from Rainbow Point and descends into canyons in the southern area of the park. Of the three backcountry campgrounds along the trail, the Riggs Spring site is conveniently located about halfway around the loop. Great hoodoo views, lots of aspen trees, and pretty meadows are highlights. A fire in 2018 burned the area of the trail near Rainbow Point; the scorched ground is now rich with flowers. Day hikers often take a shortcut that bypasses Riggs Spring and saves 0.75 mile (1.2 km).

1: hoodoo views on the Tropic Trail, which connects to Navajo Loop Trail **2:** Under-the-Rim Trail

1

2

HORSEBACK RIDING

If you'd like to get down among the hoodoos but aren't sure you'll have the energy to hike back up to the rim, consider letting a horse help you along. **Canyon Trail Rides** (Lodge at Bryce Canyon, 435/679-8665, www.canyonrides.com, Apr.-Oct.), a park concessionaire, offers 2-hour ($75) and half-day ($100) guided rides near Sunrise Point. Both rides descend to the floor of the canyon; the longer ride follows the Peekaboo Loop Trail. Riders must be at least seven years old and weigh no more than 220 pounds; the horses and wranglers are accustomed to novices.

Ruby's Horseback Adventures (435/834-5358 or 866/782-0002, www.horserides.net, Apr.-Oct.) offers horseback riding in and near Bryce Canyon. There's a choice of half-day ($100) and full-day ($145, including lunch) trips, as well as a 1.5-hour trip ($75). During the summer, Ruby's also sponsors a rodeo (7pm Wed.-Sat., $15 adults, $10 ages 5-11) across from the inn.

FOOD

The dining room at the ★ **Lodge at Bryce Canyon** (435/834-8700, www.brycecanyonforever.com, 7:30am-10am, 11:30am-3pm, and 5pm-9pm daily Apr.-Oct., $15-44) is atmospheric, with a large stone fireplace and white tablecloths, and offers food that's usually better than anything else you'll find in the area. For lunch ($10-15), the snack bar is a good bet in nice weather; the only seating is outside on the patio or in the hotel lobby. Close by, the **General Store** (by the Lodge near Sunrise Point) also serves perfectly acceptable slices of pizza (11:30am-3pm daily, $5).

If you're up for a high-volume dining experience, Ruby's Inn **Cowboy Buffet and Steak Room** (26 S. Main St., 435/834-5341, www.rubysinn.com, 6:30am-9:30pm daily summer, 6:30am-9pm daily winter, $13-41) is an incredibly busy place. It's also one of the better Ruby's-associated restaurants, with sandwiches, steaks, and pasta. Casual lunch and dinner fare, including pizza, is served in the inn's snack bar, the **Canyon Diner** (11:30am-8:30pm daily May-mid-Oct., 11:30am-7pm daily mid-Oct.-Apr., $4-12), which is not particularly recommended (the vegetarian sandwich consisted of a slice of American cheese, some lettuce, and a few cucumber slices on a hot dog bun). A third Ruby's restaurant, **Ebenezer's Barn & Grill** (7pm dinner, 8pm show daily late Apr.-mid-Oct., $27-50) features cowboy-style food and entertainment that's quite pricey for the quality.

Bryce Canyon Resort (13500 E. Hwy. 12, 435/834-5100 or 800/834-0043, www.brycecanyonresort.com), near the turnoff for the park, has an on-site restaurant, the **Cowboy Ranch House** (7am-10pm daily, $14-30), which features grilled steaks and burgers; it also serves Utah beers.

Two long-established restaurants west of the park entrance have a low-key, noncorporate atmosphere and decent food compared to what's available closer to the park. The small family-run restaurant attached to **Bryce Canyon Pines** (Hwy. 12, Milepost 10, 435/834-5441 or 800/892-7923, https://brycecanyonrestaurant.com, 7am-9:30pm daily Apr.-late-Oct., breakfast $6-9, lunch $8-10, dinner $11-27) is a homey place to stop for burgers, soup, or sandwiches. Save room for homemade fruit pie, and if you're on the go, boxed lunches are available.

Two miles (3.2 km) west of the park turnoff is **Bryce UpTop Lodge** (1152 Hwy. 12, 435/834-5227, https://bryceuptoplodge.com, 7am-11am and 5pm-9pm daily, $13-35), a steak house with an Old West atmosphere and nice views; there's also an on-site market and bakery.

ACCOMMODATIONS

Travelers may have a hard time finding accommodations and campsites April-October in both the park and nearby areas, so advance reservations are a must during these months. The rates listed below are for high season.

The Lodge at Bryce Canyon is the only lodging inside the park, and you'll need to make reservations months in advance to get a room at this historic landmark (although it doesn't hurt to ask about last-minute vacancies). Other motels are clustered near the park entrance road, but many do not offer much for the money. The quality of lodging is generally low in areas around the park; they're somewhat better in Tropic, 11 miles (17.7 km) east on Highway 12, and in Panguitch, 25 miles (40 km) to the northwest.

During the winter, it's easy to find inexpensive accommodations in this area; even guest rooms at Ruby's Inn start at about $90. The rest of the year, expect to pay twice or three times as much for the convenience of staying close to the park. Right outside the park boundary, several motels huddle along Highway 12, many of them behind on upkeep. For a more sumptuous and relaxing experience, stay at a B&B in nearby Tropic. Otherwise, the nearest towns with high-quality accommodations are an hour or more away.

$100-150

A reasonably good value for the area can be found at **Bryce View Lodge** (105 E. Center St., 435/834-5180, www.bryceviewlodge.com, $130-170), which has starkly basic guest rooms near the park entrance, across the road from (and owned by) Ruby's Inn. The lodge offers an indoor pool and hot tub. Check for deals here; rates can be as low as $60.

Although "resort" may be stretching it, **Bryce Canyon Resort** (13500 E. Hwy. 12, 435/834-5351, $100-124) is an older hotel complex with a small pool, a restaurant, and a store, offering standard motel rooms, suites, and rustic cabins that sleep up to six. While simple and a bit outdated, rooms are brightly furbished with a loose Southwestern theme.

Bryce UpTop Lodge (1152 Hwy. 12, 435/834-5227, https://bryceuptoplodge.com, $109) has pine-paneled motel rooms in what appear to be older prefab modular structures. This lodge is best suited for budget travelers who don't want to camp and don't plan to spend a lot of time in their rooms. It's 4 miles (6.4 km) west of the park entrance in a small complex with a restaurant and a supermarket.

Six miles (9.7 km) west of the park turnoff, **Bryce Canyon Pines Motel** (Hwy. 12, Milepost 10, 435/834-5441 or 800/892-7923, www.brycecanyonmotel.com, $145-150) is an older motel with standard rooms, cottages, two-bedroom suites with full kitchens, a seasonal covered pool, horseback rides, an RV park, and a restaurant with good from-scratch food (breakfast, lunch, and dinner daily early Apr.-late Oct.).

Over $150

The sprawling **Best Western Plus Ruby's Inn** (26 S. Main St., 435/834-5341 or 866/866-6616, www.rubysinn.com, $170-220) offers many year-round services on Highway 63, just north of the park boundary; winter rates are considerably lower. The hotel features many separate buildings with guest rooms, as well as an indoor pool and a hot tub. Kitchenettes and family rooms are also available; pets are allowed. In addition to offering lodging, this is the area's major center for recreational outfitters, dining, entertainment, and shopping. Many tour groups bed down here. What you'll gain in convenience, you may lose in peace and quiet.

The newest and best-appointed hotel in the area is the **Best Western Bryce Canyon Grand Hotel** (30 N. 100 E., 435/834-5700 or 866/866-6634, www.brycecanyongrand.com, $219-300). It's across the road from Ruby's, but it's actually a bit of a walk. Unlike many in the area, guest rooms have microwaves and fridges, along with a good breakfast buffet. An outdoor pool is open in summer. During winter, guests can go across the highway to use the indoor pool at Ruby's.

A considerably more pleasant option than the hubbub of the chain hotels en route to the park entrance is glamping in a dome at **Bryce Glamp & Camp** (555 W. Yellow Creek Rd., 725/270-9383, www.bryceglampandcamp.com, $250-300). Located about 25 minutes from Bryce just past the town of Tropic in a quiet red-rock setting, these luxury domes

are among the finest places to stay in the area, with AC/heat, smart TVs, a small kitchen, and an outdoor space that includes a fire pit and grill. Plus, you can stargaze through the transparent domes from your bed!

Set among ponderosa pines a short walk from the rim, the ★ **Lodge at Bryce Canyon** (435/834-8700 or 877/386-4383, www.brycecanyonforever.com, Apr.-Oct., rooms $254-271, cabins $271) was built in 1923 and is listed on the National Register of Historic Places. A division of the Union Pacific Railroad constructed the building, and a spur line once terminated at the front entrance. This is the only lodging in the park itself, and it's heavy on charm. Options include suites in the lodge, motel-style guest rooms, and lodgepole pine cabins. Rooms are clean and pleasant, though fairly basic in terms of amenities. Reserving up to a year in advance is a good idea for the busy spring, summer, and early fall season.

Activities at the lodge include horseback rides, park tours, evening entertainment, and ranger talks. A gift shop sells souvenirs, while food can be found at both a restaurant and a snack bar.

Campgrounds

Bryce Canyon Campgrounds

The park's two campgrounds, **North Campground** and **Sunset Campground**, both have water, pull-through spaces, and about 100 sites each. Both campgrounds accept reservations, which are advised. During the busy summer season, they usually fill by 1pm-2pm. If you don't have a reservation, try to arrive early.

North Campground (877/444-6777, www.recreation.gov, year-round, first-come, first-served Oct.-mid-May, tents $20, RVs $30, no hookups) is on the left, just past the visitor center. The best sites here are just a few yards downhill from the Rim Trail, with easy access to many park trails. North Campground Loop A is open year-round.

About 2.5 miles (4 km) farther on the right, across the road from Sunset Point, **Sunset Campground** (877/444-6777, www.recreation.gov, late spring-early fall, tents $20, RVs $30, no hookups) offers good hiking access. Sunset has two campsites on Loop A that are accessible to people with disabilities. **Reservations** are accepted May-October; make reservations at least two days in advance.

Basic groceries, camping supplies, showers, and a laundry room are available at the General Store (mid-Apr.-late Sept.) between North Campground and Sunrise Point. The rest of the year, you can go to Ruby's Inn for these services.

Public Campgrounds

About 20-30 minutes from the park, Dixie National Forest has three US Forest Service campgrounds. Nestled among ponderosa pines, these campgrounds often have room when those in the park are full. Sites can be reserved (877/444-6777, www.recreation.gov, $8 reservation fee) at Pine Lake, Kings Creek, and Red Canyon Campgrounds.

Pine Lake Campground (late May-mid-Sept., $19) is at 8,300 feet (2,530 m) elevation in a forest of ponderosa pine, spruce, and juniper just east of its namesake lake. From the highway junction north of the park, head northeast 11 miles (17.7 km) on gravel-surfaced Highway 63, then turn southeast and go 6 miles (9.7 km). Contact the Escalante Ranger District Office in Escalante (435/826-5499) for more information.

Kings Creek Campground (usually May-late Sept., $19) is on the west shore of Tropic Reservoir, which has a boat ramp and trout fishing. Trails for hikers and ATVs begin at the campground, which sits at 8,000 feet (2,438 m) elevation. Go 2.8 miles (4.5 km) west of the park turnoff on Highway 12, then head 7 miles (11.3 km) south on the gravel East Fork Sevier River Road.

Just off Highway 12, **Red Canyon**

1: a cabin at Bryce Canyon Lodge **2:** Bryce Glamp & Camp domes

Campground (late May-late Sept., $20) is 4 miles (6.4 km) east of US 89. It's at 7,400 feet (2,456 m) elevation below brilliantly colored cliffs. No online reservations are available; contact the Red Canyon Visitor Center (435/676-2676, www.fs.usda.gov) for more information on Kings Creek and Red Canyon Campgrounds.

Camping is available a little farther away at beautiful **Kodachrome Basin State Park** (801/322-3770 or 800/322-3770, www.reserveamerica.com, tents $35, RVs $45 with hookups, bunkhouse $95, $8 reservation fee). From Bryce, take Highway 12 east to Cannonville, then head 9 miles (14.5 km) south to the park.

Private Campgrounds

Private campgrounds in the area tend to cost $30 or more. The convenient **Ruby's Inn Campground** (26 S. Main St., 435/834-5301 or 866/878-9373, Apr.-Oct.) has spaces for tents ($32) and RVs ($50)—note that you'll pay more if your party has more than two campers. Full hookups are available, and showers and a laundry room are open year-round. There's also a few tepees (from $41) and bunkhouse-style cabins (bedding not provided, $60).

Bryce Canyon Pines Campground (Hwy. 12, Milepost 10, 435/834-5441 or 800/892-7923, www.brycecanyonmotel.com, Apr.-Oct., tents $29, RVs $50), 4 miles (6.4 km) west of the park entrance, has an indoor pool, a game room, groceries, and shaded sites.

INFORMATION AND SERVICES

The **general store** at Ruby's (26 S. Main St., 866/866-6616) has a large stock of groceries, camping and fishing supplies, film and processing, Native American crafts, books, and other souvenirs. The Bryce **Post Office** is at the store as well. Horseback rides, helicopter tours, and airplane rides are arranged in the lobby. In winter, cross-country skiers can rent gear and use trails located near the inn as well as in the park. Snowmobile trails are available (snowmobiles may not be used within the park). Western-fronted shops across from Ruby's Inn offer trail rides, chuck wagon dinners, mountain bike rentals, souvenirs, and a petting farm.

GETTING THERE AND AROUND

Bryce Canyon National Park is just south of the incredibly scenic Highway 12, between US 89 and Tropic. To reach the park from Bryce Junction (7 mi/11.3 km south of Panguitch at the intersection of US 89 and Hwy. 12), head 14 miles (22.5 km) east on Highway 12, then south 3 miles (4.8 km) on Highway 63. From Escalante, it's about 50 miles (81 km) west on Highway 12 to the turnoff for Bryce; turn south onto Highway 63 for the final 3 miles (4.8 km) into the park (winter snow occasionally closes this section). Both approaches have spectacular scenery. **Free parking** is available at the visitor center or near the shuttle bus stops by Ruby's Inn.

From Las Vegas, it's a 4-hour, 259-mile (417-km) drive to Bryce, a short stretch of which takes you through Arizona. The drive is mostly north on I-15, with the last hour on smaller highways, including Highway 20, US 89, and Highway 12. The 90-minute, 89-mile (143-km) drive from Cedar City to Bryce follows the last part of the route from Las Vegas, with a short stretch on I-15, followed by smaller highways.

You can drive your own vehicle into Bryce Canyon National Park. However, trailers aren't allowed past Sunset Campground. Trailer parking is available at the visitor center. Keep in mind that in peak season, rangers say there's about one parking space for every four cars entering the park, so you may have a more pleasant experiencing touring around via the shuttle.

Park Shuttle Bus

During the crowded summer months, the National Park Service runs the free **Bryce Canyon Shuttle** (every 15-20 minutes 8am-8pm daily mid-Apr.-mid-Oct., shorter hours early and late in the season). Wheelchair-accessible buses run during peak summer season from the shuttle parking and boarding area at the junction of Highways 12 and 63 to the visitor center, with stops at Ruby's Inn and Ruby's Campground. From the visitor center, the shuttle travels to the park's developed areas, including all the main amphitheater viewpoints, Sunset Campground, Bryce Canyon Lodge, and up to Rainbow Point. Passengers can take as long as they like at any viewpoint, then catch a later bus. The shuttle bus service also makes it easier for hikers, who don't need to worry about car shuttles between trailheads.

Vicinity of Bryce Canyon

To escape the tour-bus bustle at Bryce's rim, head just a few miles west on scenic Highway 12, where you'll find a few hiking trails, mountain biking trails, and hoodoos (although none that quite rival Bryce Amphitheater), along with a visitor center that can point you in the right direction.

RED CANYON

The drive on Highway 12 between US 89 and the turnoff for Bryce Canyon National Park passes through this well-named canyon. Because Red Canyon is not part of the national park—it's part of Dixie National Forest—many of the trails are open to mountain biking and ATV riding. Red Canyon's bike trails are spectacularly scenic and exhilarating. Ruby's Inn provides a shuttle service for Red Canyon mountain bikers, but there's also a paved recreation path that runs alongside Highway 12 that makes for an easy climb to access trails.

Staff members at the **Red Canyon Visitor Center** (Hwy. 12, between Mileposts 3 and 4, 435/676-2676, www.fs.usda.gov, 9am-6pm Fri.-Mon., 10am-3pm Tues.-Thurs.) can tell you about the trails and scenic backcountry roads that wind through the area. Books and maps are available.

Hiking

The US Forest Service maintains many scenic hiking trails that wind back from the highway for a closer look at the geology. The following trails are open to hikers only. Because this is not part of the national park, dogs are permitted.

Pink Ledges Trail

Distance: *1 mile (1.6 km) round-trip*
Duration: *30 minutes*
Elevation gain: *100 feet (30 m)*
Effort: *easy*
Trailhead: *Red Canyon Visitor Center*

The Pink Ledges Trail, the easiest and most popular trail in the area, loops past intriguing geological features. Signs identify some of the trees and plants.

Birdseye Trail

Distance: *1.6 miles (2.6 km) round-trip*
Duration: *1 hour*
Elevation gain: *150 feet (46 m)*
Effort: *easy-moderate*
Trailhead: *Red Canyon Visitor Center*

The Birdseye Trail winds by red-rock formations, offers a bird's-eye view, and connects the visitor center with the short Photo Trail and its parking area on Highway 12, just inside the forest boundary.

Buckhorn Trail

Distance: *1.8 miles (2.9 km) round-trip*
Duration: *1.5 hours*
Elevation gain: *250 feet (76 m)*
Effort: *moderate-strenuous*
Trailhead: *Red Canyon Campground, site 23*

This trail climbs to views of the interesting geology of Red Canyon. It's a good choice if you'd like to burn off a little energy and get a

1

2

sense of the surrounding country. The campground is on the south side of Highway 12 between Mileposts 3 and 4.

For a longer hike, 4 miles (6.4 km) one-way, turn left off the Buckhorn Trail after about 0.6 mile (1 km) onto the Golden Wall Trail. Follow the Golden Wall Trail south past yellow limestone walls, then north again back to Highway 12, where it exits across from the visitor center. A short spur, the Castle Bridge Trail, climbs to a ridge overlooking the Golden Wall before rejoining the Golden Wall Trail.

Tunnel Trail

Distance: *1 mile (1.6 km) round-trip*
Duration: *1 hour*
Elevation gain: *300 feet (91 m)*
Effort: *moderate*
Trailhead: *Highway 12 pullout, just west of the tunnels*

The Tunnel Trail ascends to fine views of the canyon and the two highway tunnels. The trail crosses a streambed and climbs a ridge to access the views.

Road and Mountain Biking

A wonderful paved bike path parallels Highway 12 for 8.6 miles (13.8 km) through Red Canyon, taking in scenic red-rock views and climbing at a steady yet moderate grade up the canyon. Parking lots are located at either end of the trail, at the Thunder Mountain trailhead and Coyote Hollow Road (a dirt Forest Service road that can be biked). This paved path also accesses two mountain bike rides: Casto Canyon Trail and Thunder Mountain Trail.

Casto Canyon Trail

Casto Canyon, a 5.5-mile (8.9-km) one-way trail, winds through red-rock formations and forest. This ride starts west of the Red Canyon Visitor Center, about 2 miles (3.2 km) east of US 89. Turn north from Highway 12 onto Forest Road 118 and continue about 3 miles (4.8 km) to the Casto Canyon parking lot. For part of the way, the trail is shared with ATVs, but then the bike trail splits off to the right. The usual turnaround point is at Sanford Road. While the trail's nothing to write home about, it tours beautiful scenery. This ride can be linked with other trails for a longer loop, and it also intersects with several side trails if you want a shorter ride.

1: the drive through Red Canyon 2: hoodoo views on Thunder Mountain Trail

★ Thunder Mountain Trail

Thunder Mountain is an 8.1-mile (13-km) trail that's among the best stretches of singletrack in southern Utah. The trail tours hoodoo-filled terrain rivaling Bryce. While you can pedal up Thunder Mountain, it's not a pleasant climb, so the recommended route is to bike up the Red Canyon Bike Path, pedal for a couple of miles up the dirt Coyote Hollow Road, then take Thunder Mountain back down to your starting point. While this trail is rated intermediate-difficult, the primary challenges lie in the loose dirt and exposure. Less advanced riders can easily hop off the saddle over any unnerving sections. Besides the lively riding through a variety of environments and landscapes, this trail takes in sweeping views of the surrounding hoodoo country and gets you up close with some remarkable red-rock formations.

For more information, stop by the **Red Canyon Visitor Center** (Hwy. 12, between Mileposts 3 and 4, 435/676-2676, www.fs.usda.gov, 9am-6pm Fri.-Mon., 10am-3pm Tues.-Thurs.) for more information; you can also download a map from the website.

BRYCE MUSEUM AND WILDLIFE ADVENTURE

A museum and natural history complex, **Bryce Museum and Wildlife Adventure** (1945 W. Hwy. 12, 435/834-5555, www.brycewildlifeadventure.com, 9am-7pm daily Apr.-Nov. 15, $8, $2 under age 11) is a wildlife showcase housed in a large building just west of the turnoff to Bryce Canyon. This taxidermy collection depicts more than 800 animals from around the world displayed in dioramas resembling their natural habitats. It's actually quite well done, and kids seem to love it. There's also a good collection of Native American artifacts and a beautiful butterfly display. You can also rent ATVs here.

TROPIC

Just a 15-minute drive from Bryce, the town of Tropic has some lovely inns and bed-and-breakfasts, along with a few good restaurants. It's a good base camp for the national park if you didn't manage to snag a room in the Lodge at Bryce Canyon or want to avoid the commercialized vibe of the Ruby's Inn complex in the town of Bryce. Tropic also offers a quiet back entrance into Bryce Amphitheater, via the Tropic Trail.

The town's settler history traces back to 1875, when Latter-day Saints pioneer Ebenezer Bryce homesteaded near the town site of Tropic until dealing with the rugged land became too difficult. He is remembered as saying of the area, "Well, it's a hell of a place to lose a cow." He left five years later for more promising land in Arizona. The name of Bryce Canyon National Park commemorates his efforts. Other pioneers settled six villages near the upper Paria River between 1876 and 1891. The town of Tropic, along with the even smaller communities of Cannonville and Henrieville, are still around today.

Food

There are a few dining options in town. A good bet is **Rustler's Restaurant** (141 N. Main St., 435/679-8383, 7am-9pm daily early spring-late fall, $16-27), which is part of Clark's Grocery, an all-around institution that, in addition to selling groceries, serves Mexican food, pasta, pizza, ice cream, and steaks from a variety of venues within a complex that's essentially the town center.

Hungry for brisket or pulled pork? Order at the counter at **i.d.k. Barbecue** (161 N. Main St., 435/679-8353, www.idkbarbecue.com, 11am-9pm Mon.-Sat., $9-20) and sample what some have called the state's best barbecue. Top it off with peach cobbler served in a cone.

At the Stone Canyon Inn, the **Stone Hearth Grille** (1380 W. Stone Canyon Ln., 435/679-8923, www.stonehearthgrille.com, 5pm-9pm daily Mar.-Oct., reservations advised, $28-42) has an upscale atmosphere and menu. The food is the best for miles around. In good weather, have your meal on the terrace and enjoy the lovely off-the-beaten-path setting.

i.d.k. Barbecue in Tropic

Accommodations

Travelers think of Tropic primarily for its cache of motels lining Main Street (Hwy. 12), but several pleasant B&Bs also grace the town.

$100-150

At the **Bryce Canyon Inn** (21 N. Main St., 435/679-8502 or 800/592-1468, www.brycecanyoninn.com, Mar.-Oct., $77 motel rooms, $99-199 cabins), the tidy cabins are nicely furnished and are one of the more appealing options in the Bryce neighborhood. The economy motel rooms are small but clean and a good deal. There's also a good coffee shop on the premises.

Red Ledges Inn (181 N. Main St., 435/679-8811, www.redledgesinn.com, $128-184) offers conventional motel rooms in an attractive wood-fronted Western-style motel. Pets are permitted for an additional fee.

Over $150

The ★ **Stone Canyon Inn** (1380 W. Stone Canyon Ln., 435/679-8611 or 866/489-4680, www.stonecanyoninn.com, $197-387), a couple of miles west of downtown Tropic with views of Bryce, offers the most luxurious lodging in the region inside a striking modern building. Choose from several two-bedroom cabins with kitchens or bungalows configured to sleep up to four and "tree houses" that allow you to bed down above the trees. Stone Canyon also has a notably good restaurant and a shared sauna.

At the east end of town, on a family farm, the **Bullberry Inn B&B** (412 S. Hwy. 12, 435/668-9911, https://bullberryinn.com, late Mar.-Oct., $190-195) has wraparound porches and simple yet pleasant guest rooms with private baths and rustic pine furniture.

Bryce Trails B&B (1001 W. Bryce Way, 435/231-4436, www.brycetrail.com, $204-244) is comfortably off the main drag. Every guest room has a good view as well as a stunning photograph taken by the owners, who also sometimes teach one-on-one photography classes

Campgrounds

Head east to Cannonville for **Cannonville/Bryce Valley KOA** (215 N. Red Rock Dr., Cannonville, 435/679-8988, www.koa.com, tents $33-37, RVs $43-72, camping cabins $70-79), or continue south from Cannonville to **Kodachrome Basin State Park** (801/322-3770 or 800/322-3770, www.reserveamerica.com, tents $35, RVs $45 with hookups, bunkhouse $95, $8 reservation fee).

Getting There

Tropic is 11 miles (17.7 km) east of Bryce Canyon National Park on Highway 12, and is visible from many of the park's viewpoints.

PANGUITCH

A convenient stopover between Zion and Bryce, Panguitch is one of the more pleasant towns in this part of Utah, with an abundance of reasonably priced motels and a couple of good places to eat. Pioneers arrived in 1864, but the Ute people drove them out just two years later. A second attempt by settlers in 1871 succeeded, and Panguitch (the name comes from the Paiute word for "big fish") is now the largest town in the area.

Sights

The **city park** on the north edge of town has picnic tables, a playground, tennis courts, and a visitor information cabin. A **swimming pool** (250 E. Center St., 435/676-2259) is by the high school. You can even catch a movie in Panguitch—the **Gem Theater** (105 N. Main St., 435/676-2221, www.panguitchgem.com, 4pm-10pm Mon.-Tues. and Thurs.-Sat., $8.50 adults, $6.50 children and seniors) screens a couple of films at a time, and also has a small exhibit on dinosaurs and a rock shop worth checking out before or after your show. The theater serves a limited menu of tacos and tamales, homemade ice cream, typical theater snacks, and gourmet hot chocolate.

Travelers in the area during the second weekend in June should try to swing by for the annual **Quilt Walk** (www.quiltwalk.org), an all-out festival with historic home tours, quilting classes, and lots of food. The Quilt Walk commemorates a group of seven pioneers who trudged through snow to bring food back to starving townspeople—they spread quilts on the deep, soft snow and walked on them in order not to sink.

Food

A longtime favorite in Panguitch is the mesquite-grilled meat at **Cowboy's Smokehouse Café** (95 N. Main St., 435/676-8030, www.thecowboysmokehouse.com, 8am-9pm Mon.-Thurs., 7am-10pm Fri.-Sat. mid-Mar.-mid-Oct., $12-33). Try the barbecue ribs or bone-in chicken with a cup of homemade soup—and end the meal on a sweet note with Dutch oven cobbler.

The **Flying Goat Café** (41 N. Main St., 801/891-8612, 8am-11:30am Mon.-Fri., 8am-3pm Sat.-Sun., $9-15) serves up hearty breakfasts and sandwiches and salads for lunch. The Banana Foster Crepes are a great way to start a day of hiking.

With over three decades serving up pies in Panguitch, **C Stop Pizza** (561 E. Center St., 435/676-8366, 11am-9pm Mon.-Sat., medium pizza $15-22) is a local favorite. Family owned and operated, this pizzeria serves up house specialties like a bacon cheeseburger pie, alongside build-your-own options and gluten-free crusts. It also offers sandwiches, salads, and novelty items like a pizza taco.

Accommodations

$50-100

Panguitch is the best place in greater Bryce Canyon to find an affordable motel room—there are more than a dozen older motor-court lodgings, most quite basic but well-maintained. Of these, the **Blue Pine Motel** (130 N. Main St., 435/676-8197 or 800/299-6115, www.bluepinemotel.com, $78-94) is one of the better options, with friendly staff and clean, well-furnished guest rooms that include microwaves and fridges.

Nothing to do with either Zane Grey or Jerry Garcia, the older yet well-kept **Purple Sage Motel** (132 E. Center St., 435/676-8536, www.purplesagemotel.biz, $79-129) is nothing fancy but a good value. The most expensive room is a family suite.

Over $150

Cottonwood Meadow Lodge (US 89, Milepost 123, 435/676-8950, www.brycecanyoncabins.com, Apr.-Oct., 2-night minimum, $185-325 plus one-time cleaning fee) is the exception to the modest-accommodations rule in the Panguitch area. This upscale lodge features four units, all with kitchens: a bunkhouse, an 1860s-era log cabin, a three-bedroom farmhouse, and an attractively rehabbed barn that sleeps six. The property is about 15 minutes from town and 20 minutes from Bryce Canyon National Park. Ranch animals are available for visits, and the Sevier River runs through the property, located 2 miles (3.2 km) south of Highway 12 on US 89.

Campgrounds

Hitch-N-Post Campground (420 N. Main St., 435/676-2436, www.hitchnpostrv.com, year-round) offers spaces for RVs ($42-48) and also rents out a few apartments ($120); showers and a laundry room are available. On the road to Panguitch Lake, the **Panguitch KOA Campground** (555 S. Main St., 435/676-2225, Apr.-Oct., tents $29-34, RVs $42-57, camping cabins $53, deluxe cabins $110-140) has a pool, a recreation room, laundry, and showers.

The closest public campground is in **Red Canyon** (Hwy. 12, 435/676-2676, www.fs.usda.gov, late May-late Sept., $20), with 37 first-come, first-served sites and drinking water and showers ($2) available.

Information and Services

Contact **Bryce Canyon Country** (435/676-1160 or 800/444-6689, www.brycecanyoncountry.com) for information on Panguitch and the nearby area. The **Powell Ranger District Office** (225 E. Center St., 435/676-9300, 8am-4:30pm Mon.-Fri.) of Dixie National Forest has information on campgrounds, hiking trails, fishing, and scenic drives in the forest and canyons surrounding Bryce Canyon National Park.

Panguitch has a **post office** (65 N. 100 W.), and **Garfield Memorial Hospital** (200 N. 400 E., hospital 435/676-8811, clinic 435/676-8811) is the main hospital in this part of the state.

Getting There

On US 89, Panguitch is 7 miles (11.3 km) north of Bryce Junction (Hwy. 12 and US 89). From Bryce Junction, it is 11 miles (17.7 km) east on Highway 12 to Bryce Canyon National Park.

ALONG US 89

If you're driving between Zion and Bryce, you'll probably follow US 89, at least as far as Mount Carmel Junction. Head farther south to Kanab to find a wide selection of mostly inexpensive lodging and access to the southwestern part of Grand Staircase-Escalante National Monument.

At Mount Carmel Junction, Highway 9 turns west from US 89 to Zion National Park. A good place to stay here is the **Best Western East Zion Thunderbird Resort** (435/648-2203, www.bestwestern.com, $175-210), which features a nine-hole golf course, a pool, and large guest rooms with balconies.

On Highway 9, just a few miles east of Zion National Park, are the rustic log cabins and lodge at **Zion Mountain Ranch** (E. Hwy. 9, 435/648-2555 or 866/648-2555, www.zmr.com, cabins start at $250). The cabins all have king beds and private baths plus microwaves and fridges; family lodges offer two or three bedrooms. The setting is great, with expansive views, a buffalo herd, and a decent on-site restaurant, the Bison Grill. Horseback riding and other outdoor recreation is offered.

KANAB AND VICINITY

Striking scenery surrounds this small town in Utah's far south. The Vermilion Cliffs to the west and east glow with a fiery intensity at sunrise and sunset. Streams have cut splendid canyons into surrounding plateaus. The Paiutes knew the spot as kanab, meaning "place of the willows," and the trees still grow along Kanab Creek. Latter-day Saints pioneers arrived in the mid-1860s and tried to farm along the unpredictable creek. Irrigation difficulties culminated in the massive floods of 1883. Ranching proved better suited to this rugged land.

Hollywood discovered this dramatic scenery in the 1920s and has filmed over 150 movies and TV series here since, including *The Lone Ranger, The Greatest Story Ever Told,* and *Gunsmoke.* Film crews have constructed several Western sets near Kanab, but most are on private land and difficult to visit.

While most park visitors see Kanab (pop. 4,300) as a stopover on trips to Bryce, Zion, and Grand Canyon National Parks, along with the southern reaches of the monument and trips to see the Wave, a few interesting sites around town warrant more than a sleep-eat-dash visit. In fact, the presence of several nicely refurbished hotels and great dining spots makes this one of the nicest and most affordable places to stay in southwest Utah.

Sights

Best Friends Animal Sanctuary

The largest no-kill animal shelter in the country, **Best Friends Animal Sanctuary** (5001 Angel Canyon Rd., 435/688-2327, www.bestfriends.org, 8am-5pm daily, check website for tour times, reservations required, donation) takes in unwanted or abused animals and provides rehabilitation when possible. Giant octagonal doghouses house former research animals, old dogs, sick dogs, aggressive dogs, and dogs that have been abused or neglected, alongside cats, rabbits, birds, pot-bellied pigs, and horses. Many animals are adopted out, but all are given forever homes and care.

The shelter's origins date back to the 1970s, when a group of animal lovers began trying to prevent euthanasia by rescuing animals that were about to be put to sleep by shelters. In the early 1980s, this group of rescuers bought land in Angel Canyon just north of Kanab

1
2
3
4
CAVE
Museum of
Ancient

and—with their motley crew of animals—established this sanctuary. Now over 1,600 animals live here at any given time, and the shelter is the county's largest employer, with more than 200 staff members. And volunteers spend anywhere from a day to a couple months feeding, walking, socializing with, and cleaning up after the animals. Kanab is usually full of shelter volunteers spending their vacations here.

Best Friends runs a variety of tours several times a day. Call for reservations or to learn more about volunteering. There's no charge for the tour, but donations are accepted.

Moqui Cave

The natural **Moqui Cave** (4581 US 89, 5 mi/8 km north of Kanab, 435/644-8525, www.moqui-cave.com, 9am-7pm Mon.-Sat. late May-early Sept., 10am-4pm Mon.-Sat. early Sept.-late May, $6) has been turned into a roadside attraction with a large collection of Native American artifacts. Most of the arrowheads, pottery, sandals, and burial items on display have been excavated locally. See fossils, rocks, and minerals, including what's claimed to be one of the largest fluorescent mineral displays in the country. There's even a Prohibition-era speakeasy (not open for drinks). The collections and gift shop are within a spacious cave that stays pleasantly cool even in the hottest weather.

Kanab Museum

The 1895 Queen Anne-style Victorian **Kanab Museum** (13 S. 100 E., 435/644-3966, www.kanabmuseum.org, 10am-6pm daily, free) reflects the prosperity of two of Kanab's early Latter-day Saints residents. Henry Bowman built it, lived here two years before going on a mission, then sold to Thomas Chamberlain, a leader in the Latter-day Saints' United Order with six wives and 55 children. A guide will show you around the house and explain its architectural details. Other exhibits detail the history of Kanab, stretching all the way back to its first Ancestral Puebloan inhabitants.

Little Hollywood Movie Museum

The movie-set replica **Little Hollywood Movie Museum** (297 W. Center St., 435/644-5337, www.littlehollywoodmuseum.org, 9am-5pm daily Apr.-Oct., free) shows off a bit of Hollywood's Old West in Kanab. Some of the buildings have seen actual use in movies and TV shows. Exhibits display Western and movie memorabilia, and there's a selection of Western costumes available for rent. There are also souvenir photos, a gift shop, a saloon, and chuck wagon dinners.

Tours

Kanab is central to an amazing number of sights, and if you'd like the pros to handle the logistics of your visit, turn to **Dreamland Safari Tours** (435/292-3985, www.dreamlandtours.net, from $99 adults, $79 children). Dreamland offers half-day and full-day tours of slot canyons, petroglyphs, and dinosaur tracks.

Hiking

Kanab City Trail

Distance: *1.5 miles (2.4 km) one-way*
Duration: *2 hours*
Elevation gain: *800 feet (244 m)*
Effort: *moderate*
Trailhead: *north end of 100 East, near the city park*

This well-graded path (previously called Squaw Trail, but thankfully renamed) provides a close look at the geology, plant life, and animals of the Vermilion Cliffs just north of town. To cut the hike down by 1 mile (1.6 km) and cut the elevation gain in half, turn around at the first overlook, where views to the south take in Kanab, Fredonia, Kanab Canyon, and the vast Kaibab Plateau. At the top, look north to see the White, Gray, and Pink Cliffs of the Grand Staircase. Pick up a trail guide at the **Kanab Visitor Center** (745 E. US 89, 435/644-1300, 9am-4pm Tues.-Sat.). Brochures may also be available at the

1: a cabin at Zion Mountain Ranch **2:** seasonal gnocchi dish at Zion Mountain Ranch **3:** horses at Zion Mountain Ranch **4:** Moqui Cave, outside Kanab

trailhead. Bring water, and in summer, try to get a very early start.

Entertainment and Events

A unique Kanab event is the **Sighthound Shivoo/Greyhound Gathering** (www.greyhoundgang.com, mid-May most years), when hundreds of greyhounds and other sighthounds converge on the town, accompanied by their people, a breed to themselves. Events include a parade, a race, and a howl-in. The Greyhound Gang, a nonprofit organization dedicated to the rescue, rehabilitation, and adoption of former racing greyhounds, hosts this festival.

Also during May, Kanab is the center of activity for the **Amazing Earthfest** (435/644-3735, http://amazingearthfest.com), which celebrates land and life on the Colorado Plateau with lectures, workshops, and outdoor activities delving into the area's natural and human history. Most events are free.

Shopping

Find a good selection of books, camping gear, and clothing, along with a little coffee bar, at **Willow Canyon Outdoor** (263 S. 100 E., 435/644-8884, www.willowcanyon.com).

Denny's Wigwam (78 E. Center St., 435/644-2452, www.dennyswigwam.com) is a landmark Old West trading post with a broad selection of Western jewelry, cowboy hats and boots, and souvenirs.

Food

Start the day at ★ **Kanab Creek Bakery** (238 W. Center St., 435/644-5689, https://kanabcreekbakery.com, 6:30am-5pm Tues.-Sun. summer, limited hours off-season, breakfast $9-16), a European-style bakery-café operated by a Belgian-born woman. The breads and pastries are thoroughly authentic, and you can get a heartier breakfast or lunch with omelets, quiche, and fresh sandwiches on the menu.

★ **Sego** (190 N. 300 W., 435/644-5680, www.segokanab.com, 5pm-9pm Mon.-Wed. and Fri.-Sat., $14-35) is a surprisingly good find in this little town. Located in the Canyons Boutique Hotel, it has a lively menu, with starters like artisanal toast or a pork belly and watermelon salad. Most dishes are small plates designed for sharing.

Another good bet is the ★ **Rocking V Café** (97 W. Center St., 435/644-8001, www.rockingvcafe.com, 11:30am-9:30pm Thurs.-Mon., dinner $18-48), with a casual setting and modern Southwestern food. Rocking V, which caters to vegans and steak lovers alike, pays homage to the "slow food" movement by making everything from scratch. Be sure to check out the art gallery upstairs.

It's small and often crowded, but friendly, family-run **Escobar's Mexican Restaurant** (373 E. 300 S., 435/644-3739, www.escobarskanab.com, 11:30am-9pm Sun.-Mon. and Wed.-Fri., $13-29) is the place for a Mexican lunch or dinner.

Wild Thyme Café (198 S. 100 E., 435/644-2848, https://wildthymekanab.com, 11:30am-9pm daily, $17-44) focuses on Southwest and Cajun flavors, supported by the restaurant's home-grown greens and vegetables. Pistachio chicken with poblano cream is a standout. Call to confirm winter hours.

Travelers setting out from Kanab should note that this is the best place for many miles around to stock up on groceries. **Honey's Marketplace** (260 E. 300 S., 435/644-5877, 7am-10pm Mon.-Sat.) is a good grocery store on the way out of town to the east; note that it's closed Sunday.

Accommodations

While a number of new hotels from the major chains line the edge of town, Kanab has a number of carefully refurbished vintage motor-court hotels to fit diverse tastes and budgets. They're fun and within easy walking distance of downtown. Reservations are a good idea mid-May-summer. Almost all the lodgings are along US 89, which follows 300 West, Center, 100 East, and 300 South through town.

1: a salad at Sego **2:** Canyons Boutique Hotel **3:** the dunes of Coral Pink Sand Dunes State Park

1
Canyons
HOTEL
sego
RESTAURANT
2
3

$100-150

Relive Kanab's Hollywood heyday at the **Parry Lodge** (89 E. Center St., 435/644-2601 or 877/386-4383, www.parrylodge.com, $99-193). Opened in 1892 and operated during Kanab's glory days as a moviemaking center, the Parry Lodge was where the stars and crews stayed. Nearly a century later, this is still a pleasantly old-fashioned place to spend the night, and it has lots of character. At the very least, you'll want to stroll through the lobby to see photos of the celebrities who once stayed here.

★ **Canyons Lodge** (236 N. 300 W., 844/322-8824, www.canyonslodge.com, $115-232) is an extensively renovated hotel with pleasant log cabin-style guest rooms, all with fridges and microwaves, plus an outdoor pool and breakfast included. What was once a typical mom-and-pop motel is now a stylish place to stay, though rooms tend to be on the small side. Several rooms are pet-friendly, and because it's a popular place for visitors to Best Friends Animal Sanctuary, it's best to reserve in advance. Canyons Lodge is one of several properties in town that have been renovated by local hotel group Canyons Collection (www.thecanyonscollection.com).

Another offering from Canyons Collection, the **Quail Park Lodge** (125 N. 300 W., 435/644-8700, www.quailparklodge.com, $89-119) is a tricked-out and updated 1960s motel, with a well-thought-out combination of vintage kitsch, mid-century modern, and quality linens. The motel has a pool and accepts pets. The lodge also has cruiser bicycles to rent (free to guests).

Over $150

Most of Kanab's accommodations accept dogs, but only the ★ **Best Friends Roadhouse** (30 N. 300 W., 435/644-3400, https://bestfriendsroadhouse.org, $153-339) offers dog-washing stations, a fenced dog park, snuggle zones, pet walkers (for a fee), and a shuttle to the Best Friends Animal Sanctuary. The sparse decor is attractive and includes comfy pet beds. The most expensive room is a two-story kitchenette suite. A vegan continental breakfast is included at the adjoining mercantile, which also sells snacks for pets and their people.

A Canyons Collection property, the ★ **Canyons Boutique Hotel** (190 N. 300 W., 435/644-8660, www.canyonshotel.com, $143-169) has a color scheme that echoes nearby Coral Pink Sand Dunes. But the rooms are well appointed, the decor is welcoming, and the beds are comfy. The entire top floor is taken up by a three-bedroom penthouse ($259), and most rooms have luxuriously large spa bathtubs. Breakfast is included for all guests, and dinner is available, too, at Sego, a fine restaurant located on the first floor.

Another stylish entry from Canyons Collections is **Flagstone Boutique Inn and Suites** (223 W. Center St., 435/429-1206 or 844/322-8824, www.theflagstoneinn.com, $125-189), a former 1940s motor lodge updated with contemporary pizzazz. Some rooms have full or partial kitchens and are set up for extended stays, so daily housekeeping is not provided. The on-site Peekaboo Canyon Wood-fired Kitchen (open for three meals daily) makes vegetarian and vegan pizza and other specialties. This is a perfect spot for those using Kanab as a base camp for park and monument exploration.

If you're traveling with a group that plans to spend several nights in Kanab, the **Kanab Garden Cottages** (various locations, 435/429-1206, www.kanabcottages.com, $149-189) are beautifully furnished three- or four-bedroom pet-friendly houses that can easily sleep up to eight within walking distance of town.

North of Kanab, at Mount Carmel Junction, the **Best Western East Zion Thunderbird Resort** (4530 State St., Mount Carmel, 435/648-2203, www.bestwestern.com, $175-210) has a pool, a nine-hole golf course, and a restaurant. This pleasant crossroads motel is convenient if you're heading to Zion or Bryce Canyon National Parks. All guest rooms have balconies or patios.

Northwest of Kanab, just a few miles east

of Zion National Park, are the rustic log cabins and lodges of **Zion Mountain Ranch** (9065 W. Hwy. 9, 435/648-2555 or 866/648-2555, www.zmr.com, cabins from $250). The simple and very quiet cabins all have king beds and private baths, plus microwaves and fridges. Family lodges offer two or three bedrooms, while the larger lodges sleep up to 12. The real draw here is the setting, right out of a Western movie, with expansive views and a buffalo herd, plus a good on-site restaurant. Horseback riding and other guided trips are offered.

Campgrounds

The campground at **Coral Pink Sand Dunes State Park** (435/648-2800, https://stateparks.utah.gov, $25-40) has restrooms with showers, paved pull-through sites, and a dump station. It's a pleasant, shady spot, though it can hum with ATV traffic. It's open year-round, but the water is shut off from late October until Easter in March or April; winter campers must bring their own. Reservations are recommended for the busy Memorial Day-Labor Day season. About 8 miles (13 km) north of Kanab on US 89, head west on Hancock Road for 9.4 miles (15 km), then follow Coral Pink Sand Dunes Road for 3 miles (5 km) to reach the campground. The route is well marked.

Just north of the state park, the BLM maintains **Ponderosa Grove Campground** ($12) on the north edge of the dunes. There's no water here. From Kanab, head 8 miles (13 km) north on US 89, turn west onto Hancock Road (between Mileposts 72 and 73), and continue 7.3 miles (11.7 km) to the campground.

The **Kanab RV Corral** (483 S. 100 E., 435/644-5330, www.kanabrvcorral.com, year-round, $40-55) has RV sites (no tents) with hot showers, a pool, and laundry service. The **Hitch'n Post RV Park** (196 E. 300 S., 435/644-2142, www.hitchnpostrvpark.com, tents $30, RVs $45, house $99) has showers. The **J & J RV Park** (584 E. 300 S., 435/899-1956, https://jandjrvpark.com, mid-Apr.-late Oct., RVs $47-52) is a newer campground without much shade. It's less than appealing for tent campers, but a good bet for larger RVs.

Information and Services

Staff members at the **Kane County Information Center** (78 S. 100 E., 435/664-5033, www.visitsouthernutah.com, 8am-5pm Mon.-Fri.) offer literature and advice for services in Kanab and travel in Kane County. You can also visit the **Kanab Visitor Center** (745 E. US 89, 435/644-1300, 9am-4pm Tues.-Sat.) on the east edge of town.

Getting There

Situated on US 89, Kanab is 15 miles (24 km) south of Mount Carmel Junction (Hwy. 9 and US 89), a total of 40 miles (64 km) from Zion National Park, and just 7 miles (11.3 km) north of the Arizona-Utah border. From Kanab, US 89 continues southeast, providing access to the southern reaches of Grand Staircase and Kaiparowits Plateau and, 74 miles (119 km) later, Glen Canyon Dam at Page, Arizona.

CORAL PINK SAND DUNES STATE PARK

Churning air currents funneled by mountains have deposited huge sand dunes in a valley west of Kanab. Formed from eroded Navajo sandstone, the ever-changing dunes reach heights of several hundred feet and cover about 2,000 (809) of the park's 3,700 acres (1,497 ha). Different areas in **Coral Pink Sand Dunes State Park** (435/648-2800, https://stateparks.utah.gov, day-use $10 per vehicle, camping $25-40) are reserved for hiking, off-road vehicles, and camping.

There are no defined trails or sights within the park. Think of it more like a massive sandbox where you can make your own path or adventure. The park is a great spot to visit at sunrise or sunset (easy to do if you're camping), when the pink dunes glow even rosier with the light. It's also a fun spot for families with young kids who love playing in the sand—bonus points for bringing shovels and buckets. You can also rent sand boards or sleds at the park ($25). ATV enthusiasts are free to explore 90 percent of the dunes, and guided ATV tours are also available (from $210 for 1 hour).

The canyon country surrounding the park has good opportunities for hiking and off-road vehicle travel—grab maps and info from the **Kanab Visitor Center.** Drivers with 4WD vehicles can turn south on Sand Springs Road (1.5 mi/2.4 km east of Ponderosa Grove Campground), go 1 mile (1.6 km) to Sand Springs, and drive another 4 miles (6.4 km) to the **South Fork Indian Canyon Pictograph Site** in a pretty canyon. Visitors may not enter the Kaibab-Paiute Indian Reservation, which is south across the Arizona state line.

Getting There

While the park is only 6 or so miles (9.7 km) west of Kanab as the crow flies, the shortest route by car is on US 89. Drive north about 8 miles (13 km) on US 89, turn left on Hancock Road (between Mileposts 72 and 73), and travel 9.4 miles (15 km) on the paved road to its end. Then turn left (south) and go 3 miles (5 km) on a paved road into the park. From the north, follow US 89 for 3.5 miles (5.6 km) south of Mount Carmel Junction (Hwy. 9 and US 89), then turn right (south) and go 11 miles (17.7 km) on a paved road. The back road from Cane Beds in Arizona has about 16 miles (26 km) of gravel and dirt with some sandy spots. Ask a park ranger for current conditions.

St. George

Southern Utah's largest city, St. George (pop. 93,000) sits between lazy bends of the Virgin River and rocky hills of red sandstone. The city itself will have limited appeal to most park travelers; if your focus is Zion, you'll most likely use St. George as a jumping-off point. However, St. George's abundance of hotels, a clutch of good restaurants, public art and galleries in the old downtown, and a slickrock-laden state park a few miles away make it a handy place to begin or end your Utah desert adventure.

In 1861, over 300 Latter-day Saints families in the Salt Lake City area answered the church's call to go south to start the Cotton Mission, of which St. George became the center (hence the now controversial use of the term "Dixie" to describe the area). The cotton initiative ultimately failed, but the name unfortunately stuck. Brigham Young chose the city's name to honor George A. Smith, who had served as head of the Southern (Iron) Mission during the 1850s. The title *Saint* means simply that he was an LDS member.

SIGHTS

St. George Art Museum

The **St. George Art Museum** (47 E. 200 N., 435/627-4525, www.sgcity.org/artmuseum, 11am-6pm Tues.-Sat., $5 suggested donation), housed in a renovated beet-seed warehouse, is worth a visit both for its exhibits and its design. It's also a good place to get out of the sun for a couple of hours on a summer afternoon. The permanent collection has a strong regional emphasis, and visiting shows often feature contemporary Western art.

Dinosaur Trackways

Some 200 million years ago in the early Jurassic, when the supercontinent of Pangea was just beginning to break up, lakes covered this part of Utah, and dinosaurs were becoming the earth's dominant vertebrates. Two sites southeast of St. George preserve dinosaur tracks from the era. A full museum has been built around the more recently discovered tracks at Johnson Farm, and it's been called one of the world's 10 best dinosaur tracks sites. The Fort Pearce site is good

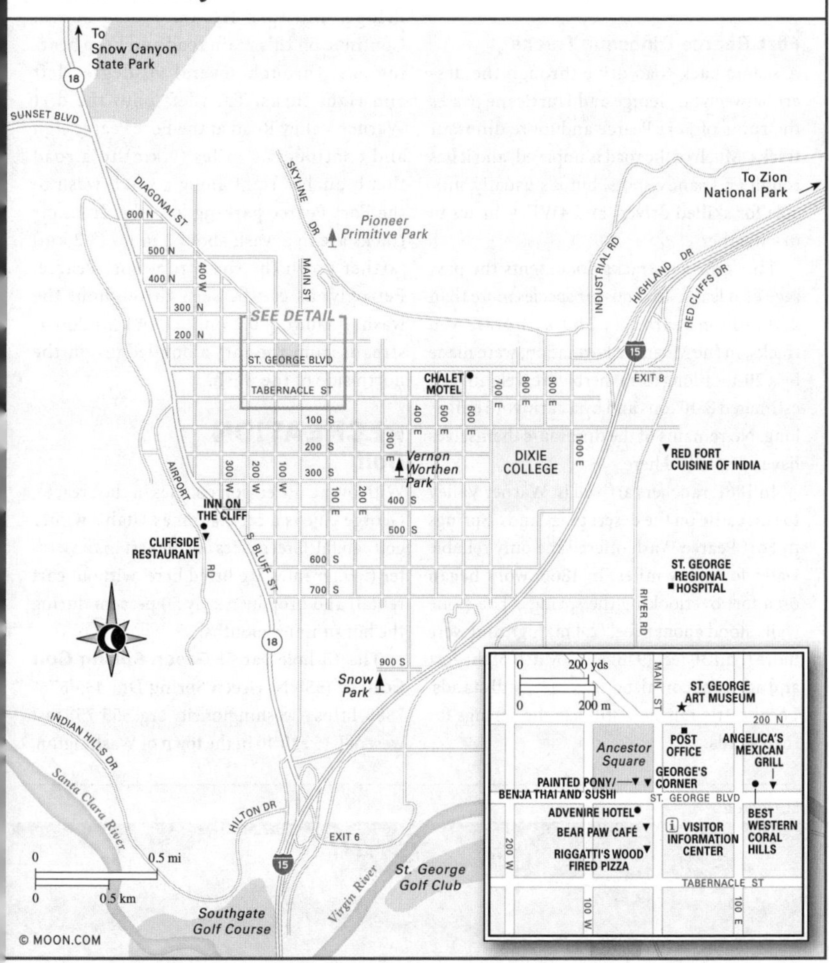

if you're hankering for back-road travel and like scouting dino tracks and petroglyphs in remote washes.

St. George Dinosaur Discovery Site at Johnson Farm

Tracks at the **St. George Dinosaur Discovery Site at Johnson Farm** (2180 E. Riverside Dr., 435/574-3466, www.utahdinosaurs.com, 10am-5pm Wed.-Mon., $8 adults, $7 seniors, $4 ages 4-17) were discovered in 2000 by a retired optometrist, and five years later, a full museum opened at this site. Since then, many more tracks have been uncovered, including those from three species of theropods (meat-eating dinosaurs), as well as important "trace fossils" of pond scum, invertebrates, and fish. Excavation work is ongoing, and a visitor center profiles exciting finds. Also quite remarkable are the "swim tracks," which settled a long-standing argument over whether dinosaurs actually swam. Johnson Farm is located about 2 miles (3.2 km) south of St. George off I-15 exit 10.

Fort Pearce Dinosaur Tracks

A scenic back-road drive through the desert between St. George and Hurricane passes the ruins of Fort Pearce and more dinosaur tracks. Much of the road is unpaved, and it has rough and sandy spots, but it's usually suitable for skilled drivers and 4WD vehicles in dry weather.

This group of tracks documents the passage of at least two dinosaur species more than 200 million years ago. The well-preserved tracks, in the Moenave Formation, were made by a 20-foot-long (6-m) herbivore weighing an estimated 8-10 tons and by a carnivore half as long. No remains of the dinosaurs themselves have been found here.

In 1861, ranchers arrived in Warner Valley to run cattle on the desert grasslands. Springs in Fort Pearce Wash offered the only reliable water for many miles. In 1866, work began on a fort overlooking the springs. The stone walls stood about 8 feet (2.4 m) high and were more than 30 feet (9 m) long. Much of the fort and adjacent corral, built in 1869, still stands. Local cattle ranchers still use the springs for their herds.

To reach this site from St. George, head south on River Road, cross the Virgin River Bridge, and turn left onto 1450 South. Continue on this main road and keep bearing east through several 90-degree left and right turns. Turn left onto the dirt Warner Valley Road at the Fort Pearce sign and continue 5.6 miles (9 km) to a road that branches right along a small wash to the Fort Pearce parking lot. The dinosaur tracks are in a wash about 2 miles (3.2 km) farther down the road from Fort Pearce. Petroglyphs can be seen throughout the wash, including 0.25 mile (0.4 km) downstream from the fort along ledges on the north side of the wash.

RECREATION

Golf

With over a dozen golf courses in the area, St. George enjoys a reputation as Utah's winter golf capital. Greens fees are highest in the winter (winter rates are listed here, without cart rental) and drop by nearly 50 percent during the hot summer months.

The 18-hole par-71 **Green Spring Golf Course** (588 N. Green Spring Dr., 435/673-7888, https://washingtoncity.org, $55-75), just west of I-15 exit 10 in the town of Washington,

St. George

has a reputation as one of the finest courses in Utah.

Professionals favor the cleverly designed 27-hole par-72 **Sunbrook Golf Club** (2366 Sunbrook Dr., 435/627-4400, www.sgcity.org, $30-60), which features lava rock and red sand traps alongside gorgeous views. The **St. George Golf Club** (2190 S. 1400 E., 435/627-4404, www.sgcity.org, $23-35) has a popular 18-hole par-73 course south of town in Bloomington Hills. The par-70 **Southgate Golf Course** (1975 Tonaquint Dr., 435/627-4440, www.sgcity.org, $23-35), on the southwest edge of town, has 18 holes. This club features a game improvement center complete with computerized golf-swing analysis and ample indoor practice space. The 18-hole par-72 **Sky Mountain** (1030 N. 2600 W., 435/635-7888, www.skymountaingolf.com, $57), northeast of St. George in nearby Hurricane, has a spectacular setting.

Mountain Biking

Mountain bikers in the know come to St. George in early spring and fall to ride single-track trails and slickrock just as good as what you'll find in Moab. One of Utah's most spectacular trails is **Gooseberry Mesa,** southeast of Hurricane, a challenging but fun 13-mile (20.9-km) ride with a mix of slickrock and single-track. A more intermediate option is the 6.4-mile (10.3-km) **Green Valley Race Course,** 10 minutes west of St. George, accessed via Bearclaw Poppy Access Road. To reach the trailhead and parking from St. George, take I-15 south and follow signs for West Dixie Drive, then turn left on West Canyon View Drive.

Less intense cycling can be found at **Snow Canyon State Park,** where the paved 6-mile (9.7-km) Whiptail Trail and the 8-mile (13-km) gravel and sand West Canyon Road are open to bikes.

ENTERTAINMENT AND EVENTS

One of St. George's biggest annual events is the early October **St. George Marathon** (www.stgeorgemarathon.com), which attracts about 4,000 runners from all over the United States. Also in October, the **Huntsman World Senior Games** (www.seniorgames.net) presents a wide variety of Olympic-type competitions for seniors—you'll be amazed at the enthusiasm and ability on display. The city fills with triathletes in early May, when the **Ironman 70.3 St. George** (www.ironman.com) is held.

FOOD

Although its dining scene has improved in recent years, chain restaurants still rule in St. George.

The best place to head for lunch or dinner is the old downtown area, known as Ancestor Square, at the intersection of St. George Boulevard and Main Street. There you'll find several blocks of locally owned restaurants and art galleries. ★ **Painted Pony** (2 W. St. George Blvd., 435/634-1700, www.painted-pony.com, lunch 11:30am-3pm daily, dinner 4pm-9pm daily, reservations advised on weekends, $30-48) is a stylish restaurant where the kitchen puts Southwestern touches on American standards; try the cocoa chili-dusted tenderloin with blackberry demi. Downstairs from the Painted Pony is another pretty good restaurant, **Benja Thai and Sushi** (2 W. St. George Blvd., 435/628-9538, www.benjathai.com, 11:30am-10pm Mon.-Sat., $13-23), one of few Thai restaurants in southern Utah.

At the corner of St. George Boulevard and Main Street is an actual pub: **George's Corner** (2 W. St. George Blvd., 435/216-7311, https://georgescornerrestaurant.com, 8am-10pm Sun.-Thurs., 8am-midnight Fri.-Sat., $11-30). The fare is an elevated take on bar grub—a lamb burger, a vegan sandwich, short-rib ragout. George's also has a solid beer and wine selection, plus a killer cocktail list, including tempting after-dinner drinks.

Bear Paw Café (75 N. Main St., 435/879-3410, https://bearpawcafe.com, 7am-3pm daily, $8-15) is a bright spot for coffee drinkers and anyone who wants a good breakfast;

Belgian waffles are the house specialty. Next door is the deservedly popular **Riggatti's Wood Fired Pizza** (974 W. Sunset Blvd., 435/674-9922, www.riggattis.com, 11am-9pm daily, medium pizza $10-17). The pies are delicious, but the dining atmosphere is a little basic; take your pizza to go if you'd rather find a scenic outdoor spot to eat.

Find excellent tacos at **Angelica's Mexican Grill** (101 E. St. George Blvd., 435/628-4399, www.angelicasmexicangrill.com, 11am-9pm Mon.-Sat., $8-14), an authentic Mexican restaurant near downtown, owned by a Mexico City native.

A little farther from the downtown hub, **Red Fort Cuisine of India** (148 S. 1470 E., 435/574-4050, https://redfortcuisine.com, 4pm-10pm Wed.-Mon., $17-25) probably has the best Indian food you'll find in this part of the state, including many vegetarian options. It's a local favorite, and often crowded.

Also worth the 2-mile (3.2-km) drive southwest of downtown is the award-winning ★ **Cliffside Restaurant** (511 S. Tech Ridge Dr., 435/319-6005, www.cliffsiderestaurant.com, 11am-3pm and 5pm-9pm Mon.-Thurs., 11am-3pm and 5pm-10pm Fri.-Sat., $19-45), where the astounding views are nearly matched by the very good food (elevated surf and turf). Drive up to the cliff on which the restaurant is perched and ask for a seat on the patio, which overlooks St. George and the surrounding red cliffs—bonus points for snagging a seat right before sunset. Inside, floor-to-ceiling windows also offer solid views.

ACCOMMODATIONS

St. George offers many places to stay, though the town fills up when events such as the early-October marathon or early-May triathlon are held. Motel prices vary wildly: They are highest during the cooler months and drop if business is slow in summer (we've listed the higher prices here). Golfers should ask about golf-and-lodging packages. You'll find most lodgings along the busy I-15 business route of St. George Boulevard (exit 8), a little less than 1 mile (1.6 km) north of downtown, and on Bluff Street (exit 6), which is a little over 1 mile (1.6 km) south of downtown.

Under $100

Near downtown, there are some decent locally owned accommodations. The **Chalet Motel** (664 E. St. George Blvd., 435/628-6272, www.chaletmotelstgeorge.com, $69-165) offers fridges and microwaves, or in larger guest rooms, efficiency kitchens. There's also a pool.

$100-150

Close to downtown is one of St. George's best: the **Best Western Coral Hills** (125 E. St. George Blvd., 435/673-4844, www.coralhills.com, $135-180), a very attractive property with indoor and outdoor pools and two spas, an exercise room, and a complimentary continental breakfast.

Over $150

Golfers and those willing to pay extra for refined desert luxury should consider the **Inn at Entrada** (2588 W. Sinagua Trail, 435/634-7100, www.innatentrada.com, $560-1,000), located near Snow Canyon State Park. A stay at the inn is the easiest way to gain access to the resort's top-notch golf course. In addition to the lovely setting, you'll find Southwestern-style suites, spa services, gorgeous pools, and a good restaurant complete with a dress code—whether or not that appeals to you.

The classy and friendly **Inn on the Cliff** (511 S. Tech Ridge Dr., 435/216-5864, www.innonthecliff.com, $150-210) is perched over the city, with the best views in St. George and boutique-style amenities, including a pool, a balcony adjoined to each room, and free breakfast delivered to the room. The inn also operates the award-winning Cliffside Restaurant, with excellent food and patio dining overlooking St. George and the cliffs beyond.

Downtown, a newer option, the **Advenire**

Hotel (25 W. St. George Blvd., 435/522-5022, www.theadvenirehotel.com, $278-500) boasts modern yet locally inspired decor, beautiful views from balcony rooms, and a rooftop pool. There's also an innovative, lauded restaurant on-site called wood.ash.rye.

Campgrounds

The best camping in the area is at **Snow Canyon State Park** (435/628-2255, https://stateparks.utah.gov, reservations 800/322-3770, www.reserveamerica.com, reservations required in spring, year-round, $40 without hookups, $45 with hookups, $8 reservation fee). The 145 RV sites and 17 multiuse sites are located in a pretty canyon, and the campground has showers. From downtown St. George, head north on Bluff Street (Hwy. 18) and follow signs about 12 miles (19.3 km) to the park.

Other public campgrounds in the area include **Quail Creek State Park** (435/879-2378, https://stateparks.utah.gov, reservations www.reserveamerica.com, year-round, $28-40), north of town off I-15. This park has 22 sites available to RVs and tents alike, plus one group site. Take exit 16 when coming from the south or exit 23 from the north. Quail Creek is on a reservoir with little shade, but it's a good option if you have a boat.

The BLM **Red Cliffs Recreation Area** (435/688-3200 or 877/444-6777, year-round, $15) is also north of St. George. The 11 campsites are available to tents and car campers alike, but vehicles over 11 feet, 9 inches (3.6 m) can't access the campground. Take I-15 exit 22 when coming from the south or exit 23 from the north. Red Cliffs is more scenic than Quail Creek and has hiking trails, including Silver Reef, which leads to dinosaur tracks.

If you need a place to park an RV for the night right in town, the 75 sites available at **McArthur's Temple View RV Resort** (975 S. Main St., 435/673-6400 or 800/776-6410, www.templeviewrv.com, year-round, tents and RVs $50) is fine but has little shade.

INFORMATION AND SERVICES

Staff at the downtown **Visitor Information Center** (20 N. Main St., 435/634-5747, https://greaterzion.com, 9am-5pm Mon.-Fri.) can tell you about the sights and events of southwestern Utah.

For information on fishing, hiking, and camping in national forest land, visit the **Dixie National Forest** office (196 E. Tabernacle St., 435/652-3100, www.fs.usda.gov, 8am-5pm Mon.-Fri.).

St. George has a **post office** (180 N. Main St., 435/673-3312), and urgent health issues can be seen at the 24-7 **St. George Regional Hospital** (1380 E. Medical Center Dr., 435/251-1000).

GETTING THERE

St. George's airport (SGU) is 5 miles (8 km) southeast of downtown off I-15 exit 2. **SkyWest Airlines,** a local partner of **Delta** (800/221-1212, www.delta.com), plus **American** (800/433-7330, www.aa.com) and **United** (800/864-8331, www.united.com) offer several daily direct flights to St. George from Salt Lake City, Denver, Phoenix, and Los Angeles.

Several of the national rental-car companies operate at the St. George airport: **Budget** (435/673-6825), **Avis** (435/627-2002), and **Hertz** (435/652-9941).

It's an easy 2-hour drive from Las Vegas to St. George, so travelers may want to consider flying into Las Vegas and renting a car there. From St. George, it's a 1-hour, 41-mile (66-km) drive to Zion National Park's main south entrance, north on I-15 and east on Highway 9; it's a 30-minute, 33-mile (53-km) drive to Zion's Kolob Canyons entrance at I-15 exit 40.

Greyhound (800/231-2222) buses depart from a Texaco station (1572 S. Convention Center Dr.) for Salt Lake City, Denver, Las Vegas, and other destinations. The **St. George Shuttle** (790 S. Bluff St., 435/628-8320 or 800/933-8320, www.stgshuttle.com) will take you to Las Vegas ($43), the Salt Lake

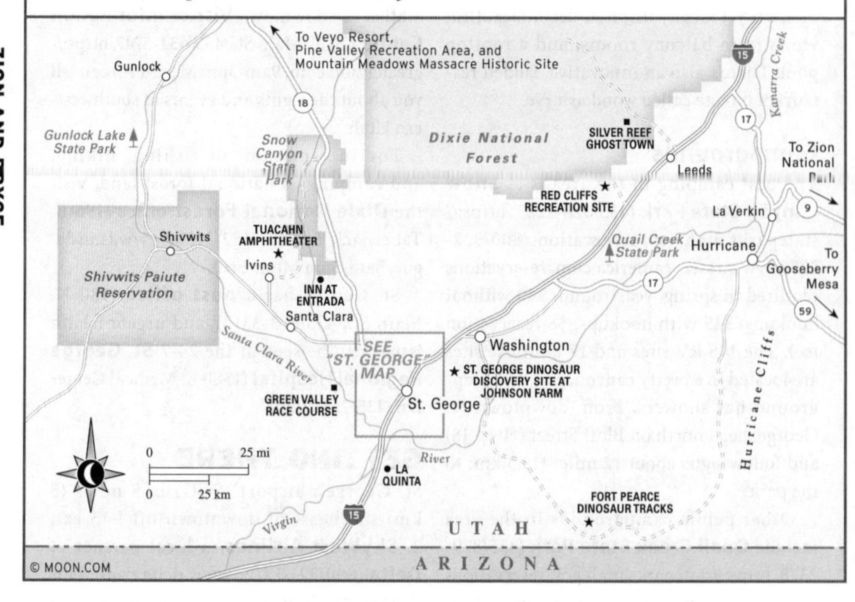

City airport ($62), or Springdale ($70) in a van.

VICINITY OF ST. GEORGE

A few good scenic drives begin at St. George. Whether you're short on time or have all day, a good choice is the 24-mile (39-km) loop through Snow Canyon State Park via Highway 18, the park road (Hwy. 300), and Santa Clara. In summer, head to the cool forests of the Pine Valley Mountains, 37 miles (60 km) northwest of town. You can make a 130-mile (209-km) drive with many potential side trips by circling the mountains on Highway 18, Highway 56, and I-15. Zion National Park, with its grandeur and color, is about 40 miles (64 km) northeast of St. George.

Snow Canyon State Park

If St. George's outlet stores and chain restaurants threaten to close in on you, head a few miles north of town to the red-rock canyons, sand dunes, volcanoes, and lava flows of **Snow Canyon State Park** (1002 N. Snow Canyon Rd., 435/628-2255, https://stateparks.utah.gov, 6am-10pm daily year-round, $10 per vehicle Utah residents, $15 nonresidents).

Walls of sandstone up to 750 feet (229 m) high enclose the 5-mile-long (8-km) canyon. **Hiking trails** trace the canyon bottom, and some lead into the backcountry; take the 1.5-mile (2.4-km) **Hidden Pinyon Trail** for a good introduction. Common plants include prickly pear cacti, yuccas, and cottonwood trees. Delicate wildflowers bloom mostly in the spring and autumn, following the wet seasons, but cacti and the sacred datura can flower in summer.

Wildlife includes sidewinder and Great Basin rattlesnakes, Gila monsters, desert tortoises, kangaroo rats, kit foxes, coyotes, and mule deer. During summer and fall thundershowers, the endangered desert tortoises may take to the roadways to drink from puddles; take extra care driving at these times. You may find some Native American rock art, arrowheads, and bits of pottery. Snow Canyon was named for Lorenzo and Erastus Snow, church leaders who lived in the area.

Snow Canyon is about 12 miles (19.3 km) northwest of St. George by either Highway 18—the faster way—or through the towns of Santa Clara and Ivins by heading north on Bluff Street to Snow Canyon Parkway, then following signs to the park. The campground here has a few lovely sites.

Hiking

There are many trails to explore in Snow Canyon State Park, from quick meanders to hikes that explore petrified dunes. Most hikes are short and perfect as a half-day activity. **Scout Cave Trail** is a great 4.4-mile (7.1-km) out-and-back hike with a trailhead right off Snow Canyon Drive, the park's main road. It gains 613 feet (187 m) in elevation and offers a tour of the area. It leads to a beautiful cave with a keyhole opening that makes for a great photo op.

Rock Climbing

Snow Canyon State Park offers many technical routes on sandstone, ranging from easy 5.7s to 5.12s. There's a good mix of trad and sport climbs, including some multi-pitch routes. Islands in the Sky is one of the more popular areas, and a couple of crowd-favorite routes are the moderately challenging Living on the Edge (5.10c, trad, 4 pitches) and the relatively easy Leopard Skin (5.7, trad/sport, 4 pitches).

Tuacahn Amphitheater

Tuacahn (1100 Tuacahn Dr., 800/746-9882, www.tuacahn.org, shows most Mon.-Sat. mid-May-mid-Oct., $30-126) is an outdoor amphitheater that seats 1,900 among towering red-rock cliffs northwest of St. George near the south entrance to Snow Canyon State Park. Tuacahn offers a three-show summer musical theater season, with performances such as *The Hunchback of Notre Dame* and *Matilda the Musical.* Tuacahn is also the place to catch a big concert. On Saturday mornings year-round, vendors set up for a crafts and food market. Between Thanksgiving and Christmas, Tuacahn hosts a free Festival of Lights.

Veyo

Warm-water springs feed a swimming pool in this pretty spot. The family-friendly **Veyo Resort** (287 E. Veyo Resort Rd., Veyo, 435/574-2300, www.veyopool.com, 9am-8pm daily May-Sept., $16 adults, free kids 2 and under) has picnic tables and a snack bar.

The resort has also developed a private rock-climbing area called **Crawdad Canyon,** which is included in the pass to the pool. There are over 260 bolted sport climbing routes ranging from 5.6 to 5.13 on 80-foot (24-m) basalt cliffs. Climbers (and other visitors) can also camp here ($40-45 per tent).

Take the Veyo Resort Road from Highway 18 southeast of town. The little village of Veyo is along the Santa Clara River, 19 miles (31 km) northwest of St. George.

Mountain Meadows Massacre Historic Site

A short trip from Highway 18 leads to the site of one of the darkest chapters of Latter-day Saints history. The pleasant valley had been a popular rest stop for pioneers about to cross the desert. In 1857, a California-bound wagon train whose members had already experienced trouble with LDS pioneers in the region was attacked by an alliance of Latter-day Saints and local Native Americans. About 120 people were killed. Only some small children too young to tell the story were spared. The close-knit LDS community tried to cover up the incident and hindered federal attempts to apprehend the killers. Only John D. Lee, who was in charge of Indian affairs in southern Utah at the time, was ever brought to justice.

After nearly 20 years and two trials, authorities took him back to this spot to be executed by firing squad. Many details of the massacre remain unknown. The major causes seem to have been a Latter-day Saints fear of invasion, aggressive LDS and Native Americans, and poor communication between LDS leadership

1

2

in Salt Lake City and southern Utah. Two monuments now mark the site of the tragedy. Take Highway 18 north and turn west onto a paved road between mileposts 31 and 32.

PINE VALLEY MOUNTAINS

A massive body of magma exposed by erosion comprises the Pine Valley Mountains, located north of St. George between Highway 18 (to the west) and I-15 (to the east). Signal Peak (elev. 10,365 ft/3,159 m) tops the range, much of which has been designated the Pine Valley Mountain Wilderness.

In 1856, pioneers established the town of Pine Valley (elev. 6,800 ft/2,073 m) to harvest the forests and raise livestock. Lumber from Pine Valley helped build many southern Utah settlements, and even went into Salt Lake City's great tabernacle organ. The town's picturesque white chapel was built in 1868 by Ebenezer Bryce, who later homesteaded at what's now Bryce Canyon National Park. Right near the chapel, the **Pine Valley Heritage Center** (132 E. Main St., 435/574-2463, 10am-4pm Mon.-Sat. Memorial Day-Labor Day) is run by the US Forest Service and has info, books, and maps.

Pine Valley Recreation Area

Three miles (4.8 km) past the town of Pine Valley are picnic areas, several popular **campgrounds,** and trails in Dixie National Forest (435/865-3700, www.fs.usda.gov). At Pine Valley Reservoir (2.3 mi/3.7 km up E. Pine Valley Rd., on the right), you can fish for rainbow and some brook trout. Fishing is fair in the Santa Clara River upstream and downstream from the reservoir. About 0.5 mile (0.8 km) past the reservoir are several large streamside picnic areas.

The 50,000-acre (20,234-ha) Pine Valley Mountain Wilderness has the best scenery of the Pine Valley Mountains, but it can be seen only on foot or horseback. A network of trails from all directions leads into the wilderness. The road from Pine Valley provides access to the **Whipple trailhead** and **Brown's Point trailhead** on the east side of the wilderness area. Trails are usually open mid-June into October. Several loops are possible, although most are too long for day hikes. **Whipple National Recreation Trail** is one of the most popular for both day and overnight trips. It ascends 2,100 vertical feet (640 m) in 6 miles (9.7 km) to the 35-mile-long (56-km) **Summit Trail,** which connects with many other trails. **Brown's Point Trail** also climbs to Summit Trail, but in 4 miles (6.4 km). Strong hikers can use Brown's Point and Summit Trails to reach the top of Signal Peak on a day hike. Generally, the trails from Pine Valley are signed and easy to follow; trails in other areas may not be maintained.

Silver Reef Ghost Town

This is probably Utah's most accessible ghost town. In about 1870, prospectors found rich silver deposits in the sandstone here, much to the surprise of mining experts, who thought such a combination impossible. From 1878 to 1882, the town boomed with a peak population of 1,500 that included a sizable Chinese community. Then a combination of lower silver prices, declining yields, and water in the mines forced the operations to close one by one, the last in 1891. Built of stone in 1877, the **visitor center** (www.silverreefutah.org, 10am-3pm Mon. and Thurs.-Sat., $3) houses a small museum. From Leeds, take I-15 exit 22 or 23 and follow signs 1.3 miles (2.1 km) on a paved road.

1: Snow Canyon State Park **2:** Tuacahn Amphitheater

Cedar City

Cedar City (pop. about 33,000), known for its scenic setting and its summertime Utah Shakespeare Festival, is a handy base for exploring a good chunk of southern Utah. Just east of town are the high cliffs of the Markagunt Plateau—a land of panoramic views, colorful rock formations, desolate lava flows, extensive forests, and flower-filled meadows. Also on the Markagunt Plateau is the Cedar Breaks National Monument, an immense amphitheater eroded into the vividly hued underlying rock.

Zion National Park's Kolob Canyons area is less than 20 miles (32 km) from Cedar City. Within an easy day's drive are the Zion Canyon section of the park to the south, and Bryce Canyon National Park and the Escalante canyons unit of Grand Staircase-Escalante National Monument to the east.

SIGHTS

Frontier Homestead State Park Museum

The **Frontier Homestead State Park Museum** (635 N. Main St., 435/586-9290, https://frontierhomestead.org, 9am-6pm daily June-Aug., 9am-5pm Mon.-Sat. Sept.-May, $4) illuminates local history through historic buildings, a horse-drawn wagon collection, and a mix of indoor and outdoor exhibits. Cedar City was a center for iron mining and processing starting in 1850, when Brigham Young, hoping to increase Utah's self-sufficiency, sent workers here to develop an "Iron Mission."

RECREATION

The main **City Park** (Main St. and 200 North) has picnic tables, a playground, and horseshoe courts. The **Cedar City Aquatic Center** (2090 W. Royal Hunte Dr., 435/865-9223) has an outdoor pool, lap pool, and lazy river. From West Canyon Park (on 400 East, halfway between Center St. and 200 South), the paved **Coal Creek Walking and Biking Trail** leads 4 miles (6.4 km) up the desert canyon.

ENTERTAINMENT AND EVENTS

Cedar City's lively **Utah Shakespeare Festival** (435/586-7880, box office 435/586-7878 or 800/752-9849, www.bard.org, $24-84 tickets) presents Shakespearean plays, contemporary theater, and musicals each summer (late June-mid-Oct.) in the **Beverley Taylor Sorenson Center for the Arts** (195 W. Center St.) on the campus of Southern Utah University.

This theater complex boasts three performance areas, including Engelstad Shakespeare Theatre, an open-air space reminiscent of Elizabethan theaters but with modern amenities and technology; a black-box studio theater staging more experimental performances; and an indoor theater for Shakespeare Festival plays and college productions. Purchase tickets in advance if you can, though you can usually find tickets to something if you didn't plan ahead.

Costumed actors stage the popular free Greenshow (7pm Mon.-Sat. late June-Aug.) before the performances, with a variety of Elizabethan comedy skits, Punch-and-Judy shows, period dances, and other 16th-century fun. Backstage tours ($12) of the costume shop, makeup room, and stage show how the festival works.

Although the Shakespeare Festival is better known, Cedar City's annual **SimonFest Theatre Co.** (105 N. 100 E., 435/267-0194, www.simonfest.org, $30) is also quite popular. It runs mid-June-mid-August.

Utah athletes compete in the **Utah Summer Games** (435/865-8421, www.larryhmillerutahsummergames.org) through much of June; events, patterned after the Olympic games, begin with a torch relay and include track and field, 10K and marathon

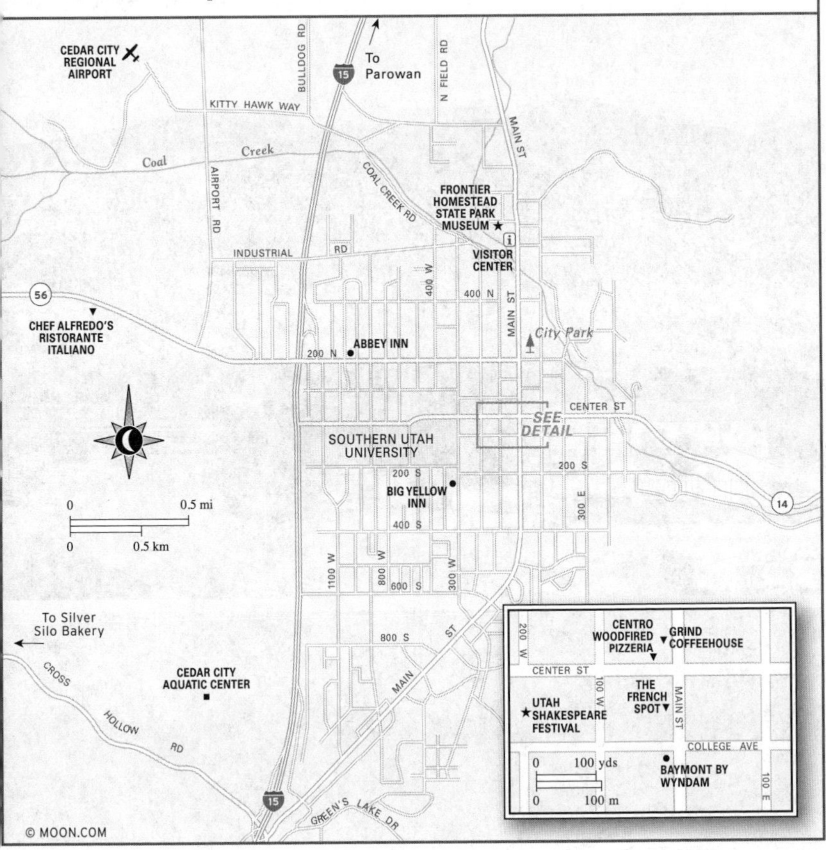

runs, cycling, boxing, wrestling, basketball, tennis, soccer, karate, and swimming.

Everyone dresses up in period clothing in mid-July for the **Utah Midsummer Renaissance Faire** (www.umrf.net), with 16th-century entertainment, crafts, and food.

FOOD

Cedar City has a few good casual restaurants with anomalously low prices. The brightest spot is ★ **Centro Woodfired Pizzeria** (50 W. Center St., 844/385-3285, www.centropizzeria.com, 11am-10pm Mon.-Sat., 11am-9pm Sun., $14-17), a stylish place with great pizza (cooked to a char unless you specify otherwise), large salads, and a decent beer and wine selection. It's a busy spot in the evening, especially when the Shakespeare Festival is in session, so plan accordingly.

Grind Coffeehouse (19 N. Main St., 435/867-5333, 7am-7pm Mon.-Sat., 9am-3pm Sun., $6-9) has the best coffee in town and a good selection of sandwiches. The cavernous space isn't especially inviting, but it does have the feeling of a community gathering place. Nearby, **The French Spot** (18 S. Main St., 435/263-0586, www.thefrenchspotcafe.com, 8am-10pm daily, $5-24) is a sweet café run by a French pastry chef and his family. Stop in for

6
1

2
Silver Silo
BAKERY & ESPRESSO
RESERVED
PARKING

an omelet, crepes, or macarons in fun flavors like "Baby Yoda."

Silver Silo Bakery (777 Cross Hollow Rd., 435/572-7070, www.silversilobakeryandespresso.com, 6am-8pm Mon.-Sat., $6-7) is a literal silo at the edge of town. Service is beyond friendly, and all the bread and pastries are made with fresh-ground locally grown wheat. Fresh sandwiches, a lively espresso drink menu, and smoothies are all on offer for a song. Get it to go and eat it at the trailhead.

Chef Alfredo's Ristorante Italiano (2313 W. 400 N., 435/586-2693, www.chefalfredos.com, 11am-2pm and 4pm-9pm Mon.-Fri., 4pm-9pm Sat., 4pm-8pm Sun., $16-40) has a wide-ranging and well-executed Italian menu and an elegance that belies its location in a strip mall some distance from downtown. Come prepared for generous servings.

ACCOMMODATIONS

During the Shakespeare Festival, Cedar City is a popular destination, so it's best to reserve a room at least a day or two in advance during the summer. A half-dozen large chain hotels cluster around the I-15 exits, alongside a bevy of fast-food restaurants and strip malls. Downtown along Main Street are even more motels, most within walking distance to the Shakespeare Festival. Many of Cedar City's B&Bs are also within a stroll of the festival grounds.

Note that the following prices are for the summer festival high season. Outside high season, expect rates to drop by about one-third.

$100-150

Conveniently located downtown, **Baymont by Wyndham Cedar City** (80 S. Main St., 435/586-6518, www.wyndhamhotels.com, $117) is an old-style motel with good amenities like a heated outdoor pool.

B&B inns and Shakespeare seem to go hand in hand. Near the festival, at the edge of the Southern Utah University campus, the **Big Yellow Inn** (234 S. 300 W., 435/586-0960, www.bigyellowinn.com, $139-249) is easy to spot: It is indeed yellow and filled with antiques. Several of the guest rooms are in a house directly across the street from the main inn.

Over $150

One of the best places to stay in Cedar City is the **Abbey Inn** (940 W. 200 N., 435/586-9966 or 800/325-5411, www.abbeyinncedar.com, $179-225), which has remodeled guest rooms, an indoor pool, and a good breakfast included.

Campgrounds

East of Cedar City on Highway 14 are a handful of campgrounds in the Dixie National Forest. The closest to town is **Cedar Canyon** (435/865-3200, www.fs.usda.gov, Memorial Day-Labor Day, $21), 12 miles (19.3 km) southeast of Cedar City. Situated along Cow Creek, the campground's 19 sites sit at 8,100 feet (2,469 m) elevation and have water. RVs are permitted, but there are no hookups.

Cedar City KOA (1121 N. Main St., 435/586-9872 or 800/562-9873, https://koa.com, year-round, tents $34, RVs $56) has cabins ($63-74 no linens, $78-145 with linens), 88 sites with full hookups, and 29 tent-only sites, showers, a playground, and a pool.

INFORMATION AND SERVICES

The **Cedar City Brian Head Tourism Bureau** (581 N. Main St., 435/586-5124, www.visitcedarcity.com, 8:30am-5pm Mon.-Fri., 9am-5pm Sat.) is just south of Frontier Homestead State Park. The Dixie National Forest's **Cedar City Ranger District Office** (1789 N. Wedgewood Ln., 435/865-3200) has information on recreation and travel on the Markagunt Plateau. The **BLM's Cedar City District Office** (176 E. D. L. Sargent Dr., 435/865-3000) is just off Main Street on the north edge of town.

1: Cedar City 2: Silver Silo Bakery

GETTING THERE

Just east of I-15, Cedar City is 52 miles (84 km) northeast of St. George and 253 miles (407 km) southwest of Salt Lake City; take I-15 exit 57, exit 59, or exit 62.

Delta (800/221-1212, www.delta.com) has flights operated by SkyWest between the small **Cedar City Regional Airport** (CDC, 2560 Aviation Way, 435/867-9408) and Salt Lake City. Rent a car from **Avis** (435/867-9898) at the airport.

From Zion National Park's main south entrance, it's 58 miles (93 km), a little over an hour's drive, to Cedar City, west on Highway 9 and north on I-15; it's a 20-minute, 19-mile (30-km) drive from Zion's Kolob Canyons entrance north on I-15 to exit 57. Coming from Bryce Canyon National Park, it's a 90-minute, 77-mile (124-km) drive to Cedar City south on US 89 and west on Highway 14.

THE MARKAGUNT PLATEAU

Markagunt is a Paiute name for "highland of trees." The large, high plateau—which mostly sits between 9,000 and 11,000 feet (2,743 and 3,353 m) in elevation—consists mostly of rolling hills, forests, and lakes. Black tongues of barren lava extend across parts of the landscape. Cliffs at Cedar Breaks National Monument are the best-known feature of the plateau, but the land also drops away in the colorful pink cliffs farther southeast.

Two scenic byways cross this highly scenic area. The Markagunt Scenic Byway (Hwy. 14) climbs up a dramatic cliff-lined canyon from Cedar City, reaching overlooks of Zion before dropping to Long Valley Junction on US 89. The Brian Head-Panguitch Lake Scenic Byway—aka the Patchwork Parkway (Hwy. 143)—departs from Parowan, climbing steeply to lofty Brian Head with its ski and recreation area, past Panguitch Lake, and down to Panguitch in the Sevier Valley.

Popular activities on the Markagunt include fishing, hiking, mountain biking, downhill and cross-country skiing, and snowmobiling. In summer, volunteers or foresters staff the **Duck Creek Visitor Center** (435/682-2432) on Highway 14 opposite the Duck Creek Campground turnoff.

Markagunt Scenic Byway

Starting at Cedar City's eastern boundary, Highway 14 plunges into a narrow canyon flanked by steep rock walls before climbing to the top of the Markagunt Plateau. This scenic route passes dramatic cliffs and distant hoodoos. Although it's not a quick drive—especially if you get caught behind a lumbering RV—the incredible vistas, which extend down into Arizona, more than repay your patience. Stop at the Zion Overlook (on the right side of the road, 16.6 mi/26.7 km from Cedar City) for sweeping bird's-eye views of the national park, and at Duck Creek Village for a lakeside picnic (signed turnout on the left side of the road, 30 mi/48 km from Cedar City).

Markagunt Byway also passes several wooded campgrounds and small mountain resorts. Topping out at 9,000 feet (2,743 m), these high-mountain getaways are popular when temperatures in the desert below soar. The route ends at US 89 in Long Valley Junction, 41 miles (66 km) east of Cedar City, and Zion Overlook sits 16.5 miles (26.6 km) east of Cedar City. In summer, you can also access Cedar Breaks National Monument by heading north on Highway 148 from Highway 14.

At the **Zion Overlook,** a sweeping panorama takes in the deep canyons and monuments of Zion National Park to the south. The easy **Bristlecone Pine Trail** (0.5-mi/0.8-km loop), graded for wheelchair access, leads to the rim of the Markagunt Plateau and excellent views. A dense spruce and fir forest opens up near the rim, where storm-battered limber and bristlecone pines cling precariously near the edge. You can identify the bristlecone pines by their short-needled "bottle brush" branches. The trailhead is 17 miles (27 km) east of Cedar City on the south side of Highway 14.

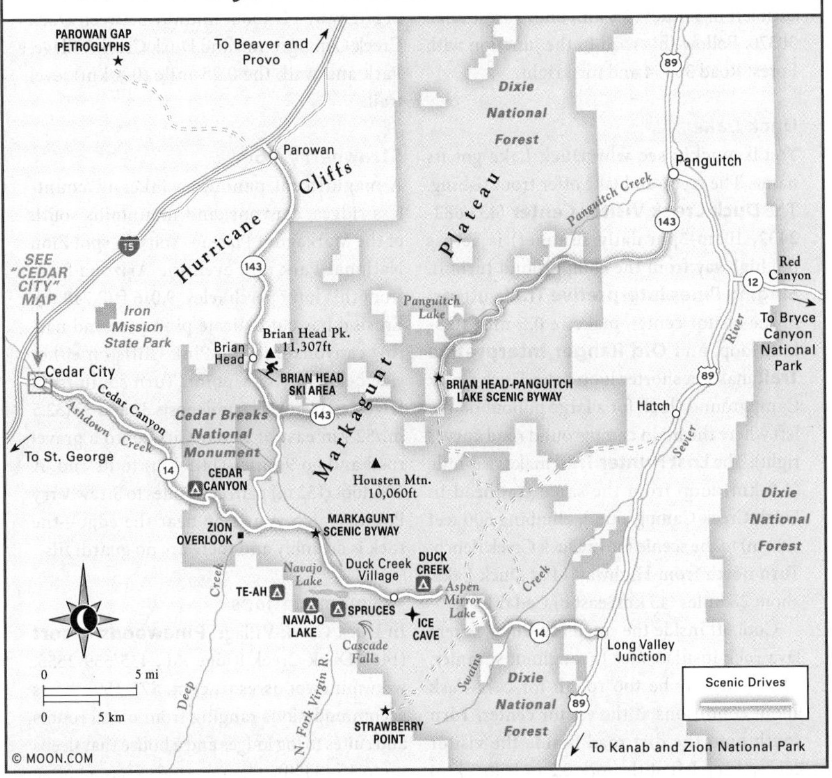

Navajo Lake

Lava flows dammed this unusual 3.5-mile-long (5.6-km) lake, which has no surface outlet. Instead, water drains through sinkholes in the limestone underneath and emerges as Cascade Falls (in the Pacific Ocean drainage) and Duck Creek (in the Great Basin drainage). From a pullout along the highway 24 miles (39 km) east of Cedar City, you can sometimes see three of the sinkholes at the east end. Anglers catch rainbow trout and the occasional eastern brook and brown trout. You can hand-launch small boats at Navajo Lake Campground or from boat ramps at Navajo Lake Lodge and Behmer Lodge and Landing. An 11.5-mile (18.5-km) trail open to hikers and mountain bikers circles the lake. Take the Navajo Lake turnoff, 25.5 miles (41 km) east of Cedar City, for the campgrounds, marina, and lodge along the south shore.

The **Virgin River Rim Trail** stretches about 38 miles (61 km) along the rim between Deer Haven Group Campground and Strawberry Point. Beautiful panoramas of the headwaters of the Virgin River reward hikers and mountain bikers on this trail. Splendid views and a waterfall make the **Cascade Falls National Recreation Trail** an exciting trip. The easy trail is 1.6 miles (2.6 km) round-trip. It begins at the south rim of the Markagunt Plateau, drops a short way down the Pink Cliffs, then winds along the cliffs to the falls. The falls gush from a cave and bounce down to the North Fork of Zion's Virgin River. Take the Navajo Lake turnoff from Highway 14, go 0.3 mile (0.5 km) on Forest Road 30053, then turn left in 3 miles (4.8 km) onto Forest Road 30370. Follow this road to the junction with Forest Road 30054 and turn right.

Duck Lake

You'll quickly see why Duck Lake got its name. The creek and lake offer trout fishing. The **Duck Creek Visitor Center** (435/682-2432, 10am-3pm daily summer) is across the highway from the campground turnoff. **Singing Pines Interpretive Trail,** just east of the visitor center, makes a 0.5-mile (0.8-km) loop, and **Old Ranger Interpretive Trail** makes a shorter loop from Duck Creek Campground (look for a large pullout on the left where the main campground road curves right). The **Lost Hunter Trail** makes a 3-mile (4.8-km) loop from the same trailhead in Duck Creek Campground, climbing 600 feet (183 m) to the scenic top of Duck Creek Bench. Turn north from Highway 14 at Duck Lake, about 28 miles (45 km) east of Cedar City.

Cool off inside the small **Ice Cave,** where lava rock insulates ice throughout summer. The road may be too rough for cars—ask about conditions at the visitor center. Turn south onto the dirt road beside the visitor center, keep left at the fork 0.2 mile (0.3 km) in, keep right at another fork 0.8 mile (1.3 km) farther, and continue 0.4 mile (0.6 km) to the cave at the end of the road; signs mark the way.

Duck Creek Village

Hollywood has used this area since the 1940s to film such productions as *How the West Was Won, My Friend Flicka,* and the *Daniel Boone* TV series. This handsome village—a collection of lodges, cabins, and log-built homes—is at the edge of a large meadow (elev. 8,400 ft/2,560 m) about 30 miles (48 km) east of Cedar City. The surrounding countryside is excellent for cross-country skiing and snowmobiling late November-March. Snowmobile rentals are available at Pinewoods Resort (435/682-2512).

Trout and scenic beauty attract visitors to pretty **Aspen Mirror Lake.** The turnoff (signed Movie Ranch Rd.) is on the north side of Highway 14, about midway between Duck Creek Campground and Duck Creek Village. Park and walk the 0.25-mile (0.4-km) level trail.

Strawberry Point

A magnificent panorama takes in countless ridges, canyons, and mountains south of the Markagunt Plateau. You can spot Zion National Park and even the Arizona Strip from this lofty perch (elev. 9,016 ft/2,748 m). Erosion has cut delicate pinnacles and narrow canyons into the Pink Cliffs on either side below the viewpoint. Turn south from Highway 14 between mileposts 32 and 33 (32.5 mi/52 km east of Cedar City) onto a gravel road and go 9 miles (14.5 km) to its end. A 500-foot (152 m) path continues to Strawberry Point. Watch your step near the edge—the rock is crumbly and there are no guardrails.

Accommodations

In Duck Creek Village, **Pinewoods Resort** (1460 Duck Creek Ridge Rd., 435/559-2555, www.pinewoodsresort.com, $75-159) offers accommodations ranging from motel rooms and suites to log lodges and a house that sleeps up to 15 ($450). The resort also has a coffee shop and a sit-down restaurant. **Duck Creek Village Inn** (Duck Creek Village, 435/990-5488, www.duckcreekvillageinn.com, May-Sept., $169-500) is a motel-cabin hybrid with pleasantly rustic rooms.

Campgrounds

All of the campgrounds in the area have water and a few sites for reservation (877/444-6777, www.recreation.gov, early June-Labor Day, $21 camping, $8 reservation fee). Sites in the **Cedar Canyon Campground** (elev. 8,100 ft/2,469 m) are along Crow Creek among aspen, fir, and spruce in a pretty canyon setting, 12 miles (19.3 km) east of Cedar City on Highway 14. **Spruces** and **Navajo Lake Campgrounds** are on Navajo Lake, where all the spruce trees have been removed due to bark beetle infestations, leaving little shade. **Te-Ah Campground** is in an aspen grove 1.5 miles (2.4 km) west of Navajo Lake. Expect cool nights at the 9,200-foot (2,804-m) elevation.

Duck Creek Campground is north from Highway 14 at Duck Lake (elev. 8,600 ft/2,621 m).

Brian Head-Panguitch Lake Scenic Byway

Beginning in Parowan, Highway 143 quickly climbs up some of Utah's steepest paved road to nearly 10,000 feet (3,048 m). The terrain changes from arid desert to pine forests to alpine aspen forests in just 14 miles (22.5 km).

At an elevation of 9,850 feet (3,002 m), Brian Head is the highest municipality in Utah, with a year-round population of about 100. Winter skiers like Brian Head for its abundant snow, challenging terrain, and good accommodations. Summer visitors come to enjoy the high country and plunge down the slopes on mountain bikes. The beautiful colors of Cedar Breaks National Monument are just a few miles south. To the east, Panguitch Lake has excellent trout fishing.

Brian Head Peak

You can drive all the way to Brian Head's 11,307-foot (3,446-m) summit by car when the road is dry, usually July-October. Panoramas from the top take in much of southwestern Utah and beyond into Nevada and Arizona. Sheep graze the slopes below. From Brian Head, follow Highway 143 about 2 miles (3.2 km) south, then turn left (northeast) and go 3 miles (4.8 km) on a gravel road to the summit. The stone shelter here was built by the Civilian Conservation Corps in the 1930s.

Brian Head Resort

Brian Head Resort (329 S. Hwy. 143, 435/677-2035, www.brianhead.com, $28-89 adults, kids 12 and under free) comes alive during skiing season (late Nov.-late Apr.). While it's not Utah's most exciting ski area, it's a good place for families and advanced skiers who like a low-key feel. Lifts (including two high-speed quads) and a skier bridge make it easy to get between the two mountains that comprise Brian Head. Navajo Peak is good for beginners, while Giant Steps has more advanced runs. Lifts carry skiers up to elevations of 10,970 feet (3,344 m) and access 71 runs across 650 skiable acres (263 ha). The

Duck Creek Campground on the Markagunt Plateau

resort also features three terrain parks, plus a tubing area.

Brian Head's second season is during summer and fall, roughly mid-June-September, when the area comes alive with mountain bikers taking advantage of great terrain and discounted accommodations. Brian Head Resort opens as a mountain bike park, complete with chairlift ($29-39 for a full-day lift pass) and trailhead shuttle services, bike wash, rentals, and repair services. Thrifty bikers can score good deals by looking for mountain bike lodging packages at nearby hotels, which combine lodging with lift tickets, shuttle service, and sometimes even food and bike rentals. Mountain bike rentals are available ($70-90, reserve online).

In addition to biking, the resort offers summer visitors scenic lift rides ($15 adult, $10 children), a mini zipline ($15 for two runs) and an 18-hole disc golf course ($15).

Food and Accommodations

Rates at Brian Head are moderate during the ski season compared to most of Utah's other ski resorts, and packages with discounts are abundant. **Brian Head Condo Reservations** (435/677-2045 or 800/722-4742, www.brianheadcondoreservations.com) offers units near both the Giant Steps and Navajo Peak lifts in five large condo developments. Units range from studios to two bedrooms and two baths, and most have a kitchen and a wood-burning fireplace. Prices run about $70-175 in summer; during the ski season, expect to pay $150-235.

Cedar Breaks Lodge and Spa (223 Hunter Ridge Rd., 435/677-3000 or 800/438-2929, www.cedarbreakslodge.com, $85-125 summer, $100-250 winter plus resort fee of $17) is at the base of Navajo Peak on the north side of town. All guest rooms come with jetted tubs, a refrigerator, in-room coffee, and cable TV; kitchens are available in some rooms. There's also an indoor pool, two hot tubs, a steam room and sauna, a day spa, and a fitness center. Lodging choices range from hotel rooms to three-bedroom suites. The lodge offers a couple of dining options plus a lounge.

The fanciest option is **Brian Head Lodge** (314 Hunter Ridge Dr., 435/677-9000, www.brianhead.com/lodging, $73-278 summer, $220-304 winter), with nicely decorated guest rooms, an on-site spa, an indoor pool, indoor and outdoor hot tubs, pool tables, and a fitness center. It's pet-friendly to boot ($30 extra).

Cedar Breaks National Monument

If you're driving between Zion and Bryce, consider stopping at Cedar Breaks. Note that this is high country, and the road is closed mid-October-late May.

Cedar Breaks National Monument (435/986-7120 winter, www.nps.gov/cebr, $10 pp, free under age 16) is a lot like Bryce, but with far fewer crowds. Here on the west edge of the Markagunt Plateau sits a giant stone amphitheater 2,500 feet (760 m) deep and more than 3 miles (4.8 km) across. A fairyland of forms and colors appears below the rim, while ridges and pinnacles extend from the steep cliffs. Traces of iron, manganese, and other minerals have tinted the white limestone a rainbow of warm hues, which blaze at **sunset** and glow even on cloudy days.

Elevation ranges from 8,100 feet (2,469 m) at Ashdown Creek to 10,662 feet (3,250 m) at the rim's highest point. Over 150 species of wildflowers brighten meadows in late June-early July, during the **Annual Wildflower Festival.** Designated an **International Dark Sky Park,** Cedar Breaks is popular for stargazing. **Star parties** are held in summer (9pm most Fri.-Sat.) and winter (check www.nps.gov/cebr).

Three easy trails (pets prohibited) near the rim provide great windows into the geology and forests. A 7.5-mile (12.1-km) scenic drive leads past four spectacular and distinct overlooks. Avoid exposed areas during thunderstorms, which are common on summer afternoons. Heavy snows close the road for much of the year. You can drive in only from about late May (sometimes later), until the first big snowstorm of autumn, usually in October. Winter visitors can ski, snowshoe, or travel by snowmobile (only on unplowed roads) from Brian Head (2 mi/3.2 km north of the monument) or Highway 14 (2.5 mi/4 km south).

Visitor Center

A log cabin **visitor center** (435/986-7120, www.nps.gov/cebr, 9am-6pm daily late May-mid-Oct.) includes an information desk and bookstore. Exhibits provide a good intro to the Markagunt Plateau and local rocks, wildflowers, trees, and animals. Staff offers nature walks, geology talks, and campfire programs; see schedules posted in the visitor center and at the campground. The Point Supreme Overlook is located west of the visitor center. The entrance fee ($10 pp) is collected near the visitor center, though there's no charge if you're just driving through the monument without stopping.

Campground Trail

Distance: *1 mile (1.6 km) round-trip*
Duration: *45 minutes*
Elevation gain: *20 feet (6 m)*
Effort: *easy*
Trailheads: *visitor center and campground*

Travel between the visitor center and the campground on this paved ADA-compliant trail that follows the rim of the amphitheater, crosses the road, and passes meadows and forested stands. Because it passes through three different habitats, it's a good place to see wildflowers. It's also the only trail in the park that allows pets.

Spectra Point/Ramparts Trail

Distance: *4 miles (6.4 km) round-trip*
Duration: *2 hours*
Elevation gain: *400 feet (122 m)*
Effort: *moderate-strenuous*
Trailhead: *visitor center*

The Spectra Point/Ramparts Trail begins at the visitor center, then follows the rim along the south edge of the amphitheater to an overlook. Hikers short on time or feeling the effects of the 10,000-foot (3,048-m) elevation can cut the distance in half by stopping after 1 mile (1.6 km) at Spectra Point, where weather-beaten bristlecone pines grow. The trail ends at an overlook.

Alpine Pond Trail

Distance: *2 miles (3.2 km) round-trip*
Duration: *1 hour*
Elevation gain: *20 feet (6 m)*
Effort: *easy*
Trailhead: *Chessmen Ridge Overlook*

The Alpine Pond Trail drops below the rim into one of the few densely wooded areas of the amphitheater. The trail winds through enchanting forests of aspen, subalpine fir, and Engelmann spruce. You can cut the hiking distance in half with a car shuttle between the two trailheads or by taking a connector trail that joins the upper and lower parts of the loop near Alpine Pond. Begin from either Chessmen Ridge Overlook or the trailhead pullout 1.1 miles (1.8 km) farther north. A trail guide ($1) is available at the start or at the visitor center. Even though this is not a strenuous trail, don't be surprised if you huff and puff your way around it due to the elevation.

Food and Accommodations

The nearest accommodations and restaurants are 2 miles (3.2 km) north in Brian Head, including **Cedar Breaks Lodge** (page 250).

Point Supreme Campground (www.recreation.gov, mid-June-late Sept., $24), east of the visitor center, offers 25 sites (10 reservable) with water. If you plan to visit in June or September, call ahead to check that it's open—some years, the season is pretty short due to snow. There's a picnic area near the campground.

Getting There

Cedar Breaks National Monument is 24 miles (39 km) east of Cedar City, 17 miles (27 km) south of Parowan, 30 miles (48 km) southwest of Panguitch, and 27 miles (43 km) northwest of Long Valley Junction (Hwy. 14 and US 89).

The Escalante Area and Capitol Reef

South-central Utah is defined by Grand Staircase-Escalante National Monument, Capitol Reef National Park, and Glen Canyon National Recreation Area. While these public lands are not as famous as other parts of southern Utah, they have much to offer anyone who loves the backcountry and a little more solitude—aside from most of Glen Canyon, that is, which has turned into quite the houseboat party resort scene, in spite of its waning water levels.

Grand Staircase-Escalante National Monument spans a spectacular stretch of nearly 2 million acres (809,371 ha) across the Colorado Plateau. It would take a literal lifetime to explore in full. From red-rock cliffs and the Escalante River to coniferous forests, you can hike, go

Highlights

Look for ★ to find recommended sights, activities, dining, and lodging.

★ **Kodachrome Basin State Park:** Explore colorful sand pipes and spires rivaling Bryce's hoodoos (page 260).

★ **Lower Calf Creek Falls:** Hike 3 miles (4.8 km) of red rock and sand to reach a breathtaking 126-foot (38-m) waterfall plunging into a shallow spring where you can cool off before hiking out (page 273).

★ **Peek-a-boo and Spooky Slot Canyons:** No ropes required—these gorgeous and accessible narrow canyons up Coyote Gulch involve squeezing and scrambling (page 273).

★ **The Wave at Vermilion Cliffs National Monument:** If you manage to get a permit to hike 3 miles (4.8 km) to this iconic feature in northern Arizona near the Utah border, you'll behold a mind-bending sight (page 277).

★ **Hell's Backbone Grill & Farm:** A James Beard Award semifinalist in the middle of canyon country? Don't skip a stop at this farm-to-table restaurant (page 285).

★ **Grand Wash at Capitol Reef National Park:** There's no trail—just the opening of a canyon with towering, awe-inducing sandstone walls that makes this journey great for little ones (page 300).

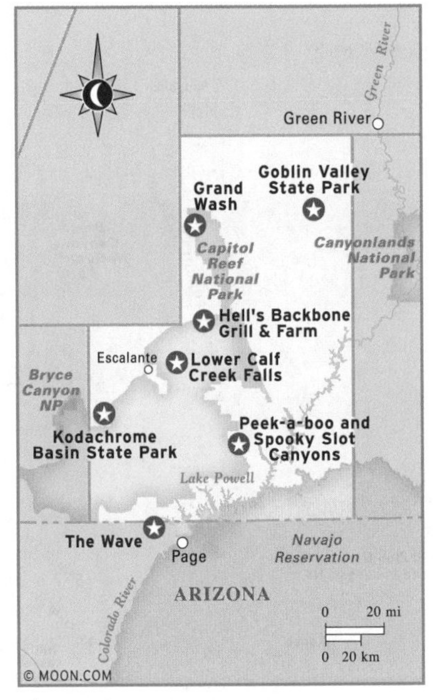

★ **Goblin Valley State Park:** The goblin-esque sandstone rocks of Goblin Valley State Park will get your imagination going (page 309).

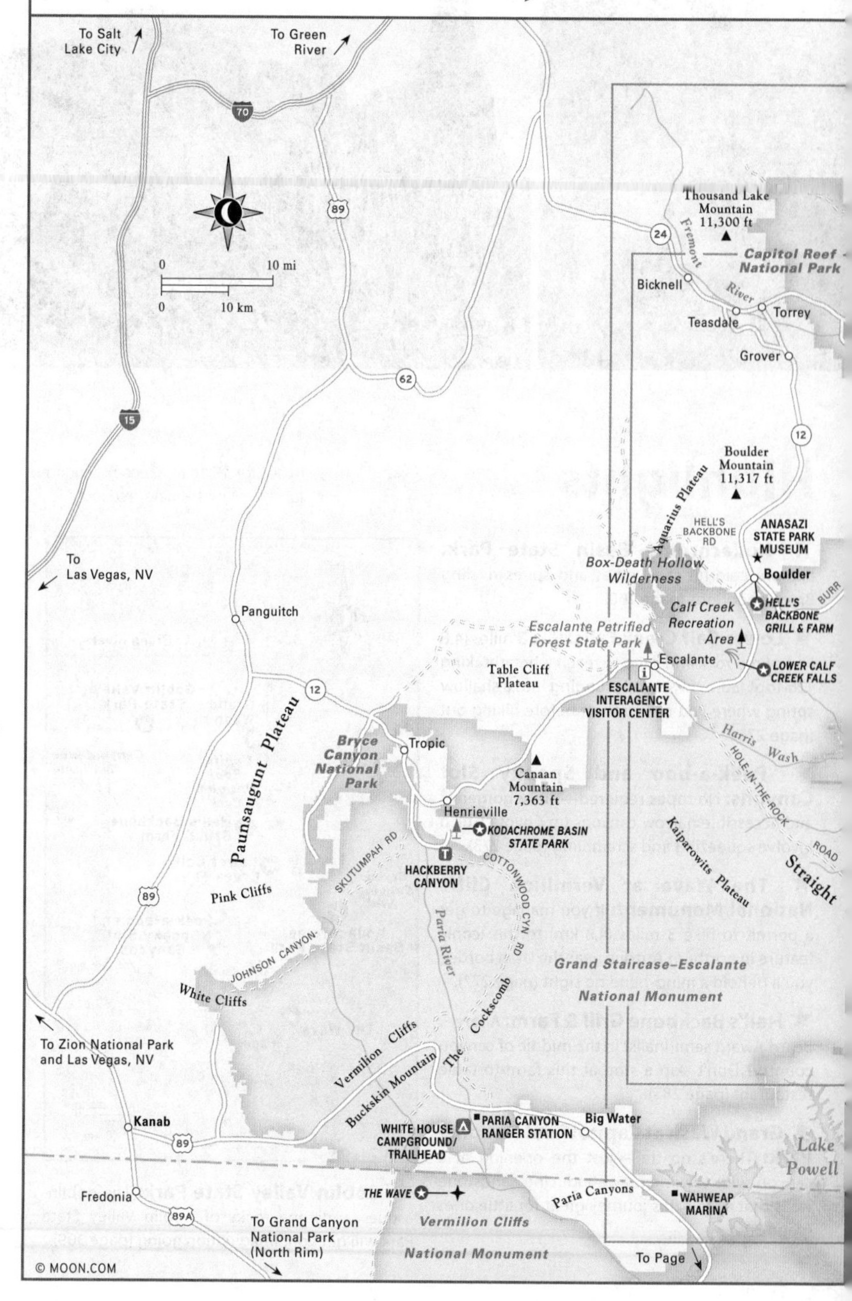

The Escalante Area and Capitol Reef
To Salt Lake City
To Green River
70
89
24
Thousand Lake Mountain 11,300 ft
Fremont
Capitol Reef National Park
Bicknell
River
Torrey
Teasdale
Grover
0
10 mi
0
10 km
62
15
12
Boulder Mountain 11,317 ft
Aquarius Plateau
HELL'S BACKBONE RD
ANASAZI STATE PARK MUSEUM
Box-Death Hollow Wilderness
Boulder
HELL'S BACKBONE GRILL & FARM
BURR
To Las Vegas, NV
Panguitch
Calf Creek Recreation Area
Escalante Petrified Forest State Park
Escalante
LOWER CALF CREEK FALLS
Table Cliff Plateau
ESCALANTE INTERAGENCY VISITOR CENTER
12
Paunsaugunt Plateau
Bryce Canyon National Park
Tropic
Harris Wash
HOLE-IN-THE-ROCK ROAD
Canaan Mountain 7,363 ft
Henrieville
KODACHROME BASIN STATE PARK
HACKBERRY CANYON
SKUTUMPAH RD
COTTONWOOD CYN RD
Kaiparowits Plateau
Straight
89
Pink Cliffs
Paria River
JOHNSON CANYON
Grand Staircase-Escalante National Monument
White Cliffs
The Cockscomb
To Zion National Park and Las Vegas, NV
Vermilion Cliffs
Buckskin Mountain
Kanab
89
WHITE HOUSE CAMPGROUND/ TRAILHEAD
PARIA CANYON RANGER STATION
Big Water
Lake Powell
Fredonia
89A
THE WAVE
Paria Canyons
WAHWEAP MARINA
Vermilion Cliffs National Monument
To Grand Canyon National Park (North Rim)
To Page
© MOON.COM

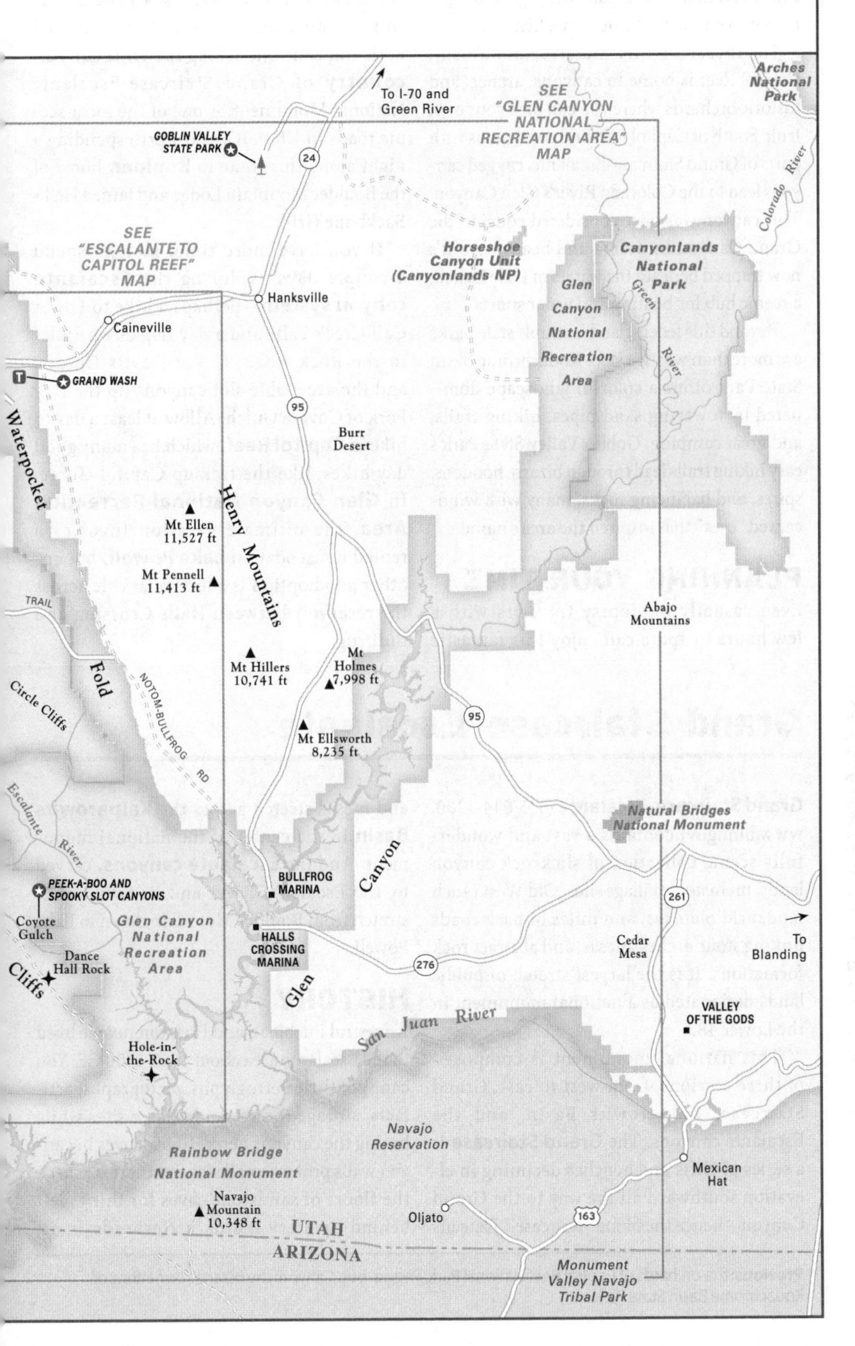

To I-70 and Green River
SEE "GLEN CANYON NATIONAL RECREATION AREA" MAP
Arches National Park
Colorado River
GOBLIN VALLEY STATE PARK
24
SEE "ESCALANTE TO CAPITOL REEF" MAP
Horseshoe Canyon Unit (Canyonlands NP)
Canyonlands National Park
Green River
Hanksville
Caineville
Glen Canyon National Recreation Area
GRAND WASH
Waterpocket
Fold
95
Burr Desert
Henry Mountains
Mt Ellen 11,527 ft
Mt Pennell 11,413 ft
TRAIL
Abajo Mountains
Mt Hillers 10,741 ft
Mt Holmes 7,998 ft
Circle Cliffs
NOTOM-BULLFROG RD
Mt Ellsworth 8,235 ft
Escalante River
Natural Bridges National Monument
Canyon
PEEK-A-BOO AND SPOOKY SLOT CANYONS
BULLFROG MARINA
261
Coyote Gulch
Glen Canyon National Recreation Area
HALLS CROSSING MARINA
Cedar Mesa
To Blanding
Dance Hall Rock
276
Cliffs
Glen
San Juan River
VALLEY OF THE GODS
Hole-in-the-Rock
Navajo Reservation
Rainbow Bridge National Monument
Mexican Hat
Navajo Mountain 10,348 ft
Oljato
163
UTAH
ARIZONA
Monument Valley Navajo Tribal Park

canyoneering, or backpack through geologic, paleontologic, and Indigenous history.

Northeast of this massive monument, Capitol Reef is home to canyons, arches, and historic orchards where you can pick your own fruit. South of Capitol Reef and contiguous with parts of Grand Staircase-Escalante, rugged canyons lead to the Colorado River's Glen Canyon. This canyon was once considered equal to the Grand Canyon in drama and beauty, but it's now trapped beneath the waters of Lake Powell, a scenic hub for boating and water sports.

Beyond this federal land, a couple state parks are more than worth a stop. Kodachrome Basin State Park offers a colorful landscape dominated by towering sand pipes, hiking trails, and great camping. Goblin Valley State Park's easy hiking trails lead through bizarre hoodoos, spires, and balancing rocks, many with wind-carved "eyes" that inspired the area's name.

PLANNING YOUR TIME

Even casually outdoorsy travelers with a few hours to spare can enjoy this fantastic landscape of desert and rock. **Highway 12,** which begins near Bryce Canyon National Park and continues along the **wild canyon country** of Grand Staircase-Escalante National Monument, is one of the most scenic roads in Utah. It's also worth spending a night along this route in **Boulder,** home of the Boulder Mountain Lodge and famed Hell's Backbone Grill.

If you have more time, plan to spend a couple days exploring the **Escalante canyon system**—perhaps a hike to Lower Calf Creek Falls and a day trip down Hole-in-the-Rock Road, to see Devils Garden and the accessible slot canyons up the Dry Fork of Coyote Gulch. Allow at least a day to hike in **Capitol Reef,** which has many good day hikes, like the trek up Capitol Gorge. In **Glen Canyon National Recreation Area,** the ultimate vacation involves a rented houseboat on **Lake Powell,** but another good option is a ferryboat ride across the reservoir between Halls Crossing and Bullfrog.

Grand Staircase-Escalante

Grand Staircase-Escalante (435/644-1200, www.blm.gov) contains a vast and wonderfully scenic collection of slickrock canyon lands, prehistoric village sites, Old West ranch land, arid plateaus, and miles of back roads linking stone arches, mesas, and abstract rock formations. It is the largest stretch of public lands designated as a national monument in the Lower 48.

This national monument is composed of three sections, from west to east: Grand Staircase, Kaiparowits Basin, and the Escalante canyons. The **Grand Staircase** is a series of cliffs and benches declining in elevation southward all the way to the Grand Canyon—hence the name "staircase." Plateaus and mesas stretch across the **Kaiparowits Basin** in the center of the national monument. And the **Escalante canyons,** carved by the Escalante River and its tributaries, stretch from Boulder Mountain down to Lake Powell.

HISTORY

Ancestral Puebloan and Fremont people lived in the Escalante area about 1050-1200 CE. You can spot their petroglyphs, pictographs, artifacts, storage rooms, and village sites while hiking the canyons here. High alcoves in canyon walls protect small stone granaries. Check the floors of sandstone caves for things left behind—pottery shards, arrowheads, mats,

Previous: the orchards of Capitol Reef National Park; Peek-a-boo Canyon; the bizarre formations of Kodachrome Basin State Park.

sandals, and corncobs. (Federal laws prohibit removal of artifacts; please leave everything for the next person to enjoy.) You can visit an excavated Ancestral Puebloan village, along with a modern replica of the original, at Anasazi State Park, just north of Boulder.

The Southern Paiute people arrived in the 1500s and stayed until white settlers took over. The nomadic Paiute had few possessions and left little behind. Latter-day Saints colonists didn't learn about the Escalante area until 1866, when a cavalry went east from Kanab in pursuit of Paiutes. Reports of the expedition described the upper Escalante, which was named Potato Valley after the wild tubers growing there.

Major John Wesley Powell's 1869 expedition down the Green and Colorado Rivers failed to recognize the mouth of the Escalante River—it seemed too shallow and narrow to be a major tributary. In 1872, a detachment of Powell's second expedition stumbled across the Escalante on an overland journey. After some confusion they realized that an entire new river had been found, and they named it for Spanish explorer and priest Silvestre Vélez de Escalante. The elusive river was the last to be discovered in the contiguous United States. LDS ranchers and farmers arrived in the upper valleys of the Escalante in 1876 from Panguitch and other towns to the west, not as part of a church-directed mission, but simply in search of better lands.

EXPLORING THE PARK

There is no entrance fee to visit **Grand Staircase-Escalante National Monument** (visitor center 435/826-5499, headquarters 435/644-1200, www.blm.gov). Free permits are required for all overnight backcountry camping or backpacking. There are fees to camp in the monument's three developed campgrounds.

Some areas within the monument require day-use fees or overnight permits—a couple of which are highly sought after. Hikers in the Paria Wilderness area—which includes Paria Canyon, Coyote Buttes, and the Wave—are required to buy a permit (day hikers $6 per day, overnight $5 per day), as are hikers at the Calf Creek Recreation Area (day-use $5 per vehicle).

It's best to have a travel strategy when visiting this huge national monument. Also important, especially for longer visits: a vehicle that can tackle rugged roads. A Subaru will be adequate in dry weather, but when the clay is wet and muddy, the back roads are virtually impassable to all but 4WD vehicles with high clearance.

Only two paved roads pass through the monument areas, both running east-west. To the north, beautiful **Highway 12** links Bryce Canyon and Capitol Reef National Parks, with access to the Escalante River canyons. *Car and Driver* magazine has rated this route one of the 10 most scenic in the country, with countless vistas and geologic curiosities. Incredible scenery also awaits on **US 89,** which runs along the southern edge of the monument between Kanab and Lake Powell. It's also the access road for the North Rim of the Grand Canyon.

Three fair-weather dirt roads, each with a network of side roads and trails, cut through the rugged heart of the monument, linking the two paved roads. Before heading out on these back roads, check with the visitor center for conditions; high-clearance vehicles are recommended.

VISITOR CENTERS

The monument's **field office** (669 S. US 89A, Kanab, 435/644-1200, 8am-4:30pm Mon.-Fri.) is in Kanab, but the regional visitor centers listed below are the best places for practical travel information.

Cannonville Visitor Center (10 Center St., Cannonville, 435/826-5640, 9am-4pm Wed.-Sun. mid-Mar.-mid-Nov.) is an attractive building at the north end of Cottonwood and Skutumpah-Johnson Canyon Roads. Even if the office is closed, stop by to see outdoor exhibits about the different cultures that have lived in the area.

Escalante Interagency Visitor Center

(755 W. Main St., Escalante, 435/826-5499, 9am-4pm Thurs.-Tues.) is housed in a sprawling building at the west end of the town of Escalante. Staff is very knowledgeable and helpful, and exhibits focus on the monument's ecology and biological diversity.

Anasazi State Park Museum (460 N. Hwy. 12, Boulder, 435/335-7308, https://stateparks.utah.gov, 9am-5pm daily, $5) has a ranger on duty at an information desk inside the museum.

Big Water Visitor Center (20 Revolution Way, Big Water, 435/675-3200, 9am-4pm Thurs.-Mon.) is home to a small yet distinctive collection of dinosaur bones and a wild mural depicting late-Cretaceous life in the area. Stop here to learn about local paleontology.

Paria Contact Station (2040 Long Valley Rd., Kanab, 435/689-0801, 8am-4:30pm daily mid-Mar.-mid-Nov.) is a small seasonal visitor center but an important stop for anyone planning to hike Paria Canyon.

Kanab Visitor Center (745 E. US 89, Kanab, 435/644-1300, 9am-4pm Tues.-Sat.) is the place to stop if you're planning to drive Cottonwood or Johnson Canyon and Skutumpah Roads from the south. Staff can give you updates on the road conditions and suggest driving and hiking strategies. A walk-in lottery for permits to hike Coyote Buttes is held at 8:30am daily. You'll also find geology and archaeology exhibits.

TOURS

For guided tours of Escalante's canyons, **Utah Canyon Outdoors** (325 W. Main St., Escalante, 435/826-4967, www.utahcanyonoutdoors.com, 9am-6pm Mon.-Sat., 9am-5pm Sun.) offers day hikes (full-day $150 pp) to less crowded slot canyons and riparian areas. They also run hiker shuttles and have a good gear shop that happens to serve up coffee in downtown Escalante.

The guides at **Excursions of Escalante** (125 E. Main St., Escalante, 435/826-4714 or 800/839-7567, www.excursionsofescalante.com) lead hikes into remote canyons, technical canyoneering adventures, and multiday backpacking trips. Straightforward hiking trips ($165 pp) are also offered, either cross-country (easiest) or in slot canyons (more challenging). A day of basic canyoneering ($225 pp) includes instruction.

Many local outfitters use pack animals. With **Escape Goats** (435/826-4652, www.escalantecanyonguides.com), you can hike with goats (and a friendly goat-loving human guide) into canyons—a great option for families. A variety of hikes are available (full-day hikes $150 pp), including backpacking trips (from $600 pp per day) and herbal walks that enlighten hikers to local wild plants and medicinal herbs (from $100 pp).

Saddle up for day rides or horse-packing trips with **Hell's Backbone Ranch and Trail** (435/335-7581, www.bouldermountaintrails.com, 1.5-2-hour ride $75), located next to the Boulder Mountain Guest Ranch up Hell's Backbone-Salt Gulch Road.

If you're in the market for a cycling outfitter, **Western Spirit Cycling** (435/259-2453, www.westernspirit.com) over in Moab offers guided rides in the area, include a 6-day beginner-friendly tour of the monument that can be done on an e-bike if desired (from $1,745 pp). But they also let you build your own custom trip if nearly a week of riding sounds like too much.

ALONG HIGHWAY 12

Scenic Byway 12 runs west to east from the town of Panguitch to the town of Torrey, 122 miles (196 km) away, through Bryce Canyon National Park, along the northwestern part of Grand Staircase-Escalante National Monument, through the monument's gateway towns of Escalante and Boulder, and north past Capitol Reef National Park. Stop at the **Cannonville Visitor Center** (10 Center St., Cannonville, 435/826-5640, 9am-4pm Wed.-Sun. mid-Mar.-mid-Nov.) for information about back-road conditions and hikes in the western part of the monument.

Geology of the Grand Staircase

the varicolored cliff bands of the Grand Staircase

This desert landscape once sat at the verge of a vast inland sea. About 300 million years ago, sandy dunes rose hundreds of feet above the waves, then sank below sea level and were covered by water. Thick layers of sediment built up one on top of the other, turning the sand dunes to stone. During the last 50 million years, powerful forces within the earth slowly pushed the entire region 1 mile (1.6 km) upward. The ancestral Colorado River began to carve the deep gorges seen today near Glen Canyon. In turn, the tributaries of the Colorado River, such as the Escalante River, were also forced to trench deeper and deeper in order to drain their watershed.

The most characteristic rocks in the monument are the ancient dunes, turned to stone called slickrock, which make up many of the sheer canyon cliffs, arches, and spires of the region. Delicate cross-bedded lines of the former dunes add grace to these features. Forces within the restless plateau have also buckled and folded rock layers into great reefs as long as 100 miles (161 km). Weathering then carved them into rainbow-hued rock monuments. The aptly named Cockscomb, visible from Cottonwood Canyon Road, which cuts through the center of Grand Staircase-Escalante, is an example of these massive rock wrinkles.

Skutumpah-Johnson Canyon Road

This backcountry drive takes you all the way from Highway 12 in the northern part of Grand Staircase-Escalante down to its southern reaches at US 89 and Kanab. The two main roads that comprise this drive are Johnson Canyon and Skutumpah. From Highway 12 to US 89, it's 46 miles (74 km), but to take this backcountry route all the way from the town of Cannonville to Kanab, it's 66 miles (106 km). This road system also links up with several other remote backcountry roads.

Where Highway 12 passes through Cannonville, turn onto Kodachrome Road, which, after a few miles, leads to Skutumpah Road. Named in part for a Paiute word for "water where rabbitbrush grows," this incredible scenic road takes in views of Bryce at its northernmost stretch and follows the White and Pink Cliff terraces, with access to excellent, less traveled trails and canyons. The best views (and worst driving conditions) are in the northernmost 20 miles (32 km) or so, above Lick Wash. Much of the rest of the way is rangeland, so watch for cattle.

Skutumpah leads to Johnson Canyon Road, which takes you to US 89 and beholds sweeping views of the Vermilion and White Cliffs of the Grand Staircase. It also provides access to more rugged roads and lesser-known canyons. After about 12.5 miles (20 km) on Johnson Canyon Road, look for a weathered set from the TV show *Gunsmoke* (it's on private land, so don't trespass).

While the last 16 miles (26 km) are paved, the unpaved portions of this drive can be rough and rutted. After rain, the roadbed's bentonite soils turn to goo. In good weather, cars with decent clearance can usually make the journey.

Cottonwood Canyon Road

Connecting Cannonville along Highway 12 with the Big Water area off US 89, 46-mile (74-km) Cottonwood Canyon Road is one of the most scenic backcountry routes in the monument. Not to be confused with Big or Little Cottonwood Canyon Roads in northern Utah (which may come up first in a Google Maps search), this mostly unpaved road offers access to dramatic Grosvenor Arch and passes along the Cockscomb, a soaring buckle of rock that divides the Grand Staircase and the Kaiparowits Plateau.

The road parallels Cottonwood Creek, a normally dry streambed that cuts through the angular rock beds of the Cockscomb. Several excellent hikes lead into the steep side canyons and narrows, where the Paria River, Hackberry Canyon, and Cottonwood Creek all meet, about 20 miles (32 km) south of Cannonville.

Check at the Cannonville or Big Water Visitor Centers for information about road conditions, especially if you plan to go beyond Grosvenor Arch. Several road crossings are susceptible to washouts after rainstorms, and the northern portion is impassable even to 4WD vehicles when wet because of the extremely unctuous roadbed.

★ Kodachrome Basin State Park

Located in a basin southeast of Bryce, **Kodachrome Basin State Park** (435/679-8562, https://stateparks.utah.gov, 8am-9:30pm daily, day-use $10) is well worth a visit. The park takes its name from an article in the September 1949 issue of *National Geographic* magazine. The story drew attention to the scenery and earned the area the name "Kodachrome Flat," for the then-experimental Kodak film used by the expedition.

At Kodachrome Basin, you'll see not only colorful cliffs but also strange-looking rock pillars that occur nowhere else in the world. Sixty-seven pillars, called sand pipes, found in and near the park range in height from 6 feet (1.8 m) to nearly 170 feet (52 m). One theory of their origin is that earthquakes caused sediments deep underground to be churned up by water under high pressure. The particles of calcite, quartz, feldspar, and clay in the sand pipes came from underlying rock formations, and the pipes appeared when the surrounding rock eroded away. Most of the other rocks visible in the park are Entrada sandstone: The lower orange layer is the Gunsight Butte Member, while the white layer with orange bands is the Cannonville Member.

Camping

The state park has three **campgrounds** (435/679-8562, reservations 800/322-3770 or https://utahstateparks.reserveamerica.com, year-round). In a natural amphitheater at an elevation of 5,800 feet (1,768 m), **Basin Campground** (tents $25, RVs $35 with hookups, $8 reservation fee) has restrooms, showers, and a dump station. In winter, restrooms and showers may close, but pit toilets are available. The campground usually has space except on summer holidays. The smaller **Bryce View Campground** ($25) is more primitive and, as its name suggests, has good views of

1: Kodachrome Basin State Park **2:** Skutumpah-Johnson Canyon Road **3:** camping at Kodachrome Basin State Park **4:** hiking at Kodachrome Basin State Park

Kodachrome
Basin
State
Park
1
2
NORTH POINT
3
4

Bryce. The campground's Oasis group site also has two bunkhouse cabins that sleep up to six (bring your own bedding; no running water, restrooms and showers adjacent, $85). And **Arch Campground** ($35) has 12 sites best for RVs and vans. Fire rings, picnic tables, toilets, and potable water are available.

Getting There

To reach the park, take Highway 12 south to Cannonville and follow signs for 7 miles (11.3 km) along paved Cottonwood Canyon Road. Adventurous drivers can also approach the park from US 89 to the south via the 46-mile (56-km) Cottonwood Canyon Road, or the 46-mile (77-km) Skutumpah Road through Bull Valley Gorge and Johnson Canyon. These routes may be impassable in wet weather but are generally okay for cars with good clearance.

Grosvenor Arch

Just 1 mile (1.6 km) off Cottonwood Canyon Road, a side road leads to the magnificent Grosvenor Arch. It takes a bit of effort to get here—the 10-mile (16.1-km) dirt road between the turnoff to Kodachrome Basin and the arch is bumpy and can be impassable in wet weather. There are actually two arches here (a rare occurrence), which jut like flying buttresses out of a soaring cliff. The larger of the two openings is 99 feet (30 m) across. A 1949 National Geographic Society expedition named the double arch in honor of the society's president at the time.

Escalante Petrified Forest State Park

Just northwest of the town of Escalante, the pleasant **Escalante Petrified Forest State Park** (435/826-4466, https://stateparks.utah.gov, 7am-10pm daily summer, 8am-10pm daily winter, day-use $10) offers camping, boating, fishing, picnicking, hiking on trails where petrified wood can be found, and a visitor center with displays of petrified wood and dinosaur bones.

Rivers of 140 million years ago carried trees here and buried them in sand and gravel. Burial prevented decay as crystals of silicon dioxide gradually replaced the wood cells. Mineral impurities added a rainbow of colors to the trees as they turned to stone. Weathering has exposed this petrified wood and the water-worn pebbles of the Morrison Formation.

For a look at some colorful petrified wood, follow the **Petrified Forest Trail** from the campground up a hillside of piñon pine and juniper. At the top of the 240-foot-high (73-m) ridge, continue on a 1-mile (1.6-km) round-trip loop to the petrified wood (allow 45-60 minutes). The steep **Rainbow Loop Trail** (0.75 mi/1.2 km) branches off Petrified Forest Trail to more areas of petrified wood.

The **campground** (reservations 800/322-3770, www.reserveamerica.com, year-round, tents $25, RVs $30 with water and electric hookups) offers drinking water, flush toilets, and showers (mid-Mar.-mid-Nov.). The adjacent 139-acre (56-ha) Wide Hollow Reservoir offers fishing, boating, and birdwatching. The park is 1.5 miles (2.4 km) west of Escalante on Highway 12, then 0.7 mile (1.1 km) north on a gravel road.

Escalante

This little community is the most bustling place for miles, and a center for ranchers and travelers. The **Escalante Interagency Visitor Center** (755 W. Main St., 435/826-5499, 9am-4pm Thurs.-Tues.) provides information on local hikes and road conditions. You'll also find accommodations, dining, and amenities.

Smoky Mountain Road

This designated scenic byway starts in Escalante and travels 78 miles (126 km) south to US 89 in Big Water. Running just west of Lake Powell, this largely dirt road is rougher than other cross-monument routes. Check conditions before setting out; a 4WD vehicle is required. This route passes across the arid Kaiparowits Plateau, then drops precipitously onto a bench, where side roads lead through badlands to Lake Powell beaches. The southern portions of the route pass through Glen Canyon National Recreation Area, and side roads lead to remote beaches and flooded canyons. The original *Planet of the Apes* was filmed in this area before it was inundated by Lake Powell.

Big Water is 19 miles (31 km) northwest from Page, Arizona, and 57 miles (92 km) east from Kanab.

Hole-in-the-Rock Road

From Highway 12 in Escalante to the namesake **"Hole-in-the-Rock"** just west of Lake Powell, this 62-mile (100-km) dirt road follows the path of a 19th-century Latter-day Saints expedition. Since the road doesn't connect to any other roads, this out-and-back journey can easily take two or more days, especially if you plan to hike or bike any trails or canyons along the way.

The story of this against-all-odds road traces back to Latter-day Saints church leaders, who organized the 1879 Hole-in-the-Rock Expedition to colonize the wildlands around Utah's San Juan River. Along with the 236 Latter-day Saints, including children, who set out on the expedition, 200 horses and over 1,000 head of cattle were brought along. Planners ruled out lengthy routes through northern Arizona or eastern Utah in favor of a straight shot via Escalante that would cut the distance in half.

Trouble started when the pioneers discovered that the Colorado River crossing was far more difficult than believed. From their start at Escalante, road-building progressed rapidly for the first 50 miles (80 km), then slowly over rugged slickrock for the final 6 miles (9.7 km) to Hole-in-the-Rock. Below this narrow notch, they faced a sheer 45-foot (14-m) drop, followed by almost 1 mile (1.6 km) of extremely steep slickrock leading to the Colorado River. The route looked impossible, but workers used picks and blasting powder to simultaneously widen the notch and construct a precarious wagon road down to the river and up the cliffs on the other side.

After six weeks, all the people, animals, and wagons made it down and were ferried across the Colorado River without serious incident. Canyons and other obstacles continued to block the way. Only after 6 months of exhausting travel did they stop at the present-day site of Bluff on the San Juan River.

Except for scattered signs of ranching, the land here remains unchanged. If the road is dry, vehicles with good clearance can drive

the stretch of Hole-in-the-Rock Road closest to the town of Escalante

close to Hole-in-the-Rock. The rough conditions encountered past Dance Hall Rock require more clearance than most cars allow. Bring sufficient gas, food, and water for the entire 124-mile (200-km) round-trip from Escalante; there are no services along this route.

Note that some of the stops along this road—including Golden Cathedral Trail and Hole-in-the-Rock at the road's end—are within the Glen Canyon National Recreation Area, which charges day-use fees. While there are no entrance booths or strict enforcement, if you want to comply, you can pay the fee in Escalante before heading out on the road or purchase it online (www.nps.gov/glca, $30 per vehicle). An interagency national parks pass also includes this recreation area, so there's no need to pay the day-use fee if you're already a passholder.

Sights

Metate Arch and other rock sculptures decorate **Devils Garden,** 12.5 miles (20.1 km) down Hole-in-the-Rock Road. Turn west and continue 0.3 mile (0.5 km) at the sign to the parking area; you can't really see the "garden" from the road. Red and cream-colored sandstone formations sit atop pedestals and tilt at crazy angles. Delicate bedding lines run through the rocks. There are no trails or markers—just wander around. The BLM manages picnic tables, grills, and outhouses here for day-use. No overnight camping is allowed.

Back in 1879, the natural amphitheater of **Dance Hall Rock** (38 mi/61 km down Hole-in-the-Rock Rd.) made a perfect gathering spot for the Hole-in-the-Rock expedition group when they had to wait three weeks at nearby Fortymile Spring for roadwork to be completed ahead. This is an enjoyable place to explore and only a short walk from the parking area. Solution holes, left by water dissolving in the rock, pockmark the sandstone structure.

At road's end, 62 miles (100 km) from Highway 12, continue on foot across slickrock to the notch and views of the blue waters of **Lake Powell** below. Rockslides have made the descent impossible for vehicles, but hikers can scramble down to the lake and back in about 1 hour. The elevation change is 600 feet (183 m). The 0.5-mile (0.8-km) round-trip hike is strenuous. After a steep descent over boulders, look for the steps of Uncle Ben's Dugway at the base of the notch. Drill holes in the rock once held stakes for logs, brush, and earth to support wagon wheels. The inner wheels followed a narrow rut 4-6 inches (10-15 cm) deep. Some of this impressive roadwork can still be seen.

Getting There

The turnoff from Highway 12 is 5 miles (8 km) east of Escalante. In addition to sweeping views, Hole-in-the-Rock Road passes many side drainages of the Escalante River to the east and some remote country of the Kaiparowits Plateau high above to the west. Staff at the **Escalante Interagency Visitor Center** (755 W. Main St., Escalante, 435/826-5499, 9am-4pm Thurs.-Tues.), just west of Escalante, can give current road conditions and suggest hikes.

Boynton Overlook and the Hundred Hands Pictograph

At the **Boynton Overlook** (at the Escalante River Bridge, Hwy. 12), 14 miles (22.5 km) east of Escalante, scan the walls on the far side of the Escalante River for the Hundred Hands pictograph (binoculars help immensely). For a closer look, take a 30-minute hike from the trailhead parking area at the bottom of the hill at the Escalante River crossing. Rather than hike along the river, go up above the house (don't stray onto fenced-in private property), scramble up the face of the first cliff, and follow faint trails and rock cairns across the bench. It is easiest if you've located the pictographs first from the overlook. The Hundred Hands are high up on a cliff face that is larger than the one you scrambled up. Follow the cliff to the right, where you'll see pictographs of goats lower on the wall.

Back down at river level, head downstream a few hundred yards and look up to the left to see an Ancestral Puebloan site known as Moki House.

Calf Creek Recreation Area

This stunning canyon and park at **Calf Creek Recreation Area** (Hwy. 12, 15 mi/24 km east of Escalante, day-use $5 per vehicle) offers the most accessible glimpse of what Escalante canyon country is all about. The trailhead to 126-foot (38-m) **Lower Calf Creek Falls** is here. If you can, make plans for the half-day hike (6 mi/9.7 km round-trip, 3-4 hours), especially if you have no time for further exploration of this magical landscape. Otherwise, stop here to picnic in the shade of willows and cottonwoods. This is also the most convenient **campground** ($15) for dozens of miles. The 13 first-come, first-served campsites have water, fire pits, and picnic tables.

Million-Dollar Road

Highway 12 between Escalante and Boulder was completed in 1935 by the Civilian Conservation Corps at a budget-busting cost of $1 million, hence the moniker "million-dollar road" for this stretch of Highway 12. Before then, mules carried supplies and mail across this wilderness of slickrock and narrow canyons. The section of Highway 12 between Calf Creek and Boulder is extraordinarily scenic—you will want to pull over and ogle the views from the **Hogback,** where the road crests a fin of rock above the canyons. Stop at sunset on a clear evening for the most memorable experience.

Boulder

Boulder is a very small yet mighty community at the base of Boulder Mountain, where the alpine air mixes with the desert breeze. The town is also home to a lovely inn, the Boulder Mountain Lodge, and its revered on-site restaurant, Hell's Backbone Grill.

Anasazi State Park Museum

One mile (1.6 km) north of Boulder is the excellent **Anasazi State Park Museum** (460 Hwy. 12, 435/335-7308, https://stateparks.utah.gov, 9am-5pm daily, $5 pp, $10 family). The exhibits, an excavated village site, and a pueblo replica provide a look into the life of the ancient Ancestral Puebloan people, who lived here for 50-75 years sometime between 1050 and 1200. They grew corn, beans, and squash in fields nearby. The village population peaked at about 200, with an estimated 40-50 dwellings.

Why the Ancestral Puebloans left or where they went isn't known for certain, but a fire swept through much of the village before they abandoned it. Perhaps they burned the village on purpose, knowing they would move on. University of Utah students and faculty excavated the village, known as the Coombs Site, in 1958-1959. In the museum you can view pottery, ax heads, and other tools found here, along with delicate items like sandals and basketry that came from more protected sites elsewhere.

The self-guided tour of the sites begins behind the museum. You'll see a range of Ancestral Puebloan building styles—a pit house, masonry walls, jacal walls (mud reinforced by sticks), and combinations of masonry and jacal. Replicas of habitation and storage rooms behind the museum show complete construction details.

Fuel up for your museum tour at the food truck parked out front.

Burr Trail Road

Originally a cattle trail blazed by stockman John Atlantic Burr, this 67-mile (108-km) road extends from the town of Boulder on Highway 12 to Notom-Bullfrog Road, which runs between Highway 24 near Capitol Reef National Park's east entrance and Lake Powell's Bullfrog Marina. Paved for the first 31 miles (50 km), this scenic backcountry route traverses the Circle Cliffs and spectacular Long Canyon.

As the road meets Capitol Reef's Waterpocket Fold, breathtaking switchbacks drop some 800 feet (244 m) in elevation in just

1

2

0.5 mile (0.8 km). These switchbacks are not considered suitable for RVs or vehicles towing trailers. Just before it exits Capitol Reef, Burr Trail Road joins Notom-Bullfrog Road, which leads to Lake Powell. The unpaved sections of the road may be impassable in poor weather. Visitors should inquire about road and weather conditions before setting out.

ALONG US 89

In this region, US 89 runs between Kanab in the west to the Utah-Arizona border in the Glen Canyon National Recreation Area. From Kanab to Page, Arizona, at the Colorado River's Glen Canyon Dam, is 80 miles (129 km).

Skutumpah-Johnson Canyon Road

Eight miles (12.9 km) east of Kanab, Johnson Canyon Road heads north in the Grand Staircase unit before joining Skutumpah Road and Glendale Bench Road. Via Skutumpah Road, you can connect with Highway 12 to the north. See the full description of this road on page 259.

Paria Canyon and Vermilion Cliffs National Monument

Paria Canyon consists of a series of magnificent slot canyons that drain from Utah down to the Grand Canyon in northern Arizona. This is a hot spot for multiday canyoneering expeditions. Paria Canyon and 293,000 acres (118,573 ha) of surrounding desert grasslands are now protected as **Vermilion Cliffs National Monument** (www.blm.gov). Although the monument spreads south from the Utah-Arizona border, access to the monument's most famous sites is from back roads in Utah.

In addition to the long Paria Canyon backpacking route, you can also explore the area through some shorter but strenuous day hikes. For more information, contact the **Kanab Visitor Center** (745 E. US 89, Kanab, 435/644-4680, 9am-4pm Tues.-Sat.) or stop at the **Paria Contact Station** (2040 Long Valley Rd., 44 mi/71 km east of Kanab, 435/689-0801, 8am-4:30pm daily mid-Mar.-mid-Nov.), near milepost 21 on US 89.

Cottonwood Canyon Road

A few miles east of the Paria Contact Station (milepost 21 on US 89), Cottonwood Canyon Road leads north, eventually intersecting with Highway 12 to the north. See page 260 for a full description of this route.

Big Water and Smoky Mountain Road

At the little crossroads town of Big Water, **a BLM visitor center** (20 Upper Revolution Way, Big Water, 435/675-3200, 9am-4pm Thurs.-Mon. Apr.-Oct., hours vary Nov.-Mar.) serves travelers to the monument and to the adjacent Glen Canyon National Recreation Area. The visitor center is definitely worth a stop—it houses bones that are 75 million years old from a giant duck-billed dinosaur.

Joining US 89 at Big Water, the long and rugged Smoky Mountain Road leads to Highway 12 at Escalante, 78 miles (126 km) north. For a full description of Smoky Mountain Road, see page 262.

HIKING AND BACKPACKING

The monuments of Grand Staircase-Escalante preserve some of the best long-distance hiking trails in the American Southwest, but there are also shorter trails that provide a taste of the slot canyons and backcountry without venturing too far afield.

Stop at local visitor centers for road and trail conditions and to get up-to-date maps. Many of the following hikes require extensive travel on backcountry roads, which can be impassable after rain and rough the rest of the time. In summer, these trails are hot and exposed—always bring plenty of water and sunscreen, and wear a hat.

1: the entrance to a kiva in its original site at Anasazi State Park **2:** roadside foliage along Burr Trail Road

Walk Softly

Only great care and awareness can preserve these pristine canyons. You can help by minimizing the trace of your passage in the area.

- Travel in groups of **12 or fewer.**
- To protect soil crust and vegetation, **park** only in already disturbed areas.
- Don't touch or disturb **Native American artifacts.**
- **Protect wildlife** by leaving your dogs at home.
- Build **campfires** in developed or designated campgrounds with fire grates, fire pits, or fire pans. Wood collection in these areas is not permitted. The National Park Service and the Bureau of Land Management recommend the use of backpacking stoves.
- Most important, **pack out all waste** and use portable human waste disposal bags.

Leave No Trace (www.lnt.org) is a national organization dedicated to awareness, appreciation, and respect for our wildlands. The organization also promotes education about outdoor recreation that is environmentally responsible.

Hiking the **Escalante River canyons** is recognized worldwide as one of the greatest wilderness treks. Most people devote 4-6 days to exploring these slickrock canyons, which involve scrambling over rocks, stream fording (and even swimming depending on water levels), and long detours around rockfall and logjams. A few day hikes are possible along the Escalante River drainage. Hikers without a week to spare can sample the landscape along the Dry Fork of Coyote Gulch, which links two fascinating slot canyons.

Paria Canyon is another famed long-distance slickrock canyon hike that covers 37 miles (60 km) between the border of Utah and the edge of the Colorado River's Marble Canyon. Several long day hikes leave from trailheads on the Paria Plateau, along the border with Arizona.

More developed hiking trails can be found off Skutumpah Road and Cottonwood Canyon Road, in the Kaiparowits Plateau unit. Otherwise, hiking is mostly on unmarked routes. To plan a hiking adventure off-trail, contact one of the visitor centers and ask for help from the rangers. Free permits are required for all overnight backpacking trips, and day-use hiking fees are charged in other areas, such as Calf Creek and Paria Canyon.

Trails Along Skutumpah-Johnson Canyon Road

The northern portions of Skutumpah-Johnson Canyon Road pass through the White Cliffs, where several steep and narrow canyons carve into the terraces. Rough hiking trails traverse these slot canyons, which should only be explored when forecasts are unequivocally dry. Flash floods—especially common in mid-late summer—can strike fast.

Willis Creek Narrows

Distance: *4.4 miles (7.1 km) round-trip*
Duration: *3-4 hours*
Elevation gain: *40 feet (12 m)*
Effort: *easy*
Trailhead: *9 miles (14.5 km) south of Cannonville along Skutumpah Road*

A great introduction to slot-canyon hiking, this relatively easy trail follows a small stream through a deep, narrow gorge. From the parking area where Skutumpah Road crosses Willis Wash, walk downstream along the wash. Follow the streambed, which quickly descends between slickrock walls. At times, the canyon is just 6-10 feet (1.8-3 m) wide, while the walls rise 200-300 feet (61-91 m). The trail follows the streambed through the canyon for nearly 2.5 miles (4 km). To return, backtrack up the canyon. Use caution when hiking during flash-flood season.

Bull Valley Gorge

Distance: *2 miles (3.2 km) round-trip*
Duration: *1-2 hours*
Elevation gain: *850 feet (259 m)*
Effort: *moderate-strenuous*
Trailhead: *10.5 miles (16.9 km) south of Cannonville along Skutumpah Road*

Approximately 1.5 miles (2.4 km) south of Willis Creek on Skutumpah Road, a narrow bridge vaults over the Bull Valley Gorge. Like the Willis Creek Narrows, this is a steep and narrow cleft in the slickrock, but scrambling along the canyon bottom here is a greater challenge. From the bridge, walk upstream along a faint trail on the north side of the crevice until the walls are low enough to scramble down. The canyon deepens quickly, and you'll have to negotiate several dry falls (a rope comes in handy). When you reach the area below the bridge, look up to see a 1950s-era pickup truck trapped between the canyon walls. Three men died in this 1954 mishap—their bodies were recovered, but the pickup was left in place. From here, the canyon continues another mile (1.6 km) before widening a bit. There is no loop trail out of the canyon, so turn back when you've seen enough.

Lick Wash

Distance: *4 miles (6.4 km) one-way to Park Wash*
Duration: *4-5 hours*
Elevation gain: *200 feet (61 m)*
Effort: *easy*
Trailhead: *20 miles (32 km) south of Cannonville along Skutumpah Road*

From Lick Wash, trails lead downstream into slot canyons to a remote arroyo (dry riverbed) surrounded by mesas, one of which contains a preserve of rare native grasses. Although this area can be reached in a day's hike, this is also a good base for a backpacking trip. The trail starts just below the road crossing on Lick Wash and follows the usually dry streambed as it plunges into a narrow slot canyon. The canyon bottom is mostly level and easy to hike. After 1 mile (1.6 km), the canyon begins to widen; after 4 miles (6.4 km), Lick Wash joins Park Wash, a larger desert canyon.

Looming above this canyon junction are mesas topped with deep sandstone terraces. Rising to the east, **No Mans Mesa** is skirted on all sides by steep cliffs. The 1,788 acres (724 ha) atop the mesa were grazed by goats for 6 months in the 1920s, but since then, the pristine grassland has been protected by the BLM as an Area of Critical Environmental Concern. Hardy hikers can scramble up a steep trail—used by the goats—to visit this wilderness preserve. The ascent of No Mans Mesa is best done as an overnight trip from the Lick Wash trailhead.

Trails Along Cottonwood Canyon Road

This mostly unpaved scenic road offers access to several excellent day hikes and backpacking trips that lead into the canyons, where the Paria River, Hackberry Canyon, and Cottonwood Creek meet. Check at the Cannonville or Big Water Visitor Centers for information about road conditions, especially if you plan to go beyond Grosvenor Arch, where road crossings are prone to post-rain washouts and impassable conditions.

Cottonwood Narrows

Distance: *3 miles (4.8 km) round-trip*
Duration: *2 hours*
Elevation gain: *minimal*
Effort: *easy*
Trailhead: *From the pavement's end at Kodachrome Basin State Park, head south on Cottonwood Canyon Road. The northern end of the Cottonwood Narrows is 15 miles (24 km) down the dirt road; the southern end is 1 mile (1.6 km) farther south. Access is easier from the southern end.*

This hike through a narrow, high-walled Navajo sandstone canyon is good for casual hikers. The sandy-bottomed wash offers an easy path through the Cockscomb and a good look at the warped rock layers. Several side canyons join the wash if you're up for some scrambling. Even on this short hike, bring water and use caution during flash-flood season.

Box of the Paria River

Distance: *7 miles (11.3 km) round-trip*
Duration: *4-5 hours*
Elevation gain: *500 feet (152 m)*
Effort: *strenuous*
Trailheads: *at the confluence of Cottonwood Creek and the Paria River, 2.5 miles (4 km) south of the lower Hackberry Canyon trailhead, and 29 miles (47 km) south of the pavement's end at Kodachrome Basin State Park; from the south, 11.5 miles (18.5 km) north of US 89*

The confluence of Paria, Hackberry, and Cottonwood Canyons provides the backdrop to an excellent day hike involving steep climbs up rocky slopes as it traverses a tongue of slickrock. The route then follows the Paria River through its "box" (a cliff-sided canyon) in the Cockscomb Formation. The trail returns by following Cottonwood Canyon upstream back to the trailhead. For an easier hike, start at the Old Paria town site, at the northern end of Movie Set Road. Hike 1 mile (1.6 km) down the Paria River, then turn east into the box. Inquire at visitor centers for maps and trail conditions.

Hackberry Canyon

Distance: *22 miles (35 km) one-way*
Duration: *3 days*
Elevation gain: *1,300 feet (396 m)*
Effort: *strenuous*
Trailhead: *southern end of BLM Road 422*
Directions: *Head south on Cottonwood Canyon Road for 7.5 miles (12.1 km), from where the pavement ends at Kodachrome Basin State Park to the crossing of Round Valley Draw. From here, turn south onto BLM Road 422.*

You can travel the 22-mile (35-km) length of this scenic canyon in 3 days, or take out-and-back day hikes from either end of the trail. The lower canyon meets Cottonwood Canyon at an elevation of 4,700 feet (1,435 m), just above the mouth of the Paria River. Cottonwood Canyon Road provides access to both ends. In the lower half of Hackberry Canyon, hikers should expect to get their feet wet in small spring-fed stream flows.

Many side canyons entice, including Sam Pollock Canyon on the west side about 4.5 miles (7.2 km) upstream from the junction of Hackberry and Cottonwood Canyons. Follow it 1.75 miles (2.8 km) to **Sam Pollock Arch** (60 ft/18 m high and 70 ft/21 m wide). Available USGS topographic maps include Slickrock Bench and Calico Peak. Michael Kelsey's *Hiking and Exploring the Paria River* contains trail information and a history of the Watson homestead, located a short way below Sam Pollock Canyon.

The Escalante River Canyon System

The maze of canyons that drain the Escalante River presents exceptional hiking, ranging from easy day hikes to challenging backpacking treks. The main Escalante canyon begins just downstream from the town of Escalante and ends at Lake Powell, about 85 miles (137 km) beyond. Only one road (Hwy. 12) bridges the river. Many side canyons provide additional access to the Escalante, and most are as beautiful as the main gorge. The river system covers such a large area that you can find solitude even in spring, the busiest hiking season. The many eastern canyons remain virtually untouched.

The Escalante canyons preserve some of the quiet beauty once found in Glen Canyon, which is now lost under Lake Powell. Prehistoric Ancestral Puebloan and Fremont peoples have left structures, rock art, and artifacts in many locations. These archaeological resources are protected by federal law; don't collect or disturb them.

Before setting out, visit the rangers at the **Escalante Interagency Visitor Center** (755 W. Main St., 435/826-5499, 9am-4pm Thurs.-Tues.) for the required free backpacking permit and to check the latest trail and road conditions. Restrictions on group size may be in effect on more popular trails. You can also obtain topographic maps that show trailheads, mileage, and other useful info. Some of the more popular trailheads have self-registration stations for permits.

The best times to visit are early March-early June and mid-September-early November. Summertime trips are possible, but be prepared for higher temperatures and greater flash-flood danger in narrow canyons. Hiking along the Escalante River involves frequent crossings, and there's always water in the main canyon, usually ankle- or knee-deep. Pools in the Narrows between Scorpion Gulch and Stevens Canyon can be up to chest-deep in spots (which you can bypass), but that's the exception. Occasional springs, some tributaries, and the river itself provide drinking water. Always purify the water first, since it carries microorganisms causing the unpleasant disease giardiasis. Don't forget insect repellent—mosquitoes and deerflies seek out hikers in late spring and summer. Long-sleeved shirts and long pants also discourage biting insects and protect against the brush.

For guided day hikes and hiking shuttles into the Escalante canyons, contact **Utah Canyon Outdoors** (325 W. Main St., Escalante, 435/826-4967, www.utahcanyonoutdoors.com).

Escalante Canyon Trailheads

All sorts of trips are possible here. One of the easiest access points is where the Highway 12 bridge passes over the river. Hikers can reach the Escalante River through western side canyons from Hole-in-the-Rock Road or eastern side canyons from Burr Trail Road. The western trailheads on Hole-in-the-Rock Road are more easily reached by car, making this a good area for vehicle shuttles. To reach eastern trailheads—with the exceptions of Deer Creek and the Gulch on Burr Trail Road—you'll need lots of time and, if the road is wet, a 4WD vehicle. Carry water for these canyons, which are usually dry, except for Deer Creek.

Escalante to Highway 12 Bridge

Distance: *15 miles (24 km) one-way*
Duration: *1-2 days*
Elevation gain: *500 feet (152 m)*
Effort: *moderate-strenuous*
Trailhead: *near the town of Escalante*
Directions: *Follow signs from Highway 12 on the east side of town (by the high school) to the trailhead.*

This section of the Escalante River offers easy walking and stunning canyon scenery. Tributaries and sandstone caves invite exploration. You'll find good camping areas the entire way (be sure to get a permit for overnight camping). Usually, the river here is only ankle-deep. Almost immediately, the river knifes its way through the massive cliffs of the Escalante Monocline, leaving the broad valley of the upper river behind. Although there is no maintained trail along this stretch of the east-flowing river, it is relatively easy to pick your way along the riverbank.

Death Hollow, which is far prettier than the name suggests, meets the Escalante from the north after 7.5 miles (12.1 km). Several good swimming holes carved in rock are a short hike upstream; watch for poison ivy among the greenery. Continue farther up Death Hollow to see more pools, little waterfalls, and outstanding canyon scenery. You can bypass some pools, but others you'll have to swim—bring a small inflatable boat, air mattress, or waterproof bag to ferry backpacks.

Some 4.5 miles (7.2 km) downstream from Death Hollow, **Sand Creek,** on the Escalante's north side, is also worth exploring. Deep pools begin a short distance up from the mouth. Another 0.5 mile (0.8 km) down the Escalante, a natural arch appears high on the canyon wall. Then Escalante Natural Bridge comes into view, just 2 miles (3.2 km) from the Highway 12 bridge.

Highway 12 Bridge to Harris Wash

Distance: *26.5 miles (43 km) one-way*
Duration: *4-6 days*
Elevation gain: *700 feet (213 m)*
Effort: *moderate*

Trailhead: *Highway 12 bridge over the Escalante River, between Escalante and Boulder*

This is where many long-distance hikers begin their exploration of the Escalante canyons, and indeed, it's one of the world's greatest wilderness treks. This section features narrows, lush side canyons, sparkling streams, great valleys, and dry washes. A good 37-mile (60-km) hike of 4-6 days begins at the Highway 12 bridge, follows the Escalante River down to Harris Wash, then travels up Harris to a trailhead off Hole-in-the-Rock Road.

From the Highway 12 bridge parking area, a trail leads to the river. Canyon access goes through private property, so cross the river at the posted signs. **Phipps Wash** comes in from the south (on the right) after 1.5 miles (2.4 km), entailing several more river crossings. Turn up its wide mouth for 0.5 mile (0.8 km) to see Maverick Bridge in a drainage to the right. To reach Phipps Arch, continue another 0.75 mile (1.2 km) up the main wash, turn left into a box canyon, and scramble up the left side (see the USGS 7.5-minute Calf Creek topographic map).

One mile (1.6 km) beyond Phipps Wash, up a north side canyon known locally as Deer Creek, you'll find **Bowington (Boynton) Arch.** Trek up the wash past three deep pools, turn left into a tributary canyon, and this feature is on your left. In 1878, gunfire resolved a quarrel between local ranchers John Boynton and Washington Phipps. Phipps was killed, but their names live on. You can also start down Deer Creek from Burr Trail Road, 6.5 miles (10.5 km) southeast of Boulder at a primitive BLM campground. Starting at the campground, follow Deer Creek 7.5 miles (12.1 km) to Boulder Creek, then 3.5 miles (5.6 km) down Boulder Creek to the Escalante. Both Deer and Boulder Creeks have water year-round.

In the next major side canyon, the waters of **Boulder Creek** come rushing into the Escalante from the north, 5.75 miles (9.3 km) below the Highway 12 bridge. The creek, along with its Dry Hollow and Deer Creek tributaries, provides good canyon walking—and sometimes swimming or climbing up on the plateau in deep areas. Below Boulder Creek, sheer sandstone walls constrict the river in a narrow channel, but the canyon widens again above the **Gulch** tributary, 14 miles (22.5 km) below the highway bridge. Hikers can head up the Gulch on a day hike.

Most springs along the Escalante are difficult to spot. One that's easier to find is in the first south bend after the Gulch, where water comes straight out of the rock a few feet above the river. Escalante Canyon widens as the river meanders along. Hikers can cut out some bends by walking in the open desert between canyon walls and riverside willow thickets.

Three miles (4.8 km) below the Gulch, a bend loops to the north just before Horse Canyon. Along with its tributaries **Death Hollow** and **Wolverine Creek, Horse Canyon** drains the Circle Cliffs to the northeast. Floods in these mostly dry streambeds wash down pieces of black petrified wood. Vehicles with good clearance can reach the upper sections of all three canyons from **Wolverine Loop Road** off Burr Trail Road. Horse and Wolverine Creek Canyons offer good easy-to-moderate hiking.

If you really want a challenge, try Death Hollow—sometimes called Little Death Hollow in contrast with the larger one near Hell's Backbone Road. Starting from the Escalante River, go about 2 miles (3.2 km) up Horse Canyon and turn right into Death Hollow. Rugged scrambling over boulders takes you back into a long section of twisting narrows. Carry water for Upper Horse Canyon and its tributaries. Lower Horse Canyon usually has water.

About 3.5 miles (5.6 km) down the Escalante from Horse Canyon, you'll enter Glen Canyon National Recreation Area and come to Sheffield Bend, a large grassy field on the right. Only a chimney remains from Sam Sheffield's old homestead. Beyond the clearing lie two grand amphitheaters up a stiff climb in loose sand. Over the next 5.5 river miles (8.9 km) to Silver Falls Creek, you'll pass long bends, dry side canyons, and a huge sand slope on the right canyon wall. Don't look for any silver waterfalls in **Silver Falls Creek**—the name comes from streaks of shiny desert varnish on the cliffs.

Harris Wash is to the right (west) side of the Escalante River, almost opposite Silver Falls Creek. When the Hole-in-the-Rock route proved so difficult, pioneers descended Harris Wash to the Escalante River, climbed part of Silver Falls Creek, crossed the Circle Cliffs, descended Muley Twist Canyon in the Waterpocket Fold, then followed Hall's Creek to Hall's Crossing on the Colorado River. Charles Hall operated a ferry there from 1881 to 1884. Old maps show a 4WD road through Harris Wash and Silver Falls Creek Canyons, before the National Park Service closed off the Glen Canyon National Recreation Area section. Harris Wash is just 0.5 mile (0.8 km) downstream and across the Escalante from Silver Falls Creek.

Harris Wash

Distance: *10.25 miles (16.5 km) one-way from trailhead to Escalante River*
Duration: *2-3 days round-trip*
Elevation gain: *700 feet (213 m)*
Effort: *moderate*
Trailhead: *Harris Wash trailhead off Hole-in-the-Rock Road*
Directions: *From Highway 12, turn south and travel on Hole-in-the-Rock Road for 10.8 miles (17.4 km), then turn left and go 6.3 miles (10.1 km) on a dirt road (keep left at the fork near the end).*

Clear shallow water glides down this gem of a canyon. High cliffs streaked with desert varnish are deeply undercut and support lush hanging gardens. Harris Wash provides a beautiful route to the Escalante River, but it can also be a destination in itself. Along the way, tributaries and caves will tempt you to explore. The sand and gravel streambed makes for easy walking. Don't be dismayed by the drab appearance of upper Harris Wash: The canyon and creek appear a few miles downstream. The Harris Wash trailhead is restricted to a maximum of 12 people per group.

★ Lower Calf Creek Falls

Distance: *3 miles (4.8 km) one-way*
Duration: *4 hours*
Elevation gain: *250 feet (76 m)*
Effort: *easy-moderate*
Trailhead: *Calf Creek Campground (day-use $5), 16 miles (26 km) east of Escalante on Highway 12*

Calf Creek is a tributary of the Escalante River, entering it near Highway 12. For many, the hike to Lower Calf Creek Falls is the highlight of a first trip to the Escalante area. And with a trailhead right off the highway (rather than miles up a backcountry road), it's one of the more accessible adventures in Grand Staircase-Escalante. From the parking area just off Highway 12, the trail winds between high Navajo sandstone cliffs streaked with desert varnish, where you'll see beaver ponds, a petroglyph of three figures holding hands, and the misty 126-foot-high (38-m) Lower Calf Creek Falls. Bring water and perhaps lunch, since the falls are a nice spot to linger. Summer temperatures can soar, but the falls and the clear pool beneath stay cool. Sheer cliffs block travel farther upstream.

Near the road, **Calf Creek Campground** (early Apr.-late Oct., $15) has 13 sites with drinking water.

Dry Fork of Coyote Gulch

Drive 26 miles (42 km) south on the Hole-in-the-Rock Road to enjoy a moderate day hike through a series of narrow and enchanting **slot canyons: Peek-a-boo, Spooky,** and **Brimstone.** Exploring these slots requires only basic canyoneering skills—namely the ability to pass through narrow (12-in/30-cm) spaces—making it a great spot for the canyoneering-curious and families with kids old enough to hike for a few hours and enjoy the adventure.

TOP EXPERIENCE

★ Peek-a-boo and Spooky Slot Canyons

Distance: *3.5 miles (5.6 km) round-trip*
Duration: *5 hours*

Lake Powell 70 mi
Escalante Natural Bridge 2 mi
Escalante Arch
Escalante 15 mi
1
2
3
4

Elevation gain: *300 feet (91 m)*
Effort: *moderate*
Trailhead: *Dry Fork of Coyote Gulch*
Directions: *From Highway 12, turn south onto Hole-in-the-Rock Road and follow it for 26 miles (42 km). Turn left at the sign for Dry Fork and continue 1.7 miles (2.7 km) along a rutted dirt road to the trailhead.*

From the trailhead parking lot, follow cairns down into the sandy bottom of the Dry Fork. The slot canyons all enter the gulch from the north. Watch for cairns and trails because the openings are easy to miss. You'll have to scramble up some rocks to get into Peek-a-boo. The slots sometimes contain deep pools of water, and choke stones and pour-offs can make access difficult. No loop trail links the three slot canyons, so follow each until the canyon becomes too narrow to continue, then return. Making a full circuit of these canyons entails about 3.5 miles (5.6 km) of hiking. A side trail from Coyote Gulch also leads to stunning 225-foot (69-m) **Stevens Arch.** Because they're relatively accessible, these canyons draw a crowd. Get an early start and do your part by packing out your garbage.

Paria Canyon and Vermilion Cliffs

The wild, twisting canyons of the Paria River and its tributaries offer a memorable experience for seasoned hikers. Silt-laden water has sculpted the colorful canyon walls, revealing 200 million years of geologic history. For an immersive experience, you can enter the 2,000-foot-deep (610-m) gorge of the Paria in southern Utah, then hike 37 miles (60 km) downstream to Lee's Ferry in Arizona, where the Paria empties into the Colorado River. A handful of shorter but rugged day hikes lead to superb scenery and geologic wonders.

Ancient petroglyphs and campsites show that Pueblo people traveled the Paria more than 700 years ago. They hunted mule deer and bighorn sheep while using the broad lower end of the canyon to grow corn, beans, and squash. The first nonnatives to see the river were part of the Domínguez-Escalante Expedition that stopped here in 1776. In 1871, John D. Lee and three companions brought a herd of cattle from the Pahreah settlement through the canyon to Lee's Ferry. After Lee began a Colorado River ferry service in 1872, he and others farmed the lower Paria Canyon. Prospectors came here to search for gold, uranium, and other minerals, but much of the canyon remained unexplored. In the late 1960s, the BLM organized a small expedition that led to the Arizona Wilderness Act of 1984, designating Paria Canyon a wilderness area, along with parts of the Paria Plateau and Vermilion Cliffs. Vermilion Cliffs National Monument was created in 2000.

The **Paria Contact Station** (435/689-0801, 8am-4:30pm daily mid-Mar.-mid-Nov.) is in Utah, 44 miles (71 km) east of Kanab on US 89 near milepost 21. It's on the south side of the highway, just east of the Paria River. Self-serve day-use permits ($6 pp, $6 per dog) are required for day hiking in Paria Canyon and to visit other sites in Vermilion Cliffs National Monument.

Paria Canyon

Distance: *38.5 miles (62 km) one-way*
Duration: *4-6 days*
Elevation gain: *1,300 feet (396 m)*
Effort: *moderate*
Trailhead: *Whitehouse Campground*
Directions: *The trailhead is 2 miles (3.2 km) south of the Paria Contact Station, on a dirt road near a campground and old homestead site called White House. The exit trailhead is in Arizona at Lonely Dell Ranch of Lee's Ferry, 44 miles (71 km) southwest of Page via US 89 and US 89A, or 98 miles (158 km) southeast of Kanab on US 89A.*

Backpacking the Paria is a beautiful, immersive canyon experience. Allow plenty of time for this trek—there are many river crossings, and you'll want to make side trips up some tributary canyons. A decent amount of backpacking experience is a must, as help may be days away. Flash floods can race through the

1: an Escalante Canyon trailhead off Highway 12
2: Lower Calf Creek Falls **3:** Navajo sandstone cliffs on the trail to Lower Calf Creek Falls **4:** Peek-a-boo Canyon

canyon, especially during summer. Rangers close Paria Canyon if they think the danger exists. Because the upper end (between mileposts 4.2 and 9.0) is narrowest, rangers require all hikers to start here so they have up-to-date weather information.

You must register at a trailhead or the **Kanab BLM Office** (318 N. 100 E., Kanab, 435/644-2672, 8am-4:30pm Mon.-Fri. year-round). **Permits** to hike the canyon are $5 pp per day. Backpackers should get a permit online up to 4 months in advance (www.recreation.gov) or at the ranger station. Competition for overnight permits is fierce, so it's best to go online at the first of the month for reservations 4 months out. Day hikers can just register and pay the fee at the trailhead. The visitor center and the office both provide weather forecasts and maps. The visitor center always has the forecast posted at an outdoor kiosk.

The full hike requires a 150-mile (242-km) round-trip car shuttle. For a list of shuttle services, ask at the **Paria Contact Station** (2040 Long Valley Rd., Kanab, 435/689-0801, 8am-4:30pm daily mid-Mar.-mid-Nov.) or the Kanab BLM Office. Expect to pay at least $200 for this service.

Visitors should minimize their impact on this beautiful canyon. Before you go, study the BLM's Paria "Visitor Use Regulations," which include no campfires, a pack-out-all-waste policy, and a requirement that latrines be made at least 100 feet (30 m) from the river and campsites. Human waste and toilet paper must be transported out in plastic bags (available at the ranger station). The Paria rangers recommend a maximum group size of 6, though regulations specify a 10-person limit. No more than 20 people per day can enter the canyon for overnight trips. The best times for this hike are mid-March-June and October-November. May—especially Memorial Day weekend—tends to be crowded.

Good drinking water is available from springs along the way (see a BLM map for locations). Avoid the river water because of possible chemical pollution from agriculture upstream. Normally the river is only ankle-deep, but in spring or after rain, it can deepen considerably. There's a good chance much of the hike will be through water, so the right footwear is paramount, especially in winter. During thunderstorms, levels can rise to more than 20 feet (6 m) in the Narrows, so heed weather warnings. Quicksand, which is most prevalent after flooding, is more a nuisance than a danger—usually it's just knee-deep. Many hikers carry a walking stick to probe opaque water before crossing.

One of Arizona's largest natural arches, **Wrather Canyon Arch** has a massive 200-foot (61-m) span and is about 1 mile (1.6 km) up a Paria side canyon. The mouth of Wrather Canyon and other points along the Paria are unsigned, so turn right (southwest) at milepost 20.6 and follow your map.

Buckskin Gulch and Wire Pass

Distance: *1.7 miles (2.7 km) one-way*
Duration: *3 hours*
Elevation gain: *300 feet (91 m)*
Effort: *moderate*
Trailhead: *Wire Pass trailhead*
Directions: *From Kanab, head 37 miles (60 km) east on US 89 to BLM Road 700 (also called House Rock Valley Rd.), between mileposts 25 and 26. Turn south for 8.5 bumpy miles (13.7 km) to the trailhead. 4WD high-clearance vehicles are strongly advised.*

The longest, deepest slot canyon in the United States and perhaps in the world, Buckskin Gulch is a tributary of the Paria, with walls reaching hundreds of feet high and narrowing to as little as 4 feet (1.2 m) in width. In places, the walls block out so much light that it's like walking in a cave. Be very careful to avoid flash floods.

Day hikers can get a taste of this incredible area along a relatively easy trail that leads into Wire Pass, a narrow side canyon that joins Buckskin Gulch. The trail runs the length of Wire Pass to its confluence with Buckskin Gulch. From here, you can explore the canyon or follow Buckskin Gulch until it meets Paria Canyon after 12.5 miles (20 km).

For the full experience of Buckskin Gulch,

long-distance hikers can begin at the Buckskin Gulch trailhead, 4.5 miles (7.2 km) south of US 89 on BLM Road 700. From here, it's 16.3 miles (26 km) one-way through Buckskin Gulch to Paria Canyon. Hikers can continue down the Paria or turn upstream and hike 6 miles (9.7 km) to exit at the White House trailhead near the ranger station. Hiking this gulch can be strenuous, with rough terrain, deep pools of water, and log or rock jams that may require ropes. Conditions vary considerably from year to year. Regulations mandate packing your waste out.

Hiking permits ($6 pp per day) are required and can be paid day-of at the trailhead. Backpackers need to obtain an overnight permit (www.recreation.gov, $5 pp per day, available up to 4 months in advance) online or at the ranger station.

★ The Wave (Coyote Buttes)

Distance: *6.4 miles (10.3 km)*
Duration: *4-6 hours*
Elevation gain: *1,233 feet (376 m)*
Effort: *strenuous*
Trailhead: *Wire Pass*
Directions: *From Kanab, head 37 miles (60 km) east on US 89 to BLM Road 700 (also called House Rock Valley Rd.), between mileposts 25 and 26. Turn south for 8.5 bumpy miles (13.7 km) to the trailhead. 4WD high-clearance vehicles are strongly advised.*

Of all the bizarre sandstone features in the desert out here, the Wave might just be the most mesmerizing. While the trailhead for this sought-after hike is in Utah, the feature itself is in Arizona, meaning you'll hike across the state border. Made of Navajo sandstone, this formation owes its existence to wind and rain calcifying and compacting dunes over deep time. While the main attraction is undoubtedly the Wave, there's more to explore besides just one iconic feature, including dinosaur tracks and landscapes resembling Salvador Dalí's surrealist settings.

The Wave is located in the Paria Canyon-Vermilion Cliffs Wilderness area, specifically within Coyote Buttes North Permit Area. From the trailhead, head east into Wire Pass Wash, and a little over 0.5 mile (0.8 km) from the trailhead, turn right at the sign for Coyote Buttes. Climb a hill and cross a sagebrush field until you reach a wash, then hike up slickrock to a saddle. When you see twin buttes, head west around them. To the south, you should see a cliff with a crack in it—head in this direction past another wash and over sand dunes to reach the Wave. There are small

the Wave

signs maintained by the BLM leading the way, and over the slickrock, you'll see cairns. But don't rely on cairns and signage alone—you must head into this area with a topo map and compass or GPS unit.

So what's the catch? A difficult permitting process and remote location mean planning ahead is all but mandatory. Ideally, you would organize your trip around this hike. The area where the Wave is located, Coyote Buttes North, requires day-use permits, which are available up to 4 months ahead through an extremely competitive online advance lottery (www.recreation.gov); notifications of successful applications occur 3 months in advance. There is also a daily lottery (a separate listing on www.recreation.gov) that you can apply for 6am-6pm two days in advance of your desired hike date; you will be notified the evening you submit your application if you obtained a permit.

While there's no camping allowed within Coyote Buttes North, there is dispersed BLM land camping at the trailhead (toilets available), or continue 1 mile (1.6 km) farther on House Rock Road past the trailhead to Stateline Campground. Note that House Rock Road can be impassable when wet, so don't attempt this adventure during or after rain, or if there's precipitation in the forecast.

MOUNTAIN BIKING

While there are no purpose-built bike trails in the park, hopping on the saddle allows you to take in the spectacular scenery at a more leisurely pace. Road bikers can cruise through views on scenic Highway 12 and US 89. Mountain bikes are allowed on all roads, but not on hiking trails, off-road, or across slickrock. But the hundreds of miles of dirt roads in the monument offer plenty of riding, with many loop possibilities for long day rides or multiday trips. A few popular routes on a mountain or gravel bike include **Burr Trail, Hole-in-the-Rock Road** (and its side roads), and **Cottonwood Canyon Road** to the south.

Visitor centers in the area can offer maps and help with planning backcountry bike adventures. If you'd rather focus on the scenic ride than planning and heavy loads, look into local outfitters. This country is remote and primitive, so cyclists must carry everything, including drinking water or purification systems, since there are few sources of potable water.

4WD EXPLORATION

Without a mountain bike or a pair of hiking boots, the best way to explore the backcountry here is with a high-clearance 4WD vehicle. However, the scale of the landscape, the primitive quality of many of the roads, and the risk of flash flooding mean you shouldn't head into the backcountry unless you're a confident driver and can perform basic mechanical repairs. Choose roads that match your vehicle's capacity and your driving ability.

The BLM has let some roads that may be marked on maps return to nature and is closing others entirely, so it's best to check access and road conditions with a visitor center before setting out. Remember that many of the roads in the monument are very slow going. If you've got somewhere to be in a hurry, these corrugated, boulder-dodging roads may not get you there in time. Be sure to take plenty of water—not only for drinking but also for overheated radiators. It's also wise to carry wooden planks or old carpet scraps to help you gain traction should your wheels get mired in sand.

RAFTING

Most of the year, shallow water and rocks make boat travel impossible on the Escalante River, but for two or three weeks during spring runoff, which peaks in mid-May-early June, river levels may rise high enough to be passable. Some years, there may not be enough water at all. Contact the **Escalante Interagency Visitor Center** for ideas on when to hit the river at its highest. A shallow draft and maneuverability are essential, so inflatable canoes or kayaks work best (they're also easier to carry out at trip's end or if water levels drop too low for floating). Rafts are too wide and bulky, and hard-shelled kayaks and canoes get banged up on all the rocks.

The usual launch is the Highway 12 bridge. Coyote Gulch—a 13-mile (21-km) hike—is a good spot to get out, as is Crack in the Wall, which is a 2.75-mile (4.4-km) hike on steep sand from the junction of Coyote and Escalante Canyons to the Forty-Mile Ridge trailhead. A 4WD vehicle is needed, and a rope is required to negotiate the vessel over the canyon rim. Hole-in-the-Rock is another pullout (a 600-ft/183-m ascent over boulders; rope suggested). You could also arrange for a friend to pick you up by boat from Halls Crossing or Bullfrog Marina. Boaters must obtain a free backcountry permit from either the Bureau of Land Management or the National Park Service.

OUTFITTERS

There aren't many places to shop for gear in this remote area. The most centrally located shops are in the town of Escalante, where you'll find **Utah Canyon Outdoors** (325 W. Main St., Escalante, 435/826-4967, www.utahcanyonoutdoors.com), which stocks books, maps, and some gear. Across the street, **Escalante Outfitters** (310 W. Main St., Escalante, 435/826-4266, www.escalanteoutfitters.com) has a little bit of everything, including a small liquor store. It's a good place to pick up a warm jacket or a guide for fishing, biking, or hiking trips.

Another shop with a good selection of clothing and gear is **Willow Canyon Outdoor** (263 S. 100 E., Kanab, 435/644-8884 www.willowcanyon.com), in Kanab, which also serves good coffee and has an excellent book shop.

Escalante

The friendly little town of Escalante (elev. 5,813 ft/1,772 m) is a natural hub for exploring the Escalante River canyons and the northeastern part of the monument. The town sits 38 miles (61 km) east of Bryce Canyon and 23 miles (37 km) south of the town of Boulder. Less than 700 people live here alongside the resident cows, horses, and chickens you'll meet a block off Main Street.

FOOD

Just about all restaurants in town close mid-November-early March. Seasonal closures vary from year to year, so check before you go, and don't expect to roll into town in December and find any viable dining options.

Escalante Outfitters (310 W. Main St., 435/826-4266, www.escalanteoutfitters.com, 8am-9pm Thurs.-Tues.) runs a little café with good espresso, sandwiches, outstanding handmade pizza ($12-26), and craft brews. The breakfast pastries are also delicious. This is also a good spot to pick up lunch to pack for your hike.

Stock up on food for the trail at the **Escalante Mercantile and Natural Grocery** (210 W. Main St., 435/826-4114, 8am-5pm Mon.-Sat.). It's a great spot to pick up fresh fruit, bottled iced tea, or kombucha. Gluten-free, vegetarian, and vegan options are available. For great pastries, quiche, and brown-bag sandwiches, stop by **Mimi's Bakery & Deli** (30 W. Main St., 435/690-0576, 8am-7pm Mon.-Sat. Mar.-Nov., $9-11) inside Griffin's Grocery.

Nemo's Drive Thru (40 E. Main St., 435/826-4500, 11am-8pm Mon.-Sat., $9-17) is the perfect place to refuel after a long hike. The tiny restaurant doesn't look too impressive from the street, but the food is far better than what you'll find at most small-town burger joints. In addition to regular burgers, they serve veggie burgers, fish-and-chips, and good milkshakes.

Escalante to Capitol Reef

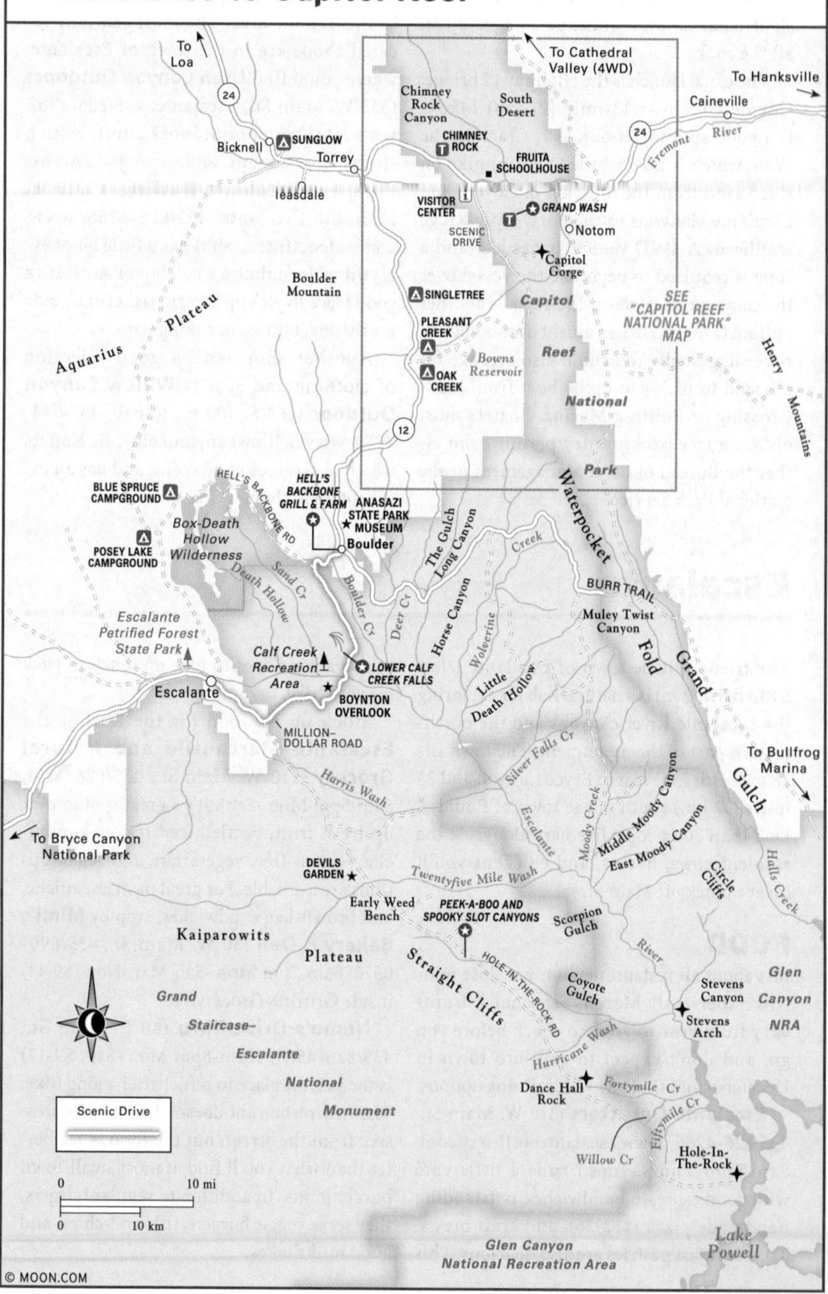

As close as you'll get to fine dining in Escalante is the ★ **Circle D Eatery** (485 W. Main St., 435/826-4125, www.escalantecircledeatery.com, 11am-9pm Wed.-Mon., 4pm-9pm Tues., $16-45), which offers local free-range beef and a variety of house-smoked meats. The steaks are dependably good, as is the smoked brisket. If you're around for breakfast, chow down on some good Mexican-style eggs.

The only true bar (at least according to Utah's liquor laws) on the entire length of Highway 12 is **4th West Pub** (425 W. Main St., 435/826-4525, 5pm-10pm Mon.-Sat., $12-17). The food is simple—sandwiches, tacos, salads—but you don't need to order food just to enjoy a cocktail (unlike at drinking establishments deemed restaurants in the state).

East of town, **Kiva Koffeehouse** (7144 Hwy. 12, Milepost 73.86, 435/826-4550, www.kivakoffeehouse.com, 8am-4pm Wed.-Sun. Apr.-Oct., $6-12) has one of the best settings in the state, with windows looking out at the landscape. It's worth a stop for a latte or a lunch of Southwestern-style fare featuring organic ingredients. There are also a few guest rooms for rent here.

ACCOMMODATIONS

Accommodations in Escalante range from simple to luxurious. Most are seasonal, closing around mid-November-early March. Seasonal closures vary from year to year, so check online or call in advance.

$50-100

The seven small yet cozy log cabins at ★ **Escalante Outfitters** (310 W. Main St., 435/826-4266, www.escalanteoutfitters.com, Mar.-mid-Nov., $55) share all-gender bathhouses and a common grassy area. A larger ADA-accessible cabin with a bath ($150) sleeps four, and a few spots for tent camping are also available ($16). These Wi-Fi-equipped cabins are conveniently located behind the store, which also houses a casual café serving pizza and a tiny liquor store. Dogs are allowed in some cabins ($10 extra).

The **Prospector Inn** (380 W. Main St., 435/826-4653, www.prospector-inn.com, $94) is a large motor lodge near the center of town, with a restaurant and a lounge on the premises. A pleasant and modern establishment, **Rainbow Country B&B** (586 E. 300 S., 435/826-4567, www.bnbescalante.com, $99-134) has four guest rooms and a hot tub, a pool table, and a TV lounge.

$100-150

On the west edge of town, the **Circle D Motel** (475 W. Main St., 435/826-4297, www.escalantecircledmotel.com, $115-130) offers hikers, cyclists, and other recreational users clean basic guest rooms. Pets are welcome in some rooms. The motel also has a good restaurant on-site.

Right on the edge of town, find cozy log cabins, vacation houses, and RV sites at **Escalante Cabins and RV Park** (680 W. Main St., 435/826-4433, www.escalantepark.com, RVs $55-70, cabins and homes $195-345). The cabins have baths and microwaves, minifridges, and coffeemakers.

A remodeled motel with a fanciful Old West theme, the **Cowboy Country Inn** (25 S. 100 W., 435/616-4066, www.cowboycountryinn.com, $110-150) is a half block off the highway and offers 22 rooms, ranging from a small "bunkhouse" with bunk beds to a two-bedroom suite.

Over $150

East of Escalante on Highway 12, Kiva Koffeehouse rents a couple of spacious, beautifully decorated rooms in ★ **Kiva Kottage** (7144 Hwy. 12, Milepost 73.86, 435/826-4550, www.kivakoffeehouse.com, Apr.-Oct., $250, breakfast included). With remarkable views, fireplaces, and jetted tubs, these rooms are wonderful places to relax after exploring—and the absence of TVs makes it even better. Located just above the spot where the Escalante River crosses Highway 12, it's also a good base for hikers. You'll have to drive to Escalante or Boulder for dinner, though the rooms do have microwaves and fridges.

One of the newer accommodations in the

Boar's Head
ESCALAN
OUTFITTE
PIZZA • BEER • CABINS
1

2

area, ★ **Yonder Escalante** (2020 Hwy. 12, 435/274-7222, www.stayyonder.com, mid-Mar.-mid-Nov.) offers cabins ($194), furnished Airstream trailers ($214), a variety of RV sites with hookups ($109), and campsites for tents or vans ($59). There's also an on-site drive-in movie theater, a pool, a hot tub, private bathhouses, laundry, and a general store with booze and food for sale. A food truck serves breakfast and dinner.

In downtown Escalante, ★ **Canyons B&B** (120 E. Main St., 435/690-8013, www.canyonsbnb.com, late Mar.-Nov., $150-190) is a modern three-bedroom bunkhouse built behind an old farmhouse that offers its own lodge room. There's nothing rustic about the guest rooms—all are nicely decorated and equipped with a TV, telephones, and Wi-Fi. Minimum-stay requirements may apply.

About 5 miles (8 km) west of Escalante on a dramatically scenic 160-acre (65-ha) ranch, ★ **Slot Canyons Inn B&B** (3680 W. Hwy. 12, 435/826-4901 or 866/889-8375, www.slotcanyonsinn.com, $190-250) has eight modern guest rooms, some with patios or balconies. A spacious pioneer cabin that sleeps six has also been moved to the property and restored ($334). Breakfast is included with your room.

Perhaps the most upscale of Escalante's hotels is the **Canyon Country Lodge** (760 E. Hwy. 12, 435/826-4545 or 844/367-3080, https://canyoncountrylodge.com, $199-209), just east of town. Rooms are large and nicely appointed, and an indoor pool and outdoor hot tub await, as does a charging station for your electric car. The on-site Canyon Grill (5pm-9pm daily, $10-15) serves dinner.

If you're traveling with a family or group of friends, consider renting the architecturally striking solar-heated **La Luz Desert Retreat** (680 W. 600 S., 888/305-4708, www.laluz.net, 2- to 3-day minimum stay, high season $210 for 4 people, plus $75 cleaning fee), in a private setting just south of town. The house, designed in the Usonian tradition of Frank Lloyd Wright, sleeps up to six.

1: Escalante Outfitters **2:** freshly made pizza at Escalante Outfitters

Campgrounds

Just northwest of the town, **Escalante Petrified Forest State Park** (435/826-4466, https://stateparks.utah.gov, reservations 800/322-3770, www.reserveamerica.com, year-round, tents $25, RVs $30) is conveniently located and full of attractions like trails passing chunks of petrified wood, along with boating and swimming in a reservoir (canoe, kayak, and paddleboard rentals available). Drinking water and showers are available, along with RV hookups.

In town, you can stay at **Canyons of the Escalante RV Park** (495 W. Main St., 435/826-4959, www.canyonsofescalantervpark.com, mid-Mar.-Oct.), which has simple and deluxe cabins (the more expensive ones have half baths, $54-83) and sites for tents ($26) and RVs ($43), plus showers and a coin laundry. **Escalante Cabins and RV Park** (680 W. Main St., 435/826-4433, www.escalantepark.com, Mar.-Nov., RVs $55-70, cabins and homes $195-345) is also a good bet for RV travelers.

A couple of miles north of town in a grove of cottonwoods and junipers, ★ **Escalante Yurts** (1605 N. Pine Creek Rd., 435/826-4222 or 844/200-9878, www.escalanteyurts.com, $289-408) offers glamping comforts in 450- to 900-square-foot (42- to 84-sq-m) yurts that sleep 4-7. Each yurt has a private bath, high-quality furnishings, and a private patio. Continental breakfast is included.

Calf Creek Campground (Hwy. 12, first-come, first-served, early Apr.-late Oct., $15) is in a pretty canyon 15.5 miles (25 km) east of Escalante on Highway 12. Lower Calf Creek Falls Trail (6 mi/9.6 km round-trip) begins at the campground and follows the creek upstream to the falls.

INFORMATION AND SERVICES

The **Escalante Interagency Visitor Center** (755 W. Main St., 435/826-5499, 9am-4pm

Thurs.-Tues.), on the western edge of town, has an information center for visitors to US Forest Service, Bureau of Land Management, and National Park Service areas around Escalante. It's also one of the best spots for information on the national monument. Hikers or bikers headed for overnight trips in the monument system can obtain permits here.

Kazan Memorial Clinic (570 E. Moqui Ln., 435/826-4374) offers medical care, but it isn't open on weekends. The nearest hospital is 70 miles (113 km) west in Panguitch.

GETTING THERE

Located on Highway 12, Escalante is 38 miles (61 km) east of Bryce Canyon and 23 miles (37 km) south of Boulder. A word of warning: Drive slowly through town. The local police have a sharp eye for out-of-towners exceeding the speed limit.

HELL'S BACKBONE

Hell's Backbone Scenic Drive

This 38-mile (61-km) drive is the longer, more scenic, and far spicier way to travel from the town of Boulder to the town of Escalante (versus the paved way on Hwy. 12). The road climbs high into the pine forests north of Escalante with excellent views of the distant Navajo, Fifty-Mile, and Henry Mountains. The highlight is the one-lane **Hell's Backbone Bridge,** which vaults a chasm between precipitous Death Hollow and Sand Creek Canyons. Stop here for photos of the outstanding vistas.

Hell's Backbone Road reaches an elevation of 9,200 feet (2,805 m) on the slopes of Roger Peak before descending to a bridge. Mule teams used this narrow ridge, with sheer canyons on either side, as a route to Boulder until the 1930s. At that time, a bridge built by the Civilian Conservation Corps allowed the first vehicles to make the trip.

To reach Hell's Backbone Road from Escalante, turn north on 300 East and follow the initially paved road out of town. The bridge is about 25 miles (40 km) from town. Alternatively, you can turn onto Hell's Backbone Road 3 miles (4.8 km) south of Boulder on Highway 12. From this corner, the bridge is 13 miles (20.9 km).

Campgrounds

Amid aspen and ponderosa pines, Posey Lake (elev. 8,700 ft/2,652 m) is stocked with rainbow and brook trout. The adjacent **Posey Lake Campground** (Forest Rd. 154, www.recreation.gov, Memorial Day-Labor Day, $14) has 21 single sites and a group site, plus drinking water. A hiking trail (2 mi/3.2 km round-trip) begins near space number 14 and climbs 400 feet (122 m) to an old fire-lookout tower, with views of the lake and surrounding country. Posey Lake is 14 miles (22.5 km) north of Escalante via Hell's Backbone Road, then 2 miles (3.2 km) west on Forest Road 154.

Nearby **Blue Spruce Campground** (Forest Rd. 145, www.fs.usda.gov, $9) is another pretty spot at an elevation of 7,860 feet (2,395 m), but it has only six sites. Anglers can try for pan-size trout in a nearby stream. The campground, surrounded by blue spruce, aspen, and ponderosa pine, has drinking water late May-early September; go north on Hell's Backbone Road 19 miles (31 km) from town, then turn left and drive 0.5 mile (0.8 km) on Forest Road 145.

Boulder

About 400 people call this unique farming community home. Long after the Ancestral Puebloans lived here, ranchers began drifting in during the late 1870s. By the mid-1890s, Boulder had established itself as a ranching center. Remote and rimmed by canyons and mountains, Boulder remained one of the last communities in the country to use pack trains for transportation, and also among the last to receive US mail by mule. Motor vehicles couldn't drive in until the 1930s, and the highway into town wasn't fully paved until 1971. Today, Boulder is worth a visit to see an excavated Ancestral Puebloan village and the spectacular scenery along the way, as well as to eat at one of the best restaurants in Utah.

FOOD

The Boulder Mountain Lodge restaurant, ★ **Hell's Backbone Grill** (20 Hwy. 12, 435/335-7464, www.hellsbackbonegrill.com, 4pm-9pm daily mid-Mar.-mid-Nov., reservations strongly advised, $28-44) has gained something of a cult following across the West. Run by two American Buddhist women, supplied with vegetables from their own farm, and typically filled with well-heeled guests from Boulder Mountain Lodge, the restaurant has a menu that's updated daily. You can count on irresistible steaks, outstanding meatloaf, fabulous vegetarian options, tasty posole, and a tempting dessert menu you'd better save room for.

It may not be award-winning, but you'll also find good fare next door, too, at **Burr Trail Grill** (10 N. Hwy. 12, 435/335-7511, www.burrtrailgrill.life, 11am-6pm Mon.-Fri., 11am-8pm Sat.-Sun. late Mar.-Oct., $12-25), at the intersection of Highway 12 and Burr Trail Road. The atmospheric dining room, sided with weathered wood planking and filled with whimsical art, serves excellent burgers and sandwiches, a tasty trout entrée, and homemade pies.

Stop by **Magnolia's Street Food** (460 N. Hwy. 12, 435/335-7589, https://magnoliasstreetfood.com, 9am-3pm daily Mar.-Nov., $5-11) for a breakfast burrito or some lunchtime tacos. It's a food truck—technically, a turquoise school bus—parked outside the Anasazi State Park Museum.

ACCOMMODATIONS

You wouldn't expect to find one of Utah's nicer places to stay in Boulder, but the ★ **Boulder Mountain Lodge** (20 Hwy. 12, 435/355-7460 or 800/556-3446, www.boulder-utah.com, $190-350), along the highway right in town, is one of the few destination hotels in the state. The buildings are grouped around the edge of a private 15-acre (6-ha) pond that serves as an ad hoc wildlife refuge. You can sit on the deck or wander paths along the pond, observing the amazing variety of birds. The guest rooms and suites are in modern Western-style lodges facing the pond. Rooms are nicely decorated, and there's a central great room with a fireplace, plus a large outdoor hot tub. One of Utah's best restaurants, Hell's Backbone Grill, is on the premises.

For no-frills (and no Wi-Fi) accommodations, head to **Pole's Place Motel** (465 Hwy. 12, 435/335-7422, www.boulderutah.com, spring-fall, $90), across the road from Anasazi State Park. While you're here, drop into the motel's gift shop and chat with the owner about local history.

Seven miles (11.3 km) from Boulder on Hell's Backbone Road, at **Boulder Mountain Guest Ranch** (3995 Hell's Backbone Rd., 435/335-7480, https://bouldermountainguestranch.com), guests have a choice of tepees with stone flooring and a queen bed, yurts, or canvas-walled tents ($65-95); simple bunk rooms with shared baths ($87); and queen-bed guest rooms with private baths ($100-125) in the main lodge. Cabins that can sleep 6-8 with full kitchens and private baths are also available ($235-265). Inside the lodge is the excellent **Sweetwater Kitchen** (5pm-9pm Thurs.-Tues. Apr.-Oct., reservations advised, $16-30), open to nonguests. Continental breakfast is included in the room rates; a box lunch is $10. This is a good base for horseback trail rides: Right next door is **Hell's Backbone Ranch and Trail** (435/335-7581, www.bouldermountaintrails.com, 1.5-2 hour ride $75).

INFORMATION AND SERVICES

A good stop for visitor information is the **Anasazi State Park Museum** (460 N. Hwy. 12, 435/335-7308, https://stateparks.utah.gov, 9am-5pm daily, museum $5 pp), where there's an info desk for the national monument.

The two gas stations in Boulder sell groceries and snack food. At **Hills and Hollows Mini-Mart** (on the hill above Hwy. 12, 435/335-7349, www.hillshollows.com, generally 8:30am-7pm daily), you'll find provisions as diverse as Ben & Jerry's, artisanal bread, and organic cashews. Every other Friday night in summer, Hills and Hollows fires up a wood oven to make pizzas alongside an acoustic music jam.

GETTING THERE

Take paved Highway 12 either through the canyon and slickrock country from Escalante or over Boulder Mountain from Torrey, near Capitol Reef National Park. Burr Trail Road connects Boulder with Capitol Reef National Park's southern district via the Waterpocket Fold and Circle Cliffs. A fourth route to Boulder is from Escalante on the dirt Hell's Backbone Road, which joins Highway 12 about 3 miles (4.8 km) west of Boulder.

BOULDER MOUNTAIN SCENIC DRIVE

East of Boulder, Highway 12 climbs high into forests of ponderosa pine, aspen, and fir on Boulder Mountain until it reaches the town of Torrey. Travel in winter is usually possible, although heavy snows can close the road. Viewpoints along the drive offer panoramas of Escalante canyon country, the Circle Cliffs, the Waterpocket Fold, and the Henry Mountains. Hikers and anglers can explore the alpine country of Boulder Mountain and seek out the 90 or so trout-filled lakes. The Great Western Trail—built with ATVs in mind—runs over Boulder Mountain to the west of the highway. The US Forest Service's Fishlake National Forest map (Teasdale District) shows the back roads, trails, and lakes.

Campgrounds

The US Forest Service has three developed campgrounds on Highway 12 between Boulder and Torrey: **Oak Creek** (18 mi/29 km from Boulder, elev. 8,800 ft/2,682 m, first-come, first-served except group sites, $16), **Upper and Lower Pleasant Creek** (19 mi/31 km from Boulder, elev. 8,600 ft/2,621 m, first-come, first-served, $12), and **Singletree** (24 mi/39 km from Boulder, elev. 8,200 ft/2,500 m, www.recreation.gov, some sites reservable online, some sites first-come, first-served, $20). Singletree is the largest of the three and the best pick for larger RVs. The season runs approximately late May-mid-September, with water available; the campgrounds may also be open in spring and fall without water.

Lower Bowns Reservoir (Forest Rd. 168, elev. 7,000 ft/2,134 m, no water, free) has primitive camping and fishing for rainbow and cutthroat trout. To get here, head east for 5 miles (8 km) on rough dirt Forest Road 168 (not recommended for cars); the turnoff from Highway 12 is just south of Pleasant Creek Campground.

Contact the **Fremont River District Office** (138 S. Main St., Loa, 435/836-2800) for information about camping or recreation on Boulder Mountain.

Capitol Reef National Park

TOP EXPERIENCE

Although **Capitol Reef National Park** (435/425-3791, www.nps.gov/care, $20 per vehicle for the scenic drive, $10 cyclists and pedestrians, $15 motorcyclists) gets far less attention than the region's other national parks, it is a great place to visit, with excellent hiking, splendid scenery, and historic orchards where you can pick your own fruit.

The Waterpocket Fold is the defining geologic feature of Capitol Reef, extending from Thousand Lake Mountain to the north toward Lake Powell to the south. Along with this monocline—the technical term for a fold—the park is home to canyons, arches, and dreamy sandstone formations.

Roads and hiking trails in the park provide access to the colorful rock layers and to the local flora and fauna. You'll also see remnants of the area's long human history—petroglyphs of the prehistoric Fremont people, a schoolhouse and other structures built by LDS pioneers, and several small uranium mines from the 20th century. Legends tell of Butch Cassidy and other outlaw members of the Wild Bunch who hid in these remote canyons in the 1890s.

Travelers short on time will enjoy a quick look at visitor center exhibits and a drive on Highway 24 through an impressive cross section of Capitol Reef cut by the Fremont River. You can see more of the park on the Scenic Drive, a narrow paved road that heads south from the visitor center. The drive passes beneath spectacular cliffs of the reef and enters Grand Wash and Capitol Gorge Canyons; allow at least 1.5 hours for the 15.8-mile (25-km) round-trip and any side trips.

For the adventurous at heart with a 4WD vehicle and a little more time, the fair-weather Notom-Bullfrog Road (about half paved, with paved segments at both north and south ends) heads south along the other side of the reef for almost 70 miles (113 km), offering fine views of the Waterpocket Fold. Burr Trail Road (dirt inside the park) in the south actually climbs over the fold in a steep set of switchbacks, connecting Notom Road with Boulder. Only drivers with high-clearance vehicles can explore Cathedral Valley in the park's northern district. All of these roads provide access to viewpoints and hiking trails.

VISITOR CENTER

At the **Capitol Reef National Park Visitor Center** (Hwy. 24, 8am-4:30pm daily mid-May-Sept., 9am-4pm daily Oct.-mid-May), start with the 15-minute film introducing Capitol Reef's natural wonders and history. Rock samples and diagrams illustrate the park's geologic formations, and photos identify local plants and birds. On display are prehistoric artifacts of the Fremont people, including petroglyph replicas, sheepskin moccasins, pottery, basketry, stone knives, spear and arrow points, and bone jewelry. Other historical exhibits outline exploration and early Latter-day Saints settlement. Hikers can also pick up trail maps here.

Rangers offer talks, campfire programs, and other special events from Easter (late Mar.-mid-Apr.) through October. The visitor center is on Highway 24 at the turnoff for Fruita Campground and the Scenic Drive.

ALONG HIGHWAY 24

From the west, Highway 24 drops from the broad mountain valley near Torrey onto Sulphur Creek, with dramatic rock formations soaring to the horizon. A huge amphitheater of stone rings the basin, with formations such as Twin Rocks, Chimney Rock, and the Castle glowing in deep reds and yellows. Ahead, the canyon narrows as the Fremont River slips between the cliffs to carve its chasm through the Waterpocket Fold.

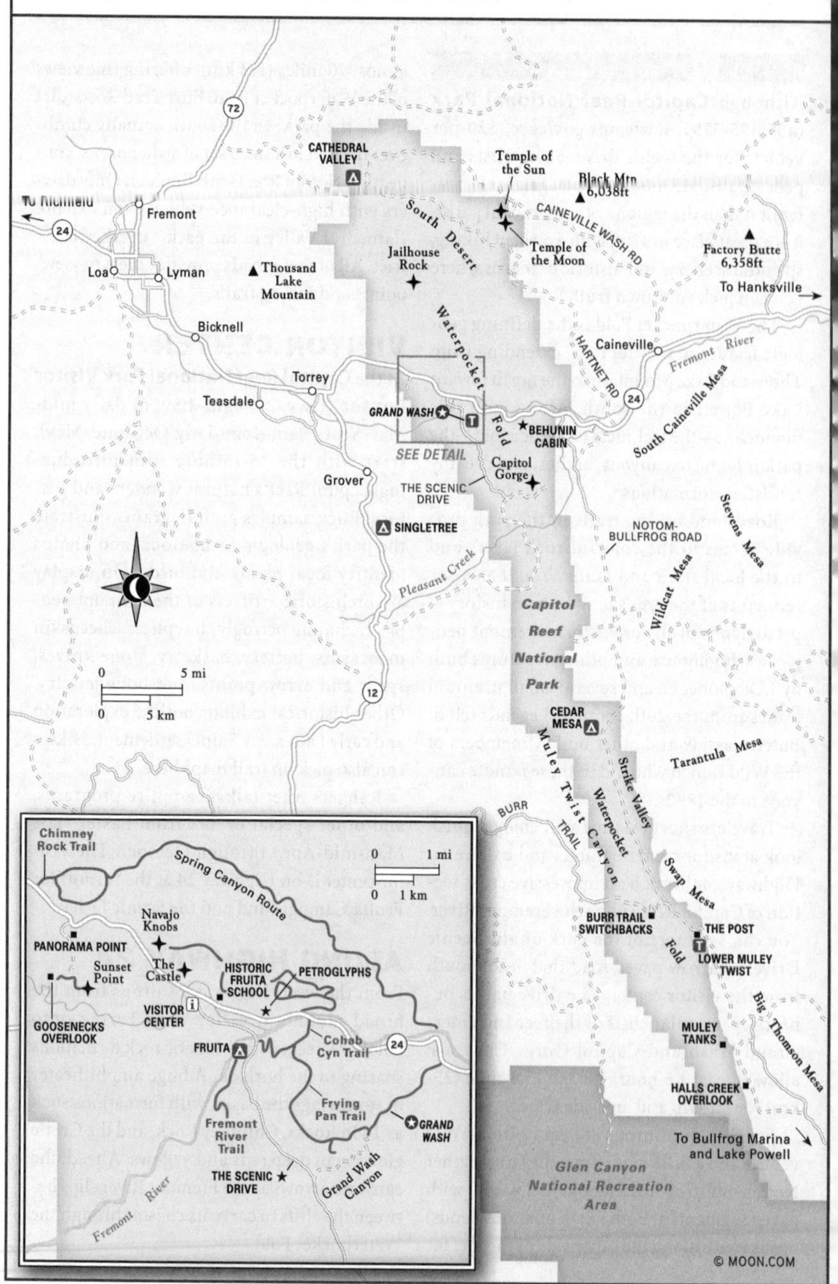
Capitol Reef National Park
72
CATHEDRAL VALLEY
Temple of the Sun
Black Mtn 6,038ft
To Richfield
Fremont
24
CAINEVILLE WASH RD
South Desert
Temple of the Moon
Factory Butte 6,358ft
Jailhouse Rock
Loa
Lyman
Thousand Lake Mountain
To Hanksville
Waterpocket
Bicknell
HARTNET RD
Caineville
Fremont River
Torrey
Teasdale
GRAND WASH
BEHUNIN CABIN
South Caineville Mesa
Fold
SEE DETAIL
Capitol Gorge
Grover
THE SCENIC DRIVE
SINGLETREE
NOTOM-BULLFROG ROAD
Stevens Mesa
Wildcat Mesa
Pleasant Creek
Capitol Reef National Park
0 5 mi
0 5 km
12
CEDAR MESA
Tarantula Mesa
Muley Twist Canyon
Strike Valley
Waterpocket
BURR TRAIL
Swap Mesa
Fold
BURR TRAIL SWITCHBACKS
THE POST
LOWER MULEY TWIST
Big Thomson Mesa
MULEY TANKS
HALLS CREEK OVERLOOK
To Bullfrog Marina and Lake Powell
Glen Canyon National Recreation Area
© MOON.COM
Chimney Rock Trail
Spring Canyon Route
0 1 mi
0 1 km
Navajo Knobs
PANORAMA POINT
Sunset Point
The Castle
HISTORIC FRUITA SCHOOL
PETROGLYPHS
VISITOR CENTER
GOOSENECKS OVERLOOK
FRUITA
Cohab Cyn Trail
Frying Pan Trail
Fremont River Trail
GRAND WASH
THE SCENIC DRIVE
Grand Wash Canyon
Fremont River

Panorama Point

Bask in the scenery from Panorama Point, 2.5 miles (4 km) west of the visitor center on the south side of Highway 24. Follow signs south for 250 yards (229 m) to Panorama Point, where you'll take in views of Capitol Reef, the distant Henry Mountains to the east, and looming Boulder Mountain to the west. The large black basalt boulders were swept down from Boulder Mountain to the reef as part of giant debris flows between 8,000 and 200,000 years ago.

Goosenecks Overlook

On a gravel road 1 mile (1.6 km) south of Panorama Point are the gracefully arcing bends—called the Goosenecks—of Sulphur Creek. A short trail leads to Goosenecks Overlook (elev. 6,400 ft/1,951 m) on the rim for dizzying views of the creek alongside colorful canyon walls.

Sunset Point

Enjoy panoramas of the Fremont River gorge, the Capitol Reef cliffs, and the distant Henry Mountains at Sunset Point. Plan your evening around viewing the sunset—it's worth hanging out for the whole show. From the Goosenecks Overlook parking area, it's an easy 0.3-mile (0.5-km) hike across the slickrock to Sunset Point. There's a sign at the trailhead. Bring a headlamp and use caution when hiking back in the dark.

Historic Fruita School

Remnants of the pioneer community of Fruita stretch along the narrow Fremont River Canyon. The Fruita Schoolhouse is just east of the visitor center on the north side of Highway 24. Early settlers completed this one-room log structure in 1896 and used it as a schoolhouse for grades 1 through 8. Latter-day Saints church meetings, dances, elections, and other gatherings took place here. A lack of students caused the school to close in 1941. Although the schoolhouse is locked, you can peer inside the windows, listen to stories about the schoolhouse on audio posts, and wander the surrounding boulders carved with names.

Fremont Petroglyphs

Farther down the canyon, 1.2 miles (1.9 km) east of the visitor center on the north side of Highway 24, are several panels of Fremont petroglyphs—the best in the park. The artwork was created 600-1300 CE, when the Indigenous Fremont people called this area home. The Fremont people were primarily hunter-gatherers who dwelled in pit houses in this valley.

Several big-horned mountain sheep and human figures with headdresses decorate the cliff. Due to fading and natural varnish, the rock art is faint, so binoculars will give you a closer look. In addition to these petroglyphs, there's also a panel up Capitol Gorge and other artwork scattered throughout the park. Fremont artifacts have been discovered along the river as well.

You can see more petroglyphs by walking to the left and right along the cliff face. Stay on the boardwalk, don't climb the talus slope, and don't touch the petroglyphs, since the oil from your hands can damage them. The area is well signed and there is a small parking area. To reach the petroglyphs, walk across a short wheelchair-accessible boardwalk.

Behunin Cabin

The historic Behunin Cabin is 6.2 miles (10 km) east of the visitor center on the south side of Highway 24. Latter-day Saints settler Elijah Cutler Behunin used blocks of sandstone to build this cabin around 1882. For several years, Behunin, his wife, and 11 of their 13 children shared this sturdy yet quite small cabin (the kids slept outside). They moved on when flooding made life too difficult. Small openings allow a look inside the dirt-floored structure, but no furnishings remain.

THE SCENIC DRIVE

Turn south from Highway 24 at the visitor center to experience some of the reef's best scenery and to learn more about its geology. A

1
2
3
4
ENTER
OPEN

The Orchards of Capitol Reef

Fruit trees and verdant farmland thriving beneath cliffs of red might catch some by surprise. A farm in the desert? The apples, peaches, and other fruit that grow in Capitol Reef are thanks to a short-lived yet persistent community that put down roots here for less than a century, and used the Fremont River for irrigation.

Capitol Reef was actually one of the last places in the West to be found by settlers. Junction (renamed Fruita in 1902) was settled around 1880. Floods and transportation difficulties forced many families to leave, but irrigation and hard work paid off with prosperous orchards and the sobriquet "The Eden of Wayne County." Although Fruita's citizens were gone by the 1950s, the National Park Service still maintains the orchards.

Visitors are welcome to pick their own fruit during the harvest season, as follows:

- **Mid-June through early July:** Cherries
- **July:** Apricots
- **August:** Peaches and pears
- **September through mid-October:** Apples
- **Hours:** 9am-5pm daily (seasonal dates above vary from year to year)

Bring your own bag to pick fruit from any tree bearing a "U-Pick Fruit" sign. Ladders and other tools are available in the visitor center, but don't climb any trees. There is a self-pay station, and your contribution will be reinvested in the orchards. The Park Service also uses a portion of the fruit harvest to make jams and pies, available in the Gifford Farmhouse amid the orchards.

quick tour of this 15.8-mile (25-km) out-and-back trip requires about 1.5 hours, but several hiking trails and spur roads may tempt you to spend a whole day exploring the drive. Right off the road, you can see sights that include an arch where Butch Cassidy allegedly once hid and what look like hoodoos in the making in the Moenkopi Formation.

It's worth picking up a brochure at the visitor center for descriptions of the geology along the road. The Scenic Drive is paved, although there are two dirt side roads: Grand Wash and Capitol Gorge. The 4WD Capitol Gorge Road once served as the main highway through the area, and you can still drive a ways up the canyon. At the end of both Grand Wash and Capitol Gorge roads, you can park and walk up each canyon to explore the rock formations and access more hiking trails. Note that drivers must pay the $20 park entrance fee to travel on the Scenic Drive.

1: Highway 24 near the entrance to Capitol Reef National Park **2:** Fruita Schoolhouse **3:** the walkway to view the Fremont Petroglyphs **4:** Gifford Homestead

Fruita

In the Fruita Historic District, you'll first pass orchards and several of Fruita's buildings. A **blacksmith shop** (on the right, 0.7 mi/1.1 km from the visitor center) displays tools, farm machinery, and Fruita's first tractor. The tractor didn't arrive until 1940, long after the rest of the country had modernized. The nearby orchards and fields are still maintained using traditional farming techniques.

Ripple Rock Nature Center, just under 1 mile (1.6 km) south of the visitor center, has activities and exhibits for kids, many centering on pioneer life. Kids can also earn certification as Junior Rangers and Junior Geologists.

The **Gifford Homestead** (9am-4:30pm Mar. 15-Oct., closed noon-12:45pm, hours may vary, free), 1 mile (1.6 km) south on the Scenic Drive, is typical of rural Utah farmhouses of the early 1900s. Cultural demonstrations along with handmade baked goods (pie!) and gifts are available. In peak season, the pie tends to sell out by midday. A picnic area with fruit trees and grass is just beyond. A short trail crosses orchards and the Fremont River to the **Historic Fruita School.**

Grand Wash

Turn east off the Scenic Drive to explore Grand Wash, a dry channel through a narrow canyon. A dirt road follows the twisting gulch for 1 mile (1.6 km), with sheer rock walls rising along the sandy streambed. At the road's end, an easy trail follows the wash 2.5 miles (4 km) to its mouth along Highway 24. This is a great hiking area for kids to wander, exploring boulders and giant huecos (holes in a rock face) along the way. You can also take a steep, challenging 1.7-mile (2.7-km) spur trail from this trailhead to reach Cassidy Arch, where outlaw Butch Cassidy is said to have absconded.

Back on the paved Scenic Drive, continue south past Slickrock Divide to where the rock lining the reef deepens into a ruby red color and forms odd columns and spires. Called the **Egyptian Temple,** this is one of the most striking and colorful areas along the road.

Note that while Grand Wash is a dry canyon, it is subject to flash flooding, so avoid this drive if summer skies threaten rain.

Capitol Gorge

Capitol Gorge lies at the end of the Scenic Drive, 10.7 miles (17.2 km) from the visitor center. Believe it or not, for 80 years, this narrow dry canyon was the route of the main state highway through south-central Utah. Latter-day Saints pioneers laboriously cleared a path so wagons could get through—a task they repeated every time flash floods rolled in a new set of boulders. Cars bounced their way down the canyon until 1962, when Highway 24 opened, but few traces of the old road remain today.

Walking is easy along the gravel riverbed, but don't enter if storms threaten, since flash flooding is a possibility. An easy 1-mile (1.6-km) saunter down the gorge will take day hikers past faded petroglyphs and a "register" rock where pioneers carved their names high on the wall. If you're lucky, you may get a glimpse of desert bighorn sheep. Native to the area and often depicted in rock art, the sheep disappeared from the park but were successfully reintroduced in the 1990s. Rock climbers can find a few trad routes and boulder problems to attempt here as well.

Pleasant Creek Road

The Scenic Drive curves east toward Capitol Gorge and onto Pleasant Creek Road (turn right 8.3 mi/13.4 km from the visitor center), which continues south below the face of the reef. After 3 miles (4.8 km), the dirt road—which can be rough in spots—passes Sleeping Rainbow-Floral Ranch (closed to the public) and ends at Pleasant Creek. South Draw Road, a rugged road for 4WD vehicles, continues on the other side, but it is too rough for cars.

Floral Ranch dates back to the early years of Capitol Reef settlement. In 1939 it became the Sleeping Rainbow Guest Ranch, from the translation of the Native American name for the Waterpocket Fold. Now the ranch belongs to the park and is used as a field research station by Utah Valley University. Pleasant Creek's perennial waters begin high on Boulder Mountain to the west and cut a scenic canyon completely through Capitol Reef. Hikers can head downstream through the 3-mile-long (4.8-km) canyon and then return the way they went in, or continue another 3 miles (4.8 km) cross-country to Notom Road.

SOUTH DISTRICT

Notom-Bullfrog Road

The 70-mile (113-km) Notom-Bullfrog Road can take you from Capitol Reef to the intersection with the Burr Trail Road, to any number of hikes and cliffs, and even all the way to Glen

1: huecos mark the walls of Grand Wash **2:** the dirt drive through Capitol Gorge

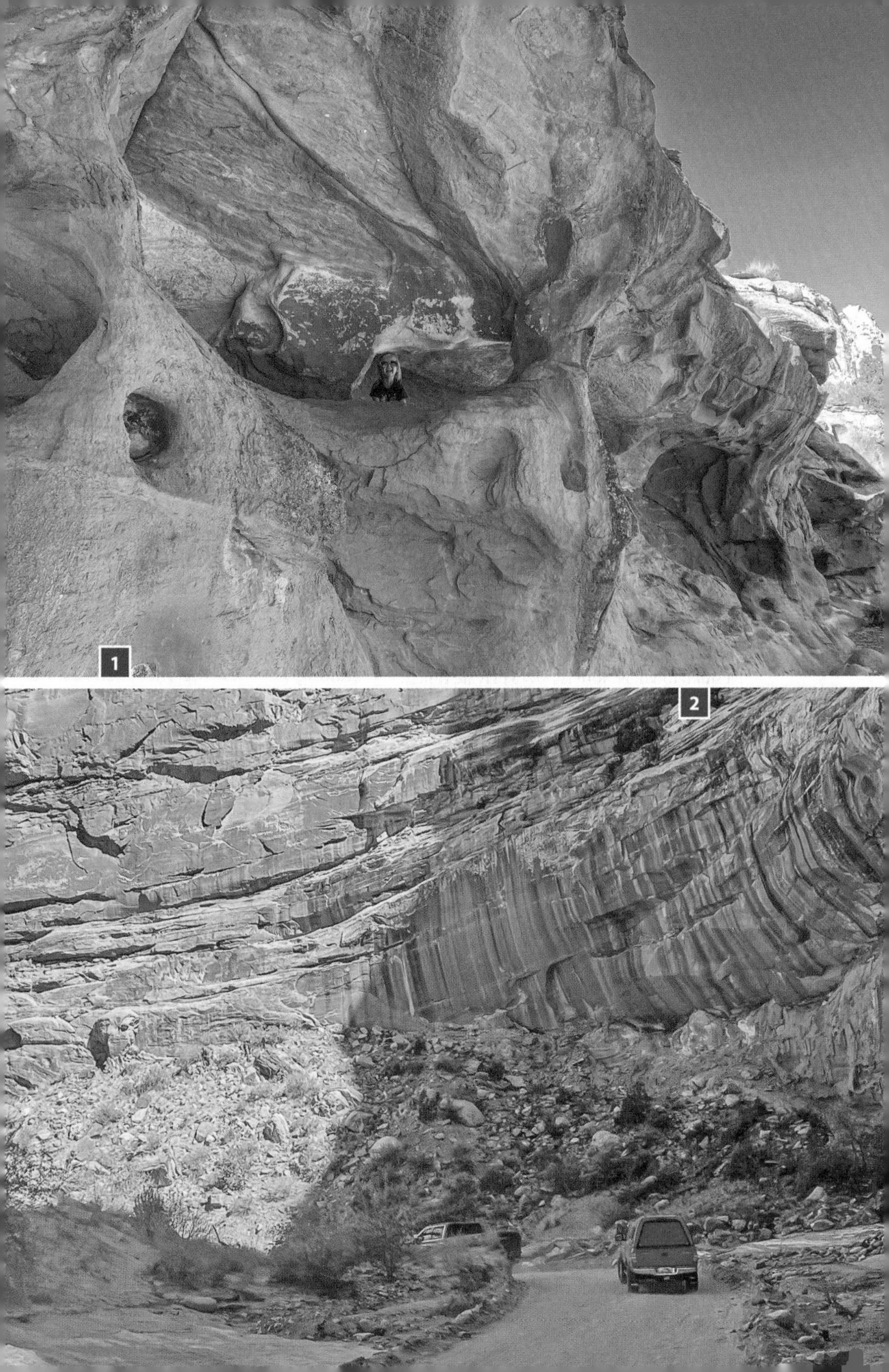

1
2

Canyon. The road crosses some of the park's younger geologic layers, like the colorful hills of the Morrison Formation. In other spots, eroded layers of the Waterpocket Fold jut up at 70-degree angles. The Henry Mountains to the east and the many canyons on both sides of the road add to the panoramas.

Have a full tank of gas and carry extra water and food; no services are available between Highway 24 and Bullfrog Marina. Stop at the visitor center for information sheets if you're planning to hike or canyoneer in the slot canyons; a permit is required for overnight backcountry camping.

Features and mileage along the drive from north to south include the following:

- **Mile 0:** The turnoff from Highway 24 is 9.2 miles (14.8 km) east of the visitor center and 30.2 miles (49 km) west of Hanksville; another turnoff from Highway 24 is 3 miles (4.8 km) east.
- **Mile 4.1:** Notom Ranch is to the west. Once a small town, Notom is now a private ranch.
- **Mile 8.1:** At Burrow Wash, experienced hikers can explore the slot canyon upstream. A 2.5-mile (4-km) hike up the sandy wash leads to narrow slots.
- **Mile 9.3:** Cottonwood Wash is a 2.5-mile (4-km) trek leading to a slot canyon hike.
- **Mile 10.4:** Five Mile Wash is yet another sandy wash. The pavement ends.
- **Mile 13.3:** Sheets Gulch leads to an upstream slot canyon. The trail goes 6.7 miles (10.8 km) and can be done as an overnight (permit required).
- **Mile 14.4:** Oak Creek crossing.
- **Mile 20.0:** Entering Capitol Reef National Park.
- **Mile 22.3:** The five-site Cedar Mesa Campground is to the west, surrounded by junipers. Free sites have tables and grills; there's a pit toilet but no drinking water. The Red Canyon Trail (5.6 mi/9 km round-trip) begins here and heads west into a box canyon.
- **Mile 26.0:** Bitter Creek Divide. Streams to the north flow to the Fremont River. Halls Creek on the south side runs through Strike Valley to Lake Powell, 40 miles (64 km) away.
- **Mile 34.1:** Burr Trail Road junction. Turn west up steep switchbacks to ascend the Waterpocket Fold and continue 36 miles (58 km) to Highway 12. Burr Trail is the only road that crosses the top of the fold, and it's one of the most scenic in Utah. Driving conditions are similar to the Notom-Bullfrog Road—fine for standard 2WD cars in dry conditions. Pavement begins at the park boundary and continues to Boulder.
- **Mile 36.0:** Surprise Canyon trailhead. This 2-mile (3.2-km) round-trip hike into this narrow, usually shaded canyon takes 1-2 hours, and is the best option for a short hike in this area of the park.
- **Mile 36.6:** Post Corral was once a small trading post serving sheepherders and cattle ranchers. Park here to hike to Headquarters Canyon (3.2 mi/5.1 km round-trip). A trailhead for Lower Muley Twist Canyon via Halls Creek is at the end of a 0.5-mile-long (0.8-km) road to the south.
- **Mile 37.5:** Leaving Capitol Reef National Park. Much of the road between here and Glen Canyon National Recreation Area is paved.
- **Mile 45.5:** Road junction. Turn right (south) to continue 25 miles (40 km) to Bullfrog Marina, or go straight (east) for 23 miles (37 km) to Starr Springs Campground in the Henry Mountains.
- **Mile 46.4:** The road to the right (west) goes to Halls Creek Overlook. This turnoff is poorly signed and easy to miss; look for it 0.9 mile (1.4 km) south of the previous junction.
- **Mile 49.0:** Colorful clay hills of deep red, cream, and gray rise beside the road. This

clay turns to goo when wet, providing all the traction of axle grease.

- **Mile 54.0:** A beautiful panorama of mesas, mountains, and canyons, including Lake Powell and Navajo Mountain to the south.
- **Mile 65.3:** Junction with paved Highway 276. Turn left (north) for Hanksville in 59 miles (95 km) or right (south) to Bullfrog Marina in 5.2 miles (8.4 km).
- **Mile 70.5:** End at Bullfrog Marina in Glen Canyon National Recreation Area.

Muley Twist Canyon

"So winding that it would twist a mule pulling a wagon," said an early visitor. This canyon has some of the best hiking in the southern district of the park. In the 1880s, Latter-day Saints pioneers used the canyon as part of a wagon route between Escalante and new settlements in southeastern Utah, replacing the even more difficult Hole-in-the-Rock route.

Unlike most canyons of the Waterpocket Fold, Muley Twist runs lengthwise along the crest for 18 miles (29 km) before turning east and leaving the fold. Hikers starting from Burr Trail Road can easily follow the twisting bends down to Halls Creek, 12 miles (19.3 km) away. Two trailheads and the Halls Creek route allow a variety of trips.

Upper Canyon

This part of the canyon has plenty of scenery. Large and small natural arches along the way add to its beauty. Upper Muley Twist Road turns north off Burr Trail Road about 1 mile (1.6 km) west from the top of a set of switchbacks. Cars can usually go in 0.5 mile (0.8 km) to a trailhead parking area; high-clearance 4WD vehicles can head another 3 miles (4.8 km) up a wash to the end of the primitive road. Look for natural arches on the left along this last section. The **Strike Valley Overlook Trail** (0.75 mi/1.2 km round-trip) begins at the end of the road and leads to a magnificent panorama of the Waterpocket Fold and beyond. Return to the canyon, where you can hike as far as 6.5 miles (10.4 km) to the head of Upper Muley Twist Canyon.

Two large arches are a short hike upstream. The second on the left, Saddle Arch, is 1.7 miles (2.7 km) away. The **Rim Route** begins across from Saddle Arch, climbs the canyon wall, follows the rim (offering views of Strike Valley and the Henry Mountains), and descends back into the canyon at a point just above the narrows, 4.75 miles (7.6 km) from the road's end. The Rim Route is most easily followed in this direction.

To see several more arches, proceed up-canyon. A narrow section of canyon about 4 miles (6.4 km) from the end of the road must be bypassed to continue; look for rock cairns showing the way around to the right. Continuing up the canyon past the Rim Route sign will take you to several small drainages marking the upper end of Muley Twist Canyon. Climb a high forested point on the west rim for views. Experienced hikers with maps can follow the rim back to Upper Muley Twist Road. There is no trail and no markers on this route. Bring all the water you'll need, as there are no reliable sources here.

Lower Canyon

Start from Burr Trail Road near the top of the switchbacks 2.2 miles (3.5 km) west of Notom-Bullfrog Road and hike down the dry gravel streambed. After 4 miles (6.4 km), you have the option of returning the same way, taking the Cut Off route east 2.5 miles (4 km) to the Post Corral trailhead (off Notom-Bullfrog Rd.), or continuing 8 miles (12.9 km) down Lower Muley Twist Canyon to its end at Halls Creek. On reaching Halls Creek, turn left (north) and travel 5 miles (8 km) up the creek bed or the old 4WD road beside it to the Post. This section of creek is in an open dry valley. With a car shuttle, the Post would be the end of a good 2-day, 17-mile (27-km) hike. Check the weather beforehand and avoid the canyon if storms threaten.

Cream-colored sandstone cliffs lie atop the red Kayenta and Wingate Formations.

BOULDER - BULLFROG SCENIC
BACKWAY
1

2

Impressively deep undercuts have been carved into the lower canyon. Spring and fall offer the best conditions; summer temperatures can exceed 100°F (38°C). Elevations range from 5,640 feet (1,719 m) at Burr Trail Road to 4,540 feet (1,384 m) at the confluence with Halls Creek and 4,894 feet (1,492 m) at the Post.

More detailed info is available at the trailheads. You'll also find this hike described in David Day's *Utah's Favorite Hiking Trails* and in the small spiral-bound *Explore Capitol Reef Trails* by the Capitol Reef Natural History Association, available at the visitor center. Carry all the water you'll need for the trip because natural sources are often dry or polluted.

NORTH DISTRICT (CATHEDRAL VALLEY)

More adventurous travelers seek the remote canyons and desert country of the park's northern district. In wet weather, the few roads cannot be negotiated by 4WD vehicles, let alone ordinary cars. In good weather, high-clearance vehicles (good clearance is more important than 4WD) can enter the region from the east, north, and west. The roads lead through the sandstone monoliths of Cathedral Valley, volcanic remnants, badlands country, many low mesas, and vast sand flats. Foot travel allows closer inspection of these features, as well as lengthy excursions into the canyons of Polk, Deep, and Spring Creeks, which cut deeply into the flanks of **Thousand Lake Mountain.**

Jailhouse Rock, Temple of the Sun, and **Temple of the Moon** are a few iconic features in this part of the park. There are multiple roads that access these monoliths, which may take you anywhere from a couple hours to a full day to explore. Jailhouse Rock requires hiking in on a trail that's not particularly well-marked. If you want to visit any of these formations, stop at the visitor center for detailed directions, current conditions, and a map.

Mountain bikers enjoy these challenging roads as well, but they must stay on established roads. Much of the north district is good for horseback riding too. And the totally unpolluted dark skies of Cathedral Valley are considered best-in-class for stargazing and night sky photography.

The district's two main roads—**Hartnet Road** and **Cathedral Road** (aka Caineville Wash Rd.)—combine with a short stretch of Highway 24 to form a loop, with a campground at their junction. The six sites at **Cathedral Valley Campground** (no reservations, no water, first-come, first-served, free) provide a place to stop for the night. The campground is on the 4WD Cathedral Valley loop road about 36 miles (58 km) from the visitor center: From the park entrance, head 12 miles (19.3 km) east on Highway 24 to milepost 91. Turn north and ford the Fremont River, then follow Hartnet Road about 24 miles (39 km) to the campground. Check road conditions at the visitor center before heading out.

Just below the campground, the 1-mile (1.6-km) **Upper Cathedral Valley Trail** offers excellent views of the Cathedrals. Backcountry hikers must have a **permit** and camp at least 0.5 mile (0.8 km) from the nearest road. Be prepared to take care of yourself in this remote district; cell phone service is limited or nonexistent. Detailed guides to this area can be purchased at the visitor center.

HIKING

Fifteen trails for day hikes begin within a short drive of the visitor center. Of these, only Grand Wash, Capitol Gorge, and the short paths to Sunset Point and Goosenecks are easy. The others involve moderately strenuous climbs over irregular slickrock. Signs and rock cairns mark the way, but it's very easy to wander off the trail if you don't pay attention.

Although most hiking trails can easily be done in a day, backpackers and hikers might want to try longer trips in Chimney

1: the entrance to Notom-Bullfrog Road near Capitol Reef **2:** the edge of Cathedral Valley in late fall

Rock-Spring Canyons to the north or Muley Twist Canyon and Halls Creek to the south. Obtain the required **backcountry permit** (free) in person at the visitor center and camp at least 0.5 mile (0.8 km) from the nearest maintained road or trail. (Cairned routes like Chimney Rock Canyon, Muley Twist Canyon, and Halls Creek don't count as trails but are backcountry routes.) Bring a stove for cooking since fires aren't permitted. Avoid camping or parking in washes at any time—torrents of mud and boulders can carry away everything.

Trails Along Highway 24

Stop by the visitor center to pick up a map showing hiking trails and trail descriptions. These trailheads are located along the main highway through the park and along the Fremont River. Note that the Grand Wash Trail cuts west through the reef to the Scenic Drive.

Chimney Rock Loop

Distance: *3.5 miles (5.6 km) round-trip*
Duration: *2.5 hours*
Elevation gain: *590 feet (180 m)*
Effort: *moderate-strenuous*
Trailhead: *3 miles (4.8 km) west of the visitor center on the north side of Highway 24*

Towering 660 feet (201 m) above the highway, Chimney Rock (elev. 6,100 ft/1,859 m) is a fluted spire of dark red rock (Moenkopi Formation) capped by a block of hard sandstone (Shinarump Member of the Chinle Formation). The trail leads nearly straight uphill from the parking lot to a ridge overlooking Chimney Rock, before leveling off a bit. Panoramic views take in the face of Capitol Reef. Along the trail, you'll see petrified wood eroded from the Chinle Formation (the same rock layer found in Petrified Forest National Park in Arizona). It is illegal to take any petrified wood.

Hickman Natural Bridge Trail

Distance: *2 miles (3.2 km) round-trip*
Duration: *1.5 hours*
Elevation gain: *400 feet (122 m)*
Effort: *easy-moderate*
Trailhead: *2 miles (3.2 km) east of the visitor center on the north side of Highway 24*

The graceful Hickman Natural Bridge spans 133 feet (41 m) across a small streambed. Numbered stops along the self-guided trail correspond to descriptions in a pamphlet available at the trailhead or visitor center. From the parking area (elev. 5,320 ft/1,622 m), the trail follows the Fremont River's green banks a short distance before climbing to the bridge. The last section follows a dry wash shaded by cottonwoods, junipers, and piñon pines. You'll pass under the bridge—eroded from the Kayenta Formation—at trail's end. Capitol Dome and other sandstone features surround the site. Joseph Hickman, for whom the bridge was named, served as principal of Wayne County High School and later in the state legislature; he and another local, Ephraim Pectol, led efforts to promote Capitol Reef.

Rim Overlook and Navajo Knobs

Distance: *4.5 miles (7.2 km) round-trip*
Duration: *3-5 hours*
Elevation gain: *1,110 feet (335 m)*
Effort: *moderate-strenuous*
Trailhead: *2 miles (3.2 km) east of the visitor center on the north side of Highway 24*

A splendid overlook 1,000 feet (305 m) above Fruita beckons hikers up the Rim Overlook Trail. Take the Hickman Natural Bridge Trail from the parking area, turn right at the signed fork, and hike for about 2 miles (3.2 km). Allow 3.5 hours from the fork for this hike.

Panoramic views take in the Fremont River Valley below, the great cliffs of Capitol Reef above, the Henry Mountains to the southeast, and Boulder Mountain to the southwest. The trail keeps things interesting with volcanic rock strewn along the path, ever-changing views, stretches over slickrock, wildflowers if the season is right, and terrain that seems to transform around every bend. The Hickman

1: Hickman Natural Bridge seen from the Rim Overlook Trail **2:** volcanic rock along Rim Overlook Trail

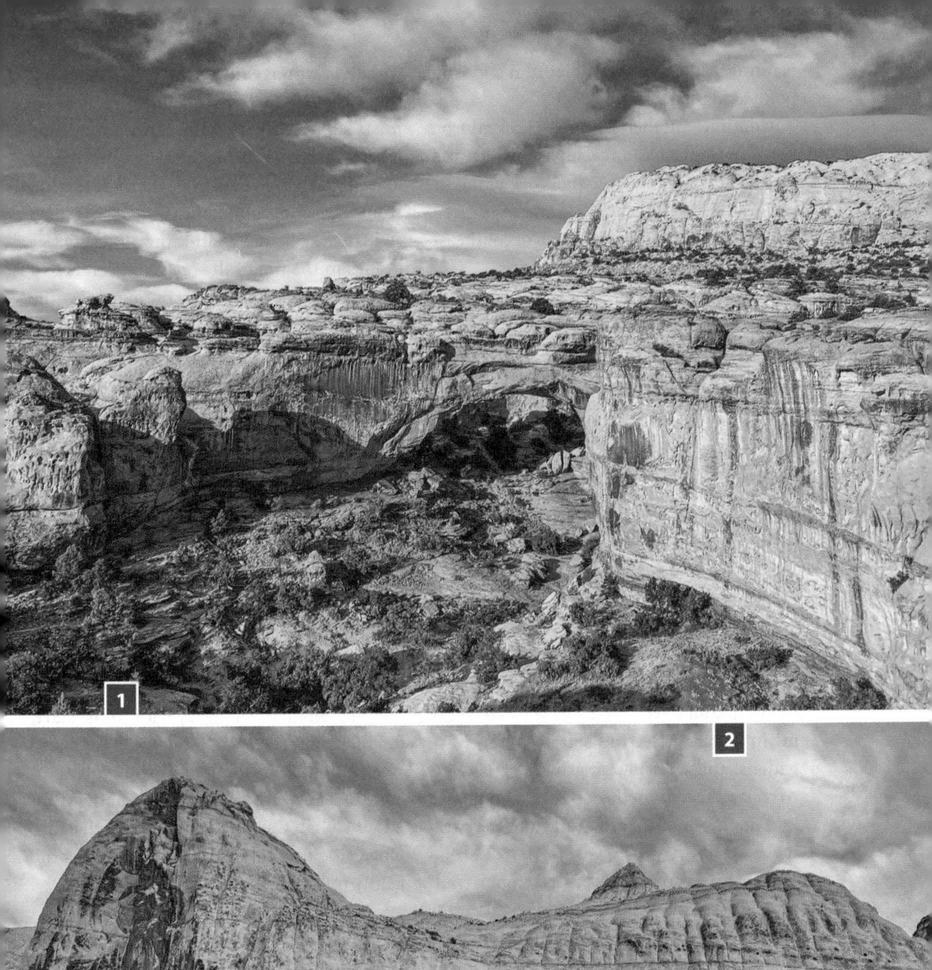
1

2

Natural Bridge is also visible from a lookout point along the trail.

Continue another 2.2 miles (3.5 km) from the Rim Overlook to reach **Navajo Knobs.** Cairns lead the way over slickrock along the rim of the Waterpocket Fold. A magnificent view at trail's end takes in much of southeastern Utah.

★ Grand Wash

Distance: *4.5 miles (7.2 km) round-trip*
Duration: *2-3 hours*
Elevation gain: *200 feet (61 m)*
Effort: *easy*
Trailhead: *4.7 miles (7.6 km) east of the visitor center on the south side of Highway 24*

One of only five canyons cutting completely through the reef, Grand Wash offers easy hiking, great scenery, and an abundance of wildflowers. There's no trail—just follow the dry riverbed. (Flash floods can occur during storms.) Only a short distance from Highway 24, canyon walls rise 800 feet (244 m) above the floor and narrow to as little as 20 feet (6 m) in width. After the Narrows, the wash widens, and wildflowers grow. The Cassidy Arch trailhead is on the left just 0.2 mile (0.3 km) up the Grand Wash Trail from the parking area.

This hike can also be started from a trailhead at the end of Grand Wash Road, off the Scenic Drive. A car or bike shuttle can make it a one-way hike of 2.2 miles (3.5 km).

Trails Along the Scenic Drive

These hikes begin from trailheads along the Scenic Drive. Drivers must pay the $20 national park admission fee to travel this road.

Cohab Canyon Trail

Distance: *3.5 miles (5.6 km) round-trip*
Duration: *2.5 hours*
Elevation gain: *440 feet (134 m)*
Effort: *moderate-strenuous*
Trailheads: *across the road from Fruita Campground (1 mi/1.6 km south of the visitor center) and across Highway 24 from the Hickman Natural Bridge trailhead*

Cohab is a pretty little canyon overlooking the campground. Latter-day Saints polygamists supposedly used the canyon to escape federal marshals during the 1880s. Trailheads exist at either end of the canyon. Starting from the campground, the trail follows steep switchbacks before continuing along gentler grades to the top of the reef. You can take a short trail to viewpoints or continue 0.75 mile (1.2 km) down the other side of the ridge to Highway 24.

Another option is to turn right at the top on Frying Pan Trail toward Cassidy Arch (3.5 mi/5.6 km one-way) and Grand Wash (4 mi/6.4 km one-way). The trail from Cassidy Arch to Grand Wash is steep. All these interconnecting trails offer many possibilities, especially if you can arrange a car shuttle. One possibility is to start up Cohab Canyon Trail from Highway 24, traverse the reef on Frying Pan Trail, make a side trip to Cassidy Arch, descend to Grand Wash, then back to Highway 24, and walk (or shuttle) 2.7 miles (4.3 km) along the highway back to the start, for 10.5 miles (16.9 km) total.

Hiking the Frying Pan Trail involves an additional 600 feet (183 m) of climbing from either Cohab Canyon or Cassidy Arch Trail. Once atop Capitol Reef, the trail follows the gently rolling slickrock terrain.

Fremont River Trail

Distance: *2 miles (3.2 km) round-trip*
Duration: *2 hours*
Elevation gain: *480 feet (146 m)*
Effort: *moderate-strenuous*
Trailhead: *Fruita Campground amphitheater*

The trail starts out quite easy, passing orchards along the Fremont River (elev. 5,350 ft/1,631 m). This part of the trail is wheelchair-accessible. After 0.5 mile (0.8 km), it climbs sloping rock to a Miners Mountain viewpoint overlooking Fruita, Boulder Mountain, and Capitol Reef. This is a good early-morning

1: the scenic trail to Cassidy Arch **2:** where the road ends up Capitol Gorge, carry on by foot
3: bouldering in Capitol Reef National Park

1
2
3

hike from the campground. Bring a thermos of coffee and enjoy the panoramic views from the top.

Cassidy Arch Trail

Distance: *3.5 miles (5.6 km) round-trip*
Duration: *3 hours*
Elevation gain: *670 feet (204 m)*
Effort: *moderate-strenuous*
Trailhead: *end of the drivable section of Grand Wash Road*
Directions: *Turn left off the Scenic Drive, 3.6 miles (5.8 km) from the visitor center, and follow Grand Wash to the trailhead*

Cassidy Arch Trail begins near the end of Grand Wash Road (just 0.2 mi/0.3 km up Grand Wash Trail), ascends the north wall of Grand Wash, then winds across slickrock to a vantage point close to the arch. The first part of the hike is most challenging, with steep switchbacks and an exposed, narrow path. The trail mellows out once you gain elevation on the switchbacks.

Energetic hikers will enjoy good views of Grand Wash, great domes of Navajo sandstone, and the sturdy arch itself, which is wide enough to walk on. The notorious outlaw Butch Cassidy may have traveled through Capitol Reef and hidden near this arch. Frying Pan Trail branches off Cassidy Arch Trail at the 1-mile (1.6-km) mark, then wends its way across 3 miles (4.8 km) of slickrock to Cohab Canyon.

Capitol Gorge

Distance: *2 miles (3.2 km) round-trip*
Duration: *1-2 hours*
Elevation gain: *100 feet (30 m)*
Effort: *easy-moderate*
Trailhead: *Capitol Gorge parking area*

Follow the well-maintained dirt road to the parking area in Capitol Gorge to begin this hike. The first mile (1.6 km) downstream is the most scenic. Fremont petroglyphs (in poor condition) appear on the left after 0.1 mile (0.2 km). The narrows of Capitol Gorge close in at 0.3 mile (0.5 km). Soon after, a "pioneer register" on the left displays names and dates of early travelers and ranchers scratched in the canyon wall.

If you scramble up a cairn-marked path, you can also see natural water tanks, about 0.8 mile (1.3 km) from the main trail. These depressions in the rock collect water and give the Waterpocket Fold its name. Back in the wash, listen for canyon wrens—their song starts on a high note, then trills down the scale. From the turnoff to the water tanks, hikers can continue another 3 miles (4.8 km) downstream to Notom Road.

BOULDERING

Rock climbing is allowed in the park, but a **permit** (at the visitor center or email care_permits@nps.gov, free) is required for each day you plan to climb. Climbers must use "clean" techniques (no pitons or bolts) and keep at least 100 feet (30 m) from rock-art panels and prehistoric structures. Because of the abundance of prehistoric rock art found here, the rock wall north of Highway 24 between the Fruita School and the east end of Kreuger Orchard (milepost 81.4) is closed to climbing. Other areas closed to climbing include Hickman Natural Bridge and all other arches and bridges, Temple of the Moon and Temple of the Sun, and Chimney Rock.

Most of the climbing is up Grand Wash and Capitol Gorge—the two spur roads from the Scenic Drive. The majority of routes are trad (using traditional gear protection) and bouldering.

The harder, fractured sandstone of the Wingate Formation is better suited to climbing than the crumblier Entrada sandstone. The rock is susceptible to flaking, however, so climbers should use caution. Chalk also must match the color of the rock; white chalk is prohibited.

CAMPGROUNDS

Fruita Campground (year-round, $25), 1 mile (1.6 km) south of the visitor center on the Scenic Drive, has 71 sites for tents and RVs, with drinking water and heated restrooms, but no showers or hookups. In winter, campers must get their water from the visitor center. The surrounding orchards and lush grass make this an attractive, though somewhat suburban, spot. It has excellent access to hiking trails. Most sites can be reserved in advance (www.recreation.gov). Five sites are wheelchair-accessible and can be reserved March-October. One group campground (www.recreation.gov, reservation required, Mar.-Oct., $4 pp, $75 minimum) and a picnic area are nearby.

Two campgrounds offer first-come, first-served primitive sites with no water. The five-site **Cedar Mesa Campground** (year-round, free) is in the park's southern district, just off dirt Notom-Bullfrog Road. Cedar Mesa has fine views of the Waterpocket Fold and the Henry Mountains. From the visitor center, go east 9.2 miles (14.8 km) on Highway 24, then turn right and go 22 miles (35 km) on Notom-Bullfrog Road—but avoid this road if it's wet.

Cathedral Valley Campground (year-round, free) serves the park's northern district. It has six sites near Hartnet Junction, about 30 miles (48 km) north of Highway 24. Take either Caineville Wash Road or Hartnet Road. Both are dirt roads and should be avoided when wet. Hartnet has a river ford that can be impassable at times.

If you're just looking for a place to park for the night, check out the public land east of the park boundary, off Highway 24. Areas on both sides of the highway about 9 miles (14.5 km) east of the visitor center can be used for free. Primitive campgrounds catering mostly to RVs are in Torrey.

Backcountry camping is allowed in the park; obtain a free **backcountry permit** at the visitor center.

GETTING THERE

Capitol Reef National Park flanks Highway 24, which by southern Utah standards is a major east-west road, roughly paralleling and south of I-70. Highway 24 intersects I-70 at the town of Green River, north and east of the park; follow Highway 24 south through Hanksville to reach Capitol Reef. This is the quickest way to get from the Moab area to Capitol Reef.

Travelers coming from the Escalante area should head north toward the town of Boulder on Highway 12. This is also the most scenic route from Zion and Bryce. Highway 12 runs past Boulder Mountain to Highway 24 at the town of Torrey; Capitol Reef is just 11 miles (17.7 km) farther east.

From Las Vegas to Capitol Reef, it's a

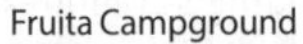
Fruita Campground

Pando: The World's Largest Living Organism

Less than an hour's drive northwest of Capitol Reef lies the world's largest living organism: an aspen grove, all grown from a single seed. Named Pando—Latin for "I spread"—this clonal colony clocks in at 13 million pounds dispersed across some 40,000 trees. Also known as "The Trembling Giant," the arboreal organism is sadly showing signs of degeneration as a result of overgrazing from deer, bark beetles, and disease.

While there are no formal hiking trails in Pando, you can drive past it on Highway 25, or just roam through the aspens. It's also located alongside Fish Lake, where you can enjoy a picnic. A particularly stunning time to visit is fall, when the aspen leaves glow yellow and orange before shaking loose. A visit to Pando can also be a nice way to seek shade and cooler temperatures midday or in the afternoon if you're visiting Capitol Reef in the summer. For more information on Pando, contact the **Fishlake National Forest** (115 E. 900 N., Richfield, 435/896-9233, www.fs.usda.gov/fishlake).

aspen trees

5.5-hour, 333-mile (535-km) drive north, almost entirely on I-15, except for short stretches at the end on Highway 20 and US 89. From Salt Lake City, it's a 3.5-hour, 224-mile (360-km) drive south on I-15 and east on smaller US 50 and Highway 24.

TORREY

Torrey (pop. 240) is an attractive little village with a real Western feel. Only 11 miles (17.7 km) west of the Capitol Reef National Park visitor center, at the junction of Highways 12 and 24, it's a friendly and convenient place to stay, with several excellent lodgings and a few good restaurants.

There are other little towns along the Fremont River, which drains this steep-sided valley. Teasdale is a small community just 4 miles (6.4 km) west, situated in a grove of piñon pines. Bicknell, a small farm and ranch town, is 8 miles (12.9 km) west of Torrey.

The **Fremont River Ranger District** (138 S. Main St., Loa, 435/836-2800, www.fs.usda.gov/r4, 8am-5pm Mon.-Fri.) of the Fishlake National Forest has information about hiking, horseback riding, and road conditions in the northern and eastern parts of Boulder Mountain and the Aquarius Plateau.

Outfitters

Hondoo Rivers and Trails (435/425-3519, www.hondoo.com), run by longtime locals, offers guided horseback riding adventures for multiday backcountry excursions. For a real treat, check out the inn-to-inn trail rides. They also provide guided hiking tours and backpacking trips, jeep tours, and shuttle services.

Entertainment and Events

The **Entrada Institute** (www.entradainstitute.org), a nonprofit organization that seeks to further understanding and appreciation of the natural, historical, cultural, and scientific heritage of the Colorado Plateau, sponsors a cultural event as part of its **Saturday Sunset Series** (7:30pm Sat. late May-late Oct., usually free). Events range from talks by local ranchers on the cattle industry to musical performances.

Food

Most restaurants in Torrey are not open year-round. Some start to close or switch to limited hours in mid-October while others end the season in November, then reopen in March or early April.

At **Hunt & Gather** (599 W. Main St., 435/425-3070, www.huntandgatherrestaurant.com, 8am-11am and 5pm-10pm Wed.-Fri., 8am-noon and 5pm-10pm Sat.-Sun., dinner entrées $20-42), you'll find meals that reflect the restaurant's name. On the "hunter" side of the menu, there's wild game, beef, and fish. Vegetarians will love the "gather" options. The chef has worked at some of Salt Lake City's finest restaurants, and this is the most upscale dining you'll find in this small town.

Great Mexican fare and a lively vibe are available at **Chak Balam Mexican Restaurant** (12 Sand Creek Rd., 435/425-2877, 7am-9pm Tues.-Sat., $15-30). Chak Balam—Mayan for "red jaguar"—serves standards like enchiladas and chiles rellenos alongside authentic Latin plates like octopus tacos, enmoladas (enchiladas with mole), and shrimp ceviche. Espresso drinks and Mexican hot chocolate are served in the morning, and you can enjoy Mexican sodas, beer, or a fine margarita with lunch or dinner.

The best greasy spoon in town is **Slacker's Burger Joint** (165 E. Main St., 435/425-3710, www.slackersburgerjoint.com, 11:30am-8pm Mon.-Sat., $9-15), serving burgers, chili, and milkshakes (vegetarian options are available). The pastrami burger is rightfully famous, and a shake hits the spot after a day of hiking in the heat.

Stop by the **Wild Rabbit Café** (135 E. Main St., 435/425-3074, https://thewildrabbitcafe.com, 8am-2pm Thurs.-Mon., $8-19) for a great cup of coffee or an expresso drink and a homemade pastry or breakfast sandwich (including vegan and gluten-free options). Wild Rabbit also serves breakfast and lunch, along with a hiker's box you can take with you for a picnic. This counter-service spot with indoor-outdoor seating fills up fast with hungry hikers—expect a line out the door on peak season mornings. But it's worth the wait! Wild Rabbit is one of the few places in town that stays open nearly year-round.

About 23 miles (37 km) east of the Capitol Reef visitor center, stop by ★ **Mesa Farm Market** (Hwy. 24, Milepost 102, Caineville, 435/456-9146, www.mesafarmmarket.com, 10am-3pm daily late Mar.-Oct.) for artisanal cheese and yogurt made with milk from goats on the farm, sourdough bread baked in a wood-fired oven, a cup of coffee, outstanding homemade pesto, and whatever produce is growing in the back 40—the best picnic fixings in southeastern Utah.

Accommodations

$50-100

A few cabins are available at the center of town at the **Torrey Trading Post** (25 W. Main St., 435/425-3716, www.torreytradingpost.com, $60-150). The smaller cabins aren't loaded with frills—toilets and showers are in men's and women's bathhouses—but the price is right, pets are permitted, and there's a place to do laundry. The larger studio cabins come fully furnished with a full bath and kitchen.

$100-150

At the east end of Torrey, the **Rim Rock Inn** (2523 E. Hwy. 24, 435/425-3398 or 888/447-4676, www.therimrock.net, Mar.-Dec., $129-229) does indeed perch on a rim of red rock; it's just about as close as you can get to the park. The motel and its two restaurants are part of a 120-acre ranch, so the views are expansive, though the rooms themselves are fairly basic. There are also two built-in restaurants—one fine-dining and a more casual spot on the patio.

In Teasdale, 4 miles (6.4 km) west of Torrey, **Pine Shadows** (195 W. 125 S., Teasdale, 435/425-3939, www.pineshadowcabins.net, 2-night minimum, $119-288) offers spacious modern cabins, equipped with two queen beds plus full baths and kitchens, in a piñon forest.

Wild Rabbit
Cafe
435-425-3074 www.thewildrabbitcafe.com
Dine In or Take Out • Pastries • Espresso
COFFEE
Espresso·Tea·Food·Drinks·Pastries·Snacks
1

2

Over $150

Stay in a 1914 schoolhouse: The **Torrey Schoolhouse Bed and Breakfast** (150 N. Center St., 435/491-0230, www.torreyschoolhouse.com, Apr.-Oct., $150-185) has been renovated but retains many period touches in each of its unique themed rooms. Modern amenities include a shiatsu massage chair in every room, memory foam mattress toppers, flat-screen TVs, and a wheelchair-accessible suite. Breakfast is served family-style at 8:30am daily.

If you're looking for nicely furnished rooms with an outdoor pool and great views, a good choice is the **Capitol Reef Resort** (2600 E. Hwy. 24, 435/425-3761, www.capitolreefresort.com, $219-269). If a hotel room seems too tame, stay in one of the air-conditioned Conestoga wagons (sleeps 6, $356-373). Tepees ($339) and cabins ($322-407) are also available.

In a pretty setting 3 miles (4.8 km) south of town, **Cowboy Homestead Cabins** (Hwy. 12, 435/425-3414 or 888/854-5871, www.cowboyhomesteadcabins.com, $159) has attractive one- and two-bedroom cabins with private baths, kitchenettes, and outdoor gas grills.

In a grove of trees immediately behind downtown Torrey's old trading post and country store is **Austin's Chuck Wagon Lodge** (12 W. Main St., 435/425-3335 or 800/863-3288, www.austinschuckwagonmotel.com, Mar.-Dec., rooms $189-289, cabins $369-389). This cute yet basic motel has recently renovated guest rooms, a newer lodge-like building, and newer two-bedroom cabins. There's also a pool, a hot tub, a general store, and a deli with a bakery on-site.

The ★ **Lodge at Red River Ranch** (2900 W. Hwy. 24, 435/425-3322, www.redriverranch.com, $244-349) is between Bicknell and Torrey beneath towering cliffs of red sandstone on the banks of the Fremont River. This wood-beamed lodge sits on a 2,200-acre (890-ha) working ranch, but there's nothing rustic or unsophisticated about the accommodations. The three-story structure is built in the same grand architectural style as old-fashioned mountain lodges. The great room has a massive stone fireplace as well as cozy chairs and couches with a splendid Old West atmosphere. There are 15 guest rooms, most decorated according to a theme, and all have private baths. Guests are welcome to wander the ranch paths, fish for trout, or meander in the gardens and orchards. Breakfast and dinner are served in the lodge restaurant but are not included in the room rates; box lunches can be ordered.

The lovely **SkyRidge Inn Bed and Breakfast** (1012 E. Hwy. 24, 435/425-3222, www.skyridgeinn.com, $179-315) is 1 mile (1.6 km) east of downtown Torrey. The modern inn has been decorated with high-quality Southwestern art and artifacts, and all six guest rooms have private baths. SkyRidge sits on a bluff amid 75 acres (30 ha), and guests are invited to explore the land on foot or by bicycle.

Campgrounds

Although most campers will try for a site at Capitol Reef National Park, the campground there fills up quickly. Torrey has a couple of private campgrounds that cater to both RV and tent campers. Right in town, the **Sand Creek RV Park** (540 W. Hwy. 24, 435/425-3577, www.sandcreekrv.com, Mar.-Oct., tents $29, RVs $55-58, camping cabins $69-86, vintage trailer $45) has shaded campsites in a pleasant grassy field. Showers (nonguests $5) and laundry facilities (wash and dry $5) are available, along with Wi-Fi.

Thousand Lakes RV Park (1110 W. Hwy. 24, 1 mi/1.6 km west of Torrey, 435/425-3500 or 800/355-8995, www.thousandlakesrvpark.com, Apr.-late Oct., tents $25, RVs $45-49 with full hookups, weekly rates available) has showers, Wi-Fi, a laundry room, and a store. Thousand Lakes also has cabins, ranging from spartan (no linens, $45) to deluxe (sleeps up to 6, linens provided, $119).

1: espresso and pastries at Wild Rabbit Café
2: Conestoga wagons at Capitol Reef Resort

The US Forest Service's **Sunglow Campground** (Forest Rd. 143, east of Bicknell, 435/836-2811, www.recreation.gov, with water, May-Oct., $16) is just east of Bicknell at an elevation of 7,200 feet (2,195 m). The surrounding red cliffs light up at sunset, hence the name. Several other Forest Service campgrounds are on the slopes of Boulder Mountain along Highway 12 between Torrey and Boulder. All are above 8,600 feet (2,621 m) and are usually not open until late May-early June.

East of Capitol Reef

Highway 24 follows the Fremont River east from Capitol Reef National Park to a junction at Hanksville. From here, you can head north toward I-70 (the best route to Moab) or south along the eastern edge of the Henry Mountains to the upper reaches of Lake Powell. Hanksville is a good place to gas up if you're exploring the remote Henry Mountains or the southern San Rafael Swell. Goblin Valley State Park is worth a visit, and it's a good place to camp.

HANKSVILLE

Even by Utah standards, tiny Hanksville (pop. just over 200) is pretty remote. Ebenezer Hanks and other LDS settlers founded this out-of-the-way community in 1882 along the Fremont River, then known as the Dirty Devil River. The isolation attracted polygamists like Hanks and other fugitives. Butch Cassidy and his gang found refuge in the rugged canyon country of Robbers' Roost, east of town. Several houses and the old stone church on Center Street, one block south of the highway, survive from the 19th century.

Travelers exploring this scenic region find Hanksville a handy if lackluster stopover, with Capitol Reef National Park to the west, Lake Powell and the Henry Mountains to the south, the remote Maze District of Canyonlands National Park to the east, and Goblin Valley State Park to the north. Because Hanksville is a true crossroads, the few lodgings here are often booked well in advance, so plan ahead.

Wolverton Mill

E. T. Wolverton built this ingenious mill during the 1920s at his gold-mining claims in the Henry Mountains. A 20-foot (6-m) waterwheel, still perfectly balanced, powered ore-crushing machinery and a sawmill. Owners of claims at the mill's original site didn't like a steady stream of tourists coming through to see the mill, so it was moved to the BLM office at Hanksville. Drive south 0.5 mile (0.8 km) on 100 West to see the mill and some of its original interior mechanism.

Food

Hanksville's restaurants—worth a stop for convenience more than culinary intrigue—cluster at the south end of town. Stop by **Outlaw's Roost** (20 N. Hwy. 95, 435/542-1763, 11am-9pm Thurs.-Mon., $7-12) for a tasty burrito or rice bowl. **Stan's Burger Shak** (150 S. Hwy. 95, 435/542-3330, www.stansburgershak.com, 10am-10pm Mon.-Sat., noon-10pm Sun., $6-12), at the Chevron station, is full of locals and represents a step up from the chains. Soak in the Western atmosphere and some good steaks, burgers, and barbecue at **Duke's Slickrock Grill** (275 Hwy. 24, 435/542-2052, www.dukesslickrock.com, 7am-10pm daily, $10-32).

Accommodations

Hanksville is a busy crossroads with just two lodging options, so rooms go fast. At **Whispering Sands Motel** (90 S. Hwy. 95, 435/542-3238, www.dukesslickrock.com, $149), you'll have a choice of rooms in the motel or in "cabins" that look a lot like garden sheds. Though by the time you arrive, you'll be glad to see them.

In the center of town, behind Duke's Slickrock Grill, there's **Duke's RV campground** (435/542-3235 or 800/894-3242, www.dukesslickrock.com, open year-round, $20 tents, $40 RVs) with showers, laundry, campfire pits, and Wi-Fi that works most of the time.

Information and Services

The **Bureau of Land Management** (380 S. 100 W., 435/542-3461, www.blm.gov) has a field station 0.5 mile (0.8 km) south of Highway 24, with information on road conditions, hiking, camping, and the buffalo herd in the Henry Mountains.

★ GOBLIN VALLEY STATE PARK

Thousands of rock formations, many with goblin-like "faces," inhabit this valley, now part of **Goblin Valley State Park** (435/259-3710, https://stateparks.utah.gov, reservations 800/322-3770, www.reserveamerica.com, year-round, day-use $20 per vehicle, camping $45, yurts $150). All of these so-called goblins were weathered out of the Entrada Formation, which consists of soft red sandstone and even softer siltstone.

Carmel Canyon Trail (1.5-mile/2.4-km loop) begins at the northeast side of the parking lot at road's end, then drops down to the desert floor and a strange landscape of rock goblins, spires, and balancing acts. Wander at your whim—this is a great place for the imagination. A 1.3-mile (2.1-km) trail connects the campground and the goblin-studded Carmel Canyon Trail. Curtis Bench Trail begins on the road between the parking lot and the campground and goes south to a viewpoint of the Henry Mountains; cairns mark the 1.5-mile (2.4-km) one-way route.

Mountain bikers can explore the five-loop Wild Horse Trail System, which consists of 7 miles (11.3 km) of single-track west of the campground and includes several overlooks and areas of the park rarely seen by hikers.

Twelve miles (19.3 km) north, the Temple Mountain Bike Trail traverses old mining roads, ridges, and wash bottoms. Popular hikes near the state park include the Little Wild Horse and Bell Canyons Loop, Chute and Crack Canyons Loop, and Wild Horse Canyon. The park is also a good base for exploring the San Rafael Swell area to the northwest (page 446).

Camping at Goblin Valley is delightful. The late evening and early morning sun makes the sandstone spires glow. If you're not much of a camper, consider booking one of the park's two yurts. They're tucked back among the rock formations, and each is equipped with bunk beds and a futon, swamp cooler, and propane stove. There are only 26 camping sites, so reserve well in advance.

The turnoff from Highway 24 for the state park is at milepost 137, which is 21 miles (34 km) north of Hanksville and 24 miles (39 km) south of I-70. Follow signs west 5 miles (8 km) on a paved road, then south 7 miles (11.3 km) on a gravel road.

LITTLE WILD HORSE CANYON

West of Goblin Valley, Little Wild Horse is a good slot canyon hike for anyone without technical experience, though a little scrambling is required. Hike in as far as you like and turn around to exit or make a loop with Bell Canyon. Hiking is best in spring and fall. Avoid the area when there's a chance of rain, which is often the case in August. Reach the trailhead by traveling south on Goblin Valley Road, but turning west on Wild Horse Road before entering Goblin Valley State Park. The trailhead is about 6 miles (9.7 km) from the park.

HENRY MOUNTAINS

Great domes of intrusive igneous rock pushed into and deformed surrounding sedimentary layers about 70 million years ago. Erosion later uncovered the domes, revealing mountains towering 5,000 feet (1,524 m) above the surrounding plateau. Mount Ellen's North Summit Ridge (elev. 11,522 ft/3,512 m) and Mount Pennell (elev. 11,320 ft/3,450 m) top

1

2

the range. Scenic views and striking geologic features abound in the Henrys. Rock layers tilt dramatically in the Waterpocket Fold to the west. Between Ellen and Pennell Mountains, sheer cliffs of the Horn attract rock climbers.

The arid land and rugged canyons surrounding the Henrys so discouraged early explorers that the range wasn't even named or described until 1869 by members of the Powell River Expedition. Buffalo brought to the Henrys from Yellowstone National Park in 1941 form one of the few free-roaming herds in the United States. They winter in the southwestern part of the mountains, then move up as the snow melts.

Countless mountain and canyon hiking routes exist in the range, most of which go cross-country or follow old mining roads. Rough, scenic roads—best-suited for high-clearance vehicles—cross the range between the peaks at Bull Creek, Pennellen, and Stanton Passes. The road through Bull Creek Pass (elev. 10,485 ft/3,196 m) is snow-free only early July-late October. Rain, which peaks in August, occasionally makes travel difficult in late summer. Roads tend to be at their best in autumn, just before deer-hunting season. Travel at the lower elevations is possible all year, though spring and fall have the best temperatures. Check in with the BLM office in Hanksville before exploring the backcountry. Bring water, food, and extra clothing, since the Henry Mountains remain a remote region.

The only easily accessible campsites in the Henry Mountains are the BLM sites at **Starr Springs Campground** (elev. 6,300 ft/1,920 m, 435/542-3461, no water, $10), off Highway 276 north of Ticaboo. The campground sits in an oak forest at the base of Mount Hillers. A good gravel road to Starr Springs Campground turns off Highway 276 near milepost 17 (23 mi/37 km north of Bullfrog and 43 mi/69 km south of Hanksville) and goes in 4 miles (6.4 km).

Glen Canyon National Recreation Area

Glen Canyon National Recreation Area (928/608-6200, www.nps.gov/glca, 24/7 year-round, $30 per vehicle, $25 per motorcycle, $15 cyclists and pedestrians, no charge for passing through Page, Arizona, on US 89) is a vast preserve covering 1.25 million acres (505,857 ha) in Arizona and Utah. At the center of the preserve is Lake Powell. When the Glen Canyon Dam was completed in 1964, conservationists deplored the loss of the remote and beautiful Glen Canyon of the Colorado River beneath the lake's waters—a canyon considered on par in magnificence with the Grand Canyon.

Today, the 186-mile-long (299-km) lake provides access to an area most had not even known existed. As far as artificial lakes go, Lake Powell is second in size only to Lake Mead, though Lake Powell has three times more shoreline (1,960 mi/3,154 km). Lately, though, Lake Powell's existence has been called into question as the waters of the Colorado River deplete due to drought exacerbated by climate change and overuse. Just a handful of roads approach the lake, so access is basically limited to boats. Bays and coves offer nearly limitless opportunities for exploration by boaters, as well as long-distance hiking trails.

HALLS CROSSING AND BULLFROG MARINAS

At **Halls Crossing Marina** (435/684-7000), you'll find a store (groceries, plus fishing and boating supplies), tours to Rainbow Bridge, boat rentals (fishing, waterskiing, and houseboats), a gas dock, slips, and storage. The **ranger station** is nearby, although rangers

1: rock formations in Goblin Valley State Park
2: Glen Canyon National Recreation Area

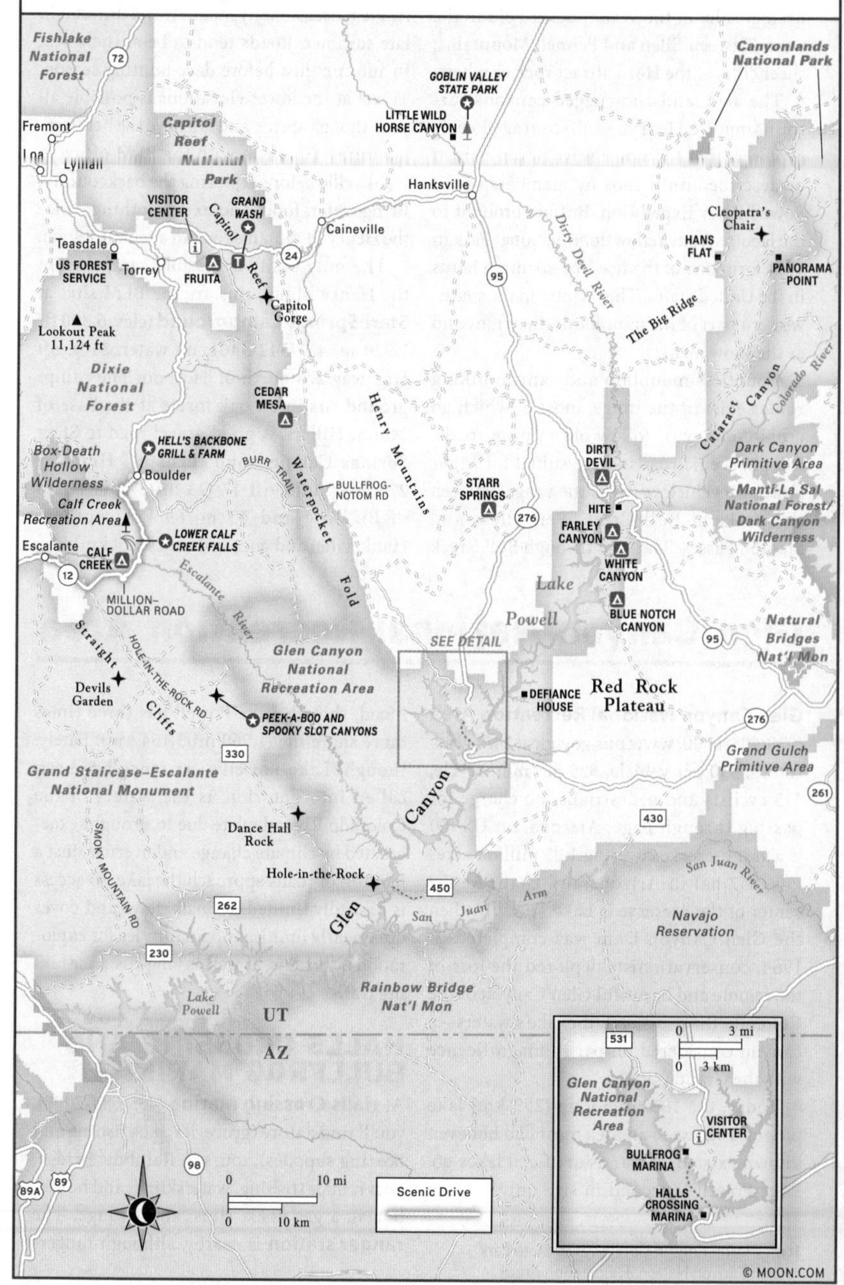
Glen Canyon National Recreation Area
Fishlake National Forest
72
Capitol Reef National Park
Fremont
Loa
Lyman
VISITOR CENTER
GRAND WASH
Capitol Reef
Teasdale
US FOREST SERVICE
Torrey
FRUITA
24
Capitol Gorge
Caineville
Hanksville
GOBLIN VALLEY STATE PARK
LITTLE WILD HORSE CANYON
Canyonlands National Park
Cleopatra's Chair
HANS FLAT
PANORAMA POINT
Dirty Devil River
The Big Ridge
95
Lookout Peak 11,124 ft
Dixie National Forest
CEDAR MESA
Henry Mountains
Colorado River
Cataract Canyon
Dark Canyon Primitive Area
Manti-La Sal National Forest/ Dark Canyon Wilderness
HELL'S BACKBONE GRILL & FARM
Box-Death Hollow Wilderness
Boulder
BURR TRAIL
BULLFROG-NOTOM RD
Waterpocket Fold
STARR SPRINGS
DIRTY DEVIL
HITE
276
FARLEY CANYON
WHITE CANYON
Calf Creek Recreation Area
LOWER CALF CREEK FALLS
Escalante
CALF CREEK
12
Escalante River
MILLION-DOLLAR ROAD
Lake Powell
BLUE NOTCH CANYON
Natural Bridges Nat'l Mon
SEE DETAIL
Straight Cliffs
HOLE-IN-THE-ROCK RD
Devils Garden
Glen Canyon National Recreation Area
DEFIANCE HOUSE
Red Rock Plateau
PEEK-A-BOO AND SPOOKY SLOT CANYONS
330
Grand Staircase–Escalante National Monument
Grand Gulch Primitive Area
261
430
Dance Hall Rock
Glen Canyon
SMOKY MOUNTAIN RD
Hole-in-the-Rock
450
San Juan Arm
San Juan River
262
Navajo Reservation
230
Rainbow Bridge Nat'l Mon
Lake Powell
UT
AZ
531
0
3 mi
0
3 km
Glen Canyon National Recreation Area
VISITOR CENTER
BULLFROG MARINA
HALLS CROSSING MARINA
98
89A
89
0
10 mi
0
10 km
Scenic Drive
© MOON.COM

are usually out on patrol; look for their vehicle in the area if the office is closed.

On the western side of the lake, **Bullfrog Marina** is more like a small town (albeit one run by Aramark), with a **visitor center** (435/684-3000, hours vary May-early Oct.), a clinic, stores, a service station, and a handsome hotel and restaurant. The marina rents boats ranging from kayaks ($50 per day) and paddleboards ($90 per day) to houseboats ($2,470-15,000 per week), but for guided boat tours of Lake Powell, you'll have to go to the Wahweap Marina near Page, Arizona.

Defiance House Lodge (888/896-3829, www.lakepowell.com, $208-228) offers comfortable lake-view accommodations and **Anasazi Restaurant** (435/684-3198, 4pm-9pm daily late May-Oct., $16-28). The front desk at the lodge also handles family units (well-equipped trailers, about $320 per night), an RV park ($47), and houseboat rentals (from about $2,000 for a week). Showers, a laundry room, a convenience store, and a post office are at **Trailer Village.** Ask the visitor center staff or rangers for directions to primitive camping areas with vehicle access elsewhere along Bullfrog Bay.

Bullfrog Marina can be reached from the north via paved Highway 276. It is 40 miles (64 km) between Bullfrog and the junction with Highway 95. Ticaboo, 20 miles (32 km) north of Bullfrog, has another good lodging option. The **Ticaboo Lodge** (844/662-2628, www.northlakepowell.com, $141-165) has a swimming pool, a restaurant, RV camping ($42, no bathhouse) and a service station that pretty much constitutes all of Ticaboo.

For reservations and information regarding lodging, camping, tours, boating, and recreation at both Halls Crossing and Bullfrog Marina, contact **Lake Powell Resorts & Marinas** (928/645-1030, www.lakepowellmarinas.com).

HITE

In 1883, Cass Hite came to Glen Canyon in search of gold. He found some at a place later named Hite City, which set off a small gold rush. Cass and a few of his relatives operated a small store and post office, which were the only services for miles. Travelers who wanted to cross the Colorado River here had the difficult task of swimming their animals across. Eventually, in 1946, resident Arthur Chaffin put through the first road and opened a ferry service. The Chaffin Ferry served uranium prospectors and adventurous motorists until the lake backed up to the spot in 1964. A steel

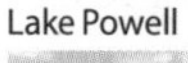
Lake Powell

bridge now spans the Colorado River upstream from Hite Marina. Cass Hite's store and the ferry site are underwater about 5 miles (8 km) down the lake from Hite Marina.

Beyond Hite, on the tiny neck of land between the Colorado River Bridge and the Dirty Devil Bridge, an unmarked dirt road turns north. The long and rugged Hite Road (also called Orange Cliffs Rd.) eventually links up with backcountry routes—including the Flint Trail—in the Maze District of Canyonlands National Park.

The uppermost marina on Lake Powell, Hite is 141 lake miles (227 km) from Glen Canyon Dam. It is hit hard when water levels drop in Lake Powell, which has been most of the time in recent years. When water is available, boats can continue up the lake to the mouth of Dark Canyon in Cataract Canyon at low water, or into Canyonlands National Park at high water. During times of low water, the boat ramp is often high above the lake and the place is pretty desolate. Facilities include a small store with gas and a primitive campground (free) with no drinking water. Primitive camping is also available nearby, off Highway 95 at Dirty Devil, Farley Canyon, White Canyon, Blue Notch, and other locations. A ranger station (435/684-2457) is occasionally open.

PAGE, ARIZONA

Although the town of Page is hot, busy, and not particularly appealing, it is the largest community anywhere near Lake Powell, and it offers access to boat tours and a number of places to stay and eat. The town overlooks Lake Powell and Glen Canyon Dam.

The largest resort in the Glen Canyon National Recreation Area, **Wahweap Resort and Marina** (100 Lakeshore Dr., 888/896-3829, www.lakepowell.com) is just 6 miles (9.7 km) northwest of Page off US 89. Wahweap is a major center for all manner of water sports, including houseboats that sleep up to 10 (from $3,939 for 5 days in high summer season), kayaks (from $55 per day), and paddleboards ($90 per day). Wahweap also offers an extensive range of boat tours and boat-assisted hiking, among other recreational activities. Wahweap's Lake Powell Resort, a hotel and restaurant complex, offers some of the most comfortable rooms in the area.

Tours

From Wahweap, several boat tours depart from the **Wahweap Marina** (928/645-2433, www.lakepowell.com) to areas including Navajo Canyon and Rainbow Bridge. There's also a dinner cruise. However, tour offerings vary depending on water levels, so call ahead to see what's available and book in advance.

The Wahweap Marina has discontinued its tours of Antelope Canyon, so if you want to explore this elusive, water-sculpted canyon, you'll need to travel by truck and foot, not boat. You can book a land-based tour that begins east of Page with **Antelope Canyon Tours** (22 S. Lake Powell Blvd., 855/574-9102, www.antelopecanyon.com, $93-120 adults, $75-112 kids), a Navajo-owned company. Tours last about 1.5 hours and run several times a day year-round.

Food

If you've been traveling through remote rural Utah for a while, dipping into Page, Arizona, can seem like a gastronomic oasis. The **Ranch House Grille** (819 N. Navajo Dr., 928/645-1420, www.ranchhouse-grille.com, 6am-3pm daily, $13-22) serves breakfast all day plus sandwiches, burgers, steaks, and chops for lunch. At **Blue Wine Bar** (644 N. Navajo Dr., 928/608-0707, 6pm-11pm Tues.-Sat., $8-16), you'll find excellent tapas and small plates, plus a great wine selection. In the same Dam Plaza complex, the stylish **Blue Buddha Sushi Lounge** (644 N. Navajo Dr., 928/645-0007, www.bluebuddhasushilounge.com, 5pm-9pm Tues.-Fri., 5pm-8pm Sat., $10-20) serves cocktails and Japanese food, including sushi. Small but classy **Bonkers Restaurant** (810 N. Navajo Dr., 928/645-2706, www.bonkerspageaz.com, 4pm-8:30pm Tues.-Thurs., 4pm-9pm Fri.-Sat., $12-46) serves good salads, steaks, pasta, and old-time favorites like chicken marsala. **Fiesta Mexicana** (125 S. Lake Powell Blvd., 928/645-4082, www.fiestamexrest.com, 11am-9pm Sun.-Thurs., 11am-10pm Fri.-Sat., $9-20) is a busy but friendly little Mexican chain out West that serves fine food and good margaritas.

Accommodations

Nearly all Page motels are on or near Lake Powell Boulevard (US 89L), a 3.25-mile (5.2-km) loop that branches off the main highway. Page is a busy place in summer, however, and a call ahead is a good idea if you don't want to chase around town looking for vacancies. Expect to pay top dollar for lake views. The summer rates listed here drop in winter (Nov.-Mar.).

In a way, the most appealing lodgings are in the small apartments-turned-motels on and around 8th Avenue, a quiet residential area two blocks off Lake Powell Boulevard. These apartments date back to 1958-1959, when they housed supervisors for the dam construction project. The remodeled **Lake Powell Motel** (750 S. Navajo Dr., 928/645-9362, www.lakepowellmotel.net, $159-209) has standard rooms and nice one- and two-bedroom apartments with kitchenettes. Another vintage spot, the **Red Rock Motel** (114 8th Ave., 928/645-0062, www.redrockmotel.com, $80-139) offers everything from small basic rooms to two-bedroom apartments with kitchen and living room. All rooms have private patios, some with grills.

If you prefer the comforts of chain motels, Page has all the usual suspects. **Courtyard by Marriott Page** (600 Clubhouse Dr., 928/645-5000, www.marriott.com, $209-241) is a good option in a great setting, with views, a restaurant, a pool, spa, and exercise room, and an adjacent 18-hole golf course.

If you want to play in the water, there's no closer spot than the **Lake Powell Resort** at Wahweap Marina (6 mi/9.7 km north of Page off US 89 at 100 Lakeshore Dr., 928/645-2433, www.lakepowell.com, $145-309), with access to recreation, tours, and lively drinking and dining right outside your door.

Moab, Arches, and Canyonlands

The Colorado River and its tributaries have

carved extraordinary landscapes into the Colorado Plateau's radiant sandstone deposits in this part of Utah. Labyrinthine canyons, improbable arches, and massive monoliths make this region seem primordial at times and lunar at others. Two national parks—Arches and Canyonlands—plus state parks and recreation areas preserve these lands of intrigue and beauty.

At Arches, you'll find a relatively compact park that can conceivably be visited in a day or less. From right-off-the-road vistas and a variety of trails to the maze-like Fiery Furnace backcountry area, several different arch-viewing experiences are possible within this popular park.

By comparison, Canyonlands is massive and sprawling. While a

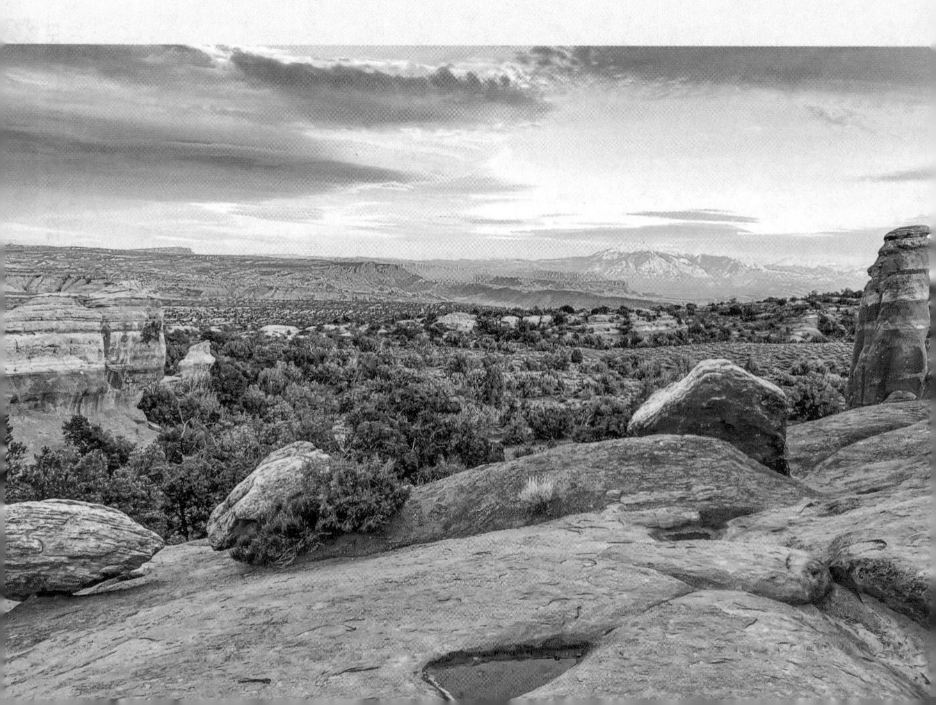

Highlights

Look for ★ to find recommended sights, activities, dining, and lodging.

★ **Corona and Bowtie Arches:** With slickrock hiking, a little scrambling, and some ladder climbing, this action-packed hike leads to phenomenal views (page 330).

★ **Moab Mountain Biking:** From the world-renowned Slickrock Trail (touristy, but worth it) to the epic Whole Enchilada descent, the riding in Moab is second to none (page 331).

★ **Delicate Arch:** While you can view Utah's "license plate arch" in the distance from your car, it's worth the trek up sand and slickrock—ideally early before the crowds—to see this legendary formation up close (page 351).

★ **Fiery Furnace:** An enchanting maze of narrow canyons and arches await in this backcountry area, which you can enter with a permit or on a guided ranger tour (page 351).

★ **Horseshoe Canyon:** In Canyonlands' remote Horseshoe Unit, the Great Gallery is a premier rock-art site accessible by a 7-mile (11.3-km) round-trip hike (page 357).

★ **Shafer Trail Road:** This formidable dirt road descends 1,500 feet (457 m) down a sandstone cliff. For confident off-road drivers and 4WD, high-clearance vehicles only (page 365).

★ **White Rim Bikepacking:** Spend a few days pedaling and camping your way up Canyonlands' dirt White Rim Road through the best of canyon country (page 366).

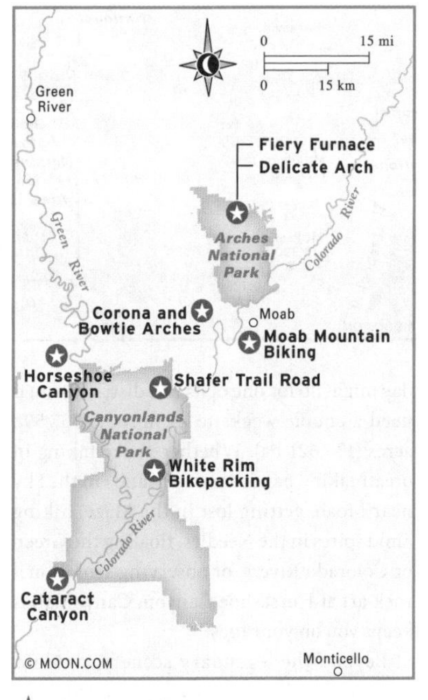

★ **Cataract Canyon:** Raft the Class III-V (depending on flow) rapids of this confluence of the Green and Colorado Rivers in Canyonlands (page 379).

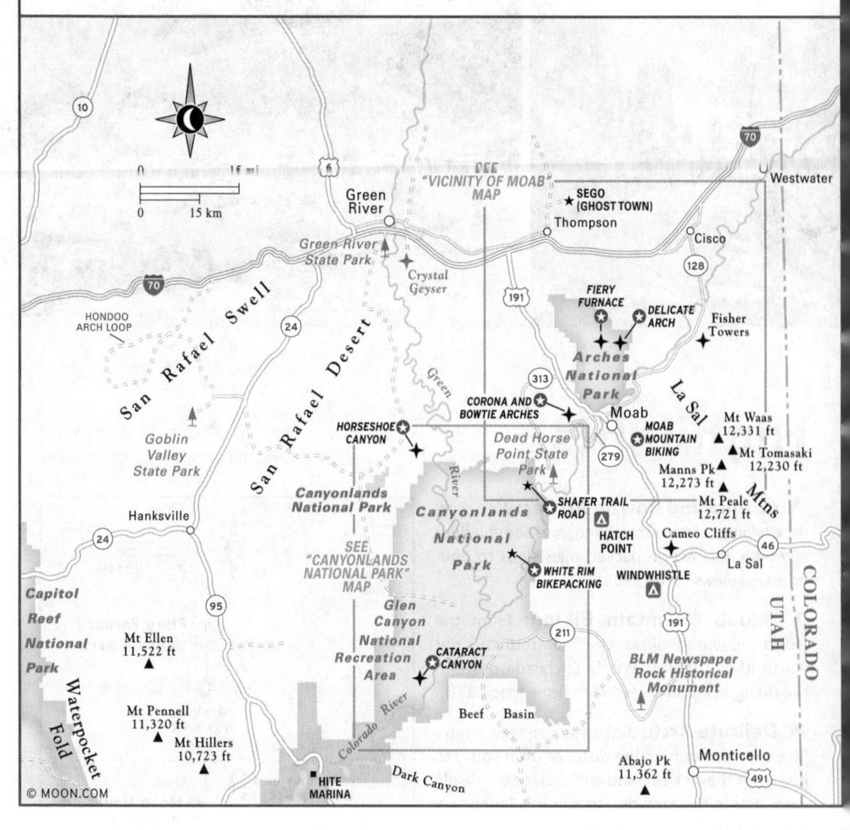

day might do for one of its five districts, you'd need a couple weeks to explore its 337,598 acres (136,621 ha). Whether you're taking in breathtaking panoramas at Islands in the Sky near Moab, getting lost in the Maze, hiking amid spires in the Needles, floating the Green or Colorado Rivers, or observing sensational rock art at Horseshoe Canyon, Canyonlands keeps you on your toes.

Beyond the legendary scenery, outdoor recreation brings many people to this corner of Utah, particularly to the Moab area. In this adventure-powered town, you'll find world-class slickrock mountain biking, desert rock climbing, off-roading, and miles of river for paddlers to navigate.

PLANNING YOUR TIME

With two national parks and myriad public lands, the hiker, mountain biker, or outdoor lover could easily fill a **week** here. Not everyone has that much time to spend, of course, but even more casual visitors should consider budgeting at least **3 days.** Each of the two **national parks** near **Moab** (Arches, plus the Island in the Sky District of Canyonlands) will

Previous: sunset in Arches National Park; Fiery Furnace; Corona and Bowtie Arches in Moab.

require a day just to drive through. Other sections of Canyonlands require more time. That leaves a single day to explore Moab itself, take a **rafting trip** down the **Colorado River,** or go on a hike or mountain bike ride.

Fall and spring are the most popular times to visit, as daytime temperatures are moderate. **Summer heat** sets in late May-early June, when temperatures soar into the 90s and 100s, although the dry air makes the heat more bearable. Early morning is the best time to schedule adventures in summer. Autumn begins after late-summer rains end and lasts into November or even December; days are bright and sunny with ideal temperatures, but nights get cold. **Winter** lasts only about 2 months at the lower elevations. With **light snow** contrasting with the red canyon walls, winter can be a nice time for a trip.

Compared to Zion and Bryce, Arches and Canyonlands don't have any dining options inside the park, and water is usually only available at visitor centers, so plan on picking up food and loading up on water in Moab before you visit.

Moab

TOP EXPERIENCE

Gateway to world-class hiking, mountain biking, rock climbing, paddling, off-roading, and even backcountry skiing, Moab is a strong contender for adventure capital of the United States. Located near the Colorado River in a green valley enclosed by high sandstone cliffs, Moab makes an excellent base for exploring the surrounding canyon country. In the Bible, Moab was a kingdom at the edge of Zion, and a lush valley surrounded by desert—sound familiar? Although some argue the name actually comes from a Paiute word, moapa, meaning "mosquito."

Today, Moab (pop. 5,300, elev. 4,025 ft/1,225 m) is the largest town in southeastern Utah. The first boom came during the 1950s when vast deposits of uranium, important fuel for the atomic age, were discovered. By the 1970s the uranium mines were largely abandoned, but all the rough roads built to access mines set the stage for exploration by 4WD vehicles, ATVs, and mountain bikes. Another legacy of the uranium boom can be seen along the highway at the north end of town, where a massive ongoing environmental cleanup is occurring by the Colorado River bridge.

Few disagree that Moab offers the best mountain biking in southern Utah, and it's an MTB (mountain biking) destination across the country and globe. The slickrock canyon country seems made for exploration by bike, and people come from all over to pedal the backcountry. A host of other outdoor adventures—rafting the Colorado River, horseback riding, off-roading, and rock climbing, to name a few—make Moab one of the most popular destinations in Utah.

As the town's popularity has grown, so have concerns that the area is getting loved to death. On busy days, hordes of mountain bikers form lineups to negotiate the trickier sections of the famed Slickrock Trail, and more than 20,000 people crowd into town on peak-season weekends to bike, hike, float, and party. As noted in an article in *Details* magazine, "Moab is pretty much the Fort Lauderdale of the intermountain West." Whether this old Latter-day Saints town and the delicate desert environment can endure such an onslaught of popularity is a question of increasing concern. Spare yourself the Fort Lauderdale vibes by coming during less crowded times, and avoid being part of the problem by minimizing your impact on the environment.

SIGHTS

With the astonishing sights of Canyonlands and Arches National Parks just minutes from

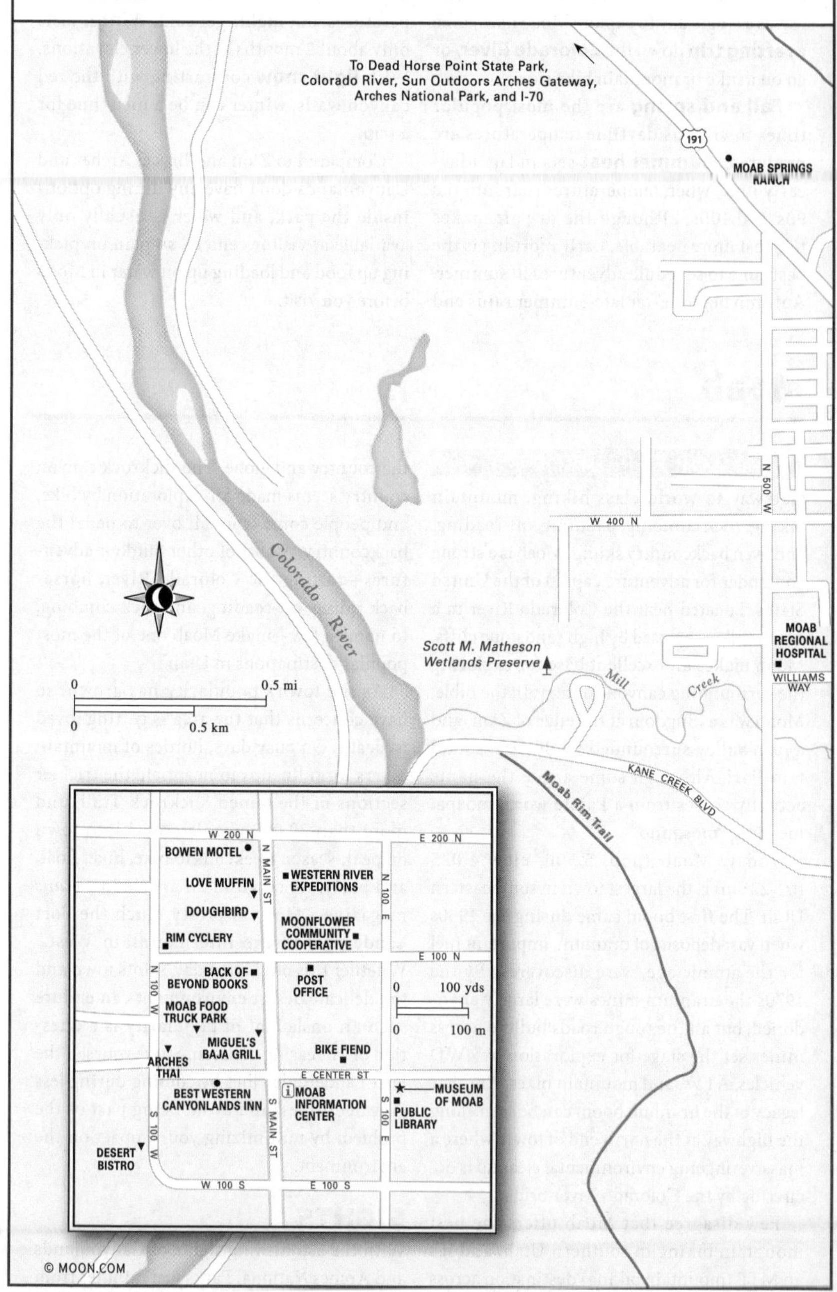
Moab
To Dead Horse Point State Park, Colorado River, Sun Outdoors Arches Gateway, Arches National Park, and I-70
191
MOAB SPRINGS RANCH
N 500 W
W 400 N
Colorado River
MOAB REGIONAL HOSPITAL
WILLIAMS WAY
Scott M. Matheson Wetlands Preserve
Mill Creek
KANE CREEK BLVD
Moab Rim Trail
0 0.5 mi
0 0.5 km
W 200 N
E 200 N
BOWEN MOTEL
N MAIN ST
WESTERN RIVER EXPEDITIONS
LOVE MUFFIN
N 100 E
DOUGHBIRD
MOONFLOWER COMMUNITY COOPERATIVE
RIM CYCLERY
E 100 N
BACK OF BEYOND BOOKS
POST OFFICE
N 100 W
0 100 yds
MOAB FOOD TRUCK PARK
0 100 m
MIGUEL'S BAJA GRILL
ARCHES THAI
BIKE FIEND
E CENTER ST
BEST WESTERN CANYONLANDS INN
MOAB INFORMATION CENTER
MUSEUM OF MOAB
PUBLIC LIBRARY
S 100 E
S MAIN ST
S 100 W
DESERT BISTRO
W 100 S
E 100 S

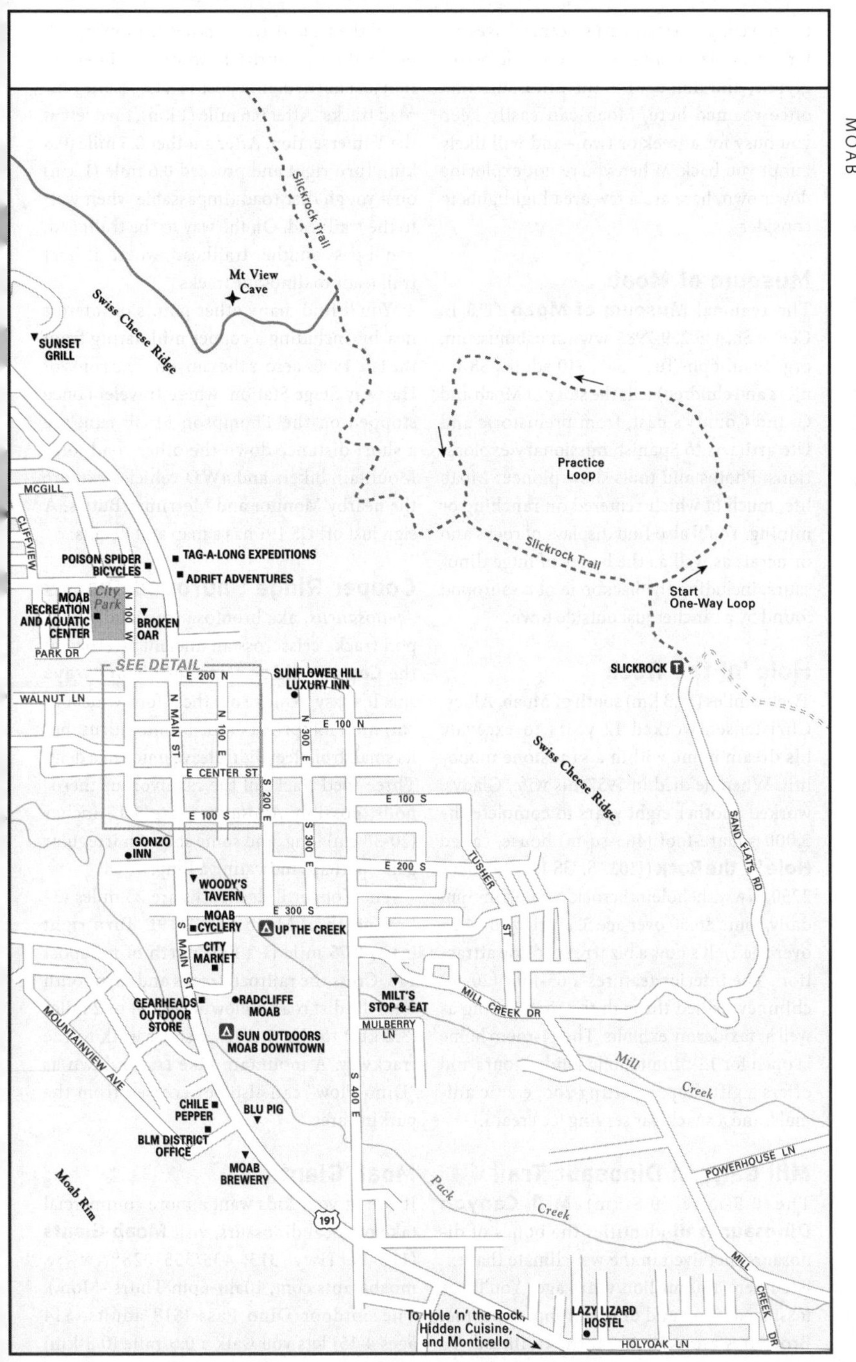
Slickrock Trail
Mt View Cave
Swiss Cheese Ridge
SUNSET GRILL
Practice Loop
MCGILL
CLIFFVIEW
POISON SPIDER BICYCLES
TAG-A-LONG EXPEDITIONS
ADRIFT ADVENTURES
Slickrock Trail
Start One-Way Loop
MOAB RECREATION AND AQUATIC CENTER
City Park
N 100 W
BROKEN OAR
PARK DR
SEE DETAIL
E 200 N
SUNFLOWER HILL LUXURY INN
SLICKROCK
WALNUT LN
N MAIN ST
N 100 E
N 300 E
E 100 N
Swiss Cheese Ridge
E CENTER ST
S 200 E
E 100 S
E 100 S
S 300 E
GONZO INN
E 200 S
TUSHER ST
SAND FLATS RD
WOODY'S TAVERN
E 300 S
MOAB CYCLERY
UP THE CREEK
S MAIN ST
CITY MARKET
MILT'S STOP & EAT
MILL CREEK DR
GEARHEADS OUTDOOR STORE
RADCLIFFE MOAB
MULBERRY LN
MOUNTAINVIEW AVE
SUN OUTDOORS MOAB DOWNTOWN
Mill Creek
S 400 E
CHILE PEPPER
BLU PIG
BLM DISTRICT OFFICE
MOAB BREWERY
Moab Rim
POWERHOUSE LN
Pack Creek
191
MILL CREEK DR
To Hole 'n' the Rock, Hidden Cuisine, and Monticello
LAZY LIZARD HOSTEL
HOLYOAK LN

town, a couple of state parks, scenic drives galore from the mining days, incredible petroglyphs, and homages to the dinosaurs that once roamed here, Moab can easily keep you busy for a week or two—and will likely tempt you back. When you're not exploring downtown, here are a few area highlights to consider.

Museum of Moab

The regional **Museum of Moab** (118 E. Center St., 435/259-7985, www.moabmuseum.org, 10am-6pm Tues.-Sat., $10 adults, $8 seniors and children) tells the story of Moab and Grand County's past, from prehistoric and Ute artifacts to Spanish missionary explorations. Photos and tools show pioneer Moab life, much of which centered on ranching or mining. You'll also find displays of rocks and minerals as well as the bones of huge dinosaurs, including the backbone of a sauropod found by a rancher just outside town.

Hole 'n' the Rock

Twelve miles (19.3 km) south of Moab, Albert Christensen worked 12 years to excavate his dream home within a sandstone monolith. When he died in 1957, his wife, Gladys, worked another eight years to complete the 5,000-square-foot (465-sq-m) house, called **Hole 'n' the Rock** (11037 S. US 191, 435/686-2250, www.theholeintherock.com, 9am-5pm daily, tours $6.50 over age 5, exotic zoo $4.25 over age 1). It's now a bizarre roadside attraction. The interior features a 65-foot (20-m) chimney drilled through the rock ceiling as well as taxidermy exhibits. The 14-room home is open for 12-minute-long guided tours and offers a gift shop, a petting zoo, exotic animals, and a snack bar serving ice cream.

Mill Canyon Dinosaur Trail

The 0.5-mile (0.8-km) **Mill Canyon Dinosaur Trail** identifies the bones of dinosaurs that lived in the wet climate that existed here 150 million years ago. You'll see fossilized wood and dinosaur footprints too. Brochures are available at the trailhead. To reach the trail, drive 15 miles (24 km) north on US 191, then turn left (west) at an intersection just north of milepost 141. Cross the railroad tracks. After 0.6 mile (1 km), turn left at the Y intersection. After another 0.5 mile (0.8 km), turn right and proceed 0.6 mile (1 km) on a rough dirt road (impassable when wet) to the trailhead. On the way to the trailhead, you'll pass another trailhead, where a short trail leads to dinosaur tracks.

You'll find many other points of interest nearby, including a copper mill dating from the late 1800s across the canyon. The ruins of Halfway Stage Station, where travelers once stopped on the Thompson-Moab run, are a short distance down the other road fork. Mountain bikers and 4WD vehicles explore the nearby Monitor and Merrimac Buttes. A sign just off US 191 has a map and details.

Copper Ridge Sauropod Tracks

Apatosaurus, aka brontosaurus, and theropod tracks crisscross an ancient riverbed at the **Copper Ridge Dinosaur Trackways** site. It's easy to make out the 2-foot-wide (60-cm) hind footprints of the brontosaurus, but its small front feet didn't leave much of a dent. Three-toed tracks of the carnivorous theropods, possibly *Allosaurus*, are 8-15 inches (20-38 cm) long, and some show an irregular gait—perhaps indicating a limp.

The Copper Ridge tracks are 23 miles (37 km) north of Moab on US 191. Turn right (east) 0.75 mile (1.2 km) north of milepost 148. Cross the railroad tracks and turn south onto the dirt road, following the signs 2 miles (3.2 km) to the site. It's a short walk to the trackway. A mountain bike trail known as "Dino-Flow" can also be accessed from the parking area.

Moab Giants

If you or your kids want a more commercial take on local dinosaurs, visit **Moab Giants** (112 W. Hwy. 313, 435/355-0288, www.moabgiants.com, 10am-6pm Thurs.-Mon.). The outdoor Dino Pass ($18 adults, $14 ages 4-15) lets you walk a 0.5-mile (0.8-km) outdoor trail flanked by more than 100 life-size dinosaur replicas, as well as check out exhibits inside the museum with a focus on fossil footprints. A visit to the prehistoric aquarium and 3-D theater here costs extra ($6 pp).

Utahraptor State Park

About 15 miles (24 km) north of Moab off US 191, about 6,500 acres (2,630 ha) recently became Utah's newest state park. Some of this brush-laden terrain was previously a popular spot for free dispersed camping. The area is also home to **Dalton Wells Quarry,** where the dinosaur *Utahraptor ostrommaysorum* was discovered in 1991. This early Cretaceous carnivore inspired the velociraptors in *Jurassic Park,* and you can see the bones found in Dalton Wells on display at the Natural History Museum of Utah in Salt Lake City.

To address overuse in the area, as well as to preserve the quarry and other historic sites, the Utah Legislature established **Utahraptor State Park** (https://stateparks.utah.gov) in 2021. While the park won't be fully operational for a few years, there is now a fee to camp ($15), which can be paid online (https://parkspass.utah.gov) or at a self-service station at the intersection of Willow Springs Road and Dalton Wells Road—the only two roads where camping access is now available. You must camp in existing sites, which means no new fire pits. Currently, camping is still primitive; there are two seasonal pit toilets, but no other amenities. The network of 4WD roads and mountain bike trails in the area remain free in the interim, though a day-use fee will likely be instituted in spring 2024. The park may also expand the trail system.

In spring 2024, the park aims to open Willow Springs Campground, which will have water, picnic tables, fire pits, and full hookups. Most campsites will be reservable in advance. A second "Dalton Wells" campground may open later, depending on funding. Dispersed camping will still be allowed on a first-come, first-served basis. Sometime in 2024, a visitor center will also open, with information about the park's namesake raptor, as well as a **Civilian Conservation Corps camp** and an **isolation center** that served as an internment camp for Japanese Americans during World War II, both located here.

While the development of the park and the new fees may frustrate some who previously loved exploring this unmanaged area, remember that the state has the best of intentions. The area was getting "over-loved," as Utahraptor State Park manager Josh Hansen explains—not to mention the pilfering occurring at the dinosaur quarry site. Ultimately, the state wants people to "come out and respect the land" and help "keep things as pristine as we can."

Dead Horse Point State Park

Just east of Canyonlands National Park's Island in the Sky District and a short drive northwest of Moab is one of Utah's most spectacular state parks. At **Dead Horse Point** (435/259-2614, https://stateparks.utah.gov, day-use $20 per vehicle), the land drops away in sheer cliffs, and 2,000 feet (610 m) below, the Colorado River twists through a gooseneck on its long journey to the sea. The river and its tributaries have carved canyons that reveal a geologic layer cake of colorful rock formations. Even in a region with impressive views around every corner, Dead Horse Point stands out for its exceptionally breathtaking panorama. The star of the view, the Colorado River, is the result of powerful underground forces. Salt, under pressure, has pushed up overlying rock layers into an anticline. This formation, the Shafer Dome, contains potash that is being processed by the Moab Salt Plant. You can see the mine buildings, processing plant, and evaporation ponds, which are tinted blue to hasten evaporation.

A narrow neck of land only 30 yards (27 m) wide connects the point with the rest of the plateau. Cowboys once herded wild horses onto the point, then placed a fence across the neck to make a 40-acre (16-ha) corral. They chose the best animals from the herd and let the rest go. According to one tale, a group of horses left behind after such a roundup became confused by the geography and circled repeatedly until they died of thirst within sight of the river below. You may also hear other stories of how the point got its name.

Besides the awe-inspiring views, the park also has a **visitor center** (9am-5pm daily), a very popular campground, a picnic area, trails, and mountain biking on the multiuse **Intrepid Trail System.** Spectacularly scenic hiking trails run along the east and west rims of the park. Rangers lead hikes during the busy spring season and on some evenings during summer, including monthly full-moon hikes. Whether you're visiting for the day or camping at Dead Horse Point, bring plenty of water. Water is available, but it's trucked in.

Dead Horse Point is easily reached by paved road, either as a destination itself or as a side trip on the way to the Island in the Sky District of Canyonlands National Park. From Moab, head northwest 10 miles (16.1 km) on US 191, then turn left and travel 22 miles (35 km) on Highway 313. The drive along Highway 313 climbs through a scenic canyon and tops out on a ridge with panoramas of mesas, buttes, mountains, and canyons.

SCENIC DRIVES

Each of the following routes is at least partly accessible to standard low-clearance vehicles. If you have a 4WD vehicle, you have the option of additional off-road exploring.

You'll find detailed information on these and other spots in Charles Wells's *Guide to Moab, UT Backroads & 4-Wheel Drive Trails.* This guide, along with a good selection of maps, is available at the **Moab Information Center** (25 E. Center St., 435/259-8825 or 800/635-6622, www.discovermoab.com, 8am-4pm daily mid-Mar.-late Nov., 9am-4pm daily late-Nov.-mid-Mar.), where staff usually know current road and trail conditions.

Utah Scenic Byway 279

Also known as Potash Road, Highway 279 heads downstream along the west side of the Colorado River canyon, across the river from Moab. The pavement runs 17 miles (27.4 km) past petroglyphs, arches, rock climbing, and hiking trails. A **potash plant** marks the end of the highway. If you've got a high-clearance 4WD vehicle, a rough dirt road continues to connect with Shafer Trail Road in Canyonlands National Park.

To reach Highway 279 from Moab, head north 3.5 miles (5.6 km) on US 191, then turn left onto Highway 279. The highway enters the canyon at the "portal," 2.7 miles (4.3 km) from the turnoff. Sandstone cliffs tower on the right, and the Colorado River drifts just below on the left.

Stop at a signed pullout on the left, 0.6 mile (1 km) past the canyon entrance, to see **Indian Ruins Viewpoint,** a small prehistoric stone structure tucked under a ledge across the river that was probably used for food storage.

Along the highway, groups of **petroglyphs** cover cliffs 5.2 miles (8.4 km) from US 191, which is 0.7 mile (1.1 km) beyond milepost 11. Look across the river to see the Fickle Finger of Fate among the sandstone fins of Behind the Rocks. A petroglyph of a bear is 0.2 mile (0.3 km) farther down the highway. Archaeologists think the Fremont people and then the Utes did most of the artwork in this area.

A signed pullout on the right, 6.2 miles (10 km) from US 191, points out **dinosaur tracks** and petroglyphs visible on rocks above. Sighting tubes help locate the features, and you can hike up the steep hillside for a closer look.

Ten miles (16.1 km) west of the highway turnoff is the trailhead for **Corona Arch Trail** (3 mi/4.8 km round-trip).

The aptly named **Jug Handle Arch,** with an opening 46 feet (14 m) high and 3 feet (1 m) wide, is close to the road on the right, 13.6 miles (21.9 km) from US 191. Ahead, the canyon opens up where underground pressure from salt and potash has folded the rock layers into an anticline.

At the **Moab Salt Plant,** mining operations inject water underground to dissolve potash and other chemicals, then pump the solution to evaporation ponds. The ponds are dyed blue to hasten evaporation, which takes about a year. You can see these colorful ponds from Dead Horse Point and Anticline Overlook on the canyon rims.

High-clearance vehicles can continue on the unpaved road beyond the plant. The road passes through canyon country, with views overlooking the Colorado River. At a road junction in Canyonlands National Park's Island in the Sky District, you can turn left for the 100-mile (161-km) White Rim Trail (4WD vehicles only past Musselman Arch) or continue up the steep switchbacks of Shafer Trail Road (4WD recommended) to the paved Canyonlands park road.

Utah Scenic Byway 128

From US 191, Highway 128 runs northeast through Grandstaff Canyon just south of the Colorado River bridge, 2 miles (3.2 km) north of Moab. This exceptionally scenic canyon route follows the Colorado for 30 miles (48 km) upstream before crossing the river at Dewey Bridge and turning north to I-70. The entire 46.7-mile (75-km) highway is paved and passes many campsites and trailheads, including Lions Park picnic area at the turnoff from US 191, and Big Bend campground and bouldering area 7.5 miles (12.1 km) up Highway 128. The rugged scenery along this stretch of the Colorado River has been featured in many films—mostly Westerns, but also *Thelma & Louise.* If you're intrigued, stop by the free **Film Museum** at Red Cliffs Ranch, a resort near milepost 14.

Make a beautiful loop by turning right on the paved **La Sal Mountains Loop Road,** after 15.5 miles (24.9 km) on Highway 128. This road takes in views of Castle Valley, Arches, Canyonlands, and Moab Rim before climbing high into the La Sals. You'll see everything from desert sage and rabbitbrush to forests of aspen, fir, and spruce. You can loop back to Moab via US 191. In total, this 62-mile (100-km) loop can easily take a full day, especially if you stop to hike, fish, or picnic. Due to its high elevation, the loop's season usually lasts May-October. Before heading out, get more info and current back-road conditions from the **Moab Ranger District** (62 E. 100 N., 435/259-7155, www.fs.usda.gov/mantilasal, 8am-4:30pm Mon.-Fri.) or the **Moab Information Center** (25 E. Center St., 435/259-8825, www.discovermoab.com, 8am-4pm daily mid-Mar.-late Nov., 9am-4pm daily late-Nov.-mid-Mar.).

A graded Bureau of Land Management (BLM) road, **Onion Creek Road,** turns southeast off Highway 128 about 20 miles (32 km) from US 191 and heads up and crosses its namesake many times. Avoid this route if storms threaten. The unpleasant-smelling creek contains poisonous arsenic and selenium. Colorful rock formations of dark red sandstone line the creek. After about 8 miles (12.9 km), the road climbs steeply to upper Fisher Valley and a junction with Kokopelli's Trail, which follows a 4WD road over this part of its route.

Some of the area's most striking sights are the gothic spires of **Fisher Towers,** which soar as high as 900 feet (274 m) above Professor Valley. Unpaved Fisher Towers Road turns southeast off Highway 128 near milepost 21, which is 21 miles (34 km) from US 191, and continues 2 miles (3.2 km) to the area. Supposedly, the name Fisher is a corruption of the geologic term *fissure* (a narrow crack). In 1962, three Colorado climbers made the first ascent of Titan Tower, the tallest of the three. The near vertical rock faces, overhanging bulges, and sections of rotten rock took an exhausting 3.5 days. Slackliners have also walked between the two tallest towers, and you'll frequently see climbers here. The BLM has a small campground and picnic area nearby, and a hiking trail skirts the base of the main towers.

The existing **Dewey Bridge,** 30 miles (48 km) up the highway, replaced a picturesque wood-and-steel suspension bridge built in 1916, which burned in 2008. Here, the BLM has built the Dewey Bridge Recreation Site, with a picnic area, a trailhead, a boat launch, and a small campground.

Upstream from Dewey Bridge, the wild

Rock Art Around Moab

The diverse petroglyphs (carvings) and pictographs (paintings) on the sandstone throughout Moab are some of the best in Utah. The fertile valley here has been home to humans for as long as 10,000 years. Prehistoric Fremont and Ancestral Puebloan peoples once farmed in the bottoms of the canyons here. Their rock art, granaries, and dwellings can still be found. By the time the first nonnative settlers arrived, nomadic Utes were adding their artistry to the area's rock-art panels. Here are a few great petroglyph destinations, organized by proximity to town:

- **Meet the "Moab Man" at Golf Course Rock Art:** Take US 191 south to the Moab Golf Course, which is about 4 miles (6.4 km) from the corner of Main and Center Streets in downtown Moab. Turn left down Spanish Trail Road. Approximately 1 mile (1.6 km) past the fire station, turn right onto Westwater Drive. Proceed 0.5 mile (0.8 km) to a small pullout on the left. An area approximately 30 feet by 90 feet (9 m by 27 m) is covered with human and animal figures, including a figure with what looks like earrings and antlers known as "Moab Man" and what is popularly referred to as the "reindeer and sled."
- **Gaze up at a series of panels right off Potash Road (Hwy. 279):** From US 191 just north of the Colorado River bridge, take Highway 279 west along the river 5.2 miles (8.4 km) to these easily accessed petroglyphs, just beyond a popular rock climbing area known as Wall Street. There's a sign ("Indian Writing") to guide you to them. Contemplate whether the ancient artists also climbed here to leave their artwork so high up the walls.
- **Contemplate unusual imagery up Kane Creek Boulevard:** Kane Creek leads to several excellent rock-art sites. To see a mastodon up Moonflower Canyon, keep left at the intersection of Kane Creek Drive and 500 West and continue along Kane Creek Drive approximately 2.3 miles (3.7 km) to the mouth of Moonflower Canyon. Just past the canyon turnoff, turn left on a dirt road and park at the top of the hill. Follow a slickrock trail to the left; at the top of the next hill, turn right toward cliffs and continue for 0.5 mile (0.8 km) to reach what appears to be a mastodon and a creature with four-toed feet. Kane Creek's most iconic petroglyph, however, is "Birthing Rock," depicting a breech birth. To reach this art-filled boulder, about 1.4 miles (2.3 km) past the cattle guard where Kane Creek turns to graded gravel—and just past the second sign for Amasa Back trail—watch for a small pullout to Birthing Rock.
- **Observe pictographs alongside petroglyphs at Courthouse Wash:** Although this site is within Arches National Park, it is accessed from a parking lot off US 191 just north of the Colorado River bridge, 1 mile (1.6 km) north of Moab. A 0.5-mile (0.8-km) hike leads to the panel, which is almost 19 feet (6 m) high and 52 feet (16 m) long. It has both pictographs and petroglyphs, with figures resembling ghostly humans, bighorn sheep, scorpions, and a large beaked bird. This panel, which was vandalized in 1980, was restored by the National Park Service; restoration work revealed older images underneath the vandalized layer.
- **See a premier rock art gallery at Sego Canyon:** Along I-70 on the way to or from Moab, consider a side trip to Sego Canyon, about 5 miles (8 km) north of I-70 exit 187 for Thompson Springs. Drive through the little town and continue up the canyon behind it; BLM signs point the way. A side road leads to a parking area where the canyon walls close in. Sego Canyon showcases rock art that's thousands of years old. The Barrier Canyon Style drawings, featuring horned ghostlike beings, may be 8,000 years old, while the more recent Fremont Style images, depicting stylized human figures in geometric form, were made in the last 1,000 years. Experts speculate that the Ute etchings of bison and hunters on horseback may have been drawn in the 1800s, when Ute villages lined Sego Canyon.

A Rock Art Auto Tour brochure is available at the **Moab Information Center** (25 E. Center St., Moab, 435/259-8825, www.discovermoab.com, 8am-4pm daily mid-Mar.-late Nov., 9am-4pm daily late-Nov.-mid-Mar.).

Vicinity of Moab

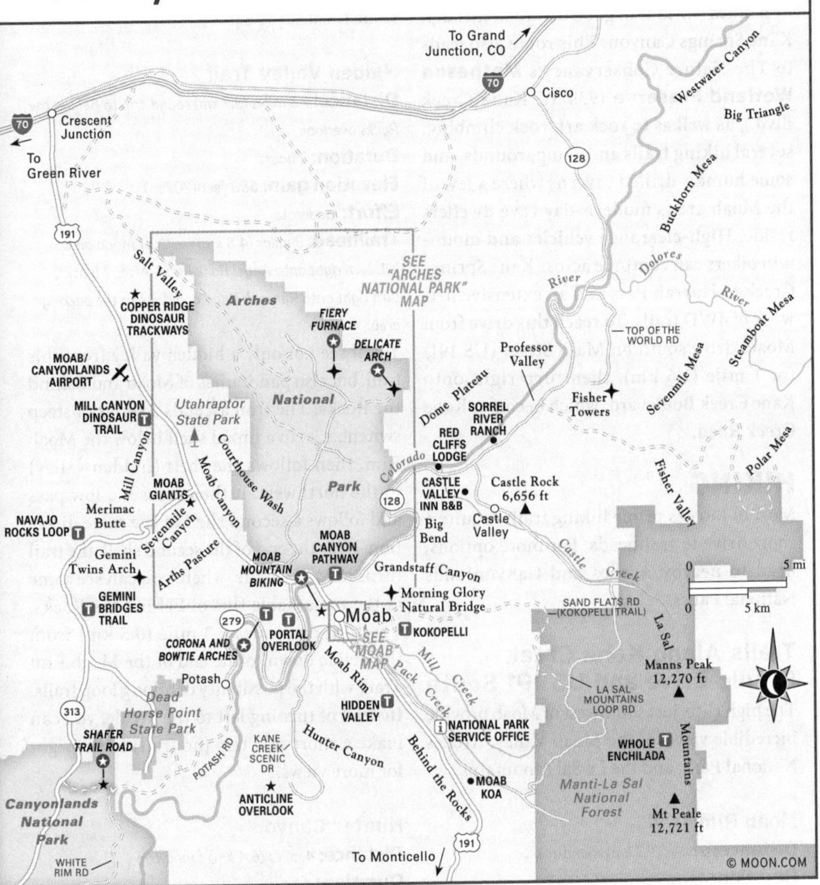

rapids of **Westwater Canyon** await in a narrow gorge that cuts through dark metamorphic rock. You can raft or kayak down the river in 1 day or a more leisurely two—many local outfitters guide here. Camping is limited to a single night. Unlike most desert rivers, this section of the Colorado also offers good river-running at low water levels in late summer and fall. Westwater Canyon's inner gorge, where boaters face their greatest challenge, is only about 3.5 miles (5.6 km) long. You can enjoy scenic sandstone canyons both upstream and downstream.

The rough 4WD **Top-of-the-World Road** climbs nearly 3,000 feet (914 m) to a 6,800-foot (2,073-m) overlook with outstanding views of Fisher Towers, Fisher Valley, Onion Creek, and beyond. Pick up a map at the **Moab Information Center** (25 E. Center St., 435/259-8825, www.discovermoab.com, 8am-4pm daily mid-Mar.-late Nov., 9am-4pm daily late-Nov.-mid-Mar.).

Kane Creek Scenic Drive

Kane Creek Road heads downstream along the Colorado River on the same side as

Moab. The 4 miles (6.4 km) through the Colorado River canyon are paved, followed by 6 miles (9.7 km) of good dirt road through Kane Springs Canyon. This route also leads to The Nature Conservancy's **Matheson Wetland Preserve** (934 W. Kane Creek Blvd.), as well as to rock art, rock climbing, several hiking trails and campgrounds, and some human-drilled caverns where a few of the Moab area's modern-day cave dwellers reside. High-clearance vehicles and mountain bikers can continue across Kane Springs Creek to Hurrah Pass and an extensive network of 4WD trails. To reach this drive from Moab, drive south on Main Street (US 191) for 1 mile (1.6 km), then turn right onto Kane Creek Boulevard, which becomes Kane Creek Road.

HIKING

Most of Moab's prime hiking trails require a short drive to trailheads. For more options, head to nearby Arches and Canyonlands National Parks.

Trails Along Kane Creek Scenic Drive and US 191 South

The high cliffs just southwest of Moab provide incredible views of the Moab Valley, Arches National Park, and the La Sal Mountains.

Moab Rim Trail

Distance: *6 miles (9.7 km) round-trip*
Duration: *4 hours*
Elevation gain: *940 feet (287 m)*
Effort: *moderate*
Trailhead: *Kane Creek Boulevard, 2.6 miles (4.2 km) northwest of its intersection with US 191 in Moab*

Hikers should expect to share this route with mountain bikers and 4WD enthusiasts. The trail climbs northeast 1.5 miles (2.4 km) along tilted rock strata of the Kayenta Formation to the top of the plateau west of Moab, with the first of several great views over town and the Spanish Valley. On top, hikers can follow 4WD roads southeast to Hidden Valley Trail, which descends to US 191 south of Moab—a 5.5-mile (8.9-km) trip one-way. Experienced hikers can also head south from the rim to Behind the Rocks, a fantastic maze of sandstone fins.

Hidden Valley Trail

Distance: *2.3 miles (3.7 km) round-trip to Behind the Rocks overlook*
Duration: *3 hours*
Elevation gain: *680 feet (207 m)*
Effort: *moderate*
Trailhead: *3 miles (4.8 km) south of Moab on US 191. Turn right onto Angel Rock Road. After 2 blocks, turn right onto Rimrock Road and drive to the parking area.*

You'll see not only a hidden valley from this trail, but also panoramas of Moab and Behind the Rocks. The trail ascends a series of steep switchbacks to a broad shelf below the Moab Rim, then follows the shelf (hidden valley) to the northwest. It then crosses a low pass and follows a second shelf in the same direction. Near the end of the second shelf, the trail turns left to a divide, where you can see some of the remarkable fins of Behind the Rocks. The trail continues 0.3 mile (0.5 km) from the divide down to the end of the Moab Rim Trail, with the possibility of hiking loop trails. Instead of turning left to the divide, you can make a short side trip (no trail) to the right for more views.

Hunter Canyon

Distance: *4 miles (6.4 km) round-trip*
Duration: *4 hours*
Elevation change: *240 feet (73 m)*
Effort: *moderate*
Trailhead: *On Kane Creek Scenic Drive, 7.5 miles (12 km) west of US 191; Hunter Canyon is on the left, 1 mile (1.6 km) beyond the switchbacks*
Directions: *To reach the trailhead from Moab, drive 8 miles (12.9 km) on Kane Creek Boulevard along the Colorado River up Kane Creek Canyon. The road is paved where it fords Hunter Creek, but the asphalt is usually covered with dirt washed over it by the creek.*

An arch and other formations along with lush creek-side vegetation are highlights of this hike. Off-road vehicles have made tracks

Odd Formations: Behind the Rocks

Behind the Rocks and the La Sal Mountains in the background

Topographic maps show something strange going on in the area known as **Behind the Rocks.** Spread across a large area are massive fins of Navajo sandstone, separated by super-narrow vertical cracks. The fins are 100-500 feet (30-152 m) high, 50-200 feet (15-61 m) thick, and up to 0.5 mile (0.8 km) long. There are also more than 20 named major arches here. And pour-offs through canyon drainages have formed sheer-walled canyons, 400-1,000 feet deep (122-305 m).

Behind the Rocks was inhabited extensively by the Ancestral Puebloan and Fremont peoples. The two cultures apparently overlapped here as well. Petroglyph panels, cave dwellings, an ancient structure, and waste heaps abound throughout the area.

No maintained trails exist, and some routes require technical climbing skills. The maze offers endless routes for exploration. If you get lost, which is very easy to do, the fins are oriented east-west. The rim of the Colorado River canyon is reached by going west, and Spanish Valley is reached by heading east. Bring plenty of water, a topographic map (USGS Moab 7.5-minute), and a compass. Access routes are the **Moab Rim** and **Hidden Valley Trails** (from the north and east) and **Pritchett Canyon** (from the west and south). Although it is only a couple of miles from Moab, Behind the Rocks seems a world away.

a short way up, though you'll walk mostly along the creek bed. Short sections of trail wind around thickets of tamarisk and other water-loving plants. Look for Hunter Arch on the right, about 0.5 mile (0.8 km) up. Most of the water here comes from a deep pool surrounded by hanging gardens of maidenhair ferns. A dry waterfall and a small natural bridge are above the pool. This pretty spot marks the hike's turnaround point and an elevation gain of 240 feet (73 m).

Trails Along Highway 279

Portal Overlook Trail

Distance: *4 miles (6.4 km) round-trip*
Duration: *3 hours*
Elevation gain: *980 feet (299 m)*
Effort: *moderate*
Trailhead: *JayCee Park Recreation Site, Highway 279, 4.2 miles (6.8 km) west of the Highway 279-US 191 junction*

The Portal Overlook Trail switchbacks up a slope, then follows a sloping sandstone ledge of the Kayenta Formation for 2 miles (3.2 km) to an overlook. A panorama (the "portal") takes in the Colorado River, Moab Valley, Arches National Park, and the La Sal Mountains. This trail is a twin of the Moab Rim Trail across the river. Expect to share it with mountain bikers.

★ Corona Arch and Bowtie Arch Trail

Distance: *3 miles (4.8 km) round-trip*
Duration: *2 hours*
Elevation gain: *200 feet (61 m)*
Effort: *moderate*
Trailhead: *Highway 279, 10 miles (16.1 km) west of the Highway 279-US 191 junction*

If you have time for only one hike, this one delivers excellent bang for your buck. The trail leads across slickrock country to two impressive Navajo sandstone arches. The trailhead and first part of the trail may feel crowded, but hikers tend to disperse quickly. The trail climbs 1.5 miles (2.4 km), crosses railroad tracks, and follows a 4WD road and a small wash to an ancient gravel bar. A third arch, called Pinto—also known as Gold Bar Arch—stands to the left, but there's no trail to it. Follow rock cairns to Corona and Bowtie Arches. Handrails and a ladder help in the few steep spots.

Despite being only a few hundred yards apart, each arch has a completely different story. Bowtie formed when a pothole in the cliffs above met a cave underneath. It used to be called Paul Bunyan's Potty before that name was appropriated for an arch in Canyonlands National Park. The hole is about 30 feet (9 m) in diameter. Corona Arch, reminiscent of the larger Rainbow Bridge, eroded out of a sandstone fin into a span of 140 feet (43 m) long and a height of 105 feet (32 m).

Trails Along Highway 128

Grandstaff Canyon

Distance: *4 miles (6.4 km) round-trip*
Duration: *3-4 hours*
Elevation gain: *330 feet (101 m)*
Effort: *easy-moderate*
Trailhead: *Highway 128, 3 miles (4.8 km) east of the Highway 128-US 191 junction*

One of the most popular hiking destinations in the Moab area, Grandstaff Canyon Trail follows a lively stream dammed by beavers and surrounded by abundant greenery and sheer cliffs. The high point is **Morning Glory Natural Bridge,** spanning 243 feet (74 m). The trail is named after William Grandstaff, the first African American to live in the area, about 1877-1881. The trailhead and parking area are on the right just after crossing a bridge 3 miles (4.8 km) from US 191. The Grandstaff Campground, run by the BLM, is on the banks of the Colorado River just across the road.

The trail follows the creek up the canyon, with numerous stream crossings. Although the crossings aren't difficult, hikers must be comfortable stepping from rock to rock. To see Morning Glory Natural Bridge, head 2 miles (3.2 km) up the main canyon to the second side canyon on the right, then follow a fairly steep side trail for 0.5 mile (0.8 km) up to the long slender bridge. The spring and small pool below keep the air cool even in summer. Ferns, columbines, and poison ivy thrive here.

Fisher Towers

Distance: *4.4 miles (7.1 km) round-trip*
Duration: *4 hours*
Elevation gain: *670 feet (204 m)*
Effort: *moderate*
Trailhead: *From Highway 128, about 21 miles (34 km) east of US 191, turn right on an improved dirt road and go 2.2 miles (3.5 km) to a parking lot.*

These spires of dark-red sandstone rise 900 feet (274 m) above Professor Valley. You can hike around the base of them on a trail accessed up a short flight of stairs from the BLM picnic area. The trail follows a small slickrock-covered ridge leading away from the main cliffs. When the ridge narrows, go left into the ravine through a small cut. From here, the trail heads steeply up, then winds directly beneath the Fisher Towers. After skirting around the largest tower, The Titan, the trail ascends and ends after 2.2 miles (3.5 km) on a ridge with a panoramic view. The Fisher Towers attract expert rock climbers, who can be fun to watch. Carry plenty of water; much of the trail is exposed and gets quite hot.

★ MOUNTAIN BIKING

The first mountain bikes came to Moab in 1982, when they were used to herd cattle. That didn't work out so well, but within a decade or so, Moab had become the West's most noted mountain bike destination. The area is best known for its challenging slickrock trails—slickrock is the exposed sandstone that composes much of the land's surface here, and despite its name, bike tires grab it nicely. There's also plenty of good gravel and road riding to be had in the Moab area. A rec path connects the downtown to Arches and Grandstaff Canyon, as well.

Cyclists can also pedal through alpine meadows in the La Sal Mountains or take nearly abandoned 4WD tracks into the surrounding backcountry. The best-known trails—like the Slickrock Bike Trail—are not for beginners, though there are good options for new riders as well, like the **Intrepid Trail System** at Dead Horse Point State Park. A good resource for trails and advice is Moab Bike Patrol (www.moabbikepatrol.com).

Before planning a trip, read up on the riding options. Numerous guides are available, and you can also hire an outfitter to introduce you to the special skills needed to mountain bike in slickrock country or join a guided tour. Some rides—like the classic Whole Enchilada—require a shuttle, which several shops in town offer. The **Moab Information Center** (25 E. Center St., 435/259-8825, www.discovermoab.com, 8am-4pm daily mid-Mar.-late Nov., 9am-4pm daily late-Nov.-mid-Mar.) also has good information about bike trails.

The best time to mountain bike here is mid-March-late May, then again in mid-September-October. Unless you're a very early riser, summer is too hot for extended bike touring in this desert environment. Be prepared for crowds, especially in mid-March during spring break. The Slickrock Trail alone has been known to attract more than 150,000 riders per year.

If you've never biked on slickrock or in the desert, take care here if venturing off-trail—it's a long way down some of the sheer cliff faces. A trail's steep slopes and sharp turns can be tricky, so a helmet is a must. Kneepads and riding gloves also protect from scrapes and bruises. In the sand, fat bald tires work best. Partially deflated knobby tires do well on slickrock. Carry plenty of water—one gallon in summer, half a gallon in cooler months. And stay on the rock to avoid riding over the fragile cryptobiotic soil.

Navajo Rocks Loop

The desert panoramas just keep on coming during this 17.5-mile (28-km) mountain bike ride. It begins with some easy climbing on Rocky Tops Trail, which leads to harder climbing on Coney Island Trail, including sections of steep slickrock, requiring power to crest without hopping off the saddle. From here, you'll get some good downhill in on the slickrock and sand of Big Lonely, followed by mellow, mostly flat pedaling on Big Mesa. All in all, you're in for 1,342 feet (409 m) of climbing. Arguably the most challenging terrain lies on Ramblin', the final stretch with more technical features over slickrock and dirt. The last half of this ride is the most scenic, leading past towering sandstone amphitheaters and walls that will make you and your bike feel awfully small.

Reach the trailhead by taking US 191 north for 11 miles (17.7 km), then turning left on Highway 313—the road to Dead Horse Point State Park and part of Canyonlands National Park. Turn right at Big Mesa Recreation Area and keep left to reach the parking lot.

Slickrock Trail

Not a touch of dirt goes under-tire on this classic local ride. The undulating slickrock in the Sand Flats Recreation Area just east of Moab challenges even the most skilled mountain bike riders. Originally, motorcyclists laid

1
2
3
4

out the route, although now most riders rely on leg and lung power. The 2-mile (3.2-km) practice loop near the trail's beginning allows first-time visitors a chance to get a feel for the slickrock. The "trail" consists only of painted white lines. Riders following it have less chance of getting lost or finding themselves in hazardous areas. Plan on 3-5 hours to do the 10.5-mile (16.9-km) loop, and expect a little hike-a-bike—bike shoes with good traction are recommended.

Side trails lead to viewpoints overlooking Moab, the Colorado River, and arms of Grandstaff Canyon. Panoramas of the surrounding canyon country and the La Sal Mountains enhance the ride.

To reach the trailhead from Main Street in Moab, turn east on 300 South and go 0.4 mile (0.6 km), turn right on 400 East and go 0.1 mile (0.2 km), turn left (east) on Mill Creek Drive and go 0.5 mile (0.8 km), then turn left on Sand Flats Road and go 2.5 miles (4 km). The trail is located in the **Sand Flats Recreation Area** (vehicle day pass $5, bicycle or motorcycle $2). Camping ($15) is available, but there is no water—bring plenty with you!

Farther up Sand Flats Road, the quite challenging, often rock-strewn **Porcupine Rim Trail** draws motorcycles, 4WD vehicles, and mountain bikers. After about 11 miles (17.7 km), the trail becomes single-track, and four-wheelers drop out. The whole trail is about 15 miles (24 km) long.

Gemini Bridges Trail

This 14-mile (22.5-km) one-way trail passes tremendous twin rock arches (the bridges) and the slickrock fins of the Wingate Formation, making this one of the most scenic trails in Moab. It's also one of the more moderate trails in terms of skill and fitness. The trail begins 12.5 miles (20.1 km) up Highway 313, just before the turnoff to Dead Horse Point State Park. It's a stiff 21-mile (34-km) uphill ride from Moab to reach the trailhead. You can shorten the ride by parking at the MOAB Brand parking area or taking a shuttle from town. Several companies, including **Coyote Shuttle** (435/260-2097, www.coyoteshuttle.com, $25), provide this service, enabling cyclists to concentrate on the fun, mostly downhill ride back toward Moab. The Gemini Bridges Trail, which is shared with motorcycles and 4WD vehicles, ends on US 191 just north of town.

1: a young hiker on the trail to Corona and Bowtie Arches 2: Navajo Rocks Loop 3: the Whole Enchilada 4: Slickrock Trail

Whole Enchilada

Alpine climbing, fast turns, techy descents, slickrock sections—this legendary 27-mile (43-km) ride gives you a taste of it all. Traditionally, the Whole Enchilada is ridden as a shuttle, and many bike shops and other outfits in town will haul you and your bike up to Burro Pass in the La Sal Mountains, where the ride begins. A short descent is quickly followed by a long climb, which will have you huffing and puffing at over 11,000 feet (3,352 m) elevation.

After the initial climb, you'll get in some fast, sharp turns through brushy terrain on Hazard County Trail, followed by a stretch along the end of **Kokopelli's Trail,** a double-track route that travels 142 miles (228 km) from Loma, Colorado, all the way to Moab. Then play on the slickrock and thrilling exposed Porcupine single-track before starting a technical yet highly scenic descent down Porcupine Rim, which ultimately drops into Grandstaff Canyon and the Colorado River. From here, take the paved 5-mile (8.1-km) rec path back into Moab.

With over 7,000 feet (2,133 m) of downhill, the Whole Enchilada is an unforgettable soul-stirring romp, but only for strong riders. The many technical sections and the relentless exposed descent make this a difficult challenge. And keep in mind that the ride still entails 1,269 feet (386 m) of climbing—some of it at quite a high altitude—so fitness is imperative too.

Most years, the season for this ride doesn't begin until mid-July, when the snow finally melts and the trails dry up at Burro Pass. The ride is usually doable through September, before the snow starts to fly again up in the La Sals. There are many variations on how to execute the Whole Enchilada, so read up before you ride to plot the best course for you. And even though this is a popular ride, it's easy to get off course as you link up different trails, so bring a map and don't blindly follow the rider in front of you.

Moab Canyon Pathway

Although Moab is great for cyclists, riding along busy US 191 is no fun. Enter the Moab Canyon Pathway, which starts at the pedestrian and bike bridge over the Colorado River on Highway 128 at the north end of town and closely parallels the highway north to Arches National Park. From the entrance to the park, the path, which is separated from the road, continues north, climbing to the junction of US 191 and Highway 313, which is the road to Dead Horse Point State Park and Canyonlands' Island in the Sky District. From this intersection, the bike path is on a relatively wide shoulder. It's a 35-mile (56-km) ride to Canyonlands' Grand View Point, or a mere 24-mile (39-km) uphill chug to Dead Horse Point.

If you don't mind taking your mountain bike to the road to extend the adventure, the paved route provides easy cycling access to the MOAB Brand trails, just off US 191, and a more challenging ride to the Intrepid trails in Dead Horse Point State Park and the Gemini Bridges Trail, which starts just outside the park.

Bike Tours

Most of the rental shops in Moab offer daylong mountain bike excursions, while outfitters offer multiday tours that vary in price depending on the difficulty of the trail. The charge for these trips is usually $200-250 per day, including food and shuttles. Inquire whether rates include bike rentals if you don't have your own.

Rim Tours (1233 S. US 191, 435/259-5223 or 800/626-7335, https://rimtours.com) is a well-established local company offering several half-day (2-3 cyclists $110-135 pp), full-day (2-3 cyclists $160-165 pp), and multiday trips, including a 5-day bike camping trip in Canyonlands' Maze District ($1,250). **Magpie Cycling** (711 N. 500 W., 435/259-4464 or 800/546-4245, www.magpiecycling.com) is a small local business running day trips, mountain biking lessons, and overnight rides mostly in Canyonlands, including a 3-day tour of the White Rim Trail ($945).

Western Spirit Cycling (478 S. Mill Creek Dr., 435/259-8732, www.westernspirit.com) offers mountain and road bike tours in the western states, many of them in Utah. Moab-area trips include the White Rim, the Maze, and Kokopelli's Trail (5 days, $1,395). Another Moab-based company with tours across the West, **Escape Adventures** (Moab Cyclery, 391 S. Main St., 435/259-5774 or 800/596-2953, www.escapeadventures.com) leads multiday mountain bike trips, including a 5-day "Best of Moab" tour (camping $1,349, inn accommodations $2,749). Some of the tours combine cycling with rafting, climbing, hiking, or plane rides.

Rentals and Repairs

Rim Cyclery (94 W. 100 N., 435/259-5333, www.rimcyclery.com, 8am-6pm daily) is Moab's oldest bike and outdoor gear store, offering road and mountain bike sales, rentals, and service. Mountain bike rentals are also available at **Poison Spider Bicycles** (497 N. Main St., 435/259-7882 or 800/635-1792, www.poisonspiderbicycles.com, 8am-7pm daily spring and fall, 9am-6pm daily winter and summer) and **Chile Pepper** (702 S. Main St., 435/259-4688 or 888/677-4688, www.chilebikes.com, 8am-6pm daily). **Moab Cyclery** (391 S. Main St., 435/259-7423 or 800/559-1978, www.moabcyclery.com, 8am-6pm daily) offers rentals, tours, shuttles, and gear. Expect to pay $60-110 per day to rent a mountain bike, a little less for a road bike, and around $130 per day for an e-bike. If you just want to tool around town, rent a basic townie ($40) at **Bike Fiend** (69 E. Center

St., 435/315-0002, www.moabbikefiend.com, 8am-6pm daily).

Shuttle Services

Several of Moab's best mountain bike trails are one-way or too long to ride as an out-and-back, so you'll need to arrange a shuttle to pick you up and bring you back to Moab or your car. Also, if you don't have a bike rack, you'll need a shuttle service to get to and from the more distant trailheads. **Coyote Shuttle** (435/260-2097, www.coyoteshuttle.com) and **Whole Enchilada Shuttle** (435/260-2534, https://wholeenchiladashuttles.com) are two good options for this service, with fares typically around $25-40 per person. Both companies also shuttle hikers to trailheads and pick up rafters.

RAFTING AND BOATING

Even a visitor with a tight schedule can get out and enjoy the canyon country on rafts and other watercraft. Outfitters offer both laid-back and exhilarating day trips, which usually require advance planning. Longer multiday trips include gentle canoe paddles along the placid Green River and thrilling expeditions down the Colorado River.

You'll need to reserve well in advance for most of the longer trips: The BLM and the National Park Service limit trips through the backcountry, and space, especially in high season, is at a premium. Experienced rafters can also plan their own unguided trips, although you'll need a **permit** for all areas except for the daylong Fisher Towers float upstream from Moab.

The rafting season runs April-September, and jet-boat tours run February-November. Most river-runners floating independently without a guide service obtain their permits by applying in January-February for a March drawing. The BLM ranger at the **Moab Information Center** (25 E. Center St., 435/259-8825, www.discovermoab.com, 8am-4pm daily mid-Mar.-late Nov., 9am-4pm daily late-Nov.-mid-Mar.) can advise on this process and provide the latest information about available cancellations.

Rafting and Kayaking Trips

For most of the following trips, full-day rates include lunch and beverages, while part-day trips throw in beverages only. On overnight trips, you'll sleep in tents in backcountry campgrounds.

The **Colorado River** offers several exciting options. The most popular day run near

kayaking the Colorado River

Moab starts upstream near Fisher Towers and bounces through several moderate rapids on the way back to town. Full-day raft trips ($110-124 pp adults) run from Fisher Towers to near Moab. Half-day trips ($85-119 pp adults) run over much the same stretch of river but don't usually include lunch.

Several outfitters offer guided **stand-up paddling** trips (half-day $75-115) on quiet stretches of the Colorado River near the boundary of Arches National Park.

The **Cataract Canyon** section of the Colorado River, which begins south of the river's confluence with the Green River and extends to Lake Powell, usually requires 4 days of rafting to complete. However, if you're in a hurry, some outfitters offer 1-day trips that motor rather than float through most of the water. This is the wildest white water in the Moab area, with big boiling Class III-IV rapids. Costs range $625-1,825, depending on craft type, number of days, and whether you fly, hike, or drive out at the trip's end.

The **Green River** also offers Class II-III rafting and canoeing or kayaking opportunities, although they are milder than those on the Colorado. Trips on the Green make good family outings. Most trips require 5 days, leaving from the town of Green River, paddling through **Labyrinth Canyon,** and taking out at **Mineral Bottom,** just before Canyonlands National Park. Costs range $1,149-1,750 for a 5-day rafting trip.

Rafting or Kayaking on Your Own

The Class II-III **Fisher Towers** section of the Colorado River is gentle enough for amateur rafters to negotiate on their own. A popular 1-day raft trip with mild rapids begins from the Hittle Bottom Recreation Site (Hwy. 128, 23.5 mi/38 km north of Moab, near Fisher Towers) and ends 14 river miles (22.5 km) downstream at Take-Out Beach (Hwy. 128, 10.3 mi/16.6 km north of US 191). You can rent rafts and the mandatory life jackets in Moab, and you won't need a permit on this section of river.

Experienced white-water rafters can run the Westwater Canyon of the Colorado River on their own. Obtain **permits** ($10) by calling 435/259-7012 two months prior to launch date. The usual put-in is at the Westwater Ranger Station, 9 miles (14.5 km) south of I-70 exit 227. Another put-in option is the Loma boat launch in Colorado, which adds a day or two, along with the sights of Horsethief and Ruby Canyons. Normal take-out is at Cisco, although it's possible to continue 16 miles (26 km) on slow-moving water to Dewey Bridge, where Highway 128 crosses the Colorado, 30 miles (48 km) north of Moab.

Wild West Voyages (422 Kane Creek Blvd., 435/355-0776 or 866/390-3994, www.wildwestvoyages.com) and **Navtec Expeditions** (321 N. Main St., 435/259-7983 or 800/833-1278, www.navtec.com) are two local rafting companies that rent out rafts ($120-140 per day). Both companies also rent kayaks ($55-75 per day) and stand-up paddleboards ($55-65) for those who would rather organize their own river adventures.

Rafting Outfitters

Moab is full of river-trip companies offering a variety of day and multiday trips. Many also combine raft trips with biking, horseback riding, hiking, or 4WD excursions. The following list includes a few major outfitters—check out more at www.discovermoab.com. Most lead trips to the main river destinations on the Colorado and Green Rivers as well as other rivers in Utah and the West. Red River Adventures runs trips in smaller self-paddled rafts and inflatable kayaks. Inquire about natural history or petroglyph tours if that's of interest.

- **Adrift Adventures** (378 N. Main St., 435/259-8594 or 800/874-4483, www.adrift.net)
- **Canyonlands Field Institute** (1320 S. US 191, 435/259-7750 or 800/860-5262, https://cfimoab.org)
- **Wild West Voyages** (422 Kane Creek

Blvd., 435/355-0776, www.wildwestvoyages.com)

- **Moab Adventure Center** (225 S. Main St., 435/259-7019 or 866/904-1163, www.moabadventurecenter.com)
- **Navtec Expeditions** (321 N. Main St., 435/259-7983 or 800/833-1278, www.navtec.com)
- **Red River Adventures** (1140 S. Main St., 435/259-4046 or 877/259-4046, www.redriveradventures.com)
- **Sheri Griffith Expeditions** (2231 S. US 191, 503/259-8229 or 800/332-2439, www.griffithexp.com)

Canoeing

Canoeists can also sample the calm waters of the Green River on multiday excursions with **Moab Rafting and Canoe Company** (2480 US 191, 435/259-7722, www.moab-rafting.com), which runs scheduled guided trips ($1,149 for a 4-day trip) to four sections of the Green and to calmer stretches of the Colorado River. It also rents canoes ($40-50 per day) and other necessary equipment.

Another good source for DIY canoe and kayak trips on the Green River is **Tex's Riverways** (691 N. 500 W., 435/259-5101 or 877/662-2839, www.texsriverways.com), which specializes in rentals, shuttles, and support for self-guided trips.

Jet Boat and Motorboat

Canyonlands by Night & Day (435/259-5261 or 800/394-9978, www.canyonlandsbynight.com, Apr.-mid-Oct., $89 adults, $79 ages 4-12, includes dinner, boat only $79 adults, $69 ages 4-12) runs open boat tours several miles upstream on the Colorado River. The sound-and-light show begins on the way back. Music and historical narration accompany the play of lights on the canyon walls. Reservations are a good idea because the boat fills up fast. This company also offers daytime jet-boat tours, including a 3-hour trip ($129 adults, $119 children) to the Colorado River canyon downstream from Moab. Trips depart from the Spanish mission-style office just north of Moab, across the Colorado River.

Stand-Up Paddleboarding (SUPing)

Upstream from Moab, sections of the Colorado River are calm enough for stand-up paddleboards, alternating with rapids more appropriate for kayaking. SUPs can put in at Dewey Bridge, about 30 miles (48 km) northeast of Moab along Highway 128, to access a 10-mile (16.1-km) stretch of mostly calm waters as the Colorado descends into its canyon; take out at the Onion Creek ramp. In contrast, Onion Creek is an excellent put-in location for kayakers, with roughly 9 miles (14.5 km) of moderately thrilling Class II-III rapids.

Most of the rafting outfitters in Moab also rent SUPs and kayaks, but for the best equipment and advice, go to **Paddle Moab** (44 W. 200 N., 435/210-4665, www.paddlemoab.com, 8am-8pm daily Mar.-Oct., 9am-6pm daily Nov.-Feb.). This outfit offers both guided paddleboard trips (starting with a 3.5-hour flat-water trip, $85 adults, $75 children) and rental-and-ride packages including two boards and a shuttle to the put-in of your choice ($165 per day). Half-day white-water kayaking trips are $80 adults, $70 kids.

AIR TOURS

You'll have a bird's-eye view of southeastern Utah's incredible landscape from Moab's Canyonlands Field with **Redtail Aviation** (435/259-7421, https://flyredtail.com). A 30-minute flight over Arches National Park is $169 per person; add Canyonlands and the rate is $319 per person. Longer tours are also available, and flights operate year-round.

SKYDIVING

If you think the Arches and Canyonlands area looks dramatic from an airplane, imagine the excitement of parachuting into the desert landscape. **Skydive Moab** (Canyonlands Field Airport, US 191, 16 mi/26 km north of Moab, 435/259-5867, www.skydivemoab.com) offers jumps for both first-time and experienced skydivers. First-timers receive 30 minutes of schooling followed by a half-hour flight before a tandem parachute jump with an instructor from 10,000 feet (3,048 m). Tandem skydives, including instruction and equipment, start at $199, and equipment and parachutes are available for rent.

4WD, ATVS, AND DIRT BIKES

Road tours offer visitors a special opportunity to view unique arches and spires, Indigenous rock art, and wildlife. An interpretive brochure and map at the **Moab Information Center** (25 E. Center St., 435/259-8825, www.discovermoab.com, 8am-4pm daily mid-Mar.-late Nov., 9am-4pm daily late-Nov.-mid-Mar.) outlines Moab-area 4WD trails—four rugged 15- to 54-mile (24- to 87-km) loops through the desert that take 2.5-4 hours to drive. You can also take an off-road 4WD tour with a private operator. Most Moab outfitters offer jeep or Hummer tours, often in combination with rafting or hiking options. The **Moab Adventure Center** (225 S. Main St., 435/259-7019 or 866/904-1163, www.moabadventurecenter.com) runs 2-hour ($98 adults, $78 youths) and half-day ($215 adults, $175 youths) guided Hummer safaris. The Adventure Center, which can book you on any number of trips, can also arrange 4WD rentals (from $290 per day).

Jeep and other 4WD-vehicle rentals are also available at many Moab outfits, including **Twisted Jeep Rentals** (446 S. Main St., 435/259-0335, www.twistedjeeps.com) and **Cliffhanger Jeep Rental** (1331 US 191, 435/259-0889, www.cliffhangerjeeprental.com). Expect to pay at least $285 per day.

Alternatives to 4WD touring, all-terrain vehicle (ATV) and motorcycle "dirt biking" typically (though not exclusively) is geared toward families. Although kids ages 8-15 may operate an ATV—if they possess an Education Certificate issued by Utah State Parks and Recreation, or an equivalent certificate from their home state—parents should research ATV safety before heading out. Much of the public land surrounding Moab is open to ATV exploration, with many miles of unpaved roads and existing trails. However, ATV and dirt bike riding is not allowed within either Arches or Canyonlands National Parks.

One particularly popular area for ATVs is **White Wash Sand Dunes,** with many miles of dirt roads in a strikingly scenic location. It is 48 miles (77 km) northwest of Moab, reached by driving 13 miles (20.9 km) south from I-70 exit 175, just east of Green River. The dunes are interspersed with large cottonwood trees and bordered by sandstone cliffs. White Wash is also a popular route around three sides of the dunes.

ATVs and dirt bikes are available from a number of Moab-area outfitters, including **High Point Hummer** (301 S. Main St., 435/259-2972 or 877/486-6833, www.highpointhummer.com) and **Moab Tour Company** (427 N. Main St., 435/259-4080 or 877/725-7317, www.moabtourcompany.com). A half-day dirt bike or ATV rental starts at around $329.

ROCK CLIMBING

There's rock climbing to be had all over the Moab area. A diversity of route types and difficulty levels can be found here, mostly on sandstone. Never climb sandstone that is wet or still holding moisture from recent rainfall, as it is very susceptible to breaking and you might damage the rock. For world-class crack climbing, head south to Indian Creek, near the Needles District of Canyonlands National Park.

Moab Desert Adventures (39 E. Center St., 804/814-3872 or 877/765-6622, www.moabdesertadventures.com) offers rock climbing and canyoneering lessons, both for beginners and experienced climbers; families are welcome. A half day of basic climbing instruction is $90 for a private lesson; rates are lower for groups of 2-4. Head out for a climbing or canyoneering trip with **Moab Cliffs & Canyons** (253 N. Main St., 435/259-3317 or

877/641-5271, www.cliffsandcanyons.com). A day of climbing is $350 for one person, $220 per person for two.

Moab has a couple of stores with rock climbing gear and informative staff: **Gearheads Outdoor Store** (471 S. Main St., 435/259-4327, 8am-9pm daily) and **Pagan Mountaineering** (211 N. Main St., 435/259-1117, 9am-8pm Mon. and Thurs., 8am-8pm Fri.-Sun.).

HORSEBACK RIDING

Head up the Colorado River to the Fisher Towers area, where **Moab Horses** (Hauer Ranch, Hwy. 128, Milepost 21, 435/259-8015, www.moabhorses.com, half-day $125 for 2 or more riders) runs guided trail rides. Also along Highway 128, **Red Cliffs Lodge** (Hwy. 128, Milepost 14, 435/259-2002 or 866/812-2002, www.redcliffslodge.com) and **Sorrel River Ranch** (Hwy. 128, Milepost 17, 435/259-4642 or 877/317-8244, www.sorrelriver.com) both offer trail rides.

GOLF

The **Moab Golf Club** (2705 E. Bench Rd., 435/259-6488, https://moabgolfcourse.com, $46-62) is an 18-hole par-72 public course amid stunning red-rock formations. To get here from Moab, go south 5 miles (8 km) on US 191, turn left onto Spanish Trail Road and follow it 2 miles (3.2 km), then go right on Murphy Lane and follow it to Bench Road and the golf course.

PARKS

City Park (181 W. 400 N.) has shaded picnic tables and a playground. It's also home to the **Moab Recreation and Aquatic Center** (374 Park Ave., 435/259-8226), a very nice community center with indoor and outdoor swimming pools, a weight room, and group exercise classes.

Two miles (3.2 km) north of town, **Lions Park** (US 191 and Hwy. 128) offers picnicking along the Colorado River. **Rotary Park** (Mill Creek Dr.) is family-oriented and has lots of activities for kids.

ENTERTAINMENT AND EVENTS

Nightlife

Woody's Tavern (221 S. Main St., 435/259-3550, www.woodystavernmoab.com, 2pm-2am Mon.-Sat., 10:30am-2am Sun.), a classic dive bar, has pool and live bands on the weekend—you might hear bluegrass, rock, or jam bands. Come for some barbecue and stay for the blues (or vice versa, since both are good) at **Blu Pig** (811 S. Main St., 435/259-3333, www.blupigbbq.com, 11:30am-10pm daily).

For a more family-friendly evening out, cruise the Colorado with **Canyonlands by Night** (435/259-5261, www.canyonlandsbynight.com, Apr.-mid-Oct., $79 adults, $69 ages 4-12). The evening cruise ends with a sound-and-light presentation along the sandstone cliffs. Dinner packages ($89 adults, $79 ages 4-12) are available, though children under age four are not allowed, per Coast Guard regulations.

Festivals and Events

To find out about local happenings, contact the **Moab Information Center** (25 E. Center St., 435/259-8825, www.discovermoab.com, 8am-4pm daily mid-Mar.-late Nov., 9am-4pm daily late-Nov.-mid-Mar.) or browse *Moab Happenings,* available free around town or online (www.moabhappenings.com).

Unsurprisingly, Moab offers quite a few annual biking events. The **Moab Skinny Tire Festival,** held in mid-March, and the **Moab Century Tour,** held in September or early October, are both sponsored road bike events that benefit the fight against cancer. For information on both, visit www.skinnytireevents.com or call 435/260-8889. The bike demo event **Outerbike** (www.outerbike.com) is held in early October, and the **Moab Ho-Down Mountain Bike and Film Festival** (https://moabhodown.com) in late October offers silly competitions, endurance races, jump contests, skills camps, and other fun events, plus an evening of bike-themed films.

Other major annual athletic events include

the **Moab Marathon** (www.moabtrailmarathon.com) in early November, which also includes a half marathon and 5K, as well as a number of running events organized by **Mad Moose Events** (www.madmooseevents.com). These include the **Canyonlands Half Marathon and Five Mile Run,** held the third Saturday in March, and a women's half marathon held in early June, the **Thelma and Louise Half Marathon.**

But Moab's most popular annual event is the **Easter Jeep Safari** (www.rr4w.com), which is the Sturgis or Daytona Beach of recreational four-wheeling. Upward of 2,500 4WD vehicles (it's not exclusively for jeeps, although ATVs aren't allowed) converge on Moab in March or April for 10 days' worth of organized backcountry trail rides. "Big Saturday" (the day before Easter) is the climax, when all participating vehicles parade through Moab. Plan well ahead for lodging if you're planning to visit Moab during this event, as hotel rooms are often booked a year in advance.

Memorial Day weekend brings artists, musicians, and art cars to the city park for the **Moab Arts Festival** (435/259-2742, www.moabartsfestival.org).

The dust gets kicked up at the **Spanish Trail Arena** (3641 S. US 191, just south of Moab) with the **Canyonlands PRCA Rodeo** (www.moabcanyonlandsrodeo.com), held the last weekend in May or first weekend in June, with a rodeo, a parade, a dance, horse racing, and a 4-H gymkhana.

The **Moab Music Festival** (435/259-7003, www.moabmusicfest.org) is first and foremost a classical chamber music festival, but every year a few jazz, bluegrass, or folk artists are included in the lineup. More than 30 artists are currently involved in the festival, held in late August-early September. Many of the concerts are held in dramatic outdoor settings. The **Moab Folk Festival** (www.moabfolkfestival.com) is the town's other big annual musical event, attracting top-notch acoustic performers to Moab the first weekend of November.

SHOPPING

Main Street, between 200 North and 200 South, has nearly a dozen galleries and gift shops with T-shirts, outdoor apparel, Native American art, and other gifts. **Back of Beyond Books** (83 N. Main St., 435/259-5154, 9am-9pm daily) features an excellent selection of regional books and maps. Pick up those missing camping items at **Gearheads Outdoor Store** (471 S. Main St., 435/259-4327, 8am-9pm daily), an amazingly well-stocked outdoor store. If you're heading out to camp or hike in the desert, Gearheads is a good place to fill your water jugs with free filtered water.

Moab's largest grocery store, **City Market** (425 S. Main St., 435/259-5181, 6am-11pm daily), is a good place to pick up supplies, and also has a pharmacy and a gas station. Stop by the **Moonflower Community Cooperative** (39 E. 100 N., 435/259-5712, 8am-8pm daily) for natural-food groceries.

FOOD

Moab has the largest concentration of good restaurants in southern Utah. No matter what else the recreational craze has produced, it has certainly improved the food. Several Moab-area restaurants are closed for vacation in February, so call ahead if you're visiting in winter.

Casual Dining

Food isn't limited to muffins at ★ **Love Muffin** (139 N. Main St., 435/259-6833, https://lovemuffincafe.com, 6:30am-1pm Fri.-Tues., $8-11), but if you decide to skip the breakfast burritos or tasty rainbow quinoa, the Shake Yo Peaches muffin may be just what you need. While you're eating breakfast, order a cubano sandwich to pack for lunch.

If you're a sucker for sweet and savory combos, check out the doughnuts and fried chicken (served after 11am) at **Doughbird** (125 N. Main St., 435/255-8510, www.doughbirdmoab.com, 7am-2pm Fri.-Mon., $5-12), which also pours delicious espresso drinks.

If the weather's fine, head to the **Moab Food Truck Park** (39 W. 100 N., 435/261-7880, www.moabfoodpark.com, 11am-9pm daily Mar.-Oct.), located just a block off Main Street. You can find everything from tacos and kung pao chicken to pizza and gelato. With picnic bench seating and shade canopies, it's a lovely spot to visit between hikes or after the day's adventures are done.

Another spot with excellent burgers and shakes is ★ **Milt's Stop & Eat** (356 S. Millcreek Dr., 435/259-7424, www.miltsstopandeat.com, 11am-8:30pm daily, $5-9) near the Sand Flats Recreation Area—it's been a local classic since the mid-1950s, and it's the place to stop and sprawl under the big tree out front after a day in the sun.

A more upscale Mexican restaurant is **Miguel's Baja Grill** (51 N. Main St., 435/259-6546, www.miguelsbajagrill.net, 5pm-9pm daily, $18-32), with well-prepared Baja-style seafood, including good fish tacos. It's a busy place, so make a reservation or be prepared to wait.

In a quaint building a block off the main drag, **Arches Thai** (60 N. 100 W., 435/355-0533, https://archesthai.com, noon-3pm and 4pm-10pm daily, $11-30) has excellent service and Thai food, with a good mix of classics like drunken noodles, Indian-inspired options like curried samosas, and more authentic Thai dishes such as nam tok salad.

The **Broken Oar** (53 W. 400 N., 435/259-3127, www.thebrokenoarmoab.com, 5pm-9:30pm Mon.-Sat. Jan.-Nov., $12-35) is just north of downtown in a large log building resembling a ski lodge. In addition to burgers, pasta, and steak, the restaurant offers a selection of meats from its smoker. The beer and wine menu veers toward local producers.

About 3 miles (4.8 km) south of downtown, ★ **Hidden Cuisine** (2740 S. US 191, 425/259-7711, www.hidden-cuisine.com, 8am-2pm Mon. and Wed., 8am-2pm and 5:30pm-9pm Thurs.-Sun., $15-38) is a rare find in Utah: a restaurant specializing in South African food. While you can get a good burger here, try the delicious South African-style ribs or the babotie (a ground beef stew baked with a savory custard). For lunch, the citrus quinoa salad is especially tasty.

Brewpubs

You'll find good beer and decent food at the **Moab Brewery** (686 S. Main St., 435/259-6333, www.themoabbrewery.com, 11:30am-10pm Sun.-Thurs., 11:30am-11pm Fri.-Sat., $8-21), although not much of a nightlife scene. The atmosphere is light and airy, and the food is good—steaks, sandwiches, burgers, and a wide selection of salads. There's deck seating when weather permits. Immediately next door, the same folks operate the Moab Distillery. There's no tasting room, but you can sample their gin and vodka in the brewery.

Fine Dining

Just off Main Street, the ★ **Desert Bistro** (36 S. 100 W., 435/259-0756, www.desertbistro.com, 5pm-10pm daily Mar.-Nov., $27-53, reservations advised) is housed in a lovely renovated building that was, when built in 1892, Moab's first dance hall. Today, it's a longtime favorite for regional fine dining. Its seasonal, sophisticated Southwest-meets-continental cuisine features local meats and game plus fresh seafood. The patio dining is some of the nicest in Moab.

Inside the Radcliffe Hotel on a quiet stretch of Main Street, **Il Posto Rosso** (Radcliffe Hotel, 477 S. Main St., 435/355-1085, www.radcliffemoab.com, 6am-11am and 5pm-10pm daily, $17-78) serves beautiful Mediterranean-inspired and New American options, including shareable sides, house-made pastas, and seasonally rotating "land and sea" dishes. There's also a good wine and spirits selection.

Inside uranium king Charlie Steen's former mansion on a hill high above town, the **Sunset Grill** (900 N. US 191, 435/259-7146, www.moabsunsetgrill.com, 5pm-10pm Mon.-Sat., $14-35) serves steaks, fresh seafood, and a selection of pasta dishes—what you'll remember is the drive up and the view. The grill now offers a free shuttle from most Moab locations (call 435/259-7777 to request a ride).

1
CAFÉ
2
Arches Thai
Authentic Thai Cuisine & Pho
3
MOAB BREWERY

ACCOMMODATIONS

Moab has been a tourist destination for generations and offers a wide variety of lodging choices, ranging from older motels to new upscale resorts. US 191 is lined with all the usual chain hotels and motels. This list focuses on the smaller local operations, most within walking distance of downtown restaurants and shopping.

Moab Property Management (435/259-5955 or 800/505-5343, www.moabproperty management.com) can make bookings at area vacation homes, which include some relatively inexpensive apartments. Another handy tool is www.moab-utah.com, which has a complete listing of lodging websites for the Moab area.

The only time Moab isn't busy is in the dead of winter: November-February. At all other times, make reservations well in advance. Summer room rates are listed here. In winter, rates typically drop 40 percent, and during spring break season, they tend to rise, especially during Easter weekend, when four-wheelers fill the town.

Under $50

The **Lazy Lizard Hostel** (1213 S. US 191, 435/259-6057, www.lazylizardhostel.com) costs just $16 (cash preferred) for simple dorm-style accommodations. You won't need a hostel membership to stay at this Moab classic. All guests share access to a hot tub, kitchen, barbecue, coin-operated laundry, and a common room with cable TV. Showers for nonguests ($3) and private guest rooms ($41 for 2 people) are also offered. Log cabins can sleep two ($47-49) to six ($64) people. If you're traveling with a big family or a lot of friends, the hostel also offers large group houses that sleep 12-30 people. Lazy Lizard is 1 mile (1.6 km) south of town, behind A-1 Storage; the turnoff is about 200 yards (180 m) south of Moab Lanes.

1: doughnuts at Doughbird 2: Arches Thai 3: Moab Brewery

$100-150

A simple yet homey spot is the **Bowen Motel** (169 N. Main St., 435/259-7132 or 800/874-5439, www.bowenmotel.com, $125-153), which has an outdoor pool. The Bowen offers a variety of room types, including three-bedroom family suites and an 1,800-square-foot (167-sq-m) three-bedroom house with a full kitchen.

Over $150

In the heart of Moab, ★ **Best Western Canyonlands Inn** (16 S. Main St., 435/259-2300 or 800/649-5191, www.canyonlandsinn.com, $257-299) has suites, a pool, a fitness room and spa, an above-average complimentary breakfast, and a bike storage area. This is one of the better spots downtown for upscale amenities.

One of the most unique accommodations in Moab is the ★ **Gonzo Inn** (100 W. 200 S., 435/259-2515 or 800/791-4044, www.gonzo inn.com, $203-249). A cross between an adobe inn and a postmodern warehouse, this Hunter S. Thompson-inspired lodge is great for families, with large colorful guest rooms, a pool, and a friendly welcome.

If you want seclusion in a quiet community 18 miles (29 km) east of Moab, stay at **Castle Valley Inn** (424 Amber Ln., Castle Valley, 435/259-6012 or 888/466-6012, www.castle valleyinn.com, $195-320). The B&B-style inn adjoins a wildlife refuge in a stunning landscape of red-rock mesas and needle-pointed buttes. You can stay in one of the main house's four guest rooms, in a cabin, or in one of the three bungalows with kitchens, all with hot tub access. To reach Castle Valley Inn, follow Highway 128 east from Moab for 16 miles (26 km), turn south, and continue 2.3 miles (3.7 km) toward Castle Valley.

Located in a lovely and quiet residential area, the ★ **Sunflower Hill Luxury Inn** (147 N. 300 E., 435/259-2974 or 800/662-2786, www.sunflowerhill.com, $309-329) offers high-quality accommodations. Choose from a guest room in one of Moab's original farmhouses, a historic ranch house, or a garden cottage. All 12 guest rooms have private baths, air-conditioning, and queen beds; there are also two suites. Guests share access to an outdoor swimming pool and a hot tub, bike storage, patios, and large gardens. Children over age seven are welcome, and the inn is open year-round.

Families or groups might want to rent a condo at **Moab Springs Ranch** (1266 N. US 191, 435/259-7891 or 888/259-5759, www.moabspringsranch.com, 2-night minimum, $293-433), located on the north end of town on the site of Moab's oldest ranch. The townhomes have a parklike setting with a swimming pool and a hot tub, and they sleep up to 10. Book well in advance.

Billing itself as an adventure boutique hotel, the ★ **Radcliffe Moab** (477 S. Main St., 435/355-1088, www.radcliffemoab.com, $399) is one of the newer lodging options in town. To play off the concept, the hotel has in-room bike storage and towels, coolers, a hot tub, and the **Gearheads Outdoor Store** adjacent to the lobby. Rooms are spacious and modern, with high-end mattresses and luxurious showers. Suites are also available, and a great dining option, **Il Posto Rosso,** is located on the first floor.

A short drive from Moab along the Colorado River's red-rock canyon is the region's most upscale resort, the **Sorrel River Ranch** (Hwy. 128, 17 mi/27 km northeast of Moab, 435/259-4642 or 877/317-8244, www.sorrelriver.com, 2- or 3-night minimum stay sometimes applies, $1,403-1,557). The ranch sits on 240 acres (97 ha) just across the river from Arches National Park and beneath the soaring mesas of Castle Valley. Accommodations are in a series of beautifully furnished wooden lodges, all with Old West-style furniture plus kitchenettes. Horseback rides are offered into the arroyos behind the ranch, and kayaks and bicycles are available for rent. The ranch's restaurant, the **River Grill** (435/259-4642, 7am-11am, noon-3pm, and 5pm-9pm daily, $35-89), has some of the best views in Utah.

Sharing a similar view of the Colorado River and Castle Valley, but 3 miles (4.8 km) closer to Moab, the sprawling **Red Cliffs Lodge** (Hwy. 128, Milepost 14, 435/259-2002 or 866/812-2002, www.redcliffslodge.com, $340-440) houses guests in "mini suites" in the main lodge and in a number of riverside cabins that sleep up to six ($379). The lodge offers the Cowboy Grill bar and restaurant, horseback rides, and mountain bike rentals, and will arrange river raft trips. The lodge is also the site of the free **Moab Museum of Film & Western Heritage,** which displays a collection of movie memorabilia from Westerns filmed in the area.

Campgrounds

Camping is convenient at ★ **Up the Creek** (210 E. 300 S., 435/260-1888, www.moabcampground.com, mid-Mar.-Oct., $26 for 1 person, $33 for 2, $40 for 3), a walk-in, tents-only campground tucked into a residential neighborhood near downtown. The shady campground, with a bathhouse and showers, picnic tables, and a few propane grills (campfires are prohibited), is right alongside a bike path.

RV parks cluster at the north and south ends of town. Two miles (3.2 km) north of Moab, **Sun Outdoors Arches Gateway** (1773 N. US 191, at Hwy. 128, 877/418-8535, www.sunoutdoors.com/utah, tents $53-73, RVs $56-84) is open year-round and has showers, a pool, a playground, and free Wi-Fi. Pets are allowed in RVs. Although this place is a conveniently located spot, it's close to a large ongoing environmental cleanup project involving removal of radioactive mine tailings; according to the Environmental Protection Agency, it's safe to camp here. The same company operates another RV park in town called **Sun Outdoors Moab Downtown** (555 S. Main St., 435/259-6848, www.sunoutdoors.com, tents $53-73, RVs $56-84), open year-round with showers, laundry, a store, a pool, and two-person air-conditioned cabins—bring your own bedding.

Moab KOA (3225 S. US 191, 435/291-1712 or 800/562-0372, https://moabkoa.com,

Mar.-Nov., tents $50-57, RVs from $56 with hookups, cabins $109-189), barely off the highway 4 miles (6.4 km) south of town, has showers, a laundry room, a store, mini golf, and a pool.

You'll also find campgrounds farther out at Arches and Canyonlands National Parks, Dead Horse Point State Park, Canyon Rims Recreation Area, and east of town in the cool La Sal Mountains.

For something a little less rugged, **Under Canvas Moab** (13748 N. US 191, 888/496-1148, www.undercanvas.com, mid-Mar.-Oct.) offers a luxury safari tent experience on 40 acres (16 ha) near the entrance to Arches National Park. Lodging is in a variety of large wall tents, all fitted with fine bedding and furniture, and some with private en suite baths—glamping at its best. Tent accommodations that sleep four start at $239, with modern plumbing and restroom facilities in group shower houses. Also available are adventure packages that customize outdoor activities to your preferences and include three camp-cooked meals a day.

INFORMATION AND SERVICES

Moab is a small town, and people are generally friendly. Between the excellent Moab Information Center and the county library—and the friendly advice of people you meet—you'll find it easy to assemble all the information you need to have a fine stay.

Information

The **Moab Information Center** (25 E. Center St., 435/259-8825, www.discovermoab.com, 8am-4pm daily mid-Mar.-late Nov., 9am-4pm daily late-Nov.-mid-Mar.) is the place to start for nearly all local and area information. The National Park Service, the BLM, the US Forest Service, the Grand County Travel Council, and the Canyonlands Natural History Association are all represented here. Visitors who need help from any of these agencies should start at the information center rather than at the individual agency offices. Free literature is available, the selection of books and maps for sale is large, and the staff is knowledgeable. The center's website is also well organized and packed with information. In addition, the center screens *Welcome to Moab,* a film introducing visitors to the wonders of the surrounding area.

The **BLM district office** (82 E. Dogwood Ave., 435/259-2100, 8am-4:30pm Mon.-Fri.) on the south side of town behind Comfort Suites sells land-use maps, and this is the place to pick up **river-running permits.**

Services

The **Grand County Public Library** (257 E. Center St., 435/259-1111, 9am-8pm Mon.-Fri., 9am-5pm Sat.) is a good place for local history and general reading.

The **post office** (50 E. 100 N., 435/259-7427) is downtown. **Moab Regional Hospital** (450 W. Williams Way, 435/719-3500) provides medical care. For ambulance, sheriff, police, or fire emergencies, dial 911.

Dogs can spend a day or board at **Karen's Canine Campground** (435/259-7922, https://karensk9campground.wordpress.com) while their people hike the no-dogs trails in Arches and Canyonlands.

GETTING THERE

SkyWest, associated with United Airlines (800/335-2247, www.united.com), provides daily scheduled air service between **Canyonlands Field Airport** (CNY, US 191, 16 mi/26 km north of Moab, 435/259-4849, www.moabairport.com) and Denver. Grand Junction, Colorado, is 120 miles (193 km) east of Moab via I-70 and has an airport with more scheduled flights; Salt Lake City is 240 miles (385 km) northwest of Moab.

Moab Express (435/260-9289, https://moabexpress.com) runs shuttles between Moab and Canyonlands Field (must book in advance, $27 pp). Moab Express shuttles also link to the Grand Junction airport in Colorado.

Arches National Park

TOP EXPERIENCE

The largest concentration of rock arches in the world is found at **Arches National Park** (435/719-2299, www.nps.gov/arch, $30 per vehicle, $15 per motorcycle, $15 pedestrians and bicyclists), one of the most popular parks in the United States.

Mazes of rock fins, balanced rocks, and tall spires add to the splendor of the 1,500-plus arches here. Thanks to unrelenting erosion, the arches are constantly changing. Every so often, there's a dramatic change, like the collapse of 71-foot (22-m) Wall Arch in 2008.

Paved roads and short moderate hiking trails (a couple wheelchair accessible) lead to some of the 1,500-plus arches here. If you're short on time, a drive to the Windows Section (23.5 mi/38 km round-trip) affords a look at some of the largest and most spectacular arches right off the road. To visit all the stops on the scenic drive and hike a few short trails easily takes a full day. Plan on bringing your own food and water, since there's no dining inside the park.

Recreational interest in Arches sparked in 1923, when a local prospector tipped off officials from the Rio Grande Railroad. This led to the first director of the National Park Service, Stephen Mather, securing the designation of two small areas as a national monument in 1929. Over the years, the monument grew and, in 1971, became Arches National Park. The park now comprises 76,519 acres (30,966 ha)—small enough to be appreciated in 1 day, yet large enough for longer stays.

VISITOR CENTER

The entrance to Arches is 5 miles (8 km) north of downtown Moab on US 191. Located just past the park entrance booth, the expansive **visitor center** (7:30am-6pm daily mid-Mar.-Sept., 8am-5pm daily Oct., 8am-4pm daily Nov., 9am-4pm daily late Nov.-mid-Mar., seasonal hours may vary from year to year) provides a good introduction to the park. A short film on park geology runs regularly, and exhibits identify the rock layers, describe the geologic and human history, and illustrate some of the wildlife and plants of the park. A large outdoor plaza is a good place to trawl for information when the visitor center is closed. If you manage to arrive at the park early, skip the visitor center to take advantage of dawn among the arches, and stop to see the exhibits on the way back.

At the visitor center, staff is available to answer questions or check you in for a ranger-led Fiery Furnace tour. Look for the posted list of special activities; rangers host campfire programs and lead a wide variety of **guided walks** (Apr.-Sept.). An audio tour of the park's scenic main road is also available for rent or purchase. An audio version of the park brochure is available on CD (or can be downloaded from www.nps.gov/arch), and you may also request large-print or braille publications at the visitor center. See the rangers for advice and the **free backcountry permit** required for overnight trips.

Desert bighorn sheep frequent the area around the visitor center and can sometimes be seen from US 191 just south of the park entrance. A sheep crossing about 3 miles (4.8 km) north of the visitor center is also a good place to scan the steep talus slopes for these nimble animals.

SCENIC DRIVE

The 18-mile-long (29-km) scenic road through Arches gets busy. Be sure to stop only in parking lots and designated pullouts. Watch out for others on the sightseeing circuit. The following are major points of interest.

Moab Fault

The park road begins with a long, steady climb from the visitor center. A pullout on the right after 1.1 miles (1.8 km) offers a good view of

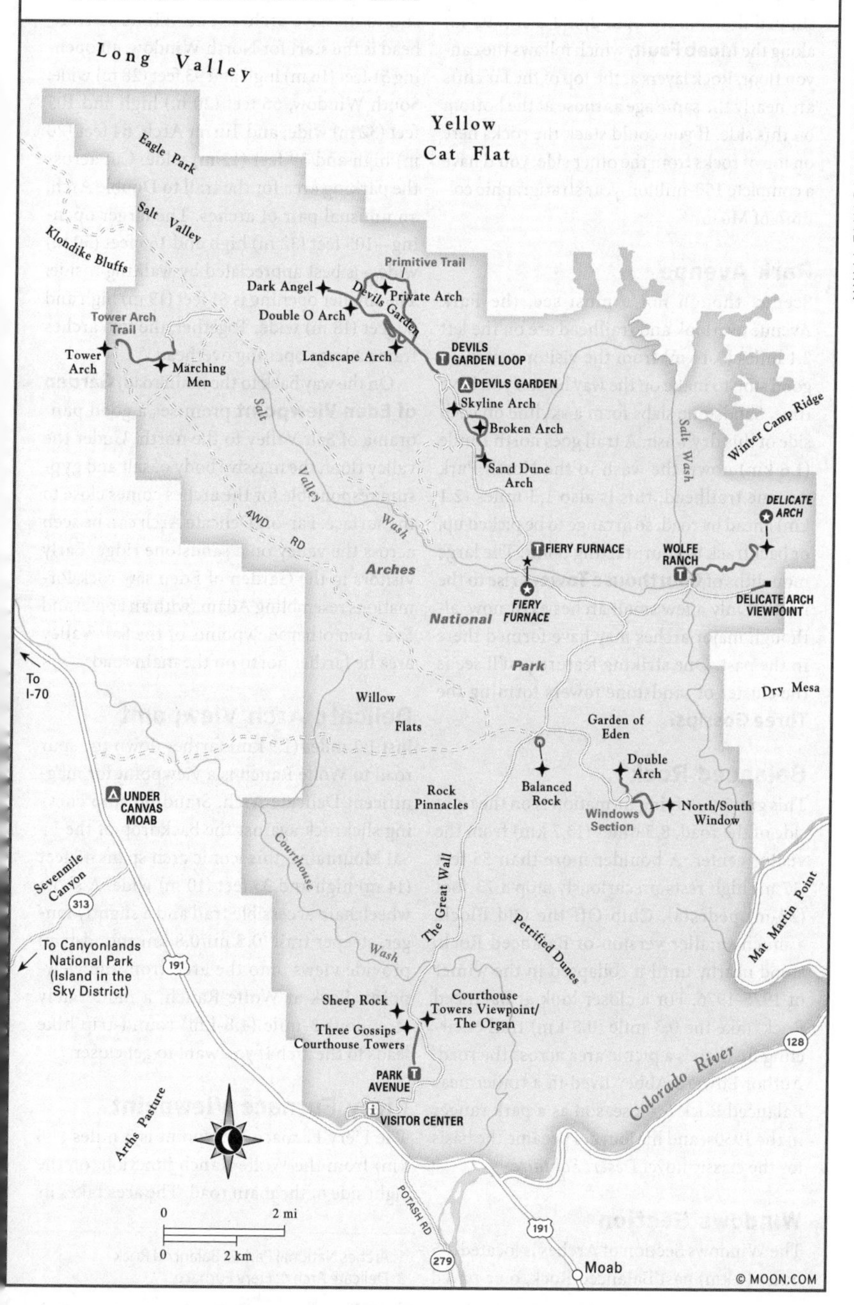
Arches National Park
Long Valley
Yellow Cat Flat
Eagle Park
Salt Valley
Klondike Bluffs
Primitive Trail
Dark Angel
Private Arch
Devils Garden
Double O Arch
Tower Arch Trail
Tower Arch
Marching Men
Landscape Arch
DEVILS GARDEN LOOP
DEVILS GARDEN
Skyline Arch
Broken Arch
Sand Dune Arch
Salt Wash
Winter Camp Ridge
Salt Valley Wash
4WD RD
DELICATE ARCH
FIERY FURNACE
WOLFE RANCH
FIERY FURNACE
DELICATE ARCH VIEWPOINT
Arches National Park
To I-70
Willow Flats
Dry Mesa
Garden of Eden
Double Arch
Balanced Rock
Rock Pinnacles
North/South Window
Windows Section
UNDER CANVAS MOAB
Courthouse Wash
The Great Wall
Petrified Dunes
Mat Martin Point
Sevenmile Canyon
313
To Canyonlands National Park (Island in the Sky District)
191
Sheep Rock
Courthouse Towers Viewpoint/ The Organ
Three Gossips
Courthouse Towers
128
Colorado River
PARK AVENUE
VISITOR CENTER
Arths Pasture
POTASH RD
0
2 mi
0
2 km
191
279
Moab
© MOON.COM

Moab Canyon. About six million years ago, the rock layers on this side of the canyon slipped down more than 2,600 feet (792 m) along the **Moab Fault,** which follows the canyon floor. Rock layers at the top of the far cliffs are nearly the same age as those at the bottom on this side. If you could stack the rocks here on top of rocks from the other side, you'd have a complete 150-million-year stratigraphic column of Moab.

Park Avenue

Scenic, though not a must-see, the Park Avenue overlook and trailhead are on the left 2.1 miles (3.4 km) from the visitor center—a good stop to make on the way back if you have time. Sandstone slabs form a skyline on each side of this dry wash. A trail goes north 1 mile (1.6 km) down the wash to the North Park Avenue trailhead; this is also 1.3 miles (2.1 km) ahead by road, so arrange to be picked up, or backtrack to your starting point. The large monoliths of **Courthouse Towers** rise to the north. Only a few small arches exist now, although major arches may have formed there in the past. One striking feature you'll see is the cluster of sandstone towers forming the **Three Gossips.**

Balanced Rock

This gravity-defying formation is on the right side of the road, 8.5 miles (13.7 km) from the visitor center. A boulder more than 55 feet (17 m) high rests precariously atop a 73-foot (22-m) pedestal. Chip Off the Old Block, a much smaller version of Balanced Rock, stood nearby until it collapsed in the winter of 1975-1976. For a closer look at Balanced Rock, take the 0.3-mile (0.5-km) trail encircling it. There's a picnic area across the road. Author Edward Abbey lived in a trailer near Balanced Rock for a season as a park ranger in the 1950s, and his journal became the basis for the classic novel *Desert Solitaire.*

Windows Section

The Windows Section of Arches is located 2.5 miles (4 km) past Balanced Rock, on a paved road to the right. Short, easy trails (0.25-1 mi/0.4-1.6 km one-way) lead from the road's end to massive arches. The Windows trailhead is the start for North Window, an opening 51 feet (16 m) high and 93 feet (28 m) wide; South Window, 66 feet (20 m) high and 105 feet (32 m) wide; and Turret Arch, 64 feet (20 m) high and 39 feet (12 m) wide. Cut across the parking area for the trail to Double Arch, an unusual pair of arches. The larger opening—105 feet (32 m) high and 163 feet (50 m) wide—is best appreciated by walking inside. The smaller opening is 61 feet (19 m) high and 60 feet (18 m) wide. Together, the two arches frame a large opening overhead.

On the way back to the main road, **Garden of Eden Viewpoint** promises a good panorama of Salt Valley to the north. Under the valley floor, the massive body of salt and gypsum responsible for the arches comes close to the surface. Far-off Delicate Arch can be seen across the valley on a sandstone ridge. Early visitors to the Garden of Eden saw rock formations resembling Adam (with an apple) and Eve. Two other viewpoints of the Salt Valley area lie farther north on the main road.

Delicate Arch Viewpoint

Just 1.2 miles (1.9 km) farther down the spur road to Wolfe Ranch is a viewpoint for magnificent Delicate Arch. Standing atop curving slickrock against the backdrop of the La Sal Mountains, this iconic arch spans 45 feet (14 m) high and 33 feet (10 m) wide. A short wheelchair-accessible trail and a slightly longer, steeper trail (0.5 mi/0.8 km round-trip) provide views onto the arch from the viewpoint. Back at Wolfe Ranch, a moderately strenuous 3-mile (4.8-km) round-trip hike leads to the arch if you want to get closer.

Fiery Furnace Viewpoint

The Fiery Furnace Viewpoint is 3 miles (4.8 km) from the Wolfe Ranch junction, on the right side of the main road. The area takes its

1: Arches National Park 2: Balanced Rock
3: Delicate Arch 4: Fiery Furnace

1
2
3
4

name from the way its sandstone fins turn flaming red when thin clouds on the horizon reflect the warm light of sunrise and sunset. The shady recesses beneath the fins provide a cool respite from the summer sun.

Closely packed sandstone fins form a maze of deep slots, with many arches and at least one natural bridge inside. For safety reasons (it's easy to get lost) and to reduce human impact on this sensitive area, which harbors several species of rare plants, hikers are encouraged to join a ranger-led hike. The hike is moderately strenuous and involves steep ledges, squeezing through narrow cracks, a couple of jumps, and hoisting yourself up off the ground. There is no turning back once the hike starts, so make sure you're physically prepared and properly equipped.

To visit the Fiery Furnace without a ranger, visitors must obtain a **permit** at the visitor center ($10 adults, $5 ages 5-12, available 2-7 days before your trip); you can reserve a self-guided permit at www.recreation.gov, but must pick up your permit in person.

Skyline Arch

This arch is on the right, 1 mile (1.6 km) past the Sand Dune-Broken Arch trailhead. In desert climates, erosion can proceed imperceptibly for centuries—but from time to time a cataclysmic event occurs. In 1940, a giant boulder fell from the opening of Skyline Arch, doubling the size of the arch in seconds. The hole is now 45 feet (14 m) high and 69 feet (21 m) wide. A short trail leads to the base of the arch.

Devils Garden

The Devils Garden trailhead, picnic area, and campground are all near the end of the main park road. Devils Garden offers fine scenery and more arches than any other section of the park. The hiking trail leads past large sandstone fins to Landscape and six other named arches. Carry water, even if you think you're just going for a short stroll—you may be tempted to hike farther than you planned! Adventurous hikers could spend days exploring the maze of canyons among these fins.

Klondike Bluffs and Tower Arch

Relatively few visitors come to the spires, high bluffs, and fine arch in this northwestern section of the park. A fair-weather dirt road turns off the main drive 1.3 miles (2.1 km) before Devils Garden trailhead, winds down into Salt Valley, and heads northwest. After 7.5 miles (12.1 km), turn left on the road to Klondike Bluffs and proceed 1 mile (1.6 km) to the Tower Arch trailhead. These roads may have washboards, but they're usually passable by most cars in dry weather. Don't drive on them if storms threaten.

The trail to Tower Arch (3 mi/4.8 km round-trip) winds past the Marching Men and other rock formations. Alexander Ringhoffer, who first recorded the arch in 1922, carved an inscription on the south column. The area is also fun to explore off-trail with a map and compass or a GPS receiver. Those with 4WD vehicles can drive close to the arch on a separate 4WD road. Tower Arch, which takes its name from a nearby tall monolith, has an opening 34 feet (10 m) high by 92 feet (28 m) wide.

4WD Exploration

A rough road near Tower Arch in the Klondike Bluffs turns southeast past **Eye of the Whale Arch** in Herdina Park to Balanced Rock on the main park road, 10.8 miles (17.4 km) away. The road isn't particularly difficult for 4WD enthusiasts, although normal precautions should be taken. A steep sand hill north of Eye of the Whale Arch is difficult to climb for vehicles coming from Balanced Rock—it's better to drive from the Tower Arch area instead. (Trust us and don't try this road in a big pickup truck, even one with 4WD!)

HIKING

Because of its popularity and proximity to Moab, Arches sees a lot of visitors: About 1.8 million visit the park yearly. Most people drive the parkways and stop at easily accessible viewpoints. You can quickly leave the crowds behind by planning a hike to farther destinations. The Arches backcountry offers magnificent rewards for hikers willing to leave the pavement behind and get dusty on a backcountry trail.

Established hiking trails lead to many beautiful arches and overlooks that can't be seen from the road. You're free to wander cross-country too, but stay on slickrock or in washes to avoid damaging the fragile cryptobiotic soil crusts. Take a map and compass (or a GPS unit) for off-trail hiking. Wear good walking shoes with rubber soles for travel across slickrock. The summer sun is very harsh—don't forget water, a hat, and sunscreen. The desert rule is to carry at least one gallon of water per person for an all-day hike.

Many trails are partially or entirely over slickrock. Be cautious on this terrain—the soft sandstone can crumble easily. Also, remember that it's easier to go up a steep slickrock slope than it is to come back down.

You can reach almost any spot in the park on a day hike, although you'll also find some good overnight camping possibilities if you want to go backpacking. Areas for longer trips include Courthouse Wash in the southern part of the park and Salt Wash in the eastern part. All backpacking is off-trail, and a **backcountry permit** must be obtained from a ranger.

Backcountry regulations prohibit fires and pets, and they allow camping only out of sight of any road (at least 1 mi/1.6 km away) or trail (at least 0.5 mi/0.8 km away), and at least 300 feet (91 m) from a recognizable archaeological site or nonflowing water source.

★ Delicate Arch Trail

Distance: *3 miles (4.8 km) round-trip*
Duration: *2 hours*
Elevation gain: *500 feet (152 m)*
Effort: *moderate-strenuous*
Trailhead: *Wolfe Ranch*

The hike to the base of Delicate Arch is one of the park's highlights. Shortly after the trail's start at Wolfe Ranch, a spur trail leads to some petroglyphs depicting horses and their riders and a few bighorn sheep. Horses didn't arrive in the area until the mid-1600s, so these petroglyphs are believed to be the work of the Ute people.

The first stretch of the main trail is broad, flat, and not especially scenic, except for a good display of spring wildflowers. After about 20-30 minutes of hiking, the trail transitions to steep slickrock and the views open up across the park to the La Sal Mountains in the distance.

Just before the end of the trail, walk up to the small, decidedly indelicate Frame Arch for a picture-perfect view of the final destination. The classic photo of Delicate Arch is taken at dawn or in the evening when the sandstone is ablaze. Standing at the base of Delicate Arch is a magical moment: The arch rises out of the barren, almost lunar, rock face, at the edge of a sandstone amphitheater overlooking the Colorado River valley.

★ Fiery Furnace Trail

Distance: *2-mile (3.2-km) loop*
Duration: *3 hours*
Elevation gain: *250 feet (76 m)*
Effort: *moderate-strenuous*
Trailhead: *Fiery Furnace Viewpoint*

The Fiery Furnace area is open only to hikers with **permits** ($10 pp, under age 5 prohibited) or to those joining a ranger-led hike. May-September, there are two daily hike options: Ranger-led **loop hikes** ($16 pp, under age 5 prohibited) are roughly 3 hours long and cover 1.5 miles (2.4 km), while ranger-led **out-and-back hikes** ($16 pp, under age 5 prohibited) are about 2.5 hours long and cover 1.25 miles (2 km). Tours are offered in the morning and in the afternoon; usually, only morning tours are reservable in advance online at www.recreation.gov. Afternoon tickets are typically only sold in person at the visitor center up to a week in advance. These hikes are popular and are often booked weeks in advance, so plan accordingly.

Especially if you plan to explore this area

1
2
3
4

without a ranger, keep in mind that hiking in the Fiery Furnace is not along a trail. Hikers navigate a maze of narrow sandstone canyons, for which there is no legitimate map. The route can be challenging, requiring hands-and-knees scrambling up cracks and ledges. Navigation is even more difficult: Route-finding can be tricky because what look like obvious paths often lead to dead ends. Drop-offs and ridges make straight-line travel impossible, and it's easy to become disoriented. Small white arrows painted on the rock lead the way, but they are sparse and sometimes confusing. Even if you're an experienced hiker, the ranger-led hikes provide the best introduction to the Fiery Furnace.

Broken and Sand Dune Arches

Distance: *1 mile (1.6-km) round-trip*
Duration: *45 minutes*
Elevation gain: *140 feet (43 m)*
Effort: *easy*
Trailhead: *on the right side of the road, 2.4 miles (3.9 km) past the Fiery Furnace turnoff*

A short, sandy trail leads to small Sand Dune Arch. Its opening is 8 feet (2.4 m) high and 30 feet (9 m) wide, tucked within fins. A longer 1 mile (1.6 km) round-trip trail crosses a field to Broken Arch, which is visible from the road and 43 feet (13 m) high and 59 feet (18 m) wide. Up close, you'll see that the arch isn't really broken, just quite attenuated. These arches can also be reached by a trail across from campsite 40 at Devils Garden Campground. And beautiful **Tapestry Arch** requires a short detour off the trail between the campground and Broken Arch.

Look for low-growing Canyonlands biscuit root, found only in areas of Entrada sandstone, colonizing the sand dunes. Hikers can protect the habitat of the biscuit root and other fragile plants by keeping to washes or rock surfaces.

1: The trail to Delicate Arch follows sand and slickrock. **2:** Fiery Furnace Trail **3:** Broken Arch **4:** Devils Garden Loop

Devils Garden Loop

Distance: *7.2 miles (11.6 km) round-trip*
Duration: *4 hours*
Elevation gain: *350 feet (107 m)*
Effort: *strenuous*
Trailhead: *Devils Garden trailhead*

From the end of the paved park road, a full tour of Devils Garden leads to eight named arches and a week's worth of scenic wonders. This is one of the park's most popular areas, with several shorter versions of the full loop hike that make the area accessible to nearly every hiker. Don't be shocked to find quite a crowd at the trailhead—it usually dissipates after the first two or three arches.

The first two arches are an easy walk via a short side trail to the right. **Tunnel Arch** has a relatively symmetrical opening 22 feet (6.7 m) high and 27 feet (8.3 m) wide. Nearby **Pine Tree Arch,** named for a piñon pine that once grew inside, has an opening 48 feet (15 m) high and 46 feet (14 m) wide.

Continue on the main trail to **Landscape Arch,** past which the trail narrows and continues to the remains of **Wall Arch,** which collapsed in 2008. A short trail branches off to the left beyond the stubs of Wall Arch to **Partition Arch** and **Navajo Arch,** where prehistoric Native Americans may have camped.

The main trail climbs up slickrock, offering views of the La Sal Mountains and Fin Canyon. At the Fin Canyon viewpoint, the trail curves left (watch for cairns) and continues northwest, ending at **Double O Arch** (4 mi/6.4 km round-trip from the trailhead). Double O has an oval-shaped opening 45 feet (14 m) high and 71 feet (22 m) wide, and a smaller hole underneath. **Dark Angel** is a distinctive rock pinnacle 0.25 mile (0.4 km) northwest; cairns mark the way. Another primitive trail loops back to Landscape Arch via **Fin Canyon.** This route goes through a different part of Devils Garden, and adds about 1 mile (1.6 km) to your trip (3 mi/4.8 km back to the trailhead instead of 2 mi/3.2 km). Pay attention to trail markers so you don't get lost.

1
2

ROCK CLIMBING

Rock climbers should stop by a kiosk outside the visitor center for a **free permit** (also available online at www.nps.gov/arch). Groups are limited to five climbers, and Balanced Rock, the "Arches Boulders," and all arches with openings greater than 3 feet (91 cm) are closed to climbing. Check at the visitor center or online for temporary closures, often due to nesting raptors. Slacklining and BASE jumping are prohibited in the park. There are still plenty of long-standing routes for advanced climbers to enjoy, although the rock in Arches is sandier and softer than in other areas around Moab.

Several additional climbing restrictions are in place. If an existing bolt or other hardware item is unsafe, it may be replaced, but if any new hardware is installed, a permit is required. This mostly restricts all technical climbing to existing routes or new routes not requiring placement of fixed anchors. And climbers should always stick to established trails on the approach and carefully avoid stepping on cryptobiotic soil. Other restrictions are detailed on the park's website (www.nps.gov/arch).

There are over 80 climbing routes, the vast majority of which are trad (protected by traditional gear) and aid, although clean techniques are required (no pitons or other gear left behind). There are also a few bouldering areas. For more information on climbing in Arches, consult *Desert Rock* by Eric Bjørnstad or *High on Moab* by Karl Kelley, or ask for advice at **Pagan Mountaineering** (211 N. Main St., Moab, 435/259-1117, www.paganclimber.com), a climbing and outdoor-gear store. You can also check out www.mountainproject.com for some good beta (information on routes).

CAMPGROUND

Devils Garden Campground (elev. 5,355 ft/1,632 m, year-round, $25) is near the end of the 18-mile (29-km) main park road. It's an excellent place to camp, with some sites tucked under rock formations and others offering great views, but it's extremely popular. Plan accordingly and reserve a site online (www.recreation.gov) as far in advance as you can; reservations are accepted between 4 days and 6 months in advance. All campsites can be reserved March-October, so campers without reservations during this time are out of luck. November-February, sites are first-come, first-served, but still quite competitive. There are two accessible sites, close to an accessible restroom. A camp host is on-site, firewood is for sale ($5), and water is available, but there are no other amenities.

If you can't score a coveted Arches campsite, all is not lost. There are many Bureau of Land Management (BLM) campsites within an easy drive of the park throughout the Moab area. Try the primitive BLM campgrounds on Highway 313, just west of US 191 and on the way to Canyonlands National Park's Island in the Sky District. Another cluster of BLM campgrounds is along the Colorado River on Highway 128, or at the Sand Flats area near the Slickrock Trail.

GETTING THERE

Arches National Park is 26 miles (42 km) south of I-70 and 5 miles (8 km) north of Moab, both off US 191. If you're driving from Moab, allow 15 minutes to reach the park, as there is often slow-moving RV traffic along the route. If you're on a bike, a paved bike path parallels the highway between Moab and the park.

1: Landscape Arch 2: Devils Garden Campground

Canyonlands National Park

TOP EXPERIENCE

Water spent hundreds of millions of years shaping Canyonlands, and those epochs of flow have paid off. Alongside the park's namesake, you'll find buttes, arches, and breathtaking rock formations spread across several districts: Islands in the Sky, the Needles, the Maze, and noncontiguous Horseshoe Canyon, along with the Green and Colorado Rivers running through the rock.

The Colorado and Green Rivers form the River District and divide Canyonlands National Park into three other regions. Island in the Sky is north, between the rivers; the Maze is to the west; and Needles is to the east. To the west, the small Horseshoe Canyon Unit preserves a canyon on Barrier Creek, a tributary of the Green River, where you'll find astounding petroglyphs and ancient rock paintings.

Each district has its own distinct character. No bridges or roads directly connect the three land districts and the Horseshoe Canyon Unit, so unless you're up for a very long hike, you'll have to leave the park to travel between them. The huge park can be seen in many ways and on many levels. Paved roads reach a few areas, 4WD roads go to more places, and hiking trails reach still more, but much of the land shows scant trace of human passage. For a bird's-eye view, you can fly over this incredible network of canyons. To know it intimately, take a river trip or a long hike.

The park can be visited in any season, but spring and autumn are the best times to go. Summer temperatures can climb past 100°F (38°C), so carrying lots of water is critical then (at least one gallon per person per day). Arm yourself with insect repellent late spring-midsummer. Winter days tend to be bright and sunny, although nighttime temperatures can dip into the teens or even below 0°F (-18°C). Winter visitors should inquire about travel conditions, as snow and ice occasionally close roads and trails at higher elevations.

EXPLORING THE PARK

Every district of **Canyonlands National Park** (425/719-2313, www.nps.gov/cany, $30 per vehicle, $25 motorcyclists, $15 bicyclists and pedestrians, no fee to enter the Maze District or Horseshoe Canyon) offers great views, spectacular geology, and a chance to see wildlife. You won't find crowds or elaborate park facilities because most of Canyonlands remains a primitive backcountry park, so bring the food and water you'll need during your stay. There are no restaurants or accommodations anywhere in the park.

Front-country camping is allowed only in the Island in the Sky Campground and Needles Campground. Car and boat campers can bring in firewood but must use grills or fire pans. Backcountry camping requires a permit, good navigation skills, and packing in your own water. No firewood collecting is permitted in the park, and backpackers must use gas stoves for cooking.

For most day hikes, the maps issued at park visitor centers will suffice. The best topographic maps for the park, with the latest trail and road information, are made by National Geographic-Trails Illustrated.

Rock climbing is allowed in some areas of the park. Permits are not required unless the trip involves overnight camping. Check in at the district visitor centers to find out where climbing is restricted. Climbing is not allowed within 300 feet (91 m) of cultural sites like the Great Gallery.

Pets aren't allowed on trails and must be leashed in campgrounds.

Visitor Centers

Because Canyonlands covers so much far-flung territory, separate visitor centers serve each district. One website (www.nps.gov/cany)

serves the whole park and is a good source for current information and permit applications. There are visitor centers at the entrances to the **Island in the Sky District** (435/259-4712, 8am-5pm daily Apr.-late Oct., 8am-4pm daily mid-Feb.-late Mar. and late Oct.-Dec., 9am-4pm Thurs.-Mon. Jan.-mid-Feb.) and the **Needles District** (435/259-4711, 8am-5pm daily mid-Feb.-Oct., 8am-4pm daily Nov.-mid-Dec., closed mid-Dec.-mid-Feb.). The **Hans Flat Ranger Station** (435/719-2218, 8am-4:30pm daily year-round) is on a remote plateau above the isolated canyons of the Maze District and Horseshoe Canyon. The River District is administered by the **National Park Service office** (2282 SW Resource Blvd., Moab, 435/719-2313, 8am-4pm Mon.-Fri. year-round). This office can generally handle inquiries for all districts of the park. For backcountry information, or to make backcountry reservations, call 435/259-4351.

If you're coming from Moab, it's easiest to stop at the **Moab Information Center** (25 E. Center St., 435/259-8825 or 800/635-6622, 8am-4pm daily mid-Mar.-late Nov., 9am-4pm daily late-Nov.-mid-Mar.), where a national park ranger or volunteers with the Canyonlands Natural History Association are often on duty to answer questions and hand out brochures and maps.

Island in the Sky District

Perhaps the most accessible area of Canyonlands, the Island in the Sky District has paved roads leading to impressive sights. Easily visited as a day trip from Moab, the "Island" is actually a large mesa, connected to the "mainland" to the north by a narrow neck. If you're on a tight schedule, it's possible to spend a few hours exploring Arches National Park, then head here for a drive to the **Grand View Point Overlook** and a short hike to **Mesa Arch** or the strange **Upheaval Dome** viewpoint. If you have a full day, add a hike along the **Neck Springs Trail.** If you have a few days, hikers, mountain bikers, or those with high-clearance 4WD vehicles can descend about 1,300 feet (400 m) in elevation from Island in the Sky on the 100-mile (161-km) **White Rim Road,** which follows the cliffs around most of the Island.

Needles District

Colorful spires inspired the name of this district, easily accessible from Highway 211 and US 191 south of Moab. Splendid canyons contain arches, strange rock formations, and archaeological sites. Overlooks and short nature trails can be enjoyed from a paved scenic drive. If you only have a day, hike the **Cave Spring Trail.** On a longer visit, take **Big Spring Trail** to **Chesler Park.** A 10-mile (16.1-km) round-trip hike will take you to the **Confluence Overlook,** a great view of the junction of the Green and Colorado Rivers. Drivers with 4WD vehicles can take on more challenging roads through canyons and other highly scenic areas amid the Needles.

Maze District

Few visitors make it over to the Maze District, which is some of the wildest country in the United States. Only the rivers and a handful of 4WD roads and hiking trails provide access. Experienced hikers can explore the labyrinth of canyons on unmarked routes. Plan to spend at least 2 or 3 days here, since even day-hike trailheads can take a long time to reach. If you don't have much time, your best bet is the hike from **Maze Overlook** to the **Harvest Scene.** If you have more than 1 day, head to the **Land of Standing Rocks** area and hike north to the **Chocolate Drops.**

★ Horseshoe Canyon Unit

This separate section of Canyonlands National Park northwest of the Maze District contains exceptional prehistoric rock art. Ghostly life-size pictographs in the **Great Gallery** provide an intriguing look into the past. This ancient artwork is reached via a series of long unpaved roads and a moderately challenging hiking trial down a canyon.

Archaeologists think that the images had religious importance, although the meaning of the figures remains unknown. The Barrier

Canyonlands National Park

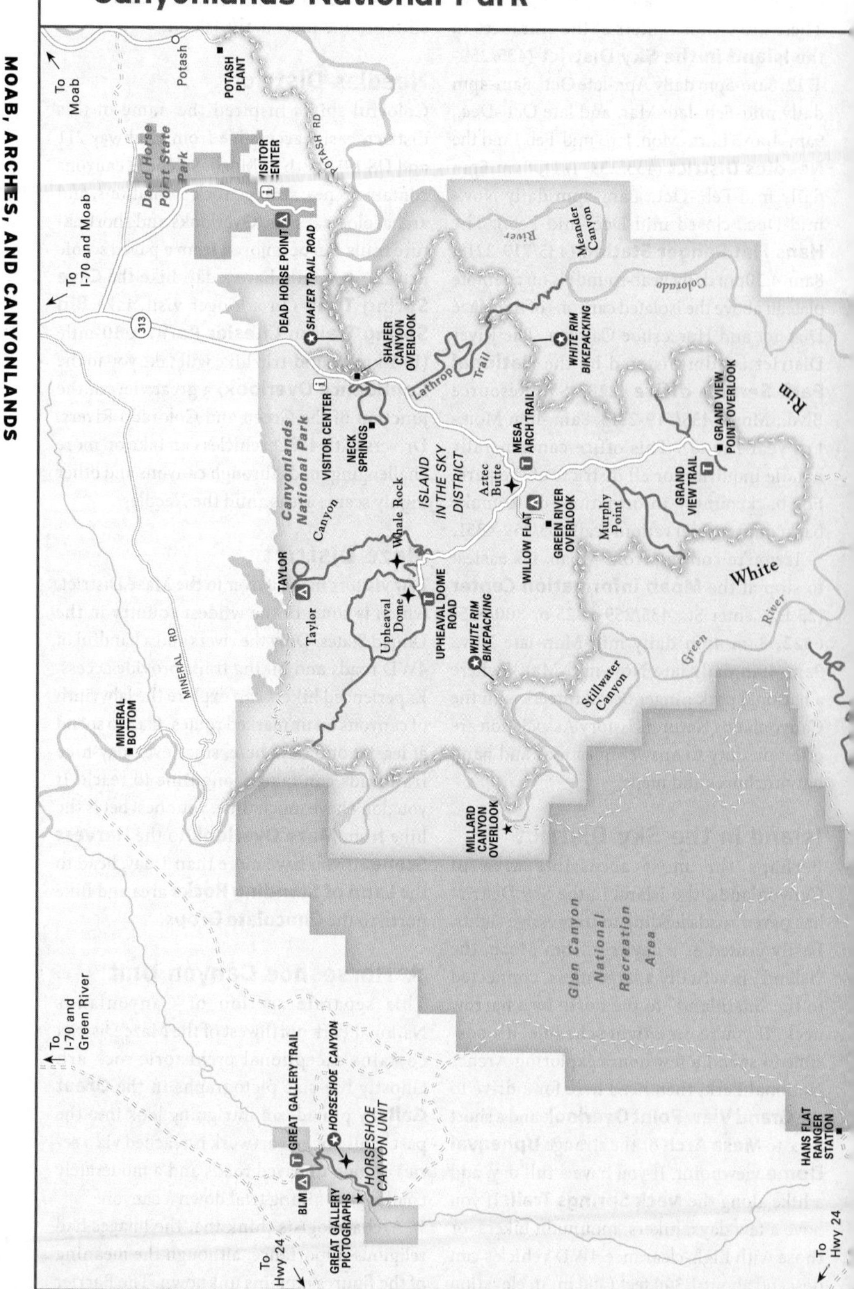

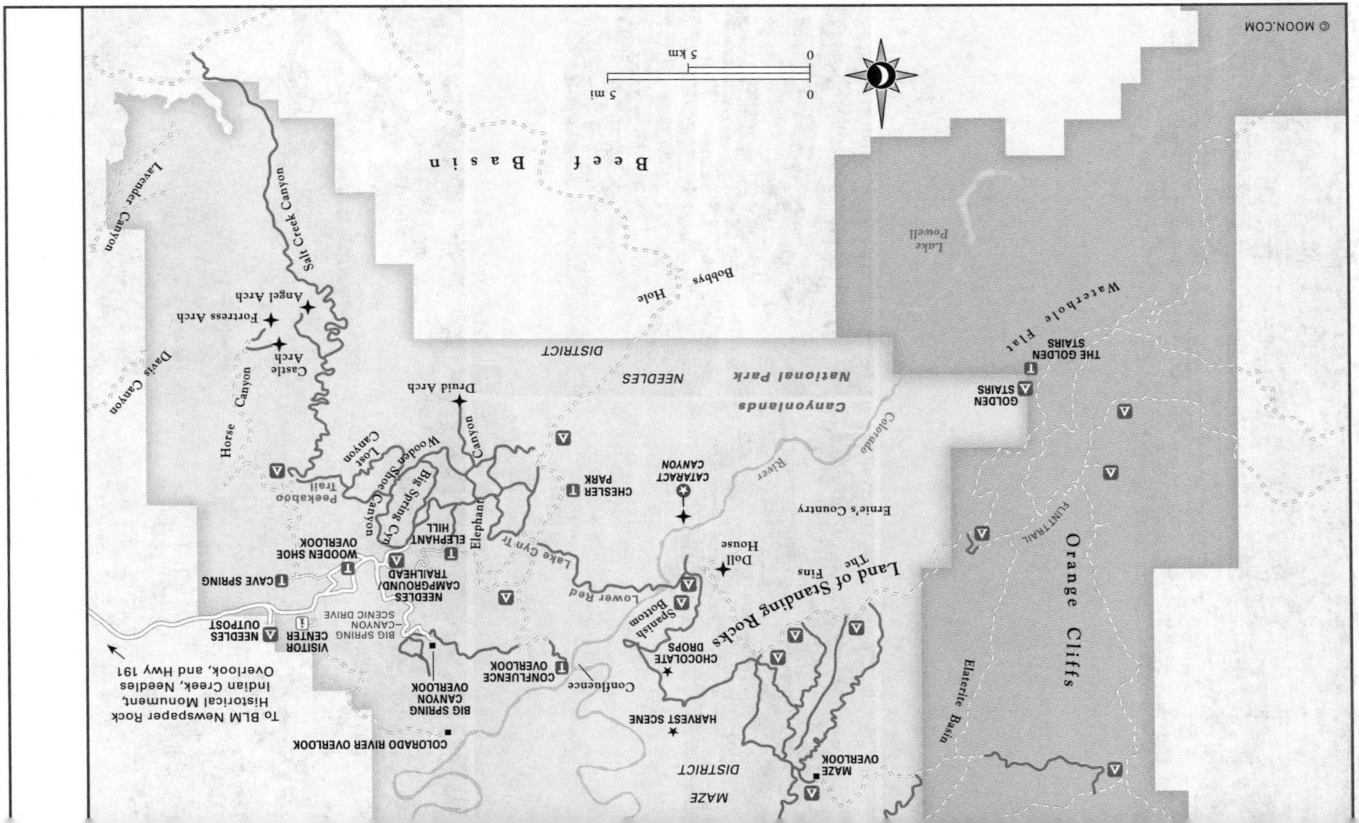

MAZE DISTRICT
MAZE OVERLOOK
HARVEST SCENE
COLORADO RIVER OVERLOOK
BIG SPRING CANYON OVERLOOK
To BLM Newspaper Rock Historical Monument, Indian Creek, Needles Overlook, and Hwy 191
Confluence
CONFLUENCE OVERLOOK
CHOCOLATE DROPS
VISITOR CENTER
NEEDLES OUTPOST
BIG SPRING CANYON SCENIC DRIVE
Land of Standing Rocks
The Fins
Spanish Bottom
Lower Red Lake Cyn Tr
NEEDLES CAMPGROUND/ TRAILHEAD
CAVE SPRING
Doll House
WOODEN SHOE OVERLOOK
ELEPHANT HILL
Elephant Canyon
Big Spring Cyn
Wooden Shoe Canyon
Orange Cliffs
Elaterite Basin
FLINT TRAIL
Ernie's Country
CATARACT CANYON
CHESLER PARK
Peekaboo Trail
Lost Canyon
Horse Canyon
Colorado River
Druid Arch
Canyonlands National Park
NEEDLES DISTRICT
GOLDEN STAIRS
THE GOLDEN STAIRS
Waterhole Flat
Castle Arch
Fortress Arch
Angel Arch
Davis Canyon
Bobbys Hole
Salt Creek Canyon
Lake Powell
Beef Basin
Lavender Canyon
0
5 mi
0
5 km

1
2
3
4

Canyon Style of these drawings has been credited to an ancient culture beginning at least 8,000 years ago and lasting until about 450 CE. Horseshoe Canyon also contains rock art left by the subsequent Fremont and Ancestral Puebloan people. The relationship between the earlier and later prehistoric groups hasn't been determined.

Call the **Hans Flat Ranger Station** (435/259-2652) to inquire about ranger-led hikes to the Great Gallery (Sat.-Sun. spring, summer, and fall); when staff are available, additional walks may be scheduled. In-shape hikers will have no trouble making the hike on their own, however. You'll need a full day to reach and explore this area.

River District

Long stretches of the Green and the Colorado Rivers make up this sector, and floating these rivers is one of the best ways to experience the inner depths of the park. Boaters can obtain helpful literature and advice from park rangers. Groups planning their own trip through **Cataract Canyon** need a permit. Flat-water permits are also required. River outfitters based in Moab offer trips ranging from half a day to several days.

Backcountry Exploration

A complex system of fees is charged for backcountry camping, 4WD exploration, and river rafting. Except for Island in the Sky Campground and Needles Campground, you'll need a **backcountry camping permit** ($5 pp plus $36 reservation fee for overnight backpacking, biking, or 4WD). **Day-use permits** (limited in quantity, $6 reservation fee) are required for vehicles, including motorcycles and bicycles, on the White Rim Road, Elephant Hill, and a couple of other areas. Each of the three major districts has a different policy for dispersed car camping, so check when you get your permit for the specifics. Backcountry permits are also needed for any trips with horses or stock; check with a ranger for details.

You can reserve backcountry permits in advance, and this is definitely advised for spring and fall travel to popular areas like Island in the Sky's White Rim or the Needles backcountry. Permit applications are available online (www.nps.gov/cany) and should be submitted at least two weeks before your trip. Phone reservations aren't accepted. Backroad travel is a popular method of exploring the park. Canyonlands has hundreds of miles of exceptionally scenic dirt roads, beloved by mountain bikers and off-roading enthusiasts alike. A 4WD vehicle with high clearance is recommended. Maneuvering tight turns can be difficult for large pickup trucks. Park regulations require all motorized vehicles to have proper registration and licensing for highway use, and all-terrain vehicles (ATVs) are prohibited in the park. Vehicles and bicycles must stay on existing roads to prevent damage to the delicate desert vegetation. Carry tools, extra fuel, water, and food in case you break down in a remote area.

Before heading out, talk with a ranger to register and to check current road conditions, which can change drastically from one day to the next. The rangers can also tell you where to seek help if you get stuck. Primitive campgrounds are available on most roads, but you'll need a backcountry permit from a ranger. Books on backcountry exploration include Charles Wells's *Guide to Moab, UT Backroads & 4-Wheel Drive Trails,* which includes Canyonlands, and Damian Fagan and David Williams's *A Naturalist's Guide to the White Rim Trail.*

One more thing about backcountry travel in Canyonlands: You may need to pack your poop out, because it's not always possible to dig a hole in the slickrock and desert conditions, and you can't leave your waste under a rock to decompose (decomposition is a very slow process out here). Bring the gear needed to do this if you're staying overnight.

1: Island in the Sky District **2:** Grand View Point Overlook **3:** Needles District **4:** Maze District at sunset

1
2

ISLAND IN THE SKY DISTRICT

High above the Colorado and Green Rivers, Island in the Sky is a 40-square-mile (104-sq-km) mesa accessed via a narrow land bridge just wide enough for the road, known as "the neck." Panoramic views of the park and southeastern Utah can be enjoyed from any point along the rim.

Short hiking trails lead to overlooks and to Mesa Arch, Aztec Butte, Whale Rock, Upheaval Dome, and other features. Longer trails make steep, strenuous descents from the Island to White Rim Road below. Elevations on the Island average about 6,000 feet (1,830 m).

Although much of the rock within Canyonlands is not suitable for climbing, there are some routes in the Island in the Sky, including Taylor Canyon in the northwest corner of the park, which is reached by lengthy and rugged 4WD roads.

Bring water for all hiking, camping, and travel in Island in the Sky. During the summer, water is only available at the visitor center.

Sights

Shafer Canyon Overlook

Half a mile (0.8 km) past the visitor center is Shafer Canyon Overlook (on the left, just before crossing the neck). The overlook has incredible views down the canyon out to the twisting **Shafer Trail Road.** Originally a Native American route for accessing stored resources on the mesa top, this trail was built up in the early 1900s by cattle ranchers Frank and John Shafer to move stock between pastures. Uranium prospectors turned it into a 4WD road in the 1950s so they could reach their claims at the base of the cliffs. Shafer Trail Viewpoint, across the neck, provides another perspective 0.5 mile (0.8 km) farther on.

Grand View Point Overlook

Perhaps the most spectacular panorama from Island in the Sky, Grand View Point Overlook lies at the end of the main road, 1 mile (1.6 km) past the Grand View Picnic Area (12 mi/19.3 km south of the visitor center). Monument Basin lies directly below, with countless canyons, the Colorado River, the Needles, and mountain ranges in the distance. The Grand View Point Overlook is wheelchair-accessible, and the easy 1-mile (1.6-km) **Grand View Trail** continues past the end of the road to more vistas.

Return to the main road to explore more overlooks and geological curiosities in the western portion of Island in the Sky.

Green River Overlook

Just west of the main junction on a paved road, wheelchair-accessible Green River Overlook beholds Soda Springs Basin and part of the Green River (deeply entrenched in Stillwater Canyon). The small Island in the Sky Campground is on the way to the overlook.

Upheaval Dome

At the end of the road, 5.3 miles (8.5 km) northwest of the junction (just over 11 mi/17.7 km from the visitor center), is **Upheaval Dome.** This geologic oddity is a fantastically deformed pile of rock sprawled across a crater about 3 miles (4.8 km) wide and 1,200 feet (366 m) deep. For many years, Upheaval Dome has kept geologists busy trying to figure out its origins. They once assumed that salt of the Paradox Formation pushed the rock layers upward to form the dome. Now, however, strong evidence suggests that a meteorite impact created the structure.

The surrounding ring depression, caused by collapse, and the convergence of rock layers upward toward the center correspond precisely to known meteorite impact structures. Shatter cones and microscopic analysis also indicate an impact origin. When the meteorite struck, sometime in the last 150 million years, it formed a crater up to 5 miles (8 km) across. Erosion removed some of the overlying rock—perhaps as much as a vertical mile (1.6

1: Horseshoe Canyon Unit **2:** the Great Gallery

1
2
3
4

km). The underlying salt may have played a role in uplifting the central section.

The easy **Crater View Trail** leads to overlooks on the rim of Upheaval Dome; the first viewpoint is 0.5 mile (0.8 km) round-trip, and the second is 1 mile (1.6 km) round-trip. There's also a small **picnic area** here.

Scenic Drives

White Rim Road

This driving adventure follows the White Rim below the sheer cliffs of Island in the Sky. A close look at the light-colored surface reveals ripple marks and cross beds laid down near an ancient coastline. The plateau's east side is about 800 feet (244 m) above the Colorado River. On the west side, the plateau meets the bank of the Green River. White Rim sandstone forms the distinctive plateau crossed on the drive.

Travel along the winding road presents a constantly changing panorama of rock, canyons, river, and sky. Keep an eye out for desert bighorn sheep. You'll see all three levels of Island in the Sky District, from the high plateaus to the White Rim to the rivers.

Only 4WD vehicles with high clearance can make the trip. With the proper vehicle, driving is mostly easy but slow and winding; a few steep or rough sections must be negotiated. The 100-mile (161-km) trip takes 2 or 3 days. Allow an extra day to travel all the road spurs. Access points are Shafer Trail Road (from near Island in the Sky), as well as Potash Road (Hwy. 279 from Moab) to the east and Mineral Bottom Road to the west.

Overnight drivers must obtain **reservations** and a **backcountry permit** ($5 pp plus $36 reservation fee) for the White Rim campsites from the Island in the Sky Visitor Center. Find applications online (www.nps.gov/cany); return the completed application at least two weeks before your planned trip. You can't reserve by phone, but you can call with questions (435/259-4351, 8am-noon Mon.-Fri.). Demand exceeds supply during the popular spring and autumn, when you should make reservations as far in advance as possible. No services or developed water sources exist anywhere on the drive, so be sure to have plenty of fuel and water.

1: Cataract Canyon 2: switchbacks on Shafer Trail 3: a hiker heads to the cusp of Shafer Canyon Overlook 4: Upheaval Dome

★ Shafer Trail Road

This 19.3-mile (31-km) challenging drive descends from the Island's mesa top via a long-traveled path—first a Native American route, then a cattle trail, later a uranium mining road, and now a recreational thrill. Considered the first section of White Rim Road, Shafer Trail Road connects the Island's mesa top with the rest of White Rim Road and Potash Road. You can drive it in either direction, depending on whether you'd rather gain or lose 1,500 vertical feet (457 m), or do it as a round-trip drive. Plan about an hour for a one-way trip.

High-clearance 4WD vehicles are required. Drive cautiously and remember that vehicles headed uphill have right of way. This is also a fun mountain bike ride if you're up for the challenge, even if you don't plan to continue on White Rim. Road conditions can vary considerably, so contact a ranger beforehand.

Hiking

Neck Springs Trail

Distance: *5.8-mile (9.3-km) loop*
Duration: *3-4 hours*
Elevation gain: *300 feet (91 m)*
Effort: *moderate*
Trailhead: *Shafer Canyon Overlook*

The trail begins near the Shafer Canyon Overlook and loops down Taylor Canyon to Neck and Cabin Springs, formerly used by ranchers (look for the remains of the old cowboy cabin near Cabin Springs). It then climbs back to Island in the Sky Road at a second trailhead 0.5 mile (0.8 km) south of the start. Water at the springs supports maidenhair ferns and other plants. Also watch for birds and wildlife attracted to this spot. Bring water, as the springs are not potable.

☆ Bikepacking White Rim Road

cyclists descend Shafer Trail to White Rim Road

It's not only off-roading enthusiasts who take to the White Rim—mountain bikers love it too. One of the most popular bikepacking trips in Utah, White Rim Road involves 100 miles (161 km) of rugged pedaling and 6,000-7,500 feet (1,828-2,286 m) of elevation gain, depending on which way you ride it. It's a beautiful way to take in a long stretch of canyon country, with sublime viewpoints along the way, like at Monument Basin.

Technically speaking, this ride is moderate, though most still choose a mountain bike to handle the dirt and rocks. There are no sections of narrow single-track—it's all road—and there are no super-tight switchbacks. The challenges lie in loose terrain, steep grades, exposure, and the length of the ride, requiring excellent fitness—it's the very definition of a grind. Still, most choose to do this ride supported with an accompanying 4WD vehicle (a friend or a paid guide) to carry water, food, and camping gear.

It takes most cyclists 3-4 days to complete this dirt century (the term for a 100-mi/161-km ride). The permitting process for camping out at the backcountry campsites along the way is the same for vehicle drivers. This is a coveted experience in high season, so reserve permits and any outfitters and equipment you'll need well in advance.

Lathrop Trail

Distance: *10.5 miles (16.9 km) one-way to the Colorado River*

Duration: *overnight*

Elevation gain: *2,000 feet (610 m)*

Effort: *strenuous*

Trailhead: *1.3 miles (2.1 km) past the neck, on the left*

This is the only marked hiking route going all the way from Island in the Sky to the Colorado River. The first 3 miles (4.8 km) cross Gray's Pasture to the rim and fantastic vistas over the Colorado. From here, the trail descends steeply, dropping 1,600 feet (488 m) over 2.5 miles (4 km) to White Rim Road, a little less than 7 miles (11.3 km) from the trailhead. Part of this section follows an old mining road past several abandoned mines, all relics of the uranium boom. Don't enter the shafts; they're in danger of collapse and may contain poisonous gases.

From the mining area, the route descends through a wash to White Rim Road, follows the road a short distance south, then goes down Lathrop Canyon Road to the Colorado River, another 4 miles (6.4 km) and 500 vertical feet (152 m). The trail has little shade and can be very hot. Vehicular traffic may be encountered along the White Rim Road portion of the trail. For a long day hike of 13.6 miles (21.9 km) round-trip, turn around when you reach the White Rim Road and hike back up to the top of the mesa.

Mesa Arch Trail

Distance: *0.25 mile (0.4 km) one-way*
Duration: *15 minutes*
Elevation gain: *80 feet (24 m)*
Effort: *easy*
Trailhead: *5.5 miles (8.9 km) from the neck, on the left*

This easy trail leads to a spectacular arch on the mesa rim. On the way, the trail crosses arid grasslands and scattered juniper trees. The rather barren, undramatic trail climbs gently until it suddenly descends toward the edge of an 800-foot (244-m) precipice, topped by a sandstone arch. The arch frames views of rock formations below and the La Sal Mountains in the distance. Photographers come here to catch the sun or the moon rising through the arch.

Murphy Point Trail

Distance: *11-mile (17.7-km) loop*
Duration: *5-7 hours*
Elevation gain: *1,100 feet (335 m)*
Effort: *strenuous*
Trailhead: *Murphy Point*
Directions: *From the Upheaval Dome junction on the main park road, head 3 miles (4.8 km) south. Turn right onto a rough dirt road and follow it 1.7 miles (2.7 km) to Murphy Point.*

Murphy Point Trail starts as a jaunt across the mesa, then drops steeply from the rim down to White Rim Road. This strenuous route forks partway down; one branch follows Murphy Hogback (a ridge) and the other follows a wash to the road 1 mile (1.6 km) south of the campground.

Aztec Butte Trail

Distance: *1 mile (1.6 km) one-way*
Duration: *1.5 hours*
Elevation gain: *200 feet (61 m)*
Effort: *moderate*
Trailhead: *Aztec Butte parking area, 1 mile (1.6 km) northwest of the road junction on Upheaval Dome Road*

It's a bit of a haul up the slickrock to the top of this sandstone butte, but once you get here, you'll be rewarded with a good view of the Island and Taylor Canyon. Atop the butte, a

Mesa Arch

loop trail passes several Ancestral Puebloan granaries—among the few archaeological sites in Island in the Sky.

Whale Rock Trail

Distance: *0.5 mile (0.8 km) one-way*
Duration: *1 hour*
Elevation gain: *100 feet (30 m)*
Effort: *easy-moderate*
Trailhead: *Upheaval Dome Road, on the right, 4.4 miles (7.1 km) northwest of the road junction*

A relatively easy trail climbs Whale Rock, a sandstone hump near the outer rim of Upheaval Dome. In a couple of places, you'll have to do some scrambling up slickrock, which is made easier and a bit less scary thanks to handrails. From the top of the rock, there are good views of the dome.

Campground

There is only one developed campground in the Island in the Sky District. **Willow Flat Campground** on Murphy Point Road has only 12 sites ($15), available on a first-come, first-served basis; sites tend to fill up in all seasons except winter. No water or services are available.

Camping is available just outside the park at **Dead Horse Point State Park** (reservations 800/322-3770, www.reserveamerica.com, $40 RV, $35 hike-in tent only, $140 yurt, plus $9 reservation fee), which is also very popular, so don't plan on getting a spot without reserving way ahead. There are also primitive Bureau of Land Management (BLM) campsites along Highway 313.

NEEDLES DISTRICT

Named for the area's distinctive sandstone spires, the Needles District showcases some of the finest rock sculptures in Canyonlands. Spires, arches, and monoliths appear in almost every direction. Prehistoric archaeological sites and rock art exist in greater variety and quantity here than elsewhere in the park. Perennial springs and streams bring greenery to the desert.

While scenic paved Highway 211 leads to the district, this area of the park has only about a dozen miles (19 km) of paved roads. Needles doesn't have a lot to offer travelers who are unwilling to get out of their vehicles and hike. However, it's the best section of the park for a wide variety of day hikes. Even a short hike opens up the landscape and leads to remarkable vistas and prehistoric sites.

The primary access road to the Needles District, Highway 211, also passes through the iconic rock climbing area of **Indian Creek,** now a unit of **Bears Ears National Monument.** Contact the BLM office in Monticello (365 N. Main St., Monticello, 435/587-1500) for information about this area.

Sights

Needles and Anticline Overlooks

Although outside the park, these viewpoints atop the high mesa east of Canyonlands National Park offer magnificent panoramas of the surrounding area. Part of the BLM's **Canyon Rims Recreation Area** (www.blm.gov), these easily accessed overlooks provide the kind of awe-inspiring vistas over the Needles District that would otherwise require a hike in the park. The turnoff for both overlooks is signed at milepost 93 on US 191, which is 32 miles (52 km) south of Moab and 7 miles (11.3 km) north of Highway 211. There are also two campgrounds along the access road.

For the **Needles Overlook,** follow the paved road for 22 miles (35 km) west to its end (turn left at the junction 15 mi/24 km in), where the BLM maintains a picnic area and interpretive exhibits. A fence protects visitors from the sheer cliffs that drop more than 1,000 feet (305 m). You can see much of Canyonlands and southeastern Utah. Look south for Six-Shooter Peaks and the Abajo Mountains; southwest for the Needles (thousands of spires); west for the confluence area of the Green and Colorado Rivers, the Maze District, and the Henry Mountains; northwest for the lazy bends of the Colorado River canyon and the sheer-walled mesas of Island in the Sky; north for the Book Cliffs; and northeast for the La Sal Mountains.

For the **Anticline Overlook,** from US 191, head 15 miles (24 km) west to the junction with the Needles road, then turn right and drive 17 miles (27 km) north on the well-maintained gravel road to the fenced overlook at road's end. You'll be standing 1,600 feet (488 m) above the Colorado River. The sweeping panorama over the canyons, the river (and the bright blue evaporation ponds at the potash factory outside Moab), and the twisted rocks of the Kane Creek Anticline is nearly as spectacular as that from Dead Horse Point, only 5.5 miles (8.9 km) west as the crow flies. Salt and other minerals of the Paradox Formation pushed up overlying rocks into the dome below. Down-cutting by the Colorado River has revealed the twisted rock layers. Look carefully at the northeast horizon to see an arch in the Windows Section of Arches National Park, 16 miles (26 km) away.

The BLM operates two campgrounds in the Canyon Rims Recreation Area. **Hatch Point Campground** (10 sites, May-mid-Oct., $20) has a quiet and scenic mesa-top setting just off the road to the Anticline Overlook, about 9 miles (14.5 km) north of the road junction. Closer to the highway in a rock amphitheater is **Windwhistle Campground** (May-mid-Oct., $20); it's 6 miles (9.7 km) west of US 191 on the paved road to Needles Overlook. Both are first-come, first-served, and no water is available at either.

Needles Outpost

The **Needles Outpost campground** (435/979-4007, https://needlesoutpost.com, Mar.-mid-Nov., tents or RVs $30, no hookups), just outside the park boundary, is a good place to stay if the campground in the park is full. A general store here has groceries, ice, gas, propane, showers (campers $3, noncampers $6), and basic camping supplies. Campsites have good privacy and great views of the park's spires. The turnoff from Highway 211 is 1 mile (1.6 km) before the Needles Visitor Center.

Scenic Drive

The main paved park road continues 6.5 miles (10.5 km) past the visitor center to **Big Spring Canyon Overlook.** On the way, you can stop at several nature trails or turn onto 4WD roads. The overlook takes in a view of slickrock-edged canyons dropping away toward the Colorado River.

Hiking

The Needles District includes about 60 miles (97 km) of backcountry trails. Many interconnect to provide all sorts of day-hike and overnight opportunities. Cairns mark the paths, and signs point the way at junctions.

You can normally find water in upper Elephant Canyon and canyons to the east in spring and early summer, although whatever remains is often stagnant by midsummer. Always ask rangers about water sources, and don't depend on their availability. Treat water from all sources, including springs, before drinking it. Chesler Park and other areas west of Elephant Canyon are very dry, so bring all your water. Mosquitoes, gnats, and deerflies can be pesky late spring-midsummer, especially in wetter places, so bring insect repellent.

To plan your trip, obtain the small hiking map available from the visitor center, or for longer and more in-depth journeys, procure the National Geographic-Trails Illustrated Needles District map or USGS topographic maps. Overnight backcountry hiking requires a **permit** ($5 pp plus $36 reservation fee). Permits become available 4 months in advance of each season and are available online (www.nps.gov/cany). Campers at sites in Chesler Park, Elephant Canyon, and Peekaboo are required to pack out their human waste.

Cave Spring Trail

Distance: *0.6 mile (1 km) round-trip*
Duration: *45 minutes*
Elevation gain: *50 feet (15 m)*
Effort: *easy*
Trailhead: *Cave Spring*

Don't miss the Cave Spring Trail, which

1
2

Pothole Ecosystems

At Canyonlands it's easy to be in awe of the deep canyons and big desert rivers. But the little details of Canyonlands geology and ecology are pretty wonderful, too. Consider the potholes: shallow depressions dusted with wind-blown dirt. These holes, which range from less than an inch to several feet deep, fill after rainstorms and bring entire little ecosystems to life.

Pothole dwellers must be able to survive long periods of dryness and then pack as much living as possible into the short wet periods. Some creatures, like the tadpole shrimp, live for only a couple of weeks. Others, like the spadefoot toad, hatch from drought-resistant eggs when water is present, quickly pass through the critical tadpole stage, then move onto dry land, returning to mate and lay eggs in potholes.

Although pothole dwellers are tough enough to survive in a dormant form during the long dry spells, most are very sensitive to sudden water-chemistry changes, temperature changes, sediment input, being stepped on, and being splashed out onto dry land. Humans should never use pothole water for swimming, bathing, or drinking, as this can drastically change the salinity or pH of a pool. Organisms are unable to adapt to these human-generated changes, which occur suddenly, unlike slow natural changes. While the desert pothole ecosystems may seem unimportant, they act as an indicator of the health of the larger ecosystems in which they occur.

introduces the geology and ecology of the park and leads to an old cowboy line camp. The second part of the hike is a good introduction to hiking on slickrock and using cairns to find your way. The loop goes clockwise, crossing some slickrock, and involves two ladders on steep sections. Native Americans first used these rock overhangs for shelter, and faint pictographs still decorate the walls. From the late 1800s until the park was established in 1964, cowboys used these open caves as a line camp. The National Park Service has recreated the line camp, just 50 yards in from the trailhead, with period furnishings and equipment. If you're not up for the full hike, or would rather not climb ladders, the cowboy camp and the pictographs are just a 5-minute walk from the trailhead.

Confluence Overlook Trail

Distance: *5.5 miles (8.9 km) one-way*
Duration: *5 hours*
Elevation gain: *1,250 feet (381 m)*
Effort: *moderate-strenuous*
Trailhead: *Big Spring Canyon Overlook*

The Confluence Overlook Trail begins at the end of the paved road and winds west to an overlook of the Green and Colorado Rivers 1,000 feet (305 m) below. The trail starts with some ups and downs, crossing Big Spring and Elephant Canyons, then following a 4WD road for a short distance. Much of the trail is through open country, so it can get quite hot. Higher points have good views of the Needles to the south. You might see rafts in the water or bighorn sheep on the cliffs. Except for a few short steep sections, this trail is level and fairly easy, though the length—11 miles (17.7 km) round-trip to the confluence—plus the hot sun can make it challenging. A very early start is recommended in summer; carry water even if you don't plan to go all the way. This enchanting country has lured many a hiker beyond their original goal.

Peekaboo Trail

Distance: *5 miles (8 km) one-way*
Duration: *5-6 hours*
Elevation gain: *550 feet (168 m)*
Effort: *strenuous*
Trailhead: *Wooden Shoe Arch trailhead*
Directions: *The road to Needles Campground and Elephant Hill is a left turn 2.7 miles (4.3 km) past the visitor center. The Wooden Shoe Arch trailhead is at the end of campground loop A.*

1: panorama from the Needles Overlook
2: mushroom-shaped rock in the Needles District

Peekaboo Trail winds southeast over rugged up-and-down terrain, including some steep sections of slickrock (best avoided when wet, icy, or covered with snow) and a couple of ladders. There's little shade, so carry water. The trail follows Wooden Shoe Canyon, climbs over a pass to Lost Canyon, then crosses more slickrock before descending to Peekaboo Campground on Salt Creek Road (accessible by 4WD vehicles). Look for Ancestral Puebloan granaries on the way and rock art at the campground. A rockslide took out Peekaboo Spring, which is still shown on some maps. Options on this trail include a turnoff south through Wooden Shoe or Lost Canyon to make a loop of 8.75 miles (14.1 km) or more.

Lost Canyon Trail

Distance: *3.25 miles (5.2 km) one-way*
Duration: *4-5 hours*
Elevation gain: *360 feet (110 m)*
Effort: *moderate-strenuous*
Trailhead: *Wooden Shoe Arch trailhead*
Directions: *The road to Needles Campground and Elephant Hill is a left turn 2.7 miles (4.3 km) past the visitor center. The Wooden Shoe Arch trailhead is at the end of campground loop A.*

Lost Canyon Trail is reached via Peekaboo or Wooden Shoe Canyon Trails and makes a loop with them. Lost Canyon is surprisingly lush, and you may need to wade through water. Most of the trail is in the wash bottom, except for a section of slickrock to Wooden Shoe Canyon.

Big Spring Canyon Trail

Distance: *3.75 miles (6 km) one-way*
Duration: *4 hours*
Elevation gain: *370 feet (113 m)*
Effort: *moderate-strenuous*
Trailhead: *Wooden Shoe Arch trailhead*
Directions: *The road to Needles Campground and Elephant Hill is a left turn 2.7 miles (4.3 km) past the visitor center. The Wooden Shoe Arch trailhead is at the end of campground loop A.*

Big Spring Canyon Trail crosses an outcrop of slickrock from the trailhead, then follows the canyon bottom to the head of the canyon. It's a lovely springtime hike with lots of flowers, including the fragrant cliffrose. Except in summer, you can usually find intermittent water along the way. At canyon's end, a steep slickrock climb leads to Wooden Shoe Canyon Trail and back to the trailhead for a 7.5-mile (12-km) loop. Another possibility is to turn southwest to the head of Wooden Shoe Canyon, then hike over a saddle to Elephant Canyon, for a 10.5-mile (16.9-km) loop.

Chesler Park

Distance: *3 miles (4.8 km) one-way*
Duration: *3-4 hours*
Elevation gain: *920 feet (280 m)*
Effort: *moderate*
Trailhead: *Elephant Hill parking area, or Wooden Shoe Arch trailhead (increases the round-trip distance by 2 mi/3.2 km)*
Directions: *Drive west 3 miles (4.8 km) past the Needles Campground turnoff (on passable dirt roads) to the Elephant Hill picnic area and trailhead at the base of Elephant Hill.*

The Elephant Hill parking area doesn't always inspire confidence: Sounds of racing engines can often be heard from above as vehicles attempt the difficult 4WD road that begins just past the picnic area. However, the noise quickly fades as you hit the trail of this favorite hiking destination. A lovely desert meadow contrasts with the red and white spires that give the Needles District its name. An old cowboy line camp is on the west side of the rock island in the center of the park. The trail winds through sand and slickrock before ascending a small pass through the Needles to Chesler Park. Once inside, you can take the Chesler Park Loop Trail (5 mi/8.1 km) completely around the park. The loop includes the unusual 0.5-mile (0.8-km) Joint Trail, which follows the bottom of a very narrow crack. Camping in Chesler Park is restricted to certain areas; check with a ranger.

Druid Arch

Distance: *5.5 miles (8.9 km) one-way*
Duration: *5-7 hours*

Elevation gain: *1,000 feet (305 m)*
Effort: *strenuous*
Trailhead: *Elephant Hill parking area, or Wooden Shoe Arch trailhead (increases the round-trip distance by 2 mi/3.2 km)*
Directions: *Drive west 3 miles (4.8 km) past the Needles Campground turnoff (on passable dirt roads) to the Elephant Hill picnic area and trailhead at the base of Elephant Hill.*

Druid Arch reminds many people of the massive slabs at Stonehenge in England, which are popularly associated with the druids. Follow the Chesler Park Trail 2 miles (3.2 km) to Elephant Canyon, turn up the canyon for 3.5 miles (5.6 km), and then make a steep 0.25-mile (0.4-km) climb, which includes a ladder and some scrambling, to the arch. Upper Elephant Canyon has seasonal water but is closed to camping.

Mountain Biking and 4WD Exploration

Visitors with mountain or gravel bicycles or 4WD vehicles can explore the many backcountry roads. More than 50 miles (81 km) of challenging roads link primitive campsites, remote trailheads, and sites with ancient cultural remnants. Some roads in the Needles District are rugged and require previous experience handling 4WD vehicles on steep inclines and in deep sand. Keep in mind that towing charges from here commonly run over $1,000.

The best route for mountain bikers is the 7-mile-long (11.3-km) Colorado Overlook Road, which starts near the visitor center. Although very steep for the first stretch and busy with 4WD vehicles spinning their wheels on the hill, Elephant Hill Road is another good bet, with just a few sandy parts. Start here and do a combination ride and hike to the Confluence Overlook. It's about 8 miles (12.9 km) from the Elephant Hill parking area to the confluence. The final 0.5 mile (0.8 km) is on a trail, so you'll have to lock up your bike and walk this last bit. Horse Canyon and Lavender Canyon are too sandy for pleasant biking.

All motor vehicles and bicycles must have a **day-use permit** ($6 fee) and remain on designated roads. Overnight backcountry trips with bicycles or motor vehicles require a permit ($5 pp plus $36 reservation fee).

Davis and Lavender Canyons

Accessed via Davis Canyon Road off Highway 211, both these canyons offer great scenery, arches, and Native American historic sites for those with high-clearance vehicles. Davis is about 20 miles (32 km) round-trip, while sandy Lavender Canyon is about 26 miles (42 km) round-trip. Allow plenty of time in either canyon to take in the scenery and many inviting side canyons. You can camp on BLM land just outside the park boundaries, but not in the park itself.

Colorado River Overlook 4WD Road

This popular route begins beside the visitor center and follows Salt Creek to Lower Jump Overlook before bouncing across slickrock to a view of the Colorado River, upstream from the confluence. Driving is mostly easy-moderate, until the last very rough 1.5 miles (2.4 km). Round-trip distance is 14 miles (22.5 km). This is also a good road for biking.

Elephant Hill 4WD Road

This rugged backcountry road begins 3 miles (4.8 km) past the Needles Campground turnoff. Only experienced drivers with sturdy vehicles should attempt the extremely rough and steep climb up Elephant Hill (coming up the back side of Elephant Hill is even worse). The loop is about 10 miles (16.1 km) round-trip.

Connecting roads go to the Confluence Overlook trailhead (the viewpoint is 1 mi/1.6 km round-trip on foot), the Joint trailhead (Chesler Park is 2 mi/3.2 km round-trip on foot), and several canyons. Some road sections on the loop are one-way. In addition to Elephant Hill, a few other difficult spots must be negotiated. The parallel canyons in this area are grabens—depressed slabs of earth—caused by faulting, where a layer of salt has shifted deep underground.

This area can also be reached by a long route south of the park using Cottonwood Canyon and Beef Basin Road from Highway 211, about 60 miles (97 km) one-way. You'll enjoy spectacular vistas from the Abajo Highlands. Two very steep descents from Pappys Pasture into Bobbys Hole effectively make this section one-way. It's possible to travel from Elephant Hill up Bobbys Hole, but much more difficult than going the other way, and it may require hours of road-building. The Bobbys Hole route may be impassable at times; ask about conditions at the BLM office in Monticello or at the Needles Visitor Center.

Campgrounds

The **Needles Campground** (Loop B only reservable Mar. 15-June and Sept.-Oct., reservations advised, year-round, $20) is about 6 miles (9.7 km) from the visitor center. It has water and 26 sites (two of which are accessible), with many snuggled under the slickrock. RVs must be less than 28 feet (8.5 m) long. Rangers present evening programs (spring-autumn) at the campfire circle on Loop A.

If you can't find a space at the Needles Campground—a common occurrence in spring and fall—the private campground at **Needles Outpost** (435/979-4007, https://needlesoutpost.com, Mar.-mid-Nov., tents and RVs $30, no hookups, showers $3), just outside the park entrance, is a good alternative.

Nearby BLM land also offers a number of places to camp. A string of campsites along **Lockhart Basin Road** are convenient and inexpensive. Lockhart Basin Road heads north from Highway 211 about 5 miles (8 km) east of the entrance to the Needles District. **Hamburger Rock Campground** (no water, $15) is about 1 mile (1.6 km) up the road. North of Hamburger Rock, camping is dispersed, with many small campsites (no water, free) at turnoffs from the road. Not surprisingly, the road gets rougher the farther north you travel. Beyond Indian Creek Falls, it's best to have 4WD. These campsites are very popular with climbers at Indian Creek.

There are two first-come, first-served campgrounds ($20) in the Canyon Rims Recreation Area (www.blm.gov). **Windwhistle Campground,** backed by cliffs to the south, has fine views to the north and a nature trail; follow the main road from US 191 for 6 miles (9.7 km) and turn left. In a piñon-juniper woodland at **Hatch Point Campground,** you can enjoy views to the north. Go 24 miles (39 km) in on the paved and gravel roads toward Anticline Overlook, then turn right and continue 1 mile (1.6 km). Bring your own water.

MAZE DISTRICT

Only adventurous and experienced travelers will want to visit this rugged land west of the Green and Colorado Rivers. To explore the least-visited district of Canyonlands, you'll need a high-clearance, low gear-range 4WD vehicle, a burly bike, a horse, or your own two feet to get around. Most visitors spend at least 3 days in the district. The National Park Service plans to keep this area primitive. If you can't come overland, an airplane flight provides the only easy way to see it.

The names of erosional forms describe the landscape—Orange Cliffs, Golden Stairs, the Fins, Land of Standing Rocks, Lizard Rock, the Doll House, Chocolate Drops, the Maze, and Jasper Canyon. The many-fingered canyons of the Maze give the district its name. It's not a true maze, but the canyons lend that impression. It is extremely important to have a high-quality map before entering this part of Canyonlands. National Geographic-Trails Illustrated makes a good one, called *Canyonlands National Park Maze District, NE Glen Canyon NRA.*

Sights

North Point

Hans Flat Ranger Station and this peninsula, which reaches out to the east and north, are at an elevation of about 6,400 feet (1,950 m). Panoramas from North Point take in the vastness of Canyonlands, including the

Maze, Needles, and Island in the Sky. From **Millard Canyon Overlook,** just 0.9 mile (1.4 km) past the ranger station, you can see arches, Cleopatra's Chair, and features as distant as the La Sal Mountains and Book Cliffs. For the best views, drive out to Panorama Point, about 10.5 miles (16.9 km) one-way from the ranger station. A spur road to the left goes 2 miles (3.2 km) to Cleopatra's Chair, a massive sandstone monolith and area landmark.

Land of Standing Rocks

Here in the heart of the Maze District, strangely shaped spires stand guard over myriad canyons. Six camping areas offer scenic places to stay (**permit** required). Hikers have a choice of many ridge and canyon routes from the 4WD road, a trail to a confluence overlook, and a trail that descends to the Colorado River near Cataract Canyon.

Getting to the Land of Standing Rocks takes careful driving, especially on a 3-mile (4.8-km) stretch above Teapot Canyon. The many washes and small canyon crossings make for slow going. Short-wheelbase vehicles have the easiest time, of course. The turnoff for Land of Standing Rocks Road is 6.6 miles (10.6 km) from the junction at the bottom of the Flint Trail via a wash shortcut (add about 3 mi/4.8 km if driving via the four-way intersection). The lower end of the Golden Stairs foot trail is 7.8 miles (12.6 km) in. The western end of the **Ernies Country route trailhead** is 8.6 miles (13.8 km) in. **The Wall** is 12.7 miles (20.4 km) in. **Chimney Rock** is 15.7 miles (25 km) in. And the **Doll House** is 19 miles (31 km) in, at the end of the road. Tall, rounded spires near the end of the road reminded early visitors of dolls, hence the name, and it's a great place to explore or access nearby trails.

If you drive from the south on Hite-Orange Cliffs Road, stop at the self-registration stand at the four-way intersection, about 31 miles (50 km) in from Highway 95; you can write your own permit for overnights.

Hiking

Maze Overlook Trail

Distance: *3 miles (4.8 km) one-way (to Harvest Scene)*
Duration: *3-4 hours*
Elevation gain: *550 feet (168 m)*
Effort: *strenuous*
Trailhead: *at the end of the road in the Maze District*

At the edge of the sinuous canyons of the Maze, the Maze Overlook Trail drops 1 mile (1.6 km) into the South Fork of Horse Canyon. Bring a 25-foot-long (8-m) rope to lower backpacks through one difficult section. Once in the canyon, you can walk around the Harvest Scene, a group of prehistoric pictographs, or do a variety of day hikes or backpacking trips. These canyons have water in some places, but check with the ranger when you get your permit. At least four routes connect with the 4WD road in the Land of Standing Rocks, shown on the Trails Illustrated map. Hikers can also climb Petes Mesa from the canyons or head downstream to explore Horse Canyon, but a dry fall blocks access to the Green River. You can stay at primitive camping areas (**permit** required) and enjoy the views.

The Golden Stairs

Distance: *2 miles (3.2 km) one-way*
Duration: *3 hours*
Elevation gain: *800 feet (244 m)*
Effort: *moderate*
Trailhead: *bottom of Flint Trail, at Golden Stairs camping area*
Directions: *Drive the challenging Flint Trail, a 4WD route, to its bottom. The top of the Golden Stairs is 2 miles (3.2 km) east of the road junction at the bottom of the Flint Trail.*

Hikers can descend this steep, exposed foot trail to the Land of Standing Rocks Road in a fraction of the time it takes for drivers to follow the roads. The trail offers good views of Ernies Country, the vast secluded southern area of the Maze District (no one seems to know who Ernie was, by the way). The eponymous stairs are not actual steps carved into rock, but a series of natural ledges.

Spanish Bottom Trail

Distance: *1.2 miles (1.9 km) one-way*
Duration: *3 hours*
Elevation gain: *1,260 feet (384 m)*
Effort: *strenuous*
Trailhead: *Doll House, near Camp 1, just before the end of the Land of Standing Rocks Road*

This trail drops steeply to Spanish Bottom beside the Colorado River; a thin trail leads downstream into Cataract Canyon and the first of a long series of rapids. **Surprise Valley Overlook Trail** branches to the right off the Spanish Bottom Trail after about 300 feet (91 m) and winds south past some figurine-esque hoodoos to a T junction—turn right for views of Surprise Valley, Cataract Canyon, and beyond. The trail ends at some well-preserved granaries, after 1.5 miles (2.4 km) one-way. From the same trailhead, the **Colorado-Green River Overlook Trail** heads north 5 miles (8 km) one-way from the Doll House to a viewpoint of the confluence.

4WD Exploration

Maze Overlook Road, Queen Anne's Bottom Road, Flint Trail, and a number of other narrow, rough 4WD roads connect the Hans Flat area with the Maze Overlook, Doll House, and other destinations below. The road, driver, and vehicle should all be in good condition before attempting this route. Winter snow and mud close the road late December-March, as can rainstorms anytime. Check conditions with a ranger before you go. If you're starting from the top, stop at the signed overlook just before the descent to scout for vehicles headed up (the Flint Trail has very few places to pass). The top of the Flint Trail is 14 miles (22.5 km) south of Hans Flat Ranger Station. At the bottom, 2.8 nervous miles (4.5 km) later, you can turn left and go 2 miles (3.2 km) to the Golden Stairs trailhead or 12.7 miles (20.4 km) to the Maze Overlook; keep straight 28 miles (45 km) to the Doll House or 39 miles (63 km) to Highway 95.

Campgrounds

The Maze District has 17 camping areas, each with 1-3 campsites (www.nps.gov/cany/planyourvisit/mazeroads.htm). Each site can accommodate up to nine people and three vehicles. As in the rest of the park, only designated sites can be used for vehicle camping. You don't need a permit to camp in the adjacent Glen Canyon NRA or BLM land.

Information and Services

Maze District explorers need a **backcountry permit** ($5 pp plus $36 reservation fee on www.recreation.gov) for overnight trips. Permits must be picked up in person at the Hans Flat Ranger Station (the Maze's visitor center, 46 miles off Highway 24 east of Hanksville, 435/719-2218, 8am-4:30pm daily year-round). Note that a backcountry permit in this district is not a reservation—you may have to share a site with someone else, especially in the popular spring months.

There are no developed sources of water in the Maze District. Hikers can get water from springs in some canyons (check with a ranger to find out which are flowing) or from the rivers; purify all water before drinking.

The National Geographic-Trails Illustrated topographic map of the Maze District describes and shows the few roads and trails here, as well as some routes and springs. Hikers experienced in desert and canyon travel can take off on cross-country routes, which are either unmarked or sparsely cairned.

Extra care and preparation must be taken for travel in both Glen Canyon NRA and the Maze. Always ask rangers for current conditions. Be sure to leave an itinerary with someone reliable who can contact rangers if you're overdue returning. Unless the rangers know where to look for you, a rescue could take weeks.

Getting There

Dirt roads to the **Hans Flat Ranger Station** (435/719-2218, 8am-4:30pm daily) and Maze District branch off from Highway 24 (across from the Goblin Valley State Park turnoff) and Highway 95. The longer, bumpier way in is the usually unmarked **4WD Hite-Orange Cliffs Road** between Dirty Devil and Hite Bridges at Lake Powell. From the turnoff at Highway 95, it's 54 miles (87 km) to the Hans Flat Ranger Station via the Flint Trail. The easiest way in is the graded (although sometimes badly corrugated) 46-mile (74-km) road from **Highway 24,** which takes you to Hans Flat Ranger Station and other areas near, but not actually in, the Maze District. From the ranger station, it takes at least 3 hours of skillful four-wheeling to drive into the canyons of the Maze.

One other way of getting to the Maze District is by river. **Tex's Riverways** (435/259-5101 or 877/662-2839, www.texsriverways.com, about $200 pp) can arrange a jet-boat shuttle on the Colorado River from Moab to Spanish Bottom. After the 2-hour boat ride, it's 1,260 vertical feet (384 m) uphill in a little over 1 mile (1.6 km) to the Doll House via the Spanish Bottom Trail.

HORSESHOE CANYON UNIT

This canyon, a separate section of Canyonlands National Park, contains exceptional prehistoric rock art. Ghostly life-size pictographs in the Great Gallery provide an intriguing look into the past. Archaeologists think that the images had religious importance, although the meaning of the figures remains unknown. The Barrier Canyon Style of these drawings has been credited to an ancient culture beginning at least 8,000 years ago and lasting until about 450 CE. Horseshoe Canyon also contains rock art left by the subsequent Fremont and Ancestral Puebloan peoples. The relationship between the earlier and later prehistoric groups hasn't been determined.

Call the **Hans Flat Ranger Station** (435/259-2652) to inquire about ranger-led hikes to the Great Gallery (Sat.-Sun. spring-fall); when staff are available, additional walks may be scheduled. In-shape hikers will have no trouble making the hike on their own, however.

Hiking

Great Gallery Trail

Distance: *3.5 miles (5.6 km) one-way*
Duration: *4-6 hours*
Elevation gain: *800 feet (244 m)*
Effort: *moderate-strenuous*
Trailhead: *parking area on the canyon's west rim*

From the rim and parking area, the trail descends 800 feet (244 m) in 1 mile (1.6 km) on an old 4WD road, which is now closed to vehicles. At the bottom, turn right and go 2 miles (3.2 km) upstream to the Great Gallery. The sandy canyon floor is mostly level; trees provide shade in some areas.

Look for other rock art along the canyon walls on the way to the Great Gallery. Take care not to touch any of the drawings because they're extremely delicate—the oil from your hands will remove the paints.

Information and Services

Horseshoe Canyon also offers pleasant scenery and spring wildflowers. Carry plenty of water. Neither camping nor pets are allowed, although horses are okay. Camping is permitted on the rim. Contact the **Hans Flat Ranger Station** (435/259-2652) or the **Moab Information Center** (435/259-8825 or 800/635-6622) for road and trail conditions.

Getting There

Horseshoe Canyon is a noncontiguous unit of Canyonlands and requires quite a bit of driving to reach. While it's only around 10 miles (16.1 km) due west of the northern part of Island in the Sky District as the crow flies, it takes 4.5 hours of driving over 170 miles (274 km) to get here from the Island in the Sky Visitor Center. The dirt access road (signed) across from the entrance to Goblin Valley State Park turns east from Highway 24 between Hanksville (14 mi/22.5 km south) and I-70 exit 149 (19 mi/31 km north). Travel 30 miles (48 km) east to Horseshoe Canyon, keeping left at the Hans Flat Ranger Station and at the Horseshoe Canyon turnoff 25 miles (40 km) in. In good weather, the road is passable by most cars, though it has many washboard sections and blowing sand can be a hazard. If you have questions, call the Hans Flat Ranger Station (435/259-2652) or another Canyonlands visitor center. Allow an hour to make the journey in from Highway 24 to the Great Gallery trailhead.

Horseshoe Canyon can also be reached via primitive roads from the east. A 4WD road runs north 21 miles (34 km) from the Maze's Hans Flat Ranger Station and drops steeply into the canyon from the east side. The descent on this road is so rough that most people prefer to park on the rim and hike the last mile (1.6 km) of road. A vehicle barricade prevents driving right up to the rock-art panel, but the 1.5-mile (2.4-km) walk is easy.

RIVER DISTRICT

The River District is the name of the administrative unit of the park that oversees conservation and recreation for the Green and Colorado Rivers.

Generally speaking, there are two boating experiences on offer here. The first is relatively gentle paddling and rafting on the Colorado and Green Rivers above their confluence. The second is white-water rafting the Class III-V rapids of the Colorado River through Cataract Canyon.

While rafting and canoeing enthusiasts can plan their own trips to any section of these rivers, the vast majority of people sign on with outfitters, often located in Moab, and let them do the planning and work. Do-it-yourselfers must start with the knowledge that permits are required for most trips and are usually not easily procured. Because these rivers flow through rugged and remote canyons, most trips involve multiple days and challenging logistics.

No matter how you execute a trip through the River District, there are several things to consider beforehand. During late summer and fall, sandbars are usually plentiful and make ideal camps. However, during high water periods in spring and early summer, camps can be difficult to find, since there are no designated campsites along the rivers. There is also no access to potable water along the river, so river-runners either need to bring along their own water or purify river water.

You'll also need to pack in your own food. While it's possible to fish in the Green and Colorado Rivers, these desert rivers don't offer much in the way of species that most people consider edible.

The park requires all river-runners to pack out their solid human waste. Specially

the Green River snaking through Canyonlands

designed portable toilets that fit into rafts and canoes can be rented from most outfitters in Moab.

Rafting

Above the Confluence

The Green and Colorado Rivers flow smoothly through their canyons above the confluence of the two rivers. Almost any shallow-draft boat can navigate these waters: Canoes, kayaks, rafts, and powerboats are commonly used. Advanced planning is required because of the remoteness of the canyons and the scarcity of river access points. No campgrounds, supplies, or other facilities exist past Moab for the Colorado River or the town of Green River for the Green River. All river-runners must follow park regulations, which include carrying life jackets, using a fire pan for fires, and packing out all garbage and solid human waste. The river flow on both the Colorado and the Green Rivers averages a gentle 2-4 mph (3-6 km/h) (7-10 mph/11-16 km/h at high water). Boaters typically do 20 miles (32 km) per day in canoes and 15 miles (24 km) per day on rafts.

The Colorado has one modest rapid, called the Slide (1.5 mi/2.4 km above the confluence), where rocks constrict the river to one-third of its normal width. This rapid is roughest during high water levels in May-June. This is the only difficulty on the 64 river miles (103 km) from Moab. Inexperienced canoeists and rafters can portage around the Slide. The most popular launch points on the Colorado are the Moab Dock (just upstream from the US 191 bridge near town) and the Potash Dock (17 mi/27 km downriver on Potash Rd./Hwy. 279).

On the Green River, boaters at low water need to watch for rocky areas at the mouth of Millard Canyon (33.5 mi/54 km above the confluence, where a rock bar extends across the river) and at the mouth of Horse Canyon (14.5 mi/23.3 km above the confluence, where a rock and gravel bar on the right leaves only a narrow channel on the left side). The trip from the town of Green River through Labyrinth and Stillwater Canyons is 120 miles (193 km).

★ Cataract Canyon

The Colorado River enters Cataract Canyon at the confluence and picks up speed. The rapids begin 4 miles (6.4 km) downstream and extend for the next 14 miles (22.5 km) to Lake Powell. Especially in spring, the 26 or more rapids give a wild ride equal to the best in the Grand Canyon. The current zips along at up to 16 mph (26 km/h) and forms waves more than 7 feet (2.1 m) high. When the excitement dies down, boaters have a 34-mile (55-km) trip across Lake Powell to Hite Marina. Most people either carry a motor or arrange for a powerboat to pick them up. Depending on water levels, which can vary wildly from year to year, the dynamics of this trip and the optimal take-out point can change. Depending on how much motoring is done, the trip through Cataract Canyon takes 2-5 days.

Outfitters

Outfitters must be authorized by the National Park Service to operate in Canyonlands. For a complete list, visit the park website (www.nps.gov/cany). Most guides are based in Moab and concentrate on river trips, but some can take you on combined adventures that include mountain biking and/or vehicle-supported tours of the White Rim 4WD Trail. Here are a few options:

- **Adrift Adventures** (378 N. Main St., Moab, 435/259-8594 or 800/874-4483, www.adrift.net)
- **Sheri Griffith Expeditions** (435/259-8229 or 800/332-2439, www.griffithexp.com)
- **Tag-A-Long Expeditions** (452 N. Main St., Moab, 435/259-8594 or 800/453-3292, http://tagalong.com)
- **Western River Expeditions** (225 S. Main St., Moab, 801/942-6669 or 866/904-1163, www.westernriver.com)

Information and Services

National park rangers require boaters to have proper equipment and to obtain a **permit** (overnight river permits $25 pp plus $36 reservation fee; day-use river permits $10 pp plus $6 reservation fee). Permits become available 4 months in advance of each rafting season, usually in mid-June and mid-December, and close 2 days before any given launch date.

Permits are available online (www.recreation.gov), at the **Moab National Park Service office** (2282 SW Resource Blvd., Moab, 435/719-2313, 8am-4pm Mon.-Fri.), at the **Canyonlands National Park Headquarters** (2282 SW Resource Blvd., Moab, 435/719-2313, 8am-4pm Mon.-Fri.), or at any Canyonlands visitor center. For more details about river permits, contact the **Canyonlands River Unit of the National Park Service** (435/259-3911, www.nps.gov/cany).

To raft stretches of the river that lie outside the Canyonlands National Park boundaries, permits are available online (www.recreation.gov) or at the **BLM office** (82 Dogwood Ave., Moab, 435/259-2100, 8am-4:30pm Mon.-Fri.), **Green River State Park** in Green River, or the **John Wesley Powell River History Museum** (1765 E. Main St., Green River, 435/564-3427, 9am-5pm Mon.-Sat.).

Information on boating the Green and Colorado Rivers is available from the National Park Service's Moab office (435/719-2313). Bill and Buzz Belknap's *Canyonlands River Guide* has river logs and detail maps covering the Green River below the town of Green River and the Colorado River from the upper end of Westwater Canyon to Lake Powell.

Getting There

Launch points include Green River State Park (in the town of Green River) and Mineral Canyon (52 mi/84 km above the confluence), reached on fair-weather BLM Road 129 from Highway 313. Boaters who launch at Green River State Park pass through Labyrinth Canyon; a free interagency permit is required for travel along this stretch of the river.

No roads go to the confluence. The easiest return to civilization for nonmotorized craft is a pickup by jet boat from Moab by **Tex's Riverways** (435/259-5101, www.texsriverways.com). A far more difficult way out is hiking either of two trails just above the Cataract Canyon rapids to 4WD roads on the rim. Don't plan to attempt this unless you're a very strong hiker and have a packable watercraft.

Southeast Utah

Round out your southern Utah trip with a visit

to one of our nation's newest national monuments: Bears Ears. Brimming with Ancestral Puebloan archaeological sites, remarkable rock-art panels, soaring natural bridges, and deep river canyons, this national monument is as compelling from a cultural perspective as it is from a recreational one. "Bears Ears is a living landscape," Deb Haaland, the first Native American cabinet secretary, says. "When I've been there, I've felt the warmth and joy of ancestors who have cared for this special place since time immemorial."

Named for two buttes resembling the ears of a bear, the monument was established in 2016 by the Obama administration, reduced drastically (by 85 percent) by the Trump administration a year later, then

Highlights

Look for ★ to find recommended sights, activities, dining, and lodging.

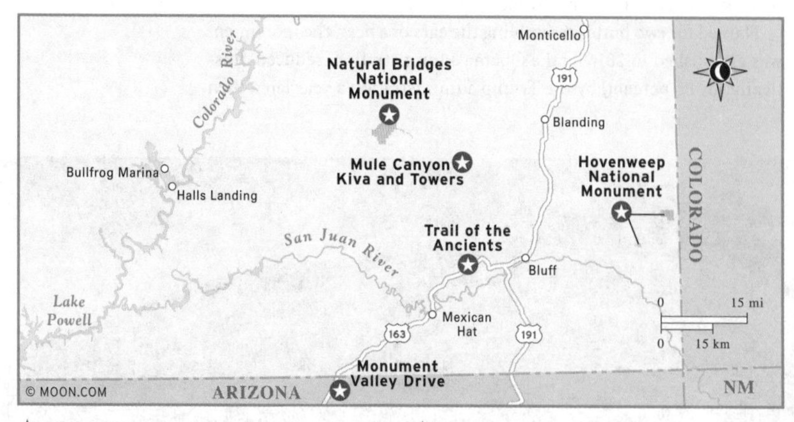

★ **Trail of the Ancients:** Spend a day seeing the best of Bears Ears human history—plus breathtaking scenery—on this loop drive through the Cedar Mesa area (page 385).

★ **Mule Canyon Kiva and Towers:** See how the Ancestral Puebloan people lived over 1,000 years ago at some of the most easily accessible sites in Bears Ears National Monument (page 388).

★ **Natural Bridges National Monument:** Like Arches National Park, but with fewer crowds, this national monument has a great scenic drive and good trails (page 399).

★ **Hovenweep National Monument:** Ponder the mysteries of the mostly unexcavated 900-year-old villages of Hovenweep National Monument, which remains relatively under the radar (page 408).

★ **Monument Valley Drive:** Experience awe (and cinematic history) with a drive through Monument Valley Navajo Tribal Park—the landscape that comes to mind when many of us think of "the West" (page 411).

Southeast Utah

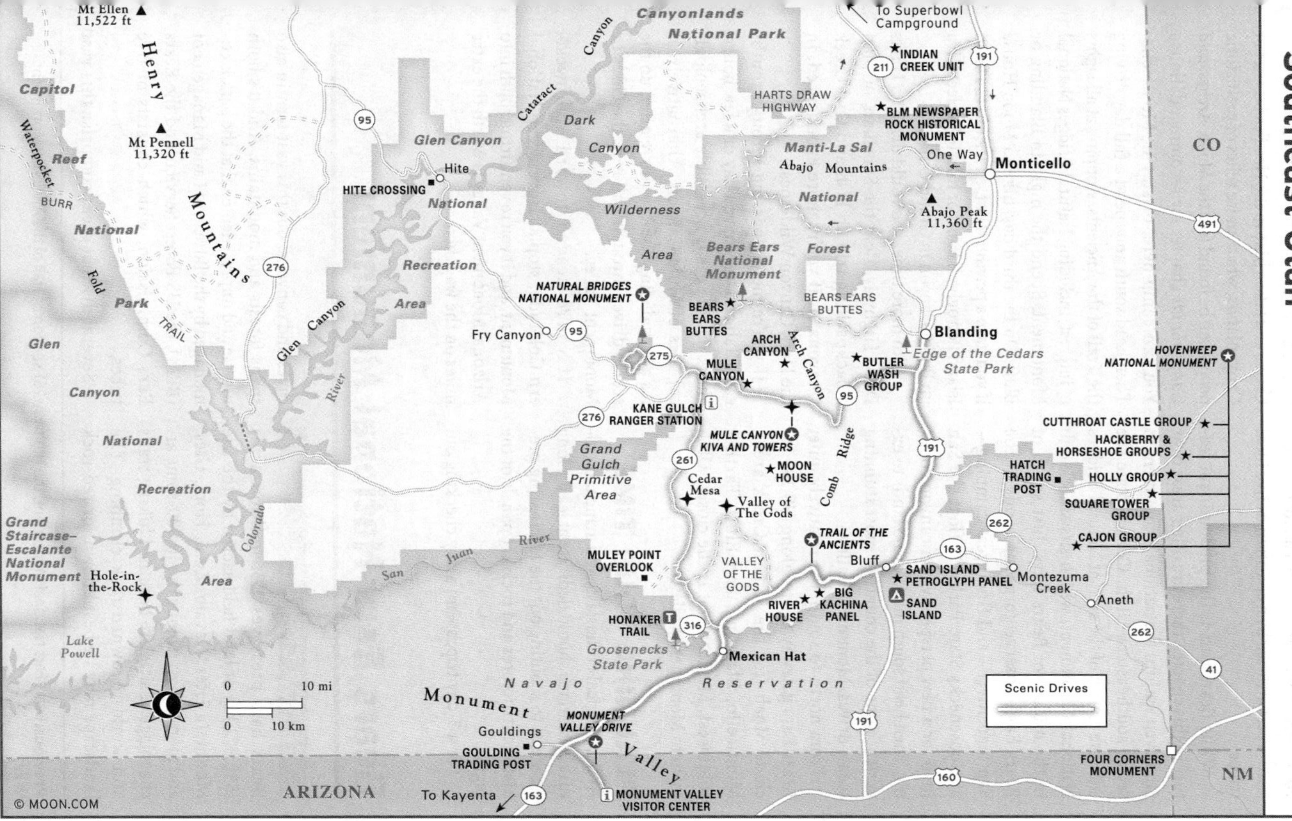

fully restored by the Biden administration in 2021. Talk about a tumultuous history—and a hard-won battle led by a coalition of five local tribes.

While Bears Ears is the predominant feature in this chapter, there are other areas near (and even within) the national monument to see in southeastern Utah. Contemplate the sublime cousin of the arch at Natural Bridges National Monument, which sits smack-dab in the middle of Bears Ears. Just south of Bears Ears, observe gorgeous bends in the San Juan River—and find great camping—at Goosenecks State Park. Or float the San Juan for a new perspective on canyon country. Then head south into Navajo lands to experience one of the country's most stunning scenic drives: Monument Valley.

From north to south, the relatively quiet Bears Ears gateway towns along US 191 include Moab (for the Indian Creek area), Monticello, Blanding, and Bluff. Farther southwest, Mexican Hat is the closest Utah town to Monument Valley.

PLANNING YOUR TIME

Archaeological enthusiasts and armchair cultural historians should dedicate at least a long weekend to scouting out the fascinating prehistoric structures and rock-art panels of the region.

For a 3-day trip, spend a day checking out the Indian Creek Unit: see the Newspaper Rock panel, gaze up at the climbers of Indian Creek, and take a hike in the Needles District of Canyonlands, where more relics of prehistoric people can be found (see the *Moab, Arches, and Canyonlands* chapter for recommendations). You can camp here, or stay in Monticello. Then head south and spend a full day driving the Trail of the Ancients, stopping at all sights of interest, including Natural Bridges National Monument. Spend the night in Blanding or Bluff. On the third day, hike to Moon House if you have a permit; if not, check out the Sand Island Petroglyph Panel or hike to Perfect Kiva up Bullet Canyon in Grand Gulch.

With more time, you could drive up Harts Draw Highway, float the San Juan, or plan a backpacking trip up Fish and Owl Creek Canyons, or if you're more experienced, in the Dark Canyon Wilderness.

If you're merely passing through southeast Utah and only have a day or a few hours, check out the easily accessible archaeological sites of Mule Canyon. Alternatively, if it's awe-inducing scenery you're after, do the scenic drives through Valley of the Gods or Monument Valley.

If you're headed toward southwestern Colorado, stop at Hovenweep National Monument, and if you're venturing south into Arizona, Monument Valley is worth the extra miles on the way there.

Bears Ears National Monument

TOP EXPERIENCE

Bears Ears preserves 1.36 million acres (550,372 ha) of land held sacred by the Ute Mountain Utes, Navajo, Zuni, Hopi, Utes, and more tribes. Among the 10,000-some archaeological sites are beautiful hiking trails and world-renowned rock climbing. The landscape may be best known for red-rock caves and canyons, but this vast terrain also spans forests and mountains. And it's both unique and unprecedented that the park is co-managed by the Bureau of Land Management (BLM), the US Forest Service, and the Bears Ears Commission, which consists of five tribes.

Several distinct areas comprise this vast

Previous: Bears Ears National Monument; the Highway 261 section of Trail of the Ancients; Monument Valley.

stretch of public lands. Massive **Cedar Mesa** stretches across the southern half of Bears Ears, encompassing the monument's most developed hiking and many of its iconic archaeological sites. North of Cedar Mesa, the **Manti-La Sal National Forest** and sprawling **Dark Canyon Wilderness** offer the possibility of longer, rugged treks—and more shade. In the southern reaches of the Manti-La Sal Forest, the eponymous twin buttes of Bears Ears can be found, just a few miles north of Cedar Mesa. Farther north, the **Indian Creek Unit** is the crème de la crème of desert crack climbing and home to the Newspaper Rock petroglyph site.

On some maps or materials, you might see reference to the **Shash Jáa Special Recreational Management Area,** a narrow stretch of land across the eastern side of Cedar Mesa. When Bears Ears was reduced by the Trump administration, this area and Indian Creek were the two units that remained preserved. Since the monument was restored, Shash Jáa, which means "Bears Ears" in Navajo, is only a distinct area from a BLM management perspective.

The best places to get the beta on Bears Ears are the **Kane Gulch Ranger Station** (Hwy. 261, 4 mi/6.4 km south of Hwy. 95, 435/587-1500, www.blm.gov/visit/kane-gulch-ranger-station, 8am-noon daily Mar.-mid-June and Sept.-Oct.), the **BLM Monticello Field Office** (365 N. Main St., Monticello, 435/587-1510, www.blm.gov/programs/recreation/permits-and-passes/lotteries-and-permit-systems), and the **Blanding Visitor Center** (12 N. Grayson Pkwy., Blanding, 435/678-3662).

Ranking ninth in size among all national monuments (including vast marine monuments), Bears Ears remains relatively undeveloped and is still in the resource management planning phase. While you won't have the same level of amenities and services you'd find in a national park, you'll be rewarded with fewer crowds and a different sort of public lands experience.

SCENIC DRIVES

If you don't have time for a long backpacking trip or day hike, scenic drives provide great access to the archaeological heritage and gorgeous landscape that are Bears Ears. These are just a few of the routes that tour Bears Ears, so if you have more time, head out with a good map and follow your curiosity down side roads—paved and dirt alike.

Some stops along these drives require short hikes or walks, but numerous vistas and sights are right off the road. Keep in mind that all of these drives include sections that will quickly become hazardous in heavy rain or snow, so check the forecast beforehand. There are limited or no facilities, gas, or water along these routes, so fuel up beforehand and bring all necessary supplies with you.

★ Trail of the Ancients

Starting point: *Bluff*
Length: *120 miles (193 km)*
Time: *Full day to make all stops, or half day for a couple stops*
Drive type: *loop*

This scenic drive tours the best of what Bears Ears is known for, linking several roads that lead to ancient structures, geologic panoramas, and the eponymous buttes of the monument. If you only have a day to spend in southeastern Utah, this drive will give you a great taste of the area.

Trail of the Ancients starts from the town of Bluff on US 163, off which you can stop to see vistas and sites including Navajo Twin Rocks (two sandstone towers huddled together), Sand Island Petroglyph Panel, and the geologic uplift that is Comb Ridge. Short detours lead to bird's-eye river views at Goosenecks State Park and the breathtaking Valley of the Gods.

Next, turn right onto Highway 261 and drive north for about 30 miles (48 km). While this stretch of the drive is beautiful, there are not as many landmarks to pull over for. You can make a short detour toward the beginning of this road to check out the sweeping view at Muley Point.

From Highway 261, travel west on Highway 275 North for 0.7 mile (1.1 km), then turn right on Elk Mountain Road (Forest Rd. 008). Six miles (9.7 km) later, you'll arrive at the closest view of the twin buttes that give this national monument its name. Return to Highway 275 North and continue west for a few miles to reach Natural Bridges National Monument, where you can observe what look like arches, but are actually natural bridges formed by running water.

The last stretch of this route is Highway 95; take 95 east to Blanding, stopping to behold Mule Canyon Kiva and the Butler Wash cliff dwellings site on the way. To return to Bluff and make this a full loop, just take US 191 south (this will add to the mileage listed above). For a map and more info on Trail of the Ancients, check out www.bluffutah.org. Note that this drive is not to be confused with the longer Trail of the Ancients route that includes Colorado and Arizona.

Bears Ears Buttes

Starting point: *Blanding*
Length: *82 miles (132 km)*
Time: *2-3 hours*
Drive type: *out-and-back*

Located in the southern cusp of the Manti-La Sal National Forest just a few miles north of Cedar Mesa, the Bears Ears Buttes are the defining feature of this place, rising to 8,700 feet (2,652 m) in elevation. As Ute legend goes, the twin buttes are the ears of a bear who went into hibernation in winter under the earth, then arose in spring to teach the Ute people the Bear Dance. After imparting the lesson, the bear reclined beneath the earth once more, keeping his head up just enough to look after the tribe.

To reach the Bears Ears from Blanding, take 95 North for 30 miles (48 km). Hang a right on Highway 275 North for .7 mile (1 km) and turn right on Elk Mountain Road, which will take you to the saddle between the buttes. This route should not be approached in wet or snowy conditions. Do not hike or climb on the buttes, which are considered sacred sites.

On the return trip, you can also stop at Mule Canyon Kiva and Butler Wash cliff dwellings site if you have time.

Harts Draw Highway

Starting point: *Monticello*
Length: *42 miles (68 km)*
Time: *2-3 hours*
Drive type: *loop*

This scenic route skirts the eastern edge of Bears Ears past excellent vistas of the national monument. This is the best drive for those looking to get up into the alpine through the Manti-La Sal National Forest, and it's particularly beautiful in fall when the aspens along the drive glow red and yellow. Other highlights include an overlook of the Needles District of Canyonlands, as well as Monticello and Foy Lakes, both of which offer good trout fishing.

The route begins in Monticello at the intersection of US 191 and West 200 South and follows the northwestern side of the Abajo Mountains. At the end of Harts Draw, turn right onto Highway 211, then make another right on US 191 to return to Monticello.

If you have more time, turn left on Highway 211 instead of right, and after just a few miles, you'll reach the Indian Creek Unit of Bears Ears and the Newspaper Rock petroglyph panel (this will add some miles and time to your drive).

Due to the high elevation of sections of Harts Draw, don't attempt this drive in snowy or icy conditions.

Valley of the Gods

Starting point: *Mexican Hat*
Length: *40 miles (64 km)*
Time: *3-4 hours*
Drive type: *loop*

If you're in the mood to drive across the set of classic Westerns of yore, the 17-mile (27-km) scenic loop through Valley of the Gods will do the trick. If you're familiar with

1: a panorama of Highway 95 where it crosses Comb Ridge on Trail of the Ancients **2:** the Bears Ears Buttes

the quintessentially Western landscape of Monument Valley (page 410), the scenery here is similar, though it's on BLM land, which means there's no entry fee and free dispersed campsites abound. Note that the mileage listed above constitutes the full loop from Mexican Hat: 17 miles (27 km) on a dirt road to tour Valley of the Gods, and the other 23 miles (37 km) on pavement.

Sitting about 1,000 feet (305 m) below and south of Cedar Mesa, the Valley of the Gods Road tours radiant sandstone formations, including Battleship Rock and Lady in the Bathtub. As you head out from Mexican Hat, look out for Mexican Hat Rock—the namesake caprock formation that lends the area its name—on your right a couple miles up US 163. If you've got a little more time, turn right on Highway 261 instead of left to check out the harrowing switchbacks of the Moki Dugway dirt road about 2 miles (3.2 km) north.

From Mexican Hat, head north on US 163 for 8 miles (13 km), then turn left onto Valley of the Gods Road. The scenic drive will spit you back out on Highway 261, which you can follow south back to Mexican Hat. The dirt road can be passable by 2WD vehicles in dry conditions, but if weather looms or the ground is wet, avoid this drive. This route also makes for a great bike ride.

SIGHTS

Bears Ears is renowned for its Indigenous cultural heritage, from granaries and dwellings to petroglyphs. Several sites, like those listed below, are easily accessible via short drives and even shorter trails. More sites and panels can be found the longer you hike. Note that to park at most of these trailheads and use these trails, you'll need to pay a day-use fee. These relics are considered sacred by tribes of the area, so never touch, climb on, or otherwise disturb any structures, artwork, or artifacts.

Archaeological Sites

River House Site

Along the southeastern edge of Cedar Mesa's Comb Ridge, Ancestral Puebloan farmers built what is now known as the River House sometime in the 11th or 12th century. This cave-based home made of sandstone and clay takes its name from its location just off the San Juan River. River House is an excellent example of prehistoric passive solar design, engineered to allow warm sunlight in during winter while maximizing shade in summer. An easy 0.5-mile (0.8-km) hike leads to the kiva dwelling and petroglyphs, including a Kokopelli (a fertility god). From Bluff, it's about a 30-minute drive to reach the trailhead and parking via US 191 South, US 163 South, and San Juan County Road 235, which turns into Comb Wash Road (keep right to reach the trailhead).

★ Mule Canyon Sites

Running from northern Comb Ridge along the eastern edge of Cedar Mesa, Mule Canyon is home to several Ancestral Puebloan sites, including ancient granaries, defensive towers, rock art, and kivas (Hopi for "circular structures"). A few notable sites include the Cave Towers, the Mule Canyon Kiva, and the enchanting House on Fire structure, all of which are within about a mile (1.6 km) of one another as the crow flies, though a bit longer to drive between trailheads and hike the various short trails leading to these sites.

Starting from the east, the first of these sites—and the hardest to find—is **Cave Towers,** constructed along Mule Canyon's rim in the 13th century. Among the seven structures here are towers and kivas built aboveground, which experts have hypothesized may have been used defensively. From Blanding, it's about a 30-minute drive to the trailhead. Take US 191 south for 4 miles (6.4 km), then turn right on Highway 95. After 18.8 miles (30.3 km), between mileposts 102 and 103, turn left on an unmarked dirt road. There may be a gate you'll need to open and close behind you. The fenced parking area is about 400 feet (122 m) up the road. Take the

1: Valley of the Gods **2:** Cave Towers **3:** inside a restored kiva at Mule Canyon **4:** a section of the Sand Island Petroglyph Panel

1
2
3
4

trail south to reach the towers. It's an easy 1.6 miles (2.6 km) out-and-back with minimal elevation gain.

Just west of Cave Towers, **House on Fire,** in spite of its name, is actually a series of granaries that once stored ricegrass and corn. Due to the way the granaries are constructed beneath a giant sandstone overhang, from afar, this structure does indeed resemble a house aflame. Constructed between 750 and 1300 CE, this structure is particularly photogenic in mid-morning, when the angle of the sun makes the sandstone glow. To reach House on Fire, drive 0.6 mile (1 km) farther north on Highway 95 past the turnoff for Cave Towers, then turn right onto a dirt road marked for Mule Canyon. This road is marked Texas Flat Road, but on Google Maps it shows up as Arch Canyon Road. Look for the small Mule Canyon trailhead sign on your left about 1,000 feet (305 m) up the road. The trail leads through the South Fork of Mule Canyon, and it's just over 1 mile (1.6 km) to House on Fire. Explore around the site to find three sets of handprints on rock.

You can turn around after you reach the site or continue for another 3 miles (4.8 km) to the trail's end (making for an 8.6-mi/13.8-km round-trip journey) to see more structures and petroglyphs.

Mule Canyon Kiva is the easiest site to reach in Mule Canyon—it's well marked and there's no hiking required. If you've explored the kivas of Mesa Verde in nearby Colorado, the site will look familiar, and indeed, shards of pottery discovered here show that Mesa Verde inhabitants may have influenced the Ancestral Puebloans of modern-day Utah. The site, which is right by the parking lot, includes a restored, excavated kiva as well as several other structures occupied as early as 750 CE. From House on Fire and Arch Canyon Road, turn right back onto Highway 95 for about 2,000 feet (610 m) until you see signs on the right for Mule Canyon Ruins.

Rock Art

Sand Island Petroglyph Panel

Just a few miles outside the town of Bluff, this remarkably long panel (300 ft/91 m) features artwork pecked into sandstone between 2,500 and 800 years ago, beginning with the Basketmaker culture. The panel, which includes Kokopelli figures and novelties like a sheep playing a flute, lies right along the banks of the San Juan River. To reach this easily accessible panel from Bluff, head south on US 191 for 4 miles (6.4 km), then turn left toward Sand Island (signed). Follow signs past the boating area to the petroglyph panel, which is just a short stroll from the roadside parking on your right.

For more petroglyphs nearby, head up Lower Butler Wash Road (Rd. 262) and park on the left side of the road when you get to the restroom and trail register. Hike down a rough dirt road and into the canyon below, and look for the petroglyphs on a wall to your left just past a cave. This 11th- to 12th-century Ancestral Puebloan artwork features life-size figures like a flute player and a wolf-man hybrid.

Big Kachina Panel (Butler Wash Panel)

A little farther downriver from Sand Island, where the San Juan meets Butler Wash, the Big Kachina Panel is named for its representation of kachinas, which are divine and spiritual beings in the Puebloan tradition. Some of the kachinas illustrated in these petroglyphs are quite large, and there are hundreds of figures represented here in good detail, making for a compelling rock-art experience.

From the town of Bluff, head west on US 163 for 3 miles (4.8 km), then turn left on San Juan County Road 235, which is a rough road requiring 4WD. This road soon turns into Comb Wash Road. Take it for 6.2 miles (10 km), staying right at any forks. The short trail leading to this panel starts about 1.5 miles (2.4 km) past the River House site. If you don't have a 4WD vehicle, you could also

Indigenous Peoples of Bears Ears

traditional Navajo hogan on display at Monument Valley

Archaeological evidence shows that people have lived across parts of Cedar Mesa within Bears Ears since 11,000 BCE, though human history may stretch back even further. Between 500 BCE and 750 CE, populations proliferated with the Basketmaker culture and the Ancestral Puebloans.

Many modern tribes trace their roots back to Bears Ears and led the charge for the establishment of a monument. The Hopi, Navajo (Diné), Utes, Zuni, and Ute Mountain Utes have a deep relationship with these lands. They gather resources, including herbal medicines, firewood, game, and food, for subsistence-based living. They hold spiritual ceremonies here to connect to their ancestors. And the 100,000-some cultural and archaeological sites that are of historical interest to non-Indigenous visitors are considered part of tribal heritage.

In a totally unique arrangement, Bears Ears is managed by a tribal-public partnership forged by the BLM and the Bears Ears Inter-Tribal Coalition (www.bearsearscoalition.org). Dozens more tribes outside the coalition also hold connections with this land, including the Uintah and Ouray Utes and the Jicarilla Apache. Both the Navajo Nation and the White Mesa Ute Reservation lands border the national monument.

As you respectfully travel across Bears Ears, remember that the lands here are not only beautiful, fascinating, and historically significant, but also continue to be culturally and materially important to many people today. Explains Octavius Seowtewa, a Zuni elder: "It provides a link to our ancestors, from long ago."

park where the road gets rough and bike the rest of the way.

Newspaper Rock Panel

In the southern part of Indian Creek Unit, Newspaper Rock is where prehistoric and Indigenous people seem to have posted their headlines (in visual form) for some 2,000 years. From the Ancestral Puebloans to the Paiute and Navajo, the proliferation of rock art here stands out against a dark desert varnish over the sandstone. Later, early settlers added their own marks to the rock. This panel is right off Highway 211 en route to the Needles District of Canyonlands. From the junction with US 191, drive 12 miles (19.3 km) on Highway 211 and look for signs for Newspaper Rock on your right.

CEDAR MESA

Sprawling some 400,000 acres (161,874 ha) across the southern Bears Ears, Cedar Mesa is the largest area of the monument and home to many of its best-known hikes and cultural heritage sites. In the northern part of Cedar Mesa, you'll find Mule Canyon and its many archaeological points of interest. To the south lie Fish Creek and Owl Creek Canyons, with good hiking and some fishing, too. To the west, Grand Gulch is a backpacker's paradise. In the southern reaches of Cedar Mesa, you'll find Valley of the Gods, which makes for a gorgeous scenic drive rivaled only by Monument Valley. Along its southern edge, Cedar Mesa is bordered by the San Juan River.

Along the eastern side of Cedar Mesa, the Comb Ridge monocline is southeast Utah's defining geologic feature. Forces have pushed the earth's crust up into an 80-mile-long (129-km) ridge stretching from the Abajo Mountain foothills into Arizona. To the west, Comb Ridge plunges some 800 feet (244 m) into a wash below. Driving west on US 163, you can cross Comb Ridge and find various spots to pull over and take in the massive panoramas all around.

A good place to start your exploration of Cedar Mesa is the BLM's **Kane Gulch Ranger Station** (435/587-1532, www.blm.gov, 8am-noon daily spring and fall), at the west end of Cedar Mesa, 4 miles (6.4 km) south of Highway 95 on Highway 261. Staff can provide trail info, hiking conditions, and the required permits. The ranger station sells maps, but has no water.

Note that dogs and pets are prohibited in many areas of Cedar Mesa, including Grand Gulch and McCloyd Canyon (where Moon House is located). Everywhere else, pets must be leashed at all times and watched carefully near archaeological sites to avoid damage.

If you'd rather leave the logistics to the professionals, **Wild Expeditions** (435/672-2244, www.riversandruins.com) guides hikes and even multiday trips into Cedar Mesa and beyond, plus offers rentals and support for personalized trips into this remote area.

Hiking

From short jaunts leading to the remains of ancient structures to multiday backpacking treks, Cedar Mesa offers a variety of trails to explore. This area is managed for primitive recreation, however, so don't expect to find the same amenities you might in hiking areas in Park City or Zion. Bring your own water and food, be prepared to pack out all waste (including human waste), and if you're attempting a longer hike, navigation skills and maps are a must.

Finally, there's a reason the peak seasons here are definitively spring and fall—summer in Bears Ears is hot, and in Cedar Mesa, shade is hard to come by. If you're hiking in late spring, summer, or early fall, bring plenty of protective layers, sunscreen, and water. July-September, flash foods are also a real threat in Cedar Mesa's canyons.

Permits and Fees

Day-use passes and backpacking permits are required year-round throughout Cedar Mesa, including in Grand Gulch, Fish and Owl Canyons, and Mule Canyon. Each day-use pass is good for a group of up to 12. The cost is $5 per day for a day-use pass, but if you're staying longer or planning to return, you can save with a weeklong $10 pass or a yearlong $40 pass. To reserve your day pass, look for "Cedar Mesa & Comb Ridge Day Hiking" on www.recreation.gov (passes available up to 6 months in advance). Day passes can also be purchased by check or cash at each trailhead.

Backpacking permits are $15 per person per trip (plus $6 online reservation fee), and only 20 backpackers can start from each trailhead each day. Group size is limited to 12 people. Permits can be reserved online up to 90 days in advance, but must be reserved at least 4 days in advance of your trip date—if any permits remain, you might be able to score one in person 1-3 days before the trip at

1: cairns mark the short trail to view Butler Wash cliff dwellings **2:** the trail through Mule Canyon **3:** Comb Ridge runs along the eastern edge of Cedar Mesa.

1
2

3

the Kane Gulch Ranger Station or Monticello Field Office.

The only hike requiring a special permit, which can be seasonally difficult to obtain due to visitation limits of 20 people per day, is Moon House ($5 pp, plus $6 reservation fee). All Moon House permits are available up to 90 days in advance.

Note that all backpacking and Moon House permits must be validated in person in spring (Mar.-mid-June.) and fall (Sept.-Oct.) at the Kane Gulch Ranger Station (spring and fall) or at the Monticello Field Office (year-round). Questions regarding permits or local guiding services can be directed to the **BLM Cedar Mesa Permit Office** (435/587-1510, blm_ut_mt_cedarmesa@blm.gov, 8am-noon Mon.-Fri.). Note that the America the Beautiful Pass does not include Bears Ears access.

Butler Wash Group

Along eastern Comb Ridge, hike a short trail into a side canyon of Butler Wash to a well-preserved dwelling (1 mi/1.6 km round-trip, 100 ft/30 m elevation gain, moderate). Find the well-marked trailhead on the north side of Highway 95, 11 miles (17.7 km) west of US 191, between mileposts 111 and 112. There is a restroom and plenty of parking at the trailhead. Follow cairns for 0.5 mile (0.8 km) through juniper and piñon pine woodlands and across slickrock to the overlook, where you can see four kivas and several other structures, portions of which have been restored. This dwelling tucked under an overhang is estimated to be about 900 years old.

Arch Canyon

This 12-mile-long (19.3-km) tributary of Comb Wash has spectacular scenery, Ancestral Puebloan sites, and some good hiking. Much of the canyon can be seen on a day hike, but 2-3 days are required to explore its upper reaches. The main streambeds usually have water, but purify it before drinking.

To reach the trailhead, turn north onto Comb Wash Road (between mileposts 107 and 108 on Hwy. 95) and go 2.5 miles (4 km) on the dirt road, past a house and water tank. Park in a grove of cottonwood trees before a stream. The mouth of Arch Canyon is just to the northwest (it's easy to miss). Look for the remains of a structure less than half a mile (0.8 km) up Arch Canyon on the right. More structures are tucked under alcoves farther up-canyon. The canyon's three namesake arches lie past the 7-mile (11.3-km) point.

A road and a short trail to the rim of Arch Canyon provide a beautiful view into the depths. From Highway 95, turn north onto Texas Flat Road (County Rd. 263, between mileposts 102 and 103), then continue 4 miles (6.4 km). Park just before the road begins a steep climb and walk 0.25 mile (0.4 km) east on an old jeep road to the rim. This is a fine place for a picnic, although there are no facilities. Texas Flat Road is dirt but passable when dry by cars with good clearance. Trucks can continue up the steep hill to other viewpoints of Arch and Texas Canyons.

Mule Canyon (North and South Forks)

Mule Canyon offers both short developed trails leading to archaeological sites, as well as the opportunity to enjoy an easy hike along the canyon bottom. For details on the short treks accessing Cave Towers, Mule Canyon Kiva, and House on Fire, all of which are within about a mile (1.6 km) of each other, see page 388.

For a longer and deeper journey, hike the relatively flat canyon bottoms of either the South Fork (8.6 mi/13.8 km out-and-back) or the North Fork (5.2 mi/8.3 km out-and-back). Both trailheads are located off Arch Canyon Road (also signed as Texas Flat Road) off Highway 95; the South Fork trailhead is 0.25 mile (0.4 km) past the cattle guard and fee station and the North Fork trailhead is 0.75 mile (1.2 km) farther up the road near a small bridge. Neither fork has a developed trail, but the going is flat and easy, allowing you to focus on spotting structures along the sandstone canyon walls, or artifacts in the sandy slickrock below.

Mule Canyon is prone to hazardous flash floods, so don't attempt these hikes if weather is in the forecast.

Moon House

Moon House is one of the most fascinating sites within Bears Ears, though it's considerably harder to reach than some of the ancient structures up Mule Canyon. Built into a cliff in approximately 1264 CE, this dwelling site includes 49 rooms, some with walls featuring depictions of what are thought to be lunar cycles or even a solar eclipse.

From Bluff, it's about an hour's drive to reach the trailhead, including long stretches on a rough dirt road suitable for 4WD vehicles only. Head south on US 191, which will turn into US 163. Turn right on Comb Wash Road (San Juan County Road 235), and after 2.3 miles (3.7 km), turn left on Snow Flats Road. Continue for 14 miles (22.5 km) and look for the McCloyd trailhead on your right. Both of these roads are dirt, but Snow Flats is particularly rough and may be impassable following precipitation or in winter.

The out-and-back hike to Moon House (3.5 mi/5.6 km round-trip, 400 ft/122 m elevation gain, strenuous) begins on a dirt road for a little over a mile (1.6 km), before turning into a cairn-marked trail that descends into McCloyd Canyon. The route down from the rim is steep and rocky, so approach it carefully. Look for Moon House tucked into the ledge on the canyon wall opposite the trail. Once you reach the canyon floor, follow the slickrock until you see cairns leading to the Moon House site. While you may enter the house to explore the rooms and see the pictographs, do not disturb or touch the structure or art.

Note that permits are required to hike to Moon House (see page 392 for details). Plan on about 3-4 hours to hike the trail and explore the site. Dogs are not permitted. A flashlight for touring the house isn't a bad idea.

Grand Gulch Primitive Area

Within this twisting canyon system, you can hike to captivating scenery and the largest concentrations of Ancestral Puebloan archaeological sites in southeastern Utah. From an elevation of 6,400 feet (1,951 m), Grand Gulch cuts deeply into Cedar Mesa southwest to the San Juan River, dropping 2,700 feet (823 m) in about 53 miles (85 km). Sheer cliffs, pinnacles, cliff dwellings, rock art, arches, and a few natural bridges line this dramatic canyon and its many tributaries.

Moon House site in Bears Ears

From the Kane Gulch Ranger Station, Kane Gulch Trail leads 4 relatively easy miles (6.4 km) to the upper end of Grand Gulch, where a camping area is shaded by cottonwood trees. **Junction Ruin,** a cave dwelling, is visible from here, and if you hike less than 1 mile (1.6 km) farther into Grand Gulch, you'll find more archaeological sites and an arch.

The largest tributary of Grand Gulch, **Bullet Canyon** provides access from the east. The Bullet Canyon trailhead is just a mile (1.6 km) off Highway 261 on Road 251. You can hike up the canyon and back for a long 12-mile (19.3-km) day, but Jailhouse Ruins and Perfect Kiva—perhaps the most compelling attractions here—are 4.5 miles (7.2 km) up-canyon, making for 9 miles (14.5 km) round-trip. Perfect Kiva is one of the only kivas in Bears Ears into which you can descend. A popular 23-mile (37-kim) backpacking trip loops Kane Gulch and Bullet Canyon, though you'll need to plan on at least a couple days, plus a shuttle to bridge the 7.5-mile (12.1-km) gap between trailheads.

Note that Grand Gulch is a permit area, and no dogs are allowed.

Fish Creek and Owl Creek

Canyon scenery, year-round pools, elusive cliff dwellings, and a magnificent natural arch make this an excellent hike. Fish Creek and its tributary Owl Creek sit east of Grand Gulch on the other side of Highway 261, and together make for a great loop (17 mi/27 km). From the trailhead (elev. 6,160 ft/1,878 m), the path descends 1,400 vertical feet (427 m) to the junction of the two creeks, before climbing back out. For all but the most ambitious hikers, this constitutes a good overnight backpacking trip. Opinions differ as to which direction to begin the loop, but either way is generally fine.

If you're not hiking the full loop, Owl Creek is better for a day hike because there's an easily accessible Ancestral Puebloan site just 0.5 mile (0.8 km) away, and Nevill's Arch lies 3.5 miles (5.6 km) farther. However you hike it, maps are essential here—it's easy to get off the route in places.

Many of the ancient structures in this area sit high in the cliffs and can be hard to spot from the canyon bottoms some 500 feet (152 m) below, so binoculars come in handy. Climbing equipment cannot be used to access these structures.

The turnoff for the trailhead along San Juan County Road 253 is between mileposts 27 and 28 on Highway 261, 1 mile (1.6 km) south of Kane Gulch Ranger Station.

MANTI-LA SAL NATIONAL FOREST AND DARK CANYON WILDERNESS

Bears Ears might bring to mind sandstone cliffs and canyons, but across the monument's middle stretch, groves of evergreen trees and a forested canyon is home to southeast Utah's only wilderness area. To the east, this part of Bears Ears meets the Abajo Mountains. And in the southern reaches of the forest, you'll find the twin buttes that give Bears Ears its name (see page 386 for details).

The Manti-La Sal National Forest—named for a city ("Manti") in the Book of Mormon and the snowcapped peaks resembling salt ("La Sal")—consists of some 1.4 million acres (566,560 ha) of Douglas fir, lodgepole pine, Engelmann spruce, and aspen trees. Just as in the southern Bears Ears, you'll find cliff dwellings across these lands, in addition to fossils and the remains of coal mines (though there is still active mining in the area).

Along the western side of the Manti-La Sal National Forest, you'll find magnificent Dark Canyon and its many tributaries. Partially designated as a wilderness area, Dark Canyon begins in the high country of Elk Ridge and extends west to Lake Powell in lower Cataract Canyon. Steep cliffs and an isolated location have protected this relatively pristine environment.

The upper canyons tend to be wide with open areas and groves of Douglas fir and ponderosa pine. Creeks dry up after spring snowmelt, leaving only scattered springs as water sources for most of the year. Farther downstream, the canyon walls close in and desert trees of piñon pine, juniper, and cottonwood thrive.

At its lower end, Dark Canyon has a year-round stream and deep plunge pools. Cliffs tower more than 1,400 feet (427 m) above the canyon floor. Springs and running water attract wildlife, including bighorn sheep, black bears, deer, mountain lions, coyotes, bobcats, ringtail cats, raccoons, foxes, and spotted skunks.

Experienced hikers come here for the solitude, wildlife, Ancestral Puebloan sites, and canyon views. Although it's possible to visit Dark Canyon on a day hike, it takes several days to get a feel for this area. Exploring the entire canyon and its major tributaries would take weeks.

The upper half of the Dark Canyon system is administered by the Manti-La Sal National Forest (435/587-2041, www.fs.usda.gov/mantilasal), while the lower half is mostly BLM land. Unlike Cedar Mesa, no permits are required to hike or backpack here.

The most popular entry point to lower Dark Canyon is **Sundance Trail.** The trailhead can be reached via dirt roads that branch off Highway 95 southeast of Lake Powell's Hite Marina turnoff; this approach can be used year-round in dry weather. Cairns mark the trail, which drops 1,200 vertical feet (366 m) in less than 1 mile (1.6 km) on a steep talus slope.

INDIAN CREEK

A world-class climbing area, Indian Creek is the farthest north unit of Bears Ears, rising above the Manti-La Sal National Forest. This is *the* destination for desert crack climbing. Near the climbing, you'll find the Newspaper Rock petroglyph panel.

Indian Creek is en route to the Needles District of Canyonlands, so it's easy to spend a morning climbing, then head into the national park for a hike, or vice versa. If you'd rather not pitch a tent and prefer high-end lodging options, Indian Creek is also the only area within Bears Ears where the bustling adventure hub of Moab makes for a reasonably close base camp (about an hour away).

Climbing

The crack routes in **Indian Creek** number close to 1,000. Most climbs here are tough (5.10 and up), although difficulty is subjective, mostly in regard to your hand size. Climbing season is best in fall and early spring. Summer afternoons are far too hot for climbing. Winter climbing may be possible depending on weather and your tolerance for cold. All routes here should be avoided after rain, when sandstone is fragile; wait until the ground and rock are fully dry to climb.

If you're planning to spend at least a couple days climbing here, pick up a copy of *Indian Creek: A Climbing Guide,* by David Bloom. If you're new to the rock, inexperienced with crack climbing, or don't have trad gear, **Moab Desert Adventures** (39 E. Center St., Moab, 804/814-3872, www.moabdesertadventures.com) offers guided climbing at Indian Creek.

The crags of Indian Creek start on Highway 211, about 15 miles (24 km) west of US 191 and 3 miles (4.8 km) west of the Newspaper Rock petroglyphs. If you're pulling up directions in Google Maps, be sure to put "Indian Creek Climbing Area" as your destination, not "Indian Creek" itself, which sits north of the crags and is quite a longer and more circuitous route from the main highways of the area.

Contact the **BLM office** in Monticello (365 N. Main, 435/587-1500) for information about this area.

CAMPING

Valle's Trading Post and RV Park (Mexican Hat, 435/683-2226, year-round, $35) has tent and RV sites with hookups. The camping area is pretty basic but surrounded by great scenery. The trading post offers groceries, showers, vehicle storage, and car shuttles. **Goosenecks State Park** has camping (Hwy. 316, 435/678-2238, https://stateparks.utah.gov, first-come, first-served, $10) with great views but no amenities.

Just past Indian Creek's cliffs, **Superbowl**

1

2

Campground (435/587-1500, year-round, hookups and toilets available but no water, first-come, first-served, $15) sits in open canyon country surrounded by beautiful views. There are 37 campsites that can accommodate tents or RVs.

GETTING THERE AND AROUND

The main access highway into Bears Ears is US 191, a north-south highway that cuts across Utah before heading down into Arizona. The Bears Ears gateway towns of Monticello, Blanding, White Mesa, and Bluff are all located along US 191. From US 191, to reach the Indian Creek unit, take Highway 211 west; this is about an hour's drive from the town of Moab. To access the Manti-La Sal National Forest, Natural Bridges National Monument, and the northern reaches of Cedar Mesa, take Highway 95 west. To reach Cedar Mesa and the southern parts of the southern Bears Ears as well as Mexican Hat, use US 163, which leads down through Monument Valley and Navajo lands, eventually into Arizona. Highway 261 cuts north-south across Cedar Mesa.

★ NATURAL BRIDGES NATIONAL MONUMENT

Natural Bridges preserves its namesakes, which are basically arches formed by running water, rather than melt-freeze cycles. The three bridges found here owe their existence to the streams of White Canyon and its tributaries, which cut deep canyons. Floodwaters sculpted the bridges by gouging tunnels in the meandering canyons.

The bridges here illustrate three different stages of development: massive, relatively nascent Kachina, middle-aged Sipapu, and delicate Owachomo. All three natural bridges will continue to widen and eventually collapse. A 9-mile (14.5-km) scenic drive has overlooks of the bridges, as well as Ancestral Puebloan sites and twisting canyons. You can follow short trails down from the rim to the base of each bridge or hike through all three bridges on a 9-mile (14.5-km) loop.

Natural Bridges National Monument (www.nps.gov/nabr, $20 per vehicle, $15 motorcyclists, $10 pedestrians and bicyclists) is 33 miles (53 km) west of Blanding and 91 miles (147 km) southeast of Hanksville, both on Highway 95. Natural Bridges is also right in the middle of Bears Ears along the northern Cedar Mesa. If you're driving the Trail of the Ancients Scenic Byway, the monument is right along the drive.

GOOSENECKS STATE PARK

The San Juan River winds through a series of incredibly tight bends 1,000 feet (305 m) below this small state park. So closely spaced are the bends that the river takes 6 miles (9.7 km) to cover an air distance of only 1.5 miles (2.4 km). The bends and exposed rock layers form exquisitely graceful curves. Geologists know the site as a classic example of entrenched meanders caused by gradual uplift of a formerly level plain. Signs at the overlook explain the geologic history and identify the rock formations.

Goosenecks State Park (435/678-2238, https://stateparks.utah.gov, $5 per vehicle) is an undeveloped area with a few picnic tables and vault toilets. A **campground** ($10) is available but has no water. From the junction of US 163 and Highway 261, 4 miles (6.4 km) north of Mexican Hat, go 1 mile (1.6 km) northwest on Highway 261, then turn left and go 3 miles (4.8 km) on Highway 316 to its end.

MEXICAN HAT AREA

Spectacular geology surrounds this tiny community perched on the north bank of the San Juan River. Folded layers of red and gray rock stand out dramatically. Alhambra Rock, a jagged remnant of a volcano, marks the southern approach to Mexican Hat. The town is named for another rock, 2 miles (3.2 km) north of

1: The Abajo Mountains are located within the Manti-La Sal National Forest. **2:** Indian Creek

1
2

town, which looks just like an upside-down sombrero.

The land has never proved useful for much except its scenery; farmers and ranchers thought it next to worthless. Stories of gold in the San Juan River brought a frenzy of prospecting in 1892-1893, but the mining proved mostly a bust.

Mexican Hat now serves as a modest tourism center, with Monument Valley, Valley of the Gods, Goosenecks State Park, and Bears Ears just short drives away. The shore near town can be a busy place in summer as river-runners on the San Juan put in, take out, or just stop for ice and beer.

Mexican Hat is 22 miles (35 km) west of Bluff and 25 miles (40 km) northeast of Monument Valley, both on US 163.

Muley Point Overlook

One of the great views in the Southwest is just south of the Bears Ears border and about a 30-minute drive northwest from Mexican Hat. Although the view of the Goosenecks below is less dramatic than at the state park, the 6,200-foot (1,890-m) elevation provides a magnificent panorama across Navajo lands to Monument Valley, including countless canyons and mountains. From Mexican Hat, travel 3.8 miles (6.1 km) north on US 163 and turn left (northwest) on Highway 261. Then turn left on Muley Point Road and follow this dirt road for 5 miles (8 km).

Honaker Trail

This challenging hike (5 mi/8 km round-trip) is unlike any other in the region, with unique views only those floating the San Juan River typically behold. Built by Henry Honaker to provide an access route for gold prospectors in 1893, this trail descends steeply down a dramatic limestone ledge to the banks of the river. The downside is that after a thrilling, scenic descent, you must climb 1,712 feet (522 m) back up.

The trailhead, near Goosenecks State Park, is a 15-minute drive from Mexican Hat, and it may take some route-finding to get there. Take US 163 north, turn left on Highway 261, and left on Highway 316. After 0.5 mile (0.8 km), bear right on the dirt Johns Canyon Road (County Rd. 244). After 2.2 miles (3.5 km), at a water tank, stay left. At the next cairn-marked split, stay left, and if your car can't handle the roughness of this subsequent road, walk the remaining 0.25 mile (0.4 km) to the trailhead, which is marked by a cairn on your left.

Monticello, Blanding, and Bluff

The three biggest communities that serve as gateways to Bears Ears all sit along US 191. From north to south, Monticello, Blanding, and Bluff may not be destinations in and of themselves, but they do offer accommodations if you're not camping, as well as dining and other amenities. Of the three, Bluff, which is the farthest south, offers the best lodging and dining options.

1: camping at Goosenecks State Park 2: an ancestral Puebloan site at Natural Bridges National Monument

MONTICELLO

This small Latter-day Saints town (pop. 1,800) is about 50 miles (81 km) south of Moab and pretty much its polar opposite: quiet and relatively untouristed. Monticello (mon-tuh-SELL-o) is at an elevation of 7,069 feet (2,155 m), just east of the Abajo Mountains. If you're curious about the town's name, it's not in honor of some hearty pioneer, but rather a tribute to Thomas Jefferson's plantation, only mispronounced.

Food and Accommodations

The local B&B, **Grist Mill Inn** (64 S. 300

E., 435/587-2597, www.thegristmillinn.com, $59-149), is indeed inside an old flour mill—though you won't be sleeping under an old millstone. Seven guest rooms are furnished in typical B&B fashion, all with private baths and TVs. An additional four rooms are found in The Cottage, a separate, adjacent building; the inn also rents two large homes for groups. The adjacent ★ **Granary Bar and Grill** (64 S. 300 E., 435/587-2597, www.granarybargrill.com, 5pm-10pm Wed.-Thurs. and Sat.-Sun., 5pm-1am Fri., $13-29) is a great addition to otherwise sleepy Monticello, serving good food and cocktails in a speakeasy atmosphere, all in a converted grain silo. With a large menu of pasta, burgers, steaks, and more well-prepared main courses, this is the best place to eat within miles.

Monticello also has a number of comfortable and affordable motels. The **Inn at the Canyons** (533 N. Main St., 435/587-2458, www.monticellocanyonlandsinn.com, $149-179) is nicely renovated and has an indoor pool, a pretty basic continental breakfast, and microwaves and fridges in the guest rooms. The **Monticello Inn** (164 E. Central St., 435/587-2275, www.monticelloinnutah.com, $75-198) is a well-maintained older motel with a pleasant in-town setting and a few guest rooms that allow pets.

Campgrounds

There are two campgrounds in the nearby Manti-La Sal National Forest. **Buckboard** (reservations at www.recreation.gov), 7 miles (11.3 km) west of town on Blue Mountain Road (Forest Rd. 105), is at 8,600 feet (2,621 m) in elevation, so it's not your best bet in early spring. But when the rest of southeastern Utah swelters in the summer, this shady campground is perfect. **Dalton Springs** (435/587-2041, first-come, first-served, $20) is along the same road, a couple of miles closer to town, at 8,200 feet (2,499 m). An abandoned ski area nearby is a good place for mountain biking.

Information and Services

Stop at the **Southeast Utah Welcome Center** (216 S. Main St., 435/587-3401, www.monticelloutah.org, 9am-6pm daily Mar.-Oct., 9am-3pm Wed.-Sun. Nov.-Feb.) for information about the area, including Canyonlands National Park.

The **San Juan Hospital** (380 W. 100 N., 435/587-2116) can help with any adventure-related injuries.

BLANDING

The largest town in San Juan County, Blanding (pop. 3,319, elev. 6,105 ft/1,861 m) is also a handy stop for travelers. Blanding is one of the few "dry" towns in Utah, meaning alcohol cannot be sold inside the municipality. In 2017, locals had a chance to vote to allow beer and wine sales in town for the first time in more than 80 years. Blanding overwhelmingly voted to keep the anti-alcohol restrictions in place. In this environment, few restaurants of note take root.

If you're heading east toward Hovenweep or west into the Cedar Mesa area, fuel up in Blanding.

Edge of the Cedars State Park

One mile (1.6 km) north of present-day Blanding, Ancestral Puebloan people built at least six groups of structures between 700 and 1220 CE. Today, this is the site of the **Edge of the Cedars State Park Museum** (660 W. 400 N., 435/678-2238, https://stateparks.utah.gov, 9am-5pm daily Mar.-Nov., 9am-3pm daily Dec.-Feb., $5 adults, $3 children), which provides a window into the life and culture of Ancestral Puebloans, with an excellent collection of pottery, baskets, sandals, jewelry, and stone tools. In addition, it serves as an introduction to the prehistoric villages at nearby Hovenweep National Monument. The museum also has exhibits and artifacts from descendants of the Ancestral Puebloans, the Utes and Navajo, as well as early Anglo pioneers.

1: downtown Monticello **2:** welcome to Bluff

ZZA
PIZZA
THANK-YOU for 30 years
of continued SUPPORT!
DRUG
MAIN STREET
BOUTIQUE
1
2
EST. 650 A.D.
BLUFF
UTAH

A short trail behind the museum leads past an excavated and partly restored site that helps one imagine the village's appearance when Ancestral Puebloans lived here. You may enter the kiva by descending a ladder through the restored roof; the walls and interior features are original.

The Dinosaur Museum

The Dinosaur Museum (754 S. 200 W., 435/678-3454, www.dinosaur-museum.org, 9am-5pm Mon.-Sat. Apr. 15-Oct., $5.50 adults, $4.50 seniors, $3.50 children) showcases the prehistoric flora and fauna of this corner of Utah. Exhibits include life-size models of dinosaurs (including the dino model used in the original *King Kong* movie) as well as fossils and skeletons. Don't miss the models of feathered dinosaurs.

Food

There are only a few restaurants in this town, with a relatively high turnover rate. Only fast-food joints are open on Sundays. Though **The Patio Diner** (95 N. Grayson Pkwy., 435/678-2177, www.patiodiner.com, 11am-8pm Mon.-Thurs., 11am-9pm Fri.-Sat., $8-11) has a local reputation as a drive-in, there are also a handful of tables and booths inside. **Homestead Steak House** (121 E. Center St., 435/678-3456, www.homesteadsteakhouseut.com, 11am-8pm Mon.-Fri., 4pm-8pm Sat., $11-30) is the local steak house, with typical American fare plus Navajo tacos.

Accommodations

With a couple exceptions, Blanding's motels are pretty generic. One exception is **Stone Lizard Lodge** (88 W. Center St., 435/678-3323, www.stonelizardlodge.com, $164-175), an older motel with remodeled, homey guest rooms, including a couple multi-bedroom suites ($204-294), and a good breakfast. Perhaps the most modern option in Blanding, the updated **Bears Ears Inn** (34 E. Center St., 435/270-4760, www.thebearsearsinn.com, $116-129) has rooms and suites, plus a great outdoor pool and continental breakfast.

Campgrounds

At the south edge of town, **Blue Mountain RV Park** (1930 S. Main St., 435/678-7840, www.bluemountainrvpark.com, $34 tents, $43-54 RVs) is also home to a trading post with Native American rugs, jewelry, and baskets. Although tent campers are welcome at the RV park, **Devils Canyon Campground** (reservations 877/444-6777, www.recreation.gov, $20, $8 reservation fee), at an elevation of 7,100 feet (2,164 m) in the Manti-La Sal National Forest, is a better bet for tent campers. It has sites with water June-September. From Blanding, go north 8 miles (12.9 km) on US 191, then turn west onto a paved road for 1.3 miles (2.1 km); the turnoff from US 191 is between mileposts 60 and 61.

BLUFF

Bluff, a sleepy community of about 250, is nestled in a striking location. In the past few years, Bluff has become a somewhat unlikely destination for recreationists and escapees from urban congestion. The quality of lodging is better than that of almost any other similarly sized town in the state, and local outfitters make it easy to explore the surrounding scenery.

As the oldest non-Native American community in southeastern Utah, Bluff was settled in 1880 by Latter-day Saints pioneers who had traveled the arduous Hole-in-the-Rock Road from the town of Escalante down into what's now Lake Powell. When LDS settlers finally reached the San Juan River valley, they founded **Bluff Fort,** which has been reconstructed at 550 East Black Locust Street (435/672-9995, 9am-6pm Mon.-Sat., 11am-6pm Sun., free).

Spend an afternoon poking around local washes or examining a large pictograph panel found along the cliff about 0.3 mile (0.5 km) downstream from the Sand Island Campground. The visitor center, located in the small fort museum, is worth a stop, and staff can provide detailed directions for hikes in the nearby washes.

Wild Expeditions (2625 S. Hwy. 191,

435/672-2244, www.riversandruins.com), based in Bluff, leads half-day, full-day, and multiday trips throughout southeastern Utah, including Bears Ears, centered on hiking, canyoneering, off-roading, or 4WD touring.

Bluff is 100 miles (161 km) south of Moab and 22 miles (35 km) south of Blanding, both on US 191. From Bluff, it's 22 miles (35 km) to Mexican Hat and 47 miles (76 km) to Monument Valley, both on US 163.

Floating the San Juan River

From the San Juan Mountains in southern Colorado, the San Juan River winds into New Mexico, enters Utah near Four Corners, and twists through spectacular canyons before ending at Lake Powell. Most river trips begin at **Sand Island Recreation Area** (roughly 3 mi/4.8 km east of Bluff) and take out at the town of Mexican Hat, 30 river miles (48 km) downstream.

Highlights of this trip include ancient archaeological sites, rock art, and a trip through Monument Upwarp and the Upper Canyon, which features fast water for thrills (Class III rapids) and weirdly buckled geology. Longer trips continue on through the famous Goosenecks—the "entrenched meanders" carved thousands of feet below the desert surface—and through more Class III rapids on the way to Clay Hills Crossing or Paiute Farms (not always accessible) on Lake Powell.

Allow at least 4 days for the full trip, though more time will allow for side canyon excursions and visits to Ancestral Puebloan sites. Rafts, kayaks, and canoes can be used. The season usually lasts year-round thanks to water flow from Navajo Reservoir upstream.

Private groups need to obtain permits ($10-30 pp) from the Bureau of Land Management's **Monticello Field Office** (365 N. Main St., 435/587-1544). Permits are issued through a preseason lottery (via www.recreation.gov) that opens about 4 months before the season starts (i.e., permits are released in Dec. for spring-summer), although boaters with flexible schedules can usually get permits close to their time of travel. Permit fees vary depending on how far you're floating.

Some people also like to run the river between Montezuma Creek and Sand Island, a leisurely trip of 20 river miles (32 km). The solitude often makes up for the lack of scenery. It's easy to get a permit for this section because no use limits or fees apply.

Several commercial river-running companies offer San Juan trips. Local **Wild Expeditions** (2625 S. Hwy. 191, 435/672-2244,

Bluff is the smallest of the gateway towns to Bears Ears, but the most charming.

www.riversandruins.com) has both day and multiday trips out of Bluff; trips run daily in summer, and only a day's notice is usually needed to join a float. Eight-hour, 26-mile (42-km) excursions to Mexican Hat cost $199 adults, $139 under age 15; motors may be used if the water level is low. This highly recommended trip includes lunch plus stops at Ancestral Puebloan sites and rock art.

Food

A longtime local hangout and a good place for a meal and friendly vibes is **Twin Rocks Café** (913 E. Navajo Twins Dr., 435/672-2341, www.twinrockscafe.com, 8am-3pm Thurs.-Tues., $9-20), next to the trading post just below the impossible-to-miss Twin Rocks. Here you can dine on Navajo tacos (fry bread with chili) or Navajo pizza (fry bread with pizza toppings) as well as more standard fare. Be sure to visit the trading post for high-quality Native American crafts, many of them produced locally by Navajo artisans.

★ **Comb Ridge Eat and Drink** (409 Main St., 435/487-8441, 4:30pm-9pm Wed.-Sat., 4:30pm-8pm Sun., $17-24), an artsy café housed in a historic trading post, is a spunky little eatery with delicious food, including vegetarian options. If it's warm enough, dine outdoors where tables surround a large central tree. Where else in this part of Utah are you going to find a wild mushroom sandwich?

On the premises of the Desert Rose Inn, **Duke's** (701 W. Main St., 435/672-2303, www.desertroseinn.com/dining, 5pm-9pm Mon.-Fri. Mar.-Oct., $20-46) has good burgers and steaks, a lovely dining room, and a nice patio (but no alcohol).

Accommodations

★ **Desert Rose Inn** (701 W. Main St., 435/672-2303 or 888/475-7673, www.desertroseinn.com, $209-240) is one of the nicest lodging options in this corner of the state. Inside a large log structure with two-story wraparound porches, guest rooms feature pine furniture, quilts, and Southwestern art. An additional wing has an indoor pool and spa and Duke's restaurant, while several handsome one-bedroom log cabins scatter across the property's edge.

Another classy place to stay is **La Posada Pintada** (239 N. 7th E. Navajo Twins Dr., 435/459-2274, www.laposadapintada.com, $155-175), a boutique inn with Southwest charm and 11 spacious rooms (one a pioneer cabin)—plus a serious breakfast buffet. All rooms come with flat-screen TVs, Wi-Fi, fridges and microwaves, private patios, large bathrooms, and high-end linens and amenities.

Recapture Lodge (220 E. Main St., 435/672-2281, www.recapturelodge.com, Mar.-Nov., $120-130) is operated by longtime outfitters whose staff can help you plan an adventure. While the guest rooms are basic, the setting is lovely, with trails out the back door, a swimming pool, hot tub, playground, and coin laundry. The Recapture also rents a couple fully equipped homes in Bluff for families and groups.

★ **Bluff Dwellings Resort and Spa** (2625 S. Hwy. 191, 435/672-2477, www.bluffdwellings.com, $199-289) is a large complex centered around a welcoming pool and patio area. The architecture echoes the ancient stone dwellings tucked into nearby cliffs. All rooms have private decks or balconies and modern amenities. Some offer kitchenettes, and a couple larger rooms accommodate 6-10 guests. The on-site Hozho Spa offers massage and body and beauty treatments by appointment.

Campgrounds

Sand Island Recreation Area (435/587-1500, www.blm.gov, piped water, $15) is a BLM camping area along the San Juan River, 3 miles (4.8 km) south of town. Large cottonwood trees shade this pretty spot, but tent campers should watch for thorns in the grass. River-runners often put in at the campground, so it can be a busy place.

1: Bluff Dwellings Resort and Spa **2:** Desert Rose Inn **3:** patio at Duke's **4:** Comb Ridge Eat and Drink

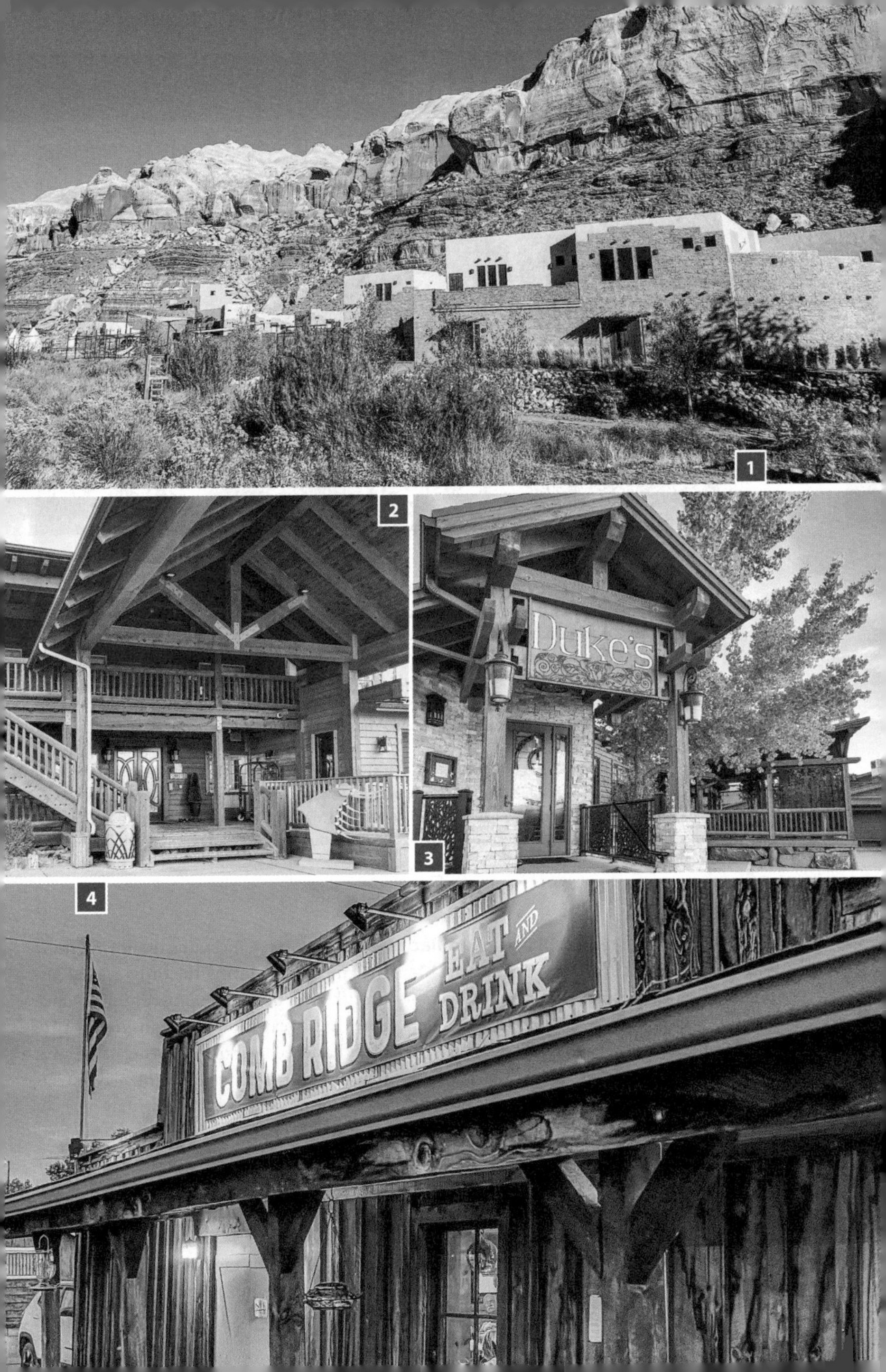
1
2
Duke's
3
4
COMB RIDGE
EAT AND DRINK

Four Corners Monument

marker of the Four Corners

A concrete slab marks the point where Utah, Colorado, New Mexico, and Arizona meet. Five national parks and 18 national monuments are within a radius of 150 miles (242 km) from this point, and it's the only spot in the United States where you can put your finger on four states at once. More than 2,000 people a day are said to stop at the marker in the summer season for an average of 7-10 minutes. Native Americans, mostly Navajo, and perhaps some Ute and Pueblo people, set up dozens of crafts and refreshment booths in summer. Navajo Parks and Recreation collects an $8 per person fee.

Getting to the Four Corners from Bluff, the closest town in Utah, is a bit indirect. Drive east from Bluff on Highway 162 for 13 miles (20.9 km), and at Montezuma Creek, turn south onto Highway 406 (Tribal Route 35) and travel 20 miles (32 km) to Red Mesa, Arizona. Turn east onto US 160 and drive 14 miles (22.5 km) to Teec Nos Pos, Arizona. The Four Corners Monument is 4 miles (6.4 km) north of Teec Nos Pos on US 160.

Two RV parks are right in town: **Cadillac Ranch RV Park** (630 Main St., 435/210-8933, www.cadillacranchrv.com, year-round, $35-48) has tent sites and a number of van-life amenities, and **Cottonwood R.V. Park** (320 Main St., 435/672-2287, http://cottonwoodrvpark.blogspot.com, Mar.-Nov. 15, $35) is at the west end of Bluff.

★ HOVENWEEP NATIONAL MONUMENT

Hovenweep National Monument (970/562-4283, www.nps.gov/hove, $20 per vehicle) preserves six groups of Ancestral Puebloan villages, including impressive stone structures built during the early-mid-1200s, near the end of their 1,300-year inhabitance here. A 25-year drought beginning in 1274 likely hastened their migration out of the area, though several centuries of intensive farming, hunting, and woodcutting may have already taken a toll on the land. Archaeologists believe the inhabitants retreated south in the late 1200s to northwestern New Mexico and northeastern Arizona.

The Ute word hovenweep means "deserted valley," a fitting name for the high desert country the Puebloans left behind. The people of Hovenweep had much in common with Mesa Verde culture, although the Dakota sandstone here doesn't form large alcoves suitable for cliff-dweller villages. The structures at Hovenweep remain essentially unexcavated, awaiting the attention of future archaeologists.

Ancestral Puebloan farmers had a keen interest in the seasons because they needed to know the best time to plant crops. To determine the equinoxes and solstices within an accuracy of 1-2 days, sun priests used astronomical stations, which have been discovered at Hovenweep Castle, at the Square Tower, and at the Cajon site. The Square Tower site, where the visitor center is, has the greatest number of remains and the most varied architecture.

Visitor Center

The **visitor center** (970/562-4282, 9am-5pm daily Apr. 21-Nov., 10am-3pm Thurs.-Sun. Dec.-Apr. 20) has a few exhibits on the Ancestral Puebloan people and photos of local wildlife. A ranger can answer questions, provide information on the monument, and give directions for visiting each of the units here. There's also a small campground at the monument (no reservations, $20).

Square Tower Group

This extensive group of Ancestral Puebloan towers and dwellings lines the rim and slopes of Little Ruin Canyon, a short walk from the visitor center. A trail guide booklet you can pick up at the visitor center has a map showing the several loop trails, with descriptions of prehistoric life, architecture, and local plants. You'll see towers (D-shaped, square, oval, and round), cliff dwellings, surface dwellings, storehouses, kivas, and rock art. Keep an eye out for the prairie rattlesnake, a subspecies of the western rattlesnake, which is active on summer nights and spring and fall days. Take care not to disturb the fragile structures and stay on the trail—don't climb walls or walk on rubble mounds.

More Hovenweep Sites

You'll need a map and directions from a ranger to find the other Hovenweep village sites, as they aren't signed. One group, the Goodman Point, near Cortez, Colorado, has relatively little to see except unexcavated mounds.

Holly Group is noted for its Great House, Holly Tower, and Tilted Tower. Most of Tilted Tower fell away after the boulder on which it

Hovenweep National Monument

sat shifted. Piles of rubble mark sites of structures built on loose ground. Look for remnants of farming terraces in the canyon below the Great House. A hiking trail connects the campground at Square Tower with Holly; the route follows canyon bottoms and is about 8 miles (12.9 km) round-trip. Hikers could also continue to sites at Horseshoe (1 mi/1.6 km farther) and Hackberry (0.3 mi/0.5 km beyond Horseshoe). All of these are just across the Colorado border and about 6 miles (9.7 km) one-way by road from the visitor center.

Horseshoe and **Hackberry Groups** are best reached by an easy trail (1 mi/1.6 km round-trip) off the road to Holly. Horseshoe House, built in a horseshoe shape similar to Sun Temple at Mesa Verde, has exceptionally good masonry work. Archaeologists haven't determined the purpose of the structure. Rubble piles and wall remnants abound in the area. The spring under an alcove here still has good flow, nurturing cottonwood and hackberry trees.

Cutthroat Castle was remote even in Ancestral Puebloan times, sitting along an intermittent stream rather than at the head of a canyon like most other Hovenweep sites. Cutthroat Castle is a large multistory structure with both straight and curved walls. Three round towers stand nearby. Look for wall fragments and the circular depressions of kivas. High-clearance vehicles can get close to the site, about 11.5 miles (18.5 km) one-way from the visitor center. Visitors without proper vehicles can drive to a trailhead then walk the rest of the way (1.5 mi/2.4 km round-trip).

The Cajon Group is at the head of a little canyon on Cajon Mesa on the Navajo Reservation in Utah, about 9 miles (14.5 km) southwest of the visitor center. The site has a commanding view across the San Juan Valley as far as Monument Valley. Buildings include a large multiroom structure, a round tower, and a tall square tower. Look for pictographs, petroglyphs, and grooves in rock (used for tool grinding). Farming terraces were located on the canyon's south side.

Getting There

One approach is from US 191 between Blanding and Bluff; head east 9 miles (14.5 km) on Highway 262, continue straight 6 miles (9.7 km) on a small, paved road to **Hatch Trading Post,** then follow signs for 16 miles (26 km). Another good way in from Bluff is to go east 21 miles (34 km) on the paved road to Montezuma Creek and Aneth, then follow the signs north for 20 miles (32 km). A scenic 58-mile (93-km) route through Montezuma Canyon begins 5 miles (8 km) south of Monticello and follows unpaved roads to Hatch and on to Hovenweep. If you're coming from Colorado, take a partly paved road west and north 41 miles (66 km) from US 491 (the turnoff is 4 mi/6.4 km south of Cortez).

MONUMENT VALLEY (TSE'BII'NDZISGAII)

Towering buttes, jagged pinnacles, and rippled sand dunes make this an otherworldly landscape that's appeared in numerous Westerns, like *Stagecoach* and *Once Upon a Time in the West*. Protected and managed by the Monument Valley Navajo Tribal Park, the area is accessible via a 17-mile (27-km) loop road and is entirely on Navajo Nation land. Monument Valley and the formations within are held sacred by the Navajo people.

Most of the natural monuments are remnants of sandstone eroded by wind and water. Agathla Peak and some lesser summits are roots of ancient volcanoes, which have dark rocks that contrast with the pale yellow sandstone of the other formations. The valley is at an elevation of 5,564 feet (1,695 m) in the Upper Sonoran Life Zone; annual rainfall averages about 8.5 inches (21.6 cm).

In 1863-1864, when Kit Carson was ravaging Canyon de Chelly in Arizona to round up Navajo people, Chief Hoskinini led his people to the safety and freedom of Monument Valley. Merrick Butte and Mitchell Mesa commemorate two miners who discovered rich silver deposits on their first trip to the valley in 1880. On their second trip, both were killed, reportedly shot by Paiutes.

Hollywood movies made the splendor of Monument Valley known to the world. *Stagecoach,* filmed here in 1938, directed by John Ford, and featuring John Wayne, became the first in a series of Westerns that has continued to the present. Aside from its appeal as the backdrop of many an iconic film, Monument Valley is a truly mystical spot of changing colors and shifting shadows.

From Mexican Hat, drive 22 miles (35 km) southwest on US 163, turn left, and go 3.5 miles (5.6 km) to the visitor center. From Kayenta, Arizona, go 24 miles (39 km) north on US 163, turn right, and go 3.5 miles (5.6 km). At the junction of US 163 is a village of outdoor market stalls and indoor shops where you can stop to buy Navajo artwork and crafts.

Visitor Center

At the entrance to the **Monument Valley Navajo Tribal Park** is a visitor center (435/727-5874, www.navajonationparks.org, 8am-5pm daily, closed major holidays, $8 pp) with exhibits and crafts. This is a good place to get a list of Navajo tour guides to lead you on driving or hiking trips into the monument. A guide is required to venture into the backcountry off the main drive, but not to follow the main scenic drive. Lots of folks along the road will also offer these services.

Tours

Take one of several guided tours leaving daily year-round from the visitor center to see sites such as a hogan, a cliff dwelling, and petroglyphs in areas beyond the self-guided drive. The trips last 1.5-4 hours and generally cost $75-100 per person. Guided horseback rides from near the visitor center cost around $90 for 2 hours; longer day and overnight trips can be arranged, too. If you'd like to hike in Monument Valley, you must hire a guide. Hiking tours of 2 hours to a full day or more can be arranged at the visitor center.

★ Monument Valley Drive

A 17-mile (27-km) **self-guided scenic drive** (8am-5pm daily, closed major holidays) begins at the visitor center and loops through the heart of the valley. Overlooks provide sweeping views from different vantage points. The dirt road is normally fine for most cars. Avoid stopping or you may get stuck in the loose sand that sometimes blows across the road. Plan on about 90 minutes for the drive. No hiking or driving is allowed off the signed

Goulding's Lodge and Trading Post

1
2
MONUMENT VALLEY & MYSTERY VALLEY
GUIDED VEHICLE
TOURS
& INFORMATION

route. Water and restrooms are available only at the visitor center.

Accommodations

Don't be surprised to find that lodging at Monument Valley is expensive—and quite popular, so book well ahead of time.

The Navajo-owned ★ **View Hotel** (Indian Rte. 42, Olijato-Monument Valley, 435/727-5555, www.monumentvalleyview.com, $159-339) in Arizona provides the only lodging within Monument Valley Tribal Park. Views are terrific from this charming modern hotel; reserve a room well in advance. Secluded cabins ($199-250) and camping ($23 tents, $45-90 RVs) are also available.

★ **Goulding's Lodge and Trading Post** (435/727-3231 or 866/313-9769, www.gouldings.com, $179-399) is another good place to stay in the Monument Valley area. Sheep trader turned entrepreneur Harry Goulding and his wife opened this dramatically located trading post in 1924. Harry later became instrumental in introducing Hollywood to this natural set.

The lodge itself is a large complex tucked under rimrock 2 miles (3.2 km) west of the US 163 Monument Valley turnoff, just north of the Arizona-Utah border. Modern rooms offer incredible views of Monument Valley. There's also a small indoor pool and dining room. A gift shop sells souvenirs, books, and Native American crafts. A nearby store has groceries and gas pumps, a restaurant is open daily for all meals, and tours and horseback rides are available. The lodge stays open year-round, and rates drop in winter and early spring. A small museum displays prehistoric and modern artifacts, movie photos, and Goulding family memorabilia. The **campground** ($84, $108-130 with hookups) is pleasant and well managed.

There are a handful of hotels about 30 minutes south in Kayenta, Arizona. The adobe-style **Hampton Inn** (US 160, 928/697-3170 or 800/426-7866, $206) is the nicest place in town, and it's only a little more expensive than others nearby.

1: Monument Valley **2:** Take a tour through Monument Valley.

Uinta Mountains and Dinosaur Country

This chapter doesn't cover a distinct region, but rather the magnificent hodgepodge of landscapes across the northeastern part of the state, including Utah's tallest mountain, domes of sandstone, dinosaur quarries, a massive reservoir, and a petroglyph-filled canyon. The longest drive between destinations covered here is about five hours.

In the state's far northeastern corner, Flaming Gorge National Recreation Area offers excellent fishing and boating in a colorful desert canyon. This region is trenched by the Green River and its tributaries, which offer lively white-water rafting.

South of the gorge, the Uinta Mountains are an alpine paradise, home to Utah's biggest mountain: Kings Peak (13,528 ft/4,123 m).

Highlights

Look for ★ to find recommended sights, activities, dining, and lodging.

★ **Mirror Lake Highway:** This scenic byway travels through the Uinta Mountains, one of the only ranges in the United States that runs east to west, past breathtaking viewpoints and trails leading to high alpine lakes and summits (page 418).

★ **High Uintas Wilderness:** Venture into the wilderness for a night or more and catch some trout for dinner via the 96-mile (154-km) Highline Trail or the path to the top of Kings Peak, Utah's highest mountain (page 420).

★ **Utah Field House Museum:** Fossils and digs at the Utah Field House Museum will delight kids and parents alike (page 423).

★ **Dinosaur National Monument:** Head toward Colorado (this monument spans both states) for more fossil fun, plus hiking and rafting (page 428).

★ **Flaming Gorge National Recreation Area:** Lake Powell gets all the attention, but this gorgeous reservoir on the border with Wyoming is a worthy destination for boating, fishing, and hiking (page 434).

★ **Nine Mile Canyon:** This 3-hour drive is filled with prehistoric relics of the past, including Fremont structures and petroglyphs (page 440).

★ **The San Rafael Swell:** Sandstone rock features, the "Little Grand Canyon," and great hiking, mountain biking, and climbing await at this under-the-radar geologic formation (page 446).

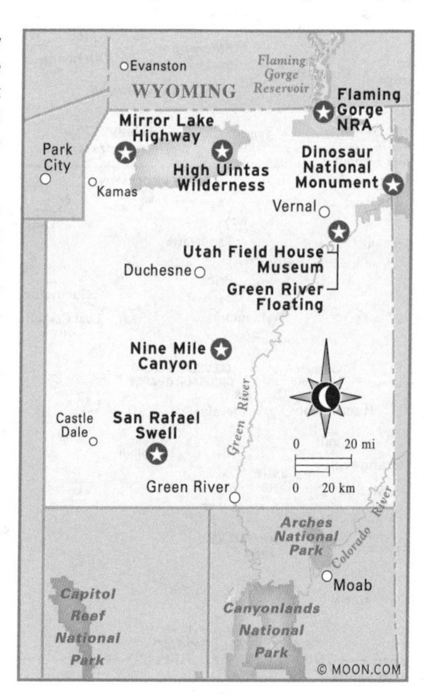

★ **Green River Floating:** Just outside Vernal, raft or kayak the Green River, which has its own state park (page 449).

Uinta Mountains and Dinosaur Country

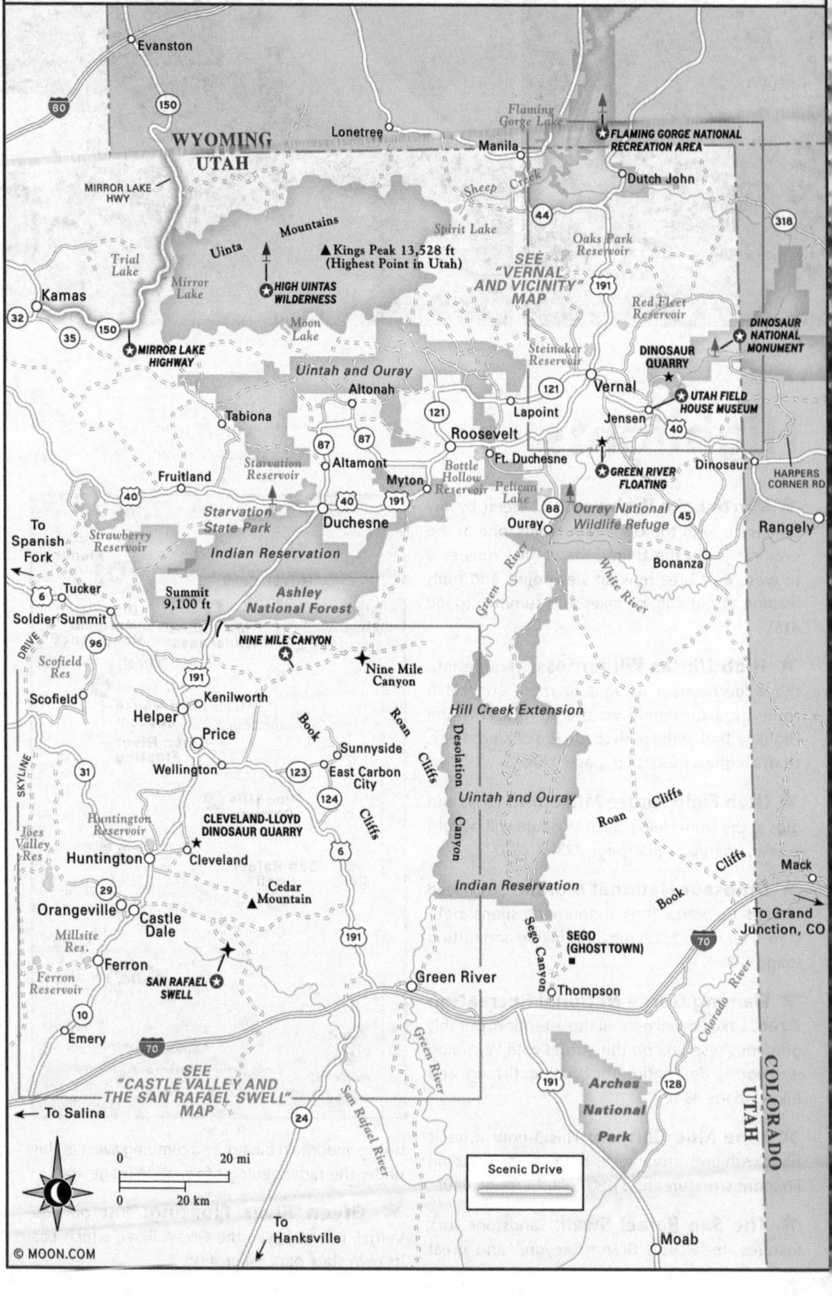
Evanston
80
150
WYOMING
UTAH
Flaming Gorge Lake
FLAMING GORGE NATIONAL RECREATION AREA
Lonetree
Manila
Dutch John
MIRROR LAKE HWY
Sheep Creek
44
318
Spirit Lake
Uinta Mountains
Kings Peak 13,528 ft (Highest Point in Utah)
Oaks Park Reservoir
SEE "VERNAL AND VICINITY" MAP
Trial Lake
Mirror Lake
HIGH UINTAS WILDERNESS
191
Red Fleet Reservoir
Kamas
32
35
150
MIRROR LAKE HIGHWAY
Moon Lake
Steinaker Reservoir
DINOSAUR QUARRY
DINOSAUR NATIONAL MONUMENT
Uintah and Ouray
Altonah
121
Vernal
UTAH FIELD HOUSE MUSEUM
Tabiona
121
Lapoint
Jensen
40
87
87
Roosevelt
Altamont
Starvation Reservoir
Bottle Hollow Reservoir
Ft. Duchesne
GREEN RIVER FLOATING
Dinosaur
HARPERS CORNER RD
Fruitland
40
40
191
Myton
Pelican Lake
88
Ouray National Wildlife Refuge
45
Starvation State Park
Duchesne
Ouray
Rangely
To Spanish Fork
Strawberry Reservoir
Indian Reservation
Green River
White River
Bonanza
6
Tucker
Summit 9,100 ft
Ashley National Forest
Soldier Summit
NINE MILE CANYON
Nine Mile Canyon
96
Scofield Res
SKYLINE DRIVE
191
Scofield
Kenilworth
Hill Creek Extension
Helper
Price
Book Cliffs
Roan Cliffs
Desolation Canyon
Sunnyside
31
Wellington
123
East Carbon City
124
Uintah and Ouray
Roan Cliffs
Huntington Reservoir
CLEVELAND-LLOYD DINOSAUR QUARRY
Cliffs
Joes Valley Res
Huntington
Cleveland
6
Indian Reservation
Book Cliffs
Mack
29
Cedar Mountain
Orangeville
Castle Dale
To Grand Junction, CO
Millsite Res.
191
Sego Canyon
SEGO (GHOST TOWN)
70
Ferron
Ferron Reservoir
SAN RAFAEL SWELL
Green River
Thompson
Colorado River
10
Emery
70
Green River
COLORADO
UTAH
SEE "CASTLE VALLEY AND THE SAN RAFAEL SWELL" MAP
191
Arches National Park
128
To Salina
24
San Rafael River
0
20 mi
0
20 km
Scenic Drive
To Hanksville
Moab
© MOON.COM

Across this range are long backpacking trails, wildflower-filled hikes, and turquoise high alpine lakes.

Considered a southeastern gateway town to the Uintas, Vernal is also the entry point to dinosaur country. Some 140 million years ago, stegosauruses, allosauruses, and other creatures roamed what was once a subtropical region. Stretching across the Colorado border, Dinosaur National Monument preserves a fossil quarry and dinosaur bones. Excavations are still underway at the Cleveland-Lloyd Dinosaur Quarry.

Head south toward the desert and stop in the Price area to explore the rock art of Nine Mile Canyon, then continue to the San Rafael Swell. This anticline—a fold in the earth like the one that defines Capitol Reef National Park—makes up the northern edge of the Colorado Plateau. At the "Swell," backcountry travelers can hike, camp, mountain bike, and explore relics of the ancient Fremont people with fewer fees and crowds than in most of Utah's desert country.

PLANNING YOUR TIME

Vernal makes a good base for exploring the **Flaming Gorge** and **Dinosaur National Monument,** although campers will find plenty of good sites in both areas. It's worth spending at least 2 days here: one at the national monument and another at Flaming Gorge. If you have an extra day, take a **rafting trip** on the **Green River.**

Another good hub is the town of **Price,** with lodging and good access to the San Rafael Swell and Cleveland-Lloyd Dinosaur Quarry.

Finally, if **hiking** or **backpacking** is your objective, the **Uintas** are the best place to spend your time, from a day trip along **Mirror Lake Highway** to a weeklong backpacking trip. However, keep in mind that you can't reliably plan a trip like this until late June, since heavy snow can block road and trail access until then.

In summer, come prepared for **hot days** and **chilly nights.** The valleys have average highs of about 90°F (32°C), but temperatures drop to the low 50s at night. The Wasatch Plateau and Uinta Mountains experience cool weather year-round. Above 10,000 feet (3048 m), summer highs rarely exceed 70°F (21°C) during the day and drop to the 30s and 40s at night. Freezing weather may occur any time of year.

Uinta Mountains

The Uintas (yoo-IN-tuhs) contain lofty peaks, lush meadows, fragrant coniferous forests, crystal clear streams, and a multitude of alpine lakes. The range takes its name from the Uintah band of the Ute Tribe, which is derived from a Ute word for "pine."

Kings Peak tops the range at 13,528 feet (4,123 m)—the highest point in the state. Unlike most other major ranges of the United States, the Uintas run east-west. Underground forces pushed rock layers up into a massive dome 150 miles (242 km) long and 35 miles (56 km) wide. Ancient Precambrian rocks exposed in the center of the range consist largely of quartzite (metamorphosed sandstone). Outcrops of progressively younger rocks are found away from the center. Glaciers have carved steep ridges and broad basins and left great moraines. Barren rock lies exposed across much of the land, including the peaks and high ridges.

Despite their great heights, the Uintas have gentler terrain than the precipitous Wasatch Range. High plateaus and broad valleys

Previous: Yellow Pine Lake; Mirror Lake Highway runs from Utah to Wyoming; Utah Field House Museum.

among the peaks hold the abundant rain and snowfall in marshes and ponds, supporting large populations of wildlife and fish.

The Uintas is home to over 1,000 natural lakes, so it's no wonder that fishing is popular. Many of these lakes are stocked, and one feisty and locally popular fish is the tiger trout, a cross between brown and brook trout.

VISITING THE UINTAS

Winding over the western side of the range from the town of Kamas to the Wyoming border, Highway 150 (Mirror Lake Highway) offers splendid panoramas and access to fishing lakes and hiking trails. To the east, US 191 and Highway 44 provide access to the Uintas and Flaming Gorge Reservoir from Vernal. Unpaved roads also lead to trailheads on all sides of the range. Developed and primitive campgrounds can be found along these highways and near many trailheads.

Most people prefer to visit the Uintas during the summer. Campers should be prepared for cold nights and freezing rain even in August. Afternoon showers are common in summer. Near lakes and marshes, arm yourself with insect repellent to ward off mosquitoes, especially in July. In the High Uintas, snow stays on the ground well into June, and snowmelt can make trails muddy until early July. The lakes and campgrounds along Highway 150 get crowded on summer weekends and holidays, although you can usually find solitude by hiking a couple miles into the backcountry.

An extensive trail system with about 20 trailheads goes deep into the wilderness and leads to many lakes. Everything from easy day hikes to long-distance backpacking treks are possible. In winter, snowmobilers and cross-country skiers come out to enjoy the snowy landscapes.

INFORMATION

The US Forest Service manages the Uintas and surrounding lands. Northern and western parts are administered by the **Uinta-Wasatch-Cache National Forest** (Heber-Kamas District, 50 E. Center St., Kamas, 435/783-4338, www.fs.usda.gov/uwcnf). Most of the southern and eastern areas are part of the **Ashley National Forest** (355 N. Vernal Ave., Vernal, 435/789-1181, www.fs.usda.gov/ashley). For specific information, it's best to contact the district office closest to the trailhead. Pick up a copy of the *Trails Illustrated High Uintas Wilderness* topo map (1:75,000 scale) online or at a ranger station.

★ MIRROR LAKE HIGHWAY

One of Utah's most spectacular alpine drives, Mirror Lake Highway (Hwy. 150) begins in Kamas at an elevation of 6,500 feet (1,981 m) and climbs to the crest of the western Uinta Mountains at Bald Mountain Pass (elev. 10,620 ft/3,237 m) before descending on the other side and continuing to Evanston, Wyoming. The first 25 miles (40 km) of the highway are pretty, but relatively flat. Shortly after passing Provo River Falls, the road climbs sharply as the views open up to include rugged mountain peaks. The highway is a great scenic drive in and of itself, but it also accesses numerous trailheads, campgrounds, off-roading, lakes for fishing, climbing areas, and more opportunities for adventure.

The nearest motels to Kamas are in Heber City (17 mi/27 km southwest) and Park City (19 mi/31 km west). The **Heber-Kamas Ranger District Office** (50 E. Center St., Kamas, 435/783-4338) can advise on road conditions, campgrounds, hiking, cross-country skiing, and snowmobiling. Bustling Evanston right off I-80 is about 75 miles (121 km) from Kamas and has several motels, fast-food restaurants, and a couple grocery stores.

Mid-November-Memorial Day weekend, Highway 150 is closed after about 14 miles (22.5 km) from Kamas, along with all back roads. Depending on the snowpack, you may not be able to make the full drive until mid-June.

1: Lake views can be found throughout the Uintas.
2: Yellow Pine Creek Trail

1
2

A $6 3-day recreation pass, available at the start of the highway and at several points along the way, is required if you're going to park and hike from an established trailhead.

Hiking

The first trailhead up Mirror Lake Highway, **Yellow Pine Creek Trail** begins just north of the Yellow Pine Campground (mile 6.7) and climbs 2,642 feet (805 m) up along the creek to Lower Yellow Pine Lake (elev. 9,600 ft/2,926 m, 4 mi/6.4 km one-way) and beyond; this is a good hike early in the season.

Provo River Falls overlook (mile 24) isn't a formal trail, but it's a great place to get out of the car and explore the river cascading over rock.

Several trails start at the **Crystal Lake trailhead,** near the Trial Lake Campground (mile 25.4). It's just 1 mile (1.6 km) from the trailhead to pretty **Wall Lake,** a good destination for families or easygoing backpackers. **Notch Mountain Trail** goes north past Wall and Twin Lakes, through the Notch to Ibantik and Meadow Lakes, to the Weber River (elev. 9,000 ft/2,743 m, 6.5 mi/10.5 km one-way), and to Bald Mountain Pass (elev. 10,678 ft/3,255 m, 10 mi/16.1 km one-way). The **Lakes Country Trail** starts at the Crystal Lake trailhead and goes west past Island, Long, and other lakes before joining the Smith-Morehouse Trail after 3 miles (4.8 km).

At **Bald Mountain Pass** (mile 29.1, elev. 10,678 ft/3,255 m), the **Bald Mountain National Recreation Trail** climbs to the summit of Bald Mountain (elev. 11,947 ft/3,641 m) with great views all the way. The 2-mile (3.2-km) each way trail climbs 1,269 vertical feet (387 m), putting you in the middle of the Uinta Range's alpine grandeur. Expect a strenuous trip because of the high elevation and steep grades. Carry rain gear to fend off the cold wind, even in summer, and possible storms. From the top, weather permitting, you'll enjoy panoramas of the High Uintas Wilderness and the Wasatch Range. **Notch Mountain Trail** also begins near the picnic area and connects with Trial Lake.

★ Backpacking

There are several excellent backpacking routes within the Uintas, but perhaps the most well-known and epic of them all is the **Highline Trail** (96 mi/154 km, 16,700 ft/5,090 m elevation gain), which tours the **High Uintas Wilderness.** From mile 34 (starting from Kamas) of the Mirror Lake Highway, the trail winds nearly 100 miles (161 km) to East Park Reservoir north of Vernal, serving as the main east-west trail in the Uintas. To hike the whole trail with a shuttle back will take about a week and is a strenuous journey.

The trail holds steady around 10,000 feet (3,048 m), and several 12,000- and 13,000-foot (3,658- and 3,962-m) mountains can be climbed via detours. Much of the trail lies above tree line, making for expansive views of the Uinta Mountains, lakes, and wildflower meadows. It's also an excellent place to spot wildlife like bears, moose, and birds of prey.

TOP EXPERIENCE

Kings Peak

While Mount Timpanogos to the west usually steals Kings Peak's thunder, there's no denying that Kings is the highest in Utah at 13,528 feet (4,123 m). Summitting **Kings Peak** (28.8 mi/46.3 km round-trip, 2 days, approx. 4,100 ft/1,250 m elevation gain, strenuous) requires an overnight backpacking trip. Henrys Fork trailhead, which accesses the most common route to the summit, is reached most quickly by driving northeast into Wyoming, then back south into Utah—about a 3-hour drive from Salt Lake City or Kamas.

The hike features moderate terrain dotted with lakes, including Dollar Lake, which is a popular dispersed camping area and stopping point. You can also find a campsite before the trail starts to climb up Gunsight Pass or near Henrys Fork Lake. Like most thirteeners, the last few miles toward the peak navigate scree and boulder fields, so expect some nontechnical scrambling.

Mountain Biking

Most of the trails in the Uintas are not purpose-built for mountain biking, though there are nearly endless miles of dirt Forest Service roads you can ride. For a very mellow tour, hit the double-track **Beaver Creek Trail** (4.5 mi/7.2 km one-way, 500 ft/152 m elevation gain), which runs parallel to Mirror Lake Highway. The best mountain biking in the Uintas can be found in a new single-track trail system being developed in the Yellow Pine area—the first trailhead on your left coming from Kamas. From the Yellow Pine trailhead, **Slate Creek Trail** (5.8 mi/9.3 km round-trip, 790 ft/241 m elevation gain) is a great moderate loop with a few technical rocky sections, a fun creek crossing, and a few optional jumps.

Rock Climbing

The Uintas offer several excellent climbing areas, featuring high-quality quartzite crags and a well-rounded mix of sport and trad, with a few top-roping areas and a little bit of bouldering. One of the most popular areas, **Ruth's Lake** offers several walls of single-pitch sport routes ranging from 5.6 to 5.12. The Ruth's Lake area is well shaded, so it's perfect for hot days. Most of the climbs are found at the **Chief Wall** and the **Good Medicine Area,** both just a 20-minute approach from the car. Another great spot is **Cliff Lake,** a gorgeous cliff above a glimmering alpine lake, where you'll find single-pitch beginner-to-moderate sport and trad climbs, ranging from 5.5 to 5.10c. Park at the Crystal Lake trailhead and start on Crystal Lake Trail until you see a small offshoot trail on your right leading to Cliff Lake, marked by a small, rusty sign.

Campgrounds

You'll find a campground just about every few miles along Mirror Lake Highway. Campgrounds usually fill on summer weekends, but some campsites can be reserved (877/444-6777, www.recreation.gov). There are also nearly endless free backpacking and dispersed camping options. Good areas to look for dispersed car camping sites include up **Norway Flats Road** and around **Soapstone Basin.** You'll see many people camping (mostly in RVs or pickup campers) in roadside pullouts, too. The campgrounds listed here are particularly lovely, with access to hiking trails and/or lakes.

Early in the season, **Yellow Pine Campground** (mile 6.7, elev. 7,200 ft/2,195 m, no water, late May-late Oct., $20) is a good bet, as is the trail that starts here. **Soapstone Campground** (mile 15.5, water early June-mid-Sept., $24, reservations available) has sites along the Provo River amid lodgepole pines at 8,200 feet (2,499 m).

Trial Lake Campground (mile 25.4, water late June-early Sept., $24) is 0.25 mile (0.4 km), to the left of the highway on Spring Canyon Road, has sites on the southeast shore of the lake in a pine and spruce forest at 9,500 feet (2,896 m). There's a parking area near the dam for anglers. Spring Canyon Road continues past the dam to Washington and Crystal Lakes and the Crystal Lake trailhead.

Mirror Lake Campground (mile 31.2, water early July-early Sept., $24, reservations available) is the largest campground (91 sites) on the Mirror Lake Highway. Sites are near the lake in a forest of spruce, fir, and lodgepole pine at 10,200 feet (3,109 m). Anglers can park at the south end of the lake and at the Mirror Lake trailhead. Boats can be hand-launched; no motors are permitted on the lake. Trails lead into the High Uintas Wilderness.

Cross-Country Skiing

Snowplows keep the highway cleared in winter up to Soapstone, 14.6 miles (23.4 km) from Kamas, to provide access for cross-country skiing, backcountry skiing, and snowmobiling. Five trails used by both skiers and snowmobilers begin along the highway and at Soapstone. Skiers using snowmobile trails will find the most solitude on weekdays.

Beaver Creek Cross-Country Trail

begins across the highway from the Yellow Pine trailhead (6 mi/9.7 km east of Kamas, $6) and parallels the highway for 6.5 miles (10.5 km) one-way with an elevation gain of 440 feet (134 m). This trail is easy; branching off from it are other cross-country ski trails rated intermediate and advanced, as well as various skintracks for backcountry skiers. Dogs are allowed only on odd-numbered days. You can obtain information and brochures for these and other skiing areas from the Heber-Kamas Ranger District Office.

Vernal

One of the oldest and largest communities in northeastern Utah, Vernal makes a handy base for travels to the many sights of the region. The perennial waters of Ashley Creek—named for mountain man William H. Ashley, who passed by in 1825—attracted the first settlers to the valley during the early 1870s.

Natural resource extraction is a major contributor to Vernal's economy. Growth of the oil industry in recent decades has been a mixed blessing because of its boom-bust cycles.

SIGHTS

★ Utah Field House Museum

The **Utah Field House of Natural History State Park Museum** (496 E. Main St., 435/789-3799, https://stateparks.utah.gov, 9am-5pm Mon.-Sat., $8 adults, $4 children, under age 5 free) is a good place for both adults and children to learn about the dinosaurs that once roamed the Uinta Basin. Full-size models stalk or fly in the Dinosaur Gardens outside, and a 90-foot-long (27.4-m) *Diplodocus* skeleton greets visitors in the museum's rotunda. The Jurassic Hall houses dinosaur fossils, including the most complete skeleton that exists of the sauropod *Haplocanthosaurus,* while the Eocene Gallery has displays of 45-million-year-old skulls of ancient mammals, crocodiles, and alligators that once roamed what is now Utah. Visitors can excavate fossils at a dig site replica.

1: mountain biking on Slate Creek Trail 2: climbers at Cliff Lake 3: Kings Peak is Utah's highest peak.

Uintah County Heritage Museum

The **Uintah County Heritage Museum** (328 E. 200 S., 435/789-7399, www.uintahmuseum.org, 9am-6pm Mon.-Fri., 10am-4pm Sat. Sept.-May, 9am-7pm Mon.-Thurs., 9am-6pm Fri., 10am-4pm Sat. June-Aug., free) is a pioneer museum and art gallery focused on Utah's outlaw heritage (real and mythical). Also housed here is the **Ladies of the White House Doll Collection,** created by a local doll maker. Each doll wears a hand-sewn reproduction of a dress worn at an Inaugural Ball.

Dry Fork Petroglyphs

Several striking petroglyph panels decorate a sharp sandstone bluff about 8 miles (12.9 km) northwest of Vernal. What makes these carvings so notable is the fact that they contain dozens of nearly life-size human figures, many with elaborate headdresses and ornamentation, and others with gory injuries. The significance of these murals is unknown, although they were probably carved by the Fremont between 1,200 and 1,600 years ago.

To reach the Dry Fork Petroglyphs (also called the McConkie Ranch Petroglyphs), drive west from Vernal on Main Street and turn north onto 500 West. Follow the main road when it turns to the left onto Highway 121 and continue until the junction with 3500 West. Turn right (north) and follow this road for 6.8 miles (10.9 km); it will head west and become Dry Fork Settlement Road. Watch for signs and follow a private ranch access road to the marked parking area.

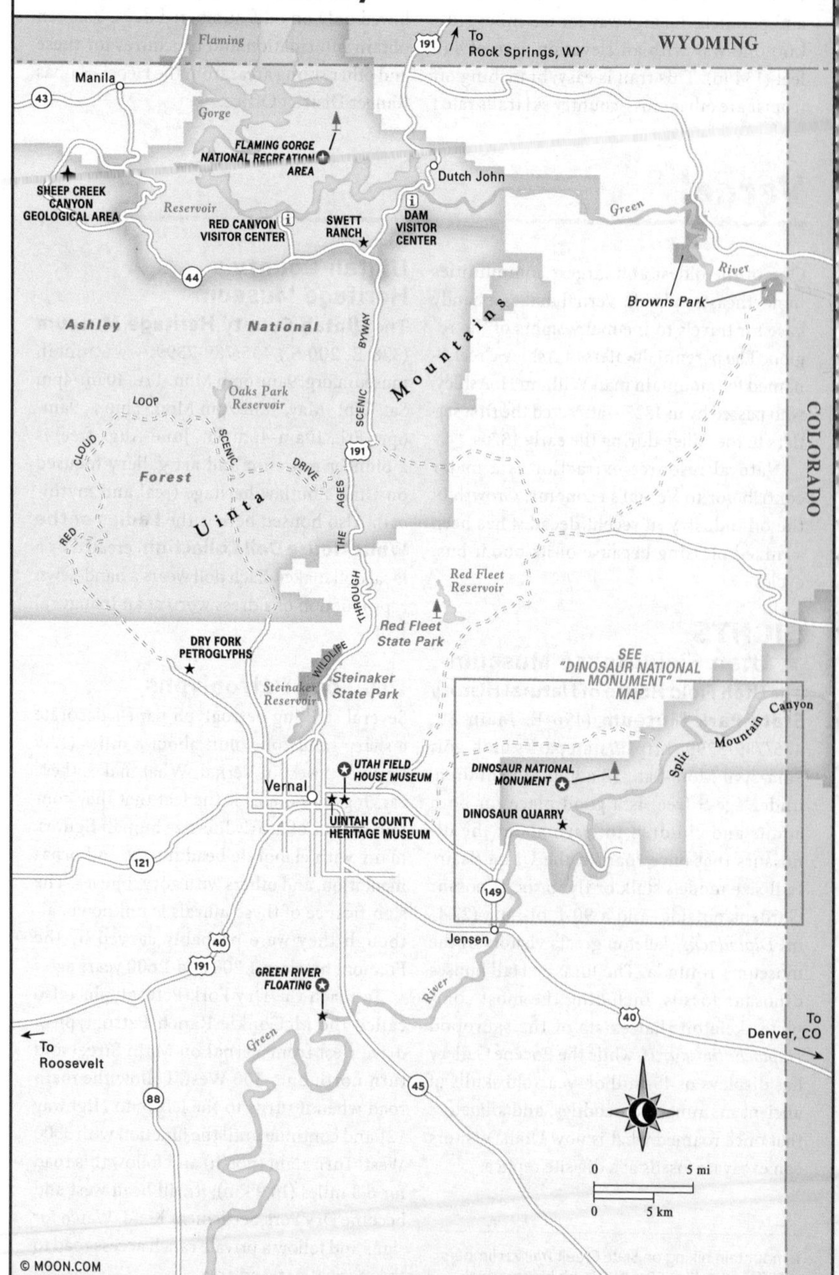
Vernal and Vicinity
To Rock Springs, WY
WYOMING
Flaming
Manila
Gorge
FLAMING GORGE NATIONAL RECREATION AREA
Dutch John
SHEEP CREEK CANYON GEOLOGICAL AREA
Reservoir
RED CANYON VISITOR CENTER
SWETT RANCH
DAM VISITOR CENTER
Green
River
Browns Park
Ashley
National
Mountains
Uinta
Forest
BYWAY
SCENIC
Oaks Park Reservoir
LOOP
CLOUD
RED
SCENIC
DRIVE
AGES
THE
THROUGH
COLORADO
Red Fleet Reservoir
Red Fleet State Park
DRY FORK PETROGLYPHS
WILDLIFE
Steinaker Reservoir
Steinaker State Park
SEE "DINOSAUR NATIONAL MONUMENT" MAP
Canyon
Mountain
Split
DINOSAUR NATIONAL MONUMENT
DINOSAUR QUARRY
UTAH FIELD HOUSE MUSEUM
Vernal
UINTAH COUNTY HERITAGE MUSEUM
Jensen
GREEN RIVER FLOATING
River
Green
To Roosevelt
To Denver, CO
0 5 mi
0 5 km

The petroglyphs are on private property, and donations are accepted; there are no facilities. Stay on the trails, and don't get discouraged—the best carvings are about 15 minutes into the cliff-side hike. This area is very rich in petroglyphs, and you could easily spend hours wandering the cliffs.

RECREATION

Mountain Biking

Vernal has good mountain biking and far less hype than other areas in Utah. The riding is so exposed that in summer, the only viable times to ride are dawn or dusk. McCoy Flats, 10 miles (16.1 km) west of Vernal, has about 35 miles (56 km) of trails, all starting from a trailhead on McCoy Flats Road. Another good trail system is in the Red Mountain area north of town, near Red Fleet Reservoir. Stop in at **Altitude Cycle** (580 E. Main St., 435/781-2595, 10am-6pm Mon.-Sat.) for info on trails. The Utah Mountain Biking website (www.utahmountainbiking.com) has good descriptions of local trails.

River Rafting

Trips down the Green River's Split Mountain Gorge through Dinosaur National Monument provide the excitement of big rapids and the beauty of remote canyons. One-day trips from the monument's Rainbow Park rafting 7 miles (11.3 km) through Split Mountain Canyon are offered by **OARS Dinosaur** (221 N. 400 E., 435/789-4316 or 800/342-8243, www.greenriverrafting.com). **Adrift Adventures** (9500 E. 6000 S., Jensen, 800/824-0150, https://adrift.com) has day trips through Split Mountain Canyon and rents inflatable kayaks ($50-75). Expect to pay about $120 adults, $99 children for guided day trips and well over $1,000 for multiday excursions.

The Yampa River, a tributary of the Colorado, joins the Green River in Dinosaur National Monument. Both are good rafting destinations. Experienced rafters will enjoy the challenge of the very technical Class III-IV run down the Cross Mountain Gorge in the Yampa River. Rent a raft or arrange a shuttle from **River Runners' Transport** (417 E. Main, 435/781-4919 or 800/930-7238, www.riverrunnerstransport.com). The company also runs fully and partially supported trips.

Permits are required for all raft trips through Dinosaur National Monument (see www.nps.gov/dino; purchase at www.recreation.gov, $20 for 1-day permit, plus $15 application fee). Outfitters will take care of permits for guided trips.

ENTERTAINMENT AND EVENTS

The **Outlaw Trail Theater** (Outlaw Trail Amphitheater, Western Park, 302 E. 200 S., 888/240-2080, www.outlawtrailtheater.org, 8pm most nights mid-June-early July, $10-14) is a community theater presenting Broadway and other shows every year.

The **PRCA Dinosaur Roundup Rodeo** (800/421-9635, www.vernalrodeo.com) in mid-July is Vernal's biggest event of the year and includes a parade and country music showdown. A parade celebrates **Pioneer Day** on July 24. The **Uintah County Fair** (435/789-7396, www.uintahcountyfair.com) comes to town the first week of June.

FOOD

The **Vernal Brewing Company** (55 S. 500 E., 435/781-2337, www.vernalbrewingco.com, 11:30am-9pm Sun.-Thurs., 11:30am-10pm Fri.-Sat., $12-33) is an upscale (for Vernal, anyway) pub across from the dinosaur museum, with beers ranging from a lager to a milk stout, decent pizza, and creative specials, including bacon confit game hen with quinoa.

For the best pizza in town, choose **Antica Forma** (251 E. Main St., 435/374-4138, www.anticaforma.com, 11am-9pm Mon.-Sat., $16-23). It's also a good place to pick up a panini or sandwich to pack for lunch or settle in for a lasagna dinner. And among the several good Mexican restaurants in town, **El Sombrero** (395 E. Main St., 435/781-0627, https://el-somrero.business.site, 9am-8pm Mon.-Fri., 10am-7pm Sat., $12-15) is a great, family-owned choice serving from-scratch Mexican

1

2
Vernal
UTAH'S DINOSAUR
LAND
VERNAL CITY
WELCOMES YOU

tacos, enchiladas, and other standard plates, alongside more authentic dishes like menudo.

ACCOMMODATIONS

A good in-town motel with reasonable rates is **Antlers Inn** (423 W. Main St., 435/789-1202, www.antlersinnvernal.com, $98-141)—make sure to ask at the desk for a breakfast voucher for the restaurant next door.

The **Dinosaur Inn** (251 E. Main St., 435/789-2660, $141-156) has a pool, a hot tub, and an exercise room. The **Springhill Suites** (1250 W. US 40, 435/781-9000, www.dinoinn.com, $114-124) is pretty stylish for Vernal, with modern decor, an indoor pool, a fitness center, and a breakfast buffet. One of Vernal's newer hotels is the **Ledgestone Hotel** (679 W. Main St., 435/789-4200, $100-119, https://ledgestonehotel.com/vernal), where all rooms have kitchenettes.

Campgrounds

Unless you really need to be in Vernal or can't drive a mile (1.6 km) farther, it's best to camp north of town toward Flaming Gorge or east in Dinosaur National Monument. But if you must stay in Vernal, or you want full hookups, **Vernal/Dinosaurland KOA Holiday** (930 N. Vernal Ave., 435/789-2148 or 800/562-7574, www.dinokoa.com, Apr.-Oct., tents $35-49, RVs $47-70, cabins $75-175) is on the north side of town. It has showers, a pool, a kitchen, laundry, and mini golf. **Fossil Valley RV Park** (999 W. US 40, 435/789-6450, www.fossilvalleyrvpark.com, open year-round, RVs $52-55) has showers and laundry.

INFORMATION AND SERVICES

The **Dinosaurland Travel Board** (800/477-5558, www.dinoland.com) provides visitor info and events.

For recreation info on the Ashley National Forest and eastern Uinta Mountains, hit up the **Vernal Ranger District Office** (355 N. Vernal Ave., 435/789-1181, www.fs.usda.gov/ashley, 8am-5pm Mon.-Fri.), which can tell you about scenic drives, camping, hiking, cross-country skiing, and snowmobiling.

Ashley Regional Medical Center (150 W. 100 N., 435/789-3342) provides hospital care.

Vicinity of Vernal

From Vernal, US 191 heads up and over the Uinta Mountains to Flaming Gorge, where a dam backs up the Green River. The drive is picturesque though not entirely pristine—views include vast phosphate mining operations and scars from off-road vehicles. For the best photos, do this drive in the evening, when the light is beautiful.

Few paved roads cross the vast area south of Vernal between US 40 and I-70. The Green River flows south from here through the spectacular Desolation and Gray Canyons. Most river-runners put in for this stretch at Sand Wash, which is accessible by dirt roads from Price, via the town of Myton (on US 40 between Roosevelt and Duchesne), or by airplane from the town of Green River (there's an airstrip at Sand Wash).

Most travelers don't linger along the US 40 corridor west of Vernal, but north of the highway, there are several jumping-off spots to the Uinta Mountains. If you want to take a break from driving on US 40, Starvation Reservoir is a good bet.

NORTH OF VERNAL

Wildlife Through the Ages Scenic Byway

This scenic interpretive route follows US 191 and Highway 44 north from Vernal to Flaming Gorge Reservoir. As the road climbs,

1: Vernal's Utah Field House Museum **2:** Vernal, land of dinosaurs

it crosses a staggering 19 geologic formations, revealing rock layers as old as the period during which the Uinta Mountains formed. The 30-mile (48-km) drive begins 4 miles (6.4 km) north of town on US 191. A tour map at a pullout details the formations ahead, and signs along the way identify each formation from the Mancos (80 million years old) to the Uinta Mountain Group (one billion years old).

Red Fleet State Park

Colorful cliffs and rock formations, including three large outcrops of red sandstone, inspired the name of Red Fleet Reservoir in **Red Fleet State Park** (8750 N. US 191, 435/789-6614, https://stateparks.utah.gov, year-round, day-use $10). Like the larger Steinaker Reservoir, Red Fleet stores water for irrigation and municipal use and has a **campground** (800/322-3770, http://utahstateparks.reserveamerica.com, $9 reservation fee, tents $15, RVs $25-28 with hookups, tepee $30). The park also rents canoes, kayaks, and stand-up paddleboards. From Vernal, go north 10 miles (16.1 km) on US 191 to milepost 211, then turn right and continue 2 miles (3.2 km) on a paved road to its end.

A moderately rigorous 2.5-mile (4-km) round-trip hike from the northern section of the park leads through desert landscape to a **dinosaur trackway** on the north shore of Red Fleet Reservoir. Three-toed upright dinos laid down these tracks in a soft mud playa (now Navajo sandstone) about 200 million years ago. It's easiest to see these sometimes elusive tracks on a cloudy day or when the sun is low in the sky. Find the turnoff from US 191 across from the big Simplot sign; follow this road 2.3 miles (3.7 km) east to the trailhead.

★ Dinosaur National Monument

Dinosaur National Monument (4545 E. US 40, Dinosaur, CO, 435/781-7700, www.nps.gov/dino, $25 per vehicle or motorcycle, $15 pedestrians and cyclists) owes its name and fame to one of the world's most productive sites for dinosaur bones.

The monument straddles the Utah-Colorado border, but only the area around the quarry at the monument's western end in Utah has dinosaur bones. The spectacular canyons of the Green and Yampa Rivers form another aspect of the monument. Harpers Corner Scenic Drive winds onto high ridges and canyon viewpoints in the heart of Dinosaur National Monument. River-running allows a close look at the geology and wildlife within the depths and provides the bonus of thrilling rapids.

Elevations range from 4,750 feet (1,448 m) at the Green River near the quarry to 9,006 feet (2,745 m) atop Zenobia Peak of Douglas Mountain. The high country is part of the east flank of the Uinta Mountains.

DINOSAUR QUARRY AREA

Visitor Center

The **Quarry Visitor Center** (11524 E. 1500 S., Jensen, 435/781-7700, 8am-6pm daily late May-mid-Sept., 9am-5pm daily mid-Sept.-late May), located 7 miles (11.3 km) north of Jensen, is the jumping-off place for a visit to the Quarry Exhibit Hall.

Quarry Exhibit Hall

Approximately 1,500 bones from 11 different dinosaur species cover a rock face at the Quarry Exhibit Hall, a short drive from the visitor center. The ranger talks at the quarry are worth catching, and this is one of the few museums where visitors are allowed to touch bones. The exhibit hall also houses reconstructions of dinosaurs whose bones were found scattered in the quarry.

The quarry was discovered in the early 1900s and excavated from about 1909 to 1924. Bones were carefully exposed, and even

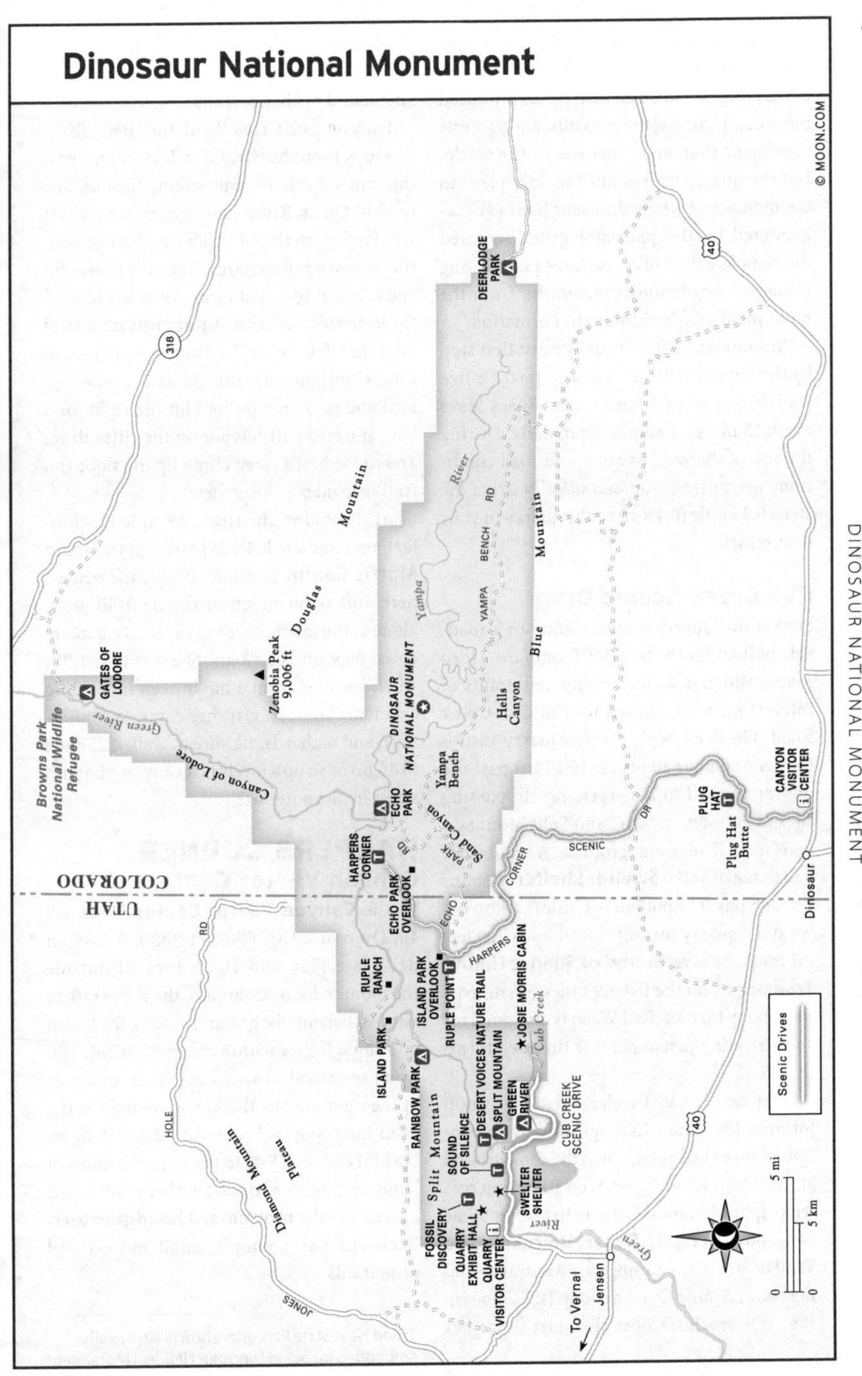
Dinosaur National Monument
© MOON.COM
Browns Park National Wildlife Refugee
GATES OF LODORE
Green River
Canyon of Lodore
Zenobia Peak 9,006 ft
Douglas Mountain
DINOSAUR NATIONAL MONUMENT
ECHO PARK
Yampa Bench
Yampa River
YAMPA BENCH RD
Blue Mountain
Hells Canyon
DEERLODGE PARK
Sand Canyon
PARK RD
HARPERS CORNER
ECHO PARK OVERLOOK
COLORADO
UTAH
RUPLE RANCH
ISLAND PARK OVERLOOK
RUPLE POINT
HARPERS CORNER SCENIC DR
ECHO
ISLAND PARK
RAINBOW PARK
DESERT VOICES NATURE TRAIL
JOSIE MORRIS CABIN
Cub Creek
SPLIT MOUNTAIN
GREEN RIVER
CUB CREEK SCENIC DRIVE
Split Mountain
SOUND OF SILENCE
SWELTER SHELTER
FOSSIL DISCOVERY
QUARRY EXHIBIT HALL
QUARRY VISITOR CENTER
Diamond Mountain Plateau
HOLE RD
JONES
To Vernal
Jensen
Green River
Dinosaur
Plug Hat Butte
PLUG HAT
CANYON VISITOR CENTER
40
318
0 5 mi
0 5 km
Scenic Drives

though some were shipped off to museums around the world, most were left in the soil as they were found. The quarry has produced more complete skeletons, skulls, and juvenile specimens than any other site in the world. But the quarry wall is not the only place in the monument where dinosaur bones are sequestered. In 2010, paleontologists discovered the complete skull of a new, large plant-eating dinosaur, *Abydosaurus mcintoshi,* from the monument's Cedar Mountain Formation.

In summer, visitors usually must first stop by the Quarry Visitor Center to board a free shuttle bus to the quarry site. Buses leave every 15 minutes 8am-5:30pm daily. During the rest of the year, weather and road conditions permitting, you can usually drive the steep 0.25 mile (0.4 km) to the quarry in your own vehicle.

Cub Creek Scenic Drive

Stop at the Quarry Visitor Center or a roadside pullout for the booklet *Tour of the Tilted Rocks,* which describes numbered points of interest for a self-driven tour of Cub Creek Road. The drive begins at the Quarry Visitor Center and goes 10 miles (16.1 km) past the quarry turnoff to a historic ranch, passing sites of Fremont rock art and Split Mountain and Green River Campgrounds. A small overhang known as the **Swelter Shelter** contains petroglyphs. The pullout is 1 mile (1.6 km) beyond the quarry turnoff; a trail leads 200 feet (61 m) to the cave. **Sound of Silence Hiking Trail** begins on the left 1.9 miles (3 km) past the quarry turnoff. Red Wash is also good for short strolls—just avoid it if thunderstorms threaten.

Keep east on Cub Creek Road to the turnoff for Split Mountain Campground, then continue 1 mile (1.6 km) down to the campground at the Green River. The Green River emerges from Split Mountain Canyon here after some of its roughest rapids. **Desert Voices Nature Trail** begins at the campground entrance and makes a 1.5-mile (2.4-km) loop (1.5-2 hours); the trail brochure near the start describes plants and geology seen along the way. A 0.25-mile (0.4-km) trail connects the Desert Voices and Sound of Silence trails.

Back on Cub Creek Road, the Green River overlook is on the left, 1.2 miles (1.9 km) past the Split Mountain Campground turnoff. The road to Green River Campground is a short way farther on the left. Cub Creek Road continues past a private ranch, then the pavement ends. When the road forks, keep left toward the Josie Morris Cabin. A **petroglyph panel** is on the left 0.7 mile (1.1 km) beyond the road fork. Continue past this panel 0.2 mile (0.3 km) and park in a pullout on the right for a look at lizard petroglyphs on the cliffs above and to the left; a steep climb up the slope (no trail) provides a closer view.

At the end of the road, 0.9 mile (1.4 km) farther, large shade trees surround the **Josie Morris Cabin.** In about 1914, Josie settled here and spent much of the next 50 years alone at the ranch, tending the fields, garden, cows, pigs, and chickens. She was in her 90s when she died from a hip broken in a riding accident. You can visit her cabin, outbuildings, and orchards. Be sure to walk 0.25 mile (0.4 km) or so up a lovely box canyon (the path starts by the outhouse).

HARPERS CORNER

Canyon Visitor Center

At the **Canyon Visitor Center** (4545 US 40, Dinosaur, CO, 970/374-3000, 9am-5pm daily late May-mid-Oct.), located outside the monument in Colorado, the River Office handles permits for groups running the Green or Yampa Rivers within the monument. You won't see any dinosaur exhibits in this part of the monument—the bones are only at the Utah quarry area. From Vernal, go 35 miles (56 km) east on US 40 to the Colorado town of Dinosaur, then continue another 2 miles (3.2 km) east to the **monument headquarters.** Dinosaur has a couple small motels and restaurants.

1: Red Fleet State Park after snowfall **2:** a skull embedded in rock at Dinosaur National Monument

1
2

Harpers Corner Scenic Drive

This scenic drive begins at monument headquarters in Colorado and winds north past many scenic overlooks. The road climbs a series of ridges overlooking Island Park, Echo Park, and the canyons of the Green and Yampa Rivers. You'll see spectacular faulted and folded rock layers and a complete range of vegetation, from the cottonwoods along the rivers to the aspens and firs of the highlands.

The paved road is 32 miles (52 km) long (one-way, open mid-Apr.-Dec. snows); allow about 2 hours for the round-trip or half a day if you also plan to hike the two nature trails. The nearest services are in Dinosaur, Colorado.

Plug Hat Trail is an easy 0.5-mile (0.8-km) loop in a piñon-juniper forest at a stop 4.3 miles (6.9 km) from the beginning of the drive. At **Island Park Overlook**, about 26 miles (42 km) along the drive, **Ruple Point Trail** heads west 4.75 miles (7.6 km) each way on an old jeep road to an overlook of the Green River in Split Mountain Canyon; carry water. The drive ends at Harpers Corner, a long, narrow peninsula. You can continue 1.5 miles (2.4 km) on foot to the very tip by taking **Harpers Corner Trail.** Cliffs on each side drop about 2,500 feet (762 m) to the Green River at the beginning of Whirlpool Canyon. Echo Park, Steamboat Rock, and the sinuous curves of the Yampa River Canyon are also visible. Allow 1.5-2 hours for the easy to moderate walk.

Echo Park

A rough dirt road branches off Harpers Corner Road 25 miles (40 km) from monument headquarters and winds down more than 2,000 vertical feet (610 m) in 14 miles (22.5 km) to Echo Park. The setting of Echo Park, near the confluence of the Green and Yampa Rivers, is one of the prettiest in the monument. The massive sandstone fin of Steamboat Rock looms into the sky across the Green River.

Echo Park offers a campground, river access for boaters (permit required), and a ranger station (summer only). Cars with good clearance can often make this side trip, although it's better to have a truck; RVs and trailers shouldn't attempt it. As with all dirt roads in Dinosaur National Monument, this one shouldn't be driven when it's wet. The clay surface becomes extremely slick after rain, but usually dries out in 2-3 hours.

RAINBOW PARK AND ISLAND PARK

Rainbow Park and Ruple Ranch are on the west shore of the Green River at opposite ends of Island Park. Both offer places to launch river boats. **Petroglyphs** are a short walk from the pullout at **McKee Springs.** Former sheep and cattle ranch Ruple Ranch still has its original corrals and loafing shed. The easiest access is from the quarry area; distances are 30 miles (48 km) to Rainbow Park and about another 5 miles (8 km) to Ruple Ranch via the rough, unpaved Island Park Road. Vehicles with good clearance may be able to drive in, but the road is impassable during wet weather.

HIKING

While hiking is not the main attraction at this monument, there are a few good desert trails, including some very short ones starting near the visitor center if you're short on time. To see fossils in situ, head out on **Fossil Discovery Trail** (2.5 mi/4 km round-trip), where you can see unexcavated dinosaur fossils. For more dynamic terrain, check out the **Sound of Silence Trail** (3.2 mi/5.1 km round-trip), which involves hiking over slickrock and a little scrambling. This unusual nature trail enters an anfractuosity (a winding channel), crosses a panorama-filled ridge, then descends through slickrock back to Red Wash and the trailhead. A map is a good idea for this hike (you can find a basic one on the monument's website, or pick up a better one at the visitor center).

RIVER-RUNNING

Trips down the Green or Yampa Rivers feature outstanding scenery and riveting rapids. All boaters in the monument must have permits or be with a licensed river-running company, even for day trips. Applications for a **permit lottery** are accepted December 1-January 31 and are available online (www.recreation.gov, application fee $15, permit fee $20 for 1 day and $185 for multiday trips). If you miss the lottery, visit www.recreation.gov or call the monument's **River Office** (970/374-2468, 8am-noon Mon.-Fri.) to check on available launch dates. One-day permits are the easiest to get. The *Dinosaur River Guide,* by Laura Evans and Buzz Belknap, has maps and descriptions of both rivers in the monument. Neither river is for novice rafters, with rapids as high as Class IV.

Guided trips are often best for first-time visitors. The following raft companies are among those authorized to guide one-day and multiple-day trips in the monument: **Adrift Adventures** (9500 E. 6000 S., Jensen, 435/789-3600 or 800/824-0150, www.adrift.com), **OARS Dinosaur** (221 N. 400 E., 435/789-4316 or 800/342-8243, www.greenriverrafting.com), and **Dinosaur River Expeditions** (800/345-7238, www.dinosaurriverexpeditions.com). The most popular 1-day run on the Green River begins at Rainbow Park or Ruple Ranch. Rafters bounce through the Class I-III rapids of Split Mountain Canyon for 9 miles (14.5 km) to take-outs at Split Mountain Campground. Commercial day trips run about $100-120 for adults, $75-100 children.

Longer trips usually begin on the Green River at Gates of Lodore in the north end of the monument. Echo Park marks the end of Lodore Canyon. The Yampa River, the last major undammed tributary of the Colorado River system, joins the Green here and noticeably increases its size and power. Trips usually end with a series of rapids through Split Mountain Canyon. A 4-day commercial trip costs about $950.

CAMPGROUNDS

Dinosaur National Monument has two pleasant riverside campgrounds—Green River and Split Mountain—within about a mile (1.6 km) of each other. **Green River Campground** (year-round, water seasonally, $18) is 5 miles (8 km) east of the Quarry Visitor Center in Jensen. **Split Mountain Campground** (water early Apr.-early Oct.) is a group campground ($40) during the high season. It serves as a general-purpose campground from the first week of October to mid-April, when there is a $6 fee (no water). It's 4 miles (6.4 km) east of Dinosaur Quarry, then 1 mile (1.6 km) north on Split Mountain Road.

There are several other campsites in the monument. One of the nicest is **Echo Park Campground** (year-round, water seasonally, $6-10), 38 miles (61 km) north of monument headquarters, with several walk-in tent sites. The last 13 miles (21 km) of the road to Echo Park are unpaved and impassable when wet. RVs and trailers are not recommended. A small campground at **Gates of Lodore** (year-round, water seasonally, $6-10) has a boat launch. At the east end of the monument, **Deerlodge Park Campground** (year-round, water seasonally, $6-10) sits upstream from the Yampa River Canyon, where river trips often begin. Deerlodge is 53 miles (85 km) from monument headquarters by paved roads. A small primitive campground at **Rainbow Park** (year-round, no water, tents only, $6) is 26 miles (42 km) from Dinosaur Quarry on an unpaved road.

All campsites in the monument are available on a first-come, first-served basis.

★ Flaming Gorge National Recreation Area

Just south of the Wyoming border, Flaming Gorge Dam impounds the Green River, backing up a reservoir through 91 miles (148 km) of gentle valleys and fiery red canyons. The rugged land is filled with spectacular scenery where the Green River cuts into the Uinta Mountains—cliffs rising as high as 1,500 feet (457 m), twisted rock formations, and sweeping panoramas. Although much of the lake is in Wyoming, most of the campgrounds and other visitor facilities, as well as the best scenery, are in Utah.

A $5 recreation pass is required if you do anything besides drive through the area. Purchase a pass at the US Forest Service offices in Manila or Vernal, at the Flaming Gorge Dam, the Red Canyon Visitor Center, or at one of several self-service pay stations.

FLAMING GORGE DAM AND VISITOR CENTER

Nearly one million cubic yards of concrete went into this massive dam, which was completed in 1964. The **visitor center** (435/885-3135, www.fs.usda.gov/ashley, tours 9am-5pm daily Apr. 15-Oct. 15, free) has a large 3D map of the area, exhibits, and video programs. The dam and visitor center are 6.5 miles (10.5 km) northeast from the junction with Highway 44 on US 191, and 2.8 miles (4.5 km) southwest of Dutch John.

RED CANYON VISITOR CENTER

The **Red Canyon Visitor Center** (435/676-2676, 9am-6pm Fri.-Mon., 10am-3pm Tues.-Thurs. Memorial Day-Labor Day, $5 recreation pass required) has what may be Utah's best window onto sheer cliffs dropping 1,360 feet (415 m) to the lake below. Nearby viewpoints—connected by a trail along the canyon rim—offer splendid panoramas of the canyon and the lofty Uinta Mountains in the distance. The visitor center is 3.5 miles (5.6 km) west on Highway 44 from the junction with US 191, then 3 miles (4.8 km) in on a paved road.

SHEEP CREEK CANYON GEOLOGICAL AREA

Canyon walls on this scenic loop drive reveal rock layers deformed and turned on end by immense geological forces. The earth's crust broke along the Uinta North Fault, and the south side rose 15,000 feet (4,572 m) relative to the north. Fossils of trilobites, corals, sea urchins, gastropods, and other marine animals show that the ocean once covered this spot before the uplifting and faulting. Rock layers of yet another time preserve fossilized wood and tracks of crocodile-like reptiles.

The road through Sheep Creek Canyon is paved but has some narrow and rough places; it's closed in winter. The 13-mile (20.9-km) loop branches off Highway 44 south of Manila between mileposts 14 and 15 and rejoins Highway 44 at milepost 22. The loop can be done in either direction, and a short nature trail at the northern end of the loop is a good place to look for bighorn sheep. The *Wheels of Time* geology brochure, available at visitor centers, describes geologic formations at marked stops. Two primitive campgrounds (outhouses but no water or established sites) are just off Highway 44 along lower Sheep Creek, a short way from the entrance to the scenic loop.

SWETT RANCH

At just 16 years old, Oscar Swett homesteaded near Flaming Gorge in 1909, then built up a

1: the Flaming Gorge 2: Sheep Creek Canyon Geological Area

large cattle ranch in this isolated region. With the nearest store days away, Oscar ran his own blacksmith shop and sawmill and did much of the ranch work. His wife, Emma, tended the garden, made the family's clothing, raised nine children, and helped with ranch chores. You can get a taste of the early homestead life on a visit to **Swett Ranch** (435/789-1181, 10am-4pm Thurs.-Sun. Memorial Day-Labor Day, free). Drive north 0.3 mile (0.5 km) on US 191 from the Highway 44 junction (or south 1.6 mi/2.6 km from Flaming Gorge Lodge), then turn west and follow the signs 1.3 miles (2.1 km) on a dirt road.

RECREATION

Some of northeastern Utah's best **hiking** and **mountain biking** can be found around the Flaming Gorge area. **Boating** on the clear blue waters of the lake or the river is always a joy. Water-skiers have plenty of room on the lake's 66 square miles (171 sq km). **Swimming** and **scuba diving** are also popular. **Anglers** regularly pull trophy trout and smallmouth bass from the lake and trout from the river. The US Forest Service and private concessions offer boating facilities and about two dozen campgrounds in the recreation area.

Peace, quiet, and snow prevail in winter. Dedicated anglers still cast their lines into the Green River or fish through the lake ice. Cross-country skiers and snowmobilers make their trails through the woods. Campgrounds are closed, although snow campers and hardy RVers can stop for the night in parking areas.

Hiking and Biking

The **Canyon Rim Trail** is a popular hike or mountain bike ride (4.2 mi/6.8 km one-way), with trailheads at Red Canyon Visitor Center and Greendale Overlook, a short distance from the junction of US 191 and Highway 44. **Browne Lake** is a popular starting point for hikes outside the recreation area. Trail 005 goes to the **Ute Mountain Fire Lookout Tower,** a national historic site (2 mi/3.2 km one-way). Trail 016 goes to **Hacking Lake** (7 mi/11.3 km one-way). Trail 012 goes to **Tepee Lakes** (5 mi/8 km one-way) and **Leidy Peak** (elev. 12,028 ft/3,666 m, 8 mi/12.9 km one-way). And Trail 017 goes to **Spirit Lake** (15 mi/24 km one-way). Browne Lake is 4.5 miles (7.2 km) west of the Sheep Creek loop drive on unpaved Forest Road 221, then 1.5 miles (2.4 km) southeast on Browne Lake Road; see the Ashley National Forest map.

Stop by **Altitude Cycle** (580 E. Main St., Vernal, 435/781-2595, 10am-6pm Mon.-Sat.) for a guide to mountain bike trails in northeastern Utah. Rentals are available at the Red Canyon Lodge. Visitor centers and US Forest Service offices have maps of hiking and mountain bike trails and can suggest dirt roads suitable for either activity.

Flaming Gorge Reservoir

Marinas along the lake offer rentals, fuel docks, guides, and supplies. Free paved boat ramps at these and several other locations are maintained by the Forest Service. **Cedar Springs Marina** (2675 N. Cedar Springs Rd., Dutch John, 435/889-3795, www.cedarspringsmarina.com, 8am-6pm daily mid-Apr.-mid-Oct.) is 2 miles (3.2 km) south of the dam at the lower end of the lake, and **Lucerne Valley Marina** (1 Lucerne Valley Recreation Rd., Manila, 435/784-3483, www.flaminggorge.com, Mar.-mid-Nov.), 8 miles (12.9 km) east of Manila, provides services and watercraft rentals ranging from paddleboards to houseboats.

The Green River

Below the Flaming Gorge Dam, the Green River bounces back to life in the Little Hole Canyon, providing enjoyment for boaters, anglers, and hikers.

Rafting Trips

Visitors with canoes, kayaks, and dories can float all sections of the Green River between the dam and Gates of Lodore, although river experience is needed. Raft rentals and shuttle services are provided by **Flaming Gorge Resort** (435/889-3773, www.flaminggorgeresort.com) and **Dutch John Resort** (435/848-8000, www.dutchjohn

resort.com). Rentals typically cost $200-250 per day, depending on the size of the raft; vehicle shuttles cost about $45 to Little Hole, a 2.5-hour river trip. The 10 Class II rapids between the dam and Little Hole lend some excitement to the trip, but aren't usually dangerous, although the water is quite cold. No motors are allowed between the dam and Indian Crossing. Water flow varies according to power needs; allow more time if the flow is small. Call the Bureau of Reclamation (435/885-3121) for present conditions. **Dinosaur River Expeditions** in Vernal (800/345-7238, www.dinosaurriverexpeditions.com) runs multiday trips in Flaming Gorge.

The put-in is at the end of a 1.4-mile (2.3-km) paved road that turns off US 191 (it may not be signed), 0.3 mile (0.5 km) east of the dam. The parking area at the river is small and for unloading boats and passengers only. The main parking areas are 0.7 mile (1.1 km) back up the road. Drivers can take either of two foot trails that descend from the parking lots to the river. The shuttle to Little Hole is only 8 paved miles (12.9 km) via Dutch John.

Fishing

Anglers can follow **Little Hole National Recreation Trail** along the north bank of the Green River through Red Canyon for 7 miles (11.3 km) between the main parking area below the dam and Little Hole. Many good fishing spots dot the way. No camping, horses, campfires, or motorized vehicles are allowed. The Green River downstream from the dam has a reputation for some of the West's best river fishing. Special regulations apply here to maintain the high-quality fishing (check current regulations). Anglers using waders should wear life jackets in case the river level rises unexpectedly; neoprene closed-cell foam waders are recommended for extra flotation and protection against hypothermia.

FOOD AND ACCOMMODATIONS

The nicest place to stay in the Flaming Gorge area is **Red Canyon Lodge** (2450 Red Canyon Rd., Dutch John, 435/889-3759, www.redcanyonlodge.com, $149-199), which sits beside Greens Lake, a short distance from the Red Canyon Visitor Center. The lodge has an assortment of cabins that sleep up to four, some with kitchenettes, some with microwaves and fridges. A restaurant opens daily for breakfast, lunch, and dinner limited hours and days in off-season, ($14-19); a store offers fishing supplies, a few groceries, bike rentals, horseback riding, and boat rentals on Greens Lake.

Flaming Gorge Resort (1100 E. Flaming Gorge Resort, Dutch John, 435/889-3773, www.flaminggorgeresort.com, $179-299), 7 miles (11.3 km) southwest of Dutch John, offers motel rooms and condos year-round and a popular restaurant serving breakfast, lunch, and dinner daily year-round. The lodge also has an RV park, a store, raft rentals, shuttles, and guided river fishing trips.

Campgrounds

Three campgrounds (435/784-3445 or 877/444-6777, www.recreation.gov, mid-May-mid-Sept., $25) are near the Red Canyon Visitor Center: **Red Canyon, Canyon Rim,** and **Greens Lake.** At 7,400 feet (2,256 m), expect cool evenings and mornings. **Lucerne Campground** (877/444-6777, www.recreation.gov, May-Sept., $25-36), 8 miles (12.9 km) east of Manila, is on the shores of the Flaming Gorge Reservoir. Several primitive campgrounds on the lake can be reached only by boat or trail. In Manila, the **Flaming Gorge KOA** (320 W. Hwy. 43, 435/784-3184, www.koa.com/campgrounds/flaming-gorge, mid-Apr.-Nov., tents $35, hookups $52, cabins $59-130) has showers, laundry, a pool, a playground, and cabins (bring sleeping bags).

GETTING THERE

Flaming Gorge NRA can easily be reached by heading north 35 miles (56 km) on US 191 from Vernal. In Wyoming, head south on Highway 530 from the town of Green River or on US 191 from near Rock Springs.

Price

In the beginning, Price was a typical LDS community. Ranchers and farmers had settled on the fertile land surrounding the Price River in 1879. Four years later, everything changed when the railroad came through. A flood of immigrants from all over the world arrived to work in the coal mines and other growing enterprises (an informal census taken in a pool hall at nearby Helper in the 1930s found 32 different nationalities in the room). Coal mining has had its ups and downs over the last 100 years but continues to be the largest industry in the area. Price (approximate pop. 8,000) is a good base for exploring the surrounding mountains and desert.

SIGHTS

USU Eastern Prehistoric Museum

Focused on natural and human history, **Utah State University Eastern Prehistoric Museum** (155 E. Main St., 435/613-5060, http://usueastern.edu/museum, 9am-5pm Sun.-Wed., 9am-7pm Thurs.-Sat., $6 adults, $5 seniors, $3 ages 2-12) has simple, old-school displays and is a must-stop for anyone interested in the prehistoric creatures and the people who lived in Utah thousands of years ago. Displays include the skeleton of a fierce, flesh-eating allosaurus, Huntington Canyon mammoth bones discovered nearby, colorful gemstones, and artifacts of the prehistoric Fremont and the modern Utes. Kids can explore hands-on displays in the Children's Room.

FOOD

A number of cafés and diners along Main Street serve standard American fare, but two of the best local restaurants are just out of town. Venture a short distance north toward Helper to **Grogg's Pinnacle Brewing Co.** (1653 N. Carbonville Rd., 435/637-2924, www.groggspinnaclebrewing.com, 11am-9pm Mon.-Thurs., 11am-10pm Fri.-Sat., 11am-8pm Sun., $14-37), the local taproom, with burgers, sandwiches, and full dinners to accompany a decent selection of beers. Just southeast of Price, in Wellington, the local's favorite **Cowboy Kitchen** (31 E. Main

bird's-eye view of Price

St., 435/637-4223, www.cowboyclubut.com, 7am-10pm Sun.-Thurs., 7am-11pm Fri.-Sat., $12-38) serves up steak, sausages, and home-grown lamb.

In downtown Price, **Farlaino's Cafe** (87 W. Main St., 435/637-9217, 8am-7pm Tues.-Fri., 8am-3pm Sat., $8-12) is an old-fashioned diner that's a good spot for a full breakfast (sit on a spinning stool at the counter and get to know the regulars). At lunch, both Italian and American food is served.

ACCOMMODATIONS

Price has the Castle Valley's best lodging and most reasonable prices, making it a good, if relatively unexciting, base for exploring this part of Utah. Aside from a reliably generic Holiday Inn Express, most of Price's motels are a bit older.

At the west end of Main Street is a shopping center complex that includes the **National 9 Price River Inn** (641 W. Price River Dr., 435/637-7000, www.national9price.com, $65-140). Just to the north is the friendly, family-run ★ **Legacy Inn** (145 N. Carbonville Rd., 435/637-2424, www.legacyinnutah.com, $74-85), with an adjoining RV park ($25-40).

At the east end of town near a clutch of fast-food restaurants and the local supermarket mall, the somewhat dated **Greenwell Inn** (655 E. Main St., 435/637-3520 or 800/666-3520, www.greenwellinn.com, $70-110) has a pool, an exercise room, a bar, and a decent restaurant.

INFORMATION AND SERVICES

Castle Country Travel Office (751 E. 100 N., 435/636-3701, www.castlecountry.com) offers info and ideas for travel in Price and elsewhere in Carbon and Emery Counties from a booth in the USU Eastern Prehistoric Museum (155 E. Main St., 435/613-5060). The **Manti-La Sal National Forest Office** (599 W. Price River Dr., 435/636-3500, www.fs.usda.gov/mantilasal, 8am-4:30pm Mon.-Fri.), across from the Creekview Shopping Center on the west edge of town, has information about recreation in the beautiful alpine country of the Wasatch Plateau to the west.

Staff at the **Bureau of Land Management** (125 S. 600 W., 435/636-3600, www.blm.gov/ut) can tell you about exploring the San Rafael Swell, Cleveland-Lloyd Dinosaur Quarry, and Nine Mile Canyon as well as about boating the Green River through Desolation, Gray, and Labyrinth Canyons.

Castleview Hospital (300 N. Hospital Dr., 435/637-4800) is on the west edge of town.

GETTING THERE

Amtrak (800/872-7245, www.amtrak.com) runs its *California Zephyr* trains via nearby Helper, once daily in each direction, on their way between Denver and Salt Lake City.

VICINITY OF PRICE

Helper

North of Price, just as the highway enters a narrow canyon, the town of Helper has a colorful mix of decrepitude, history, and art. In 1883, the Denver and Rio Grande Western Railroad began building a depot and other facilities here for its new line. Trains traveling up the long grade to Soldier Summit needed extra locomotives, or "helpers," based at the little railroad community—hence the name. Miners later settled here, and the two groups still comprise most of the 2,500 residents. Helper's early 20th-century commercial and residential buildings are designated as national historic sites. The local economy has suffered downturns from the railroad and coal industries, and this is still reflected in vacancies in town.

However, these old downtown buildings have begun to attract artists who need inexpensive studio space, and an arts community is taking hold. Come by for **First Friday art walks** (Main St., 6pm-9pm Fri.) or the excellent **Helper Arts Festival** (www.helperartsfestival.com), held in mid-August.

Western Mining and Railroad Museum

A venerable red caboose and examples of coal-mining machinery sit outside in downtown Helper next to the **Western Mining and Railroad Museum** (294 S. Main St., 435/472-3009, www.helpercity.net/museum, 10am-5pm Mon.-Sat. spring-fall, 11am-4pm Mon.-Sat. winter, $5 donation suggested). Inside, you'll see two elaborate model railroad sets and photos of old steam locomotives. A mine room has models of coal mines and equipment worn by the miners. Other exhibits illustrate Utah's two great mine disasters—the 1900 Scofield tragedy, in which 200 men and boys died, and the 1924 Castle Gate explosion, which killed 173. Other bits of history include ghost town memorabilia, a Butch Cassidy exhibit, and maps. The brick building housing the museum dates from about 1914, when it was Hotel Helper.

Price Canyon Recreation Area

The **Price Canyon Recreation Area** (435/636-3600, camping $15) makes a good stopping place for a picnic or camping. From the turnoff 8.2 miles (13.1 km) north of Helper, follow a steep, narrow paved road 3 miles (4.8 km) to the picnic area, a canyon overlook, and the campground (elev. 8,000 ft/2,438 m). **Bristlecone Ridge Trail** (2 mi/3.2 km round-trip, 700 ft/213 m elevation gain) begins at the far end of the campground loop and winds through forest to a ridgetop filled with bristlecone pines and views of surrounding mountains, as well as Price and Crandall Canyons. Take US 6 north from Helper and turn left at the sign for the recreation area.

★ Nine Mile Canyon

A **scenic drive** through this canyon takes you back in time to when Fremont Indians lived and farmed here, about 900 years ago. Although their pit-house dwellings can be difficult for a non-archaeologist to spot, the granaries and rock art stand out clearly. The canyon is especially noted for its abundant, striking **petroglyphs** and smaller numbers of **pictographs.**

You'll find an especially large concentration of rock art and Fremont sites at the eastern end of Nine Mile, up Daddy Canyon (mile 43.8) and Cottonwood Canyon (miles 45-46). You'll also see several ranches and the small **ghost town** of Harper. In the late 1800s and early 1900s, these roads through Nine Mile Canyon formed the main highway between Vernal and the rest of Utah.

Although the distances may discourage the casual traveler, the road from the south (Wellington area) is now completely paved, and the approach from the north (Myton) is mostly paved, with a short stretch of good gravel. There are no services out here; bring food and water and don't expect cell phone service.

Download a brochure on Nine Mile Canyon's rock-art sites, ancient villages, and historic relics at www.castlecountry.com, or pick one up at the **Castle Country Travel Office** (751 E. 100 N., Price, 435/636-3701, www.castlecountry.com), the USU Eastern Prehistoric Museum (155 E. Main St., Price, 435/613-5060), or the BLM office (600 Price River Dr., Price, 435/637-4591, www.blm.gov/ut).

No camping is allowed on the public land in the canyon, but the **Nine Mile Ranch** (435/637-2572, http://9mileranch.com) offers B&B lodging in its ranch house ($110-135), camping ($20), and four simple cabins ($80-130). The proprietors can also take you on a guided full-day trip through the canyon ($175 minimum for up to 6 people).

Getting There

Nine Mile Canyon is more than 40 miles (64 km) long (why it's been dubbed "nine mile" remains somewhat mysterious). The drive is about 120 miles (193 km) round-trip from Price and takes most of a day, but it's a day well spent. From Price, drive 10 miles (16.1

1: entering Nine Mile Canyon
2: a petroglyph panel up Nine Mile Canyon

1

2

km) southeast (3 mi/4.8 km past Wellington) on US 6/191 and turn north onto 2200 East (Soldier Creek Rd.) at a sign for Nine Mile Canyon. The road passes Soldier Creek Coal Mine after 13 miles (20.9 km), continues climbing to an aspen-forested pass, then drops into the canyon.

Nine Mile Canyon can also be reached from the north, from near Myton (on US 40/191) in the Uinta Basin, via Wells Draw and Gate Canyon. Gate Canyon is the roughest section and may be impassable after rain. The marked turnoff for the northern approach from US 191 is 1.5 miles (2.4 km) west of Myton. In about 2 miles (3.2 km), bear right and continue south. It's 26 miles (42 km) from US 191 to the bottom of Nine Mile Canyon.

Range Creek Archaeological Remains

In 2001, rancher Waldo Wilcox sold his ranch in the Book Cliffs canyons, some 30 miles (48 km) east of Price, to the nonprofit Trust for Public Land. The ranch, which stood in the rugged and remote Range Creek Canyon, was transferred to the State of Utah to be preserved for its incredible wealth of Fremont archaeological sites, including pit houses, petroglyphs, and stone granaries.

The site contains more than 400 Fremont sites that went untouched for some 700 years. The Fremont, who lived in south-central Utah from around 200 to 1300 CE, evolved from a hunter-gatherer culture to farming. And like the Ancestral Puebloans to the south, the Fremont abruptly disappeared from Range Creek, possibly due to a megadrought that swept the Southwest. Though Fremont archaeological sites are relatively common in Utah and western Colorado, few are as large and intact as those found here.

The Range Creek Ranch is now open to a limited number of visitors. Under a program of the **Utah Museum of Natural History** (801/581-6927, http://umnh.utah.edu), 28 visitors per day are allowed between May 15 and Nov. 30. Visitors can apply for an individual permit, which costs $1 and allows 5 days' admission, but provides no guides or tour.

To reach the ranch trailhead from Price, you're looking at 2 hours of rugged backcountry driving with a 4WD, high-clearance vehicle. From the trailhead, you can continue by foot or horseback. For most, it's best to schedule a tour with an outfitter. **Tavaputs Ranch** (435/637-1236, www.tavaputsranch.com, late June-early Sept., $175 pp) runs trips to Range Creek several days per month. You can also arrange to spend the night at the guest ranch ($200 pp). Overnight tours with an archaeologist are run by **Canyonlands Field Institute** (1320 S. US 191, Moab, 435/259-7750 or 800/860-5262, http://cfimoab.org). Three-day camping trips are offered a couple times a year ($900 pp) and include meals, tents, and transportation to and from the town of Green River; reserve well in advance. **Carbon County Outdoor Recreation** (30 E. 200 S., Price, 435/636-3702, www.carbonutah.com/range-creek-canyon, $85) also offers several trips a year.

From Price, head southeast through Wellington and turn east (left) onto Highway 123. Turn south onto Highway 124 and follow it for 10 miles (16.1 km), past Horse Canyon Mine. About 1 mile (1.6 km) past the mine, turn left and drive 9 miles (14.5 km) to the North Gate entrance to Range Creek. Camping is permitted here, and a trail leads into the archaeological area. Bring plenty of water.

Castle Valley and the San Rafael Swell

The high cliffs of the Wasatch Plateau rise like a fortress to the west above Castle Valley. These 10,000-foot-high (3,048-m) uplands wring all the moisture out of eastward storm systems, creating rain shadows. Perennial streams flow down the rugged canyons, enabling verdant desert orchards and crop fields. To the east lies some of Utah's best less-traveled canyon country: the San Rafael Swell, or "the Swell," as it's locally referred to.

Backcountry explorers can follow unpaved roads east to the San Rafael Swell, an area of geologic beauty rife with a variety of adventures. The Swell boasts slot canyons, slickrock, hoodoos, and other dramatic features, but—perhaps since it's not a national or state park—has avoided the heavy traffic found elsewhere in Utah's canyon country. A few highlights include dinosaur fossil quarries, remote vista points, desert mountain biking, rock climbing, and scenic hiking and camping.

Along the southern stretch of Highway 10, the barren mesas and badland formations make for captivating scenery. But the real attraction of this area is the backcountry routes leading to wild and undeveloped destinations. Unpaved roads wind west into the Wasatch Plateau, heading up steep canyons to pretty lakes and alpine country.

HUNTINGTON

This small town at the mouth of Huntington Canyon dates from 1878 and has a population of a little over 2,000. The town gained attention in 2007 when a mine collapsed, trapping six miners. A few days later, three rescue workers were killed in another collapse. Travelers can head west on paved Highway 31 and soon be in the cool forests and meadows of the Wasatch Plateau, or head east to the Cleveland-Lloyd Dinosaur Quarry and the San Rafael Swell. The town has services, a few restaurants, and a few limited lodging options (mostly RV parks).

Huntington State Park

Located 1 mile (1.6 km) north of Huntington on Highway 10, the 250-acre (101-ha) Huntington Reservoir at **Huntington State Park** (435/687-2491, https://stateparks.utah.gov, day-use $10) is a popular spot for picnicking, camping, swimming, fishing, boating, and waterskiing. Lots of grass, shade trees, and a swimming beach make the park especially enjoyable in summer. Anglers catch mostly largemouth bass, bluegill, and some trout; crayfishing is also good. At the **campground** (800/322-3770, http://utahstateparks.reserveamerica.com, Mar.-Oct., water and showers available, $30-33), reservations are a good idea for summer weekends. In winter, the park is open for ice skating and ice fishing.

Huntington Canyon

From the north edge of town, Highway 31 turns west up Huntington Canyon. Beyond the giant Huntington power plant, the canyon narrows as the road climbs up to groves of spruce, fir, and aspen. Forest roads branch off the highway to reservoirs and scenic spots. Highway 31 continues 10 miles (16.1 km) down the other side of the plateau to Fairview on US 89. Snowplows keep Highway 31 open in winter, although drivers must have snow tires or carry chains November-March.

Skyline Drive

Near the top of the Wasatch Plateau, Skyline Drive traverses expansive meadows and groves of fir and aspen and accesses several great campgrounds, as well as fishing. There are two access points from Highway 31 (Huntington Canyon Rd.): on the left side between mileposts 14 and 13 (southward), and 5 miles (8 km) farther west along the highway (northward). Roads branch off the northern section of Skyline Drive to **Gooseberry Campground** (1.5 mi/2.4 km, $14), **Electric**

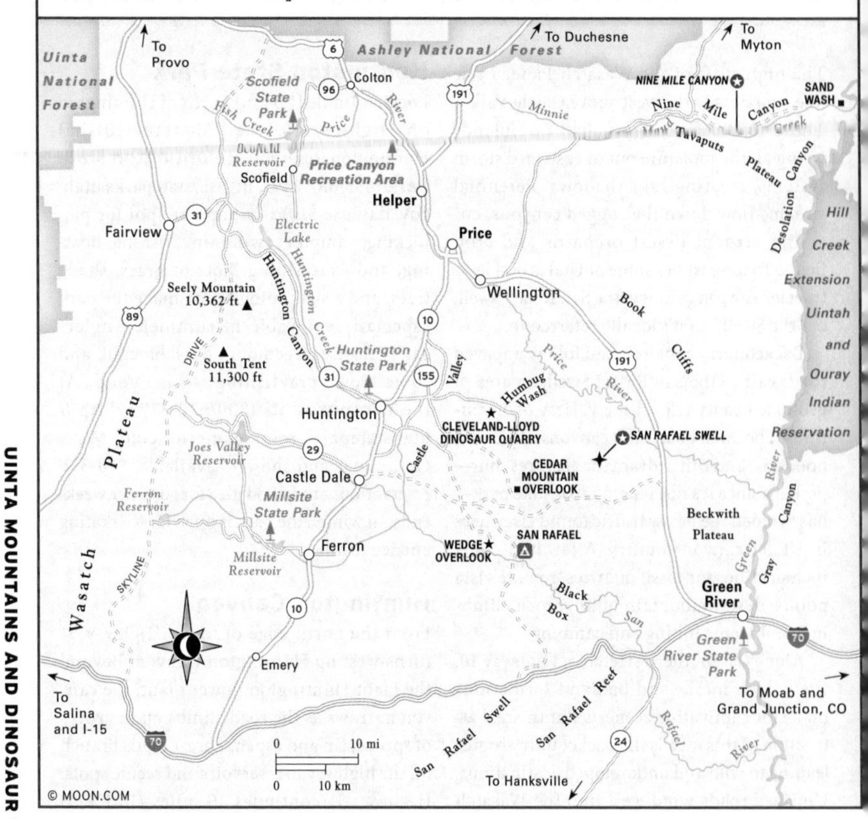

Lake (6 mi/9.7 km), and **Scofield** (17 mi/27 km). To reach **Gooseberry Reservoir Campground** (435/283-4151 or 877/444-6777, www.recreation.gov, June-Oct., no water, $10), take the north Skyline Drive turnoff and follow signs 1.5 miles (2.4 km) to this scrubby open spot. **Flat Canyon Campground** (435/283-4151 or 877/444-6777, www.recreation.gov, May-Oct., $10) also provides a good base for high-country fishing, although there's little shade. Campsites are available via a 5.5-mile (8.9-km) paved road from the north Skyline Drive turnoff at 8,800 feet (2,682 m) elevation. Boulger Reservoir is 0.25 mile (0.4 km) from the campground, Electric Lake is 1 mile (1.6 km), and Beaver Dam Reservoir is 2 miles (3.2 km).

CLEVELAND-LLOYD DINOSAUR QUARRY

You can learn more about dinosaurs and see their bones in a desert excavation site 22 miles (35 km) east of Huntington (or 30 mi/48 km south of Price via Hwy. 10). Dinosaurs roamed this land about 147 million years ago, when it had a wetter, warmer climate. Mud in a lake bottom trapped some creatures and preserved their bones. The mud layer from this site,

1: stars over Huntington State Park **2:** the San Rafael Swell

1

2

which later became the rock of the Morrison Formation, has yielded more than 12,000 bones of at least 14 different dinosaur species. Local ranchers discovered the bones, and the University of Utah began digging in 1928.

The BLM has a visitor center, quarry exhibits, a nature trail, and picnic sites at **Cleveland-Lloyd Dinosaur Quarry** (125 S. 600 W., Price, 435/636-3600, www.blm.gov/ut, 10am-5pm Thurs.-Sun. Apr.-Oct., $5 over age 16). Inside the visitor center, you'll see exhibits on dinosaurs, techniques for excavating and assembling skeletons, and local flora and fauna. A fierce allosaurus skeleton cast gazes down on you. The enclosed quarry, about 100 yards behind the visitor center, contains excavation tools and exposed allosaurus, stegosaurus, *Camptosaurus,* and *Camarasaurus* bones. The 1.4-mile (2.3-km) **Rock Walk Nature Trail** begins outside.

The long, slow drive in is on graded dirt roads, which occasionally close for rain. From Price, drive south 13 miles (20.9 km) on Highway 10, turn left and go 17 miles (27 km) on Highway 155, and follow the unpaved roads. From Huntington, go northeast 2 miles (3.2 km) on Highway 10 and turn right at 20 miles (32 km) onto Highway 155 and unpaved roads. Signs at the turnoffs from Highway 10 indicate the days and hours the quarry is open. Visitors are not allowed to collect bones at the quarry or on other public lands, since these bones have higher scientific value when researchers can examine them in situ.

CASTLE DALE

Housed in a pretty building diagonally across from Castle Dale's courthouse, the **Museum of the San Rafael** (70 N. 100 E., 435/381-3560, www.museumofthesanrafael.org, 10am-4pm Mon.-Fri., 10am-2pm Sat., $5 adults, $2 age 16 and under) includes a paleontology room with life-size skeletons of dinosaurs, such as a 22-foot (6.7-m) *Albertosaurus.* The dinosaurs displayed include only species found in Emery County. There are also exhibits of the prehistoric Fremont and Ancestral Puebloan peoples, including a rabbit-fur robe, pottery, baskets, tools, jewelry, and the famous Sitterud Bundle (a bow maker's kit).

Joe's Valley Bouldering

This world-class bouldering destination in the middle of just about nowhere features over 700 problems on gorgeous sandstone boulders in a high alpine valley. Every October, climbers flock to the area for the **Joe's Valley Festival.** There are problems across a variety of grades, and a few classics include The Angler (V2) and Planet of the Apes (V7). The nearest amenities lie in Castle Dale (a little less than a 20-minute drive away) and Orangeville (10 minutes away). But the pro move is to pack in your own food and water, and camp close to the boulders at the **Joe's Valley Reservoir Campground** (late Apr.-mid-Nov., campsites reservable online early May-early Oct., www.recreation.gov, $10), where you can cool off in the shade and water.

★ THE SAN RAFAEL SWELL

About 65 million years ago, immense underground forces pushed rock layers into a dome about 80 miles (129 km) long (north-south) and 30 miles (48 km) wide. Erosion has exposed the colorful layers and cut deep canyons into this formation. I-70 divides the Swell into roughly equal north and south halves. Today, the Swell stretches across a mix of BLM land and wilderness. In the north, a 29-mile (47-km) scenic drive, passable by cars in dry weather, branches off the road to Cedar Mountain. This scenic drive heads south past the Wedge Overlook, descends through Buckhorn Wash, crosses the San Rafael River, then winds across the desert to I-70.

Wedge Overlook

An impressive panorama takes in surrounding mountains and canyons and the 1,000-foot (305-m) sheer drop into what's known as Little Grand Canyon. Don't be fooled by the name—this canyon appears anything but little from overlooks. Rain and snowmelt on the Wasatch Plateau feed tributaries of the San Rafael River, which has cut this deep canyon through the San Rafael Swell. Downstream from Little Grand Canyon, the river plunges through narrow canyons of the Black Boxes and flows across the San Rafael Desert to join the Green River.

From Highway 10 just north of Castle Dale (between mileposts 39 and 40), follow signs east on the well-maintained dirt Green River Cutoff Road for 13.7 miles (22 km) to a four-way intersection. Turn south and stay on the main road for 6.1 miles (9.8 km) to the Wedge Overlook. Campsites are scattered around the Wedge area.

The Wedge Overlook is also the site of good mountain biking, including easy dirt-road riding suitable for families or novice riders.

Floating Little Grand Canyon

The 15-mile (24-km) trip on the San Rafael River through this canyon provides one of the best ways to enjoy the scenery. The swift waters have a few riffles and small sand waves, but no rapids. Inflatable kayaks and rafts can do the excursion in 5-6 hours with higher spring flows. An overnight trip will allow more time to explore side canyons. The best boating conditions occur during the spring runoff in May-June. Some people float through with inner tubes later in the summer. Life jackets should always be worn.

No permits are needed for boating or floating, but check with the **BLM office** (125 S. 600 W., Price, 435/636-3600, www.blm.gov/ut, 8am-4:30pm Mon.-Fri.) for advice on hazards, flow, and road conditions. Put-in is at Fuller's Bottom; the turnoff is near the one for Wedge Overlook, then it's 5.4 miles (8.7 km) to the river. Take-out is at the San Rafael Bridge Campground. Extremely dangerous rapids and waterfalls lie downstream from the campground in the Black Boxes—don't attempt these sections unless you know what you're doing.

Mountain Biking

With hundreds of miles of trail and dirt road to explore, there are many good options for short rides and multiday bikepacking trips alike, with a good mix of easy and intermediate trails. The **Wedge Trail** (also known as Goodwater Rim, 14.6 mi/23.5 km, 773 ft/236 m elevation gain) is a good moderate ride with massive views. Unlike many of the other routes here, Wedge is all single-track, with some slickrock sprinkled in for good measure. For a longer, more ambitious adventure, consider **A (San Rafael) Swell Night Out** (73 mi/118 km, 8,000 ft/2,438 m elevation gain), which starts at the North Temple Campground and tours dirt roads throughout the area. Plan on a very long day, or stagger the ride over a couple days.

Climbing and Canyoneering

For those looking to escape the crowds of Indian Creek and Moab crags, the 500-plus climbs and dozens of canyoneering routes found in the Swell are a great option. For roped rock climbing, **Buckhorn Wash** is a popular area with about 150 routes, many of which feature Wingate cracks. A couple Buckhorn classics include Private Pizza (a 5.9, 70-foot/21-m trad crack) and Old Bushmills (a 5.10+ trad route). In the **San Rafael Reef** area (also nicknamed the "Sandstone Alps"), you'll find long, multi-pitch slab routes across a range of grades, towering between 200 feet (61 m) and 2,000 feet (610 m). There are also many canyoneering routes in the canyons of the "Swell," which won't require the permitting process required in other areas, like Zion. There aren't guides specifically to this area, but www.mountainproject.com is a good resource for rock climbs, and www.canyoneeringusa.com has helpful beta on canyoneering here.

Buckhorn Draw Rock-Art Panel

Notable and striking rock-art panels in Utah can be found in the Swell right off the unpaved yet well-maintained Buckhorn Draw Road. The area features both pictographs (painted) and petroglyphs (chipped), and includes some of the best representation of the 2,000-year-old Barrier Canyon tradition anywhere. You'll also find Fremont-style artwork that's about 1,000 years old.

Camping

The small primitive **San Rafael Bridge Campground** (435/636-3600, no water, $6) at the San Rafael River makes a handy (though barebones) base for a back-roads exploration of the San Rafael Swell. The road descends into the main canyon via Buckhorn Wash to the camping area. The swinging bridge, built by the Civilian Conservation Corps in 1937, isn't open to motor vehicles, but it's safe to walk across; a newer bridge is open to cars and trucks. Hikers can explore the canyons above and below the campground on day and overnight trips. Autumn has the best temperatures and lowest water levels; wear shoes suitable for wading.

From Highway 10 north of Castle Dale, head east on the well-maintained dirt Green River Cutoff Road for 13.7 miles (22 km) to a four-way intersection. Continue 12 miles (19.3 km) past the Wedge Overlook turnoff to the bridge and campground. From the campground, the road continues south 20 miles (32 km) to I-70 at exit 129 for Ranch.

You can also find free, dispersed camping throughout the Swell. Look for sites up Buckhorn Wash and along Mexican Mountain Road.

Green River and Vicinity

The town of Green River rests midway between two popular rafting areas: Desolation and Gray Canyons upstream, and Labyrinth and Stillwater Canyons downstream. Several river companies organize day and multiday trips here.

GREEN RIVER

Green River (population about 950) is, except for a handful of motels and a lively tavern, pretty rundown, but it's the only real settlement on the stretch of I-70 between the tiny Utah town of Salina and the Colorado border. Travelers can stop for a night or a meal, set off on a trip down the Green River, or use the town as a base for exploring the nearby San Rafael Swell.

Green River is known for its melons. In summer, stop at roadside stands and partake in wondrous cantaloupes and watermelons. The blazing summer heat and ample irrigation water make such delicacies possible. **Melon Days** (3rd weekend in Sept.) celebrates the harvest with a parade, a city fair, a canoe race, and lots of melons.

John Wesley Powell River History Museum

Stop by the fine **John Wesley Powell River History Museum** (1765 E. Main St., 435/564-3427, http://johnwesleypowell.com, 10am-5pm Tues.-Sat., $6 adults, $2 ages 3-12) to learn about Powell's daring expeditions down the Green and Colorado Rivers in 1869 and 1871-1872. An excellent multimedia presentation about both rivers uses Powell's own reflections during his trips. Historic riverboats on display include a replica of Powell's *Emma Dean*.

Desolation and Gray Canyons

The Green River leaves the Uinta Basin and slices deeply through the Tavaputs Plateau, emerging 95 miles (153 km) downstream near the town of Green River. River-runners can enjoy the canyon scenery, hikes up side canyons, a chance to see wildlife, and visits to Fremont rock-art sites. John Wesley Powell named the canyons in 1869, designating the lower 36 miles (58 km) Gray Canyon. Boaters usually start at **Sand Wash,** the site of a ferry that operated here from the early 1920s to 1952; a 42-mile (68-km) road (36 mi/58 km unpaved) south from Myton is the best way in. Another road turns east from Gate Canyon near Nine Mile Canyon. Some people save the 200-mile (320-km) car shuttle by flying from the town of Green River to an airstrip on a mesa above Sand Wash.

★ Rafting and Kayaking

A few Class III rapids are interspersed with flat water, making for a good family adventure. Outfitters normally fly rafting parties to a remote airstrip at Sand Wash, south of Myton, and take 5-7 days to complete the 85-mile (137-km) trip. Outfitters also offer daylong canoe trips through the lower sections of Gray Canyon, usually for around $75.

For guided one-day or multiday Desolation and Gray Canyon float trips, contact one of the following local companies: **Holiday River Expeditions** (801/266-2087 or 800/624-6323, www.bikeraft.com, 5 days $1,446, 6 days $1,541) or **Adrift Adventures** (435/259-8594, www.adrift.net, 5 days $1,320, you row). A 5-day trip with **Sheri Griffith Expeditions** (435/259-8229 or 800/332-2439, www.griffithexp.com, $1,599 adults, $1,399 youth) is geared toward families.

Experienced kayakers or rafters can make the trip on their own. Drive in from Price or Myton or arrange a flight to the put-in at Sand Wash with Moab-based **Redtail Aviation** (435/259-7421, www.flyredtail.com, $219-359 pp, 2-person minimum). You need both a permit and river-running experience to float the canyons on your own. Contact the **BLM Price Field Office** (125 S. 600 W., Price, 435/636-3600, www.blm.gov/ut, 8am-4:30pm Mon.-Fri. or www.recreation.gov, lottery runs Dec. 1-Jan. 31) for permitting information. The BLM also has a complete list of licensed outfitters.

Labyrinth and Stillwater Canyons

The Green River's Labyrinth and Stillwater Canyons are downstream, between the town of Green River and the river's confluence with the Colorado River in Canyonlands National Park. Best for canoeing and kayaking, the Green River at this point is calm and wide as it passes into increasingly deep, rust-colored canyons. This isn't a wilderness river—powerboats can also follow the river below town to the confluence with the Colorado River and head up the Colorado to Moab, two or three days and 186 river miles (299 km) away.

The most common trip on this portion of the Green River begins just south of town and runs south through Labyrinth Canyon, ending at Mineral Bottom, a distance of 68 river miles (109 km). **Moab Rafting and Canoe Company** (2480 S. Hwy. 191, Moab, 435/259-7722, http://moab-rafting.com, 4-day guided trip $1,000 pp) offers this trip in canoes, including self-guided trips in rental canoes. **Tex's Riverways** (435/259-5101 or 877/662-2839, www.texsriverways.com) provides canoe and touring kayak rentals ($55-70 per day) and equipment to outfit a self-guided multiday trip, plus shuttle services ($215 pp) to and from the river. Permits are required to paddle in Labyrinth Canyon; they're free and available on the BLM website (www.blm.gov) or at the **BLM Field Office** (82 Dogwood Ave., Moab, 435/259-2100, 8am-4:30pm Mon.-Fri.) in Moab.

Crystal Geyser

With a little luck, you'll catch the spectacle of this cold-water geyser on the bank of the Green River. The gusher shoots as high as 60 feet (18 m), but only 3-4 times daily, so you may have to spend half a day here to see it. The eruption, typically lasting 7 minutes, is powered by carbon dioxide and other gases. A 2,267-foot-deep (691-m) petroleum test well drilled in 1935-1936 concentrated the geyser flow, but thick layers of old deposits of travertine (a form of limestone) prove that mineral-laden springs have long been active here. Colorful, newer travertine creates delicate terraces around the opening and down to the river. The orange and dark

1
2
3
4

red of the minerals and algae make this a pretty spot, even if the geyser is only quietly gurgling.

Crystal Geyser is 10 miles (16.1 km) south of Green River by road; boaters should look for the geyser deposits on the left, about 4.5 river miles (7.2 km) downstream from Green River. From downtown, drive east 1 mile (1.6 km) on Main Street, turn left, and go 3 miles (4.8 km) on signed Frontage Road (near milepost 4), then turn right and drive 6 miles (9.7 km) on a narrow paved road just after going under a railroad overpass. The road goes under I-70; keep right at a fork near some power lines. Some washes have to be crossed, so the drive isn't recommended after rain. When the weather is fair, cars shouldn't have a problem.

Food

Other than motel restaurants and fast food, the one notable place to eat in Green River is ★ **Ray's Tavern** (25 S. Broadway, 435/564-3511, 11am-9pm daily, $10-29). Ray's doesn't look like much from the outside, but inside you'll find a welcoming vibe, tables made from tree trunks, and great steaks, chops, and burgers. Don't expect haute cuisine, but the food is good, and the atmosphere is truly Western. Beer lovers will enjoy the local beer selection after a long day navigating the river or desert roads.

Grab a taco from **Taco La Pasadita** (215 E. Main St., 435/564-8159, 8am-9:30pm daily, $7-13), a taco truck in the parking lot of an old gas station. The food is good, and there are picnic tables set up by the truck.

Directly adjacent to the River Terrace hotel, **Tamarisk** (1710 E. Main St., 435/564-8109, 7am-10pm daily, $13-21), is a decent American-style restaurant with riverfront views and good Southwestern touches (including Navajo fry bread).

1: Green River's Desolation Canyon **2:** Crystal Geyser, alongside the Green River **3:** paddling into the Labyrinth Canyon **4:** Sego Canyon prehistoric rock art

Accommodations

Green River has a few rather shabby older motels as well as newer chain motels. Unless noted, each has a swimming pool—a major consideration in this often-sweltering desert valley.

The **Holiday Inn Express & Suites** (1050 Main St., 435/564-8444, www.ihg.com, $216-224) is a fine, dependable option just west of town with an indoor pool and complimentary breakfast. The **Super 8** (1248 E. Main St., 435/363-0055 or 800/454-3213, www.wyndhamhotels.com/super-8, $93-110), out by I-70 exit 162, offers good value, with spacious, comfortable guest rooms.

The nicest place to stay in town is the ★ **River Terrace** (1740 E. Main St., 435/564-3401 or 877/564-3401, www.river-terrace.com, $140-300), with dated but spacious and comfortable guest rooms, some of which overlook the Green River and some with balconies. Breakfast is included, with a restaurant adjacent to the hotel. The very pleasant outdoor pool area is flanked by patios, gardens, and shaded tables.

Campgrounds

Several campgrounds, all with showers, offer sites for tents and RVs year-round. **Green River State Park** (150 S. Green River Blvd., 435/564-3633 or 800/322-3770, https://stateparks.utah.gov, year-round, $7 day-use, $45 campsites, $75 cabin) has a great setting near the river; it's shaded by large cottonwoods and has a boat ramp. All campsites have hookups. **Shady Acres RV Park** (690 E. Main St., 435/564-8290 or 800/537-8674, www.shadyacresrv.com, year-round, $26-30 tents, $51-61 RVs, $51-55 cabin) is not all that shady and may be a bit too close to the noisy road for tent campers; it has a store, showers, and a laundry. **Green River KOA** (235 S. 1780 E., 435/564-5734, $43-48 tents, $76-102 RVs, $108-179 cabins) has campsites and cabins (bring sleeping bags) across from the John Wesley Powell Museum and next to Tamarisk restaurant.

SEGO CANYON

Prehistoric rock art and the ruins of a coal-mining town lie within scenic canyons of the Book Cliffs, just a short drive north from Thompson Springs and I-70.

Sego Canyon is a showcase of **prehistoric rock art,** preserving rock drawings and images that are thousands of years old. The Barrier Canyon-style drawings may be 8,000 years old, while the more recent Fremont-style images were created in the last 1,000 years. Compared to these ancient pictures, the Ute etchings are relatively new, perhaps created as recently as the 1800s, when Ute villages still lined Sego Canyon. Interestingly, the newer petroglyphs and pictographs are less representational than the older ones. The ancient Barrier Canyon figures are typically horned, ghostlike beings that look like aliens from early sci-fi flicks. The Fremont-style images depict stylized human figures made from geometric shapes. The Ute images are of buffaloes and hunters on horseback.

To reach Sego Canyon, take I-70 exit 185 for Thompson, which is 25 miles (40 km) east of Green River or 5 miles (8 km) east of the US 191 turnoff to Moab, and drive 1 mile (1.6 km) north to Thompson. The small railroad community has a café and convenience store near I-70. Continue north across the tracks on a paved road, which becomes dirt after 0.5 mile (0.8 km), into Thompson Canyon. At the first creek ford, 3.5 miles (5.6 km) from town, look for petroglyphs and pictographs on cliffs to the left.

A ghost town is 1 mile (1.6 km) up Sego Canyon. Both the Sego and Thompson Canyon Roads lead deeper into the rugged Book Cliffs. Drivers with 4WD vehicles and hikers can explore more of this land, seldom visited except in deer season.

Background

The Landscape

GEOGRAPHY

Utah's 84,990 square miles (220,123 sq km) place it 11th in size among the 50 states. The varied landscape is divided into three major physiographic provinces: the **Basin and Range** in the northwest; the soaring Uinta, Wasatch, and Bear River Ranges of the **Middle Rocky Mountains** in the north and northeast; and the **Colorado Plateau's** high desert landscape to the south.

The Basin and Range

Rows of fault-block mountain ranges follow a north-south alignment in this province in the Great Basin, west of the Wasatch Range and the high plateaus. Most of the land is at elevations of 4,000-5,000 feet (1,219-1,524 m). Peaks in the Stansbury and Deep Creek Mountains rise more than 11,000 feet (3,353 m) above sea level, creating "biological islands" inhabited by cool-climate plants and animals.

Erosion has worn down many ranges, forming large deposits of gravel, sand, and sediment in the basins below. Many of these broad valleys lack effective drainage, and none flow to the sea. Terraces mark the hills along what was once the shore of the prehistoric and massive Lake Bonneville. Few perennial streams originate in these mountains, but rivers from eastern ranges end their voyages in Great Salt Lake, Sevier Lake, and silt-filled valleys.

The Middle Rocky Mountains

The Wasatch Range and the Uinta Mountains provide some of the most dramatic alpine scenery in the state. In both mountainous areas, you'll find cirques, arêtes, horns, and glacial troughs carved by massive rivers of ice during glaciation periods. Structurally, however, the ranges have little in common.

The narrow Wasatch runs north-south for about 200 miles (320 km) between the Idaho border and central Utah. Slippage along the still-active Wasatch Fault has resulted in a towering western face with few foothills. Most of Utah's ski resorts are in the Wasatch.

Northeast of the Wasatch, the Uinta Mountains rise broadly about 150 miles (242 km) west-east and 30 miles (48 km) across. Twenty-four peaks exceed 13,000 feet (3,962 m), including Utah's highest: Kings Peak (elev. 13,528 ft/4,123 m). An estimated 1,400 small lakes dot the glacial moraines of the Uintas.

The Colorado Plateau

World-famous for its scenery and geology, the Colorado Plateau covers nearly half of Utah, not to mention stretches across the border well into Colorado, New Mexico, and Arizona. Elevations are mostly 3,000-6,000 feet (914-1,829 m), but some peaks reach nearly 13,000 feet (3,962 m). The Uinta Basin forms the northern part of this vast complex of plateaus.

Although most of the basin terrain is gently rolling, the Green River and its tributaries carved spectacular canyons into the Roan and Book Cliffs. Farther south, the Green and Colorado Rivers sculpted remarkable canyons, buttes, mesas, arches, and badlands.

Uplifts and foldings have formed such features as the San Rafael Swell, the Waterpocket Fold, and the Circle Cliffs. The rounded Abajo, Henry, La Sal, and Navajo Mountains are examples of intrusive rock—an igneous layer that is formed below the earth's surface and later exposed by erosion.

The high plateaus in the Escalante region drop in a series of steps known as the Grand Staircase. Exposed layers range from the relatively young rocks of the Black Cliffs (lava flows) in the north to the increasingly older Pink Cliffs (Wasatch Formation), Gray Cliffs (Mancos Shale), White Cliffs (Navajo sandstone), and Vermilion Cliffs (Chinle and Wingate Formations) toward the south.

GEOLOGY

The land now contained in Utah began as undersea deposits when North America sat near the equator, about 500 million years ago. The spectacular canyon country, now known as the Colorado Plateau, began as a basin of silt and sand deposits at the verge of a shallow sea. This basin sat on a continental plate that rose and fell, so sometimes it sat below the waters of ancient seas, which is when early marine life fossils were deposited across the landscape. During more arid periods, this vast land of sand dunes rose above sea level.

Previous: Shafer Trail at Canyonlands' Island in the Sky District.

The Colorado Plateau

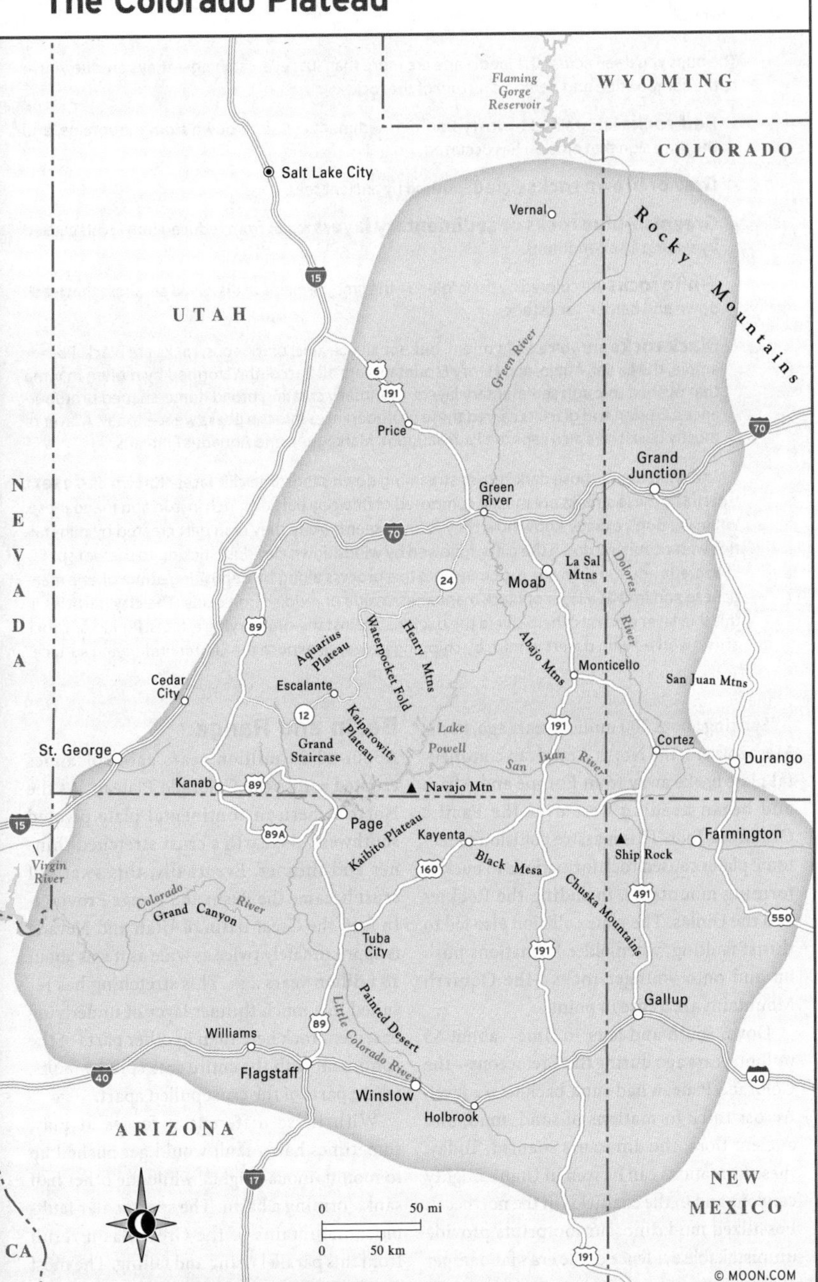

Colorful Clues

The hues you'll see across the landscape are more than just eye-catching—they can clue you in to the composition and geologic history of the rock.

- **Red rocks** are stained by rusty iron-rich sediments washed down from mountains, and they're a sign that erosion has occurred.
- **Gray or brown rocks** were deposited by ancient seas.
- **Greenish-blue rocks or sedimentary layers** result from reduced iron levels caused by swamp-like conditions.
- **White rocks** are colored by their "glue"—the limey remains of dissolved seashells that leach down and harden sandstone.
- **Black rocks** are volcanic in origin, but not all volcanic, or igneous, rocks are black. For example, the La Sal, Abajo, and Henry Mountains are all "laccoliths," formed by molten magma that pushed through sedimentary layers, eventually creating broad dome-shaped protuberances. Erosion and glaciers carved these protuberances into the peaks we see today. A layer of mostly basalt lava also caps the Paunsaugunt, Markagunt, and Aquarius Plateaus.

And what about those dark stripes streaming down sandstone cliff faces? Known as **desert varnish,** these streaks are mostly composed of fine clay particles, rich in iron and manganese. While we don't exactly know how they form, it seems likely they're in part created by mineral-rich water coursing down the cliffs, followed by wind-blown clay dust sticking to the wet spots.

Bacteria and fungi on the rock may help this process along by depositing atmospheric manganese and iron as a layer of black manganese oxide or reddish iron oxide. The clay particles in this thin layer of varnish help shield the bacteria against the sun's drying effects. Prehistoric rock artists worked with desert varnish by chipping it away to expose the lighter underlying surface.

Starting about 200 million years ago, in the Mesozoic era, the North American continental plate broke away from Europe and Africa and began heading west over the Pacific Ocean seafloor. This massive collision of tectonic plates caused rock formations to buckle, forming mountains, including the Rockies and the Uintas. The plate collision also led to thrust faulting, when older formations push up and onto younger rocks—the Oquirrh Mountains are a case in point.

Down south and later in time—about 65 million years ago during the Cretaceous—the Colorado Plateau had sunk back to sea level. Across thick formations of sand, mud, and ancient flora, the dinosaurs roamed. Today, these formations can be seen in Utah's mighty canyons and in the coalfields in the northeast. Fossilized mud dinosaur footprints provide unmistakable evidence of the era's far damper climate.

Basin and Range

About 20-30 million years ago, volcanoes erupted across the Colorado Plateau. As the North American continental plate pivoted southwest, the earth's crust stretched thinner and thinner. Eventually, this swath of crust became the Basin and Range Province. In fact, the Great Basin of Utah and Nevada is approximately twice as wide as it was about 18 million years ago. This stretching has resulted in a much thinner layer of underlying basement rock here than in other parts of the continent, with the entire area split by faults, where parts of the crust pulled apart.

With these differential forces at play, sometimes half a fault would get pushed up to mountainous heights, while the other half sank, forming a basin. The spectacular fault-block mountains of the Great Basin result from this parallel rising and falling. The most famous instance of this type of formation is the rugged Wasatch Mountains, which rise directly above the basin of Great Salt Lake.

To the east of this mountain building action, the Colorado Plateau remained relatively undisturbed—that is until the last 10 million years, when the whole region rose, as much as 5,000 feet (1,524 m) in Utah's corner of the plateau. As the land lifted, rivers cut ever-deeper canyons. The erosive power of the Green, Colorado, San Juan, and other rivers and streams have cut down through hundreds of millions of years of rock.

The Ice Age in Utah

During the geologically recent Pleistocene, ice-age mountain glaciers and climatic changes brought an abundance of moisture to Utah. Runoff and meltwater flooded the basins of fault-block mountain ranges, forming enormous lakes. The largest was Lake Bonneville, which was the predecessor of the Great Salt Lake. At its largest, Lake Bonneville covered nearly all of northern and west-central Utah and was nearly 900 feet (274 m) deeper than today.

After the ice ages ended, about 10,000 years ago, Lake Bonneville diminished in size and dropped below the level necessary to drain into a river system, resulting in the saline Great Salt Lake. You can easily see the old Bonneville shorelines along the Wasatch Front, on the outskirts of cities like Logan, Provo, and Salt Lake City. Much of the old lake bottom west of Salt Lake City is salt desert and extremely flat. In the Bonneville Salt Flats, the valley is so flat and unbroken that the curvature of the earth is visible.

CLIMATE

Most of Utah is dry, with an average annual precipitation of about 12 inches (30.5 cm). Precipitation varies greatly from place to place due to topography and storm pattern irregularities. Deserts cover about 33 percent of the state, and the driest areas are in the Great Basin, the Uinta Basin, and on the Colorado Plateau, where annual precipitation is around 5-10 inches (12.7-25.4 cm). At the other extreme, the highest peaks of the Wasatch Range receive hundreds of inches of annual precipitation, mostly as snow. In the record winter of 2022-2023, the Wasatch received over 900 inches of snowfall in places—that's over 75 feet (23 m).

Winter and Spring Weather Patterns

Periods of high-pressure systems broken by Pacific storm fronts shape most of Utah's winter weather. These high-pressure systems cause inversions when dense cold air flows down the snow-covered slopes into the valleys, where it traps moisture and smoke. The blanket of smog maintains even temperatures but is the bane of Salt Lake City. Skiers, however, enjoy bright sunny days and cold nights in the clear mountain air. Reprieve comes to the valley when cold fronts roll in from the Pacific, cleaning out the stagnant air. When skies clear, the daily temperature range returns to its normal variability.

Most winter precipitation arrives as snow across the state. Fronts originating over the Gulf of Alaska typically arrive every 6-7 days and trigger most of Utah's snowfall.

Summer and Fall Weather Patterns

During summer, the valleys still experience inversions of cold air on clear dry nights but much less dramatically than in winter. Canyon country has higher daytime temperatures than equivalent mountain elevations because there's no source of cold air in the canyons to replace the hot rising air. Also, canyon walls act as an oven, reflecting and trapping heat.

Thunderstorms are most common in summer, when moist warm air rises in billowing clouds. The storms, which can produce heavy rain and hail, tend to be concentrated in small areas less than 3 miles (4.8 km) across. Southeastern Utah sees the first thunderstorms of the season, often in mid-June. By mid-July, these storms have spread across the entire state. They lose energy as autumn approaches, and by October they're supplanted by low-pressure systems at high altitudes and Pacific storm fronts, which can cause long periods of heavy precipitation. The highest mountain peaks can get snow even in midsummer.

Storm Hazards

Rainwater runs quickly off the rocky desert surfaces into gullies and canyons. Flash floods can sweep away anything in their path, including boulders, cars, and campsites. Do not camp or park in potential flash-flood areas. If you come to a section of flooded roadway—a common occurrence on desert roads post-storm—wait until the water goes down before crossing (it shouldn't take long). Summer lightning causes forest and brush fires, posing a danger to hikers foolish enough to climb mountains when storms threaten.

ENVIRONMENTAL ISSUES

Like many other western states, Utah is deeply conflicted about environmental issues. One of the most conservative states in the nation, Utah has always been business-oriented, especially toward the historic extractive industries such as mining, logging, and agriculture. Utah has also proved to be very friendly to the military. Large portions of northwestern Utah are under Pentagon-controlled bases, weapons research areas, and munitions dumps.

On the other hand, tourism and high-tech industries breathe life into Utah's economy. Tourism brings in millions of visitors (17.8 million in 2021, for example), making it the single largest employer in Utah. The greater Salt Lake area is experiencing a phenomenal boom in population growth and new industries. Many people move to Utah for its quality of life—public lands and world-class outdoor recreation are available right out the backdoor. The interests of the tourism and recreation industries are often at odds with the interests of the state's traditional power base.

Redrawing Utah National Monuments

A couple of Utah's national monuments have seen their share of political tumult in recent past. Both the 1.9 million-acre Grand Staircase-Escalante National Monument (designated by President Bill Clinton in 1996) and the 1.35 million-acre Bears Ears National Monument (created by President Barack Obama in 2016) were slashed in size and divided into smaller units in 2018 by the Trump administration. Thankfully, a coalition of Native American tribes, environmentalists, and recreationists challenged the move in court. In 2021, the Biden administration fully restored both monuments and eliminated the division split.

Climate Change

Many places are on the "climate vulnerable" list, and Utah is among them for many reasons. The potential downfall of the ski industry, pivotal to the local economy, is one of them. It should come as no surprise that the ski industry depends on snow. During bad snow years, opening dates get delayed. Closing dates move up. More snow must be manufactured at a cost.

More gravely, as the second-driest state in the nation, Utah has much to worry about in a hotter, drier world. Planners are already raising red flags about the conflict inherent in projected population growth and the reality of the current and future water supplies. Lack of water not only has implications for drinking water supplies, agriculture, and the resources to produce fake snow for skiing, but also for how long and devastating wildfire season is each year.

A combination of drought fueled by climate change and water overuse is also leading to the demise of the Great Salt Lake—a phenomenon that's made national news several times. New initiatives are in place to try to protect the lake, and its disappearance would be a true catastrophe, releasing toxic lakebed dust into the Salt Lake area and destroying the habitat of hundreds of birds that inhabit or migrate through this important ecosystem.

Water Use

The early Mormon settlers came from well-watered New York and New England and the rich Midwestern prairies. When they arrived in Utah, they set about transforming the desert, following the scripture that says the desert will blossom as a rose. Brigham Young encouraged this endeavor, saying that God would change the climate, providing more water if the settlers worked to establish agriculture.

So the settlers planted fruit orchards, shade trees, and grass, turning the desert into an oasis. They built dams and created reservoirs. They dug canals, piping water from farther and farther away, turning the desert green.

According to a 2015 survey, Utah has the second-highest water consumption rate in the country, despite having experienced many years of drought and being the second-driest state in the United States.

Water conservationists maintain that Utah residents, including state officials in charge of water-use policy, have not let go of 19th-century ideals about water development and conservation. Meanwhile, many individuals view the drought as a wake-up call and see water conservation and native-plant landscaping as Utah's future.

ATV Impacts

Off-road vehicles, or ATVs (all-terrain vehicles), are one of the fastest-growing recreational markets in the country. ATVs are prohibited in national parks but allowed on many adjacent public lands, including BLM land.

Both due to the rapid rise of ATVs as well as to their greater power and dexterity, ATVs can be highly destructive to the delicate natural environment of the Colorado Plateau, including the ecosystem-critical cryptobiotic soil, as well as other plant and animal life.

Organizations like the Southern Utah Wilderness Alliance (www.suwa.org) continue to work with the BLM to regulate the use of ATVs in the interest of the environmental stewardship of public land.

While ATVs can be quite damaging, if used responsibly on established dirt roads and double-track, they are a fine way to explore. Set out safely by riding with caution and ensuring all riders are wearing helmets—Utah ranks number one in the country for child injuries by ATV, with several deaths per year.

Oil and Gas Drilling

In addition to ranking highly in terms of public land acreage, Utah is also among the top 15 states when it comes to oil and gas production (www.geology.utah.gov). Active and abandoned oil fields and pipelines exist across the state—and the contentious question of whether to drill more looms large. For example, untapped potential exists just half a mile (0.8 km) away from Arches and Canyonlands, and within 10 miles (16 km) of Bears Ears National Monument.

Environmentalists and recreationists are generally opposed to drilling near such a special swath of public lands. Somewhat famously, in 2008, a 27-year-old activist named Tim DeChristopher (aka "Bidder 70") outbid the competition on 14 oil and gas leases near Arches during a Bureau of Land Management auction—without the funds or intent to actually close the $1.8 million deal. Tim spent a couple years in jail for his creative act of civil disobedience. Another contentious lease sale literally on top of Moab's famed Slickrock Trail was shut down by protests in 2020.

If you're interested in learning more about these issues, check out the resources from the nonpartisan, nonprofit Southern Utah Wilderness Alliance (www.suwa.org).

Leave No Trace

With the surge in visitors coming to experience the beauty of Utah, we must all do our part to keep these public lands in good shape. The best way to do this is by following the seven "Leave No Trace" principles, developed by a nonprofit of the same name to support the protection and enjoyment of nature for all.

A few of these principles include **traveling and camping on durable surfaces** (e.g., not trampling vegetation or cryptobiotic soils), **packing out and responsibly disposing of waste** (probably the most obvious), **respecting wildlife,** and **not taking anything found in nature home** with you (whether that's a stick, a rock, or an arrowhead).

You can find the full list and resources on how to follow each at www.lnt.org.

Plants and Animals

A wide variety of plants and animals find homes within Utah's great range of elevations (more than 11,000 ft/3,353 m). Regardless of precipitation, the environment is harsh, and most plants and animals have had to adapt to endure the challenging climate.

PLANTS

Desert

In the southern Utah deserts near St. George, fewer than 8 inches (20.3 cm) of rain fall yearly. Creosote bush dominates the plant life, although you're also likely to see rabbitbrush, snakeweed, blackbrush, saltbush, yuccas, and cacti. Joshua trees grow on some of the higher gravel benches. Flowering plants tend to bloom after winter or summer rains.

In the more temperate areas of the Great Basin, Uinta Basin, and canyon lands, shadscale—a plant resistant to both salt and drought—grows on the valley floors. Commonly growing with shadscale are grasses, annuals, Mormon tea, budsage, gray molley, and winterfat. In salty soils, more likely companions are greasewood, salt grass, and iodine bush. Nonalkaline soils, on the other hand, may have blackbrush as the dominant plant.

Sagebrush, the most common shrub in Utah, thrives on higher terraces and in alluvial fans of nonalkaline soil. Grasses are commonly found mixed with sagebrush and may dominate the landscape. Piñon pine and juniper—small trees often found together—can grow only where at least 12 inches (30.5 cm) of rain falls annually; the lower limit of their growth is sometimes called the arid timberline. In the Wasatch Range, scrub oaks often grow near junipers.

Mountain

As elevation rises and rainfall increases, you'll see growing numbers of ponderosa pines and chaparral in the forest. The chaparral association includes oak, maple, mountain mahogany, and sagebrush. Gambel oak, juniper, and Douglas fir commonly grow among the ponderosa pines in the Uintas and the high plateaus.

Douglas fir is the most common tree on the slopes of the Wasatch Range, the high plateaus, and the northern slopes of the Great Basin ranges. In the Uintas, however, lodgepole pine dominates. Other trees include ponderosa pine, limber pine, white fir, blue spruce (Utah's state tree), and aspen.

Strong winds and a growing season of fewer than 120 days prevent trees from reaching their full size at higher elevations. Often gnarled and twisted, Engelmann spruce and subalpine fir grow in the cold heights over large areas of the Uintas and Wasatches. Limber and bristlecone pines live in the zone, too. Lakes and lush subalpine meadows are common.

Only grasses, mosses, sedges, and annuals can withstand the rugged conditions atop Utah's highest ranges. Freezing temperatures and snow can blast the mountain slopes even in midsummer.

Bark Beetles and the Death of Utah Forests

In many of Utah's forests, you'll likely observe miles and miles of dead trees. Since the early 2000s, forests in the western United States have been increasingly infested with small, native boring insects known collectively as bark beetles. These beetles live and reproduce in the inner bark, the tree layer responsible for providing moisture and nutrition. The beetles drill in through the tree's outer bark and, if present in sufficient numbers, destroy the life-giving inner bark as part of their reproductive cycle. The tree dies, and a new generation of bark beetles swarm on to other healthy trees. There's a bark beetle species for each type of tree: the spruce beetle, the lodgepole pine beetle, the piñon pine beetle, and so on.

The bark beetle infestation is of epic proportions. In New Mexico, bark beetles have destroyed 90 percent of piñon pines, the state tree. In Utah, about 2.2 million acres of the state's 3.5 million acres of pine, fir, and spruce forests in the state are under attack by bark beetles, and entire forests are currently dead or dying. Especially hard hit is the north slope of the Uinta Mountains.

Of course, with millions of standing dead trees in the forests, wildfire risk is hugely amplified, which is why the state is investing in clearing out affected trees. These weakened trees can also fall without warning, so don't linger or camp under red, dead trees.

Although bark beetles are native to western forests, environmental factors and forest management practices have created a perfect bark beetle storm. Climate change in the western United States has meant that bark beetle infestation is spreading faster and farther north; for the first time, beetles are decimating Canadian forests above 60 degrees latitude. Traditionally, bark beetles have a two-year reproductive cycle. In the past decade, warmer temperatures, prolonged drought, and longer seasons have instigated yearly reproductive cycles, and in some areas, bark beetles are reproducing twice a year.

Another factor in bark beetle infestation is US Forest Service fire suppression practices. Traditionally, wildfires cleared forests of mature trees, which were more affected by bark beetles than younger trees, and burned the colonies of bark beetles. But the prevention of wildfires in the last half of the 20th century has fostered thick conifer forests with abundant mature trees, perfect conditions to explode the bark beetle population.

One thing is certain: The iconic western forests that our generation has known won't be here for the next generation, if ever again. According to forest scientists, lodgepole pine forests will require 50-80 years to grow back, and spruce forests could take 150-350 years to recover. If climate change is indeed part of the problem, future replacement forests may not find the Utah mountains a hospitable home.

ANIMALS

Desert

Most desert animals retreat to a den or burrow during the heat of the day, when ground temperatures can reach 130°F (54.4°C). Look for wildlife in early morning, during late afternoon, or at night. You may see kangaroo rats, desert cottontails, black-tailed jackrabbits, striped and spotted skunks, kit foxes, ringtail cats, coyotes, bobcats, mountain lions, and several species of squirrels and mice. Birds include the native Gambel's quail, roadrunners, red-tailed hawks, great horned owls, cactus wrens, black-chinned and broad-tailed hummingbirds, and rufous-sided towhees. The desert tortoise lives here, too, but faces extinction in a losing battle with human activity, which has destroyed and fragmented its habitat.

The rare Gila monster, identified by its beadlike skin with black and yellow patterns, is found in the state's southwest corner. Sidewinder, Great Basin, and other western rattlesnakes are occasionally seen. Also watch for other poisonous creatures; scorpions, spiders, and centipedes can inflict painful stings or bites. It's a good idea when camping to check for these unwanted guests in shoes and

Cryptobiotic Soil

Over much of the Colorado Plateau, the soil is alive. What looks like a blackish-brown crust is actually a dense network of blue-green algae intertwined with soil particles, lichens, moss, green algae, and microfungi. This slightly sticky, crusty mass holds the soil together, slowing erosion. Its sponge-like consistency allows it to soak up and retain water, reducing runoff and evaporation.

This biological soil plays a critical role in the resilience of desert ecosystems. Plants growing in cryptobiotic soil have a great advantage over plants rooted in dry sandy soil. In addition to retaining moisture, cryptobiotic soil helps prevent erosion from wind and water.

The upshot? Watch where you step. Cryptobiotic soils can take centuries to fully develop and are extremely fragile. Make every effort to avoid treading on this incredible desert resource by sticking to trails, slickrock, or rocks.

other items left outside. Be careful also not to reach under rocks or into places you can't see.

In the more temperate areas, you'll see plenty of desert wildlife, although you might also see Utah prairie dogs, beavers, muskrats, black bears, desert bighorn sheep, desert mule deer, and the antelope-like pronghorn, as well as rattlesnakes and other reptiles.

Marshes of the Great Basin have an abundance of food and cover that attract waterfowl; species include whistling swans, Great Basin Canada geese, lesser snow geese, great blue herons, seagulls (Utah's state bird), common mallards, gadwalls, and American common mergansers. Chukars (from similar desert lands in Asia) and Hungarian partridge (from Eastern Europe and western Asia) thrive under the cover of sagebrush in dry-farm areas. Sage and sharp-tailed grouse also prefer the open country.

Not surprisingly, few fish live in the desert. The Great Salt Lake is too salty to support fish life; the only creatures that can live in its extremely saline water are bacteria, a few insect species, and brine shrimp, which are commercially harvested. The Colorado River, which cuts through southeastern Utah, supports a number of fish species, several of which are endemic to the river and are now considered endangered.

Mountain

In the thin forests of the high plateaus and Uintas, squirrels and chipmunks rely on pinecones for food; other animals living here include Nuttall's cottontails, black-tailed jackrabbits, spotted and striped skunks, red foxes, coyotes, mule deer, Rocky Mountain elk (Utah's state mammal), moose, black bears, and mountain lions. Moose did not arrive until the 1940s, when they crossed over from Wyoming; now they live in northern and central Utah.

Merriam's wild turkeys, originally from Colorado, are found in oak and ponderosa pine forests of central and southern Utah. Other birds include Steller's jays, blue and ruffed grouse, common poorwills, great horned owls, black-chinned and broad-tailed hummingbirds, gray-headed and Oregon juncos, white-throated swifts, and the common raven. Most snakes, such as the gopher, hognose, and garter, are harmless, but you may also come across western rattlers.

Utah has more than 1,000 fishable lakes and numerous fishing streams. Species range from rainbow and cutthroat trout to large mackinaw and brown trout to striped bass, walleye, bluegill, and whitefish. Bear Lake in extreme northern Utah is home to the Bear Lake whitefish, Bonneville whitefish, Bonneville cisco, and Bear Lake sculpin—all are unique to Bear Lake and its tributaries. Because of their restricted range, they are vulnerable to extinction from habitat alteration due to water management of Bear Lake and its tributaries.

Deer and Rocky Mountain elk graze in the lower mountains but rarely higher. Smaller animals of the high mountains include northern flying squirrels, snowshoe rabbits, pocket gophers, yellow belly marmots, pikas, chipmunks, and mice.

At the highest elevations, on a bright summer day, the trees, grasses, and tiny flowering alpine plants are abuzz with insects, rodents, and visiting birds. Come winter, though, most animals will have moved to lower, more protected areas. Few animals live in the true alpine regions. White-tailed ptarmigan live in the tundra of the Uinta Mountains.

History

PRE-SETTLEMENT UTAH

Indigenous Roots

Archaeologists have evidence that Paleo-Indians began to wander across the region that would become Utah about 15,000 years ago, hunting big game and gathering plant foods. The climate was probably cooler and wetter. Edible plants and game animals would have been more abundant than they are today. Early groups continued hunting and gathering despite climate changes and the extinction of many big-game species about 10,000 years ago.

The first attempts at agriculture were introduced from the south about 2,000 years ago and triggered a slow transition to settled village life. Fremont culture emerged in the northern part of the Colorado Plateau, and Ancestral Puebloans took hold to the south. Although both groups developed crafts such as basketry, pottery, and jewelry, only the Ancestral Puebloans constructed masonry buildings in their villages. Their corn, beans, and squash enabled them to be less reliant on migration and to construct year-round village sites. Thousands of stone dwellings, ceremonial kivas, and towers built by the Ancestral Puebloans still stand.

Both groups also created intriguing rock art, both pecked (petroglyphs) and painted (pictographs). The Ancestral Puebloans and the Fremont people departed from this region about 800 years ago, perhaps because of drought, warfare, or disease. Some of the Ancestral Puebloans moved south and joined the Pueblo people of present-day Arizona and New Mexico. The fate of the Fremont people remains a mystery.

About the same time, perhaps by coincidence, the nomadic Shoshoni in the north and the Utes and Paiutes in the south moved through Utah. Relatives of the Athabaskans of western Canada, the seminomadic Navajo, wandered into New Mexico and Arizona between 1300 and 1500 CE. These adaptable people learned agriculture, weaving, pottery, and other skills from their Pueblo neighbors and became expert horse riders and sheepherders with livestock obtained from the Spanish.

The size of prehistoric populations has varied greatly in Utah. There were probably few inhabitants during the Archaic period (before 500 CE) but many more during the time of the Ancestral Puebloan and Fremont cultures (500-1250 CE), rising to a peak of perhaps 500,000. Except for the Athabaskan-speaking Navajo, all of Utah's historic Native Americans spoke Shoshonian languages and had similar cultures.

Explorers and Colonizers

In 1776, Spanish explorers of the Dominguez-Escalante Expedition were the first Europeans to visit and describe the region during their unsuccessful attempt to find a route west to California. Utes guided the Spanish expedition through the Uinta Basin.

Retreating to New Mexico, the explorers encountered great difficulties in the canyons of southern Utah before finding a safe ford across the Colorado River. This spot, known as the Crossing of the Fathers, now lies under Lake Powell. Later explorers established the Old Spanish Trail through this area of Utah to connect New Mexico with California.

Adventurous mountain men seeking beaver pelts and other furs entered northern Utah in the mid-1820s. They explored the peaks, the rivers, and the Great Salt Lake, blazing most of the trails later used by wagon trains, the Pony Express, and the railroads. By 1830, most of the mountain men had moved on to better trapping areas and left the land to the Native Americans. Some, however, returned to guide government explorers and groups of settlers.

In 1843, John C. Frémont led one of his several government-sponsored scientific expeditions into Utah. Frémont determined the salinity of Great Salt Lake and laid to rest speculation that a river drained the lake into the Pacific Ocean. Two years later, he led a well-prepared group across the heart of the dreaded Great Salt Lake Desert, despite warnings from the local Native Americans that no one had crossed it and survived. His accounts of the region described not only the salty lake and barren deserts, but also the fertile valleys near the Wasatch Range. LDS leaders planning a westward migration from Nauvoo, Illinois, carefully studied Frémont's reports.

Langsford Hastings, an ambitious politician, seized the opportunity to promote Frémont's desert route as a shortcut to California. Hastings had made the trip on horseback but failed to anticipate the problems of a wagon train. On this route in 1846, the Donner-Reed wagon train became so bogged down in the salt mud that many wagons were abandoned. Moreover, an 80-mile (129-km) stretch between water holes proved too far for many of the oxen, which died from dehydration. Today, motorists can cruise in comfort along I-80 on a similar route between Salt Lake City and Wendover.

Native Americans Versus Settlers

The Paiutes and Utes befriended and guided the early settlers, but troubles soon began when they saw their lands taken over by farmers and ranchers. The white population eventually drove them from the most desirable lands and settled them on the state's five reservations.

The Navajo resisted, raiding neighboring communities and white settlements. In 1863-1864, the US Army drove the Navajo from their lands, killing many and forcing the survivors on the Long Walk from Fort Defiance in northeastern Arizona to a camp in eastern New Mexico. This internment was a dismal failure and the Navajo were released four years later.

In 1868, the federal government settled the Navajo on land that has since grown into a giant reservation spreading from northeastern Arizona into adjacent Utah and New Mexico.

LATTER-DAY SAINTS SETTLEMENT

The short answer to why the Latter-day Saints went west to Utah is persecution. Previously, the church had been headquartered in Nauvoo, Illinois, where they were the victims of mob violence culminating in the assassination of their leader, Joseph Smith, in 1844.

That was the final straw for Brigham Young, who decided that it was high time to find a new home. They packed up the wagons and handcarts, and headed west, wintering in Nebraska. Cold, illness, and death marked the journey, and Young was even famously afflicted with Rocky Mountain fever toward the end.

On July 24, 1847, after 111 days on the go, Young and his caravan arrived in the Salt Lake Valley. When Young emerged from Emigration Canyon and gazed out upon the valley from what we now call the Salt Lake Foothills, he declared, "It is enough. This is the right place." Today, July 24 is celebrated as Pioneer Day, an official state holiday.

Young and others briefly questioned that certainty in the year that followed as difficulties arose. A particularly memorable one involved a cricket infestation of the settler's crops. But seagulls swooped in at the last viable moment, devouring the pests and saving the crops in an event now known as the Miracle of the Gulls.

Ever since, LDS have flocked to Utah to live and visit. In the two decades following Young's arrival, over 60,000 LDS individuals relocated to the Utah Territory. Members of the Church of Jesus Christ of Latter-day Saints continue to dominate the population, accounting for well over 60 percent of its total residents. And every year, as many as five million people make the pilgrimage to the LDS headquarters at Temple Square.

MODERN HISTORY

Rooted in Indigenous cultures and carved by LDS pioneers, the story of Utah is also plotted around the industries that have boomed, busted, and in some cases persisted. One of the oldest professions in the modern economy is mining. Many relocated to Utah to work in mines, some of which still operate today. The railroad industry also significantly influenced the development and culture of Utah for about a century beginning in the early 1860s. In addition to mining, religion, and trains, the military and aerospace industries have also shaped the state, along with higher education.

For the first couple decades of the railroad's heyday, Utah was not even an official state, mostly due to clashes between the federal government and the church-controlled state government led by Brigham Young. President James Buchanan even declared a short-lived Mormon War in response to Young ruling the state as a theocracy that embraced polygamy. But shortly after the state government banned polygamy and made some other concessions, Utah became the 45th state on January 4, 1896.

While mineral extraction persists today, outdoor recreation has risen out of the ashes of the mines of yore, particularly in Park City, the Cottonwood Canyons, and Moab. The 20th-century dawn of ski resorts, the 1919 establishment of its first national park (Zion), the 2002 Winter Olympics—these phenomena and more have shaped Utah into a destination for skiers, hikers, bikers, climbers, and many more outdoors enthusiasts.

There's no doubt that the Church of Jesus Christ of Latter-day Saints continues to play a dominating role in everything from politics to bars to downtown culture—the church purchased parts of Salt Lake City's Main Street in 1999 for over $8 million. But over time, the church's growth has slowed and parts of Utah have become less homogenous, with more immigrants arriving, liquor laws loosening, and more "gentiles" joining governing bodies.

The development of ski resorts and the designation of five national parks, along with national monuments, state parks, and other recreation areas, has brought a growing stream of visitors to the state. Today, tourism is the state's largest industry.

People and Culture

One of the oddest statistics about Utah is that it's the most urban state in the United States. According to the US Census Bureau in 2015, 88.4 percent of Utah's nearly three million residents live in cities and towns, instead of unincorporated areas. To put it another way, 9 out of 10 Utahns live on 1 percent of the state's land (nearly all along the Wasatch Front).

A relatively young population, combined with the LDS' emphasis on family life and clean living, has resulted in Utah having the highest birth rate and the second-lowest death rate in the country. Racially, the state largely reflects the northern European origins of LDS settlers; in 2010 the state was 84-89 percent white. The state's population includes Hispanics (10 percent), Pacific Islanders (7 percent), Native Americans (2.5 percent),

Anasazi or Ancestral Puebloan?

As you travel through the Southwest, you may hear reference to the Anasazi, also known as Ancestral Puebloans. The word *anasazi* is actually a Navajo term used by archaeologists who thought it meant "old people." A more literal translation is "enemy ancestors." For this reason, some consider the name inaccurate or even offensive. The terminology is in flux, and which name you hear depends on whom you're talking to or where you are. The National Park Service now uses the more descriptive term Ancestral Puebloan, and that's the term used in this book. These prehistoric people built masonry villages and eventually moved south to Arizona and New Mexico, where their descendants, including the Acoma, Cochiti, Santa Clara, Taos, and Hopi Mesas, live in modern-day pueblos.

Asians (2 percent), and African Americans (2.5 percent).

UTAH'S NATIVE AMERICANS

Shoshoni

Nomadic bands of Shoshoni (or Shoshone) lived in much of northern Utah, southern Idaho, and western Wyoming for thousands of years. Horses obtained from the Plains people—who had obtained them from the Spanish—allowed hunting parties to cover a large range. The great Chief Washakie led his people for 50 years and negotiated the Shoshoni treaties with the federal government. The Washakie Indian Reservation, in far northern Utah, belongs to the Northwestern band of Shoshoni, though few live there now. Headquarters are in Rock Springs, Wyoming, south of the large Wind River Indian Reservation.

Goshute (Gosiute)

This branch of the Western Shoshoni—more isolated than other Utah Native American groups—lived in the harsh Great Basin. They survived through intricate knowledge of the land and temporary shelters. These peaceful hunters and gatherers ate almost everything they found—plants, birds, rodents, crickets, and other insects. Because the Goshute had to dig for much of their food, early explorers called them Digger Indians. The newcomers couldn't believe these people survived in such a barren land of alkaline flats and sagebrush. Also known as the Newe, the Goshutes now live on the Skull Valley Indian Reservation in Tooele County and on the Goshute Indian Reservation along the Utah-Nevada border.

Ute

Several bands of Utes, or Núuci, ranged over large areas of central and eastern Utah and adjacent Colorado. Originally hunter-gatherers, they acquired horses around 1800 and became skilled raiders. Customs adopted from Plains people included the use of rawhide, tepees, and the travois, a sled used to carry goods. The discovery of gold in southern Colorado and the pressures of farmers there and in Utah forced the Utes to move and renegotiate treaties many times. They now have the large Uintah and Ouray Indian Reservation in northeast Utah, the small White Mesa Indian Reservation in southeast Utah, and the Ute Mountain Indian Reservation in southwest Colorado and northwest New Mexico.

Southern Paiute

Six of the 19 major bands of Southern Paiutes, or Nuwuvi, lived along the Santa Clara, Beaver, and Virgin Rivers and in other parts of southwest Utah. Historically, extended families hunted and gathered food together. Fishing and the cultivation of corn, beans, squash, and sunflowers supplemented the diet of most of the communities. Today, Utah's Paiutes have their headquarters in Cedar

City and scattered parcels of reservation land. Southern Paiutes also live in southern Nevada and northern Arizona.

Navajo

Also known as Diné (meaning "the people"), the Navajo moved into the San Juan River area around 1600. The Navajo have proved exceptionally adaptable in learning new skills from other cultures. Many Navajo crafts, clothing, and religious practices have come from other Native Americans and Spanish settlers, for example. The Navajo were the first in the area to move away from hunting and gathering, relying instead on the farming and shepherding techniques they learned from the Spanish. The Navajo are one of the largest Native American groups in the country, with 16 million acres of exceptionally scenic land in southeast Utah and adjacent Arizona and New Mexico. The Navajo Nation's headquarters is at Window Rock, Arizona.

THE LDS CHURCH

With over 16 million worldwide members, the "local religion," as the Church of Jesus Christ of Latter-day Saints is often referred to, continues to thrive and dominate the affairs of Utah. While the church is still expanding and has often been named the fastest-growing religion, that growth has started to slow.

Within the Wasatch especially, the religious dynamic is changing. As of 2018, LDS is no longer the majority religion of citizens in Salt Lake County. Indeed, in many parts of Salt Lake City, not to mention Ogden and Park City, the presence of the church is scarcely felt.

Over the years, the church has also inched toward a more progressive identity. Several decades ago, it allowed Black men to aspire to priesthood. And as of 2019, same-sex couples are no longer considered heretics. The church attributes such changes to what it describes as missives from God.

In addition to changing its policies, the church has rebranded itself over the years. It's changed its name to Reorganized Church of Jesus Christ of Latter-day Saints, to Saints of Community of Christ, and back again. It's asked for its members to be referred to as "LDS" instead of "Mormon."

The best way to learn about Utah's local religion is to head to Temple Square or This Is The Place Park in Salt Lake City.

The Arts

MUSIC

There are many excellent venues for music in Salt Lake City, Park City, and beyond. In Salt Lake, glittering Abravanel Concert Hall is home to the noted Utah Symphony, and the Tabernacle at Temple Square is often filled with concerts and recitals. The famed Mormon Tabernacle Choir performs here, as do various other church-related music groups. Best of all, all performances at Temple Square are free, making this a great opportunity for travelers to soak up culture at an unbeatable price.

Salt Lake City is also the state's major venue for rock and alternative music. A number of lively clubs host both local bands and traveling acts from both coasts.

Come summer, there's fine music at more out-of-the-way places. Venues at Park City offer a full summer schedule ranging from rock concerts at Park City Mountain Resort to the Utah Symphony at Deer Valley Resort and national parks. In Logan's sparkling Capitol Theatre, the Utah Festival Opera puts on a summer season of grand opera and classic musicals.

THEATER AND DANCE

Again, Salt Lake City is Utah's center of theater. Several year-round troupes dish up

Summer Music Festivals

You might not come to Utah for the music, but between summer concert series, the Salt Lake Tabernacle, and the Utah Symphony, there are plenty of ways to enhance your trip with a show.

SALT LAKE CITY

The variety of live music available in Salt Lake City in the summer is great. In addition to ongoing music performances at the **Tabernacle,** there is the LDS-sponsored **Concert Series at Temple Square** and concerts of classical and religious music, some of which take place outdoors.

The Roman Catholic Cathedral of the Madeleine presents the **Madeleine Arts and Humanities Program,** which offers classical music in a stunning 1909 place of worship.

For more modern music in an outdoor setting, head to **Gallivan Center** in the heart of downtown, where, in addition to free summer weekday noontime and Thursday evening concerts, there's a big-band dance on Tuesday evenings. Big acts come on the weekends.

PARK CITY

During summer, the **Utah Symphony** and other classical performers grace the stage at Deer Valley's outdoor amphitheater.

The **Beethoven Festival Park City** brings classical music to the Park City area year-round, with an emphasis on concerts in July.

LOGAN

In summer, Logan is Utah's music festival center. This lovely small city in a verdant valley plays host to the **Utah Festival Opera,** with fully staged professional operas in an intimate performing arts center that was once a movie palace and vaudeville hall (the season runs late June-early Aug.).

Another historic theater in Logan serves as home base for the **Lyric Repertory Company,** which produces musicals and other theatrical productions in June, July, and August.

SPRINGDALE

At the outdoor **O. C. Tanner Amphitheater,** you'll find a summertime series of concerts ranging from bluegrass, jazz, and folk to classical music.

ST. GEORGE

Once devoted to LDS-themed musicals, the **Tuacahn Amphitheater** features Broadway musicals and other music events July-December, all amid 1,500-foot cliffs near St. George.

MOAB

The **Moab Music Festival** offers concerts of classical chamber music, traditional music, vocal music, works of living composers, and jazz performed by acclaimed artists late August-mid-September. Performances take place in indoor and outdoor venues ranging from historic Star Hall in Moab to the banks of the Colorado River.

Outside the summer season, Moab offers the **Moab Folk Festival** in November.

everything from Broadway musicals to serious plays like Tony Kushner's *Angels in America.*

In the summer, Cedar City's Utah Shakespeare Festival (www.bard.org) offers eight different plays performed by a professional repertory company. Both Shakespearean and contemporary plays are featured; the Bard's works are presented under the stars in an outdoor theater.

Salt Lake City supports several dance troupes. Ballet West performs a mix of classical and contemporary pieces, while the

Ririe-Woodbury Dance Company has a more eclectic approach.

CINEMA

While you'll be able to see most first-run films and some art-house fare in Salt Lake City and, to a lesser extent, in smaller cities in Utah, the real cinematic event in Utah is Sundance Film Festival, held every January in Park City. Founded by actor Robert Redford as a forum for little-seen documentary and independent films, the festival has grown into an internationally renowned showcase of new high-quality cinema and now offers films in Salt Lake City and surrounding communities as well. Make lodging and ticket reservations well in advance if you want to attend. For more information and email updates, visit the festival's website (www.sundance.org/festival).

MUSEUMS

Utah residents are proud of their past, and nearly every community in the state has a Daughters of Utah Pioneers (DUP) museum, which recounts the story of local LDS settlement. In fact, church history and state history are so closely interconnected that the primary state history museums are the various Temple Square institutions and the LDS-dominated Pioneer Memorial Museum. Salt Lake is also home to good cultural museums, including Utah Museum of Contemporary Art and The Leonardo.

Utah has great museums dedicated to dinosaurs and other forms of ancient life. The area around Price and Vernal is rich in fossils, and both towns have good dinosaur museums; additionally, there are fossil digs with visitor centers at Dinosaur National Monument and at the Cleveland-Lloyd Dinosaur Quarry. The Museum of Ancient Life at Lehi's Thanksgiving Point has one of the largest collections of complete dinosaur skeletons in the country.

Ogden has converted its large and handsome railroad depot into a multi-museum complex with collections of minerals, fine art, firearms, and historic automobiles and train cars.

ART GALLERIES

Utah isn't exactly known for its fine art collections, but the Utah Museum of Contemporary Art has a changing lineup of traveling shows that focus on regional artists. The universities in Salt Lake City, Provo, and Logan each have art galleries, and Ogden boasts the Myra Powell Art Gallery in the historic train depot. If you're feeling spendy, the fine art galleries along Main Street in Park City will more than fit the bill—and are also fine to peruse on a summer evening.

FESTIVALS AND EVENTS

Throughout Utah, the biggest summer event is **Pioneer Day** on July 24, with parades and fireworks in almost every Utah community. It commemorates the day in 1847 when Brigham Young first saw the Salt Lake Valley and declared, "This is the place."

To most of the outside world, the most followed event is January's **Sundance Film Festival** in Park City, when you can see the best independent films alongside actors, directors, and press. Tickets are hard to score, but it's possible. Likewise, be sure to book your room way in advance.

In June, the **Utah Shakespeare Festival** begins its summer-long run in Cedar City. July brings the **Utah Festival Opera** to Logan, and for 6 days in August, the Bonneville Salt Flats are the site of **Speed Week,** when vehicles ranging from motorcycles to diesel trucks "shoot the salt."

Essentials

Transportation

Although Salt Lake City is well connected with the rest of the world and has a good public transportation system, to really explore the state, a car is the most realistic choice (although a case can be made for a bike and strong legs). However, if you're planning a winter trip to ski the Wasatch Mountains, consider skipping the car rental and relying on shuttles or city buses.

GETTING THERE

Air

Salt Lake City is a hub for **Delta Airlines** (800/221-1212, www.delta.com), and all other major airlines have regular flights into **Salt Lake City International Airport** (SLC, 776 N. Terminal Dr., 801/575-2400, https://slcairport.com). The airport is an easy 7 miles (11.3 km) west of downtown, reached via I-80 or North Temple Street or by TRAX light rail service (www.rideuta.com).

If you're heading to southern Utah's parks, consider flying in to Las Vegas's **Harry Reid International Airport** (LAS, 5757 Wayne Newton Blvd., Las Vegas, NV, 702/261-5211, www.harryreidairport.com), which is served by all major airlines, often with cheaper airfares than to SLC.

Ogden and Provo also have small airports served by Allegiant.

Train

Amtrak (800/872-7245, www.amtrak.com) runs one passenger train across Utah three times a week in each direction. The *California Zephyr* runs between Oakland and Chicago via Salt Lake City, Provo, Helper, and Green River.

Bus

Greyhound (800/231-2222, www.greyhound.com) offers interstate service to Utah on its routes along I-15, I-70, and I-80.

RVs and Vans

Many foreign travelers enter Utah in RVs, which they rent to drive on a tour of the western national parks. It takes more planning to line up a rental RV than a car, but there are plenty of agencies in Los Angeles, Phoenix, Las Vegas, and Salt Lake City at the ready. Most travel agents can help, or you can contact the local travel office in the city of your departure. In Salt Lake City, **Basecamper Vans** (177 2100 S., www.basecampervans.com) offers several lines of camper vans.

GETTING AROUND

Air

Regional airlines connect Salt Lake City with other communities in the state. Regular scheduled flights link Salt Lake to/from St. George, Cedar City, and Moab.

Train

Amtrak (800/872-7245, www.amtrak.com) can get you to Green River, Helper, Provo, and Salt Lake City, but that's about all. Public transportation to other points of interest, such as the national parks, is notably absent.

Bus

Greyhound (800/231-2222, www.greyhound.com) provides bus service along Utah's interstate highways and US 6 (between Green River and Provo), but these routes really don't get you close to the sorts of sights that most people come to Utah to see. The Wasatch Front area (from Provo to Ogden and from Salt Lake City out to Tooele) is served by the **Utah Transit Authority** (UTA, 801/287-4636, www.rideuta.com), a regional bus company with excellent service. Park City and other Salt Lake City ski areas are accessible via several ski-bus operations, some of which pick up at the airport.

Car

Public transportation serves cities and some towns but very few of the scenic, historic, and recreational areas. Unless you're on a tour, you really need your own transportation. Cars are easily rented in any large town, although the Salt Lake City Airport offers by far the greatest selection, including all the major rental-car companies, including **Enterprise** (801/715-1617, www.enterprise.com) and **Thrifty** (877/283-0898, www.thrifty.com).

Four-wheel-drive vehicles can be rented, too, and will be a must for extensive travel on back roads. In winter, if you rent a car or bring your own, **four-wheel drive** or **snow**

Previous: salt flats.

Utah Driving Distances

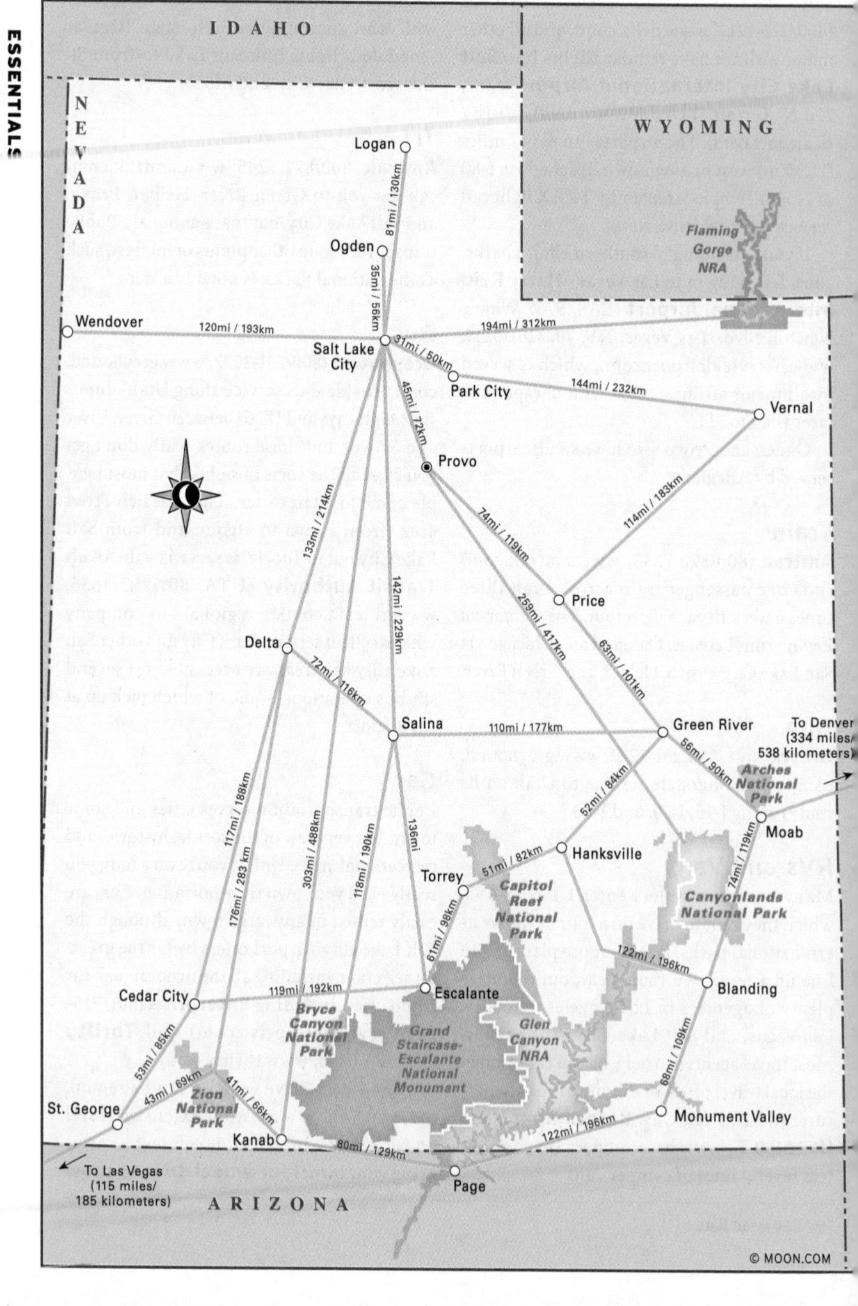

tires may be necessary or even required in the mountains, including on roads leading to ski areas. In any season, a high-clearance vehicle allows for easier travel on unpaved back roads, though rainstorms and snowmelt can easily render these roads impassable.

Most tourist offices carry the Utah road map published by the **Utah Department of Transportation** (801/965-4000, www.udot.utah.gov); it's one of the best available and is free.

Charging Your Electric Car

Electric vehicle (EV) charging stations are abundant in the Wasatch Valley and present along I-15 and I-80 as well in Zion and Bryce National Parks and Moab, but if you plan to explore far-flung destinations, a little planning is in order.

EV charging stations are available at St. George, Cedar City, Springdale, the visitor center at Zion National Park, Ruby's Inn (near Bryce Canyon National Park), Green River, Kanab, Moab, Blanding, and Page, Arizona. That leaves big areas of southeast Utah with no EV charging services.

Bicycle

Pedaling through Utah is a great way to see the state, whether you choose a route across its many backcountry roads or hug the shoulder of a scenic drive. An extra-low gear (30 inches or less) takes the strain out of long mountain grades. Utah has almost every kind of terrain and road condition imaginable. Mountain bikers find the Moab area in the southeast especially challenging and scenic. Note that designated wilderness areas are closed to cycling.

Recreation

The best place to begin looking for information on outdoor adventure in Utah is the comprehensive www.utah.com website. The site contains information on most sports and activities and provides lots of links to outfitters and more resources.

CAMPING, HIKING, AND BACKPACKING

Utah has extensive backcountry for those interested in exploring the scenery on foot. One increasingly popular activity is canyoneering—exploring mazelike slot canyons. Hundreds of feet deep but sometimes only wide enough for a hiker to squeeze through, these canyons are found in the southern part of the state, particularly near Escalante and in the Paria River area. You'll need to be fit to explore these regions—and watch the weather carefully for flash floods.

Hikers find great trails in almost all parts of the state. The rugged Wasatch Range near Salt Lake City is a popular day-hike destination for urban residents of the Wasatch Front, while the lofty lake-filled Uintas in northeastern Utah are perfect for long-distance trips. Much of the canyon lands of southern and southeastern Utah are accessible only by foot; visits to remote Ancestral Puebloan ruins and petroglyphs reward the long-distance hiker.

Campers are in luck in Utah. The state has a highly developed network of campgrounds. During peak summer season, make reservations or arrive at your destination early.

FISHING

The Wasatch and Uinta Ranges are dotted with lakes and drained by streams that are rich in rainbow and cutthroat trout. Fly fishing is a major sport in many mountain communities, and most towns have at least one fly shop and an outfitter anxious to take you out to a stream. Favorite fishing spots include Bear Lake, with good fishing for lake and cutthroat trout; Flaming Gorge Reservoir on the Green River, offering good fishing for lake trout, smallmouth bass, and kokanee salmon;

and Lake Powell, with good fishing for catfish, striper, and bass.

GOLF

There are dozens of golf courses across Utah. Notable courses dot the Salt Lake City area and are also near Ogden, Logan, Provo, and Park City. The state's greatest concentration of courses, though, is in St. George, in the southern part of the state.

MOUNTAIN BIKING

Mountain biking has done much to put Utah on the recreation map. Trails in the slickrock canyon country near Moab attract more than 180,000 biking enthusiasts a year, and now nearly all corners of the state promote their old Forest Service or mining roads as a biking paradise. There's good info for planning bike trips at www.utah.com/bike, and excellent biking guidebooks are available from bookstores or bike shops.

Peak mountain biking seasons in Moab and other parts of southern Utah are March-May and September-November. In the desert during summer, mountain bikers ride in the early morning or late evening to beat the heat. To the north in the Park City area, however, summer is the best time for a wildflower-filled ride.

WATER SPORTS

River-running is a favorite activity for visitors. The most notable float trip is down the Colorado River between Moab and the backwaters of Lake Powell. This multiday trip passes through Cataract Canyon, which is second only to trips through the Grand Canyon. The Green and San Juan Rivers are also popular. For these trips, plan well in advance, as spaces are limited and demand more than outstrips availability. In towns like Moab, Green River, Vernal, and Bluff, numerous outfitters provide exciting day trips that can usually take people with only a day's notice.

Utah also offers opportunities for **stand-up paddleboarding** (SUP), **kayaking,** and **sailing.** East of the Wasatch peaks, Jordanelle Reservoir and Deer Creek Reservoir both have nonmotorized sections where kayakers and stand-up paddlers can enjoy calm waters and beautiful scenery. Utah Lake near Provo, the state's largest freshwater lake, is a great spot to SUP. The Colorado River upstream from Moab is calm enough for most stand-up paddlers, though some of the rapids are best attempted in kayaks. Perhaps the state's top destination for SUP, kayaking, and sailing is Lake Powell, where warm, calm waters give access to hundreds of miles of flooded canyons and cliff-lined channels.

ROCKHOUNDING

Utah is rich in stones, fossils, and gems. The lack of vegetation and the high level of erosion make rockhounding relatively simple. One of the best places to plan a rock-hunting expedition is the Delta area, where you can explore for geodes, agates, garnets, and more.

SKIING AND WINTER SPORTS

The secret has been out about skiing in the Wasatch Mountains since the 2002 Winter Olympics. Utah's powder skiing is among the best in North America. Generally, ski season runs from around Thanksgiving until mid-April, though dates vary from resort to resort. For a good overview of Utah's ski areas and information on special package deals, check www.skiutah.com. Other winter sports include Nordic skiing, winter hiking, and dogsledding.

NATIONAL PARKS AND MONUMENTS

Utah is home to five major national parks, nearly a dozen national monuments, two national recreation areas, and one national historic site. The most popular destinations are Zion, Arches, and Bryce. These national park areas and national monuments are the state's largest tourist attraction.

The parks are all open year-round, although spring and fall are the best times to visit—you'll avoid the heat and crowds of high summer. If you're planning on making the rounds of the Utah national parks, purchase an America the Beautiful Pass ($80), which covers admission costs at national parks and other federal recreation sites.

STATE PARKS

Utah boasts 44 state parks, ranging from golf courses to fishing holes, from historic forts to Ancestral Puebloan ruins. Entry fees to state parks vary, but in general there's a $5-9 per vehicle day-use fee at these parks. Many have campgrounds; you can make **reservations** (800/322-3770, www.reserveamerica.com, $8 reservation fee in addition to camping fee).

For general information on Utah's state parks, contact **Utah State Parks** (801/538-7220, http://stateparks.utah.gov).

WILDERNESS TRAVEL

Utah has an abundance of designated wilderness areas, which are closed to mechanized vehicles (including mountain bikes) to protect both the environment and the experience of solitude. Most designated areas are within national forests or Bureau of Land Management lands, and many are free to visit without a permit; some have fees or require permits. The national parks and monuments require backcountry permits for overnight stays.

Travel Tips

BUSINESS HOURS

In Utah, most commercial businesses are open 9am-6pm Monday-Saturday. The biggest surprise to many travelers is that many businesses in Utah—and almost certainly those outside Salt Lake City, Park City, and the national park gateway towns—are **closed on Sunday.** This includes many restaurants. Plan well ahead so you don't get stranded hungry.

Note that most museums, recreation areas, and other attractions close on Thanksgiving, Christmas, New Year's Day, and other holidays. These closings are not always mentioned on websites, so call ahead.

WHAT TO PACK

Unless you want to return from Utah looking like a leather bag, remember to use lots of **sunscreen.** Prepare for wide variations in temperature. Nights in the desert can be very chilly even when summer highs soar above 100°F (38°C).

There's little need to pack clothes to dress up. **Casual clothes** are acceptable nearly everywhere, although if you want to break out your $300 jeans, you'll feel good about doing it in Park City. If you're visiting **religious sites** in Salt Lake City or elsewhere, modest casual clothing will be fine.

Alcohol presents another issue. If you want a drink, especially away from larger cities or in small towns near national parks, it may be easiest to pack your own—especially if you have discerning tastes. While drinking laws have relaxed tremendously and many restaurants in larger towns now offer a selection of alcoholic beverages (including good wine and Utah beers), Utah is not a drinking destination, to put it mildly.

And don't count on cell phone reception in remote mountains or canyons.

INTERNATIONAL VISITORS

Entering the United States

Citizens of Canada must provide a passport to enter the United States. However, a visa is not required for Canadian citizens.

Citizens of 28 other countries can enter under a reciprocal visa-waiver program. These citizens can enter the United States for up to 90 days for tourism or business with a valid passport; no visa is required. These countries include most of Western Europe, plus Japan, Australia, New Zealand, and Singapore. For a full list of reciprocal visa countries (and other late-breaking news for travelers to the United States), check out www.travel.state.gov. Visitors on this program who arrive by sea or air must show round-trip tickets back out of the United States dated within 90 days and must be able to present proof of financial solvency (credit cards are usually sufficient). If citizens of these countries are staying longer than 90 days, they must apply for and present a visa.

Citizens of countries not covered by the reciprocal visa program are required to present both a valid passport and a visa to enter the United States. These are obtained from US embassies and consulates. These travelers are also required to offer proof of financial solvency and show a round-trip ticket out of the United States within the timeline of the visa.

Once in the United States, foreign visitors can travel freely among states without restrictions.

Customs

US Customs allows each person over the age of 21 to bring one liter of liquor and 200 cigarettes into the country duty-free. Non-US citizens can bring in $100 worth of gifts without paying duty. If you are carrying more than $10,000 in cash or traveler's checks, you are required to declare it.

Money and Currency Exchange

Except in Salt Lake City, there are few opportunities to exchange foreign currency or traveler's checks in non-US funds at Utah banks or exchanges. Traveler's checks in US dollars are accepted at face value in most businesses without additional transaction fees.

By far the best way to keep yourself in cash is by using bank, debit, or cash cards at ATMs (automated teller machines). Not only does withdrawing funds from your own home account save on fees, but you also often get a better rate of exchange. Nearly every town in Utah has an ATM. Most ATMs at banks require a small fee to dispense cash. Most grocery stores allow you to use a debit or cash card to purchase food, with the option of adding a cash withdrawal. These transactions are free to the withdrawer.

Credit cards are accepted nearly everywhere in Utah. The most common are Visa and MasterCard. American Express, Diners Club, and Discover are also used, although these aren't as ubiquitous.

Say It Right!

The following place names are easy to mispronounce. Say it like a local!

- **Duchesne:** du-SHANE
- **Ephraim:** EE-from
- **Escalante:** es-kuh-LAN-tay
- **Hurricane:** HUR-ken
- **Kanab:** kuh-NAB
- **Lehi:** LEE-high
- **Manti:** MAN-tie
- **Moab:** Moe-AB
- **Monticello:** mon-ta-SELL-o
- **Nephi:** NEE-fi
- **Panguitch:** PAN-gwich
- **Tooele:** too-WILL-uh
- **Uinta:** you-IN-tuh
- **Weber:** WEE-ber

ACCESS FOR TRAVELERS WITH DISABILITIES

Travelers with disabilities will find Utah quite progressive when it comes to accessibility issues, especially in Salt Lake City and the heavily traveled national parks in southern Utah. Most parks offer all-abilities trails, and many hotels advertise their fully accessible facilities. The **National Ability Center** (435/649-3991, www.discovernac.org), based in Park City, provides recreational opportunities for people of all ages and abilities, including a skiing program at nearby Park City Mountain Resort.

LGBTQ+ TRAVELERS

Outside of Salt Lake City and Park City, LGBTQ+ travelers may find Utah less welcoming to openly gay people than other western states like Colorado, for example. Salt Lake City's gay newspaper, **Q** (www.qsaltlake.com), is a good place to get the read on the Utah scene. Aside from the Utah Pride Center (www.utahpridecenter.org), many of the support groups that exist in the state are concerned with supporting gay LDS individuals.

SENIOR TRAVELERS

The national and state parks, and Utah in general, are hospitable for senior travelers. The long-standing National Park Service-issued Golden Age Passport has been replaced by the America the Beautiful—National Parks and Federal Recreational Lands Senior Pass. This is a lifetime pass for US citizens or permanent residents age 62 or older. The pass provides access to, and use of, federal parks and recreation sites that charge an entrance fee or standard amenity. The pass admits the pass holder and passengers in a noncommercial vehicle at per-vehicle fee areas, not to exceed four adults. The pass costs $80 and can only be obtained in person at the park. There is a similar discount program at Utah state parks.

CONDUCT AND CUSTOMS

If you've never traveled in Utah before, you may find Utah residents don't initially seem as welcoming and outgoing as people in other western states. In smaller towns, visitors from outside the community are a relatively new phenomenon, and not everyone in the state is anxious to have their towns turned into tourism or recreational destinations. The LDS are very family- and community-oriented, and if locals initially seem uninterested in travelers, don't take it as unfriendliness.

The LDS are usually orderly and socially conservative people. Brash displays of rudeness or use of foul language in public will not make you popular.

Alcohol and Nightlife

Observant members of the Church of Jesus Christ of Latter-day Saints don't drink alcoholic beverages and **Utah's liquor laws** may confuse outsiders. Changes to Utah's once prohibitive rules have made it easier to buy and consume alcohol. Note that it's no longer necessary to be a member of a private club in order to consume alcohol in a bar—previously, you had to purchase a temporary membership or sign in on someone else's membership to enjoy a drink. A few pointers:

- Any beer you order on tap in Utah is **limited to 5 percent ABV (alcohol by volume),** while canned or bottled beers are full-strength. Any alcohol purchased in a grocery store is also limited to 5 percent ABV.
- Cocktails can contain a maximum of **2.5 ounces of total alcohol** content, which means they're not very strong. This is not a good place to order a martini.
- Utah's liquor stores—which are almost entirely state-run—only sell **unrefrigerated beer** and other booze, so buy in advance so you have time to chill in a cooler or fridge.
- Utah liquor stores are also **closed on Sundays** and all federal holidays.

Several different kinds of establishments are licensed to sell alcoholic beverages in Utah, and the rules vary at each:

Taverns, which include brewpubs, can sell only 5 percent beer (beer that is 5 percent ABV) on tap. You don't need to purchase food to have a beer in a tavern.

Licensed restaurants can sell beer, wine, and hard liquor, but only with food orders (usually an appetizer qualifies). In some parts of Utah, you'll need to specifically ask for a drink or the drink menu to begin the process. In Salt Lake City, Moab, and Park City, most restaurants have liquor licenses.

In small towns, many eating establishments don't offer alcohol.

Cocktail bars, lounges, live music venues, and nightclubs serve alcohol, but no one under the age of 21 is allowed inside. ID checks are usually routine, even if you haven't been IDed elsewhere in a decade or two. Occasionally, establishments with this license also serve food, but kids are still not allowed.

Nearly all towns will have a state-owned **liquor store.** Blanding is the exception. They can be difficult to find. Five percent beer is available in most grocery stores and gas station minimarts. Many travelers find that carrying a bottle of your favorite beverage to your room is the easiest way to enjoy an evening drink.

In southern Utah, only Moab offers much in the way of nightspots. Outside Moab, many restaurants in southern Utah don't serve alcohol.

Smoking

Smoking is prohibited in almost all public places. You're also not allowed to smoke on LDS church grounds. Obviously, take care when smoking in national parks and pick up your own butts. Besides the risk of fire, there's nothing that ruins a natural experience more than windblown piles of cigarette filters.

ACCOMMODATIONS

Utah is a major tourism destination, and you can plan on finding high-quality, reasonably priced motels and hotels in most cities and towns. Reservations are a good idea in major centers like Salt Lake City, Park City, and Moab, especially on weekends and during peak seasons. Along the national parks loop, it can be tough to find a last-minute room in high season—be sure to book well in advance—and off-season guest rooms are limited (some establishments are seasonal), so call ahead to make sure there's a room at the inn.

Hostels are available only in Salt Lake City, Park City, and Moab. They are open to travelers of all ages and don't require membership cards. You may need to provide your own sheets or sleeping bag. Utah also offers some comfortable bed-and-breakfast accommodations; contact the **Utah Travel Council** (800/200-1160, www.utah.com) for a general list of B&Bs.

Guest Ranches

Utah has fewer guest ranches than other western states, but some have sprung up here and there. Most are family ranches that take in guests during the summer. These tend to be authentic horse-powered operations, where you'll work alongside the family and stay in no-frills cabins or bunkhouses. Others are more upscale and offer a dude-ranch atmosphere with recreational options.

Most guest ranches require minimum stays, and prices include all meals and lodging. Advance reservations are usually required. If you're contemplating staying at a guest ranch, be sure to ask specific questions about lodging and work requirements. Expectations of the guest and host can vary widely. The Utah Travel Council can provide a full listing of Utah guest ranches.

Health and Safety

Utah has one of the lowest crime rates in the United States. Although parts of Salt Lake City look scruffy, there's little reason to fear random violence unless you put yourself in unwise situations.

In the event of sickness or injury, hospital emergency rooms offer the quickest help but cost more than a visit to a doctor's office or clinic.

DRIVING SAFETY

Summer heat in the desert puts an extra strain on both cars and drivers. Double-check your vehicle's cooling system, engine oil, transmission fluid, fan belts, and tires to make sure they are in top condition. Carry several gallons of water in case of a breakdown or radiator trouble. Never leave children or pets in a parked car during warm weather—temperatures inside can cause fatal heatstroke in minutes.

At times the desert has too much water, when late-summer storms frequently flood low spots in the road. Wait for the water level to subside before crossing.

Dust storms can completely block visibility but tend to be short-lived. During such storms, pull completely off the road, stop, and turn off your lights so as not to confuse other drivers.

In winter, use a vehicle with AWD or 4WD and snow tires, especially on mountain passes. However, even state highways can get dicey enough that you wouldn't want to drive on them in a storm with regular tires.

If stranded, either on the desert or in the mountains, stay with your vehicle unless you're positive of where to go for help, then leave a note explaining your route and departure time. Airplanes can easily spot a stranded car (tie a piece of cloth to your antenna), but a person walking is more difficult to see. It's best to carry emergency supplies: blankets or sleeping bags, a first-aid kit, tools, jumper cables, a shovel, traction mats or chains, a flashlight, rain gear, water, food, and a can opener.

GIARDIA

Giardia, a protozoan that has become common in even the remotest mountain streams, is carried in animal or human waste that is deposited or washed into natural waters. When ingested, it begins reproducing, causing an intestinal sickness in the host that can become very serious and may require medical attention.

You can take precautions against giardia with a variety of chemicals and filtering methods or by boiling water before drinking it. The various chemical solutions on the market work in some applications, but because they need to be safe for human consumption, they are weak and ineffective against the protozoan in its cyst stage of life (when it encases itself in a hard shell). Filtering may eliminate giardia, but there are other water pests too small to be caught by most filters. The most effective way to eliminate such threats is to boil all suspect water. A few minutes at a rolling boil will kill giardia even in the cyst stage.

HANTAVIRUS

Hantavirus is an airborne infectious disease agent transmitted from rodents to humans when rodents shed hantavirus particles in their saliva, urine, and droppings and humans inhale infected particles. It is easiest for a human to contract hantavirus in a contained environment, such as a cabin infested with mouse droppings, where the virus-infected particles are not thoroughly dispersed.

Simply traveling to a place where the hantavirus is known to occur is not considered a risk factor. Camping, hiking, and other outdoor activities also pose low risk, especially if steps are taken to reduce rodent contact.

The very first symptoms can occur

anywhere between 5 days and three weeks after infection. They almost always include fever, fatigue, and aching muscles (usually in the back, shoulders, or thighs) and other flu-like conditions. Other early symptoms may include headaches, dizziness, chills, and abdominal discomfort (such as vomiting, nausea, or diarrhea). These are shortly followed by intense coughing and shortness of breath. If you have these symptoms, seek medical help immediately. Untreated infections of hantavirus are almost always fatal.

HYPOTHERMIA

The greatest danger outdoors is one that can sneak up and kill with very little warning. Hypothermia—a lowering of the body's temperature below 95°F (35°C)—causes disorientation, uncontrollable shivering, slurred speech, and drowsiness. The victim may not even realize what's wrong. Unless corrective action is taken immediately, hypothermia can lead to death. Hikers should therefore travel with companions and always carry wind and rain protection. Space blankets are lightweight and cheap and offer protection against the cold in emergencies. Remember that temperatures can plummet rapidly in Utah's dry climate—a drop of 40 degrees between day and night is common. Be especially careful at high elevations, where sunshine can quickly change into freezing rain or a blizzard. Simply falling into a mountain stream can also lead to hypothermia and death unless proper action is taken. If you're cold and tired, don't waste time: Seek shelter and build a fire, change into dry clothes, and drink warm liquids. If a victim isn't fully conscious, warm the person by skin-to-skin contact in a sleeping bag. Try to keep the victim awake and offer plenty of warm liquids.

HEAT EXHAUSTION

Utah in summer is a hot place. Be sure to use sunscreen, or else you risk having a very uncomfortable vacation. Heat exhaustion can also be a problem if you're hiking in the hot sun. Drink plenty of water; in midsummer try to get an early start if you're hiking in full sun.

WILDERNESS TRAVEL

Part of the attraction of Utah's vast wilderness backcountry is its remoteness. And if you're hiking in the canyon country in the southern part of the state, you'll spend most of your time hiking at the bottom of narrow and twisting canyons. It's easy to get lost, or at least disoriented. Always carry adequate and up-to-date maps and a compass (a GPS unit may not work in canyon country)—and know how to use them if you're heading off into the backcountry. Always plan a route. Planning usually saves time and effort.

Tell someone (like a family member or a ranger) where you are going and when you'll be back, so they know where and when to start looking for you in case you get into trouble. Always take at least one other person with you: Do not venture into the desert alone. Parties of four people (or two vehicles) are ideal. It's a good idea to carry your cell phone in case you need to make an emergency call.

Thunderstorms can wash hikers away and bury them in the canyons and washes of the Southwest. Flash floods can happen almost any time of year but are most prevalent in the summer months. Before entering slot canyon areas like Paria or the Escalante Canyons, check with rangers or local authorities for weather reports. And while you're hiking, read and heed the clouds. Many washes and canyons drain large areas, with their headwaters many miles away. The dangerous part is that sometimes you just can't tell what's coming down the wash or canyon because of the vast number of acres that these canyons drain, and because the cliff walls are too high to see out to any storms that may be creating flood potential upstream.

At any sign of a threat, get out of the canyon bottom—at least 60 vertical feet (18 m) up—to avoid water and debris. Since many of these canyons are narrow, there are places where it's not possible to get out of the canyon on short notice. Never drive a vehicle into a flooded wash. Stop and wait for the water to recede, as it usually will within an hour.

WILDLIFE

To avoid poisonous rattlesnakes and scorpions when hiking or climbing in desert areas, never put your hand onto a ledge or into a hole that you can't see. While snakebites are rarely fatal anymore, they're no fun. If you are bitten, immobilize the affected area and seek immediate medical attention.

If you do much hiking and biking in the spring, there's a good chance you'll encounter ticks. While ticks in this part of the United States don't usually carry Lyme disease, there is a remote threat of Rocky Mountain spotted fever, spread by the wood tick. If a tick has bitten you, pull it off immediately. Grasp the tick's head parts (as close to your skin as possible) with tweezers and pull slowly and steadily. Do not attempt to remove ticks by burning them or coating them with anything. Removing a tick as soon as possible greatly reduces your chance of infection.

Utah is home to black bears, which aren't as menacing as their grizzly bear cousins. However, black bears weigh more than most humans and have far sharper claws and teeth. An encounter with a black bear is rarely fatal, but it's something to be avoided.

If you encounter a bear, give it plenty of room and try not to surprise it. Wearing a fragrance while in bear country isn't a good idea because it attracts bears, as does food. Always store food items outside the tent, and if you're in bear territory, sleep well away from the cooking area. Waking up with a bear clawing at your tent is to be avoided. Hanging food in a bag from a tree is a long-standing and wise precaution. If a bear becomes aggressive, fight back, concentrating your strikes around its face. Taking precautions and having respect for bears will ensure not only your continued existence, but theirs as well.

In recent years, as humans have increasingly moved into mountain lion habitat (and as their numbers have increased), they have become a threat to humans, especially small children. Never leave children unattended in forests, and never allow them to lag far behind on a family hike. Nearly every summer, newspapers in the western states carry tragic stories of children stalked and killed by mountain lions, which are also known as cougars. Safety is in numbers.

Information and Services

MONEY

Prices of all services mentioned in this guide were current at press time. You're sure to find seasonal and long-term price changes, so don't use what's listed here to argue with the staff at a motel, campground, museum, airline, or anywhere else.

Banks and ATMs

ATMs are available throughout Utah, even in the smallest towns. It's hard to exchange foreign currency or traveler's checks outside of central Salt Lake City, so foreign travelers should exchange all they'll need before setting out for rural parts of the state. Credit cards are generally accepted at most businesses.

Taxes

A sales tax, which varies from 5.95 to 8.7 percent, is added to most transactions on goods, food, and services. Additional room taxes are also tacked on; these vary by community and can be quite steep.

Tipping

It's customary to tip food and drink servers 20 percent; tips are almost never automatically added to the bill. Taxi drivers receive a 15-29 percent gratuity; bellhops get $1-2 per bag.

COMMUNICATIONS AND MEDIA

Normal post office hours are 8:30am-5pm Monday-Friday and sometimes 8:30am-noon Saturday. US post offices sell stamps and postal money orders. Overnight express service is also available.

Utah has three area codes: 801 and 385 are the codes for the greater Salt Lake City area, which includes suburbs as far south as Provo and as far north as Ogden. The rest of the state has the area code 435.

Toll-free numbers in the United States have an 800, 888, 877, or 866 area code. To obtain directory assistance, dial 411.

Even in small towns, most hotels (and even most budget motels) offer wireless internet access.

Depending on your cellular provider, cell phone coverage can be very spotty in rural areas, and nonexistent in canyons.

MAPS AND VISITOR INFORMATION

General tourist literature and maps are available from the **Utah Travel Council** (800/200-1160, www.utah.com). Utah's many chambers of commerce also have free material and are happy to help with travel suggestions in their areas. (See the "Information" sections throughout this guide for contact information.) Also listed are national forest offices and other government agencies that have information on outdoor recreation in their areas.

Utah Department of Transportation (801/965-4000, www.udot.utah.gov) prints and distributes a free, regularly updated map of Utah. Ask for it when you call for information or when you stop at a visitor information office. If you're planning on extensive backcountry exploration, be sure to ask locally about conditions. Backcountry enthusiasts or back-road explorers should also pick up Benchmark Maps' *Utah Road and Recreation Atlas*.

Obtain literature and the latest information on all of Utah's state parks from the **Utah State Parks and Recreation office** (801/538-7220 or 877/887-2757, http://stateparks.utah.gov). If you're planning a lot of state park visits, ask about the $75 annual state park pass. Reservations for campgrounds and some other services can be made at 800/322-3770 or www.reserveamerica.com; a reservation fee of $9 (online) or $10 (phone) applies.

WEIGHTS AND MEASURES

Time Zones

Utah is in the mountain time zone and goes on daylight saving time (advanced 1 hour) March-November. Nevada is in the Pacific time zone, 1 hour earlier; all other bordering states are in the mountain time zone. An odd exception is Arizona, which stays on mountain standard time all year (except for the Navajo Reservation, which goes on daylight saving time to keep up with its Utah and New Mexico sections).

Electricity

Like the rest of the United States, electricity is 110 volts, 60 hertz. Plugs have either two flat prongs or two flat prongs plus one round prong. Older homes and hotels may only have two-prong outlets, and you may well be traveling with computers or appliances that have three-prong plugs. Ask your hotel or motel manager for an adapter; if necessary, you may need to buy a three-prong adapter, but the cost is small.

Resources

Suggested Reading

ARCHAEOLOGY

Jones, Kevin T., and Layne Miller. *Standing on the Walls of Time: Ancient Art of Utah's Cliffs and Canyons.* Salt Lake City: University of Utah Press, 2019. With sumptuous photos, this book about Utah's rock art is written by a former Utah state archaeologist.

Lister, Robert, and Florence Lister. *Those Who Came Before.* Tucson: Southwest Parks and Monuments, 1993. A well-illustrated guide to the history, artifacts, and ruins of prehistoric Southwestern people. The author also describes parks and monuments containing archaeological sites.

Simms, Steven R. *Traces of Fremont: Society and Rock Art in Ancient Utah.* Salt Lake City: University of Utah Press and Price, UT: College of Eastern Utah Prehistoric Museum, 2010. Great photos accompany this story of Fremont culture.

Slifer, Dennis. *Guide to Rock Art of the Utah Region: Sites with Public Access.* Albuquerque: University of New Mexico Press, 2000. The most complete guide to rock art, with descriptions of more than 50 sites in the Four Corners region. Complete with maps and directions, plus an overview of rock-art styles and traditions.

GUIDEBOOKS

Benchmark Maps. *Utah Road & Recreation Atlas.* Medford, OR: Benchmark Maps, 2017. Shaded relief maps emphasize landforms, alongside abundant recreational information. Use the atlas to locate campgrounds, back roads, and major trailheads, though there's not enough detail to rely on it for hiking.

Huegel, Tony. *Utah Byways: 65 of Utah's Best Backcountry Drives.* Berkeley, CA: Wilderness Press, 2006. If you're looking for off-highway adventure, this is your guide. The spiral-bound book includes detailed directions, human and natural history, outstanding photography, full-page maps for each of the 65 routes, and an extensive how-to chapter for beginners.

Wells, Charles A. *Guide to Moab, UT Backroads & 4-Wheel Drive Trails.* Monument, CO: Funtreks Inc., 2008. Good descriptions and GPS waypoints for Moab-area four-wheelers.

Zwinger, Ann. *Wind in the Rock: The Canyonlands of Southeastern Utah.* Tucson: University of Arizona Press, 1986. Well-written accounts of hiking in the Grand Gulch and nearby canyons, including history, archaeology, wildlife, and plants.

HISTORY

Dellenbaugh, Frederick S. *A Canyon Voyage: The Narrative of the Second Powell Expedition.* Tucson: University of Arizona Press, 2017. A well-written account of John Wesley Powell's second expedition down the

Green and Colorado Rivers (1871-1872). The members took the first Grand Canyon photographs and obtained valuable scientific knowledge.

Krakauer, Jon. *Under the Banner of Heaven: A Story of Violent Faith.* New York: Doubleday Books, 2003. The story of two fundamentalist polygamous brothers who killed their sister-in-law and nephew upon receiving what they considered to be a message from God.

McPherson, Robert S. *Stories from the Land: A Navajo Reader about Monument Valley.* U.S., 2021. Drawing heavily upon interviews with Navajos in Monument Valley, McPherson weaves together a window into life in the area, from Navajo culture and trading post life to the dawn of Hollywood films.

Stegner, Wallace. *Beyond the Hundredth Meridian: John Wesley Powell and the Second Opening of the West.* New York: Penguin Books, reprinted 1992 (first published in 1954). Stegner's book tells the story of Powell's wild rides down the Colorado River, then points out why the United States should have listened to what Powell had to say about the Southwest.

Trimble, Stephen. *Red Rock Stories: Three Generations of Writers Speak on Behalf of Utah's Public Lands.* Salt Lake City, UT: Torrey House Press, 2017. This anthology of nonfiction focused on protecting wild Utah features the voices of politicians and Indigenous people alike.

MEMOIRS

Abbey, Edward. *Desert Solitaire.* New York: Ballantine Books, 1991. A meditation on the red-rock canyon country of Utah. Abbey tells riveting stories that bring the American outback to life, while excoriating the commercialization of the West.

Childs, Craig. *The Secret Knowledge of Water.* Boston: Back Bay Books, 2000. Childs looks for water in the desert, and finds plenty of it.

Meloy, Ellen, and Stephen Strom. *The Desert Hides Nothing.* Salt Lake City, UT: Torrey House Press, 2020. This reflection on desert landscapes features the posthumously published writing of southern Utah resident Meloy alongside the photography of Strom.

Williams, Terry Tempest. *Refuge: An Unnatural History of Family and Place.* New York: Vintage Books, 1992. A memoir of a family devastated by cancer (caused by federal government atomic testing), overlain with a natural history of birdlife along the Great Salt Lake. Haunting, deeply spiritual, and beautifully written.

Zwinger, Ann. *Run, River, Run: A Naturalist's Journey Down One of the Great Rivers of the American West.* Tucson: University of Arizona Press, 1984. An excellent description of the author's experiences along the Green River, from its source in the Wind River Range of Wyoming to the Colorado River in southeastern Utah. The author weaves geology, Native American ruins, plants, wildlife, and her personal feelings into the narrative and drawings.

NATURAL SCIENCES

Chronic, Lucy, and Felicie Williams. *Roadside Geology of Utah.* Missoula, MT: Mountain Press Publishing, 2014. This layperson's guide tells the story of the state's fascinating geology as seen on major roadways.

Fagan, Damian. *Canyon Country Wildflowers.* Helena, MT: Falcon Publishing, 2012. A comprehensive field guide to the diverse flora of the Four Corners area.

Williams, David. *A Naturalist's Guide to Canyon Country.* Helena, MT: Falcon Publishing, 2000. If you want to buy just one field guide, this is the one to get. It's well written, beautifully illustrated, and a delight to use.

RECREATION

Adkison, Ron. *Hiking Grand Staircase-Escalante & the Glen Canyon Region: A Guide to 59 of the Best Hiking Adventures in Southern Utah.* Helena, MT: Falcon Publishing, 2011. The vast Escalante-Glen Canyon area of southern Utah is nearly roadless, so hiking is about the only way to visit these beautiful canyons. This guide includes detailed information on 59 hikes, including Paria Canyon and Grand Gulch, in addition to Grand Staircase-Escalante National Monument.

Allen, Steve. *Canyoneering: The San Rafael Swell.* Salt Lake City: University of Utah Press, 2000. Eight chapters each cover a different area of this exceptional, though little-known, canyon country. Trail and route descriptions cover adventures from easy rambles to challenging hikes. The author provides some climbing notes, too. Detailed road logs help you get there, whether by mountain bike, car, or truck.

Belknap, Buzz, and Loie Belknap Evans. *Belknap's Waterproof Dinosaur River Guide.* Evergreen, CO: Westwater Books, 2008. Topo maps show the canyons and points of interest along the Green and Yampa Rivers in Dinosaur National Monument of northeastern Utah and adjacent Colorado. Includes Lodore, Whirlpool, and Split Mountain Canyons of the Green River. The Belknaps' other river guides are also go-to guides.

Bjørnstad, Eric. *Desert Rock I: Rock Climbs in the National Parks.* Helena, MT: Falcon Publishing, 1996. One of several excellent climbing guides by one of Utah's most respected climbers. Also see Bjørnstad's *Rock Climbing Desert Rock IV: The Colorado Plateau Backcountry: Utah* for information on climbing outside Utah's national parks.

Brinkerhoff, Brian, and Greg Witt. *Best Easy Day Hikes Salt Lake City.* Helena, MT: Falcon Publishing, 2009. More than 20 short hikes in the Wasatch Front canyons near Salt Lake City.

Bromka, Gregg. *Mountain Biking Utah.* Helena, MT: Falcon Publishing, 1999. Detailed route descriptions of more than 100 rides, from the Salt Lake City area through Moab and Brian Head. Easy-to-use maps and elevation profiles included.

Crowell, David. *Mountain Biking Moab.* Helena, MT: Falcon Guides, 2019. A guide to the many trails around Moab, from the most popular to the little explored, in a handy size—small enough to take on your ride.

Day, David. *Utah's Favorite Hiking Trails.* Provo, UT: Rincon Publishing, 2002. Good simple maps and detailed descriptions of trails all over the state, including many in southern Utah's national parks and monuments.

Green, Stewart M. *Rock Climbing Utah.* Helena, MT: Falcon Publishing, 2012. Beta on climbs in all of Utah's national parks, including many line drawings and photos with routes highlighted.

Kelsey, Michael R. *Canyon Hiking Guide to the Colorado Plateau.* Provo, UT: Brigham Distributing, 2018. One of the best guides to hiking in southeastern Utah's canyon country. Geologic cross sections show the formations you'll be walking through.

Lambrechtse, Rudi. *Hiking the Escalante.* Salt Lake City: University of Utah Press, 2016. "A wilderness guide to an exciting land of buttes, arches, alcoves, amphitheaters, and deep canyons," this introduction to history, geology, and natural history of Utah's Escalante region contains descriptions and trailhead information for 42 hiking destinations.

Matson, Mike. *Moon Utah Camping.* Berkeley, CA: Avalon Travel, 2009. The best guide to public and private campgrounds across the state. A great resource if you're planning on doing any backcountry exploration.

Molvar, Erik. *Best Easy Day Hikes Zion and Bryce Canyon National Parks.* Helena, MT: Falcon Publishing, 2014. Concise descriptions and easy-to-follow maps for 22 easily manageable hikes in two of Utah's most popular national parks.

Probst, Jeffrey. *Hiking Utah's High Uintas: 99 Day and Overnight Hikes.* Helena, MT: Falcon Publishing, 2006. Nearly 100 hiking trails, from easy to long-distance, and information on the area's 600 lakes.

Schneider, Bill. *Best Easy Day Hikes Canyonlands and Arches.* Helena, MT: Falcon Publishing, 2017. The 20 hikes covered in this guide are geared toward travelers who are short on time or can't explore the canyons on more difficult trails.

Sjogren, Morgan. *The Best Bears Ears National Monument Hikes.* Golden, CO: Colorado Mountain Club, 2018. Hikes range from easy strolls suitable for families to extended adventures into remote corners of this new national monument.

Online Resources

NEWS

Deseret News

www.deseret.com

One of Salt Lake's major newspapers, the *Deseret News* has good regional and LDS coverage.

Salt Lake Tribune

www.sltrib.com

The *Salt Lake Tribune* is the state's newspaper of record.

Salt Lake City Weekly

www.cityweekly.net

Salt Lake City's alternative weekly newspaper has online event listings and in-depth articles on city issues.

RECREATION

The American Southwest

www.americansouthwest.net/utah

An overview of national parks, national recreation areas, and some state parks.

Canyoneering USA

www.canyoneeringusa.com

Created and maintained by a canyoneering enthusiast who's also the maker of gear for the sport, Tom's Utah Canyoneering Guide offers detailed beta on routes throughout southern Utah, including in Zion and the Escalante region.

Desert USA

www.desertusa.com

Desert USA describes places to visit and what plants and animals you might meet there. Here's the best part of this site: You can find out what's in bloom at www.desertusa.com/wildflo/nv.html

Federal Recreation Reservations

www.recreation.gov

If a campground is operated by the federal government, this is the place to make a reservation. You can expect to pay $8 for this convenience ($9 if you choose to use the phone to make the reservation).

National Park Service
www.nps.gov

The National Park Service offers pages for all its parks. Trail conditions, maps, accessible features, and other helpful information are included. You can also enter this address followed by a slash and the first two letters of the first two words of the place (first four letters if there's just a one-word name); for example, www.nps.gov/brca takes you to Bryce Canyon National Park and www.nps.gov/zion leads to Zion National Park.

Reserve America
www.reserveamerica.com

Use this website to reserve campsites in state campgrounds. It costs a few extra bucks to reserve a campsite, but compare that with the cost of being skunked out of a site and having to resort to a motel room.

US Forest Service
www.fs.usda.gov/r4

Utah falls within US Forest Service Region 4. From this site you can navigate to each of the national forests in Utah.

Utah State Parks
http://stateparks.utah.gov

The Utah State Parks website offers details on the large park system.

TRAVEL

Ghost Towns
www.ghosttowns.com/states/ut/ut.html

Histories and photos of Utah's loneliest towns.

Moab Area Travel Council
www.discovermoab.com

Upcoming events, mountain bike trails, local restaurants and lodging, and outfitters are all easy to find at this comprehensive site.

Ski Utah
www.skiutah.com

If you're coming for the snow, head to Ski Utah, where you'll also find summer activities at the ski resorts.

Utah Travel Council
www.utah.com

The Utah Travel Council is a one-stop shop for all sorts of information on Utah. It takes you around the state to sights, activities, events, and maps and offers links to local tourism offices. The accommodations listings are the most up-to-date source for current prices and options.

Visit Salt Lake City
www.visitsaltlake.com

Find the scoop on all aspects of visiting Salt Lake City, including accommodations (sometimes with deals), events, and activities ranging from genealogical research to birdwatching. It's also a good place to find deals on ski passes.

Index

C

D

E

K

L

M

N

O

P

QR

S

T

U

VW

XYZ

List of Maps

Front Map

Welcome to Utah

Salt Lake City and Northern Utah

Park City and the Wasatch Back

Zion and Bryce

The Escalante Area and Capitol Reef

Moab, Arches, and Canyonlands

Southeast Utah

Uinta Mountains and Dinosaur Country

Background

Essentials

Photo Credits

All photos © Maya Silver, except page 1 Kojihirano | Dreamstime.com; page 14 © (top) Noamfein | Dreamstime.com; page 16 © (bottom) Deepfrog17 | Dreamstime.com; page 22 © Rinus Baak | Dreamstime.com; page 29 © (top) Larry Gevert | Dreamstime.com; page 34 © Deer Valley Resort; page 43 © (top left) Zrfphoto | Dreamstime.com; (top right) Robert Cliff | Dreamstime.com; page 51 © (top) Jovannig | Dreamstime.com; (bottom) Helena Bilkova | Dreamstime.com; page 58 © (top right) Ritu Jethani | Dreamstime.com; page 75 © (bottom) Judy Jewell; page 85 © (left middle)Judy Jewell; (bottom) Jeremy Christensen | Dreamstime.com; page 97 © (top) Christiannafzger | Dreamstime.com; (bottom) Roman Tiraspolsky | Dreamstime.com; page 109 © (top) Valentin M Armianu | Dreamstime.com; (bottom) Bruce Jenkins | Dreamstime.com; page 115 © (left middle) Fashionstock.com | Dreamstime.com; (right middle) Jennifer Thompson | Dreamstime.com; page 119 © (top) Sue Smith | Dreamstime.com; page 135 © (top right) Deer Valley Resort; (bottom) Roman Tiraspolsky | Dreamstime.com; page 145 © Visit Park City; page 168 © (top) Sean Pavone | Dreamstime.com; (bottom) Walter Arce | Dreamstime.com; page 173 © (top right) Stephen Moehle | Dreamstime.com; page 187 © (top right) Robert Bohrer | Dreamstime.com; page 208 © Victorianl | Dreamstime.com; page 234 © Chon Kit Leong | Dreamstime.com; page 240 © (top) Mehmet Dilsiz | Dreamstime.com; (bottom) Junko Barker | Dreamstime.com; page 244 © (top) K. Bradley Washburn | Dreamstime.com; page 253 © (top left) Gregdedman | Dreamstime.com; (top right) Cayla Vidmar; page 277 © Thomas Vieth | Dreamstime.com; page 310 © (top) Jonmanjeot | Dreamstime.com; page 329 © Colin Young | Dreamstime.com; page 332 © (right middle) Adam Wheeler; (bottom) Victoria Wickline; page 335 © Robert Crum | Dreamstime.com; page 360 © (bottom) Arlene Waller | Dreamstime.com; page 362 © (top) Cynthia Mccrary | Dreamstime.com; (bottom) Cynthia Mccrary | Dreamstime.com; page 364 © (top) Lhb Companies | Dreamstime.com; page 366 © Dave Coyne; page 378 © Paul Lemke | Dreamstime.com; page 389 © (left middle) William Cosby | Dreamstime.com; page 395 © Colin Young | Dreamstime.com; page 408 © Tang90246 | Dreamstime.com; page 409 © Natalia Bratslavsky | Dreamstime.com; page 415 © (top left) Tristan Brynildsen | Dreamstime.com; (top right) Chris Casanova | Dreamstime.com; page 422 © (bottom) Jeremy Christensen | Dreamstime.com; page 426 © (top) Chris Casanova | Dreamstime.com; (bottom) Mkopka | Dreamstime.com; page 431 © (top) Sdbower | Dreamstime.com; (bottom) Zrfphoto | Dreamstime.com; page 435 © (top) Galyna Andrushko | Dreamstime.com; (bottom) Gerwin Schadl | Dreamstime.com; page 438 © Jiawangkun | Dreamstime.com; page 441 © (top) Donald Fink | Dreamstime.com; (bottom) Saltcityphotography | Dreamstime.com; page 445 © (top) Junko Barker | Dreamstime.com; (bottom) Oleksandr Buzko | Dreamstime.com; page 450 © (top) Lhb Companies | Dreamstime.com; (left middle)Judy Jewell; (right middle) Judy Jewell; (bottom) Mudwalker | Dreamstime.com; page 470 © Valentin M Armianu | Dreamstime.com

MAP SYMBOLS

Expressway
Primary Road
Secondary Road
Unpaved Road
Trail
Ferry
Railroad
Pedestrian Walkway
Stairs

City/Town
State Capital
National Capital
Highlight
Point of Interest
Accommodation
Restaurant/Bar
Other Location

Information Center
Parking Area
Church
Winery/Vineyard
Trailhead
Train Station
Airport
Airfield

Park
Golf Course
Unique Feature
Waterfall
Camping
Mountain
Ski Area
Glacier

CONVERSION TABLES

°C = (°F - 32) / 1.8
°F = (°C x 1.8) + 32
1 inch = 2.54 centimeters (cm)
1 foot = 0.304 meters (m)
1 yard = 0.914 meters
1 mile = 1.6093 kilometers (km)
1 km = 0.6214 miles
1 fathom = 1.8288 m
1 chain = 20.1168 m
1 furlong = 201.168 m
1 acre = 0.4047 hectares
1 sq km = 100 hectares
1 sq mile = 2.59 square km
1 ounce = 28.35 grams
1 pound = 0.4536 kilograms
1 short ton = 0.90718 metric ton
1 short ton = 2,000 pounds
1 long ton = 1.016 metric tons
1 long ton = 2,240 pounds
1 metric ton = 1,000 kilograms
1 quart = 0.94635 liters
1 US gallon = 3.7854 liters
1 Imperial gallon = 4.5459 liters
1 nautical mile = 1.852 km

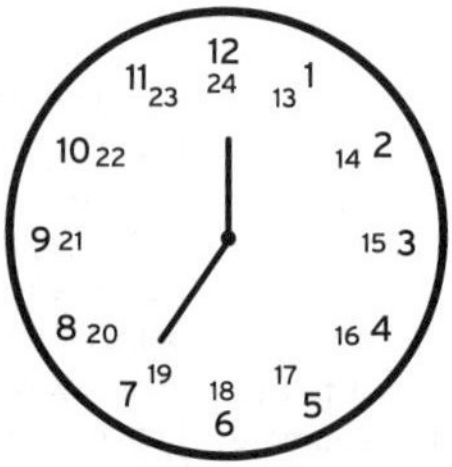

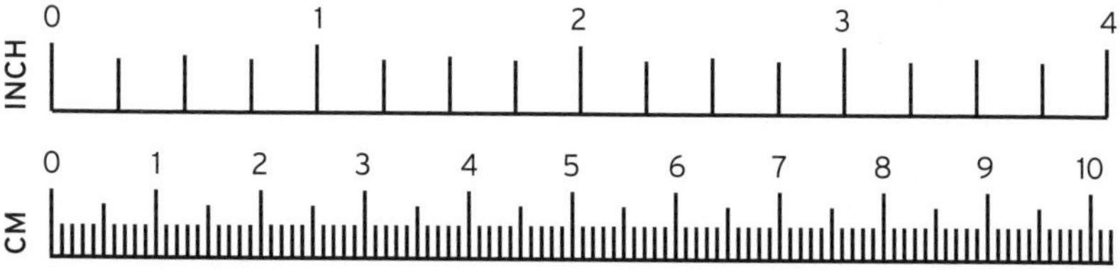

12 24 1 13 2 14 3 15 4 16 5 17 6 18 7 19 8 20 9 21 10 22 11 23

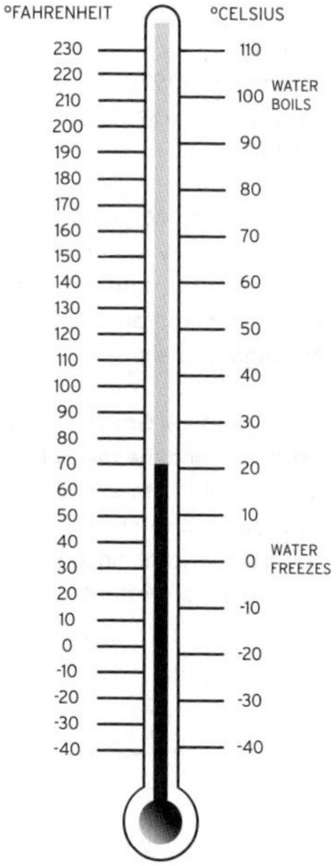

°FAHRENHEIT
230 220 210 200 190 180 170 160 150 140 130 120 110 100 90 80 70 60 50 40 30 20 10 0 -10 -20 -30 -40

°CELSIUS
110 100 WATER BOILS 90 80 70 60 50 40 30 20 10 0 WATER FREEZES -10 -20 -30 -40

INCH
0 1 2 3 4

CM
0 1 2 3 4 5 6 7 8 9 10

MOON UTAH
Avalon Travel
Hachette Book Group
555 12th Street, Suite 1850
Oakland, CA 94607, USA
www.moon.com

Editor: Vy Tran
Managing Editor: Courtney Packard
Copy Editor: Ann Seifert
Graphics and Production Coordinator: Darren Alessi
Cover Design: Toni Tajima
Interior Design: Avalon Travel
Map Editor: Kat Bennett
Cartographers: Abby Whelan, Erin Greb, Mike Morgenfeld, Kat Bennett, Brian Shotwell
Proofreader: Ashley Benning
Indexer: Greg Jewett

ISBN-13: 9798886470147

Printing History
1st Edition — 1988
15th Edition — September 2024
5 4 3 2 1

Front cover photo: Angels Landing viewpoint, Zion National Park © Maurizio Rellini / Sime / eStock Photo
Back cover photo: a skier getting fresh tracks at Alta © Robert Fullerton | Dreamstime.com

Printed in China by RR Donnelley APS

Avalon Travel is a division of Hachette Book Group, Inc. Moon and the Moon logo are trademarks of Hachette Book Group, Inc. All other marks and logos depicted are the property of the original owners.